THE ILLUSTRATED
ENCYCLOPEDIA
OF THE
PREHISTORIC
WORLD

This edition published in 2006 by
CHARTWELL BOOKS, INC.
A division of BOOK SALES, INC.
114 Northfield Avenue
Edison, New Jersey 08837
USA

Copyright © 2006 Marshall Editions
A Marshall Edition
Conceived, edited, and designed by Marshall Editions
The Old Brewery, 6 Blundell Street, London N7 9BH, UK
www.quarto.com

Consultant Editor: **Dr. Douglas Palmer**
Professor of Earth Sciences, Cambridge University, UK

Consultants:
Professor Barry Cox
Department of Biology, King's College London
Professor Brian Gardiner
Professor of Vertebrate Paleontology, King's College London
Dr. Colin Harrison
Former Principal Scientific Officer, Sub-Department of Ornithology,
British Museum (Natural History), London
Professor R. J. G. Savage
Department of Geology, University of Bristol, UK
Kevin Padian
University of California, Berkeley

ISBN-13: 978-0-7858-2086-4
ISBN-10: 0-7858-2086-8

Originated in Singapore by Master Image and Chroma Graphics;
and in Hong Kong by Modern Age
Printed in China by SNP Leefung Printers Limited

THE ILLUSTRATED
ENCYCLOPEDIA
OF THE
PREHISTORIC
WORLD

CONSULTANT EDITOR DR. DOUGLAS PALMER

PROFESSOR BARRY COX, PROFESSOR R.J.G. SAVAGE,
PROFESSOR BRIAN GARDINER, DR. COLIN HARRISON, KEVIN PADIAN

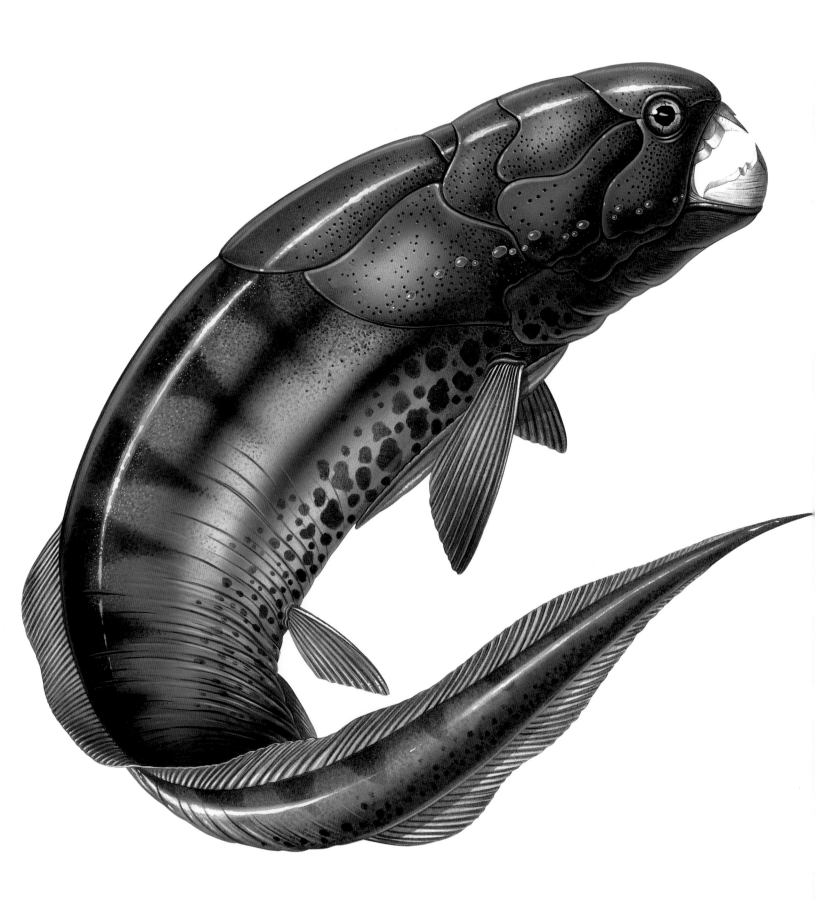

Contents

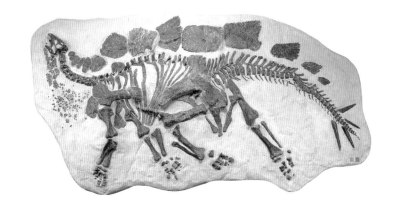

160 Animal Fact File

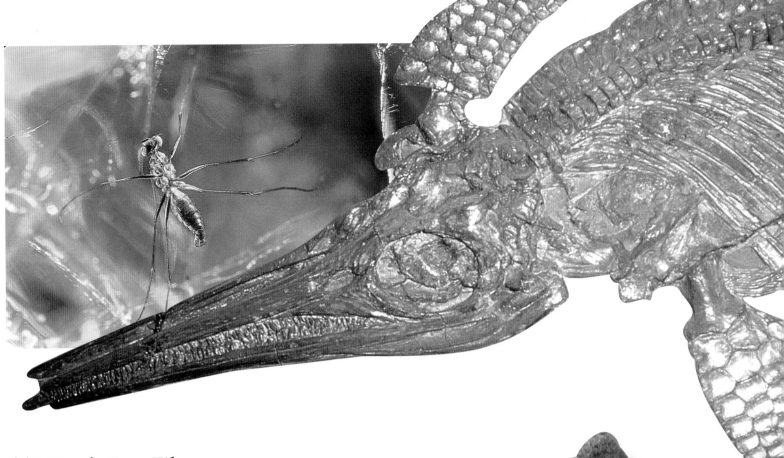

442 Earth Fact File

Introduction

For four and a half billion years or more, the Earth has been circling the Sun. Our planet hasn't always looked like it does now, of course. In fact, almost like a living thing, the Earth's face has changed continually as it has aged. Its oceans and atmospheres have evolved, mountain ranges have risen and crumbled, seas have opened and dried, rivers have run their course and cut great canyons in ancient rocks. And through it all, life on Earth has evolved to keep up with these monumental changes. It seems that whatever changes the Earth goes through, the plants, animals, and microbes manage to change along with it. How do we learn about these changes? Geology and paleontology (the scientific study of fossils) give us the history of how the Earth and its life came to be.

The Earth and all its life bear the marks of its history. Mountain ranges are former seafloors upthrust by tectonic processes, eroded by wind and water, raked by glaciers, shattered by earthquakes. In the same way, humans bear the marks of our evolution. We have elaborate organ systems, notably our kidneys and parts of our hormonal system, that function to simulate our ancestral watery home internally for us. Our forearm and lower leg bones are paired, reflecting their use in rotating the limbs during early land locomotion. Human fetuses even have gills for a while during the early stages of development.

The Illustrated Encyclopedia of the Prehistoric World allows you to follow these changes as they occurred through Earth's long history. First, a series of magnificent maps based on painstaking geological research shows how the continents have moved around the world over the last 620 million years. These maps are then related to the fossils that tell you about the plants and animals that lived in the ancient seas and on the unfamiliar lands shown in the maps. Next, a fascinating catalog introduces you to prehistoric creatures, including the fishes of the past; the first amphibians; the mammal-like reptiles; the ancient masters of the air, in the form of flying reptiles and the first birds and bats; and the mammals that were our predeccessors. Finally, a comprehensive Fact File clearly explains the complex ideas and principles of geology and paleontology.

The Western world began to study the Earth in the modern sense approximately two centuries ago. At this time there were many "theories" that tried to account for the shapes and character of rocks and their contents. It was accepted that fossils were the remains of past organic life, not artifacts or accidents of nature. The presence of fossil seashells on mountainsides, first thought to be remnants of Noah's flood, were revealed to be a succession of strata distributed all over the world, as William Smith and many others in England, then through continental Europe and elsewhere, established the science of stratigraphy.

The next step was to figure out how old the Earth's rocks were. Clearly the lower strata were deposited before the higher ones, but most places in the world had only a few pieces of the entire succession. It was not until the discovery of radioactivity and the measurement of isotope decay that the age of rocks could be calibrated in millions of years, though Darwin and many geologists had made reasonable guesses decades earlier. Finally, how did all of these disjunct pieces of rock reach their far-flung corners? This was the problem of continental drift, first a notion, then a hypothesis, then an established theory that developed into plate tectonics, the unifying concept of geology. An understanding of the movements of continents, the shifting and bucking of plates, and the openings and closings of oceans, led to the understanding that earthquakes, volcanoes, hot spots, and mountain building were all parts of the same general phenomenon of tectonics. This helped to test ideas about the origin and evolution of the atmosphere, the oceans, the Earth itself, and of course its life.

This book is a natural history of times past, featuring real creatures that lived, breathed, reproduced—then disappeared from the face of the Earth. It tells you not so much where things are, but where things were; not so much about the Earth's present day inhabitants, but much about those of the past, including their peculiar "habits" and "customs." Above all, it is a book about how these things came to be. How plants evolved; how a mass extinction wiped out most of the marine life 250 million years ago; how India moved from the southern to the northern hemisphere, throwing up the Himalayas in the process. It is also a book about the amazing creatures that have populated the Earth since the dawn of time. Although the animals featured may look fantastic, they are

by no means the creations of the imagination. In recreating each animal, artists have held faithfully to the fossil record and made realistic reconstructions of physical features, postures, and colorations.

The Illustrated Encyclopedia of the Prehistoric World is an informative digest of what we know about the world of the past. Its illustrations are meant to inform and delight its readers, and its text contains many key words that will open the doors to further knowledge in libraries and on the internet.

Though relative newcomers on Earth, the human species has done much to change its face. We have been instrumental in causing the extinction or near-extinction of many species. By paying tribute to the beauty and diversity of the past, this book reminds us of our responsibilities to the many fascinating animals with whom we share our planet today.

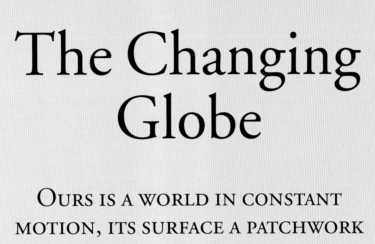

The Changing Globe

Ours is a world in constant
motion, its surface a patchwork
of interlocking tectonic plates
that carry the continents. The
maps in this section trace the
movements of the Earth's plates
over the last 620 million years,
revealing how the continents
arrived at their present positions.
We see how mountain ranges mark
where ancient continents
collided and how lands now
separated by wide oceans were
once clustered together as a
giant supercontinent.

The Changing Face of the Earth

VENDIAN TIMES 620 MILLION YEARS AGO (MA)

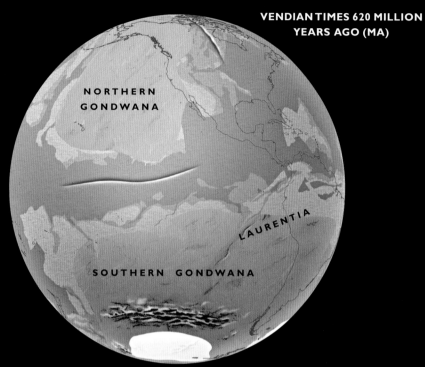

NORTHERN GONDWANA

LAURENTIA

SOUTHERN GONDWANA

Throughout its long geological history, the Earth has undergone vast changes that have affected the distribution and shapes of its continents, its climate, its lifeforms, and the extent and depths of its oceans. The maps on the following 34 pages illustrate these alterations.

The reason for many of these changes has been movement of tectonic plates—large pieces of the Earth's surface layer. These movements are in turn driven by huge flows of hot semi-molten material within the Earth's interior. Plates consist of continental crust, oceanic crust (seafloor), or both. New oceanic crust is continuously formed at structures called spreading ridges at the bottoms of the oceans. When new oceanic crust is added to a plate that also contains a continent, the continent is pushed away from the formative ridge. Over hundreds of millions of years, sequences of such movements have caused continents to move thousands of miles over the Earth's surface and in some cases to rotate.

Plate movements sometimes cause continents to collide, and the result may be the formation of vast mountain ranges. They also cause oceanic crust to be forced down into the Earth's interior at some plate boundaries, which can cause earthquake and volcanic activity, with widespread effects including climatic change. Climatic fluctuations in turn affect factors such as sea levels and the world distribution of plants and animals.

DEVONIAN TIMES 360 MA

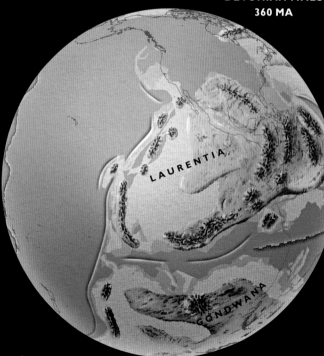

LAURENTIA

GONDWANA

LATE CRETACEOUS TIMES 65 MA

NORTH AMERICA

ATLANTIC OCEAN

PACIFIC OCEAN

AFRICA

SOUTH AMERICA

THREE STAGES IN PREHISTORY

The maps on this page show the hemisphere of the Earth now occupied by the Americas at three stages in history. About 620 million years ago or MA (top), two main landmasses existed. By 360 MA (above), these had joined up and rotated to the south, but a separate continent, Laurentia, had broken off to the north. By 65 MA (right), the landmasses were beginning to resemble their present form. Laurentia eventually gave rise to North America and to parts of Europe and Asia, while Gondwana had split up to form most of the other continents.

HOW TO READ THE MAPS

TIMELINE
At the top of each page is a timeline, divided into periods of 50 MA (millions of years). The small globe marks the point in the Earth's history shown by the maps on that page.

I. MODERN CONTINENTAL OUTLINE
The purple lines represent the modern coasts of continents and islands. They indicate what part of the globe you are looking at, and from what direction (whether looking down on the equator or on one of the poles).

2. ANCIENT CONTINENTAL SEAS
The light blue regions represent areas of the continents covered by shallow seas at the time of the map. Ancient continents were often widely flooded by the sea. The shape of the dry land changed continuously as sea levels rose and fell.

WHOLE WORLD PROJECTION

WHOLE WORLD PROJECTION
A small map for each period shows the whole ancient world in one view, making it easy to see how the face of the Earth has changed.

3. ANCIENT MOUNTAIN RANGE
Mountains are shown as they are on physical maps of the modern world— as raised brown areas. Mountains generally form either as a result of volcanic activity or continental collision. Huge mountain ranges of the distant past have since been eroded away to become gentler, more rounded hills.

4. ANCIENT LAND
The green, brown, and yellow regions indicate ancient dry land. The further back into the past, the less these regions resemble the shapes of modern continents.

5. ARID REGIONS
These areas, shown in yellow, contain evaporites (minerals formed by the evaporation of water from salty shallow seas and lakes).

NORTH AMERICA

EUROPE

ATLANTIC OCEAN

TETHYS OCEAN

AFRICA

SOUTH AMERICA

EARLY TERTIARY TIMES 45 MA

6. COAL-FORMING REGIONS
The darker green areas represent lowland forested or swampy regions where peat and coal were deposited.

8. SUBDUCTION ZONE
Solid curved lines in the oceans mark subduction zones, regions where plate movement is causing seafloor to be pushed down beneath a continental crust or (sometimes) other oceanic crust at a plate boundary. Subduction zones are often associated with earthquakes and volcanic activity.

7. SPREADING OCEAN RIDGE
Mid-ocean spreading ridges, marked on the maps as raised, jagged lines, are regions where new oceanic crust (seafloor) is created. The creation of new seafloor, which is pushed slowly away from a mid-ocean ridge as it is formed, is the main driving force for plate movement.

Vendian Times

Maps of the earth some 620 million years ago, at the beginning of Vendian times and at the end of the long Precambrian era, show a planet with an unfamiliar face. Land fills much of the area now covered by the Pacific Ocean, while ancient seas fill the hemisphere where Europe, Asia, and Africa now lie. Two main continents dominate the globe: the northern one (northern Gondwana) is made up of what is now India, Antarctica, and Australia, while the landmass in the south consists of what is now Africa, the Americas, and parts of Asia. Areas that are tropical in modern times, such as West Africa and parts of South America, were clustered then near the South Pole and were heavily glaciated.

I. PASSIVE MARGINS
The coasts of what are now northwestern Australia (in northern Gondwana), northeastern North America (Laurentia), and northeastern Siberia were all "passive margins," zones forming the edges of crustal plates but without the earthquake activity associated with such regions. Extensive sediments built up on the beds of shallow seas in these locations in Vendian times.

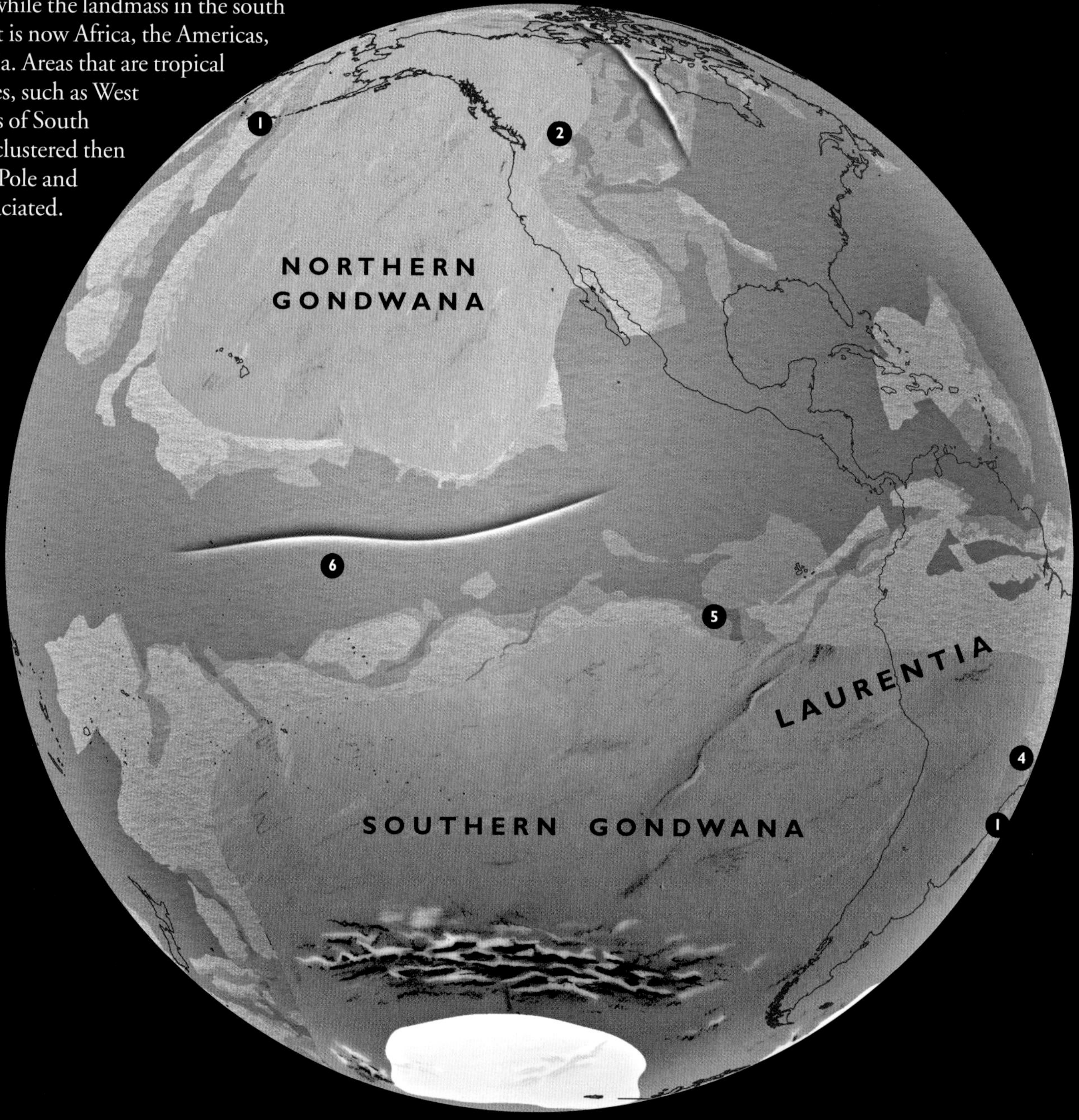

NORTHERN GONDWANA

SOUTHERN GONDWANA

LAURENTIA

6. DISAPPEARING OCEAN
The ocean between the northern and southern parts of what would one day become the supercontinent of Gondwana was rapidly narrowing. About 580 million years ago, the northern coast of southern Gondwana collided with the southern coast of northern Gondwana to form a landmass called Pannotia, which seems to have lasted for only a few million years.

5. WARM NAMIBIAN WATERS
Namibia, now in southwest Africa, lay in warm shallow equatorial waters for a long period during Vendian times. It is now one of the most famous localities in the world for Ediacaran fossil traces (although they are somewhat younger in age, mostly less than 600 million years old, than the times shown on this map).

2. FLINDERS RANGE, SOUTH AUSTRALIA

Australia lay in the northern hemisphere in Vendian times. It contains excellent examples of the sandstone that is typical of the period, originally laid down on a shallow, sandy seafloor swept by tidal currents. Vendian sandstone preserves the best-known fossils of the period, the Ediacarans. These soft-bodied animals were named for the Ediacara Hills in the Flinders Range of South Australia, where they were first found. They thrived in the shallow seas, anchored to the seabed or burrowed into the sand.

WHOLE WORLD PROJECTION

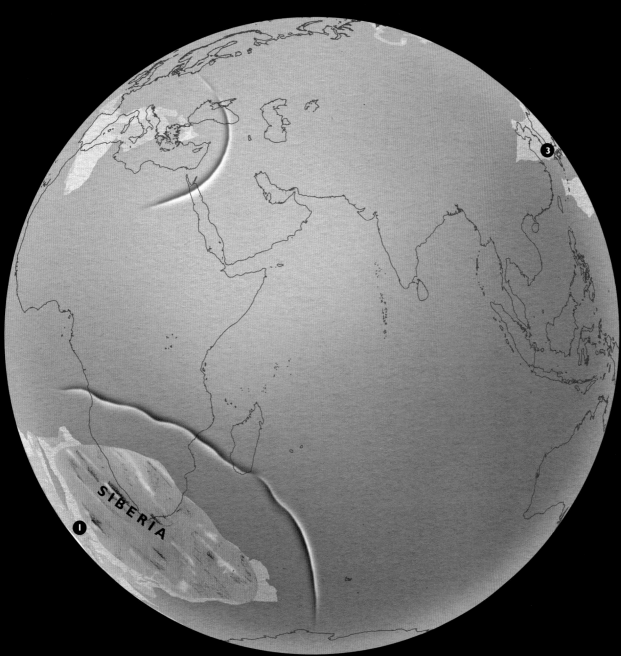

4. NEWFOUNDLAND

The Vendian sandstone rocks of Newfoundland are finer grained than those of Australia. The sediments may have been deposited by successive underwater avalanches called turbidity currents, possibly triggered by submarine earthquakes. Ediacaran fossils are also found here, at locations such as Mistaken Point.

3. CHINESE STRATA

The Nantuo Formation in southern China is made from "tillites," a mixture of mud, sand, large stones, and rock brought together and carried along by ancient glaciers. The presence of tillites in this region shows that it was glaciated in late Vendian times (20 million years after the situation shown in this map, once sea levels had fallen). How much of the world was covered by glaciers is hotly debated. Some specialists theorize that the Earth was almost completely frozen over, while others refute this claim.

Early Cambrian Times

Soon after the start of the Cambrian age, 540 million years ago, the world had already experienced major changes. All the continents of the previous Vendian world had come together briefly to form a supercontinent called Pannotia, which had then broken up. By the early Cambrian times shown in these maps, a remnant of Pannotia, called Gondwana, still stretched almost from pole to pole. It was made up of modern China, India, Australia, Antarctica, Africa, and South America. Two major lands not part of this continent were Laurentia (including most of North America) and Siberia. A growing mid-oceanic ridge between these islands and Gondwana pushed them on a long journey northward.

1. LIMESTONE OF LAURENTIA

Laurentia, including much of North America, part of Newfoundland, Scotland, and Greenland, was surrounded by calm seas, which provided the right environment for limestone to form. This limestone contains fossils of tiny, shelled creatures. Conditions in Siberia also fostered the formation of limestone during this period, but the fossils found there are different from those found in Laurentia, indicating that the two landmasses were widely separated.

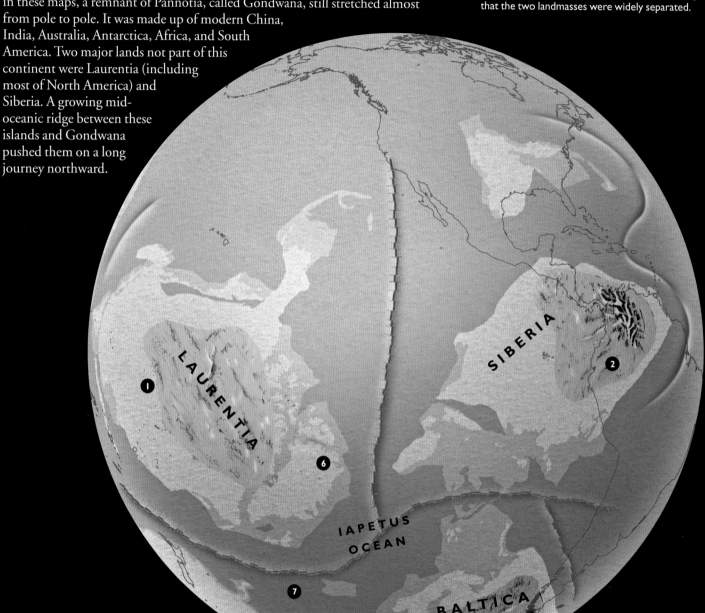

7. IAPETUS OCEAN

In early Cambrian times, a body of water known as the Iapetus Ocean separated Laurentia from Gondwana, Avalonia, and Baltica (which included Scandinavia and eastern Europe). Florida and parts of Central America were on the shores of Gondwana, split off from the rest of North America. East and west Newfoundland also lay on opposite sides of the ocean.

6. TROPICAL GREENLAND

Peary Land, now in the far north of Greenland within the Arctic Circle, lay in much warmer waters during early Cambrian times. Evidence for this comes from limestone and muddy sediments in the region, which contain fossils of arthropods, sponges, brachiopods, and worms, all inhabitants of calm, warm seas.

2. SIBERIAN MOVEMENTS

When rocks form, some of them record the Earth's magnetic field. The record in the rocks of Siberia shows that, during Cambrian times, it moved northward from its previous position near the South Pole. The data also show that the Siberian continental plate was upside-down compared to its present position.

3. NORTH AND SOUTH CHINA

China at this time consisted of two separate and submerged continental masses that lay in warm tropical waters off the coast of the large continent of Gondwana. Both parts of China were slowly moving southward during Cambrian times.

WHOLE WORLD PROJECTION

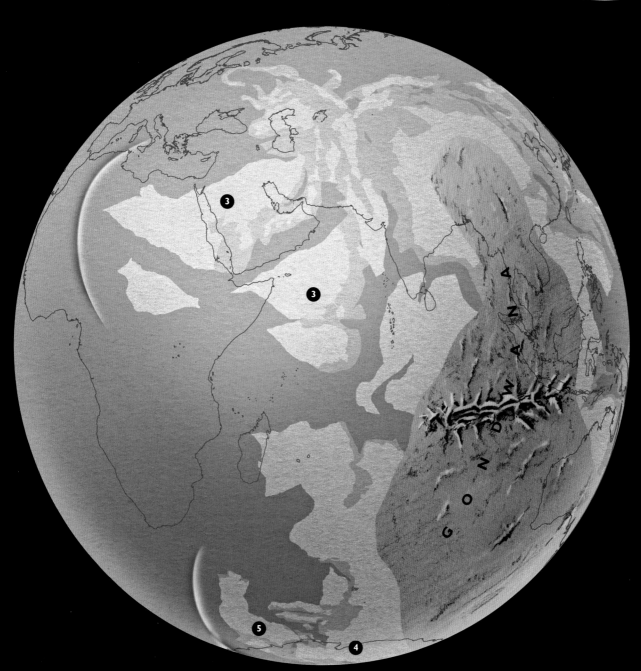

5. CAMBRIAN AVALONIA

Wales was part of Avalonia, a continental fragment off the coast of Gondwana that also carried England, parts of Newfoundland and New England, and Nova Scotia. Cambrian strata were first mapped in Wales, but strata in Newfoundland are now used to define the beginning of the period. The starting point is marked by distinctive trace fossils.

4. NORTH AFRICAN ENIGMA

Analyzing the magnetic field of rocks from Morocco suggests that North Africa lay near the South Pole in early Cambrian times, as shown on this map. Fossil evidence in coral reefs and sandstone, however, suggests that the region was hot during this period and may have lain closer to the equator. This conflict has not been satisfactorily resolved.

LATE CAMBRIAN TIMES

THE EARTH'S POLES, AS SEEN 500 MILLION YEARS AGO, PRESENT A surprising view. Today the northern hemisphere (this page, viewed looking down on the pole) is crowded with land, but half a billion years ago it was almost empty, except for a submerged fragment of modern Russia close to the North Pole. The southern hemisphere contained further surprises. Near the South Pole, located underwater off the coast of Gondwana, were Avalonia (parts of Britain, Ireland, and the eastern American seaboard), Iberia (Portugal and Spain), and Armorica (other fragments of western Europe), about 8,000 miles (13,000 kilometers) away from their present positions.

I. AUSTRALIAN BUILDUP
The area that is now eastern Australia was on the northern coast of the great landmass known as Gondwana. It contained a series of mountain belts formed as the ancient core of the continent collided with thin slivers of continental shelf called "microcontinents" beginning about 500 million years ago.

8. BRITISH COLUMBIA
During these times, Laurentia straddled the equator (the perimeter of the globes on these pages). Rising sea levels flooded more and more of the continent during the Cambrian, so that by the end of the period half of the land was under the sea. In the eastern part of modern British Columbia, underwater mudslides trapped the famous fossils of the Burgess Shale.

7. ALASKAN ACCRETION
Laurentia is the ancient continent that now forms the core of North America. In late Cambrian times, what is now the west coast of North America looked different than it does today. Alaska was just a small peninsula. Slivers of land called terranes collided with the coast of Laurentia south of Alaska. Plate movement then pushed these north until they reached Alaska, which gradually increased in size.

2. ROCK OF AGES

Strata from scattered regions of ancient Avalonia and Armorica show how sea levels changed during Cambrian times: the coarser the grains in a sedimentary rock formed underwater, the closer to shore it formed. The earliest Cambrian rock in the region is coarse sandstone. Later rock is mostly mudstone, made of much smaller particles. This shows that sea levels rose during Cambrian times.

3. NAMING TIME

The Cambrian period is named for the Roman word for Wales, "Cambria," because early mapping of rocks from this period took place in north Wales early in the 19th century. These strata consist of slate, sandstone, and some volcanic rocks, and contain fossils of worms and early shellfish.

WHOLE WORLD PROJECTION

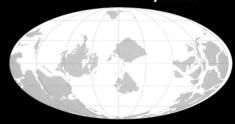

4. MUD DEPOSITS

Piles of sediment, mud, and sand up to 3 miles (5 kilometers) thick were deposited in deep marine basins in north Wales and southeast Ireland. The marine mud of north Wales was later compressed into slate, which is extensively used today as roofing material.

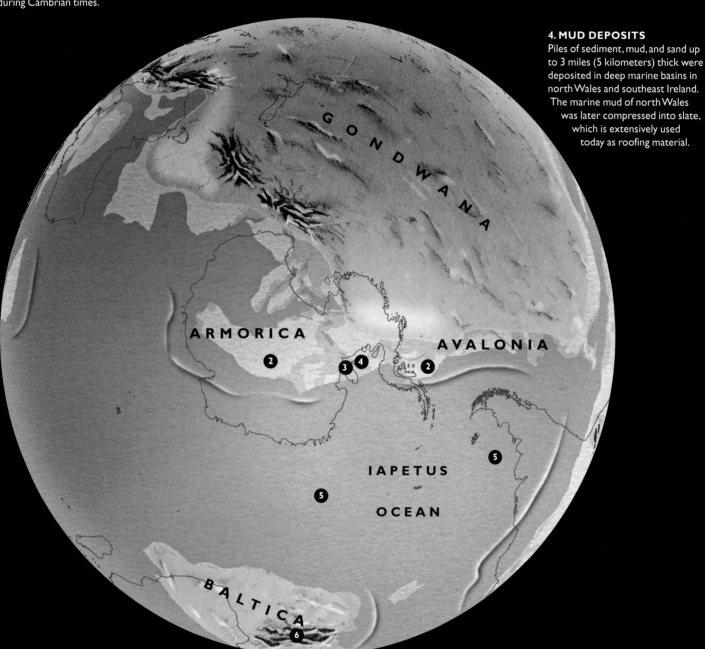

6. BUILDING UP

At the end of the Cambrian period, 495 million years ago, a mountain chain started to appear in Baltica, in the northernmost parts of what is now Scandinavia. The mountains formed as Baltica collided with a series of volcanic islands, the start of a process that later led to the building of the Caledonian Mountains in Scotland and the Appalachian chain in America.

5. OCEAN CROSSING

By late Cambrian times, the Iapetus Ocean was a huge body of water separating Gondwana, Baltica, and Laurentia. Over the next few million years, plate movements detached Avalonia, Armorica, and Iberia from the coast of Gondwana and carried them toward Laurentia, closing Iapetus while at the same time opening up a new sea, the Rheic Ocean.

ORDOVICIAN TIMES

Toward the end of the Ordovician period, 460 million years ago, one ancient sea, the Iapetus Ocean, was beginning to close, while another, the Rheic Ocean, was starting to open. These seas were on either side of thin strips of land close to the South Pole that now form the eastern seaboard of North America. Parts of Gondwana began to break away from the rest of the supercontinent. The remaining parts moved to the south, so that what is now North Africa lay directly over the South Pole. The land areas of many of the continents were growing; episodes of intense volcanic activity added land to the east coast of Australia as well as to parts of Antarctica and South America.

1. NORTHERN ENGLAND

The mountains and hills of the English Lake District are made of rocks that formed about 450 million years ago. They are resistant to erosion and are a mixture of slatelike mudrock, gritty sandstone, and volcanic rocks including lava, ash, and basalt. The ash from erupting volcanoes washed into shallow seas and lakes and settled over time to form rocks. During the last ice age, glaciers carved this bedrock into picturesque hills and wide valleys.

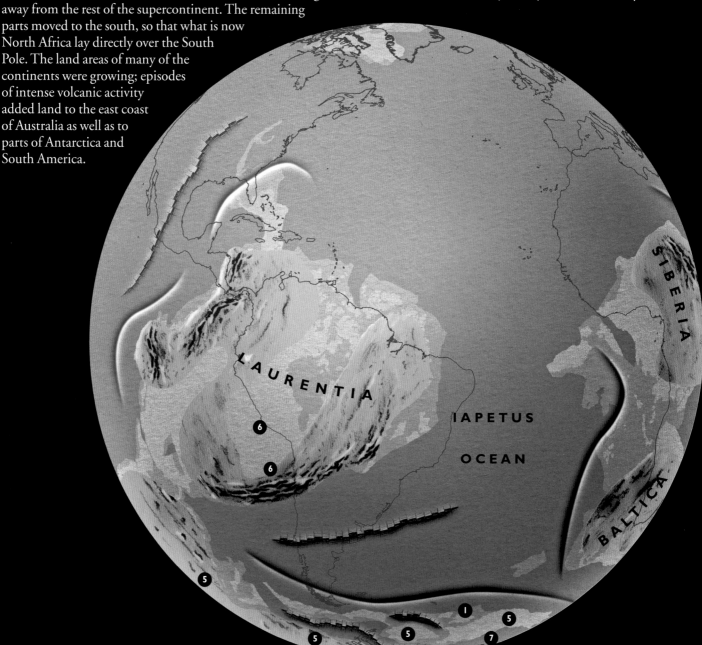

7. AN OCEAN IS BORN

During Ordovician times, Avalonia and Armorica, continental fragments that are now parts of North America and Europe, split away from the ancient supercontinent of Gondwana (which consisted of Africa, South America, Antarctica, Australia, and India). As the fragments moved north, a new ocean appeared behind them, known as the Rheic Ocean.

6. EVIDENCE OF A CATASTROPHE

Near Hagen, Virginia, a layer of volcanic ash dating from the Ordovician period can be seen. The layer stretches all the way from Minnesota and contains 500 times more ash than that created by the eruption of Mount St. Helens in 1980. The huge eruption that produced the ash led to the extinction of many species, with all local echinoderms (ancestors of modern starfish) and cephalopods disappearing.

2. CHINA

At the beginning of the Ordovician period, seas flooded across the several crustal plates that were part of western Gondwana and now make up China. Sediments accumulated to form deposits of limestone, half a mile thick in places. These rocks contain the world's most complete marine fossil record of the period, including corals, trilobites (which resembled king crabs), and nautiloids (relatives of today's squid and octopuses). From time to time, shallow lagoons in the area dried up, leaving behind deposits of minerals such as salt and gypsum.

3. FORGOTTEN SEAS

About 460 million years ago, Australia lay astride the equator. Ordovician sandstone found near Alice Springs in the middle of present-day Australia shows that Australia was partly flooded by shallow seas during Ordovician times. The sediment contains some of the oldest known fish remains.

WHOLE WORLD PROJECTION

4. SOUTH AFRICA

Late Ordovician strata, some 440 million years old, from Clanwilliam in Cape Province, South Africa, are interesting on two counts. They provide evidence for a late Ordovician glaciation and for the body form of the extinct conodonts (eel-like animals with tiny toothlike fossils). The strata contain rocks carrying scratchmarks from glaciers. Above the glacial deposits lies shale that formed in shallow seas. The occasional dropstone (a pebble that has dropped from or through sea-ice) in the shale shows that these waters were sometimes covered by sea-ice or icebergs. The fossil fauna in the shale consists of trilobites and other arthropods, as well as cephalopods (early ancestors of squid), brachiopods (primitive shelled animals), and conodonts. Recent finds show that conodonts had eyes and a notochord (primitive spinal cord).

5. SIGNS OF GLACIATION

Several sites scattered from the Amazon Basin in Brazil, across North Africa and through to Saudi Arabia contain tillites—compacted rock rubble and mud carved out by late Ordovician glaciers. These indicate that part of Gondwana, near the South Pole, was heavily glaciated in Ordovician times. Other signs of glaciation, such as dropstones, are found in many regions, such as France and Spain, which were off the coast of Gondwana at the time.

SILURIAN TIMES

Viewing the earth from an angle almost above the poles (the South Pole on this page, the North Pole opposite), it is clear that 420 million years ago, during the Silurian period, most of the continents lay in the southern hemisphere. The great continent of Gondwana, including modern South America, Africa, Australia, and India, was situated around the South Pole. Avalonia, a continental fragment including much of the eastern seaboard of America, closed up the Iapetus Ocean as it approached Laurentia, which makes up most of modern North America. South of Avalonia, the Rheic Ocean opened up. Greenland and Alaska, lands now near the North Pole, were on the equator during the Silurian period.

I. DEFINING AN AGE

The crossover between the Ordovician and Silurian periods of Earth's prehistory is defined in rock strata at Dob's Linn, Scotland. During Silurian times, the area was at the edge of Baltica, a large island that also took in Scandinavia and parts of Northern Europe. Layers of sandstone and shale formed on the seabed, and the boundary between two of these strata marks the changeover point between earlier Ordovician and later Silurian rocks.

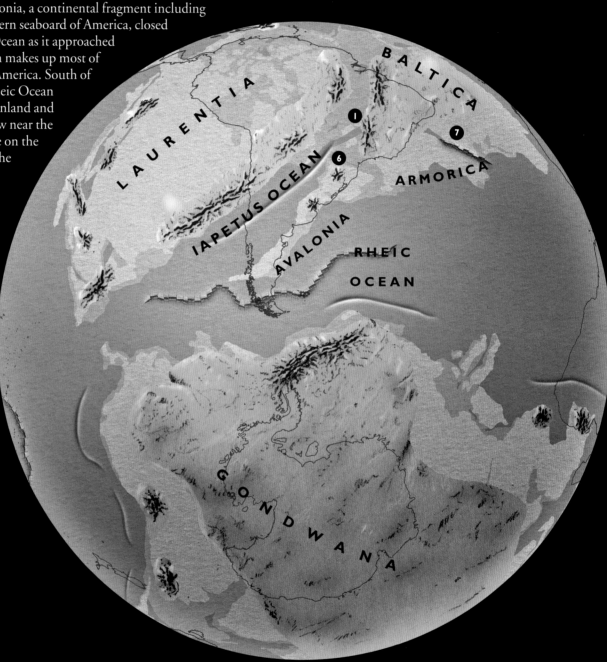

7. CZECH BOUNDARY

Shale and limestone strata at Klonk, near Prague in the Czech Republic, are the youngest Silurian rocks, and mark the transition into the next period of geologic time, the Devonian. The rocks in this region contain many fossils, including several thousand species of shellfish, particularly trilobites.

6. WALES AND SOUTHERN IRELAND

In Silurian times, the continental fragment of Avalonia was a series of islands just off the coast of Laurentia. Rocks in Wales and Ireland—then parts of Avalonia—are characterized by fossils of the first plants to colonize the land. These fossils are found in rocks formed on the bed of a shallow sea, not far from the ancient shorelines where the plants once grew.

2. EASTERN AUSTRALIA

Subduction (the movement of one plate under another) on the eastern margins of Gondwana led to the development of active volcanoes as ocean floor rocks were pushed down toward the Earth's mantle and melted. The melted rock forced its way to the surface, erupting to form volcanoes, which spewed out lava and ash. In eastern Australia, extensive volcanic eruptions occurred from mid-Silurian times into the Devonian.

3. THE FOSSIL CLOCKS OF SOUTH CHINA

Silurian strata in southern China contain many different types of fossils called graptolites. Graptolites were tiny creatures that lived in oceans around the world and evolved quickly into different forms. Successive types of graptolites form evolving and well-defined timelines that can be used as yardsticks to match the Silurian strata of China with graptolitic rocks elsewhere in the world.

WHOLE WORLD PROJECTION

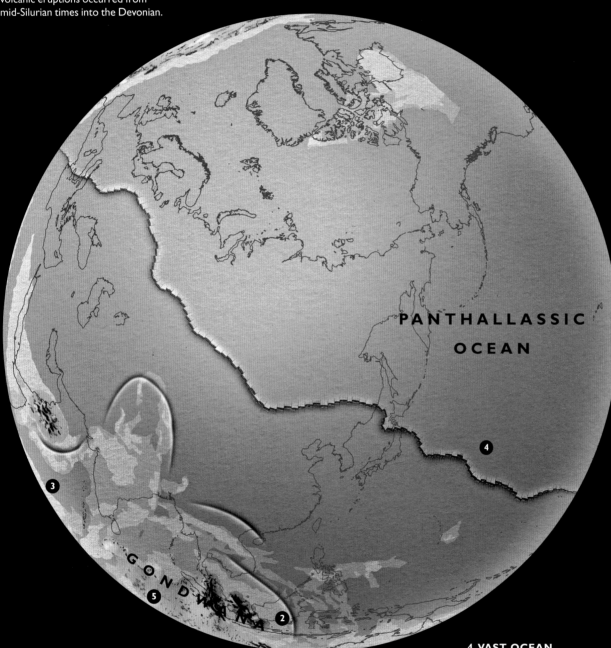

PANTHALLASSIC OCEAN

GONDWANA

5. TRACKS IN THE DUNES

Trace fossils in the late Silurian sandstones of Kalbarri, Western Australia, tell us much about early land environments there. Trace fossils—the solidified tracks and scratches left by small animals as they moved—were left on the sandy riverbeds and sand dunes. They show that there was no vegetation in the region at the time. The creatures that left the tracks fed instead on a thin film of algae and bacteria.

4. VAST OCEAN

The ocean that covered half the globe from Silurian times through to the Mesozoic era is called the Panthallassic Ocean. It was so vast that from some views in space the Earth would have looked as if it were covered by sea. The growth of the Panthallassic Ocean, and movements of the continental plates on which it lay, must have been controlled by ocean floor spreading from a mid-oceanic ridge; however, the exact location of the ridge shown on this map is not known.

DEVONIAN TIMES

A LOOK AT THE EARTH 360 MILLION YEARS AGO SHOWS two massive supercontinents drifting slowly toward each other. In the south is Gondwana, a clustering of the lands that today are called Australia, Antarctica, India, Africa, and South America. The northern supercontinent is Laurentia, which includes the modern lands of North America and northern Europe. The land shape of this continent is not at all familiar, however. Shallow seas flood the area that is the modern American Midwest, while Iberia (modern Spain and Portugal) is an island off Laurentia's south coast.

I. COLLISION ZONE

About 360 million years ago, Baltica (containing modern Scandinavia) collided with Laurentia (modern North America). In the process, great mountain chains were thrown up in Scandinavia. When they first formed, these mountains were many thousands of feet high. The rocks forming the deep roots of the mountains, several miles down, were compressed and heated to form metamorphic rocks such as schists and gneisses. Today, the mountains have been so heavily eroded that these metamorphic rocks are at the surface.

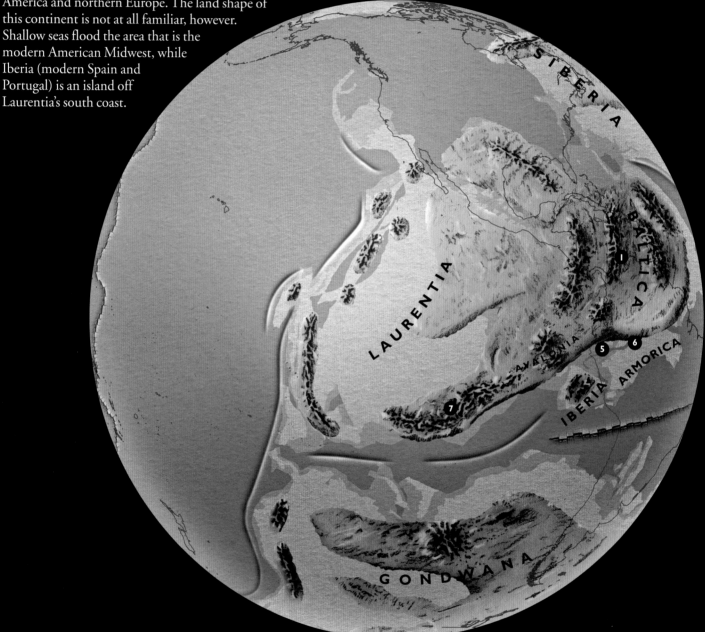

7. AMERICAN MOUNTAINS

About 380 million years ago, an episode of mountain building, or orogeny, took place along the length of the Appalachian mountains in eastern North America. It was called the Acadian orogeny. By late Devonian times, 360 million years ago, rivers had swept eroded rock from these new mountains into deep basins on either side of the range. Over time, these sediments have compacted to form characteristic red rocks.

6. OPENING AND CLOSING SEAS

Armorica (parts of western Europe) collided with Avalonia (England, Wales, and parts of eastern North America) during the Silurian age, but by early Devonian times the lands had again parted. As the gap reopened, a small ocean basin formed. Sediment gradually filled this basin and was compressed to become rock.

2. CHINESE SEAS AND MOUNTAINS

At the beginning of the Devonian period, extensive mountain building took place in China. In most parts of China, which in those times consisted of a series of islands, the process lifted the land above sea level. The northeast and southeast remained covered by shallow seas. They are marked today by Devonian limestone (old, compressed marine sediments), which contain fossils of coral reefs. Elsewhere in China, red sandstones from the Devonian period show that these regions were hot and dry at the time.

3. AUSTRALIA GROWS

During Devonian times, mountain building continued in Australia. The southeast coast of the continent collided with a chain of volcanic islands, forming a chain of mountains. New rivers flowing from these mountains carried sediment to basins in the center of the continent, forming distinctive Devonian rocks.

WHOLE WORLD PROJECTION

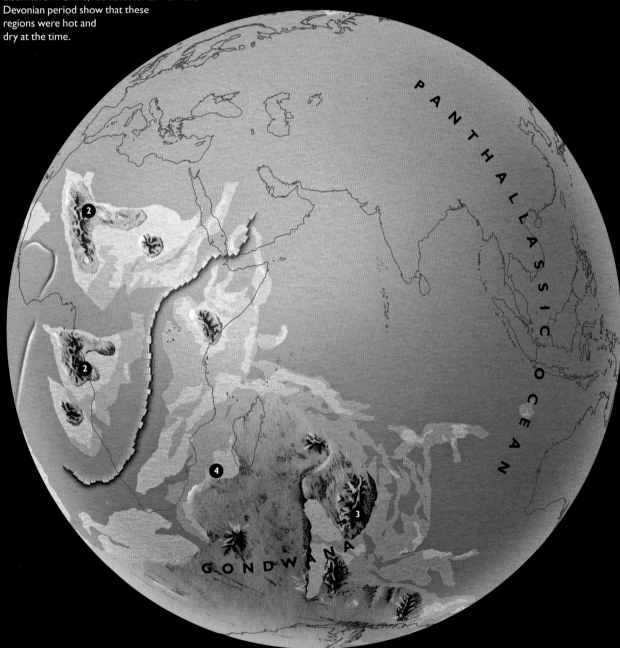

5. NAMING THE DEVONIAN

The Devonian period was named in 1839 for rock strata in the county of Devon in southwest England. The geologists Adam Sedgwick and Roderick Murchison mapped some distinctive layers of rocks found in the county. These rocks, built up from marine sediments, contained fossils different from those found in older Silurian strata and younger Carboniferous strata.

4. WESTERN AUSTRALIAN REEFS

In Devonian times, Australia was part of the southern supercontinent, Gondwana. Parts of Western Australia were covered by shallow seas. Over time, the sea-floor sediments have been compressed to form characteristic reef limestone and mudstone. Fossils of extremely diverse communities of fish and other marine life can be found within these rocks.

CARBONIFEROUS TIMES

THE CARBONIFEROUS PERIOD BEGAN 354 MILLION YEARS AGO. FOR the first time the greatest supercontinent of them all, Pangea, can be discerned. Pangea was forming at this time from the collision of Laurentia (North America and Europe) with the old southern supercontinent of Gondwana. Before the collision, Gondwana had rotated clockwise, so that its eastern part (India, Australia, and Antarctica) moved south while its western part (South America and Africa) moved north. This rotation opened a new ocean, the Tethys Ocean, in the east and closed an old one, the Rheic, in the west. At the same time the ocean between Baltica and Siberia was closing, paving the way for another collision of continents.

I. BUILDING CALIFORNIA

Most of North America existed in prehistoric times as the continent of Laurentia. The west coast, however, was not originally part of the continent. It built up by the collision of strings of volcanic islands, formed in the Panthallassic Ocean, with Laurentia's western edge. These islands were drawn toward the coast as seafloor was pushed into the Earth's interior at a subduction zone. During Carboniferous times, the collision of the eastward-moving Antler volcanic island arc with Laurentia prompted a period of rock formation known as the Antler orogeny. The effects of this impact can still be seen in California and Nevada.

7. FLORIDA JOINS AMERICA

Most of what is now North America was once part of ancient Laurentia. But Florida was originally part of the southern supercontinent, Gondwana. When Gondwana and Laurentia first collided at the end of the Carboniferous period, Florida became joined to the North American continent. It remained there when Gondwana and Laurentia later separated again as the Atlantic Ocean opened.

6. COAL FIELDS

The Joggins coal field in what is now Nova Scotia formed from the remains of a swampy forest that stood in the region during Carboniferous times. Some trunks of giant clubmoss trees from the forest are still preserved in the coal deposits. Similar coal fields lie in what was then a continuous band running from Alabama along the Appalachians and through to Germany.

2. CHINA IN THE CARBONIFEROUS

China in Carboniferous times remained mostly below sea level. Parts of the country were dry land, sometimes inundated by shallow seas. Rocks in the north of the country that date from Carboniferous times are a succession of layers of coal-bearing rocks—formed in swamps on land—and limestone formed from compact sediments that collected on the floor of a shallow sea.

3. AUSTRALIA HEADS SOUTH

In early Carboniferous times, the north of Australia was lapped by seas warm enough for coral reefs to grow. These reefs are visible today as limestone. Dense forests in the eastern part of the continent laid down thin layers of coal. In later Carboniferous times, Gondwana moved south and the climate cooled. Glacial deposits in southeastern Australia are evidence for this movement. In 30 million years Australia moved south by 20 degrees of latitude.

WHOLE WORLD PROJECTION

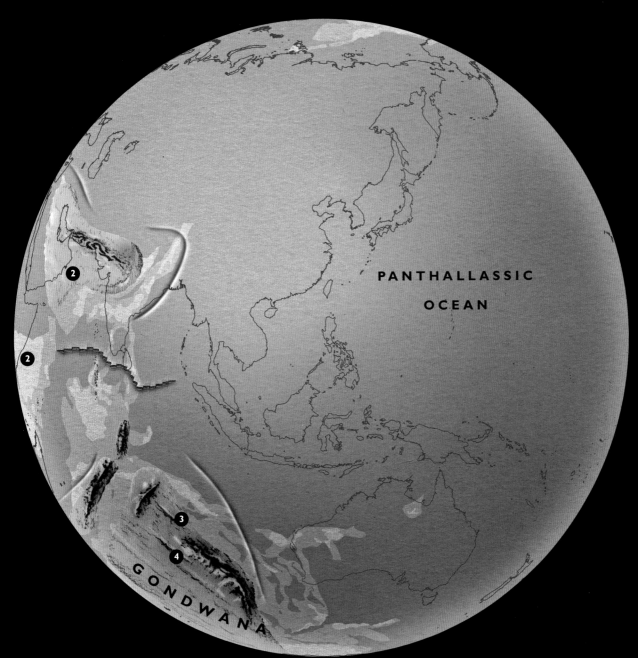

PANTHALLASSIC OCEAN

GONDWANA

5. EUROPE IN COLLISION

The collision of Armorica (now part of western Europe) and Iberia (Portugal and Spain) with the southern coast of Avalonia (England and Wales) resulted in the Variscan orogeny, the building of a chain of mountains that passed from modern Germany through southern Britain to Ireland. A similar collision between Gondwana and Laurentia in late Carboniferous times produced the Allegheny orogeny, an episode of mountain building that added to the Appalachians.

4. GONDWANA ROTATES

From late Devonian times, Gondwana began to rotate in a clockwise direction. This movement must have been caused by a mid-ocean ridge creating new seafloor to the north and pushing eastern Gondwana south. The location of the ridge shown on this map to the north of Gondwana is not certain.

PERMIAN TIMES

THE PERMIAN PERIOD LASTED FROM 290 TO 248 MILLION YEARS ago. During this time the great supercontinent of Pangea was finally assembled when the ancient island continent of Siberia joined up with the rest of the world's major landmasses. The enormous jigsaw of crustal plates, which also included Laurentia, Baltica, and Gondwana, thus stretched almost from pole to pole. The end of the Permian was marked by the biggest mass extinction in the history of life. This was probably caused by a sharp fall in sea levels that killed off much of the life in the shallow shelf seas. Huge lava flows in Siberia would also have speeded up climate change.

I. FORMATION OF THE URALS

With the final closure of the ocean separating Siberia and Baltica, the two landmasses collided. The impact compressed the rocks at the edges of the continents, folding and faulting them to form the Ural mountains (the Permian period was named for the city of Perm in the Urals). Rock strata laid down during the building of the Urals are famous for their fossils of ancient relatives of mammals.

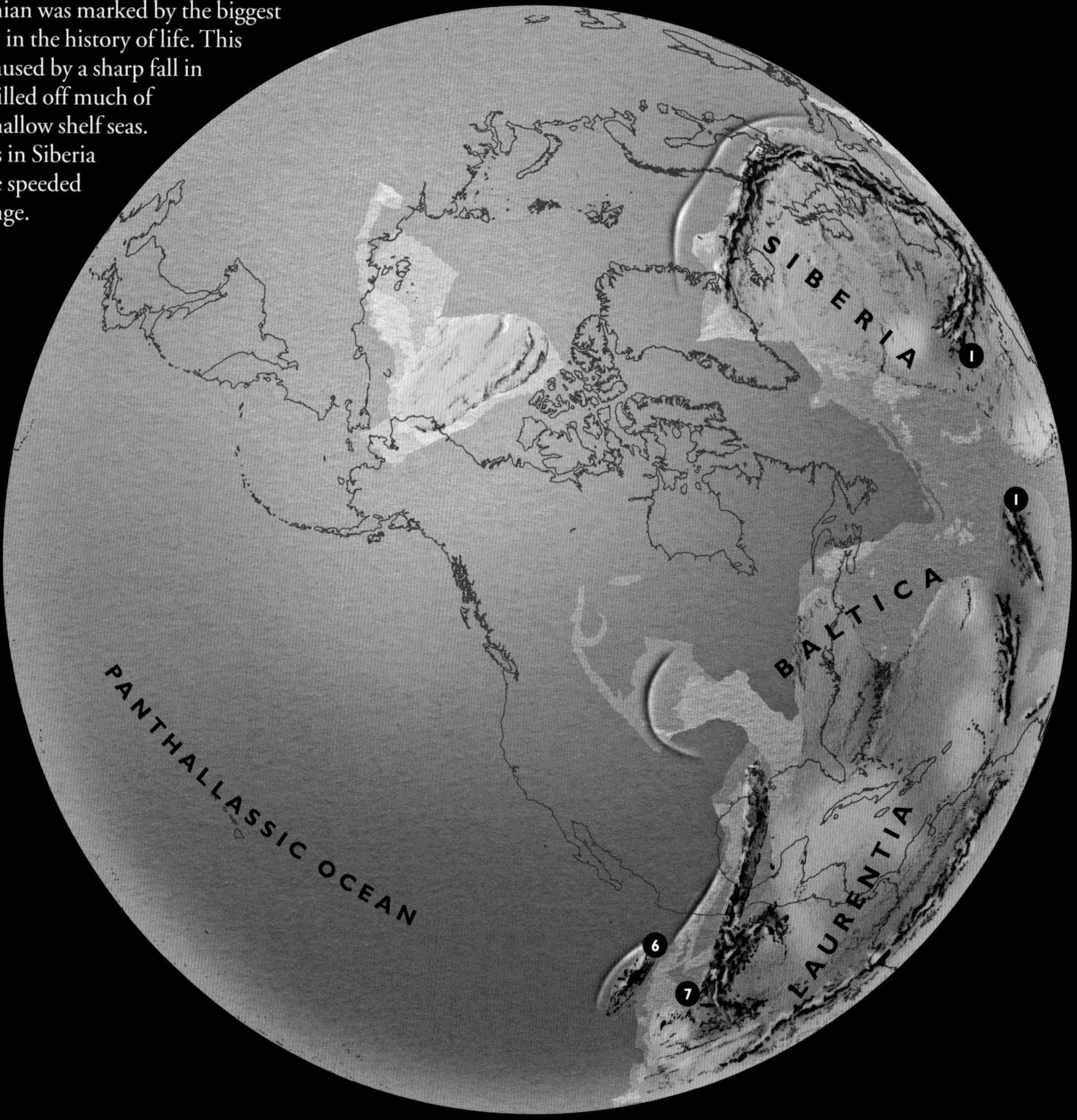

SIBERIA

BALTICA

LAURENTIA

PANTHALLASSIC OCEAN

7. SHALLOW SEAS OF AMERICA

At times during the Permian period, shallow seas covered the interior of Laurentia (the core of modern North America). Reefs that built up in these seas from sponges and algae formed the massive Permian limestone of west Texas. At the end of Permian times, temperatures rose, and many of these shallow seas dried out.

6. WEST COAST BUILD-UP

Fragments of continental crust continued to be added on to the west coasts of North and South America, which during Permian times formed the western parts of Laurentia and Gondwana. Ocean floor was subducted (pushed down) below the edges of these continental landmasses to produce a line of volcanoes.

2. GONDWANA BREAKS UP

Just as the supercontinent of Pangea finished forming, fragments began to break off one of its constituent parts, the southern continent of Gondwana. An active ocean ridge opened up, creating new ocean floor. As a newly created sea widened during Permian times, parts of the edges of Gondwana were pushed away from the mainland. The microcontinents that formed and traveled northward in this way included places such as modern-day Tibet and Malaysia.

3. GLACIATION

There is good geological evidence for an extensive southerly icecap during late Carboniferous and early Permian times before the global warming of the mid-Permian. Glacial deposits have been found in South America, southern Africa, Antarctica, and Australia.

WHOLE WORLD PROJECTION

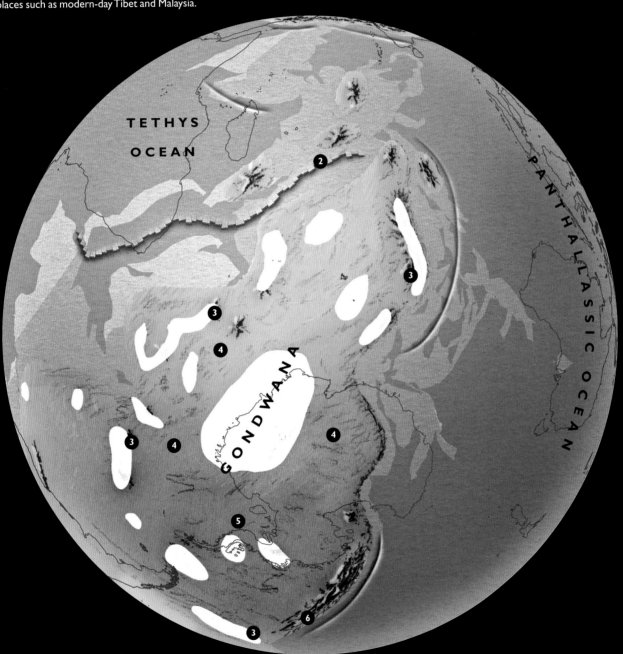

5. SEDIMENTS OF THE KAROO

Huge amounts of sediment built up in the Karoo basin of southern Africa in late Permian times. During this period, the region had a cool climate and was home to a great diversity of animals, including the likely ancestors of mammals. The Karoo basin contained river flood plains crossed by shifting channels that laid down large amounts of sediment. This provided excellent conditions for the preservation of fossils.

4. COOL CLIMATE PLANTS

Permian rock strata in the modern lands that once made up Gondwana contain the remains of plants that are characteristic of cool climates. These prove that the landmasses that are now South America, Africa, India, Antarctica, and Australia were grouped closely together near the South Pole at the time.

TRIASSIC TIMES

TWO VIEWS OF THE EARTH 240 MILLION YEARS AGO SHOW ONE hemisphere dominated by a vast ocean and another by a great supercontinent, Pangea. This great landmass included all of what is now North America, Europe, North Asia, Africa, South America, India, Australia, and Antarctica. During Triassic times, Pangea moved gradually northward. At the end of the Permian period, very low sea levels and climate change coincided with a major extinction event. Since then sea levels had risen again allowing a slow recovery of marine life such as corals; on land, tropical coal-forming forests and swamps diminished as climates got warmer and drier.

I. SEAFLOOR CREATION

In Triassic times, a long mid-ocean ridge is thought to have existed in the Panthallassic Ocean. Ridges of this type continuously create new seafloor, which is then pushed sideways from the ridge. At the same time (and approximately the same rate), existing seafloor is forced into the Earth's mantle at subduction zones near the edges of continents. Although seafloor moves away from ridges at a rate of only 0.4 to 4 inches (1 to 10 centimeters) a year, enough time has elapsed since the Triassic for all new seafloor created during the period to have since been destroyed at subduction zones.

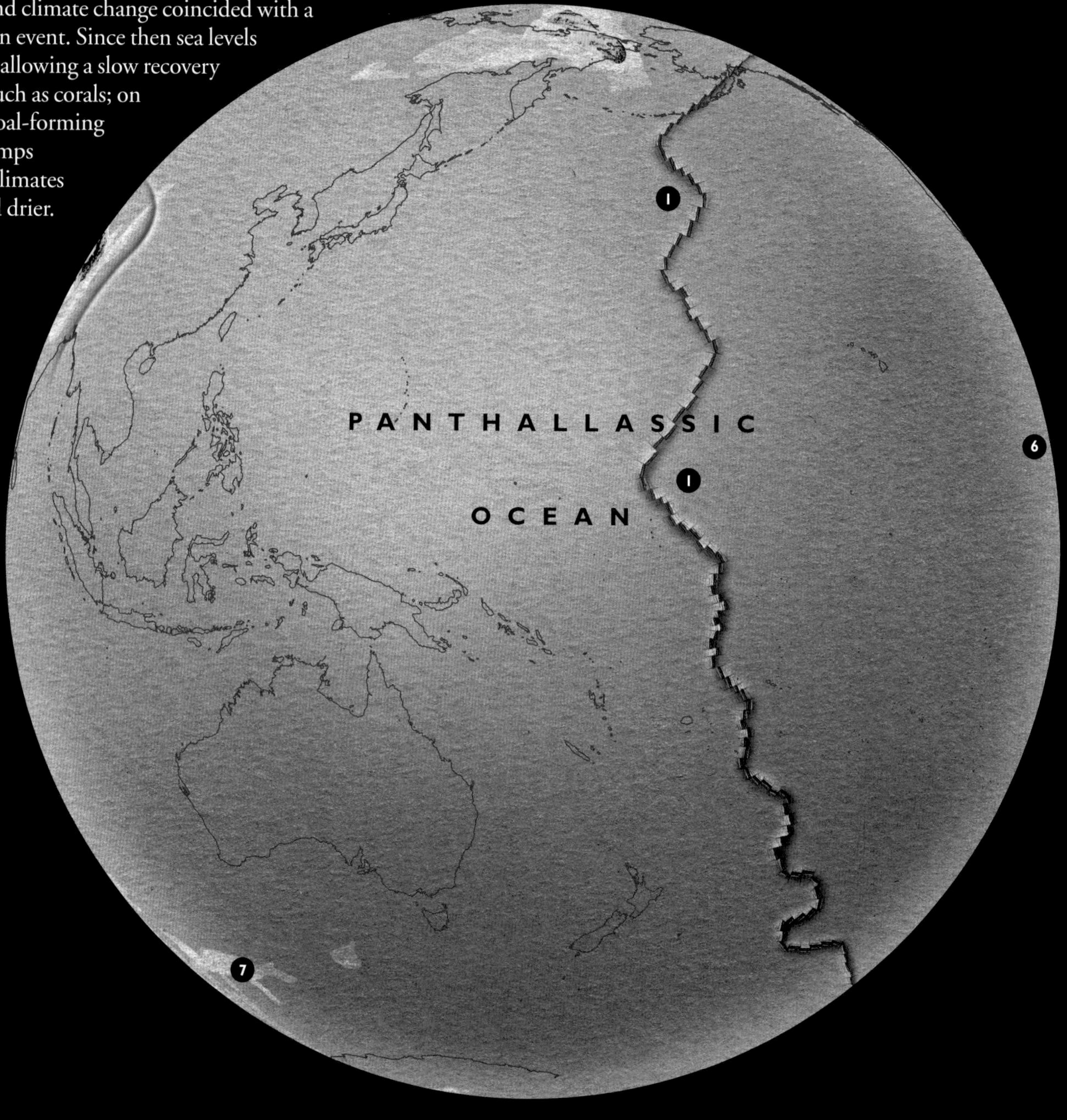

PANTHALLASSIC

OCEAN

7. SEA LEVELS FALL

At this time, sea levels across the globe were high. However, the end of the Triassic was marked by many extinctions among sea creatures, especially corals. The cause may have been climate change and a marked fall in sea levels. Many of the shallow continental seas in which corals and communities of other creatures thrived became exposed.

6. BUILDING THE WEST COAST

On the eastern edges of the Panthallassic Ocean, a sliver of continental crust consisting of marine sediments and material of volcanic origin impacted with western Laurentia to form today's western Nevada and northern California. Inland, semi-arid climates produced reddened terrestrial sediments such as the Chinle Formation in southern Utah.

2. RISE AND SPREAD OF REPTILES

Triassic times saw an enormous development of reptiles on land and in the air and sea. The first ichthyosaurs (swimming reptiles, similar in shape to modern dolphins) evolved in Triassic times and some grew to 13 feet (4 meters) long in shallow seas off the coasts of Laurentia. Fossil records also exist of early dinosaurs in areas as far apart today as New Mexico (at that time southwestern Laurentia), western Europe (eastern Laurentia), and southern Africa (part of Gondwana).

3. SALT MINES

Warm continental climates dried up the shallow seas of Europe to produce salt lakes and evaporites (minerals deposited from the evaporation of seas and lakes). These are still mined in England, Germany, and Poland. The Triassic is named for strata with salt deposits that have been mined for centuries. These deposits have three distinct divisions, hence the term Triassic, or "three-layered."

WHOLE WORLD PROJECTION

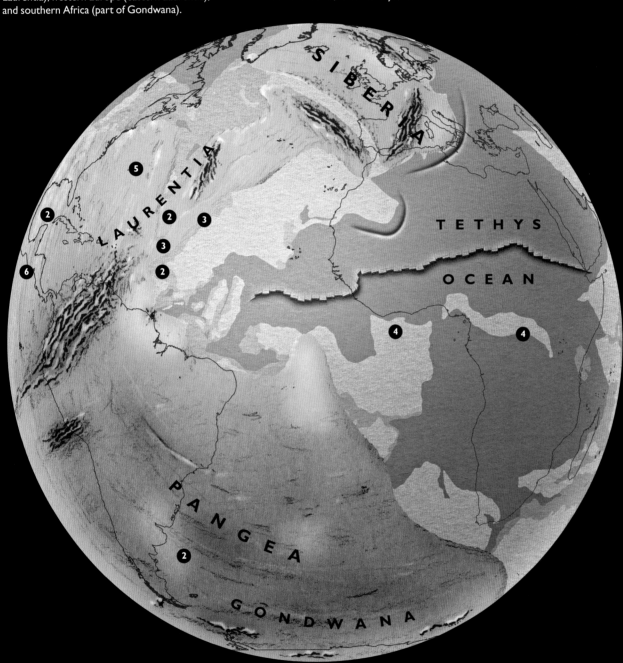

5. IMPACT IN CANADA

A large meteorite smashed into the Earth toward the end of Triassic times, about 209 million years ago, close to the beginning of the Jurassic period. The collision is marked by the Manicouagan impact crater in Quebec, Canada. There is no evidence of any disastrous global effects arising from this impact.

4. GONDWANA BREAKS UP

The edges of Gondwana continued to break up, and crustal fragments such as Tibet, Malaya, and southern China moved northward across the Tethys Ocean. Eventually they collided with Siberia and built up to form Asia. In late Triassic times, southern China collided with northern China, forming a range of mountains (the Qin Ling) that is still spectacular today.

Jurassic Times

Seen from above the poles, the earth 170 million years ago, during the Jurassic period, was a warmer, less varied place than it is today. There were probably no ice caps at the poles for much of the period, and the mild conditions made for much higher sea levels, resulting in a smaller area of dry land but extensive shallow continental seas, which teemed with life. The huge supercontinent of Pangea was splitting up, and familiar modern landmasses such as North America and Eurasia were beginning to appear. Both the South and the North Atlantic Oceans began to open up. At the same time, the ancient Tethys Ocean began to close.

I. WARM POLES
Although no evidence has been found for polar icecaps during the Jurassic period, there was almost certainly winter snow and ice. Dinosaur and plant fossils found in Siberia and Alaska suggest that even lands close to the poles had relatively mild climates. The types of plant fossils, especially, reveal that annual temperatures averaged between 35° and 45°F (2 to 8°C). Even though the world was warm, the short days of the polar winter would still have meant that plant food was scarce for parts of the year.

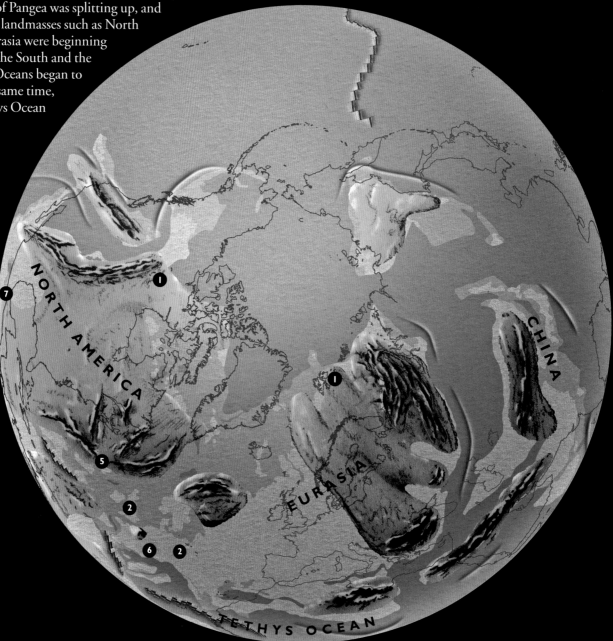

7. THE AMERICAS GO THEIR OWN WAY
During the Jurassic period, the landmasses of North and South America began to split, having previously both been part of Pangea. In the west, rising sea levels resulted in a new sea separating the two continents, while farther east, the Tethys Ocean extended to form the Gulf of Mexico. Marine lifeforms flourished on developing reefs in the shallow seas around the Americas, especially in subtropical regions.

6. NAMING THE JURASSIC
The Jurassic period is named for the limestone hills of the Jura located between France and Switzerland. This limestone formed from the sediment that accumulated in the shallow seas covering the area during that time, and contains an abundance of marine animal fossils, especially ammonites.

2. SHALLOW SEAS OVER EUROPE

Some of the most famous fossils of marine reptiles, such as ichthyosaurs and plesiosaurs, have come from the early Jurassic limestone and shale of England and Germany. The strata were deposited in shallow seas that flooded parts of Europe at this time. The seas formed when a series of rifts in the Earth's crust separated the ancient continent of Laurentia into North America and Eurasia.

3. OPENING THE SOUTH ATLANTIC

During Jurassic times, a plume of hot molten rock rose up from the Earth's mantle. It stretched the crust of the southern supercontinent, Gondwana, in the area of what now comprises southern Africa and eastern South America. This was the prelude to a rift forming and opening up the South Atlantic.

WHOLE WORLD PROJECTION

5. VOLCANIC TURMOIL IN GONDWANA

Massive volcanic eruptions producing huge outpourings of basalt lava occurred in Antarctica, South Africa, and eastern North America at the end of the Jurassic period. The eruptions would have pumped large quantities of smoke and dust into the Earth's atmosphere. The Sun's rays would have been partially blocked, and the global climate would have altered. This could have caused the mass extinction that marked the end of the Jurassic and onset of the Cretaceous periods.

4. PANGEA HEADS NORTH

During Jurassic times, Gondwana moved north. Much of Antarctica, then part of Gondwana, was a considerable distance away from the South Pole. Vegetation flourished on the continent and was sufficiently abundant in places to form thin coal seams. Dinosaur fossils have been discovered in rock layers that are now 2.5 miles (4 kilometers) high in the Antarctic mountains.

EARLY CRETACEOUS TIMES

THE CRETACEOUS PERIOD SPANNED ALMOST 80 MILLION YEARS from 142 to 65 million years ago. During this time the world began to take on a familiar look as lands that had once made up the supercontinent of Pangea pulled apart. The newly formed Atlantic Ocean extended north and southward, separating Africa and Eurasia from the Americas. The continents of Africa, India, Antarctica, and Australia began to move apart about 120 million years ago as new oceans formed between these constituents of ancient Gondwana. Asia still had an unfamiliar form, with lands that are now part of its southern edge, such as Indochina and India, still separate islands.

1. OCEAN CONNECTIONS

The Atlantic Ocean had first begun to open in the Jurassic period. During Cretaceous times, the process continued. The new ocean connected with the western part of the ancient Tethys Ocean (between Eurasia and Gondwana), while at the same time the eastern end of the Tethys Ocean began to close. At the start of the Cretaceous period, land animals could move between the Americas and between Africa and Eurasia. By later Cretaceous times all the connections between these lands had been flooded.

7. THE ATLANTIC CONTINUES TO OPEN

The long process that created the Atlantic Ocean continued through the Cretaceous period. Early Cretaceous flood basalts—rocks created by vast outpourings of lava—are found in rocks in southwest Africa and South America. Similar events occurred at the ocean's northern end, so that by late Cretaceous times 60 million years later, the Atlantic had extended far northward.

6. MAKING OIL IN THE GULF

The shallow shores along the Tethys Ocean supported a flourishing community of sea creatures during the Cretaceous age. In deeper marine basins, vast quantities of decaying planktonic organisms accumulated in muddy sediments. In time these sediments, such as those in the Gulf of Mexico, became black-shale deposits, rich sources of crude oil vital to the modern world.

2. TIBET COLLIDES WITH ASIA

In the early Cretaceous, the land that is now Tibet was made up of separate land fragments, with one of them (at the time shown on this map) still an island. Ocean crust was consumed at a subduction zone to the south of Asia, pulling this island toward an eventual collision with the continent. During the Cretaceous, other fragments of the ancient continent of Gondwana, such as Indochina, also moved northward, continuing the assembly of Asia.

3. CHINA EMERGES FROM THE SEA

During the late Jurassic age and into Cretaceous times, the continental crust of China emerged from the sea. The land that is now the west of modern China became a low-lying region rich in vegetation. It was home to a large variety of dinosaurs, as shown by the many fossils that have been found in the region.

WHOLE WORLD PROJECTION

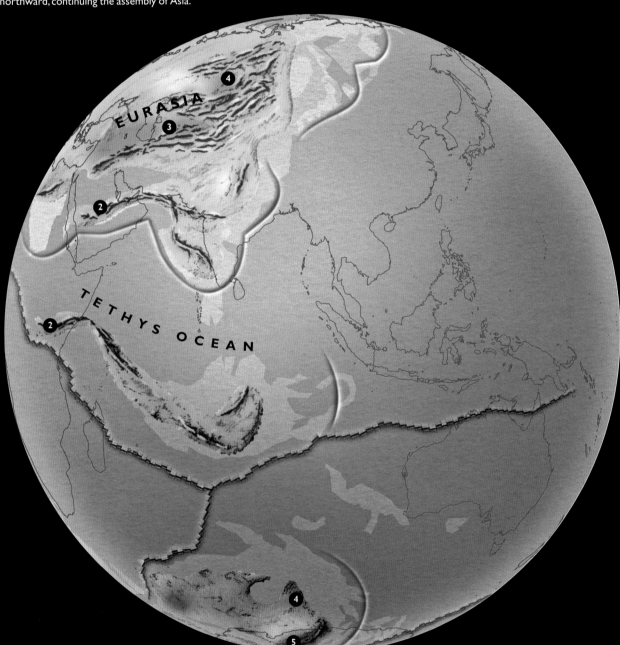

5. COLD EXTREMITIES

Early Cretaceous fossils from Koonwarra, Australia, show signs of fish having died from inadequately oxygenated water. Such conditions occur when a lake is completely covered by a layer of ice. If this was the case, it suggests that despite relatively mild climates farther north, winters in this part of Australia could be extremely cold—a phenomenon that would tally with Australia's position close to the South Pole during the Cretaceous period.

4. WARMER TIMES THAN NOW

Many coal deposits around the world date from the early Cretaceous period. They are found in places that were quite close to the poles at that time, such as Antarctica, New Zealand, northern Australia, Canada, and Siberia. Coal forms from trees and plants that grow in swampy, relatively warm conditions. The coal deposits therefore show that the globe was relatively warm during Cretaceous times.

LATER CRETACEOUS TIMES

B Y AROUND 90 MILLION YEARS AGO, THE DISTRIBUTION OF
the continents was looking more familiar. The maps shown here
depict the Earth as viewed from above the North Pole (this page) and
South Pole (opposite). The Atlantic Ocean separated the New World
of the Americas from the Old World of Europe, Asia, and Africa.
Much of Asia was assembled except for one very important
part of the continental "jigsaw" puzzle—India.
Australia still languished in the deep south,
attached to Antarctica, and India was
still attached to Madagascar.

1. FROM CALIFORNIA TO ALASKA

Subduction (movement of ocean crust down into the
Earth's mantle at a plate boundary) continued on the west
coast of the Americas. A terrane (fragment of continental
crust) collided with the west coast of North America
in the region of Baja California. It was then forced
northward along the western edge of North America.
Some terranes have been moved as much as 1,000 miles
(3,000 kilometers) by such faults, ending up in Alaska.

7. SEAS ACROSS THE MIDWEST

Sea levels were high during mid-Cretaceous
times, and the sea flooded through North
America from the Gulf of Mexico to the Arctic
Ocean. The formation of the mid-American
seaway separated the Rockies in the west from
the plains and mountain ranges in the east.

6. OCEAN CONNECTIONS

The Atlantic was connected to the Pacific at its
western edge by a tropical seaway between the
Americas. At its eastern edge, the Atlantic joined
up with the Tethys Ocean. Thus, South America
was isolated from North America and Africa was
isolated from both Europe and Asia.

2. AUSTRALIA ON ITS OWN

The formation of the Southeast Indian Ridge (a mid-ocean spreading ridge) between Antarctica and Australia began the opening of an ocean between the two continents. Australia was slowly pushed northward as new ocean floor was created and spread on either side of the ridge.

3. MALVINAS MIGRATION

The Falkland Islands are moving between continents. The geology of the islands today clearly shows that they were originally attached to the southwest tip of South Africa but in mid-Cretaceous times were being pulled toward South America. As the South Atlantic and Southern Oceans opened the islands were rotated through 180 degrees.

WHOLE WORLD PROJECTION

5. ISOLATION OF ANTARCTICA

By the middle of the Cretaceous period, the old southern supercontinent of Gondwana had mostly broken up. Three continents—South America, Africa, and India—that were once joined together were now separate, while Australia and Antarctica remained joined only by tenuous land bridges. The break-up of Gondwana had its origin in a series of spreading ridges that gradually encircled Antarctica, pushing the other continents northward.

4. MADAGASCAR BECOMES AN ISLAND

Madagascar was still joined to India, which had separated from Africa. A rising plume of hot molten material in the Earth's mantle under Madagascar began to stretch the crust. Eventually the crust rifted apart and lava poured onto the surface. This rifting began the separation of India from Madagascar.

K-T Times

THE BOUNDARY BETWEEN THE END OF CRETACEOUS TIMES 65 million years ago and the beginning of the Tertiary period is often referred to as the K-T Boundary. It was marked by a catastrophic meteorite impact at Chicxulub in Mexico that is believed to have contributed to the global extinction of some groups of animals and plants. A coincidental outpouring of lava over the west of India, global cooling, and a significant fall in sea levels, which exposed vast areas of continental shelf, may also have played major parts in the extinction of both marine and land species.

1. RIDGES OPEN THE ATLANTIC

The widening Atlantic Ocean put an ever-greater distance between the New World and Old World. The mid-Atlantic ridge extended into the North Atlantic, the opening of which stretched the western edge of the European crust, causing some areas of continental shelf around the British Isles to sink.

7. EVIDENCE OF A TSUNAMI

A sand layer at the K-T Boundary along the Brazos River, Texas, is thought to have been deposited by a giant tsunami that was generated by the Chicxulub impact. The tsunami wave is estimated to have been over half a mile (1 kilometer) high. It tore up sediment from the floor of the Gulf of Mexico before smashing its way inland all around the Caribbean.

6. CHICXULUB METEORITE

A meteorite about 6 miles (10 kilometers) in diameter slammed into Chicxulub in Mexico. The impact threw up a mountainous rim 5 miles (8 kilometers) high. The rim soon collapsed, creating concentric ridges across the landscape that extended over 90 miles (145 kilometers) from the center of impact. Today, the impact crater is hidden beneath younger sediments that are over half a mile (1 kilometer) thick.

2. SIGNS OF A DISASTER

Marine ocean floor sediments, now preserved at Gubbio in Italy, contain a thin layer of clay at the K-T Boundary. The clay is enriched with the rare metallic element iridium and traces of other metals in a ratio that suggests they came from an asteroid or comet. This iridium-enriched layer, found by Walter Alvarez in the late 1970s, was the first evidence that a large meteorite had hit Earth during K-T times.

3. VOLCANISM IN INDIA

A rising current of hot mantle material under western India produced vast outpourings of lava over the Deccan Plateau in India at the end of the Cretaceous. It is likely that associated global climate changes were partly responsible for the major extinctions that mark the K-T Boundary.

WHOLE WORLD PROJECTION

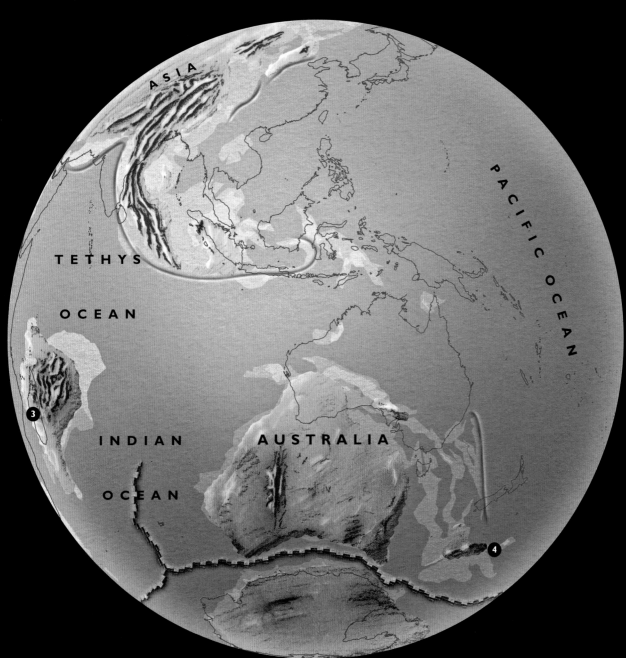

5. EVIDENCE OF GLOBAL COOLING

The rock strata now found on Seymour Island, off the coast of Antarctica, were sediments of a shallow sea in late Cretaceous times. The record of fossils trapped in these rocks shows a gradual reduction in the number of species from a time well before the impact at Chicxulub. Such a steady rate of extinctions over a long period suggests that global cooling was already happening at the end of the Cretaceous, making survival difficult for species that lived in polar regions.

4. NEW ZEALAND ESCAPES

In New Zealand, the record of tiny fossils of marine creatures shows no signs of a mass extinction at the end of the Cretaceous period. In fact, the number of species increased in the region. Possibly, a beneficial change occurred in ocean currents, brought about by the same cooling that doomed animal species in other parts of the globe.

Early Tertiary Times

The end of the cretaceous period also marks the end of the Mesozoic era of geological time and the beginning of the Tertiary era (from the Latin for third). These maps show the world as it appeared 45 million years ago, with the Atlantic Ocean still widening as the connection between Norway and Greenland severed and the Americas moved westward. Africa slowly pushed in a northeastly direction crumpling southern Europe to form the mountain belts of the Pyrenees and Alps. India continued its progress north, crossing the Equator, while Australia separated completely from Antarctica.

1. SEAS RETREAT IN AMERICA

During the previous Cretaceous period, a shallow sea had filled the midwest of North America. A small remnant, known as the Cannonball Sea, survived into the early Tertiary era. The continuing plate movements that were building up the Rocky Mountains stretched and faulted the land exposed by the retreating seas to form lake basins. One of these, Lake Uinta in Wyoming, accumulated layers of sediment, which now form the rocks of the Green River formation, famous for its exquisite fish fossils.

7. ARABIA PARTS FROM AFRICA

The Red Sea began to rift open as the Earth's crust near northeastern Africa domed and stretched. In the late Eocene age (40 million years ago) lava poured out over a vast area of the Ethiopian plateau and a line of volcanoes appeared along the rift valley.

6. SPAIN AND ITALY JOIN EUROPE

The Bay of Biscay opened as Iberia (Spain and Portugal) rotated counterclockwise. It collided with southern France, crumpling the intervening strata to form the mountains of the Pyrenees. Italy moved north toward southern Europe, pushing the Alps upward in the process.

2. VOLCANISM IN THE ATLANTIC

A "plume" of hot magma from the Earth's interior rose in the North Atlantic between Britain and Greenland. It pushed the crust in the region upward, stretching and rifting it, and in the process huge amounts of lava poured out onto the surface to form new landscapes. Signs of these great eruptions can be seen at the Giant's Causeway in Northern Ireland and Fingal's Cave on the island of Staffa, Scotland.

3. HOT SPOT IN THE PACIFIC

A hot spot in the Pacific produced a chain of volcanic islands, known as the Hawaiian-Emperor seamount chain, as the Pacific plate moved over it. The first volcano erupted from the ocean floor 70 million years ago. Plate movement has now carried the volcano to the northern Pacific. About 43 million years ago, there was a change in the Pacific plate's direction of movement, and this is preserved as a "dog-leg" in the line of volcanoes.

WHOLE WORLD PROJECTION

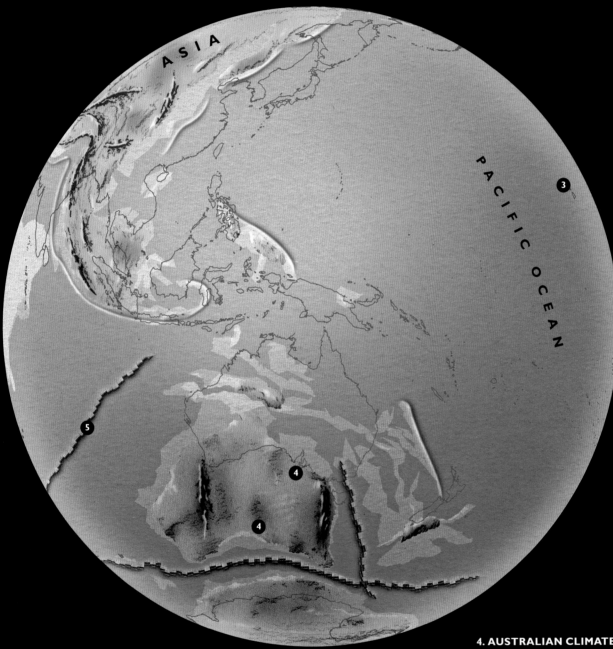

5. RIDGE RAISER

In early Tertiary times, the Ninetyeast Ridge was an active transform fault—a region where two tectonic plates slide past each other. The movement between the Indian and Australian Ocean floor plates that produced the ridge stopped when India eventually collided with Tibet. Today, the ridge is inactive but still rises 2 miles (3 kilometers) from the floor of the Indian Ocean.

4. AUSTRALIAN CLIMATE CHANGES

Rocks in South Australia and Queensland show that during the early Tertiary era, the climate in Australia changed. Around 55 million years ago it was wet and humid, allowing swampy forests to form that later became reserves of brown coal and oil shale. Layers of sediment from 40 million years ago are thinner, indicating a less rich environment. The rocks that they form are sandstonelike, a sign that the region had become much drier.

Mid-Tertiary Times

AS AFRICA APPROACHED EUROPE SOME 20 MILLION YEARS AGO, during Miocene (mid-Tertiary) times, the Tethys Ocean that separated the two continents was squeezed and narrowed. The north-south compression threw up a mountain chain that extended east-west from Turkey through the Balkans. As the ocean floor was pushed down beneath southern Europe, volcanic islands were thrown up as well as mountain belts in the Carpathians and Caucasus (on either side of what is now the Black Sea). Italy, which had been attached to northern Africa as part of Gondwana, was driven into southern Europe, buckling and uplifting the Alps.

I. HAWAII RISES FROM THE WAVES

The volcanic island of Hawaii appeared from the ocean over 5 million years ago. It is the youngest of a chain of volcanic islands that also includes Maui, Oahu, Kauai, and scores of smaller islands that extend for over 3,800 miles (6,100 kilometers) to the northwest. Hawaii rises over 3 miles (5 kilometers) from the ocean floor and a further 13,700 feet (4,170 meters) above sea level, making it the highest mountain on Earth in terms of elevation above base. A new island is currently forming to the southeast of Hawaii, but its summit is still over 3,000 feet (900 meters) below the surface and it is not expected to emerge from the waves for thousands of years.

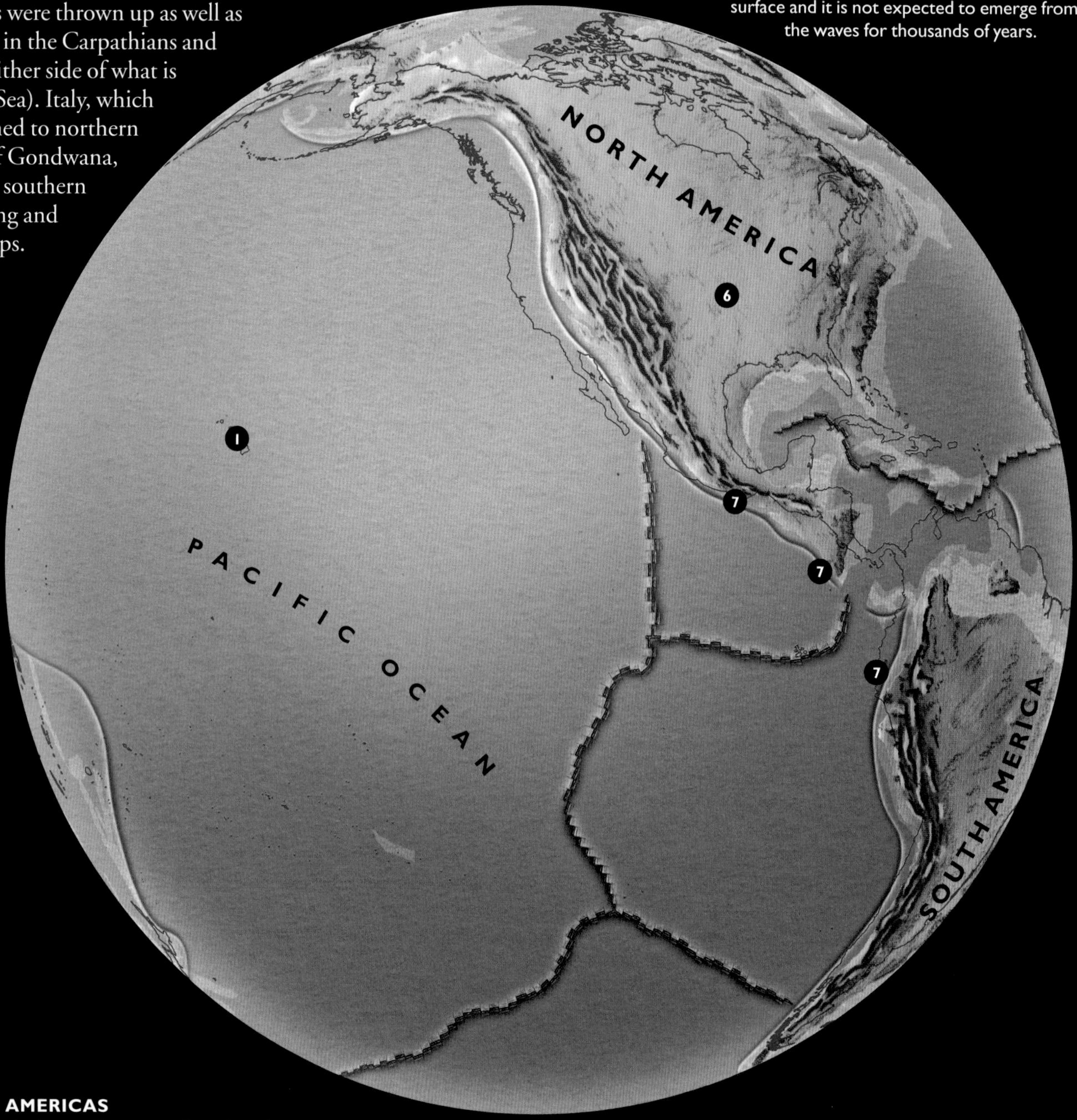

NORTH AMERICA

PACIFIC OCEAN

SOUTH AMERICA

7. LINKING THE AMERICAS

Plate movements pushed ocean floor crust down into the Earth's mantle in the eastern Pacific, resulting in explosive volcanic eruptions and mountain building along the western edge of Central America and northwestern edge of South America. Some 3 million years ago, sea levels fell and the northern Andes were uplifted, allowing a land corridor between North and South America to form. The two continents are still moving relative to one another and will eventually separate again.

6. CLIMATE CHANGE IN AMERICA

In mid-Tertiary times, the uplift of the Sierra Nevada, Cascade, and Rocky Mountains led to a cooler and drier climate in North America, especially to the east of the mountains. Tropical vegetation was displaced southward, and temperate forests and grasslands replaced them. Increased grass cover led to the evolution of grazing mammals, especially horses, which were very diverse at this time in North America.

2. FORMING THE MEDITERRANEAN

The area between North Africa and southern Europe was pushed down to form a long east-west basin to the south of the newly forming mountain belts of the Alps and Carpathians. The basin filled with seawater to form the Mediterranean. This connected with remnants of the Tethys Ocean that persisted in the Black Sea and Caspian Sea.

3. TAIWANESE ROCK

In Tertiary times, the island of Taiwan alternated between being flooded by the sea and being uplifted to form low-lying swampy land. The rock strata preserve several cycles, alternating between marine and terrestrial deposits with coal seams and layers of volcanic ash and lava.

WHOLE WORLD PROJECTION

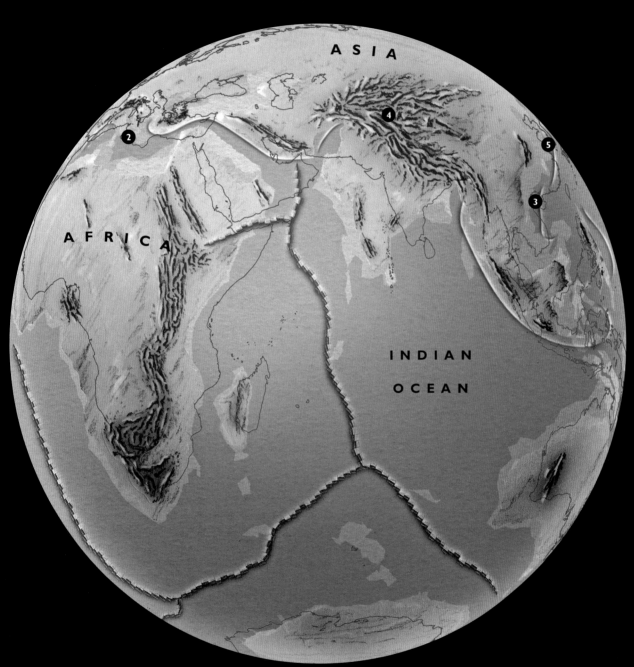

5. JAPAN MOVES EAST

The string of volcanoes forming the Japanese islands was pushed away from the Asian mainland eastward into the Pacific by the opening of the Japan Sea. A deep sea trench off the Pacific coast of the islands marks a subduction zone where ocean floor is being pushed down below the islands. The subduction generates numerous earthquakes in the region. Since their formation, the Japanese islands have moved back and forth from the Asian mainland, pushed and pulled by plate movements.

4. FORMING THE HIMALAYAS

The northward movement of the Indian plate drove India into the southern flank of Asia. The collision crumpled the intervening floor of the Tethys Ocean, pushing it down into the mantle below and up to form the Himalayas. The formation of this great east-west barrier radically changed the regional climate and initiated the seasonal Southeast Asian monsoon.

LATE TERTIARY TIMES

B Y THE END OF THE TERTIARY ERA, 5 MILLION YEARS AGO, THE world appeared almost as it does now, with all of the continents more or less in their present positions. A new island, Iceland, had appeared in the middle of the North Atlantic, where the huge ridge at the center of the ocean rose above the surface. The Earth's crust stretched and split in East Africa, where the Great Rift Valley, Red Sea, and the Gulf of Aden were slowly widening. India's northern drive into Asia continued, pushing up the Himalayas and raising the Tibetan plateau. Australia continued its movement northward to reach the tropics.

I. YELLOWSTONE TRAIL

The hot springs and geysers of the Yellowstone National Park in Wyoming are the most recent sign of volcanic activity that has shaped the American northwest for the last 18 million years. At this time, a hot spot—a rising stream of hot magma—forced its way through the North American crust, pouring out lava to form the "layer-cake" landscapes of the Snake River Plateau in Idaho. Due to movements of the North American plate, the hot spot has burned a track some 50 miles (80 kilometers) wide into Wyoming. In 20 million years' time it will cross the Canadian border.

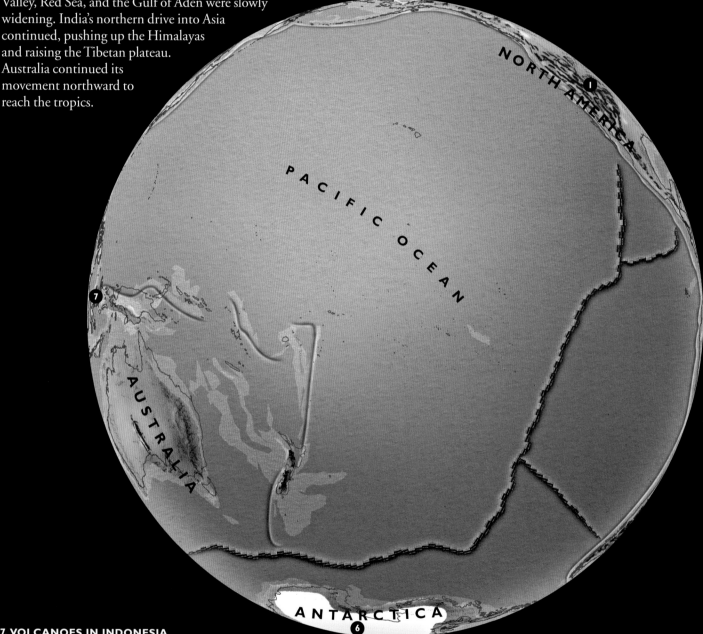

7. VOLCANOES IN INDONESIA

The northward movement of Australia has been a major influence on the development of the Indonesian islands. Over the last 15 million years Australia has moved some 500 miles (800 kilometers) northward. Many volcanic islands have formed near deep ocean trenches to the north, where the oceanic crust is pulled into the Earth's interior. The collision 5 million years ago between the Australian continental plate and Timor resulted in further mountain building.

6. ANTARCTICA FREEZES

By 5 million years ago, Antarctica was completely isolated from the other continents. Plate movement separated South America from Antarctica and allowed the cold circum-Antarctic current to form. The supply of warm water to the region became blocked, so that the land cooled and an icecap formed. The ice caused further cooling because it reflected sunlight so well.

2. THE MEDITERRANEAN DRIES OUT

Less than 7 million years ago, a fall in sea level cut off the Mediterranean Sea from the Atlantic Ocean in the west. During the next 2 million years, the Mediterranean repeatedly reflooded and dried out. Seawater evaporation has left salt deposits over 6,500 feet (2,000 meters) thick in places, while the occasional presence of dry land allowed animals to migrate from Africa into southern Europe. Then, 5 million years ago, a rise in sea level allowed Atlantic waters to flood back into the Mediterranean basin either through the Strait of Gibraltar or across the lowlands of southwest France.

3. ONE STEP UP, ONE STEP DOWN

The Indian plate thrust into the Asian plate at a rate of 2 inches (5 centimeters) a year—nearly 3 miles (5 kilometers) in total after 100,000 years—and pushed up the Himalayas. Although the mountains continued to grow, their total height was kept constant by an increased rate of weathering, which stripped mountain surfaces away.

WHOLE WORLD PROJECTION

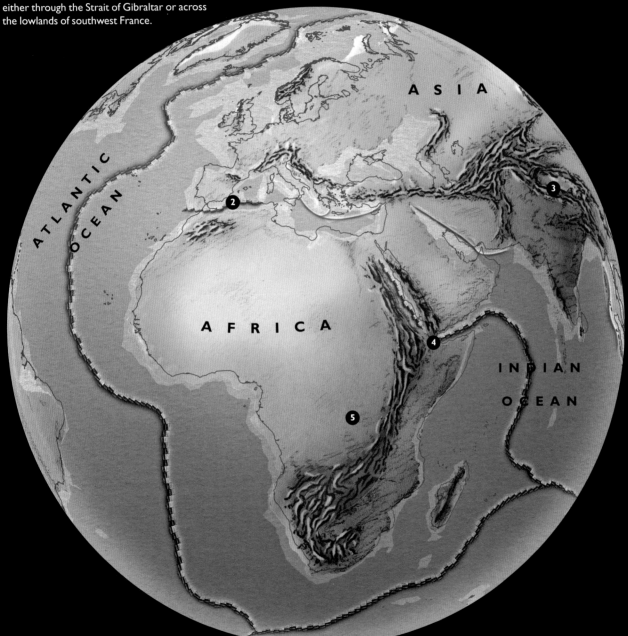

5. AFRICAN CLIMATE CHANGE

The onset of drier and cooler climates 5 million years ago caused important changes in the plant cover of Africa. The woodlands and forests retreated and were broken up into smaller patches with less dense growth. They were replaced by more extensive savanna grasslands. Such changes in vegetation had far-reaching implications for the evolution of African mammals and especially primates. They had to move out of the protection of woodlands into more dangerous open grasslands.

4. RIFTING EAST AFRICA

At the end of the Tertiary era, volcanic rifting was well under way in East Africa. The Red Sea and Great Rift Valley of East Africa are areas of continental crust which then, as now, were breaking apart due to a plume of hot rising magma under Ethiopia that domed and cracked the region. Eventually East Africa will break away from the rest of the continent and move east into the Indian Ocean.

QUATERNARY TIMES

THE MOST SIGNIFICANT GEOLOGICAL FORCE IN RECENT TIMES
has been the climate. The Quaternary period, from 1.8 million
years ago to the present, has been a long ice age. This does not mean
that temperatures have remained constantly colder than average.
Instead, fluctuating global temperatures have promoted the
growth and retreat of polar icecaps, continental ice sheets,
and mountain glaciers, with dramatic effects on
the landscape. In the coldest periods, so
much water was frozen that sea levels
dropped by 330 feet (100 meters),
turning shallow seas into
extensions of the land.

I. NORTH AMERICAN ICECAP
The North American ice sheet covered 5 million
square miles (13 million square kilometers).
Its slow, grinding movement scoured the landscapes
of northern Canada down to the bedrock created
in the Paleozoic and Precambrian eras. The ice and
meltwater ploughed the debris southward, dumping
it in formations around the Great Lakes.

8. GLACIATION IN AUSTRALASIA
The high mountains of Tasmania, New
Zealand, and southeast Australia show signs
of intense glacial sculpting. Features include
U-shaped valleys, cirques (deep semicircular
basins), arêtes (sharp ridges of erosion-
resistant rock), and horns (peaks formed
from the intersection of the walls of three
cirques). These provide clear evidence
of glaciation during the coldest periods
of the last ice age.

7. BERING LAND BRIDGE
With lowered sea levels, Eurasia and America were
interconnected by a long, narrow isthmus of land.
The opening of this "Beringian freeway" enabled land
animals to migrate in both directions. However, the
land bridge also prevented the exchange of marine
organisms between the Arctic and Pacific Oceans.

2. SCANDINAVIA

The icecap over Scandinavia reached depths of 2.5 miles (4 kilometers), compressing the land beneath. Coasts now lifted clear of the sea show that Scandinavia has "rebounded" upward since the ice melted.

3. EURASIAN ICECAP

The interior of the Eurasian landmass had a climate that was too dry to support a large build-up of ice. Icecaps and sheets were restricted to the coasts and mountains of northwest Europe and a strip along the Arctic coast of Siberia. The total volume of ice and snow is estimated to have been about 4 cubic miles (17 cubic kilometers).

WHOLE WORLD PROJECTION

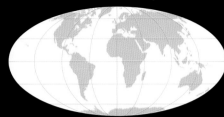

4. MAMMOTH TUNDRA

The vast interior of northern Asia was permanently frozen, but largely free of thick layers of snow and ice. Summer surface melts allowed vegetation to flourish, feeding large migratory herds of mammoth.

6. GLACIATION IN SOUTH AMERICA

Even today, the mountains of the Andes are high enough for glaciers to form on their slopes. At the height of the last ice age, these glaciers carved some of the most spectacular peaks in the world. In southern Chile and Argentina, the glaciers flowed down the mountains to cover much of the southern tip of the continent.

5. LOESS

Fine sand and dust blown from cold, dry plains that fringed areas of permafrost accumulated in parts of Central Europe, Tunisia, Pakistan, Tibet, Central Asia, Patagonia, New Zealand, and the Mississippi valley in America. Called loess, the dust covered the original landscapes and is now shaped into cliffs, which have sometimes been excavated for human dwellings.

Ancient Worlds

OVER THE LAST 4.6 BILLION YEARS,
THE EARTH HAS CHANGED FROM A
COLLECTION OF MOLTEN SPACE DEBRIS
TO THE BLUE OCEAN PLANET THAT WE
KNOW TODAY. THESE CHANGES—THE
APPEARANCE OF WATER AND AN
ATMOSPHERE, THE FIRST STIRRINGS OF
MICROSCOPIC LIFE, THE EVOLUTION OF
A VAST ARRAY OF COMPLEX ANIMALS
AND PLANTS—HAVE LEFT THEIR MARK
ON EARTH, PARTICULARLY IN ROCKS.
OVER THE PAST 200 YEARS, SCIENTISTS
HAVE BEEN ABLE TO RECONSTRUCT
AND MAP THE ANCIENT GEOLOGICAL
AND BIOLOGICAL HISTORY OF OUR
PLANET. THIS CHAPTER EXPLAINS
WHAT WE NOW KNOW.

The Origin of Life

THE EARLY HISTORY OF THE EARTH IS A STORY OF SLOW BUT DRAMATIC CHANGE, AS ITS FIERY SURFACE COOLED AND PRODUCED THE FIRST SIGNS OF MICROSCOPIC LIFE.

During the formation of our Solar System, the Earth was created by the coalescence of large fragments of rock and ice, along with dust and gas. As these pieces collided 4.6 billion years ago, they released enormous amounts of energy, heating the Earth to 9,000° F (5,000° C).

A "meltdown" followed, lasting 100 million years, during which the Earth's interior assumed its present form. Heavy iron and nickel minerals sank to form a hot, dense core 2,200 miles (3,470 kilometers) in radius. Lighter minerals moved to the surface and formed a rocky outer crust about 4.5 billion years ago. Between the core and the crust, a mass of hot rock, 1,800 miles (2,900 kilometers) thick, called the mantle, formed. Heat convecting upward from this hot interior still shapes the Earth's surface, through, for example, volcanoes and earthquakes.

ATLANTIC SMOKER
Hydrothermal vents have been found on the seabed of the Atlantic Ocean, pumping out mineral-rich water. Early bacteria fed on these minerals.

The planets of the Solar System may have been formed by pieces of orbiting dust and rock colliding and joining together.

The Universe began with the "Big Bang" about 12 billion years ago, when an infinitely small volume of matter with an infinitely large density exploded.

GENESIS OF THE EARTH
About 8 billion years separated the "Big Bang" that created the Universe from the emergence of life on Earth. It would take another 3 billion years for more complex organisms to begin to appear.

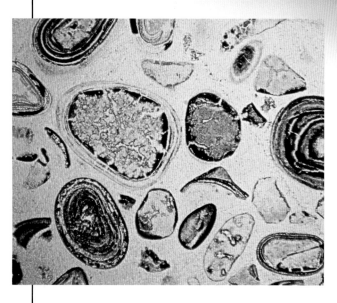

About 6 billion years ago, a spinning disc-shaped cloud of gas and dust collapsed inward to create our Solar System.

GUNFLINT ROCK
The 1.9 billion-year-old, silica-rich flint sedimentary rocks (flints) of western Ontario contain some of the best-preserved Precambrian microfossils in the world. Detailed cross-sections of the rocks reveal the different structures of the bacteria that lived at the time.

LAND, SEA, AND LIFE
Large-scale volcanic eruptions of gas and steam formed the early atmosphere and the first surface water on the Earth, but geologists are still not sure how the land, or continental crust, grew. The lighter silicate rocks of the crust may have risen high enough to form land "islands" about 4 billion years ago. Collisions between these "islands" are believed to have formed the first large landmasses, about a billion years later.

By 4 billion years ago, the crust had cooled sufficiently for microscopic life to appear. How exactly life originated remains one of the most debated questions in science today. In the early

1950s, Stanley Miller of the University of Chicago showed experimentally that it was possible to create amino acids, one of the basic building blocks of life, given a primitive atmosphere, some water, and a few flashes of lightning. More recently, scientists have speculated that the first organic molecules may have originated elsewhere in the Solar System, and have been brought to the Earth's surface by meteorites that bombarded the Earth about 4 billion years ago. Whatever their origins, the first microbes had to survive extreme conditions, with no oxygen and no protection from the Sun's ultraviolet rays.

THE MOON

Rocks brought back from the Moon by the Apollo missions have been dated as 4.5 billion years old, just younger than the Earth. The Moon is probably a chunk of rock knocked out of the Earth following collision with another planet, but it may be an unrelated body captured by the Earth's gravitational pull.

IRON FORMATION

The red color of this 1.8 to 2.5 billion-year-old iron strata in Western Australia is caused by rust. Iron removed oxygen from the early atmosphere to form rust through a process called oxidation.

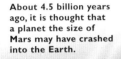

About 4.5 billion years ago, it is thought that a planet the size of Mars may have crashed into the Earth.

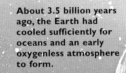

About 3.5 billion years ago, the Earth had cooled sufficiently for oceans and an early oxygenless atmosphere to form.

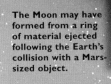

The Moon may have formed from a ring of material ejected following the Earth's collision with a Mars-sized object.

Aquatic Microbes: Life Begins

THE OLDEST KNOWN FOSSIL REMAINS OF life on Earth have been found in sedimentary rocks deposited on the seabed about 3.5 billion years ago. These microscopic organisms existed in an environment devoid of oxygen and subject to extremes of temperature and acidity.

LIVING IN EXTREMES

The discovery, since the 1980s, of modern-day primitive organisms living in a variety of extreme conditions has provided valuable insight into how ancient microscopic organisms survived. The springwaters of Yellowstone National Park in Wyoming are home to "thermophilic" bacteria, which thrive in water as hot as 185°F (85°C). At the other extreme, "psychrophile" bacteria prefer Antarctic sea-ice, where the temperature is about 40°F (5°C). "Alkaliphiles" thrive in alkaline lakes and "acidophiles" in acid waters.

The discovery of hot springs at the bottom of the oceans has also revealed the existence of "chemosynthetic" bacteria, which reproduce their cells without the need for sunlight. These bacteria are single-celled and can tolerate temperatures of over 212°F (100°C). They survive on mineral salts dissolved in the boiling water.

All of these "extremophile" bacteria belong to the most primitive group of organisms known,

the Archaebacteria. The Archaebacteria and Eubacteria (including the blue-green algae) are both groups of primitive organisms with small cells and no cell nucleus. This differentiates them from more complex lifeforms (such as animals and plants), which have large, nucleated cells. The Archaebacteria are able to survive the extremes of boiling water, ice, acids, alkalines, and darkness. Archaebacteria are also "anaerobes," which means that they can survive without oxygen. In the early

LIVING FOSSILS

In warm shallow seas, such as Mexico's Sea of Cortez, structures called stromatolites are being built today exactly as they were by early lifeforms billions of years ago. Sediments and bacteria bind together to form the curious structures.

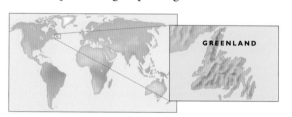

GREENLAND

EARLY SIGNS OF LIFE

By 3.5 billion years ago, primitive algae and bacteria had extensively colonized the margins of shallow, warm seas, growing as mats over the surface of the seabed sediment. When these mats were periodically covered by sediment, the primitive organisms migrated upward toward the light, creating a new mat at a higher level. This process eventually formed distinctive "stromatolitic" mounds. These mounds would have been the only visible sign of life in the bare, volcanic early Precambrian scene.

Volcanic hills

Seabed sediment

Precambrian age, the Earth's atmosphere consisted almost entirely of nitrogen and carbon dioxide, so all lifeforms were anaerobic.

STROMATOLITES

The earliest fossil remains visible to the naked eye are stromatolites, curious laminated structures that grew in the shallow, lime-rich, continental shelf seas. The first stromatolites are over 3 billion years old—they are the most common early Precambrian fossils. The stromatolites were built by photosynthesizing blue-green algae, which initially formed mats on the seabed. As the mats were covered in sediment, the organisms would migrate upward, forming a succession of layers that would build into a laminated mound up to 3 feet (1 meter) high and 1 foot (30 centimeters) wide. Similar mounds are still being built today in warm tropical waters. The mounds are very distinctive and easily preserved as fossils.

OXYGENATING THE ATMOSPHERE

All photosynthesizing bacteria produce oxygen, a by-product of using carbon dioxide, water, and sunlight to replicate their cells. The build-up of atmospheric oxygen did not become significant until about 2.5 billion years ago, when these bacteria became more abundant. Until then, the only significant atmospheric gases were carbon dioxide and nitrogen.

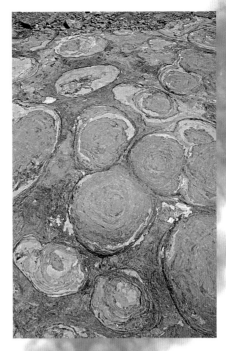

FOSSIL STROMATOLITES
These stromatolite specimens come from Precambrian marine strata located in Glacier National Park, Montana.

CARBON TRACES

Although the earliest body fossils are 3.5 billion years old, rocks dating back another 200 million years may reveal traces of even older organisms. These rocks formed when the Earth was still relatively young and so were subjected to the high temperatures and pressures that existed at the time. Fossils could not survive these processes and none exist beyond the 3.5-billion-year limit. However, some of the chemical components of life can survive high temperatures and pressures. So it is possible to find chemical traces of life, even if bodily remains cannot be recovered.

Very few rocks older than 3.5 billion years are visible at the Earth's surface. One of the few places where they are exposed is at Isua, in west Greenland. These 3.7-billion-year-old rocks contain traces of carbon that are believed to be the remains of microscopic photosynthetic bacteria, called photoautotrophs. They lived in the surface waters and their remains dropped down to the seabed, accumulating in the sediments there.

Today, planktonic organisms similar to the ancient photoautotrophs form the basis for most water-based food chains.

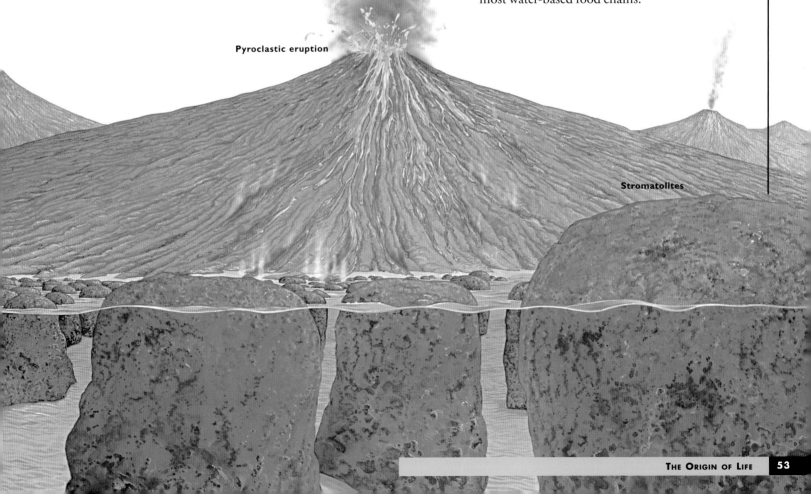

Pyroclastic eruption

Stromatolites

The Vendian Period

FOSSIL EVIDENCE SHOWS THAT MULTICELLED ORGANISMS CAME INTO EXISTENCE IN THE OCEANS OF PRECAMBRIAN TIMES, ONCE REGARDED AS DEVOID OF COMPLEX LIFE.

The Vendian period, which ended 545 million years ago, marked the last section of the Precambrian age. This long period of Earth history was a time of shifting continents and changing atmospheric and ocean chemistry. The continents grew as sedimentary rock accumulated and plates collided and combined. Geologists have good evidence to show that in Vendian times most of the continents were clustered in the southern hemisphere, with northwest Africa situated over the South Pole. Toward the end of the Vendian period the continental plates came together to form a short-lived supercontinent, which has been called Pannotia.

CHANGING CONTINENTS

The Vendian period was once regarded as a geological wasteland of complex and barren rocks, devoid of life. Landscapes did indeed consist of bare rock, rushing rivers, lakes, and vast tracts of sterile rock waste and sediment—an unpromising environment for the development of life. But the oceans were a different matter. Seawater is more protective of life: damaging light rays are filtered out and delicate cell walls are kept moist and supported by the relatively dense water.

That complex life developed and diversified in the Vendian oceans is now clear both from direct fossil evidence and from the diversity of lifeforms found in rocks from the succeeding early Cambrian period, which must have been the result of a long period of evolution in Vendian times.

SOUTH AUSTRALIAN ORGANISM
Spriggina is one of the Ediacaran fossils found in the Flinders Range in South Australia. The Ediacarans were diverse in form and were the first complex organisms to leave a trace in the fossil record, despite having no hard parts. *Spriggina* may have resembled a trilobite.

NORTHERN GONDWANA

LAURENTIA

SOUTHERN GONDWANA

NAMIBIAN SANDS
The Vendian sandstone of Namibia in southwest Africa contains some of the best-preserved Ediacaran fossils in the world. They were originally deposited in shallow-water seas, and their fossils have not been deformed by later folding or metamorphism of the rocks.

THE FIRST LARGE LIFE

Current research suggests that, in fact, most groups of complex multicelled organisms, apart from the higher plants, must have come into existence in the Vendian oceans. Unfortunately, however, the majority of these animals have left no trace in the fossil record.

The great exception is the Ediacarans, the first larger organisms of which traces have been found, fossilized in seafloor sediments. The Ediacarans had no shells or other hard parts, but they were nonetheless preserved as impressions in the

PRECAMBRIAN OIL

Traces of oil and gas around 2 billion years old have recently been discovered in Australia and South Africa. Since oil and gas are created by the decay of minute marine lifeforms, their presence shows that primitive microorganisms must have been much more abundant in the oceans during Precambrian times than had previously been thought. This microbiota formed a vast potential food resource within the ancient seas and oceans. It is surprising that it took so long for bigger multicellular life, capable of consuming this food, to evolve.

SACLIKE ORGANISM
Among the strangest of the Ediacarans from Namibia, these *Pteridinium* are preserved in a three-dimensional form. They may have lived buried in the seabed, their saclike bodies filled with sand. The small coin provides a sense of scale.

SIBERIA

ancient seafloor deposits. They had a wide range of different forms, although many of them looked superficially like jellyfish or worms. The exact place of the Ediacarans in the story of evolution remains a matter of dispute.

LACK OF OXYGEN
The oxygen levels that existed in the Vendian period, 620 million years ago, were still far too low to support life outside water. Primitive forms of bacteria had lived in the oceans from at least 3.8 billion years ago, securing light energy from the Sun and producing oxygen from photosynthesis. But this oxygen was taken up by dissolved iron and deposited as insoluble iron minerals, forming layers of iron-rich sediments, known as "banded iron formations." This oceanic process persisted for nearly a billion years before oxygen levels in the Earth's atmosphere were able to build up to any great extent. By Vendian times, oxygen had risen from 0.2 percent to 17 percent of the atmosphere, close to today's 21 percent level.

EDIACARAN ORGANISM
The flat discs of *Dickinsonia* grew to a length of 2 feet (60 centimeters), making it one of the first "large" creatures. The body is segmented and has a midline symmetry that divides it in two. Its body tissue may have been denser than that of jellyfish or worms.

COMPLEX ORGANISMS EMERGE

THE FIRST CONVINCING FOSSIL EVIDENCE FOR the existence of complex organisms in late Precambrian times was discovered in the 1940s in South Australia. These "Ediacaran" fossils—named for the Ediacaran Hills in the Flinders Range in Australia where they were first found—are small impressions found in sandy sediments. Hundreds of Ediacarans have now been found all over the world, from Siberia to Namibia, in rocks of Vendian age within the late Precambrian era. They appear as variously shaped blobs, ribbed fronds, and ribbons, ranging in length from about 0.4 inches (1 centimeter) to 3.3 feet (1 meter). Entirely soft-bodied, they apparently had no preservable hard parts, such as shells.

PRECAMBRIAN "JELLIES"

Originally, the Ediacarans were identified as the ancestors of the main groups of invertebrates (animals without backbones). They were shoe-horned into more or less familiar groups of many-celled invertebrates, such as jellyfish, worms, and seapens. Now this view of their role in evolution has been questioned. Some experts conclude that the Ediacarans as a whole are an extinct group, a failed evolutionary experiment that was neither plant nor animal. Other paleontologists disagree. They claim that some Ediacarans at least may

have genuinely belonged to various groups of invertebrates that still exist today. The Ediacarans *Charnia* and *Pteridinium* could be ancestors of the living seapen, while others may be ancestors of the arthropods and annelid worms.

EVOLUTIONARY MYSTERY

The mystery of the true nature of the Ediacarans is part of the wider mystery surrounding the timing of the evolution of the first multicelled

FLINDERS RANGE

The Ediacaran Hills in the Flinders Range in South Australia were made famous in the 1940s by the geologist R. C. Sprigg, who discovered a variety of Precambrian fossils, ranging from 0.4 inches (1 centimeter) to 3.3 feet (1 meter) long.

Adelaide •
• Melbourne

THE VENDIAN SEAWORLD

The organisms that lived in the shallow-water seas of Vendian times have puzzled paleontologists for many years. They were all completely soft-bodied—no trace of any hard parts have been found. At first they were thought to be jellyfish and wormlike creatures. But the way their bodies are preserved suggests they were made of tougher material. Some of them seem to have lived within the seabed and had saclike bodies filled with sand. However, some of the plume-shaped forms, such as *Charnia*, are similar to living seapens and sea-anemones.

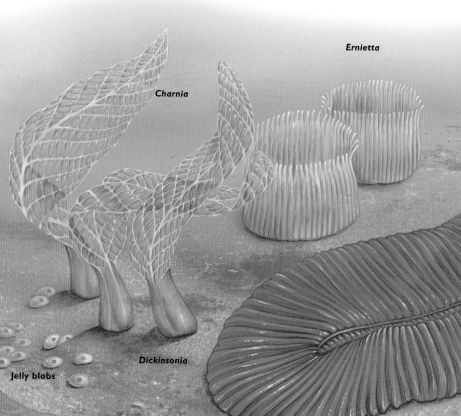

Ernietta

Charnia

Dickinsonia

Jelly blobs

Spriggina

creatures, or metazoans. There is good fossil evidence to suggest that single-celled organisms capable of sexual reproduction have been around for a billion years or more. It is argued that Cambrian fossils, from the period after 545 million years ago, are so diverse that they must have begun evolving back in Precambrian times.

Another recent approach to the mystery employs the so-called "molecular clock." Based on known rates of genetic change and the genetic "distance" between major animal groups still in existence today, this theory estimates the origin of the metazoans and the beginning of the divergence of major groups at between 600 million and a billion years ago.

In 1997, fossil evidence to support this idea was uncovered in southern China. Clusters of tiny balls, less than a twentieth of an inch (a

FOSSIL EMBRYO
Less than one twentieth of an inch (0.1 millimeters) across,
this is the embryo of an unknown early organism. Fossilized
about 570 million years ago, it was discovered in Vendian strata in China.

MAKING EDIACARAN FOSSILS

Generally, soft-bodied creatures tend to be missing from the fossil record because they do not fossilize in sediment. The Ediacaran fossils are especially puzzling because the creatures' body forms are molded and preserved as squashed but essentially three-dimensional impressions in sandstone. Researchers have carried out experiments in which they buried jellyfish in an effort to replicate the

process by which Ediacarans were preserved. These experiments have, however, failed to produce similar traces. This has led many experts to suppose that the bodies of the Ediacarans must have been made of a much tougher material than the bodies of modern jellyfish. Some even suggest that the only organism living today that could be preserved in this way would be a lichen.

tenth of a millimeter) in diameter, were discovered within Precambrian rocks 570 million years old. The balls had a delicate cellular structure that had never before been seen in fossils of such a great age.

The fossils astonishingly turned out to be exquisitely preserved fossil embryos, caught by the processes of fossilization only hours, or even minutes, after fertilization. Just how they were turned to stone remains a mystery. The cellular form of the embryos closely resembles that of early invertebrates, such as metazoan flatworms and arthropods. Their presence in 570-million-year-old strata proves that complex animals must already have been in existence at that time. The fossil remains of adults from similar species have been found only in strata from considerably later geological times.

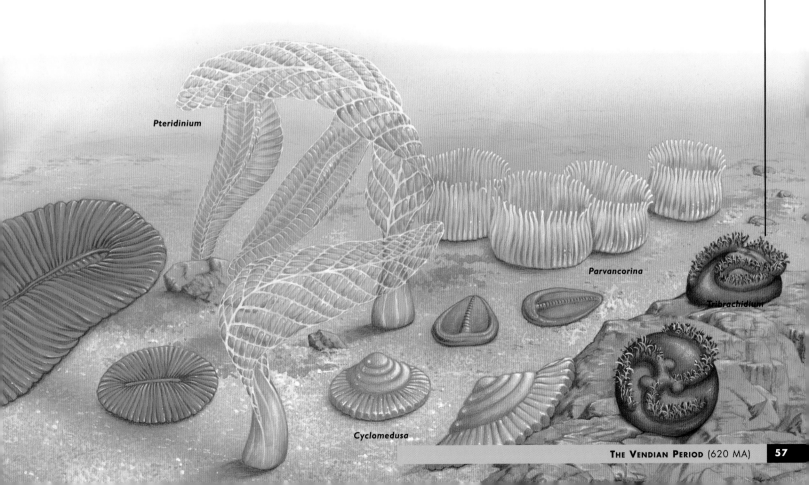

Pteridinium

Parvancorina

Tribrachidium

Cyclomedusa

Cambrian Explosion

EARLY CAMBRIAN TIMES BROUGHT A DEFINING MOMENT IN THE HISTORY OF LIFE ON EARTH—A BURST IN THE EVOLUTION OF MARINE LIFE, WHICH WE KNOW FROM A WEALTH OF FOSSIL SHELLS.

The Cambrian period, beginning 545 million years ago and lasting for around 50 million years, marks the beginning of a major division of geological time, known as the Paleozoic (meaning "ancient life"). The start of the Cambrian age witnessed the rapid growth of an amazing diversity of lifeforms.

After an incredibly long Precambrian phase of early development—lasting over 3 billion years—a range of fossil forms, unknown in earlier rocks, suddenly appeared in sedimentary rocks in the sea. This important evolutionary event coincided with major environmental changes. There was global warming and sea levels steadily rose following the end of the Vendian glaciation. Seas began to flood the old continents, and in shallow equatorial waters, such as those covering much of the Siberian plate, small fossils composed of calcium carbonate were deposited as limestone. The Sauk Transgression, in the late Cambrian period, was such a time when seas flooded large areas of the continents.

NAMING TIME

The Cambrian period was first defined in 1835 by an English professor of geology, Adam Sedgwick. He mapped a series of marine strata in North Wales and showed that they lay above older rocks (called Precambrian) and below younger Silurian strata. He named them after the Latin for Wales—Cambria.

HOLLOW SHELL
The tiny, hollow cap-shaped shells of the lapworthellids have been extracted from early Cambrian strata in Canada. Lapworthellids may have been a kind of snail-like mollusk.

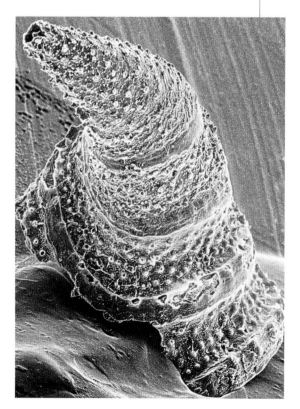

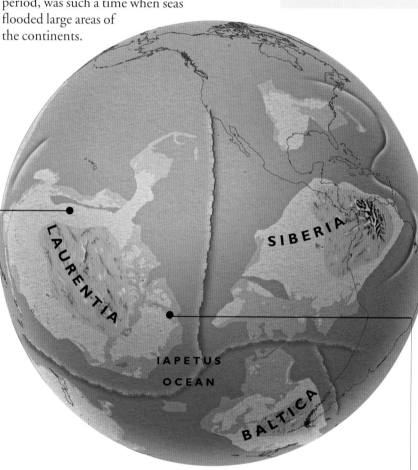

LAURENTIA

SIBERIA

IAPETUS OCEAN

BALTICA

ODD BODY
Halkiera (right), a fossil from early Cambrian strata in Greenland, has a very strange anatomy. The flat, wormlike segmented body, with a brachiopod-like shell at either end, is covered in scales. The mixture of body structures may indicate ancestry to a number of different animal groups.

EVIDENCE OF LIFE

The fossil record shows that, time and again, groups of organisms have evolved and diversified only to become extinct and be replaced by other organisms. The start of the Cambrian period witnessed such a phase of origination and diversification. Evidence of animal activity found in seabed sediment (called trace fossils) show that increasingly complex animals were evolving. Traces include scratch marks of animals with hardened skins (exoskeletons), which were probably the first arthropods—invertebrates with jointed limbs and segmented bodies. Further

LIMPET OR BURROWER
Mobergella, a tiny cap-shaped shell from Sweden, is one of the puzzling small shelly fossils found in earliest Cambrian strata worldwide. The paired indentations are thought to be the sites of muscle attachment for a limpetlike animal.

evidence comes from the 40 different kinds of shelled creatures, no bigger than a millimeter, which have been discovered in marine limestone deposited on top of Precambrian rocks.

Many of these fossils—usually known simply as small shelly fossils—are thought to represent primitive mollusks at an early evolutionary stage. These fossils are mostly simple cones, similar in appearance to today's limpet shells, except that some of them have a curious snorkel-like tube protruding from the side of the cone. It is thought that this tube might represent an early attempt to separate inhalant currents, which bring in water

needed for respiration and sometimes filter feeding, from exhalant currents, which are used for passing waste products and reproductive cells out into the sea. Along with these small shelly fossils are slightly bigger conical fossils with porous walls, known as archaeocyathans, which are probably related to the sponges.

These fossils represent the first wave of the Cambrian explosion. Although they eventually declined, to be replaced by other animals, they were widely distributed, with sequences of marine strata around the world revealing comparable remains of these early sea-dwelling creatures.

TINY FOSSIL SPINE
This millimeter-sized fossil, *Zhijinites*, was removed chemically from the earliest Cambrian strata found in Sichuan province, China. It was probably one of a number of protective spines embedded in the skin of a larger, and as yet unknown, marine animal.

EARLY CAMBRIAN MARINE LIFE

THE FOSSILS OF EARLY CAMBRIAN STRATA record a curious submarine world, inhabited by minuscule creatures. Organisms had become significantly smaller compared to the earlier Vendian fauna, which had grown up to 3 feet (1 meter) in length. By comparison, the largest organisms of early Cambrian times were small cone-shaped creatures called archaeocyathans, only a few inches high. These animals formed widespread reeflike structures in the shallow tropical waters where they lived. The surrounding seafloor sediment was ploughed by smaller snail-like animals, covered by tiny conical shells. Small worms also lived in the sediment in burrows a few inches deep. Visible life did not exist more than 3 inches (7.5 centimeters) above the seabed.

FIRST SHELLS

Shells were an innovation of early Cambrian times. The fossils that mark the boundary between Precambrian and Cambrian strata are trace fossils—the preserved forms of tracks, worm casts, and burrows. However, in strata not far above this boundary, the first fossil shells appear. They fall into two clearly distinct groups: the shells of the archaeocyathans, which were porous cones, and the shells of the so-called "small shelly fossils," a variety of solid-walled cone shapes only 0.2 inches

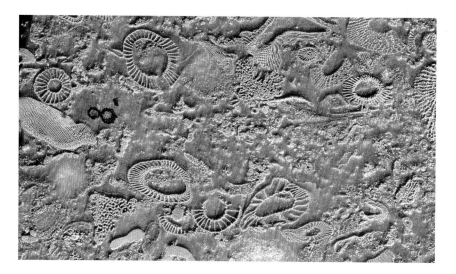

(5 millimeters) in size. In addition, a variety of fossilized spines, studs, and scalelike plates appear, which must originally have been embedded in the skins of different small creatures.

Hard spines, scales, and shells are all familiar defensive devices, suggesting a need for protection. Their appearance in the strata implies that life at this time had suddenly become much more dangerous than in previous ages. If this is true, then a revolution had taken place in the relationships between the organisms of the time. On a miniature scale, a global arms race had begun.

EARLY SHELLED CREATURES

Archaeocyathans were among the earliest fauna with hard parts, producing inner and outer calcareous walls, perforated and porous like a sponge. This double-walled structure can be clearly seen in a cross-section of the fossilized remains of a group of archaeocyathans (above).

SIBERIAN STEPPE

A SMALL WORLD UNDER THE SEA

Tiny mineralized fossil shells and plates from earliest Cambrian sediments show that seabed micro-communities thrived. They included many different kinds of animals that lived on, and perhaps in, the top layer of sediment. Some of these animals belonged to known groups such as the mollusks (*Yochelcionella, Latouchella, Hyolithellus*), brachiopods with bivalved shells, and spongelike archaeocyathans. But others are hard to categorize, such as *Microdictyon*, a soft-bodied arthropod with curious plates embedded in its skin, and *Tommotia*, a strange-shaped mollusk.

Hyolithellus

Yochelcionella

Latouchella

Brachiopods

CONTRASTING FUNCTIONS

The shells of the archaeocyathans and the shells of those animals represented by the small shelly fossils had quite different functions. Archaeocyathans primarily used theirs to anchor themselves to the seabed. From here they would grow upward, as sponges and corals do today. They almost certainly also used their shells as feeding devices. The porous walls of the shell would have filtered out microscopic food from the surrounding seawater. Providing protection against predators was probably a less important function.

By contrast, the tiny shells of the small shelly fossils were probably primarily a protective device. The inhabitants of these small shells lived on the seabed and fed by grazing on organic material from the surface of the sediment. There may have been some risk associated with feeding, however. Their exposed fleshy bodies may have made them easy targets for predators swimming in the water above.

Although the archaeocyathans quickly spread worldwide, they did not last for long by geological standards—only some 35 million years—and by late Cambrian times, they were extinct. The animals that lived in the small shells, however, are thought to be related to today's mollusks.

ARTHROPOD ARMOR
Named for their three-lobed shell, trilobites first appeared around 545 million years ago. Trilobites are among the earliest known arthropods, and account for a third of all fossils found in Cambrian rocks. They were some of the first animals to develop an external skeleton.

The "Lilliputian" early-Cambrian seaworld was short-lived. With the rapid formation of shells and other external hard structures, the organisms of that period evolved a great deal in a relatively short time. It was not, however, enough to guarantee their survival. By the end of the early Cambrian period (520 million years ago) an extinction event had wiped many of them out and another wave of diversification was underway.

SHELL THEORIES

Why did early Cambrian organisms evolve shells? The obvious answer is that they needed protection. But it has been pointed out that there were no known predators armed with teeth at this time—so what exactly were these tiny organisms protecting themselves against? One possibility is that predators used other means of attack, such as stinging cells, which left no trace in the fossil record. But it is possible that the shells were not for protection at all. They may have been energy stores, a response to chemical changes in seawater or an anchor for soft body parts.

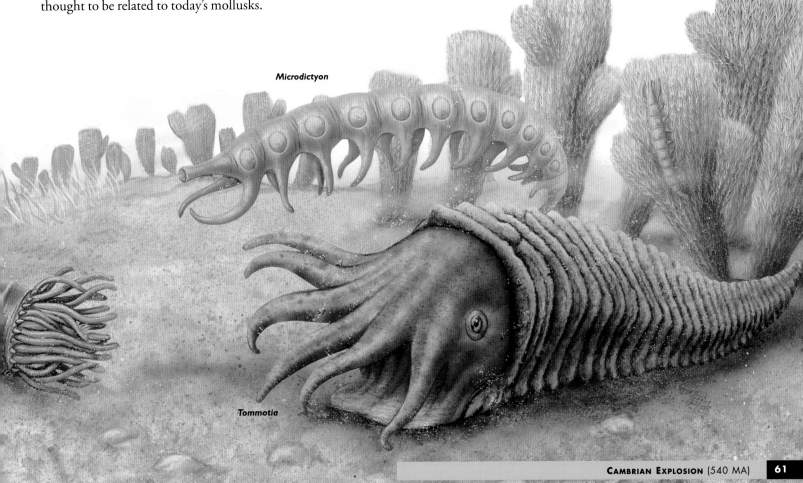

Microdictyon

Archaeocyathans

Tommotia

Late Cambrian Period

THIS PERIOD WAS MARKED BY THE CONTINUING SUCCESS OF ARTHROPODS, SUCH AS THE TRILOBITES, AND THE EMERGENCE OF A POSSIBLE ANCESTOR OF THE VERTEBRATES.

As the world emerged from the "icehouse" state of the glaciated late Precambrian era, the supercontinent of Pannotia, made up of the southern continent of Gondwana, Laurentia (North America), Baltica (Eurasia), Siberia (Asia), and Avalonia (western Europe), continued to break up, creating the Iapetus Ocean, the forerunner of today's Atlantic. Climates warmed to well above today's average temperatures and became humid. The general rise in sea level, which had started at the beginning of the Cambrian age, continued, and lasted into late Cambrian times. By then over half of the North American continent was flooded by shallow seas.

EXTINCTION EVENTS

These warm, light-filled waters were an ideal environment for life to expand and diversify, but progress was not smooth. There were two large-scale extinction events, one at the end of the Precambrian age,

and a more drastic one at the beginning of mid-Cambrian times, some 530 million years ago, when up to 70 percent of species disappeared.

Although creatures such as the numerous cone-shaped archeocyathans became extinct, other more

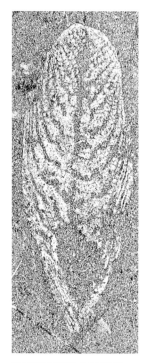

LEAF-SHAPED ANIMALS
This 8-inch (20-centimeter) *Thaumaptilon* fossil, from the Burgess Shale, is very similar to some Vendian leaf-shaped Ediacarans, such as *Charnia*. Some scientists argue that the two are related. It may also be a 560-million-year-old ancestor of the living seapens, which are colonial animals related to the corals.

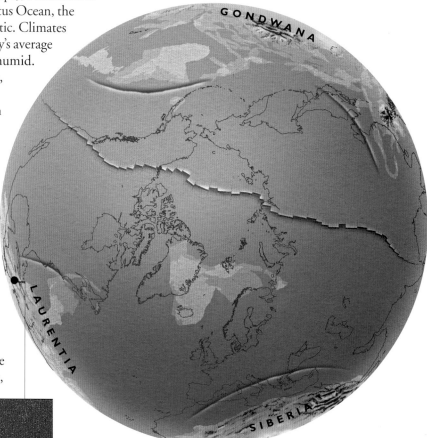

ARMORED SLUG
Scaly armor-plating covers this sluglike creature, *Wiwaxia*, 1.5 inches (4 centimeters) long, from the Burgess Shale, Canada. The scales are hollow and covered with a lattice of intersecting ribs. They may have been iridescent, flashing color signals to attract mates.

MASS EXTINCTION

The mass extinction event that occurred halfway through the Cambrian period seems to have been caused by fluctuating sea levels. As sea levels rose from the low levels of the late Precambrian age, marine animals colonized the expanding shelf seas. Mid-Cambrian sea levels fell again, destroying the shallow-water environments and wiping out large numbers of marine species.

successful and aggressive predatory creatures had evolved by mid-Cambrian times, such as *Anomalocaris* and *Laggania*, which had actively biting mouths. Other carnivorous predators were mostly worms, which swallowed their prey whole.

Arthropods, including the trilobites, were the most common marine organisms of the period, and continued to develop and thrive. Many had increasingly armored bodies, often covered in spines and chainmail-like "sclerites," for defending themselves against predators. Eventually the arthropods covered themselves in hard shells, constructed from the carbonates and phosphates present in the seawater.

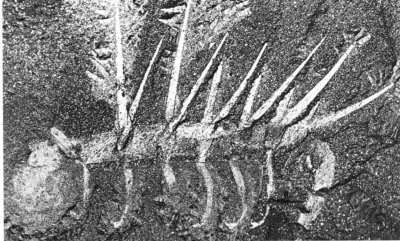

STRANGE, SPIKED CREATURE
This Burgess Shale animal is very strange, as its name, *Hallucigenia,* suggests. The stiff spikes on top were initially thought to be its legs and the flexible appendages underneath its feeding apparatus, but scientists have since turned the creature the other way up. However, it is still not clear which end is the head and which end is the tail.

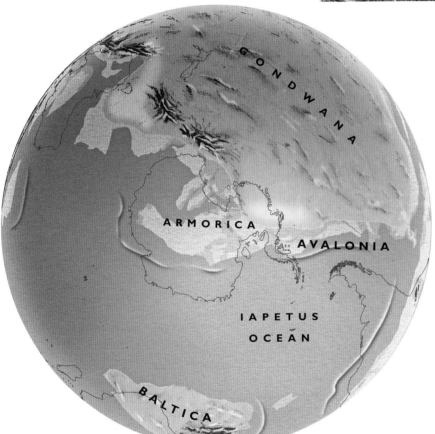

DETAILED LEG FOSSILS
Trilobites like *Olenoides* were among the most successful arthropods of the time. This Burgess Shale fossil shows *Olenoides*' legs in fine detail, projecting from underneath its hard, crablike covering.

PIKAIA AND THE BURGESS SHALE
The mollusks and brachiopods (two-shelled invertebrates), which had appeared during the early Cambrian period, continued to diversify. But perhaps the most important development of this time, at least in retrospect, was the appearance of a small swimming animal called *Pikaia* (see page 66). This was the first animal to possess the early characteristics of a backbone, in the form of a long, stiffening rod and spinal nerve cord. It is thought that *Pikaia* was the ancestor of all vertebrate animals, including ourselves.

Like animal life, other forms of life were still restricted to the seas. These lifeforms included blue-green algae (single-celled organisms) as well as early multicellular algal seaweeds (green, red, and brown algae).

Information on the creatures of this period has grown enormously since the 1980s. The detailed information from the famous Burgess Shale of Canada has now been added to by information from localities such as Chengjiang in Yunnan Province, China and Sirius Passet, Greenland.

THE BURGESS SEAWORLD

THE BEST PICTURE OF THE CAMBRIAN SEAWORLD is provided by the 530-million-year-old mudstone of the Burgess Shale in British Columbia, Canada. This site has now yielded thousands of exceptionally well-preserved fossils, many of them completely intact. Taken together, they provide a vivid insight into life in the Cambrian seas at the time when the arthropods were the dominant lifeform.

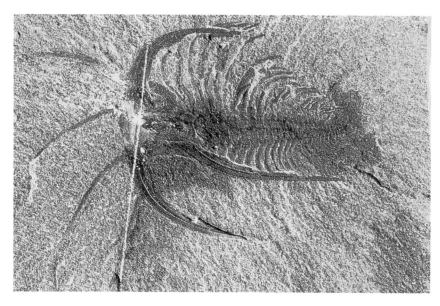

DISCOVERING THE BURGESS SHALE

The American paleontologist Charles Doolittle Walcott discovered the Burgess Shale by chance on August 31, 1909, as he was making his way across a high ridge in the Rockies that connected Mount Field and Mount Wapta. Walcott spotted a profusion of fossils in a block of hard shale and immediately recognized its importance. Not only were the usual hard parts of the animals preserved, but the soft tissue was also present. Walcott had stumbled upon the largest find of perfectly preserved fossils from any era.

It is generally thought that the creatures in the Burgess Shale were buried by a mudslide from a submarine cliff. The extraordinary anatomical detail present in the fossils, including delicate appendages, indicates that they were buried rapidly, possibly in mud that was low in oxygen.

In the absence of oxygen, tissues decompose more slowly and are consequently better preserved.

For eight years after his lucky find, Walcott systematically quarried into the mountainside, excavating thousands of specimens, which he then shipped to the Smithsonian Institute in Washington, DC. Work by paleontologists at the University of Cambridge, England, and the Royal Ontario Museum, Canada, has subsequently revealed the full significance of the find.

PERFECTLY PRESERVED
This *Marrella* fossil is one of many finely preserved specimens found in the Burgess Shale. Antennae, legs, and delicate gills are clearly visible. Walcott named this creature the "Lace Crab," but it was in fact a primitive shrimplike arthropod.

THE LIFE OF THE BURGESS SHALE

Burgess arthropods had many different lifestyles. The trilobite *Olenoides* lived on the seabed, but *Marrella* was a swimmer. Both ate organic detritus. *Laggania*, like *Anomalocaris*, was an active swimming predator. Numerous sponges, such as *Pirania*, grew up from the seabed, as did an Ediacaran survivor, *Thaumaptilon*. Many kinds of worms hid in the sediment, including the predatory *Ottoia*. Other worms, such as *Canadia*, lived on the seabed. The mollusk-like *Wiwaxia* ploughed across the mud, protected by spikes and scales. The swimming *Pikaia* is thought to be a vertebrate ancestor. Some Burgess creatures, such as the strange *Hallucigenia* and the plantlike animal *Dinomischus,* remain totally unclassifiable.

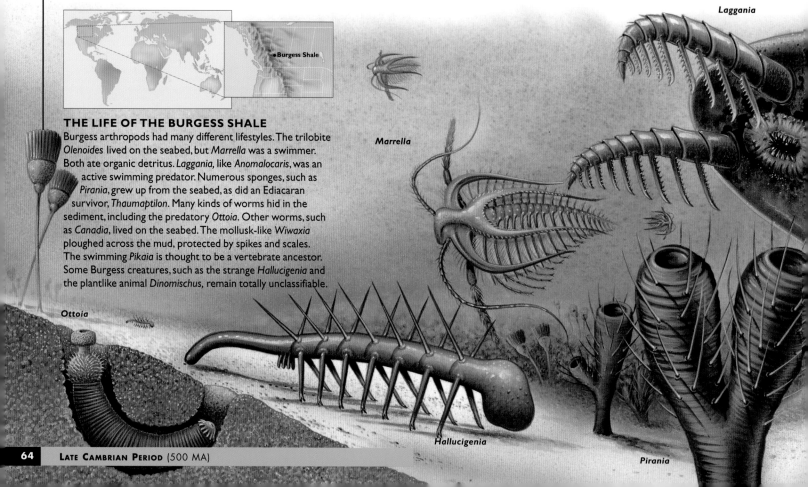

Laggania

Marrella

Ottoia

Hallucigenia

Pirania

CAMBRIAN SEAWORLD

Study of the fossils found in the Burgess Shale has revealed that approximately 40 different kinds of arthropods accounted for about half of all the preserved animals. A further 30 percent were echinoderms (the family of which the starfish are members), sponges, and priapulid worms. The remainder included brachiopods, mollusks, and a curious swimming creature called *Pikaia*, which may be related to living vertebrates.

There were also "hairy" worms living on the surface of the seabed, such as *Canadia* and *Burgessochaeta*. They literally bristled with thousands of tiny hairlike fibers. These bristles, and many of the finely ridged scales and plates of the Burgess animals, are thought to have acted as reflectors to create display lighting. In the dim light that filtered down from the surface of the

THREE-IN-ONE ANOMALOCARIS

The most awesome of the Burgess creatures was the free-swimming predator Anomalocaris, which grew to around 24 inches (60 centimeters) in length. For over 100 years it was known only from fragmentary remains, and these were thought to belong to three quite different animals, a jellyfish, a shrimp, and a sponge. Finally, in 1985, British paleontologists reassembled the pieces as one animal, and named it Anomalocaris, meaning "unusual shrimp."

IDENTIFICATION
The mouth (left) of *Anomalocaris* was thought to be a jellyfish, the limb (below), a shrimp.

FIERCE WORM
The carnivorous *Ottoia* is one of many priapulid worms found in the shale. They lived in burrows on the seabed and had retractable proboscises with hooks and teeth for grasping their unsuspecting prey.

water, the reflectors and hairs would have flashed silver as the animals moved about, enabling them to recognize each other. These appendages would also have made them visible to predators, but their spines and scales would have defended them.

The wide variety of creatures in the sea at this time suggests that a structured food web, similar to that found in modern marine ecosystems, had already evolved. Discovering this remarkable diversity and high level of ecological sophistication so early in animal evolution has led scientists to conclude that there must have been a lengthy earlier development of multicelled animals, stretching back to Precambrian times.

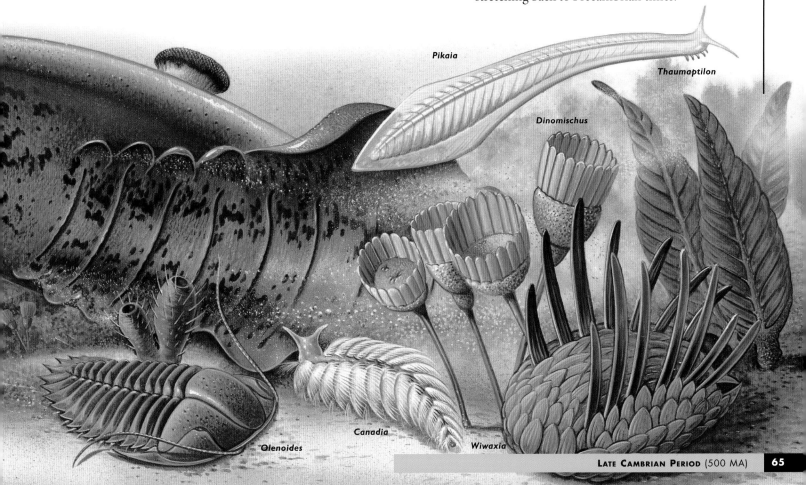

Pikaia

Thaumaptilon

Dinomischus

Canadia

Wiwaxia

Olenoides

PIKAIA—OUR ANCESTOR?

A PRIMITIVE CREATURE WITHOUT A WELL-defined head and less than 2 inches (5 centimeters) long, which swam in the seas during mid-Cambrian times, is close to the ancestor of all backboned animals (vertebrates), from fish to birds to mammals. Called *Pikaia*, it is one of the most interesting of the myriad animal fossils found in the famous Burgess Shale in the mountains of British Columbia.

UNLIKELY ANCESTOR

At first glance, *Pikaia* does not seem like a human ancestor. It looks like a worm that has been flattened sideways. But in detail, these fossils compressed within the Burgess Shale clearly show chordate features such as traces of an elongate notochord, dorsal nerve cord, and blocks of muscles down either side of the body—all critical features for the evolution of the vertebrates.

The notochord is a flexible rod that runs along the back of the animal, lengthening and stiffening the body so that it can be flexed from side to side by the muscle blocks for swimming. In the fish and all subsequent vertebrates, the notochord forms the backbone (or vertebral column). The backbone strengthens the body, supports strut-like limbs, and protects the vital dorsal nerve cord, while at the same time allowing the body to bend.

Surprisingly, a *Pikaia* lookalike still exists today, the lancelet *Branchiostoma*. This curious little animal was familiar to biologists long before the *Pikaia* fossil was discovered. With notochord and paired muscle blocks, the lancelet and *Pikaia* belong to the chordate group of animals from which the vertebrates have descended. Molecular studies have confirmed the lancelet's status as the closest living relative of the vertebrates.

While the lancelet is an advanced chordate, other living and fossil groups, such as sea squirts and graptolites, are more primitive. Called the hemichordates, they have only a notochord at an early stage of their lives.

The presence of a creature as complex as *Pikaia* some 520 million years ago reinforces the controversial view that the diversification of life must have extended back well beyond Cambrian times, deep into the Precambrian era.

SEA SQUIRT

The sea squirt, like the *Branchiostoma*, is a most unlikely looking close relation to the vertebrates. Adult sea squirts live permanently attached to the seabed and superficially look like sponges. Their free-swimming larvae, which look like tadpoles, have a body structure that relates them to vertebrates. A long stiffening rod allows the tail to flex for swimming. The larvae attach themselves head first to the seabed and transform into adults.

Tentacle

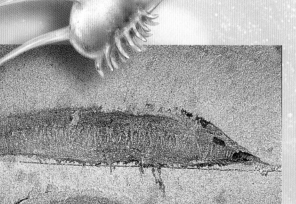

PIKAIA FOSSIL

This primitive marine creature shows the essential prerequisites for making backboned animals. The flattened body is divided into pairs of segmented muscle blocks, seen as faint vertical lines. The muscles lie either side of a flexible rod which runs from the tip of the head (bent round at the left) to the tip of the tail (the larger tapering structure to the right.)

PIKAIA ALIVE

Alive, *Pikaia* was a sideways-flattened, leaf-shaped animal. It swam by throwing its body into a series of S-shaped, zig-zag bends, much as snakes do. Fish inherited the same swimming movement, but they generally have stiffer backbones. *Pikaia* has a pair of large head tentacles and a series of short appendages, which may be linked to gill slits, on either side of its head. In these ways, it differs from the living lancelet. Paleontologists are still researching details of *Pikaia*'s anatomy.

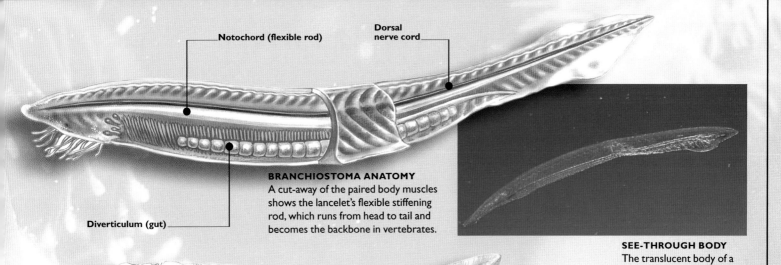

Notochord (flexible rod)

Dorsal nerve cord

Diverticulum (gut)

BRANCHIOSTOMA ANATOMY
A cut-away of the paired body muscles shows the lancelet's flexible stiffening rod, which runs from head to tail and becomes the backbone in vertebrates.

SEE-THROUGH BODY
The translucent body of a *Branchiostoma* clearly shows its internal anatomy, which closely resembles the internal structure of *Pikaia*.

Notochord

Paired muscle blocks

HEADS FOR VERTEBRATES
Development of the head resulted from a long body shape, swimming habit, and a mouth at the end that came into contact with the environment first as the animal swam forward. The search for food required ways of continually testing what lay ahead. Anatomical structures for seeing, feeling, and smelling developed around the mouth. The information they gathered was processed by a swelling of the nerve cord—the brain. Altogether these front-end structures formed the distinct part of the vertebrate body known as the head. The first sign of head development is seen in chordates such as *Branchiostoma* and *Pikaia*.

VERTEBRATE RELATIONSHIPS

Understanding the details of animal biology allows scientists to determine how different creatures are related. There are some surprises. For although the connection seems unlikely, starfish (echinoderms) and sea squirts (tunicates) turn out to be closely related to all backboned animals (vertebrates), ranging from fish to humans. The embryos and larvae of sea squirts and echinoderms, before they change to their adult forms, have close similarities to those of the vertebrates. On this biological "family tree" of relatedness, those closest to the vertebrates are chordates with a body stiffening rod (notochord) throughout their lives, as represented by the living lancelet. The 520-million-year-old fossil Pikaia is sufficiently similar to the lancelets to suggest that it, too, is a chordate, and thus our most distant known ancestor.

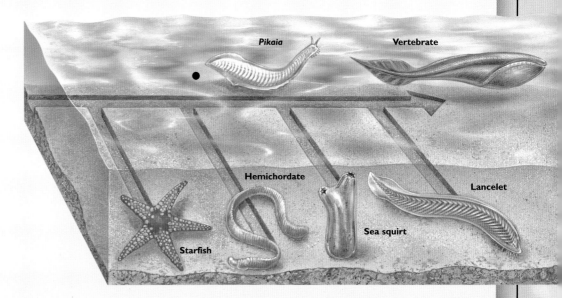

Pikaia

Vertebrate

Hemichordate

Lancelet

Sea squirt

Starfish

The Ordovician Period

ORDOVICIAN TIMES SAW THE EXPANSION OF MARINE LIFE, UNTIL CLIMATIC CHANGES DESTROYED THE ENVIRONMENT ON WHICH SO MANY SPECIES DEPENDED.

Throughout Ordovician times, the pace of global change quickened. During the period of just over 50 million years that the Ordovician lasted, from 495 to 443 million years ago, Siberia and Baltica moved north, the Iapetus Ocean began to close, and the Rheic Ocean gradually opened to the south. The supercontinent of Gondwana continued to dominate the southern hemisphere, with North Africa at the South Pole.

Much of our knowledge of changes in the Ordovician climate and the position of continents is derived from fossils of small creatures that lived in the seas and oceans. Although primitive plants, along with a few small arthropods, began to invade the land in Ordovician times, life was still concentrated in the sea.

MINIATURE LIFE
Fish had begun to evolve, but most marine life was still remarkably small, with few organisms growing larger than an inch or two. The most common shellfish were the clamlike brachiopods, mostly about 1 inch (2 to 3 centimeters) in size. Altogether, over 12,000 fossil species of brachiopods have been recorded. They lived on the seabed or attached to other creatures, such as sea lilies. Because their shell form varied depending on local conditions, their fossils help reconstruct past environments.

CREATING THE BLUE RIDGE
A collision between the landmasses of Avalonia and Laurentia triggered the formation of what are now the Blue Ridge Mountains of Virginia, deforming earlier sedimentary rocks.

LAURENTIA

SIBERIA

IAPETUS

OCEAN

BALTICA

DOB'S LINN ROCK
A shale rock at Dob's Linn marks the boundary between the end of Ordovician time and the start of the Silurian period. This rock, containing well-defined graptolite fossils, was discovered by schoolmaster Charles Lapworth in 1879 in the Southern Uplands of Scotland. Lapworth mapped the complicated succession of ancient marine strata and suggested the identification of a new period between the Cambrian and the Silurian. He named this new period "Ordovician" after a Romano-British hilltribe, the Ordovices.

TRILOBITES AND GRAPTOLITES

Other fossils that help us to understand the Ordovician world include trilobites and graptolites. There were over 4,000 trilobite species, most of them less than 4 inches (10 centimeters) in length. Although trilobites spread through the seas of the world, some regions featured their own particular kinds. The global distribution of trilobite fossils has helped scientists reconstruct the positions of the Earth's crustal plates at the time.

Graptolites were strange creatures that were once even thought to be plants. These once common

TUNING FORKS

So-called "tuning-fork" graptolites were small creatures that lived in organized colonies. Each individual animal lived in one of the "cups" formed by the serrated edge of the skeleton. Small tentacles used for filtering food would have projected from the skeleton. This fossil was found in Wales.

organisms floated in the seas and consisted of numerous tiny individual, yet interconnected, creatures living in a hollow tubular skeleton and filter-feeding from the plankton.

MASS EXTINCTION

The wonderfully diverse marine life of Ordovician times—with over 600 different families of marine organisms—was not destined to last. The global climate became progressively wetter and cooler, descending into an ice age at the end of the period that drove many organisms to extinction. As ocean water was locked up in the polar icecaps, sea levels fell by as much as 1,000 feet (330 meters). The shallow seas of the continental shelves turned into dry plains, killing off many of the creatures that lived there, especially those that could not migrate from the seabed.

GONDWANA

GRAPTOLITE BIOZONES

The shape of graptolite skeletons changed as they rapidly evolved. These changes can be used to achieve a precise dating of Ordovician, Silurian, and early Devonian marine strata. In 1879, a Scottish schoolmaster, Charles Lapworth, worked out the correct chronological sequence of graptolites in southern Scotland and used it to establish the correct sequence of strata. Lapworth's graptolite "biozonation" has since been used all over the world.

HORSESHOE FOSSIL

Fossils of horseshoe crabs first appear during the Ordovician period. Like the trilobites, they were aquatic arthropods that lived on the sea bottom. Although modern-day horseshoe crabs are sometimes referred to as "living fossils" because they so closely resemble their prehistoric ancestors, none of the species living today date back to Ordovician times.

LIFE IN THE ORDOVICIAN SEAS

THE ORDOVICIAN PERIOD MARKED A TURNING point in the evolution of marine life. Many organisms were increasing in size, strength, and speed of movement. Jawless organisms called conodonts, which are extinct today but were common in the Ordovician seas, were particularly significant as they were closely related to the first vertebrates. The appearance of the first fishlike jawless vertebrates was followed by the evolution of the first sharklike vertebrates, which had jaws and teeth, more than 450 million years ago. During this period, there is also evidence that animals began to move onto land.

CONODONT MYSTERY

Two questions puzzled paleontologists for a long time—what were the conodonts and who were their closest relatives? Until the 1990s, these were difficult questions to answer, since the only fossil remains of the animals were tiny toothlike structures found in rocks from late Cambrian to late Triassic times (520–210 million years ago). No one knew what kind of creature these teeth belonged to until the first conodont with preserved soft tissue was found in Carboniferous rocks in Scotland, and then later in South Africa. These finds have shown that the teeth were indeed a feeding apparatus, positioned below a pair of well-developed eyes. The presence of a nerve cord, a notochord (a flexible rod), and muscle blocks, all located in its back, shows that these animals were actively swimming chordates, closely related to the backboned vertebrates. They also have vertebrate features such as a head and paired eyes moved by muscles. Consequently, some experts argue that conodonts are more advanced chordates than the Cambrian vertebrate ancestor *Pikaia,* and may be closely related to the fishlike jawless vertebrates.

TINY TEETH

These comblike strands are the tiny fossilized feeding apparatus from the mouth of a conodont (*Promissum*), one of the larger creatures from Ordovician seas. Conodonts are thought to be related to the chordates, including the true backboned creatures, the vertebrates.

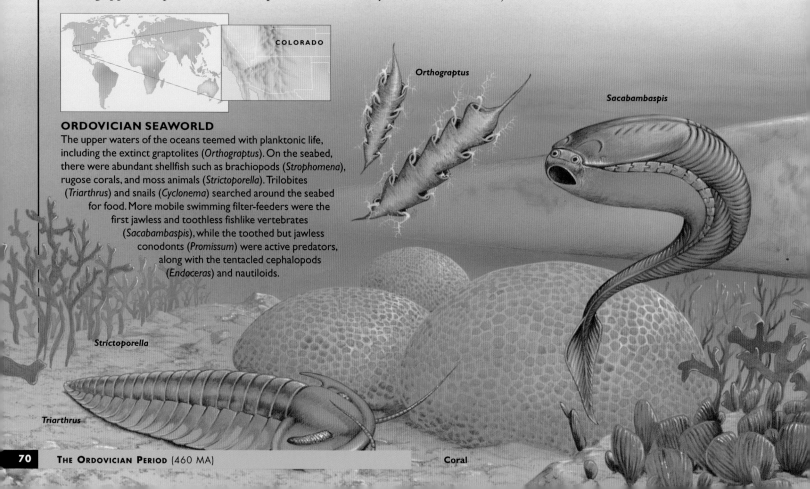

COLORADO

ORDOVICIAN SEAWORLD

The upper waters of the oceans teemed with planktonic life, including the extinct graptolites (*Orthograptus*). On the seabed, there were abundant shellfish such as brachiopods (*Strophomena*), rugose corals, and moss animals (*Strictoporella*). Trilobites (*Triarthrus*) and snails (*Cyclonema*) searched around the seabed for food. More mobile swimming filter-feeders were the first jawless and toothless fishlike vertebrates (*Sacabambaspis*), while the toothed but jawless conodonts (*Promissum*) were active predators, along with the tentacled cephalopods (*Endoceras*) and nautiloids.

Orthograptus

Sacabambaspis

Strictoporella

Triarthrus

Coral

SETTING FOOT ON LAND

Animals gained a foothold on land at this time, not directly from the sea, but through the "backdoor" medium of freshwater. Sets of parallel trackways, a centimeter wide, have been found in 450 million-year-old late Ordovician freshwater deposits in northern England. They were probably made by a millipede-like arthropod, an animal with a segmented body, numerous jointed legs, and an exoskeleton. No body fossils have yet been found for this creature. Arthropods were ideally suited to make the transition from the supportive environment of water to dry land, with its desiccating air and primitive vegetation.

and *Arandaspis*, from Australia. They are younger, but still Ordovician in age. Their wide geographical separation reinforces the view that their ancestry lies much further back than previously thought, possibly in Cambrian times.

The fossil remains indicate that Ordovician agnathans were very different to the few jawless vertebrates that survive today—the lampreys and hagfish. Typically, they had heads and bodies that were covered with tough leathery plates made of bonelike material. Only the scaly tail had flexibility for swimming. Without jaws and teeth, they must have fed on food that was small and numerous, such as planktonic microorganisms.

ORDOVICIAN JAWLESS VERTEBRATES

Fossils of the very early fishlike jawless vertebrates (agnathans) are rare at first in Ordovician strata but become more common in rocks from the succeeding Silurian and Devonian periods. There is no question, however, that agnathans did exist in Ordovician times.

In 1892, American paleontologist Charles Walcott, famous as the discoverer of the Burgess Shale (see page 64), found a fragmentary agnathan in the Harding Sandstone, Colorado. These strata are over 450 million years old. The same rocks have produced other remarkable vertebrate remains, including the scales of jawed sharklike gnathostomes. The oldest complete agnathan fossils are *Sacabambaspis*, from Bolivia,

CLAM-SHAPED BRACHIOPODS

The most common and successful Ordovician shellfish were the brachiopods. Most brachiopods, like these orthids, were permanently anchored to the seabed or to other shells by a short fleshy stalk called a pedicle, though some lay freely on the seafloor sediment. They lived by drawing seawater through their open shells and filtering out microscopic particles of food. Although they resemble clams, they are not related to them.

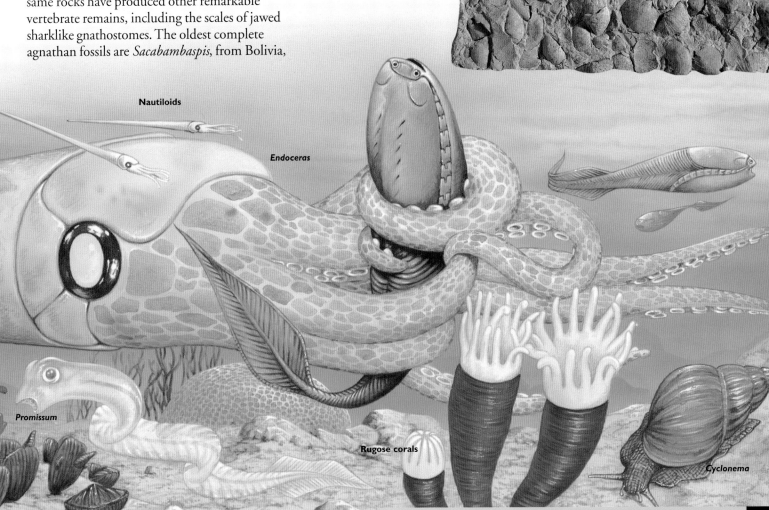

Nautiloids

Endoceras

Promissum

Strophomena

Rugose corals

Cyclonema

The Silurian Period

IN SILURIAN TIMES LIFE RECOVERED AFTER THE MASS EXTINCTION OF THE ORDOVICIAN PERIOD AND THE LAND WAS COLONIZED BY NEW PLANTS AND ARTHROPODS.

The Silurian age began about 443 million years ago. Although it lasted a mere 26 million years, the strata and fossils from this period in Britain and North America are among the most intensely studied in the world. They were already well known by the mid-nineteenth century, thanks to the efforts of geologists such as Sir Roderick Murchison in Europe and James Hall in North America.

The Silurian period marked a pivotal point in evolution. Following the setback to life caused by the late Ordovician glacial extinction, some animals, including the trilobites, conodonts, and graptolites, never fully recovered. In general, however, there was a major revival as oceans became warmer and sea levels rose. This was the period when plants and invertebrate animals first became solidly established on land, even if the seas remained a far easier environment for life.

SEA CHANGES

In Silurian times, the old Iapetus Ocean gradually closed, as the landmasses of Laurentia (North America), Baltica (northern Britain and Scandinavia), and Avalonia (southern Britain, Nova Scotia, and Newfoundland) approached one

SILURIAN AGNATHANS

Birkenia was a 1.5-inch- (4-centimeter-) long agnathan (jawless fish). This example was found in Scotland, but many similar fish have been discovered in the Baltic region of Europe.

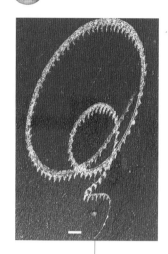

COLONIAL GRAPTOLITE
Monograptus proteus, was a coiled colony of 118 tiny creatures in a 0.75-inch- (2-centimeter-) wide skeleton. When the colony died, it sank and was buried, becoming flattened as the seabed was compressed to form shale now found in Germany.

another on a collision course. Another ocean then opened up to the south, separating the newly forming northern continent from the southern continent of Gondwana.

The closure of the Iapetus Ocean created a new environment of shallow seas and basins, providing new habitats and ecological niches in which Paleozoic marine life once again flourished and diversified. Vast coral reefs spread throughout the equatorial waters of Laurentia and Baltica.

Many of the shells washed up on a Silurian beach would be generally recognizable to us today.

HOW THE SILURIAN AGE GOT ITS NAME

The Silurian period was first identified in 1835 by British former army officer and geologist, Sir Roderick Murchison. Together with the Reverend Adam Sedgwick, a young professor at the University of Cambridge, England, Murchison mapped the strata of Wales, thought to be the oldest stratified rocks lying above the first formed igneous rocks. By studying the positions of various fossils within the sedimentary strata, Murchison distinguished strata that he called Silurian lying above Sedgwick's Cambrian. Murchison named the Silurian period for the Silures, a tribe that lived in Wales at the time of Ancient Rome.

SPINY TRILOBITE
The large headshield of this very distinctive Silurian trilobite, *Dalmanites myops*, shows evidence of well-developed eyes and long protective ribs extending down the sides of its body. It grew to 2.5 inches (6 centimeters) long and, like many other trilobites, foraged on the seabed for its food. This fine example comes from Dudley in England.

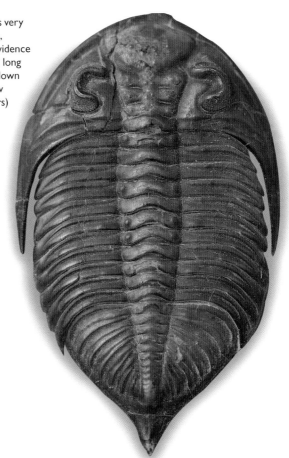

PANTHALLASSIC

OCEAN

GONDWANA

They were larger than shells from earlier ages, typically up to 1.5 inches (4 centimeters) long. A few were much larger still, such as the conical shells of the squidlike nautiloids, which reached 4 inches (10 centimeters) or more. Brachiopods, clams, snails, echinoderms (such as starfish and sea lilies), and fish continued to diversify.

The shallow seas and basins of the northern continent became progressively shallower and broke up, eventually becoming isolated from one another as lakes. Jawless fish prospered in these warm waters and grew larger than their Ordovician predecessors, reaching a size of up to 8 inches (20 centimeters). New jawed fish and water scorpions preyed upon the jawless fish, which evolved bizarre forms of heavy armor as a defense against this predation.

Most important for the long-term evolution of life on Earth was the spread of plants that were notably more complex than the mosses typical of Ordovician times. Through the mechanism of photosynthesis, they eventually created an oxygen-rich atmosphere that was capable of supporting a complex range of terrestrial animal life.

BRACHIOPOD GRAVE
Numerous rhynchonellid brachiopod fossils litter the surface of this Silurian rock slab. When alive, these shellfish were attached to hard surfaces by fleshy stalks. After they died, their shells were swept together by currents running along the seabed. These fossils were found in Wales, close to the border with England.

LIFE ON LAND AND IN THE SEA

LIFE ON LAND IS TOUGH COMPARED WITH LIFE in water. Animals and plants need to evolve special equipment to make use of the light mixture of gases we know as air. To survive, they must withstand alternate freezing and boiling, drying out, and solar radiation. Yet in Silurian times the land was increasingly colonized.

Although pioneering bryophyte plants such as mosses had already occupied the land since Ordovician times, they were very limited in form. The Silurian period saw the evolution of the first upright vascular plant that has left a fossil record. Called *Cooksonia*, it featured strengthened stems and tubes for conducting water and nutrients.

Cooksonia was quite unlike modern flowering plants (angiosperms), having no flowers, leaves, or seeds. A *Cooksonia* consisted of tiny upright stems, up to 1.5 inches (4 centimeters) high, which forked into two equal branches, ending in club-shaped reproductive sacs full of spores. The plant's primitive method of reproduction depended on living in wet conditions, so that the male gametes could swim to fertilize the female ones.

The evolution of these upright plants was essential to the formation of a terrestrial food chain. Their photosynthesized tissues provided vegetation for plant-eating animals (herbivores) to eat. Once herbivores had established

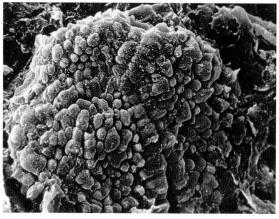

EARLY HERBIVORY
Scattered among the early plant fossils, remains of centipede-like arthropods have been found, along with tiny droppings full of tough plant spores. It is thought that these arthropods did not eat fresh plant material, but rather decaying remains of the primitive *Cooksonia* plants.

themselves in numbers, carnivorous animals could then evolve to prey on them.

Digestion of raw plant food is difficult for animals, however. The first herbivores to appear were arthropods that fed on decaying plants. Partly broken down by bacteria, this material was easier to digest. It also incidentally introduced important microorganisms into the herbivore gut that were capable of breaking down plant matter.

CORAL COMMUNITIES
Silurian corals (above and opposite), which formed the first extensive reefs, look similar to ones alive today, but belong to extinct groups.

SILURIAN SEASHORE
The shorelines of late Silurian times were crowded with biological innovations, as well as already familiar shellfish, such as trilobites and snails. The most important developments were in the vertebrates and the land plants. Jawless fishlike vertebrates such as *Ateleaspis* were armored, while *Birkenia*, *Loganellia*, and *Jamoytius* were covered in smaller scales. Their days were numbered as predators such as the jawed fishlike vertebrates and eurypterids (including *Pterygotus*) became more abundant. On land, tiny *Cooksonia* was the first upright-growing plant.

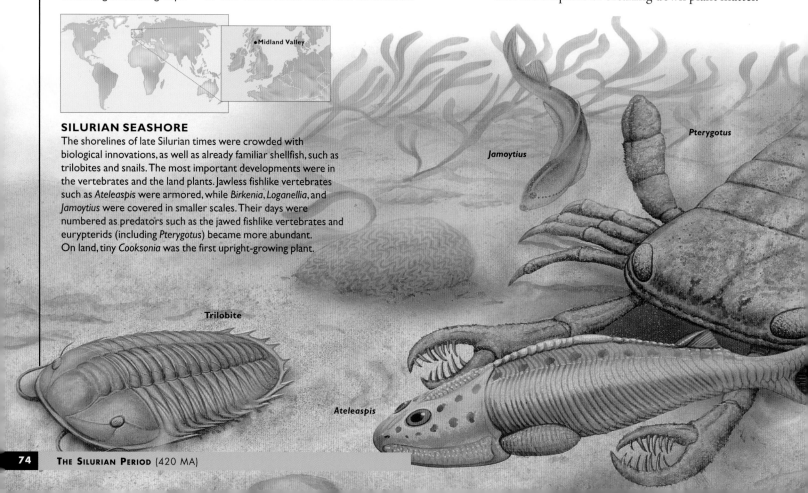

•Midland Valley

Pterygotus

Jamoytius

Trilobite

Ateleaspis

SEA SCORPIONS

The first giants of the Earth, living in the Silurian period, were the eurypterids or "sea scorpions," which evolved in Ordovician times and survived until Permian times. They were scorpionlike in shape, and some had large pincers. Their elongated, articulated bodies were covered in a tough exoskeleton, making them one of the best-armored animals of the time. However, because they were arthropods, they had to shed their exoskeleton periodically to allow for growth, a process which left them vulnerable to attack. The eurypterids evolved a variety of lifestyles. Some could swim, some were scavengers, but others were active predators. *Eurypterus*, found in the Silurian strata of New York, grew up to 6.5 feet (2 meters) in length. Eurypterids were one of the first animals to make the transition from a marine to a freshwater environment.

TEEMING WITH LIFE

Many creatures living in Silurian seas would seem unfamiliar today. Some belong to extinct groups such as the Paleozoic corals, mobile trilobite arthropods, graptolites, or free-swimming armored agnathans, eurypterids, conodonts, and straight-coned cephalopods. Others, such as brachiopod shellfish and sea lilies, still exist today but are far less common than they used to be in Ordovician and Silurian times, when they populated the seas of the continental shelf in great numbers and diversity.

THE RISE OF THE VERTEBRATES

The most common vertebrates in Silurian times were the jawless agnathans. They ranged from *Jamoytius*, an eel-shaped, free-swimming creature without scales or body armor, to *Ateleaspis*, a bottom-living creature with its head enclosed in a horseshoe-shaped bony shield. The curious-shaped thelodonts, another type of agnathan, had bodies covered in tiny spiky scales, as sharks have today. There were also more familiar fish-shaped agnathans, such as *Birkenia*.

The biological event that did the most to transform life in the oceans was the evolution of jaws in fishlike vertebrates. The first fishlike jawed vertebrates were the now-extinct acanthodians, which had distinctive spines in front of all their fins. These bony spines are almost all that is fossilized of these small animals, but they are known to have had toothed jaws.

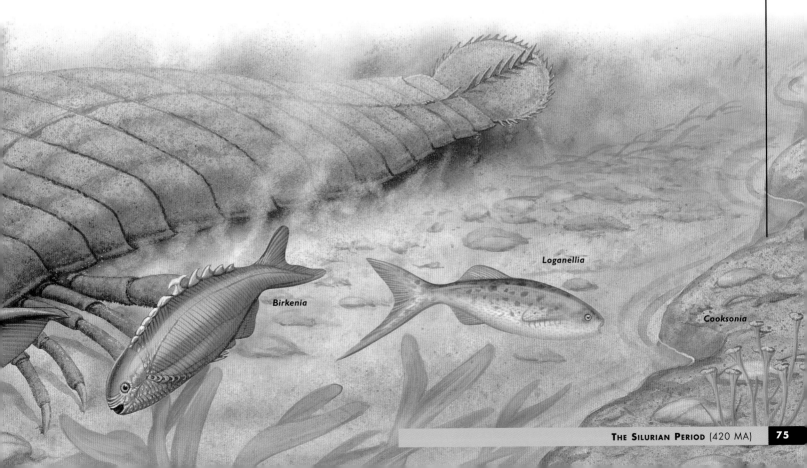

Birkenia

Loganellia

Cooksonia

The Devonian Period

OFTEN CALLED THE "AGE OF FISHES," DEVONIAN TIMES FEATURED AN ABUNDANCE OF DIVERSE LIFEFORMS IN RIVERS, INLAND SEAS, AND FRESHWATER LAKES.

The Devonian period lasted for 63 million years, from 417 million to 354 million years ago. During this time, the closure of the Iapetus Ocean was finally completed, as North America and Greenland (Laurentia) collided with the southern British Isles (Avalonia) and Scandinavia (Baltica) to form a single continental mass. A central mountain belt stretched from Scandinavia, through Britain, to Newfoundland and Canada. Meanwhile, the supercontinent of Gondwana moved steadily northward from its polar position.

Global climates remained warm during this period. The formation of new landmasses resulted in ever bigger and drier continental interiors, where vast deserts developed. The continents were traversed by huge rivers flowing into inland seas and lakes that were home to the first extensive freshwater life. By mid-Devonian times, sea levels had risen as the icecaps melted, allowing extensive reefs to develop in Laurentia and Australia.

"WINGED" BRACHIOPODS
The spiriferids were one of the groups of Paleozoic brachiopods. These wing-shaped shells from upstate New York housed a spiral structure used for filtering microscopic food from seawater.

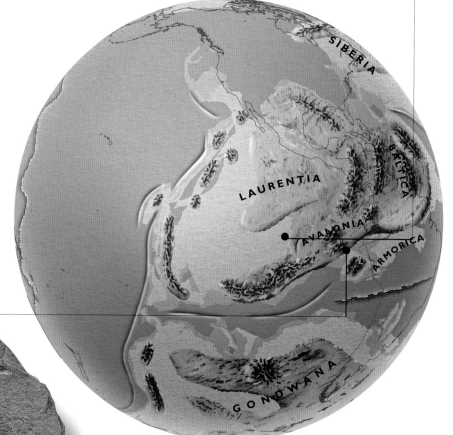

SIBERIA

BALTICA

LAURENTIA

AVALONIA

ARMORICA

GONDWANA

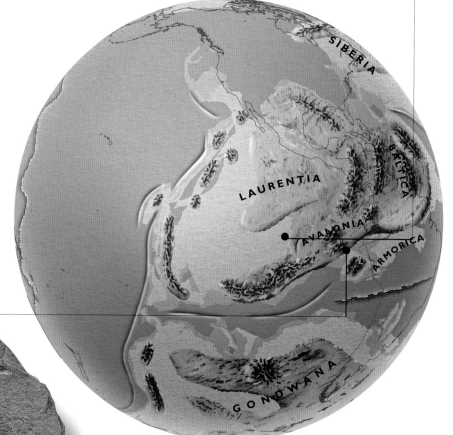

ANCESTORS OF THE FIRST TETRAPODS
The paired fins of this *Eusthenopteron foordi* fish have a single bone and are joined to the body in a similar way to the upper arm or leg bone of a tetrapod (four-legged animal). This fossil was found in Quebec, Canada.

THE "AGE OF FISHES"
The Devonian inland waterways were dominated by predators. The jawless agnathans were the first to invade freshwaters, but they were soon pursued by their jawed predators. By the end of the Devonian period, these predators had wiped out most agnathans. Only the lampreys and the hagfish survived. The jawed group, by contrast, evolved into a new array of groups—placoderms, ray-finned fishes, lobe-fins, true sharks, and lungfishes, some of which were active predators that grew up to 18 feet (6 meters) in size.

SANDSTONE FIGURES

Sandstone typically creates a bare and semi-arid landscape. Originally, storms and flash-floods generated huge rivers that transported and deposited stones into deep sedimentary basins. Erosion of the resulting rock on this Scottish cliff face has created a statuelike sculpture known locally as the Old Man of Hoy.

MARINE EXPANSION

The remarkable expansion in Devonian vertebrate diversity has become clearer as well-preserved evidence of the period, such as the marine seabed deposits of Gogo in Western Australia, have opened. These deep deposits contain one of the most diverse collection of animals of the age, including over 25 varieties of armored placoderms, ray-finned fishes, lobe-fins, and lungfishes.

The placoderms were primitive jawed forms, growing up to 2 feet (60 centimeters) in length, with a head and trunk enclosed in a boxlike structure of bony plates. Some had long, bony, winglike arms protruding from either side. They evolved in the Silurian age and dominated both the freshwater and marine environments, diversifying into over 200 genera. They looked similar to primitive sharks, but unlike the sharks they died out at the end of the Devonian period.

The lungfishes are a particularly interesting group of primitive air-breathing fish that evolved and flourished in Devonian times. They originally lived in the sea and did not invade freshwaters until the Carboniferous age. Their paired fins and ability to breathe air were thought to link lungfish with landgoing vertebrates, but it is now known that they are not ancestral.

Other creatures in Devonian waters, however, evolved in the direction of terrestrial vertebrates. As plant species continued to develop on land, fish groups such as panderichthyids become almost indistinguishable from the future tetrapods that would eventually leave the water for the land.

PANTHALLASSIC OCEAN

GONDWANA

OLD RED SANDSTONE

Periodically, the hot Devonian climate evaporated the waters of inland seas, rivers, and lakes, leaving behind mineral salt deposits that reddened when oxidized by the air. These red and brown strata, known as Old Red Sandstone, are prevalent in Britain and the American Catskills. Old Red Sandstone made excellent building material and was extensively quarried in the 18th and 19th centuries. As quarrymen opened the layers of the strata, they revealed the well-preserved remains of the creatures that had lived in the original rivers and lakes.

FISH FOSSIL

Osteolepis panderi was a mid-Devonian-age fish with muscular paired fins like the lungfish. Mostly small fish that grew to about 8 inches (20 centimeters) long, they were first discovered in the 19th century by quarrymen in the Old Red Sandstone of Scotland.

EQUIPPING LIFE FOR LAND

WHEN THE FIRST TETRAPOD (FOUR-LEGGED) fossil was found in Upper Devonian lake and river deposits in Greenland, the animal it represented was thought to be a salamander-like amphibian, capable of crawling out of the water and walking. *Ichthyostega*, as the creature was called, seemed to combine limbs and a deep ribcage for air-breathing lungs with its many fishlike features. In effect, *Ichthyostega* appeared to fill the evolutionary gap between fishes and land-going animals.

This original theory has now been revised, however. The limbs of *Ichthyostega* and its contemporary, *Acanthostega*, were better adapted for swimming than walking. Also, these animals retained gills and may have breathed in both air and water. They were gradually adapting toward the final difficult transition from water to land.

Terrestrial vertebrates had to overcome a number of problems in order to survive. Take a fish out of water and it will soon die. It will fall on its side and flap without moving any distance. It will gasp for oxygen but its gills collapse out of water. Having no ears, it will not be able to hear anything and will become blind as the eyes dry out. The skin will lose moisture. Land-living animals also had to be able to move around. Most have evolved legs for this purpose. The first

terrestrial creatures, the centipede-like Ordovician arthropods, had inherited many pairs of jointed legs from their aquatic ancestors, but the vertebrates had to make the best of a very different evolutionary heritage. From paired fins, they had to evolve jointed, muscular limbs strong enough to lift the body and propel it forward on land.

The main means of propulsion for fish is the sideways flexing of the body in a series of S-shaped waves. Although this kind of movement works

MUDSKIPPER
The mudskipper is a modern bony fish that can leave the water to find food on exposed mudbanks, using its long, bony pectoral fins to prop itself up and wriggle across soft, wet mud. However, it has to remain wet and cannot stay out of the water for long.

GREENLAND

GREENLAND WATERWAYS

The oldest tetrapod fossils, of *Ichthyostega* and *Acanthostega*, have been found in late Devonian river and lake deposits from Greenland. These first four-limbed vertebrates were aquatic creatures. They used their muscular limbs, hands, and feet for additional propulsion, holding on to plants and perhaps digging for shellfish. Growing to about 3 feet (1 meter) long, these early tetrapods were powerful predators, capable of attacking small fish. However, the tetrapod young were probably preyed on by fish, such as the lobe-finned fish, *Holoptychius*, the lungfish, *Dipterus*, and the placoderm *Bothriolepis*, as well as adult tetrapods.

Dipterus

Acanthostega

FROM FINS TO LEGS

Terrestrial vertebrates had to evolve legs out of fins. But not all forms of fin are suitable to develop into limbs. The panderichthyids had two pairs of narrow-based fins and, as in the leg structure of most tetrapods, each of these fins was supported by a single bone that joined the shoulder or hip girdle. The girdles in turn are joined to the backbone. At the outer end of each limb bone was a pair of wrist bones and then a number of rays (the spines of the fin). By contrast, today's true fishes have fan-shaped fins that are supported by a number of bones, and a lot of rays. Of the two types of fin, only the former, as found in the panderichthyids, was suitable to develop into a leg strong enough to lift a body.

site of Lode, in Latvia, is a remarkable animal. Along with tetrapodlike paired fins at the front and back of the body, it has a skull that is almost indistinguishable from that of the first four-legged animals, with a flat head, closely spaced eyes, and a large mouth. The ribs are also joined to the backbone in the same way. When the remains of *Elpistostege*, one of the panderichthyids, was first discovered, it was thought to be a tetrapod.

effectively on land, as demonstrated by snakes, it cannot lift a body off the ground. Many land vertebrates, such as lizards, evolved a compromise solution, where the body still moves in S-shaped waves but is also lifted up onto stiltlike legs. This movement puts new pressure on the backbone, however, so land vertebrates' skeletons had to become stronger and more flexible—an evolutionary process that took a long time.

TETRAPOD ANCESTORS

So what animals did *Acanthostega* and *Ichthyostega* evolve from? Research has revealed that the panderichthyids, a group of fish with paired muscular fins, are anatomically closest to the tetrapods and are their most likely ancestors. *Panderichthys* itself, found at the late Devonian

ACANTHOSTEGA FOSSIL

By disentangling the jumbled skeletal remains of this early tetrapod fossil, scientists have revised ideas about how backboned animals evolved for life on land. Found high on a remote mountainside in Arctic Greenland and entombed in hard sedimentary rock, the fossil required many days of careful preparation to unveil its secrets. The fossil shows that *Acanthostega* had a flattened skull with eye sockets placed close together on the top surface.

Holoptychius

Bothriolepis

Ichthyostega

Carboniferous Age

THE AGE OF COAL SAW THE GROWTH OF THE FIRST EXTENSIVE FORESTS ON EARTH. FOUR-LEGGED ANIMALS EMERGED FROM THE WATER, EVOLVING INTO AMPHIBIANS AND REPTILES.

The period from 354 to 290 million years ago is called the Carboniferous, meaning coal-bearing. In this time, the great mass of the southern continents that made up Gondwana rotated clockwise. The eastern part of the super-continent (Australia) moved south and became colder, while the western side (South America) rotated north into warmer latitudes. Laurentia (North America) was assaulted on all sides, folding the Appalachians and forcing up the ancestral Rockies. These impacts among Gondwana, Laurentia, and Baltica marked a major step in the amalgamation of the supercontinent of Pangea.

SEA LEVELS AND CLIMATES

The Carboniferous period is divided into the earlier Mississippian or Lower Carboniferous and the later Pennsylvanian or Upper Carboniferous. In Mississippian times, sea levels rose sharply, further flooding and drowning the old Devonian continents. But in the Pennsylvanian, sea levels fell and landscapes reemerged.

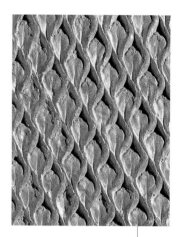

LEPIDODENDRON FOSSIL TRUNK
This fossilized trunk of the clubmoss tree *Lepidodendron*, from a coal forest in Scotland, shows a pattern of diamond-shaped scars and leaf cushions where leaf fronds were attached before being shed during growth.

SIBERIA

BALTICA

PANTHALLASSIC OCEAN

LAURENTIA

TETHYS

OCEAN

GONDWANA

FERN FROND
This fossil fragment of a Carboniferous fern frond from Jerada in Morocco looks similar to living ferns. However, the ferns of the coal forests were more varied in size, with some growing into tree-sized plants. Ferns are still successful today, with over 12,000 living species.

From its hot "global greenhouse" state of the Siluro-Devonian periods (440 to 360 million years ago), the Earth cooled. By mid- to late Carboniferous times, it had become as seasonal as it was during the ice age in the Quaternary (18,000 years ago) and polar icecaps had formed. An extensive glaciation got under way that persisted into the Permian age.

Global rainfall and humidity fluctuated drastically. Climates had become extremely humid by the beginning of the Carboniferous period. They stayed exceptionally wet for a few million

MEASURING OXYGEN LEVELS

The study of plants allows us to measure the relative levels of carbon dioxide and oxygen in the atmosphere in prehistoric times. Plants use pore cells called stomata for gas exchange with the atmosphere. They regulate their intake of carbon dioxide by altering the density of stomata on their leaves. When carbon dioxide levels are high, plants produce fewer stomata. They produce more when levels are low. By comparing the density of stomata on fossil leaves from different ages, scientists can measure how carbon dioxide and, by implication, oxygen levels varied. Devonian plants had lower stomatal densities than Carboniferous plants.

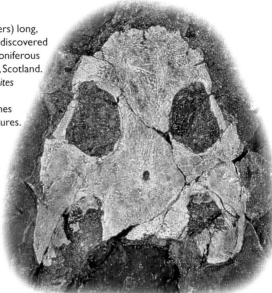

EUCRITTA
Three inches (8 centimeters) long, this is the skull of a newly discovered early tetrapod from Carboniferous limestone at East Kirkton, Scotland. Called *Eucritta melanolimnites* ("creature from the black lagoon"), the fossil combines amphibian and reptile features.

PANTHALLASSIC

OCEAN

GONDWANA

Devonian low of 15 percent to a peak of 35 percent in the late Carboniferous, higher than at any other time in the Earth's history.

The plants also provided the material for the formation of the vast coal deposits of Europe and North America during the Pennsylvanian. Ferns, which flourished at this time, were the most important contributors to this process.

LIFE ON LAND AND SEA

On land, true egg-laying (amniote) tetrapods evolved. Arachnids and insects, which had evolved in Silurian times, increased in size and diversified. The shallow equatorial seas of the Mississippian produced extensive reefs occupied by a wide diversity of marine life. Sharks and bony fishes dominated the seas, though both often took different forms from the ones familiar today. Deposits of shells and other parts of sea creatures formed extensive areas of marine limestone.

years. Then, as temperatures dropped and glaciers formed during the late Carboniferous, levels of rainfall and humidity declined.

CREATING A BREATHABLE ATMOSPHERE

Atmospheric oxygen levels increased dramatically thanks to the growth of extensive lowland forests. These huge forests offered new habitats and new sources of food for a thriving animal population, including insects, amphibians, and reptiles. Through photosynthesis, the plants increased the level of oxygen in the atmosphere from a mid-

FOSSIL TREE ROOTS
These are the fossilized roots of a coal-forest clubmoss tree, *Lepidodendron*, now in Manchester, England. Because the roots are normally found separately from the trunk and foliage of this tree, they have been given a different name—the roots are called *Stigmaria*. Some of these trees grew as high as 130 feet (40 meters).

THE FIRST TETRAPODS

SOME OF THE MOST INTERESTING FOSSILS FROM the Mississippian (Lower Carboniferous) period found in recent years have come from a limestone quarry in East Kirkton, Scotland. The fossil fauna includes the first of several different early tetrapod groups: amphibians like *Balanerpeton woodi* and *Silvanerpeton*; an animal known as *Eucritta* that combined amphibian and reptilian features; and *Westlothiana lizziae*, an almost true reptile. The tetrapods of East Kirkton formed the world's oldest known vertebrate terrestrial community.

UNDER THE VOLCANO

The limestone of East Kirkton is unusual because it came from freshwater rather than saltwater, originally deposited in a small lake at the foot of volcanically active hills. The mineral-rich soils that formed on the ash and lava promoted the growth of a lush vegetation of clubmosses (lycopsids), horsetails (sphenopsids), ferns (pteridosperms), and seed plants (gymnosperms). The forest provided food and shelter for the variety of terrestrial animals, including vertebrate tetrapods and invertebrate scorpions, myriapods,

eurypterids, and harvestmen. Storms, forest fires, and even flooding periodically devastated the area, washing plant fragments and a sample of the animals into the lake where they perished and were quickly covered by a protective layer of sediment, forming well-preserved fossils.

TERRESTRIAL FOOD CHAIN

The terrestrial food chain still relied on arthropod detrivores—animals that fed on rotting vegetation—such as mites and millipedes. But there were many additions to the fauna, including the oldest known harvestman (opilionid arachnid) and the first air-breathing scorpion, *Pulmonoscorpius*, a large, active predator, growing up to 28 inches

TREE-FERN
The few living tree-ferns look just like their Carboniferous ancestors. They are crowned with numerous fronds 10 feet (3 meters) in length that would produce an unstable plant but for the growth of massive roots.

TETRAPOD FOSSIL
The salamander-like *Silvanerpeton*, approximately 16 inches (40 centimeters) long, was one of the oldest of the anthracosaurs, an extinct group of tetrapods with a number of reptilian features.

FIRST VERTEBRATE LAND COMMUNITY
The wealth of fossils recovered from the freshwater limestone of East Kirkton in Scotland offers a remarkable glimpse of the past. A dense tropical forest of clubmosses, seed plants, and tree-ferns covered the lower slopes of volcanoes and the shores of small lakes. The water was full of fish, amphibious tetrapods such as *Balanerpeton*, and eurypterids. Other tetrapods, such as *Westlothiana*, were more at home on land, and had to compete with large and dangerous scorpions for food.

East Kirkton

Gymnosperms and ferns

Balanerpeton woodi

Lungfish

AQUATIC LIFE

The waters of the Carboniferous lake in East Kirkton supported a remarkable variety of fish. Six species of bony (actinopterygian) fish were accompanied by two species of spiny (acanthodian) ones, as well as members of two shark families. The most probable explanation for this impressive diversity of life is that the lake was originally linked to a much larger body of water. An infilling of volcanic ash from the surrounding area may have created a natural barrier that cut creatures off from their original habitat, trapping them without the possibility of escape.

(70 centimeters) long. Even this impressive beast was dwarfed by one of the three eurypterids known from the locality. *Hibbertopterus scouleri* looked like a huge, flattened, streamlined lobster. It had a headshield 26 inches (65 centimeters) wide and must have been around 10 feet (3 meters) long. Although it may have been the biggest arthropod ever, it only scavenged small prey.

Westlothiana lizziae, a vertebrate tetrapod that grew to 8 inches (20 centimeters) in length, was once thought to be the world's oldest reptile fossil. It turned out not to be a reptile, however, because it had a number of features, especially in the ankle and palate, more characteristic of primitive tetrapods than true egg-laying (amniote) reptiles.

OTHER KIRKTON FINDS

Several small amphibians growing to around 20 inches (50 centimeters) were among the other vertebrates found at East Kirkton. Some, like *Balanerpeton woodi*, resembled modern salamanders. The structure of the limbs and ankles show that *Balanerpeton* lived mostly on land, but like all amphibians, it was severely constrained by the need to return to water to breed. It also shows crucial changes in skull structure that allowed the development of earbones that detect sound in air. With a mouth full of small sharp teeth, it was an active predator on the lakeshore.

Smaller reptilelike anthracosaurs, which grew to about 12 inches (30 centimeters), were also present. With poorly developed wrists and ankles, these creatures were really better suited to swimming than walking. Other amphibians included the *Ophiderpeton*, an unusual snakelike creature. With 200 vertebrae in its backbone, it probably grew to about 3 feet (1 meter) in length, and was another terrestrial predator.

LAND SCORPION

This well-preserved fossil from East Kirkton is of the oldest known land scorpion, *Pulmonoscorpius kirktonensis*. The scorpion's unusual structures for air-breathing, called "book-lungs," can still be seen.

Westlothiana lizziae

Millipede

Harvestman

Pulmonoscorpius

COAL AND REPTILES

IT TOOK TWENTY MILLION YEARS FOR THE low-lying wetland forests and the peat bogs of late Carboniferous times to build up the bulk of the world's coal supplies. Since the Industrial Revolution in the late 18th century, it has taken the human race a mere 200 years to burn up most of these resources. One of the few positive aspects of this rapid exploitation of coal is that it has provided us with an invaluable view of life in the late Carboniferous period. Most important, it has revealed that by that time a group of tetrapods had evolved that could lay shelled eggs—the reptiles had arrived.

THE FORMATION OF COAL

The environmental change from Mississippian (Lower Carboniferous) times, dominated by marine limestone, to Pennsylvanian (Upper Carboniferous) times was marked. After 20 million years of an expanding sea world and diminishing landscapes, sea levels and global temperatures finally peaked and began to fall sharply. Organic deposits, made from plant debris, accumulated in the vast forests, swamps, and bogs that grew over the slowly emerging new land. These accumulations of debris formed the first extensive coal measures (seams), which in places can be hundreds of yards thick.

COAL DEPOSITS OF NOVA SCOTIA

Important information on the life of the coal measures has been provided by the 310-million-year-old coal deposits of Joggins, Nova Scotia. The deposits consist of Pennsylvanian strata, originally deposited in a near-equatorial floodplain environment near the coast.

With a seasonally wet climate, sand and mud sediment was carried down from highlands. Plant fossils found scattered in these sediments show that the floodplains, river banks, and sand bars supported different kinds of plant growth, depending on the nature of the soil. The ground above the floodplains was home to tall, tree-sized gymnosperms called cordaiteans, with strap-shaped leaves and stems up to 20 inches (50 centimeters) in diameter, while the drier parts of the peat swamps had equally high tree-sized clubmosses.

By comparison, only low growth of ferns with an occasional taller *Lepidodendron*, another large clubmoss, could survive on the waterlogged riverside swamps. An abundant growth of *Calamites* (a horsetail) formed on the channel banks and edges of the swamps, which also provided a suitable habitat for the first land snails.

FOSSIL HORSETAIL
This fossil shows the jointed stems and circlets of leaves characteristic of a horsetail. Many of the Carboniferous horsetails grew into tree-sized plants, unlike their small modern survivors.

COAL SWAMPS
Fossils found in the coal deposits at Joggins, Nova Scotia, have given us a picture of the near-equatorial riverside swamp that existed there in Carboniferous times. The dense plant life included horsetails (*Calamites*) at the margins of channels, and tall clubmosses, such as *Sigillaria* and *Lepidodendron*. Large insects provided food for the first reptiles, including *Hylonomus lyelli*. The fossilized remains of reptiles have been found inside hollow trunks.

Sigillaria

Lepidodendron

Hylonomus

Calamites

NOVA SCOTIA
• Joggins
• Halifax

BODIES IN THE TRUNK

More than 190 fossil skeletons of small amphibians and reptiles have been recovered from about 30 tree-sized stumps of large Carboniferous plants preserved in deposits at Joggins, Nova Scotia. Various explanations have been put forward for the occurrence of the vertebrates in the hollow stumps. It has been suggested that they lived there or that they were natural "bottle traps" into which the animals fell and were trapped and eventually died. Another recent theory is that the animals hid there to escape the fires that swept the swamps.

CARBONIFEROUS REPTILES

One of the most remarkable features of the Joggins site is the presence of numerous tree-sized stumps and trunks of the larger plants preserved in the sediment. Even more surprising is the occurrence inside these stumps of the fossil remains of the oldest known true egg-laying (amniote) reptiles, *Hylonomus lyelli* and *Paleothyris*.

These first reptiles were small—about 8 inches (20 centimeters) long—and looked like modern insectivorous lizards. They probably hatched from a tiny egg, about 0.4 inches (1 centimeter) in diameter. The reptile head was only a fifth of the body length, compared with a third in the earlier tetrapods. The structure of the skull showed an advance on the older amphibians since it allowed more space for larger and stronger jaw muscles.

The reptiles were able to live on land because food—in the form of small arthropods, such as millipedes, spiders, and insects—was abundant. With their small, sharp teeth, the reptiles could pierce these creatures' tough exoskeletons.

A layer of charcoal is often found within the stumps and there are layers of charcoal fragments in the surrounding sediments. The charcoal originated from periodic natural wildfire, suggesting that the animals may have sought shelter in the trunks, only to suffocate and die.

FOREST DRAGONFLY
Giant dragonflies, like this *Namurotypus* with a 24-inch (60-centimeter) wingspan, inhabited the Carboniferous forests. They were the first creatures to fly and were then, as now, predators on smaller insects.

Lepidodendron trunk

Lepidodendron

Sigillaria stump

Hylonomus lizard in tree stump

Medullosa

Young *Sigillaria*

Lepidodendron

The Permian Age

THE FORMATION OF THE SUPERCONTINENT OF PANGEA PROVIDED AN ENVIRONMENT FOR THE GLOBAL EXPANSION OF TERRESTRIAL LIFE.

The Permian period started 290 million years ago, when the northern continents of Eurasia and Laurentia joined the southern continent of Gondwana to form Pangea.

This event had a drastic effect on climates and on life, and marked a turning point in the development of global environments. The late Carboniferous icecap that had formed over Gondwana diminished as the continent moved north toward the equator. In the northern part of Pangea, the climate generally became hot and dry within the vast continental interiors, although in the southern part they remained cooler and wetter.

CHANGES IN PLANT LIFE

As temperatures rose, many of the shallow seas and lakes of late Carboniferous times evaporated, leaving extensive deposits of salt minerals across Laurentia. Inevitably, plant life responded to these environmental changes. The humid Carboniferous Coal Measure forests, dependent on damp ground conditions, shrank on a global scale, persisting only in wetter regions, such as China, Siberia, and parts of Gondwana, such as Australia, India, and Antarctica. The lush clubmoss and horsetail trees were replaced by more adaptable seed-bearing plants as the ground dried. In the northern hemisphere, newly evolving conifers, such as *Walchia*, spread rapidly, while as

EL CAPITAN
Permian reef limestone forms the El Capitan Peak in the Guadelupe Mountains of Texas and New Mexico.

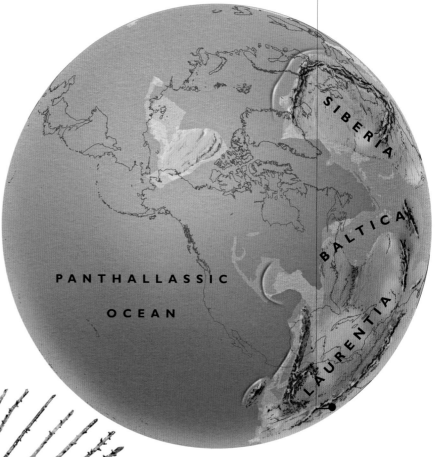

SIBERIA

BALTICA

PANTHALLASSIC

OCEAN

LAURENTIA

"SAILBACKED" REPTILES
The pelycosaur reptiles such as this *Edaphosaurus* found in Texas emerged in early Permian times. The elongated spines supported a web of skin that functioned as a heat exchanger. As a cold-blooded reptile, it basked with its side facing the Sun to heat up in the morning. To cool off, the pelycosaur turned into the wind.

CONTINENTAL DRIFT

The discovery of fossil flora and fauna of the same type and age in countries that are now widely separated has been used by geologists as evidence that vast landmasses such as Gondwana and Pangea once existed. It is unlikely that life could have spread so successfully on land if the different continents had not at one time been joined together. The first theory that continents move, or "drift," was developed in the early 20th century by the German meteorologist Alfred Wegener, after he recognized that similar late Carboniferous glacial deposits appear on all the continents of today's southern hemisphere.

SEED-FERN LEAVES
The distinctive elongated leaves of this extinct seed-fern called *Glossopteris* have been found in Permian and Triassic strata throughout India, Australia, South Africa, South America, and Antarctica. This distribution has long been seen as evidence that these landmasses were once joined as the supercontinent of Gondwana.

TETHYS OCEAN

PANTHALLASSIC OCEAN

GONDWANA

the ice age gradually waned in the cooler southern hemisphere, the seed-fern *Glossopteris* emerged as the dominant flora.

MAMMAL CHARACTERISTICS
A group of tetrapods called the synapsids became more diverse and widespread, moving from the northern to the southern hemisphere by the end of the Permian period. Some species began to evolve characteristics that pointed in the direction of the future evolution of mammals. One of the synapsid groups, called the cynodont therapsids, eventually become warm-blooded, because their lineage includes the first mammals and their living descendants.

Life in the seas was decimated by another extinction event at the end of the period. About 90 percent of the marine invertebrates disappeared, including the brachiopods and trilobites. The reason for this event is unclear, although overspecialization and the resulting inability to cope with environmental change may have been a factor. Life on land generally had greater adaptability and mostly survived.

FILTER-FEEDING SPONGE
This Texan reef-building sponge, *Girtyocoelia*, used its linked pea-sized chambers to filter food from the sea by drawing in water through tiny holes in its sides. The walls of the sponge were made from chalky carbonates present in the seawater.

ANCIENT MAMMAL RELATIVES

Life on land evolved rapidly once the early tetrapods were able to lay eggs that could hatch on land. In Carboniferous times, these amniote tetrapods evolved into two branches—the reptiles, and a group called the synapsids, which eventually gave rise to the mammals. Previously known as "mammal-like reptiles," synapsids were never true reptiles.

PELYCOSAURS

The first synapsids were the pelycosaurs. These were so successful in early Permian times that they made up nearly three-quarters of all tetrapods. An important feature of the pelycosaurs was tooth differentiation, which allowed some to become plant eaters and others carnivores. Two types of pelycosaurs developed a "sail," consisting of long spines covered by a thin web of skin, that stood up from their backs. It may have acted as a heat exchanger, helping to raise the animal's body temperature in the early morning and prevent overheating at noon. Calculations have shown that the sail could have quartered the basking time a large pelycosaur needed before it became active in the morning.

THERAPSIDS OF THE KARROO

The early Permian pelycosaurs became extinct in late Permian times and were replaced by a more advanced group of synapsids, the therapsids.

DICYNODONT EGGS
These fossil eggs, among the oldest known, were found in Permian strata of southern Africa. The eggs are thought to have been laid by reptilelike dicynodont therapsids.

PERMIAN KARROO
The semi-arid scrub of the Karroo desert in South Africa resembles the Permian landscape of over 250 million years ago. Then, the desert was dominated by the forerunners of mammals and reptiles.

PERMIAN LIFEFORMS
The Karroo strata show that during Permian times South Africa was home to many reptilelike forerunners of the mammals, such as the cynodont *Procynosuchus*. Landscapes were dominated by plant-eaters such as the pig-sized *Dicynodon* and the smaller *Robertia*, pursued by carnivores such as *Lycaenops*. Armored amphibians, including *Peltobatrachus*, existed alongside the lizardlike *Milleretta*. Horsetails, ferns such as *Dicroidium*, seed-ferns such as *Glossopteris*, and the first cycads and ginkgos vegetated the land.

Glossopteris

Lycaenops

Peltobatrachus

Lystrosaurus

Milleretta

EARLY SYNAPSID
This *Dimetrodon* is a sail-backed pelycosaur from North America. It was one of the first backboned land animals that could kill other beasts of its own size.

TEETH

Early tetrapods had simple undifferentiated teeth. Food could not be chewed, it was just torn off and swallowed. The stomach extracted nutrients from the unchewed food. But therapsids began to differentiate incisor, canine, and molarlike teeth, suggesting a varied diet of food that may have been chewed and pre-digested in the animal's mouth before being swallowed.

Fossils of over 100 kinds of therapsids, as well as thousands of reptile, amphibian, fish, and plant fossils have been found in the red sandstone of the late Permian Karroo basin of South Africa since its discovery in the 1840s. They include many varieties of dicynodont therapsid, animals with two large canine teeth. The dicynodonts included the 8-inch- (20-centimeter-) long *Oudenodon*, which lived in corkscrew-shaped vertical burrows, hog-sized animals, such as *Lystrosaurus*, with beaklike bony mouths, and hippo-sized herbivores such as *Kannemeyeria*.

CYNODONTS

More interesting, from the evolutionary point of view, are the cynodont therapsids, which evolved at the end of the Permian age and gave rise to the first mammals in late Triassic times. These cynodonts, such as *Procynosuchus*, evolved shorter tails, elbows that flexed backward, knees that flexed forward, more powerful jaws, and diversified teeth, which shows their close relationship to the mammals. The cynodonts survived through a large part of the Jurassic, living alongside the dinosaurs, and then became extinct.

Dicynodon

Lycaenops

Robertia

Procynosuchus

Dicroidium

MASS EXTINCTIONS

THE HISTORY OF LIFE ON EARTH HAS BEEN punctuated by a series of extinction events. Perhaps the best known is the one that occurred at the end of the Cretaceous, about 65 million years ago, marking the end of the reign of the dinosaurs. Life on Earth suffered its greatest setback, however, at the end of the Permian, around 248 million years ago, when organisms were struck down on a massive scale, both on land and in the seas. Although the organization and evolution of marine organisms had been drastically altered before, this was the first time that life on land had known such devastation.

Terrestrial vertebrates were severely hit. Some 21 families of therapsid reptiles (63 percent of the total number of tetrapod families) and 33 percent of amphibian families disappeared. But hardest hit of all were sea-dwelling creatures. Marine diversity was reduced from about a quarter of a million species to less than 10,000. Altogether some 60 percent of marine families became extinct. Casualties included some important Paleozoic fossil groups such as the trilobites.

Several different mechanisms have been proposed for why mass extinctions occur. The first and most spectacular is the impact of a large asteroid or a comet with the Earth. In addition to the lifeforms killed by the impact itself and the earthquakes and tidal waves it would trigger, such an impact would throw huge amounts of dust and debris high into the atmosphere, blocking out the Sun's radiation and creating cold,

RUGOSE HORN CORAL
Aulophyllum (left) is just one of many Carboniferous corals that made up the vast reefs of the tropical seas of the time. All the rugose and tabulate corals were replaced in mid-Triassic times by a new group of corals (the scleractinians).

CAUSES OF THE EXTINCTIONS
This chart shows that mass extinctions often mark the major divisions in geological history and coincide with significant meteorite impacts, volcanic eruptions, or sea-level changes. The largest extinction, at the Permo-Triassic boundary, occurred at the same time as a fall in sea levels, which killed off much of shallow marine life, and volcanic eruptions in Siberia, leading to global climate change. The Cretaceous-Tertiary boundary is associated with sea-level change, volcanic eruptions, and a layer of iridium (a rare metallic element) in rocks that is clearly linked to a meteorite impact.

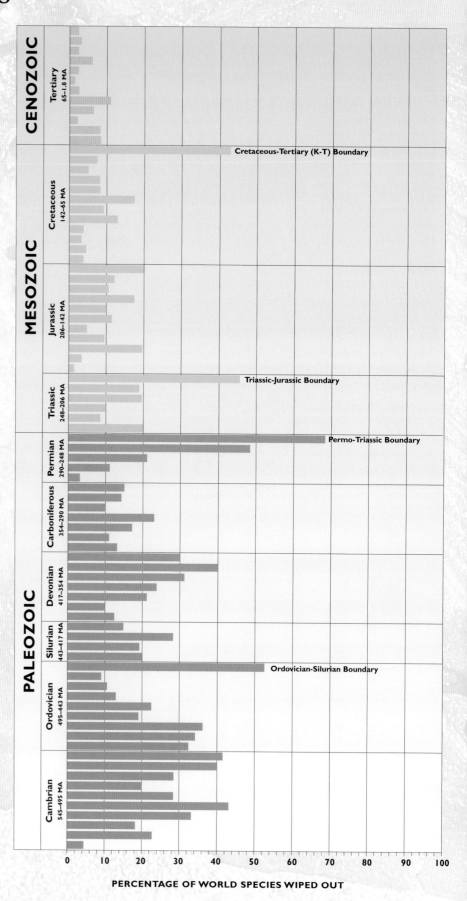

RECORD OF EXTINCTIONS

CENOZOIC — Tertiary 65–1.8 MA

MESOZOIC — Cretaceous 142–65 MA; Jurassic 206–142 MA; Triassic 248–206 MA

Cretaceous-Tertiary (K-T) Boundary

Triassic-Jurassic Boundary

PALEOZOIC — Permian 290–248 MA; Carboniferous 354–290 MA; Devonian 417–354 MA; Silurian 443–417 MA; Ordovician 495–443 MA; Cambrian 545–495 MA

Permo-Triassic Boundary

Ordovician-Silurian Boundary

0   10   20   30   40   50   60   70   80   90   100

PERCENTAGE OF WORLD SPECIES WIPED OUT

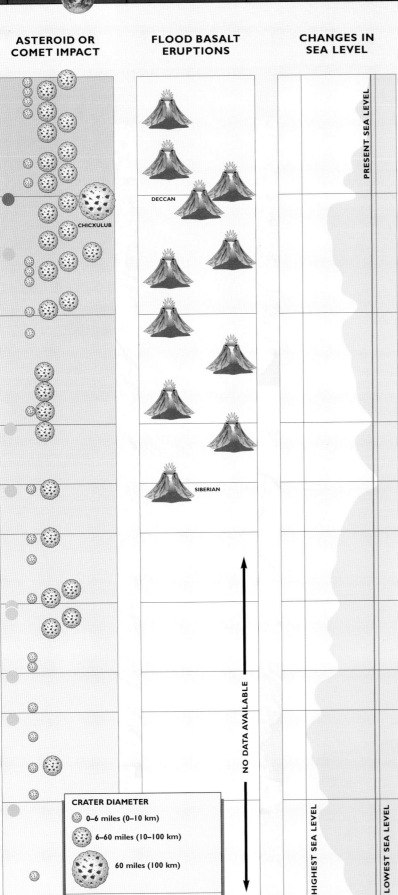

ASTEROID OR COMET IMPACT

CHICXULUB

FLOOD BASALT ERUPTIONS

DECCAN

SIBERIAN

CHANGES IN SEA LEVEL

PRESENT SEA LEVEL

NO DATA AVAILABLE

HIGHEST SEA LEVEL

LOWEST SEA LEVEL

1800   900   0

Feet above present sea level

CRATER DIAMETER

0–6 miles (0–10 km)

6–60 miles (10–100 km)

60 miles (100 km)

Iridium linked to an extraterrestrial impact

Iridium from volcanic eruptions

THERAPSID SKULL

Titanophoneus was one of the therapsids that replaced the sailbacked pelycosaurs in late Permian times, only to become extinct themselves at the end of the Permian period.

dark conditions. If the impact was big enough, living conditions would become so severe that few species would survive.

Another possible cause for mass extinction is an episode of massive volcanic eruptions. Flood basalts are layers of volcanic rock laid down by volcanic eruptions much bigger than any seen in modern times. Eruptions can alter global climates in dramatic ways and since eruption episodes can happen repeatedly, adverse conditions can persist long enough to affect animal and plant species.

The third mechanism for a mass extinction is sea-level change, caused by climate change and movements of the Earth's crustal plates. Throughout Permian times sea levels had been steadily falling. But in the early Triassic they dropped to an all-time low in the last 545 million years. Communities such as coral reefs, which thrive in warm, shallow coastal waters, become stranded and die off when sea levels fall.

The final mechanism for a mass extinction is global climate change. Although they are more gradual than the rapid changes in climate brought about by eruptions or impacts, the Earth's weather patterns can undergo major changes in very short times in geological terms.

Recently scientists have begun assessing the causes of the great extinction events of prehistory. A huge meteorite impact in Mexico's Yucatan peninsula, for example, is certainly implicated in the late Cretaceous extinctions. But there was also volcanic eruption, climate change, and a fall in sea level. No major meteorite impact has been found that correlates to the dramatic loss of species at the end of the Permian period. In most extinctions, the story does not appear to have been simple. Rather it seems that such extinctions are precipitated by a combination of factors.

The Triassic Period

AS LIFE SLOWLY RECOVERED FROM THE PERMIAN
EXTINCTION, REPTILES, INCLUDING THE FIRST DINOSAURS,
BECAME THE DOMINANT ANIMALS.

The Triassic period lasted for over 40 million years, from 248 to 206 million years ago. At first, as the supercontinent of Pangea crept northward to straddle the equator, much of its vast landmass became increasingly warm and arid. By the end of the period, however, Pangea was beginning to break up and global climates had become cooler and wetter.

During the early Triassic, there was a marked recovery in the percentage of oxygen in the atmosphere, but later oxygen levels declined. Sea levels also fluctuated. They plunged to a new low in the early Triassic, then rose again around the middle of the period, only to fall once more toward the end of the age.

LIFE ON LAND AND IN THE SEA

These environmental changes signaled major developments in the vertebrates (backboned animals). The mammalian relatives that had dominated the land in Permian times declined (although one group, the cynodonts, spread and diversified). Instead, a new wave of reptiles, the archosaurs, emerged. Later, at the end of Triassic times, some famous archosaur descendants, the dinosaurs, came to the fore.

Terrestrial ecosystems became more complex and diverse, with the rise of the first gliding and flying reptiles, the first turtles, and the first frogs. Plant life also changed significantly. Forests of

FISH-HUNTERS

The nothosaurs were marine predators that evolved from land-based reptiles during Triassic times. They had a long slim body, tail, and neck and preyed exclusively upon fish. This fossil is from Switzerland.

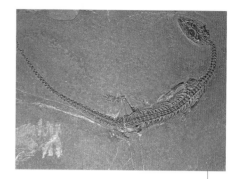

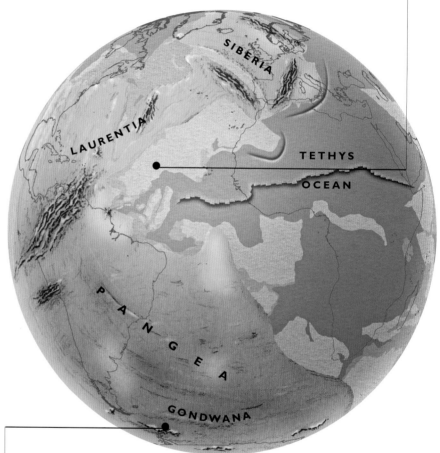

primitive conifers clothed the dry hillsides. Savanna-like open spaces supported smaller conifers, such as *Woodworthia*, tree-ferns, cycads, and cycadophytes. The ancient treelike glossopterids went into final decline, as modern-looking horsetails flourished.

CYNODONT SKULL

The cynodont *Cynognathus* from South Africa was a predator of the early to mid-Triassic. It had a mammal-like posture, possibly a covering of hair, and differentiated teeth: incisors, canines, and ridged cheek teeth for fast chewing.

BIOZONES

The rapid evolution of Triassic ammonoid shellfish resulted in constant changes in the details of their shells. Experts have used these changes to identify levels called biozones within marine fossil-bearing strata. Deposits on land are similarly zoned using pollen, plant spores, and terrestrial vertebrate remains. Detailed pictures of life within biozones have been built up and correlated from different parts of the world.

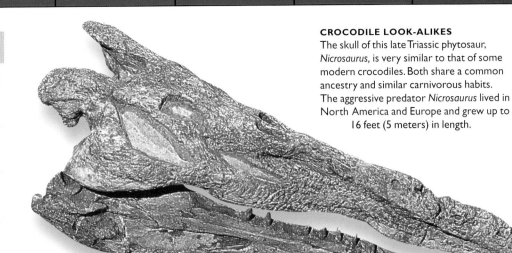

CROCODILE LOOK-ALIKES
The skull of this late Triassic phytosaur, *Nicrosaurus*, is very similar to that of some modern crocodiles. Both share a common ancestry and similar carnivorous habits. The aggressive predator *Nicrosaurus* lived in North America and Europe and grew up to 16 feet (5 meters) in length.

PANTHALLASSIC OCEAN

in the seas as swimming predators. The Triassic also saw the arrival of modern-looking corals, an extremely diverse and successful group of colonial organisms that form the largest living structures known—coral reefs. All living corals, known as hexacorals, are structurally different from the Paleozoic corals that existed before the extinction event at the end of the Permian period. Modern corals appear to have evolved from survivors of that mass extinction. The first reefs built in Triassic times were small compared with today's, however. Constructed by no more than 20 different types of coral, they grew about 3 feet (1 meter) above the seafloor. Large reefs were not established until the end of the Triassic period.

Mollusk bivalves and gastropods were able to exploit an enormous range of niches in the Triassic seas. Some were permanently attached to the seabed, others were burrowers and free-swimmers. They also invaded freshwater and, in the case of snails, eventually took to the land as well. By comparison, the superficially similar but more limited brachiopods were already in decline and would eventually be largely eclipsed.

The ecosystems in the sea were also transformed. The Triassic period saw the rise of groups of bony fish, that although more modern-looking, still differed greatly from sea life today. Some common living marine animals such as crab- and lobsterlike crustaceans did not evolve until Jurassic times. Ammonoids (coiled shellfish) flourished after the devastation wreaked by the late Permian extinction. From only a few survivors, such as *Ophiceras*, there were soon 100 genera. They, and their distant relatives the belemnite cephalopods, played an increasing role

EARLY PTEROSAUR
This fossil of one of the oldest flying reptiles, the fish-eating *Eudimorphodon*, displays two types of teeth: plain conical spikes at the front and three-pointed ones at the back. It was discovered in late Triassic strata of northern Italy.

DAWN OF THE DINOSAURS

ONE OF THE RICHEST DINOSAUR DEPOSITS ever found was at the evocatively named Ghost Ranch in the New Mexican desert. It was discovered in 1947 by American paleontologists George Whitaker and Edwin H. Colbert, from the American Museum of Natural History. Over a thousand 220-million-year-old skeletons of small two-footed dinosaurs, many of them complete, were huddled together within a narrow band of sandstone. The Ghost Ranch skeletons are all of the same kind of animal but include specimens of different sizes, from hatchlings less than 3 feet (1 meter) in size to older individuals up to a maximum size of 10 feet (3 meters).

FAST-MOVING HUNTER

Named *Coelophysis*, the Ghost Ranch dinosaur had all the hallmarks of a fast-moving, hunting meat-eater. It had a slender, muscular body, with hollow, light bones and long legs, and its narrow skull was armed with numerous dagger-shaped teeth with sharp cutting edges.

What were such a large number of predatory meat-eaters doing together? *Coelophysis* was probably a pack hunter, roaming the upland forests, lakes, and rivers of the late Triassic world, preying on small reptiles and, possibly, shrewlike mammals. Today, most big vertebrates that move around in large numbers are plant-eaters, which herd together for safety. There are no living pack hunters that operate in such large groups. But all of our modern-day examples are mammals—for reptilian dinosaurs it was presumably different.

Details of the mass of skeletons made it clear that the dinosaurs must have died together, overwhelmed by some catastrophe. The most

DINOSAUR BADLANDS
The rocky ridges around Ghost Ranch, New Mexico, expose a sequence of fossil-rich strata, from the Triassic red hills in the foreground, through Jurassic yellow cliffs, to the Cretaceous Dakota sediments of the skyline.

TRIASSIC NEW MEXICO

The plant-eating reptile *Desmatosuchus* was 16 feet (5 meters) in length with heavy armor, including 18-inch spines projecting from its shoulders, but it would have been no match for large carnivores such as the crocodile-like *Rutiodon* and the land-living archosaur *Postosuchus*. *Coelophysis* pack hunters ate anything they could catch and kill. Plant-eating *Placerias* was a shy animal living in upland woods. *Metoposaurus* was a large amphibian that fed on fish, as did the flying reptile *Eudimorphodon*.

Gymnosperm forest

Placerias

Cycads

Eudimorphodon

Rutiodon

likely cause is a flash-flood which may have swept along a river valley, carrying many of the herd away and drowning them. Even today, herds of wildebeest can be similarly overcome in Africa.

PREY AND PREDATORS

Coelophysis was far from being the only predator in this environment. In the streams and rivers, *Rutiodon*, a crocodile-like representative of a new reptile group, the phytosaurs, was top predator. The land was dominated by a large archosaur reptile, *Postosuchus*, with a long skull similar to the later tyrannosaurs. It was probably too slow to catch the swift *Coelophysis* and preyed instead on plant-eating reptiles, such as *Desmatosuchus*, *Typothorax*, and *Calyptosuchus*. These were

DINOSAUR CANNIBALS

Some of the Coelophysis *skeletons found at Ghost Ranch, New Mexico, were discovered to have smaller dinosaurs of the same species within their body cavity. At first scientists thought that these must have been unborn young, showing that* Coelophysis *gave birth to live offspring, rather than laying eggs like most reptiles. It is now known, however, that the* dinosaur's hip bones were too narrow for live birth—it simply must have laid eggs. Experts believe it is more likely that *Coelophysis practised cannibalism. One theory is that dominant males may have killed and eaten offspring sired by other displaced males. Similar behavior has been observed in such modern-day meat-eaters as lions.*

DEATH THROES

The heads of these *Coelophysis* skeletons were pulled back by contraction of the neck muscles after death. The posture indicates some delay before the corpses were buried.

slow-moving but heavily armored. They moved on all fours, with sturdy legs to support the weight of their body plates and neck and tail spikes. Another plant-eater was the ox-sized *Placerias*, a dicynodont with a short tail, a large broad skull, a pair of sharp tusks, and pointed beaklike jaws covered in horny sheaths. The skies may have been home to the first true flying pterosaur reptile, *Eudimorphodon*, and in the forests the gliding lizardlike *Icarosaurus* swooped from tree to tree. Last but not least, *Dinnetherium*, a small shrewlike descendant of the cynodonts (reptiles with doglike teeth), was living a nocturnal life, feeding off insects. This seemingly insignificant creature was, it is now thought, a possible direct ancestor of humans.

Coelophysis

Postosuchus

Desmatosuchus

Horsetails

Metoposaurus

REPTILIAN DOMINATION

THE GLOBAL DEVELOPMENT AND SPREAD OF the reptiles during the Mesozoic era was astonishing. As much of the world's climate became hotter and drier, the reptiles, who could lay their eggs on land, took advantage of the new niches available to them, venturing into new territories and returning to old ones. For the first time they took to the air, and they also returned to the water from where their tetrapod ancestors had originated.

FLYING REPTILES

The remarkable adaptability of the reptiles is highlighted by the repeated evolution of species that took to the air. The first of these, *Coelurosauravus,* whose remains have been found in Europe and Madagascar, was Permian in age. Closely resembling the living flying lizard *Draco volans* of Southeast Asia, *Coelurosauravus* was a highly effective glider and an excellent example of convergent evolution (in which similar patterns of evolution are seen in unrelated species). It grew to a length of 16 inches

GLIDING LIZARD

This late Triassic, long-legged reptile, *Kuehneosaurus,* could glide through the air using a membrane-covered wing that spanned more than 12 inches (30 centimeters) and was supported by elongated ribs. A similar technique is used by the living lizard *Draco volans,* and both can fold the wing when at rest.

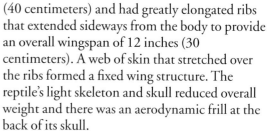

(40 centimeters) and had greatly elongated ribs that extended sideways from the body to provide an overall wingspan of 12 inches (30 centimeters). A web of skin that stretched over the ribs formed a fixed wing structure. The reptile's light skeleton and skull reduced overall weight and there was an aerodynamic frill at the back of its skull.

Like *Draco volans, Coelurosauravus* and the unrelated but similar *Kuehneosaurus* from the late Triassic probably lived in trees and used the novel trick of gliding to escape predators. *Draco volans* can glide for 200 feet (60 meters) and lose only about 6 feet (1.8 meters) in altitude.

By late Triassic and early Jurassic times, other winged reptiles called pterosaurs were evolving. Unlike *Coelurosauravus,* these had wings stretched between the limbs and body rather than attached to ribs. They had well-developed powers of sight and wing control and light but strong skeletons.

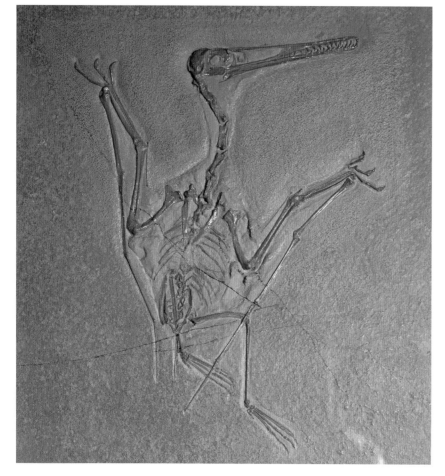

FLYING REPTILE

A well-preserved specimen of the pterosaur *Pterodactylus kochi* (left) from the Jurassic Solenhofen limestone strata of Bavaria still retains an imprint of the wing membrane.

MARINE REPTILES

During the Mesozoic, several reptile groups reverted to their ancestral habitat—water. The placodonts, resembling large iguanas, grew to 6½ feet (2 meters) long and featured broad, armored bodies. They fed on shellfish from the seafloor, grubbing up clams with their forelimbs or pulling them from the rocks with peglike front teeth.

The dolphinlike ichthyosaurs were highly specialized marine reptiles able to swim at speeds of up to 25 miles per hour (40 kilometers per hour). The first ones were about 3 to 6 feet (1 to 1.8 meters) long. Their diet consisted of fish and belemnites (swimming mollusks, a bit like cuttlefish), as we know from their stomach contents and coprolites (fossilized feces). The prey was snatched and swallowed whole.

Shonisaurus of the late Triassic, from Nevada in North America, is the largest known ichthyosaur. It grew to a length of 50 feet (15 meters), with the head and neck, the body, and the tail divided approximately into equal lengths. The backbone bent downward into the lower lobe of the fishlike tail—a feature of later ichthyosaurs. It must have swum in schools, because one deposit contained several dozen specimens. This particular group did not survive the end of the Triassic, but ichthyosaurs as a whole went on to even greater success in the Jurassic.

FOSSIL ICHTHYOSAUR

Ichthyosaurs made many adaptations to aquatic life, including giving birth to live young underwater. This fossil of a species of *Stenopterygius* is 6 feet (2 meters) long. Its elongated jaws, flippers, backbone, and vertical tail are all clearly visible.

CONVERGENT EVOLUTION

Ichthyosaurs are a classic example of convergent evolution, the process by which two lines of evolutionary development bring about superficially similar end-points. When different groups of organisms are subjected to the same environmental selection pressures, they tend to evolve similar design features. The streamlined body form of the reptilian ichthyosaurs is similar to that of living mammalian dolphins. Like dolphins, ichthyosaurs had powerful muscular bodies and keen eyesight. However, dolphins have a horizontal tail and a bigger brain.

SPOTTED DOLPHINS The reduced limbs have been specially adapted for steering.

NOTHOSAUR Found in mid-Triassic strata throughout Asia, Europe, and North Africa, *Nothosaurus* grew to 10 feet (3 meters) in length. With webbed feet and a long, flexible neck and tail, they probably lived like seals, fishing at sea and resting up on land.

The Jurassic Period

ALTHOUGH POPULARLY KNOWN AS THE "AGE OF THE DINOSAURS," THIS WAS ALSO A TIME WHEN MARINE LIFE FLOURISHED AND FLOWERING PLANTS EVOLVED.

The 64-million-year period in the Earth's history from 206 to 142 million years ago is known as the Jurassic. It is named for rock formations found in the Jura Mountains in western Europe. Although some forms of life had suffered in the extinction event at the end of the preceding age, the Triassic, the diversity of plants and animals had recovered to its previous level by mid-Jurassic times. This recovery marked the start of a long period of growth, which continued through the remainder of the Mesozoic era.

GLOBAL CHANGES

During the Jurassic period, the global super-continent of Pangea began to break up. Gondwana moved back south, opening a westward extension of the Tethys Ocean through the Panama region. Laurasia (North America and Eurasia) was separated from Gondwana and the land link between North and South America was broken. These changes had far-reaching effects on the development of differing environments and the evolution of animals and plants in the northern and southern hemispheres.

LARGE PREDATOR

The enormous dagger-shaped teeth, and scissor cut of the jaw made the *Allosaurus* a very effective predator. Remains of the dinosaur, which grew to a length of 40 feet (12 meters), are found in late Jurassic strata of the American Midwest.

SEED CONE

The reproductive seed cones of conifers are often fossilized, after being carried by streams far from the parent plant. This cone fell from a monkey-puzzle-like conifer in Patagonia, South America.

NORTH AMERICA

CHINA

EURASIA

TETHYS OCEAN

At the start of the period, global temperatures and humidity levels fell. After early Jurassic times, however, the trend reversed, with the rapid development of a much warmer "greenhouse" global climate by the end of the period. Sea levels rose and fell, but gradually rose to maintain overall higher levels than during the Triassic period. This activity drowned the coastal regions of continents, and as these new waters flooded inland, widespread shallow shelf seas developed. These warm, sunlight-filled bodies of water were ideal breeding grounds for increasingly diverse

JURASSIC SNAKESTONES

Jurassic limestone and shale sweep in gentle hills and vales across much of western Europe, from the Alps to western Scotland. They have been quarried for building materials since medieval times, giving up fossils that entered folklore as "snakestones," "thunderbolts," or "devil's toenails." Not until the early 19th century, however, was it realized that the fossils could be used to identify the Jurassic strata as representing a distinct geological period.

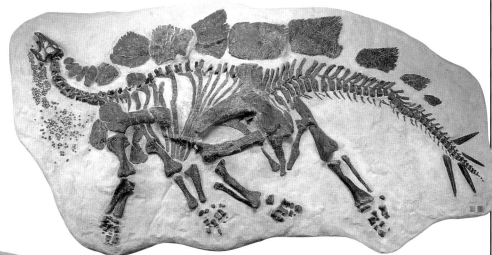

PLATED DINOSAUR
Stegosaurus, from the late Jurassic of western North America, was the largest of the plant-eating stegosaurids. A double row of diamond-shaped plates ran along the neck and back, and the tail had two pairs of spikes.

of the Jurassic seas, the predatory ichthyosaurs (fish-lizards) and plesiosaurs (near-lizards).

THRIVING FLORA AND FAUNA
On land, several groups of Triassic reptiles had died out. Mammals thrived, albeit in the shadows, but synapsids (ancient relatives of the mammals) became extinct during this age.

The airways became increasingly busy as more and more flying reptiles (pterosaurs) evolved and diversified to fill different ecological niches. In late Jurassic times these pterosaurs were joined by dinosaurs that had feathers, and some of these could fly—the birds were beginning to evolve.

Landscapes were gradually transformed and colored by the evolution of new plant life. A key event of the Jurassic age was the growth and diversification of sophisticated flowering plants, the angiosperms, which eventually came to dominate the terrestrial vegetation.

and complex marine life. From early Jurassic times, large reefs were re-established in the shallow seas. Phytoplankton, the microscopic, plantlike organisms that still form the basis of most food chains, enjoyed a new lease on life with the evolution of many of the groups that still dominate the microlife of the oceans today—the dinoflagellates and the nanoplankton.

By the end of the period, bony fishes (teleosts) had become increasingly similar in appearance to the fish we are familiar with today. They were hunted down by the spectacular "sea monsters"

AMBER TOMB
Some species of pine trees have produced amber resin since Jurassic times. Insects accidentally trapped in the amber resin become preserved, like this specimen from the Baltic Sea in Europe.

REPTILES OF THE JURASSIC SEAS

THE DISCOVERY OF FOSSIL SKELETONS of marine reptiles at Lyme Regis, in southwest England, in the early 19th century, was one of the key events that helped promote the novel idea that creatures which existed in the past might have become extinct. The fossil skeletons were once ichthyosaurs (fish-lizards) and plesiosaurs (near-lizards) that were unlike any living creatures known to the scientists of the time. They had evidently lived in the seas of the distant past, since they were found alongside the shells of typically marine clams, starfish, ammonites, and other squidlike cephalopods. Presented by early popularizers of paleontology as "sea dragons" and "denizens of the abysmal slime," these large marine reptiles immediately took a permanent hold on the popular imagination.

MONSTERS OF THE DEEP

The ichthyosaurs grew up to 50 feet (15 meters) long. Some specimens had a large skull and a distinctive dolphinlike jaw set with a fearsome array of typically reptilian teeth. These small, sharp, cone-shaped teeth were probably ideal for

MARINE STRATA
The early Jurassic strata of the cliffs around Lyme Regis in southwest England are full of fossilized marine shells, such as ammonites, clams, cephalopods, fish, and some rare reptiles.

snatching and holding fish before swallowing them whole. Fossilized stomach contents reveal fish scales and large numbers of tentacle hooks.

The ichthyosaurs were adapted for deep diving, with large, light-gathering eyes for hunting in dark waters. Rings of bones around the eyes protected against the pressure deep underwater. With their streamlined bodies, many ichthyosaurs looked like living dolphins, and they were clearly adapted for high speed cruising and the pursuit of small, fast-swimming fish.

It was initially thought that these magnificent marine reptiles went ashore to lay their eggs. It was only when a specimen was found with juveniles within the body cavity that scientists realized that like mammals, these reptiles retained fertilized eggs within the body, until the embryos were sufficiently well developed to be born directly into the sea.

Plesiosaurs ranged in size from 6 to 45 feet (2 to 14 meters) and were very well adapted for swimming, with four large, paddle-shaped limbs and long, flexible necks. Most large plesiosaurs possessed small skulls and long snouts, and had to

JURASSIC MARINE PARK
In Jurassic times, life under water was just as "nasty, brutish, and short" as life on land. The seas were populated with swimming cephalopods, and fish, including coelacanths, which were preyed upon by large marine reptiles. These predators were beaked ichthyosaurs (*Ichthyosaurus*), long-necked plesiosaurs (*Plesiosaurus*), and short-necked pliosaurs (*Rhomaleosaurus*). The coiled, shelled ammonites also preyed on small fish.

Lyme Regis

Plesiosaurus

Rhomaleosaurus

Ammonites

FINDING SEA MONSTERS

Some of the most important fossil finds of the early 19th century were made by a self-educated woman, Mary Anning, and her family, from the coastal cliffs of Lyme Regis, England. The Annings eked out a precarious existence scouring the cliffs for fossils to sell to genteel tourists. Between 1811 and 1830, they uncovered complete flattened skeletons of early marine "monsters." These ichthyosaur and plesiosaur discoveries helped revolutionize our view of life in the prehistoric past.

come to the surface to breathe. Their jaws were full of closely interlocking crocodile-like teeth, helpful for catching and holding slippery fish. Given their huge size and slow swimming speed, the plesiosaurs may have been ambush hunters, using their long necks to snatch fish from passing shoals.

There is also a separate group of short-necked plesiosaurs, known as pliosaurs. The pliosaurs had relatively massive skulls, armed with long, sharp teeth that often stuck out from the jaws. They were faster-moving predators than the other, long-necked plesiosaurs. Since some grew to around 40 feet (12 meters) long, they probably hunted such large prey as ichthyosaurs and other smaller plesiosaurs as well as fish.

GRACEFUL HUNTER

A fast-swimming marine reptile up to 6 feet (2 meters) long, *Ichthyosaurus* hunted fish and squidlike cephalopods. The beaklike jaws and sharp, conical teeth were used for snatching and holding prey.

JURASSIC FISH

The marine reptiles shared the seas with a great diversity of fish. Like Jurassic fish, most living fish are called teleosts. In Jurassic times, the teleosts had begun to evolve, but were still overshadowed by an older group of fish, the holosteans, which had deep bodies and heavy, bony scales. Many holosteans became extinct in the Cretaceous age, but some, including the garpike, still thrive today.

Another ancient group of bony fish were the chondrosteans, of which sturgeons are survivors.

Sharks and rays, such as *Squaloraja*, also gradually increased in number and diversity.

Pterosaur

Ichthyosaurus

Coelacanth

DISCOVERING EXTINCTION AND DEEP TIME

MODERN, SCIENCE-BASED UNDERSTANDING of the fossil record is little more than 200 years old. During the European Renaissance, in the 1400s and 1500s, the collection and illustration of fossils became an accepted pastime for wealthy patrons and collectors. But it was not until the middle of the 17th century that fossils began to be recognized as the remains of dead creatures, rather than objects formed by some force or fluid within the ground.

QUESTIONING THE BIBLE

The study of fossils could be justified as a worthy one in Christian Europe because, within the Christian tradition, the natural world was seen as the prime example of everything glorious created by God. But the pursuit was acceptable only so long as it did not conflict with the biblical story of the Creation. It was generally held that all the creatures on Earth had been created in a few days, in their current form. They had neither changed through time nor become extinct. In 1650, the date of this creation was estimated as 4004BC by James Ussher, the Protestant Archbishop of Armagh in Ireland.

The discovery of fossils resembling sea creatures far inland and high up on mountains, if

anything, confirmed the traditional Christian view of the past. The story of the Flood allowed these fossils to be passed off as the bodies of creatures that had either been drowned in the deluge or stranded on land once the waters receded.

By the early 1800s, however, great thicknesses of fossiliferous strata were discovered. It became clear that they could not all have been produced by a single flood, however catastrophic. Furthermore, the duration of the Earth's early prehistoric development could no longer be confined to a duration of a few thousand years.

DRAGONS

Dragons were familiar in the mythology of pre-modern cultures from China to Western Europe. Their ferocious image was based on features drawn from snakes and lizards. Not surprisingly, perhaps, the image of the dragon formed the basis for the original reconstructions of the first fossil reptilian "serpent" such as the *Iguanodon*.

BEFORE THE FLOOD

Animals line up two-by-two to enter Noah's Ark in this engraving by an unknown artist. The influence of this Old Testament story was so great that early 19th-century geologists thought fossils might be the remains of creatures drowned by the deluge. The idea was abandoned as fossils were found in more and more geological strata.

As an understanding of the slowness of the rates of many geological processes such as erosion and sedimentation developed, the age of the Earth had to be extended into millions, rather than just thousands, of years. What became clear was that during this long history there had been continual burial of organic remains within several layers of sediment, and that the types of fossils found varied throughout the different rock strata.

A NEW VIEW OF THE WORLD

By the late 18th century, fossil finds of large and often unrecognizable animals were being made in different parts of the world. Elephant-like bones were found on the banks of the Ohio River in North America (1739, named *Mastodon* in 1806). In 1796, fossil remains from Paraguay were described as those of a giant sloth. A giant marine reptile, the "Beast of Maastricht," was found in

1786 (see page 120). With the discovery of the "sea-dragons" *Ichthyosaurus* and *Plesiosaurus* at Lyme Regis in England in the early 19th century, naturalists had to face up to the idea that animals that had once existed had become extinct.

Evidence was also growing that individual species and groups of animals and plants appeared in the geological record at different times but with progressive modifications, which raised questions over just how fixed in form species were.

From the mid-19th century, a bitter debate was engaged between defenders of the traditional Christian view of the Creation and proponents of a new scientific view of the world that focused on the slow evolution of life and shifts in the surface of the Earth over almost unimaginable periods of time. In the 20th century, it was finally recognized that the Earth's age had to be measured in billions of years—a concept referred to as "deep time."

DRAGON LOOK-ALIKE

The awesomely toothed skull of this magnificent Cretaceous mosasaur, *Tylosaurus proriger*, resembles that of the mythical dragon. The reason is that the image of the dragon's head is based on folk knowledge of lizards, and mosasaurs are extinct marine lizards. Their jaws were nearly 3 feet (1 meter) long, and their total body length was about 32 feet (10 meters).

VALUABLE CATCH

The coelacanth is an animal that, until recently, was known only from the fossil record. It was common from Devonian to Jurassic times (370 to 150 million years ago) but was thought to have died out in Cretaceous times. In 1939, a scientist came across a specimen by chance off the South African coast, but he failed to preserve the fish properly and it disintegrated. Thirteen years later in 1952 a second specimen was identified in the Comoros Islands, off the east coast of Africa. Unknown to scientists, fishermen from the Comoros had for a long time regularly seen coelacanth in their catches. Since the fish were inedible, they had no value and were simply discarded. The islanders were unimpressed by the excitement about the coelacanth, but glad that the fish they called "Kombessa" had now become a valuable catch.

LIVING FOSSIL FISH

Coelacanths belong to an ancient group of creatures that were related to four-legged animals. First found in rocks of Devonian age, they were thought to be extinct until a specimen of *Latimeria chalumnae* was identified in the Indian Ocean in 1939. Scientists have now been able to observe them in their living habitats.

LIFE TAKES TO THE AIR

IN LATE JURASSIC TIMES, A LARGE lagoon, dotted with low-lying islands and sheltered from the Tethys Ocean by a reef, occupied an area of what is now Bavaria in southern Germany. The fine-grained limestone deposited on the bed of this Solenhofen lagoon proved an excellent medium for the preservation of fossils. The bodies of land animals and plants were washed into the water, settled on the lagoon bed, and covered with chalky mud. Solenhofen limestone holds the delicate remains of insects, such as dragonflies, flying pterosaurs, small dinosaurs, and, most famous of all, *Archaeopteryx*.

EARLY BIRD

In 1861, when the debate over Charles Darwin's new theory of evolution by natural selection was at its most intense, the fossil skeleton of *Archaeopteryx* was discovered. This feathered fossil was classified as the first bird, although it actually showed some reptilian characteristics as well. The connection between *Archaeopteryx* and reptiles was reinforced by the discovery later in the decade of a small bipedal (walking on hind legs only) dinosaur,

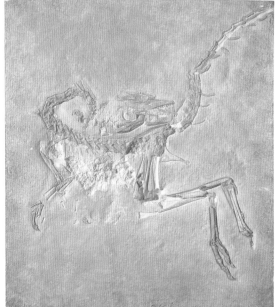

FAST RUNNER
Compsognathus was only 28 inches (70 centimeters) long. It had distinctive two-clawed hands and was a fast-running predator or scavenger. Its skeleton is very similar to *Archaeopteryx*.

Compsognathus, found in the same deposits. *Compsognathus*, one of the tiniest of predatory dinosaurs, bore a remarkably close physical resemblance to *Archaeopteryx*, although without the feathers.

SENSES AND CLAWS

Archaeopteryx was a medium-sized bird, like a magpie, about 20 inches (50 centimeters) long from the tip of its snout to the end of its long tail, and stood approximately 10 inches (25 centimeters) high. The bird's skull housed large eyes and well-developed optic lobes in the brain, showing that sight was a key sense. The pointed, beaklike jaws were armed with widely spaced sharp teeth and the forelimbs had three greatly elongated fingers, each ending in a curved claw. The hind limbs were particularly birdlike, with the inner toe situated at the rear of the foot as in living birds. There has been much debate about the living

SOLENHOFEN LAGOON

The waters and shorelines of a shallow, late Jurassic lagoon in southern Germany were vegetated with horsetails, small conifers, and palmlike cycads. The area was a good hunting ground for small reptiles such as *Compsognathus*. There were numerous flying pterosaurs, including the long-toothed, fish-eating *Rhamphorhynchus* and the smaller *Pterodactylus*, an agile flyer that may have caught insects on the wing. Most famous of all is the early bird *Archaeopteryx* which, with its long tail, was probably a fairly slow and cumbersome flyer.

Solenhofen

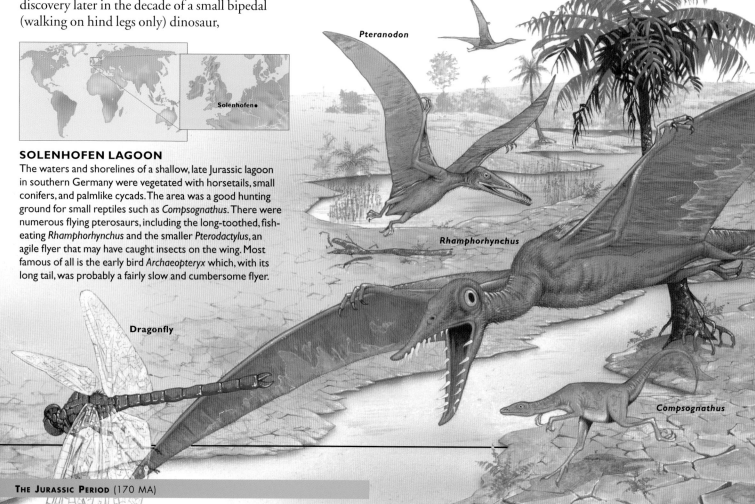

Pteranodon

Rhamphorhynchus

Dragonfly

Compsognathus

habits and flying ability of *Archaeopteryx*. Traditionally, it has been portrayed as climbing trees and then gliding from tree to tree to find food. Gliding could then have evolved over time into wing-powered flight. But, in fact, birds evolved from swift little predatory dinosaurs, so flight could well have begun from the ground up.

It is now known that the lagoon environment in which the bird lived did not include many tall trees, and thus was not the ideal place for a glider to prosper. Nevertheless, the asymmetric arrangement of the primary wing feathers suggests that *Archaeopteryx* could indeed fly. Flightless birds do not have this arrangement.

JURASSIC SHRIMP
With its long antennae and five pairs of walking legs this *Aeger*, 8 inches (20 centimeters) long, is clearly a shrimp (decapod crustacean). It is preserved in fine-grained limestone of late Jurassic age.

FLYING REPTILES

Archaeopteryx shared the Jurassic airways with flying reptiles, the pterosaurs. The earliest pterosaurs appeared during the late Triassic age, and they evolved throughout the Jurassic period. Their hollow, light skeleton was ideal for flight, but their most striking feature was an extra-long fourth finger on their forelimbs, which was the spar of the wing. Three shorter fingers were retained on the wing's front edge.

Originally, the pterosaurs had long tails that provided stability during flight at the expense of maneuverability. During the late Jurassic age, pterosaur tails became considerably shorter, making the creatures more agile hunters. The smaller species of these later pterosaurs had wingspans of up to 16 inches (40 centimeters) and were probably able to feed on insects while on the wing. The larger species were fish-eaters, diving to scoop their prey out of the sea. The wingspan of some pterosaurs grew as large as 35 to 40 feet (11 to 12 meters).

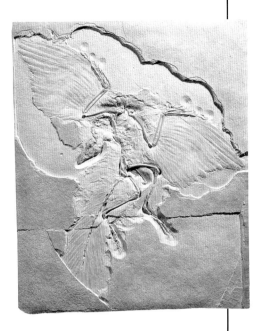

ARCHAEOPTERYX
One of the world's most famous fossils, *Archaeopteryx* has many of the features of a small dinosaur, with a long bony tail and toothed jaws. Wings and flight feathers suggest, however, that it was a bird and could fly.

Archaeopteryx

Pterodactylus

Compsognathus

EARLY MAMMALS

Today's mammals are easy to recognize, with their shared traits of hair, warm blood, and live-born young that suckle. These familiar features, however, did not evolve simultaneously, but rather over a long period of time. It is difficult to know when each manifested, since they are soft-tissue features not preserved in the fossil record.

The first mammal-like characteristics were seen in small, late Carboniferous, lizardlike reptiles. They showed the beginnings of tooth differentiation (a range of different teeth for different purposes) and skull modifications that were part of the mammalian trend.

By mid-Triassic times, mammal relatives called cynodonts ("dog teeth") had mouths that were filled with teeth with many cutting edges. They also had a bony roof plate (secondary palate) in the mouth that allowed them to continue breathing while chewing food. Changes to their jaw allowed a larger brain case, as well as the development of an ear that allowed them to distinguish sounds in a more complex way than reptiles. The small cynodonts were able to burrow, and this life in dark places led to the evolution of whiskerlike structures around the head, designed for feeling a way through tunnels.

FIRST TRUE MAMMALS

Although early cynodonts such as *Adelobasileus* from North America or *Sinoconodon* from China may not be the direct ancestors of today's mammals, they tell us a lot about early mammalian history. However, the fossil remains of the American and Chinese specimens are incomplete, so scientists have used more recent mammals to deduce the probable lifestyle of these animals. *Megazostrodon*, found in southern Africa, was the size and shape of a shrew, small enough to curl up in a matchbox. Its body was long and low, with a flexible backbone and long limbs, which were held out to the side in a primitive squatting posture that is still assumed by some small mammals today.

OPAL TEETH

This fossil is a jaw fragment of an early Cretaceous mammal from Australia. The teeth have features that link the creature to egg-laying mammals (monotremes) such as the living echidnas. After burial in sediment, the original bone material was dissolved away and the cavity infilled with opal, a silica mineral similar in composition to flint.

SOUTH AFRICAN INSECT-EATER
Megazostrodon, from late Triassic strata in southern Africa, was 5 inches (12 centimeters) long. This insect-eating, shrewlike animal may have been nocturnal.

RATLIKE MAMMAL
Ptilodus was a primitive rodentlike mammal that lived in early Tertiary times in North America. It belonged to an extinct group of mammals called the multituberculates and probably ate nuts and seeds.

IDENTIFYING EARLY MAMMALS

Land is an inhospitable environment for the preservation of animal remains. Small vertebrates with delicate bones, such as the early mammals, were likely to have been eaten whole by scavengers. However, the fecal remains (coprolites) left by the scavengers sometimes contain undigested fragments of the animals they ate, especially teeth. The fossil record of small mammals is thus mostly made up of their teeth and bits of their jawbones. Fortunately, the pattern of cusps, ridges, and furrows on the surface of mammalian cheek teeth changed rapidly over time and is distinctive for each species. Consequently, even though there is an almost complete lack of skeletal remains of these early mammals, it is possible to identify the different species on the basis of their teeth alone.

DENTAL RECONSTRUCTION

A single tooth is all that remains of this earliest mammalian primate, *Purgatorius*. Found in late Cretaceous rocks in Montana, USA, the tooth belonged to an insect-eater, about 4 inches (10 centimeters) long. The reconstruction above is based on an understanding of other primitive primates.

The skeleton of another animal, *Morganucodon*, also showed how the first true mammals lived. *Morganucodon* grew to a length of 6 inches (15 centimeters) and was found in early Jurassic strata in both England and China. It reflected all the mammalian traits of *Adelobasileus* but had a more advanced ear structure.

The teeth of *Morganucodon*, in particular, were typically mammalian. The juvenile milk teeth were followed by a single set for adult life, unlike reptiles whose teeth are replaced several times in a lifetime. The cheek teeth were also developed into premolars and molars, as in all later mammals. Chewing involved a triangular movement of the lower jaw rather than the simpler up and down, back and forth movement of the advanced cynodonts. The teeth suggest that *Morganucodon* was carnivorous, probably feeding on insects and worms at night, when predatory lizards were less active.

The morganucodonts were agile animals capable of fast movement but not sustained running. Their nocturnal habits required them to generate body heat internally. This was achieved by means of their teeth and jaws, which worked to break down food before it reached the stomach, allowing the rapid release of energy from a high-protein diet. To conserve body heat during the night, they would have needed a covering of hair, but so far the fossil record has not revealed this critical soft-tissue evidence. As a group, these small mammals survived for 40 million years.

Altogether within the Mesozoic era, while the dinosaurs dominated the land, 20 or more families of mammals evolved to live in a hidden coexistence with the massive reptiles.

MONGOLIAN PLACENTAL MAMMAL

One of the earliest placental mammals (which could bear well-developed live young) was *Zalambdalestes* (above). This shrewlike animal lived in Mongolia in late Cretaceous times and, like the living elephant shrew, had long back legs.

ELEPHANT SHREW

The fossil record of *Elephantulus* (right) and other elephant shrews extends back to early Tertiary times. They used to be regarded as primitive insectivores, but surprisingly they are closer related to the elephants.

Early Cretaceous Period

THE BREAK-UP OF THE SUPERCONTINENT OF PANGEA LED TO DIVERGENT ANIMAL AND PLANT DEVELOPMENT ON LANDMASSES SEPARATED BY BROAD SEAS.

By 130 million years ago, the North Atlantic had started to open up, breaking North America and Europe apart, although a link was probably maintained in northerly regions for another 25 million years. As Pangea fragmented, Africa and South America also began to pull apart, starting the formation of the Central and South Atlantic. The Tethys Ocean extended westward until an east-west tropical marine corridor divided North America and Eurasia in the north from Gondwana in the south, shutting down the exchange of animals and plants.

RING OF FIRE

Along the western margin of the Americas a great volcanic mountain chain developed, extending from Chile to Alaska. It survives today as the eastern flank of the Pacific Ring of Fire. During early Cretaceous times, these mountains formed a fertile ground for the evolution of terrestrial life.

The level of carbon dioxide in the Earth's atmosphere was high, producing warm, dry global climates in a greenhouse effect. Sea levels, which had been falling from a late Jurassic high, rose rapidly as temperatures increased and the polar

CHALK CLIFFS
The cliffs of southern England and northern France are formed from Cretaceous limestone, made of tiny skeletons of planktonic organisms called coccoliths.

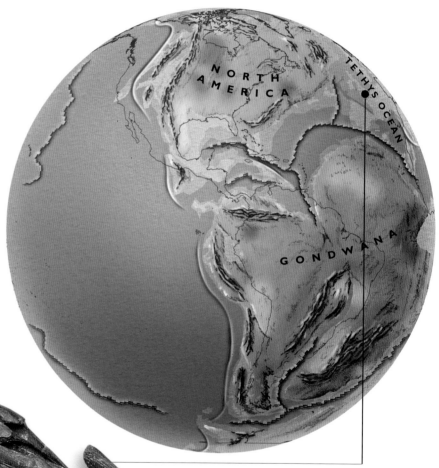

NORTH AMERICA · TETHYS OCEAN · GONDWANA

icecaps melted, flooding great areas of the continents with shallow seas, especially in North America, southern Europe, and Antarctica. These shelf seas abounded with marine life, including reefs with rich populations of fish, preyed upon by large marine reptiles and sharks. Vegetation was gradually changing. As early Mesozoic ferns declined, more modern types of ferns became dominant. Seed-ferns, cycads, ginkgos, and the older groups of conifers were in decline, being replaced by cedars and redwoods. Most important for the future was the appearance

IGUANODON SKULL
The beaklike snout and long rows of similar-shaped cheek teeth show that this early Cretaceous ornithopod dinosaur, *Iguanodon*, was a plant-eater. This iguanodon lived on what is now the Isle of Wight, in southern England, when sea levels were lower than those shown in these maps.

NEW LIFEFORMS

Recent fossil finds show that the Cretaceous was a period of remarkable biological innovation. While the reptiles continued to dominate, other fauna developed new forms. Fossils from China, Mongolia, and Spain have shown that several groups of toothed birds evolved in the early

Cretaceous age. Small, primitive mammals also diversified. Most of the birds and many of the mammals were wiped out in the mass extinction at the end of the Cretaceous period, along with the dinosaurs. But enough survived to provide the basis for the evolution of modern terrestrial life.

PARROT-JAW DINOSAUR

The parrotlike, toothless beak and jaws of *Psittacosaurus*, a ceratopsian dinosaur from early Cretaceous strata in Mongolia, were adapted for eating tough plant material. A bony ridge on top of the rear of the skull subsequently evolved into the bony frill that protected the neck of later ceratopsians.

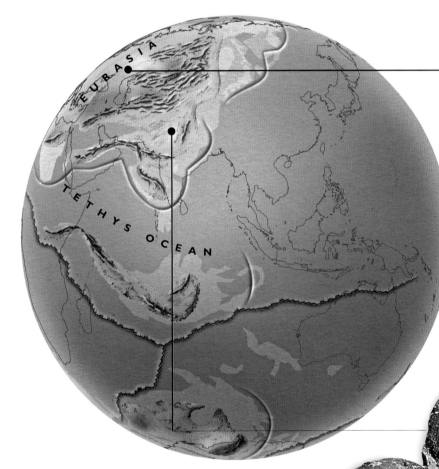

EURASIA

TETHYS OCEAN

the link between the continents was broken, by mid-Cretaceous times, the dinosaur groups diverged. In North America, a massive hypsilophodont called *Tenontosaurus* became dominant among the ornithopods (plant-eating dinosaurs that predominantly walked on two legs). In Europe, the ornithopod group called iguanodonts continued to thrive.

NORTH-SOUTH DIVIDE

Tetrapod faunas in the northern and southern hemispheres also began to show marked differences. In the north, the number of species of sauropods (giant plant-eating dinosaurs) and stegosaurs declined. Concurrently, the armored ankylosaurs and the iguanodonts increased in diversity and numbers, and the first ceratopsian dinosaurs, such as *Psittacosaurus*, appeared. By contrast, in the southern hemisphere the sauropods remained the dominant plant-eaters.

of angiosperms, the flowering plants that dominate and color modern landscapes. The air was buzzing with flying reptiles, birds, and ever-growing numbers of insects. The insects and the angiosperm plants benefited mutually from the development of flowers and pollen.

The dinosaurs continued to dominate the land while small mammals became increasingly diverse and numerous. Dinosaurs such as *Iguanodon* and some hypsilophodonts (a group of swift, bipedal, plant-eaters) were able to migrate from Europe to North America in earliest Cretaceous times. But as

DINOSAUR EGGS

The tough mineralized shells of some dinosaur eggs, like these Cretaceous eggs from China, have been preserved in nest clutches similar to those laid by turtles and crocodiles today. These eggs are 5 inches (13 centimeters) in diameter.

THE WORLD OF THE IGUANODON DINOSAUR

ONE OF THE WORLD'S most exciting fossil finds was made by two Belgian coalminers in 1878. Working in the Sainte-Barbe pit near Bernissart, southwest Belgium, they found complete skeletons of large plant-eating dinosaurs. The skeletons all belonged to *Iguanodon*, a dinosaur that had already been named on the basis of fragmentary remains.

RECONSTRUCTING IGUANODON

Excavation of the find was handed over to the scientists of the Royal Museum of Natural History in Brussels, led by Louis De Pauw and Louis Dollo. The problem the Belgian scientists faced was how to rebuild the skeletons in their original life positions. The structure of the hip bones and hind legs was distinctly birdlike, so Dollo and De Pauw used an emu skeleton as a model. But they also realized that *Iguanodon* had important differences from birds, especially in its long muscular tail, strong forearms, wrists, and hands. To account for these features, they also used a kangaroo as a model. They ended up with a cross between a kangaroo and a flightless bird— an upright bipedal dinosaur with a birdlike neck

and a tail resting on the ground. This model has been radically revised in the late 20th century. Evidence suggests that *Iguanodon* was primarily four-legged. Although its forearms were significantly shorter than its hind limbs, they were powerful, with strong wrists. The middle three fingers of the large hands could be splayed into a weight-supporting foot for walking. The tail bones of *Iguanodon* were actually strapped together by bonelike ligaments that would have made the tail stiff—it could not have been flexed as the kangaroo-based model devised by Dollo

FAST-MOVING HERBIVORE
The bipedal *Hypsilophodon* was a small 5-foot- (1.5-meter-) long fast-running, gazellelike herbivore. In the early Cretaceous, it lived in Europe and North America.

THUMB SPIKE

On the end of its thumb, Iguanodon had a sharp, bony spike that might have formed a very effective weapon against predators. In the earliest reconstructions of Iguanodon, the thumb spike was mistakenly seen as a rhinoceros-like nose horn.

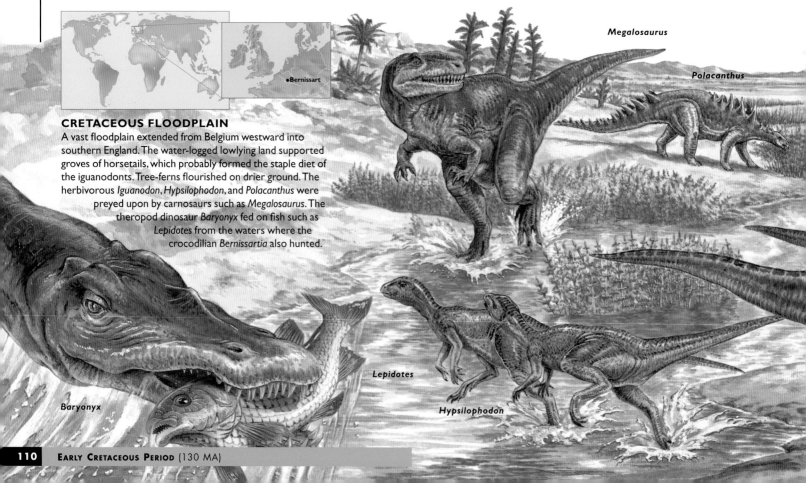

CRETACEOUS FLOODPLAIN

A vast floodplain extended from Belgium westward into southern England. The water-logged lowlying land supported groves of horsetails, which probably formed the staple diet of the iguanodonts. Tree-ferns flourished on drier ground. The herbivorous *Iguanodon*, *Hypsilophodon*, and *Polacanthus* were preyed upon by carnosaurs such as *Megalosaurus*. The theropod dinosaur *Baryonyx* fed on fish such as *Lepidotes* from the waters where the crocodilian *Bernissartia* also hunted.

•Bernissart

Megalosaurus

Polacanthus

Baryonyx

Lepidotes

Hypsilophodon

and De Pauw required. Young *Iguanodons* were probably more likely to stand on two legs, while the much heavier adults usually walked on four legs, only raising themselves on their hind legs for feeding, fighting, and mating.

Iguanodon was large, about 2 tons in weight, and needed to be an efficient feeder. A herbivore, its food consisted of cycads, horsetails, and conifers, plants tough to chew and low in nutrition. To break down the coarse cellulose fibers for digestion, herbivores need powerful jaw muscles and strong cheek teeth to grind the plant material up as much as possible before swallowing it. The front of *Iguanodon*'s jaws lacked teeth but were covered with a turtlelike horny beak, ideally suited for cropping vegetation. Cheek teeth formed parallel, interlocking rows of about 100 leaf-shaped teeth with serrated edges. Using its flexible mouth, *Iguanodon* could grind its upper teeth from side to side against its lower ones.

LIVING ALONGSIDE IGUANODON

Hypsilophodon, another plant-eating, "bird-footed" (ornithopod) dinosaur, existed alongside *Iguanodon* in early Cretaceous times. Surprisingly, this small bipedal animal was highly successful. It used to be thought that *Hypsilophodon* lived in trees because one specimen had a foot that appeared to have a birdlike, "perching" toe on the back of the foot. This reconstruction was later found to be incorrect, and other features show

that *Hypsilophodon* was built for speed and agility. It was the dinosaur equivalent of today's gazelle. Another herbivore was the four-legged *Polacanthus,* which used armor for defense.

The top predators of the time were carnosaurs (meat-eating dinosaurs), although not much is known about them. British strata of this age have also produced evidence of a large fish-eating theropod dinosaur, *Baryonyx*. The lakes and rivers of the locality were populated with turtles (*Plesiochelys*) and crocodiles (*Bernissartia*), as well as fish, clams, and snails.

TRIASSIC SURVIVOR
Crocodylus, the modern crocodile, is a survivor of a reptile group that originated in the late Triassic age. Dinosaur reconstructions were orginally based on crocodiles, until it was determined that many dinosaurs were either two-legged, or simply too big to maintain a lizardlike posture.

Iguanodon

Tree-ferns

Baryonyx

Bernissartia

INVENTING AND PICTURING THE DINOSAURS

DINOSAURS HAVE TAKEN THE PLACE OF THE dragons and monsters of myth and legend, playing an enduring role in the modern imagination. These terrible lizards were a 19th-century invention of the newly emerging science of paleontology. As icons of popular science, they have gone through a number of transformations over the years, before ending up as the fleet-footed, colorful creatures depicted in dinosaur books and movies today.

The story starts some time before 1818, when part of a fossil jawbone with large, bladelike teeth was found in the mid-Jurassic strata of Oxfordshire, England. It was estimated that *Megalosaurus*, as the dinosaur was named, would have stood about 8 feet (2.5 meters) high. Further puzzling fossil bones were unearthed in 1825 in lower Cretaceous limestone. Naturalists of the time, such as Gideon Mantell, were puzzled by these fossils and had little idea about the real shape of the animal. It was clear from the size of the fossil remains that they were dealing with a gigantic land reptile, but living lizards, such as the iguana and crocodiles, were the only models that these early investigators had. Mantell imagined *Iguanodon*, as he called it, as a four-legged and lizardlike creature with a very long tail.

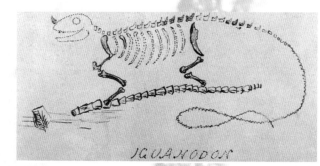

FIRST DRAFT
This unpublished sketch of 1833 (above) by Gideon Mantell was the first attempt to reconstruct the dinosaurs. Mantell had only a very incomplete jumble of bones of his new *Iguanodon* fossil and mistakenly positioned the thumb spike as a rhinoceros-like horn.

IGUANID ROLE MODEL
The living iguana lizard (left) provided the model for the first attempts to reconstruct a dinosaur. But growing to only a few feet long, it is not possible that the iguanas are just a miniature version of much larger dinosaurs, such as *Iguanodon*.

JURASSIC PARK

Michael Crichton's novel and Steven Spielberg's film of Jurassic Park have played an important part in changing the popular perception of dinosaurs. Their reputation as dim-witted, cold-blooded, and slow-moving creatures has now been reassessed, with studies of their living habits and behavior showing that they were as diverse as mammals.

In the film, the predatory, carnivorous velociraptors are portrayed as aggressive fast-running creatures, capable of intelligent thought and displaying acute senses. In a frightening chase scene, a Tyrannosaurus rex nearly outruns a jeep. Quite a few of the dinosaurs featured in the film are, however, actually Cretaceous, rather than Jurassic, in age.

CELLULOID STEGOSAURS
In an early scene from the film *Jurassic Park: The Lost World*, two enormous, plated stegosaurs make their first appearance crossing a dry river bed.

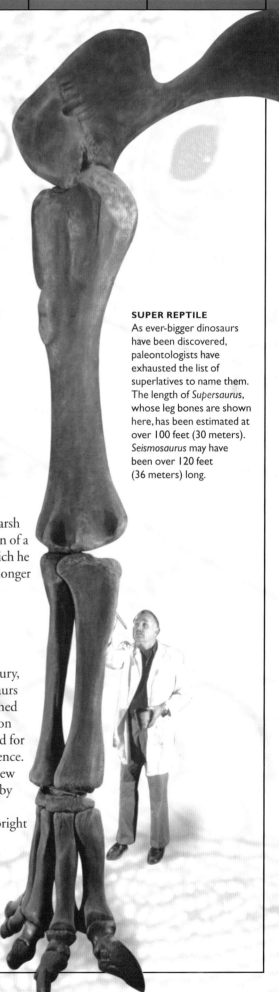

SUPER REPTILE
As ever-bigger dinosaurs have been discovered, paleontologists have exhausted the list of superlatives to name them. The length of *Supersaurus*, whose leg bones are shown here, has been estimated at over 100 feet (30 meters). *Seismosaurus* may have been over 120 feet (36 meters) long.

DINOSAURS ARE NAMED
The name dinosaur was first coined in 1842 by a British professor of anatomy, Richard Owen. He advocated the creation of a whole new division of animals—the class Dinosauria—to distinguish anatomically between recently discovered fossil reptiles and known living reptiles.

Owen's vision of the dinosaurs was a huge popular success, and by the 1860s dinosaur research had taken off in a big way in the United States. America had already been the site of a major discovery. In 1802, some fossil footprints were uncovered on a farm in Massachusetts. Edward Hitchcock, a local naturalist, claimed that the curious three-toed footprints must have been made by giant birds. In fact, they had been made by a dinosaur. The discovery was the first evidence that some dinosaurs walked on two rather than four legs, although the right connection was not finally made until 70 years later.

In the 1870s, the United States was the scene of the "dinosaur wars"—a bitter rivalry between two experts, Professor Othniel Charles Marsh of Yale University and Edward Drinker Cope of Philadelphia. Their competing expeditions led to the discovery and description of some 130 new species of dinosaur. In 1883, Marsh produced the first reconstruction of a giant plant-eating dinosaur, which he called *Brontosaurus* (a name no longer used). The image of these huge sauropods captured public imagination the world over.

REVAMPING THE IMAGE
In the first half of the 20th century, the popular image of the dinosaurs was as slow-moving, small-brained creatures, a byword for extinction through the failure to adapt, and for lumbering size without intelligence. In the 1960s, however, a new view of the dinosaurs was promoted by Dr. Robert Bakker and others. Intelligent, diverse, arrayed in bright colors and patterns, the new dinosaurs were shown as highly successful creatures whose extinction is still interestingly problematic. These new dinosaurs have proved even more popular than the old.

Later Cretaceous Period

OCEANIC CHANGES DURING THE MID- AND LATE CRETACEOUS LED TO A HOTHOUSE ENVIRONMENT IN WHICH LIFE CONTINUED TO DIVERSIFY RAPIDLY.

Approximately 100 million years ago, during the mid-Cretaceous, the movement of the Earth's crust was being driven by the opening up of new oceans in the southern hemisphere, such as the Southern Ocean and South Atlantic Ocean. These oceans and the formation of new ocean floor were in turn driven by changing convection patterns within the Earth's mantle.

Gondwana continued to break up. Madagascar split away from India, which then moved northward. New Zealand rifted from Australia as the Tasman Sea opened. In the Far East, the final collision of landmasses such as Tibet and Southeast Asia formed new mountain belts and completed the eastern margin of Eurasia. In Europe, the northward rifting of the Atlantic opened the Bay of Biscay and split Britain, Labrador, and Newfoundland, followed by the separation of Norway and Greenland.

OCEANIC CHANGES
Geological evidence points toward an unusually high rate of volcanic activity during the mid-Cretaceous, especially at mid-ocean ridges. Ridge systems rose high above the old ocean depths and

VELOCIRAPTOR SKULL
A small late Cretaceous dinosaur whose remains have been found in Mongolia, *Velociraptor*'s large eye sockets and sharp curved teeth are typical of a highly active carnivore.

PACIFIC OCEAN

NORTH AMERICA

ARCTIC OCEAN

ASIA

ATLANTIC OCEAN

EUROPE

TETHYS OCEAN

TYRANNOSAURUS REX
Tyrannosaurids such as *T. rex* were at large in North America and Central Asia during the late Cretaceous. This photograph of a *T. rex* skull amply depicts the curved and serrated bladelike teeth.

lifted the neighboring deep ocean floors with them. As a result, sea levels rose worldwide up to 650 feet (200 meters) higher than present levels, causing worldwide flooding. Sea levels had fallen again by the end of the Cretaceous.

Ocean water temperatures saw a sharp rise, fall, and partial rise again before falling toward the end of the period. These changes were prompted by fluctuating patterns of ocean circulation as the continents moved apart. Periods of rapid ocean warming (and oxygen depletion) appear to have caused extinctions among marine life.

MAIASAURA

This fossil of a hadrosaur hatchling was found in Montana. It is so small that, for survival, its parents must have cared for it just as adult birds look after their chicks. Parental care is reflected in the dinosaur's name which means "good mother."

HOTHOUSE SHIFT

Extensive submarine volcanic activity during the mid-Cretaceous period released massive amounts of carbon dioxide into the ocean and atmosphere. This caused warming due to the greenhouse effect. In fact, the mid-Cretaceous was perhaps the warmest episode of Earth's entire history. As global warming peaked, temperate forest vegetation spread to high latitudes, shifting more than 1,250 miles (2,000 kilometers) from the equator toward the poles.

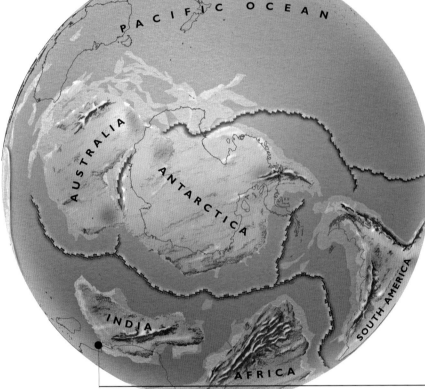

species diversity in the mid-Cretaceous hothouse. Mammals ranged from shrew- to cat-sized, and were mainly nocturnal. The earliest angiosperms (flowering plants) were very probably shrubby weeds. In time they increased in range and variety, filling in as smaller trees beneath the forest canopy of conifers. Flora of the late Cretaceous included figs, willows, poplars, magnolias, and plane trees. Insects diversified rapidly worldwide in parallel with the spread of the angiosperms.

In the water, the top predators were a group of massive, flippered lizards known as mosasaurs. Plesiosaurs and the giant turtle *Archelon* roamed the oceans, and the first teleost fishes (today's dominant fish group) appeared. Ammonites, bivalves such as clams, and gastropods became widespread. Marine planktonic microorganisms flourished and the accumulation of their remains in seabed sediments laid down the hydrocarbon basis for much of the world's present oil supply.

LIFE DURING THE MID- TO LATE CRETACEOUS

Dinosaurs continued to diversify and dominate the land. Theropods of the mid- and late Cretaceous ranged from the huge tyrannosaurids such as *T. rex* and smaller predators such as *Deinonychus* and *Velociraptor* to the ostrichlike ornithomimosaurs. Also in evidence were duck-billed hadrosaurs such as *Maiasaura*, ankylosaurs, and ceratopsians such as *Triceratops*.

The organisms that dominate our modern terrestrial ecosystems, the flowering plants, birds, and mammals, underwent explosive growth in

CLAM FOSSILS

Trigoniid clams were common in the warm waters of the Tethys Ocean in Mesozoic times. Their strong, ribbed shells protected them against battering waves. One tropical group of trigoniids has survived to the present day.

THE MAMMALS AND DINOSAURS OF MONGOLIA

THE REMOTE DESERTS OF MONGOLIA, IN THE heart of central Asia, have produced some of the most exciting fossil finds of the 20th century. In Cretaceous times, Mongolia was often swept by desert dust storms that buried the remains of hundreds of lizards, mammals, and dinosaurs in the sandstone hills. The fossil skeletons are often complete, with even the smallest, most delicate bones preserved. They provide fascinating, if often controversial, evidence about life around 90 million years ago.

During the latter part of Cretaceous times, two groups of bird-hipped (ornithischian) dinosaurs, the hadrosaurids and the ceratopsians, evolved new species and spread across the globe. This is reflected in the wide range of dinosaur fossils found in Mongolia, which also include many reptile-hipped (saurischian) dinosaurs, such as theropods, dromaeosaurs, and oviraptors.

"EGG-STEALER" DINOSAUR

The most famous reptile-hipped dinosaur fossil discovered in Mongolia is *Oviraptor philoceratops*, identified and named in the 1920s by Roy Chapman Andrews. A lightly built, two-legged dinosaur, it was originally thought to prey on the eggs of the ceratopsian dinosaur *Protoceratops*—hence its name, *Oviraptor,* or "egg-stealer." Since

the remains of an *Oviraptor philoceratops* was found within what was believed to be a *Protoceratops* nest, Andrews jumped to the conclusion that it had died while feeding on the eggs. Recent research has shown, however, that the *Oviraptor* does not live up to its name. Using new techniques to examine the fossilized embryos inside the eggs, experts have revealed that the embryos belonged to the *Oviraptor*. In other words, the *Oviraptor* died sitting on its own nest.

MONGOLIAN MORTUARY

The arid deserts of Mongolia have revealed some of the richest dinosaur-bearing strata known. Thousands of specimens have been recovered from these Mesozoic deposits over the last 80 years.

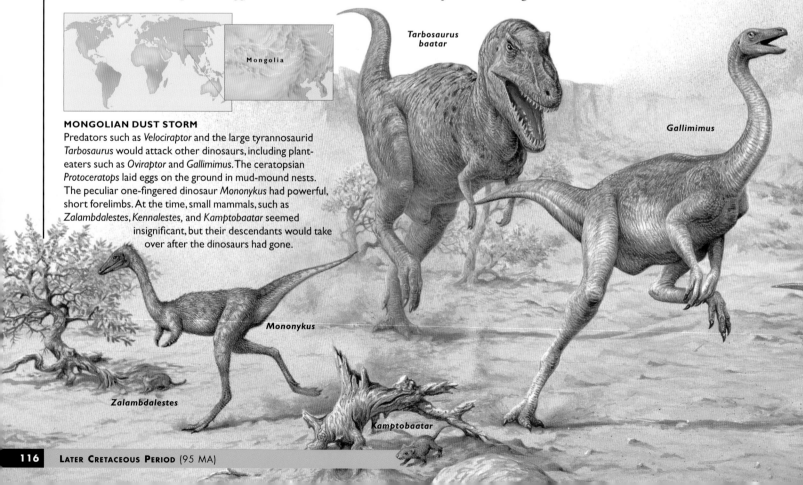

MONGOLIAN DUST STORM

Predators such as *Velociraptor* and the large tyrannosaurid *Tarbosaurus* would attack other dinosaurs, including plant-eaters such as *Oviraptor* and *Gallimimus*. The ceratopsian *Protoceratops* laid eggs on the ground in mud-mound nests. The peculiar one-fingered dinosaur *Mononykus* had powerful, short forelimbs. At the time, small mammals, such as *Zalambdalestes, Kennalestes,* and *Kamptobaatar* seemed insignificant, but their descendants would take over after the dinosaurs had gone.

Mongolia

Tarbosaurus baatar

Gallimimus

Mononykus

Zalambdalestes

Kamptobaatar

WITNESSING A LOST WORLD

Excavating Mongolia's fossil riches has been an exciting experience for paleontologists. In 1994, an expedition from the American Museum of Natural History found the well-preserved remains of more than 500 Cretaceous animals in the hills of Ukhaa Tolgod. The expedition's leader, Professor Michael Novacek, has written: "It was almost as if we had stumbled upon a giant graveyard where, just a few moments before, these animals had given their last gasp. It was as close as we will ever come to stepping back in time, walking into that world, and seeing a community of extinct animals…"

LIVING IN THE DINOSAURS' SHADOW

Although the dinosaurs still dominated the land in late Cretaceous times, small mammals were increasing in number and diversity. There were four types of mammal: placentals (whose young are born reasonably mature), marsupials (the young are born immature and nourished in a pouch), monotremes (egg-layers), and a group that is now extinct, multituberculates.

The multituberculates were at the time by far the most abundant type of mammal. They were probably plant-eaters, in contrast to placentals, marsupials, and monotremes, who were insect-eaters. It was once thought that multituberculates were tree-climbers, but Mongolian forms, such as *Nemegtbaatar*, have an anatomy close to that of living gerbils. It is now believed that they were nocturnal animals, adapted for running and burrowing rather than tree-climbing.

Examination of a well-preserved pelvis of another of the Mongolian multituberculates, *Kryptobaatar*, has proved that these creatures gave birth to live young, rather than laying eggs like the monotremes. The young must have been very undeveloped at birth, like those of the marsupials, because the creature's birth canal was very small. Looking after such helpless young would have been a further reason for living in a burrow, which could be used as a nursery.

The multituberculates died out only about 35 million years ago, in the late Eocene age. The placental mammals, represented in late Cretaceous times by creatures such as the shrewlike, insect-eating *Kennalestes*, and the slightly larger *Zalambdalestes*, survived. A few marsupials and monotremes have also survived up to the present day, but the placentals have proved by a long way the most successful mammals. This probably reflects the advantages to be gained by giving birth to far more developed young.

CAREFUL HANDLING
Part of *Protoceratops*, a ceratopsian dinosaur, is carefully cleaned before being extracted from the rock matrix. Even large dinosaur bones need gentle handling to preserve them for the future.

Protoceratops

Velociraptor

Oviraptor

Protoceratops

Kennalestes

HADROSAURS AND CARNOSAURS

MORE THAN 300 DINOSAUR skeletons have been unearthed along the Red Deer River in Alberta, Canada, now the site of the Dinosaur Provincial Park. Upper Cretaceous sediment, around 75 million years old, was exposed by the erosive power of meltwaters pouring out of the retreating glaciers some 13,000 years ago. No other rocky landscape of similar size on Earth has produced as many individual skeletons of different dinosaurs, including a wealth of late Cretaceous hadrosaurs (herbivores with a ducklike beak and webbed feet) and carnosaurs (bipedal carnivores).

The original discovery was made in 1909 when a rancher from Alberta, Canada, told the famous dinosaur collector, Barnum Brown of the American Museum of Natural History, that some bones discovered on his ranch were similar to those on display in the museum. Brown wasted no time and immediately established a camp alongside the Red Deer River. He worked the area from 1910 to 1915, recovering a spectacular variety of unusually

UNEARTHING A GIANT
The rare find of a complete tyrannosaurid skull and some bones is painstakingly excavated by a team of paleontologists.

complete skeletons with skulls. The sedimentary strata in Dinosaur Provincial Park represent a rich variety of environments, from offshore through foreshore, barrier, lagoon, swamp, and delta to river channel and floodplain. And the fossils from within these strata reflect the diversity of Cretaceous life. The total number of fossils found includes an astonishing 300 articulated large skeletons, representing 36 species of dinosaur and another 84 species of other vertebrates, including fish, amphibians (salamanders and frogs), reptiles (turtles, lizards, crocodiles, and pterosaurs), birds, and mammals. These specimens are currently exhibited in museums around the world.

THE DINOSAUR ROLL CALL

A plentiful water supply produced lush vegetation in the area in Cretaceous times, allowing plant-eating hadrosaurs to flourish, including *Corythosaurus* and *Lambeosaurus,* with their characteristic crested skulls. There are thin layers of chewed-up plant debris in the Cretaceous strata that have been

CRETACEOUS LIFE

Late Cretaceous environments in Alberta, Canada, supported many different kinds of dinosaurs, as well as other animals and plants. The bulk of the vertebrates at the base of the food chain were plant-eaters such as the ceratopsians (*Styracosaurus*), hadrosaurs (*Parasaurolophus, Maiasaura, Corythosaurus*), and ankylosaurs (*Euoplocephalus*). They adopted different modes of defense, including body armor, herding, and weapons in the form of horns and clubs. The meat-eaters included the mighty tyrannosaurids (*Daspletosaurus*) and the troodontids, who were fast pack hunters.

•Red Deer

Styracosaurus

Pachycephalosaurus

Parasaurolophus

Euoplocephalus

Troodon

Troodon

Parasaurolophus

interpreted as dung from the herds of large herbivores. Most of the hadrosaurs and other ornithopod ("bird-footed") dinosaurs weighed over 2,200 pounds (1,000 kilograms), but the fauna also included some smaller dinosaurs, such as the ankylosaurs (armored dinosaurs), pachycephalosaurs (thick-headed dinosaurs), and hypsilophodonts. The latter were so small, at 22 to 220 pounds (10 to 100 kilograms), that they probably had high metabolic rates and needed high-energy, specialized plant diets. Likewise, the small mammals of the time must have consumed high-energy food such as fruits and seeds.

GIANT FLESH-EATERS

The most numerous of the carnivorous residents of the Red Deer area in Cretaceous times were *Troodon formosus,* a birdlike theropod, the dromaeosaur *Saurornitholestes langstoni,* and the tyrannosaurid *Gorgosaurus libratus.* The tyrannosaurids, "tyrant lizards," were the largest of the theropods, growing up to 46 feet (14 meters) long and standing over 18 feet (5.5 meters) high. These awesome creatures had enormous heads on short muscular necks, and stiff tails balanced on top of long, powerful legs. The tiny arms, with short, two-fingered hands, are puzzling as they seem to have been almost useless. They could not even reach as far as the mouth.

Tyrannosaurids have popularly been portrayed as fast runners, but recent discoveries suggest that they were not so speedy after all. English biologist Robin McNeil Alexander calculated from body weight, leg length, and gait, that *Tyrannosaurus rex* had a maximum speed of 19 miles (30 kilometers) per hour. Another specialist, the American Jim Farlow, has pointed out that if an animal of this height and weight tripped, its head would hit the ground hard enough to smash its skull. So large tyrannosaurids could not have run fast because of the risk of a fatal fall.

SCAVENGERS

Although the popular image of Tyrannosaurus rex is as an actively hunting predator, this huge carnivore may in fact have been a scavenger that fed on carrion. Such a lifestyle would have required much less speed and involved less risk of injury. However, this is still an unsettled issue.

Daspletosaurus

ARMORED DINOSAUR
Euoplocephalus was one of the largest ankylosaurs. Its skull was protected by bony plates and even its eyelids were armored. Bony spines and plates protected the back of the head, neck, and shoulders.

Maiasaura

Corythosaurus

THE BEAST OF MAASTRICHT

CHALK DEPOSITS, FORMED BY THE TINY calcareous skeletons of planktonic microorganisms, are particular features of the late Cretaceous period, especially in Europe. People have quarried this soft limestone rock for thousands of years in search of flints, and more recently the chalk has been worked for lime. All this mining activity has uncovered many spectacular fossils—none more impressive, however, than the "Beast of Maastricht," named for the town in Holland where it was found.

THE TERROR OF THE CRETACEOUS SEAS

The creature, *Mosasaurus hoffmani*, was one of the last and most advanced of the mosasaur marine reptiles. It was also the largest. The mosasaurs were a group of carnivorous lizards that had left land and returned to the sea, filling a niche left by the decline of the earlier predatory marine reptiles, the ichthyosaurs.

Mosasaurus hoffmani grew to over 50 feet (15 meters) in length and had enormous jaws. Its skull was stronger and more rigid than that of its ancestors. Its eyes were quite large, indicating relatively good sight, although its binocular vision was limited, so depth perception would have been poor. There are also indications that the animal's sense of smell was not particularly good.

The creature's jaws, which were lined with numerous large, curved, and serrated cone-shaped teeth, were powerful and effective. The jawbones had a flexible joint that helped absorb the impact and stress of biting large prey. The teeth's cutting edges were the most advanced of any marine reptile—each tooth crown had numerous cutting and crushing facets. The fearsome jaws and the huge size of the animal meant that most marine animals of the time were potential prey.

To add to these capabilities, *Mosasaurus hoffmani* was a fast swimmer. Propulsion was produced by side-to-side undulations of the tail, while the shape of the paddlelike limbs indicates that they were used as rudders to steer the massive body through the water.

DISCOVERY
This engraving shows the discovery of a set of massive *M. hoffmani* jaws within a chalk mine in St. Pieter's Mount, Maastricht, in 1786. The find was to become a scientific sensation throughout Europe.

TAIL POWER
M. hoffmani was a fast-swimming surface hunter. Enormous power was generated by side-to-side undulations of the huge tail.

IDENTIFICATION PROBLEMS

Mosasaur fossil remains were a cause for some concern in the pre-Darwinian era, at a time when people had no idea that animals could become extinct. The initial concern, however, was over the animal's identity. Dutch naturalist Pieter Camper concluded in 1786 that it was a whale. His theory provoked further debate, especially with French scholar

Faujas de Saint-Fond, who thought it was a crocodile. But in 1800, Camper's son, Adriaan, claimed that it was a giant lizard. He communicated his ideas to the French paleontologist Baron Georges Cuvier, who named the fossil Mosasaurus, or "lizard from the River Meuse."

MORE JAWS

Although the "Grand Beast of Maastricht" referred to the single specimen discovered in 1786, with jaws more than 3 feet (1 meter) long, other large fossil jawbones had been discovered previously in the area. Since then, mosasaur jaws up to 5 feet (1.6 meters) in length have been found.

SHORT-LIVED PREDATOR

Tooth marks on a fossilized shell of the giant turtle *Allopleuron hoffmani* and healed jawbone fractures in a number of mosasaur fossil specimens show that they were indiscriminate predators. It has also been suggested that they engaged in potentially fatal male-to-male combat with other members of their own species. The fact that some of them survived jaw fractures shows they had an ability to recuperate rapidly, in much the same way that crocodiles do today.

As a group, these awesome animals spread successfully throughout the oceans of the late Cretaceous world, producing some gigantic forms and evolving into 20 different genera with some 70 species worldwide. But they had an extraordinarily brief existence of only about 25 million years, becoming extinct before the end of the Cretaceous age, about 65 million years ago. Their place in the world's oceans was soon taken up, during Tertiary times, by marine mammals.

WAR BOOTY

The actual jaws of the Maastricht beast, broken up by the process of fossilization, are held in the Natural History Museum in Paris. They were brought there in 1795 by Napoleon's troops.

The K-T Boundary

THE END OF THE CRETACEOUS HERALDED DRAMATIC CHANGES ON A GLOBAL SCALE, CULMINATING IN THE EXTINCTION OF MANY LIFEFORMS ON LAND AND SEA.

No dinosaur remains have been discovered in rocks younger than 65 million years old, the boundary between the Cretaceous and Tertiary periods. Along with their distant reptilian relatives the marine plesiosaurs, the mosasaurs, and the flying pterosaurs, dinosaurs had become extinct by the end of the Cretaceous, as had the most numerous fossil group of the Mesozoic era, the ammonites. By contrast, mammals and birds increased in abundance during Tertiary times. This dramatic turnover of animals was first recognized by scientists more than 100 years ago. The change in time periods is referred to as the K-T Boundary, K for Kreide (the German word for chalk) and T for Tertiary.

CLUES TO EXTINCTION

The cause of the K-T Boundary extinction was for many years a mystery. Then in the 1970s, an American geologist, Walter Alvarez, found significant traces of the element iridium in a thin clay layer that marks the exact boundary between sediments of Cretaceous and Tertiary times. This layer can be detected in many parts of Europe and North America. Iridium, one of the platinum metals, is found in meteorites and meteoric

BOUNDARY LAYER
The thin clay layer in this sequence of strata from Colorado marks the Cretaceous-Tertiary boundary. The clay is enriched with iridium from atmospheric fallout from the Chicxulub meteorite.

NORTH AMERICA

EUROPE

PACIFIC OCEAN

ATLANTIC OCEAN

AFRICA

SOUTH AMERICA

CHASMOSAURUS
This ceratopsian, from the Red Deer River in Alberta, had a bony extension to the back of the skull that was covered in skin. It may have been used for sexual display in males and for defense against predators. *Chasmosaurus* disappeared toward the end of the Cretaceous period.

TSUNAMI DEPOSIT

K-T Boundary sediments at Brazos River, Texas, contain an unusual hard sandy layer that is exactly at the boundary and clearly distinct from the softer sediments above and below. Some scientists think that the sand layer was deposited by a tsunami, a huge wave, set in motion by the Chicxulub impact 65 million years ago.

SHOCKED QUARTZ

Viewed in polarized light under a microscope, the crystal lattice of this quartz grain from Montana, has been distorted by pressure shock waves. Mineral grains of this kind are found in strata immediately above the K-T Boundary. They were shocked by the K-T impact and scattered over a wide area, along with molten glass drops called tektites, as part of the ejecta from the impact.

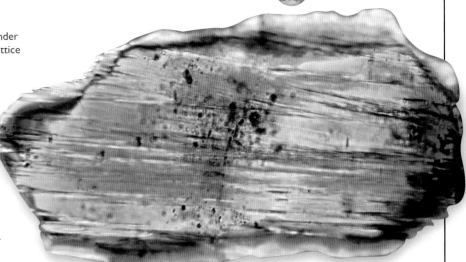

MASSIVE VOLCANISM

Despite the coincidence of the meteorite impact with the K-T Boundary, it was not necessarily the primary cause of the extinctions. Plants do not show massive extinctions at the K-T Boundary, dinosaurs were declining gradually, and many environmentally sensitive animals, such as amphibians and turtles, survived with few losses.

There were also large-scale volcanic eruptions at the time, accompanied by the emission of huge quantities of carbon dioxide. This would have boosted global warming and promoted the extinction of plants and animals, especially on land. So this volcanic event may have caused a background wave of extinctions, with the meteorite impact then delivering the final blow.

dust. Alvarez suggested that many changes occurring at the K-T Boundary had been precipitated by the impact of a large meteorite—an asteroid or comet.

Some scientists have suggested that the impact of such a collision could have had a catastrophic effect on the Earth's climate, throwing up dust and debris into the atmosphere that would have blotted out sunlight for several years and may have caused mass extinction. A buried crater that could have been the site of the K-T meteorite impact was eventually pinpointed at Chicxulub, in Yucatan, Mexico, extending many miles into the Gulf of Mexico.

THE DECCAN TRAPS

A river gorge cut into the Panna Hills in India exposes the plateau lava of the Deccan Traps. A deep "hot spot" in the Earth's mantle produced the outpouring of this basaltic lava during late Cretaceous times as India rifted from Madagascar. The accompanying volcanic fumes and emissions may have contributed to climatic change and mass extinctions.

THE LAST OF THE DINOSAURS

THE END OF THE CRETACEOUS PERIOD WAS A critical time in the history of life, the point at which the dinosaurs and a wide range of other creatures disappeared forever. Many different theories have been put forward to explain the extinction of the dinosaurs ranging from disease to the effect of a large meteorite impact 65 million years ago. But there are no great fossil graveyards piled with bones to be found at the K-T Boundary between the Cretaceous and the Tertiary periods. When the fossil record of these times is examined in detail, the changeover is not as clear-cut as might be expected if extinction had been caused by a single catastrophic event.

DINOSAURS IN DECLINE

Several of the main dinosaur groups, such as the large herbivorous sauropods, ankylosaurs, and hypsilophodonts, were in decline before the end of the Cretaceous period. This can be clearly seen by comparing the fossil record of two sites in western North America, the 75-million-year-old Judith River sediments of southern Alberta, Canada, and the 65-million-year-old sediments of Hell Creek in northeastern

Montana. The older Judith River sediments preserve 32 different kinds (genera) of dinosaur; the Hell Creek sediments, from the very end of the Cretaceous, preserve only 19 different kinds. This decrease in diversity suggests that dinosaurs were already in decline before the impact event.

The last dinosaurs found in North America included large herbivores such as the rhinoceros-like ceratopsians. But *Triceratops* (30 feet/9 meters long and up

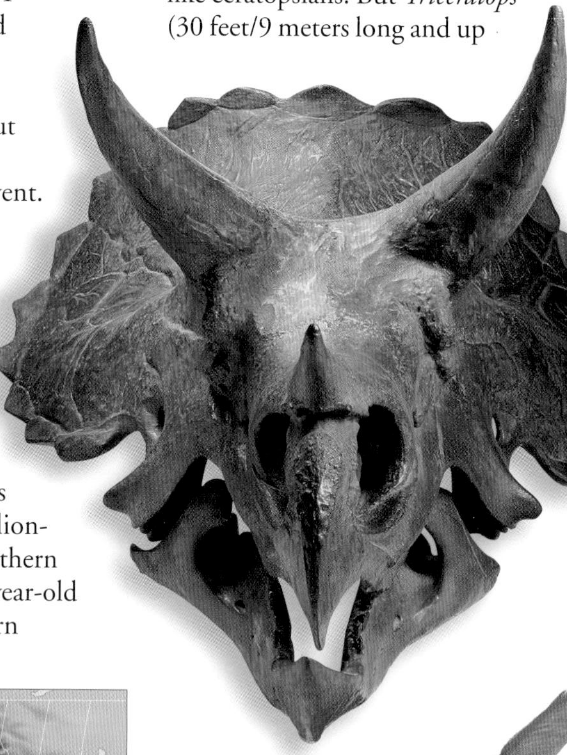

HORNED HERBIVORE
Triceratops, whose name means "three-horned face," roamed in herds across the west of North America. The horns and large neck frill were used for attack and defense in fights, most often between rival males for herd dominance.

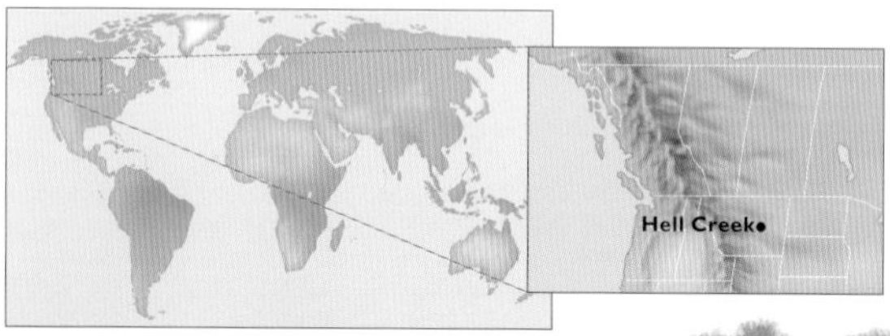

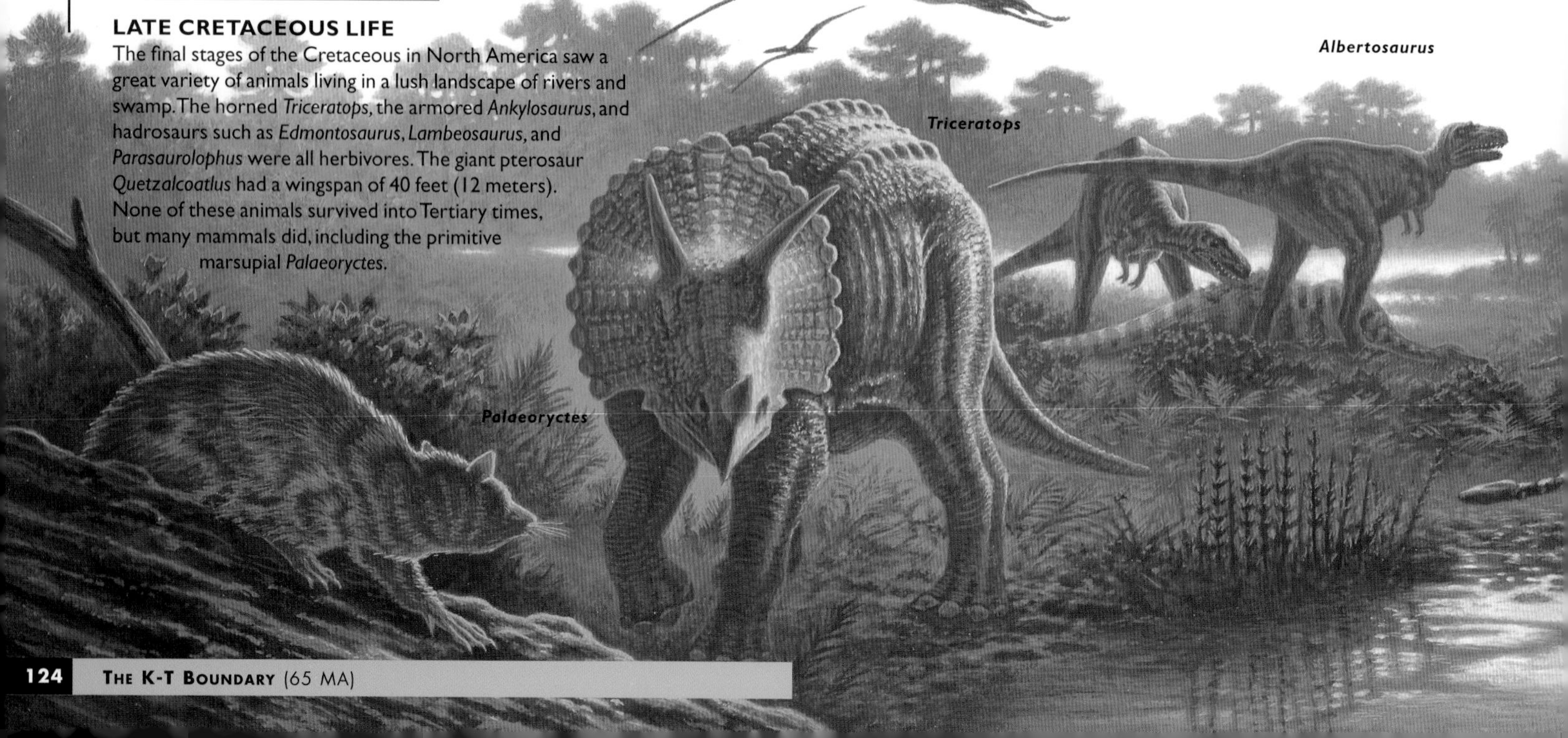

Quetzalcoatlus

Albertosaurus

LATE CRETACEOUS LIFE

The final stages of the Cretaceous in North America saw a great variety of animals living in a lush landscape of rivers and swamp. The horned *Triceratops*, the armored *Ankylosaurus*, and hadrosaurs such as *Edmontosaurus*, *Lambeosaurus*, and *Parasaurolophus* were all herbivores. The giant pterosaur *Quetzalcoatlus* had a wingspan of 40 feet (12 meters). None of these animals survived into Tertiary times, but many mammals did, including the primitive marsupial *Palaeoryctes*.

Triceratops

Palaeoryctes

Hell Creek•

to 9 tons in weight) and *Torosaurus* (25 feet/7.6 meters long) were the only two out of five ceratopsians that persisted to the end of Cretaceous times. Likewise, there were only two "duck-billed" hadrosaurids (large bipedal/ quadrupedal plant-eaters with large, flat heads), *Anatotitan* and *Edmontosaurus*, at Hell Creek, compared with seven in the earlier Judith River strata.

The last of the smaller plant-eating dinosaurs included the spiny-skinned *Ankylosaurus*. This creature was armored, with heavy nodes and spikes of bone set in its leathery skin, and wielded a massive, bony club at the end of its tail. It was accompanied by *Stegoceras*, a thick-skulled, head-butting pachycephalosaurid ("thick-headed lizard") that grew to just over 6 feet (2 meters) long.

These were all bird-hipped (ornithischian) dinosaurs. The other major dinosaur group, the reptile-hipped saurischians, included the giant plant-eating sauropods and the predatory theropods. Sauropods had disappeared from most of North America by late Cretaceous times, although a few survivors existed elsewhere—for example, *Nemegtosaurus* in Mongolia. The theropods, by contrast,

HELL CREEK
When the last dinosaurs roamed its landscape some 65 million years ago, Hell Creek (part of modern Montana) was situated on a coastal plain to the east of the Rockies.

were flourishing, especially the tyrannosaurids. Not all of them were as large as *Tyrannosaurus rex*, which weighed in at up to 8 tons (elephants weigh up to 5 tons). *Albertosaurus* was about 2 tons and the smaller *Aublysodon* a mere 450 pounds (200 kilograms), which is similar to a modern-day adult male lion.

Some theropod groups did decline in numbers and diversity during the last few million years of the Cretaceous period, notably the fleet-footed, ostrichlike ornithomimids, which grew to 13 feet (4 meters) long, including their long stiff tails. Only one of three ornithomimid genera persisted near to the end. Other small theropod dinosaurs, such as the active, fast-running predatory dromaeosaurids, *Dromaeosaurus* and *Velociraptor*, had disappeared by the end of the Cretaceous period.

Looking beyond the dinosaurs, flying reptiles were in steep decline by the late Cretaceous, and so were marine reptiles. The ichthyosaurs and plesiosaurs died out long before K-T times. A change was already well under way when Earth was struck by a meteorite 65 million years ago.

Lambeosaurus

Edmontosaurus

Ankylosaurus

Parasaurolophus

Presbyornis pervetus

IMPACT FROM OUTER SPACE

At THE END OF THE CRETACEOUS PERIOD, 65 million years ago, a massive object crashed into Earth with devastating effect. It was not the first such extraterrestrial collision, nor will it be the last. There have been five hundred or so major impacts from outer space over the last 500 million years. But the meteorite that impacted close to what is now the village of Chicxulub on the coast of Mexico's Yucatan peninsula was to mark a turning point in the history of life. Before the cataclysmic impact, dinosaurs and their reptile relatives ruled the land, seas, and skies. Their subsequent extinction left the way clear for the mammals and birds to take over.

ZERO HOUR AT CHICXULUB

The meteorite, measuring about 6 miles (10 kilometers) wide, blasted a hole 60 miles (100 kilometers) across and 7.5 miles (12 kilometers) deep, and must have immediately annihilated all life for many thousands of square miles around the impact site. About 12,000 cubic miles (50,000 cubic kilometers) of pulverized limestone rock were blasted into the atmosphere as dust, droplets of molten rock, and microdiamonds. Tiny grains of Chicxulub rock have been found in K-T Boundary sediments thousands of miles away. The impact also threw hundreds of millions

DOOMSDAY
One estimate is that the impact at Chicxulub released energy equivalent to the explosion of 100 million hydrogen bombs. The rock excavated by the impact was blasted back through the atmosphere as a huge mushroom cloud.

CHICXULUB SITE
The search for the site of the K-T Boundary impact took many years. Eventually the distribution of shocked (physically distorted) grains of quartz and deposits from tsunamis (giant waves) around the Caribbean helped to confirm the site at Chicxulub.

PATH TO DESTRUCTION
Geophysical analysis shows the meteorite, traveling at about 19 miles (30 kilometers) a second, approached at a low angle from the southeast (right). In late Cretaceous times, South America was still separate from North America.

Earthquakes

Wildfires

Worldwide darkness

SHORT- AND LONG-TERM EFFECTS

It has been calculated that the impact caused earthquakes of magnitude 10 on the Richter scale and huge tsunamis. Other short-term effects (days to weeks) probably included fires that poured soot into the atmosphere. It is speculated that longer-term effects included global darkness and acid rain.

CRATER CROSS SECTION

The impact pushed up a mountainous rim 5 miles (8 kilometers) high around the crater. The unstable rim collapsed soon after and fell back into the crater, creating massive earthquakes and further crater collapse rings up to 90 miles (150 kilometers) from the epicenter.

of tons of sulfur into the atmosphere. Mixing with water droplets, this would have generated vast quantities of acid rain (dilute sulfuric acid).

One scenario envisages that ten minutes after the impact, a searing blast of heat from the explosion swept across the Americas. Forests would have spontaneously ignited, blackening the sky with smoke and soot—so much vegetation was burned that particles of charcoal were blown around the world and are found as layers of soot in rock strata. The combination of dust from the impact and smoke from the fires would have darkened skies, causing temperatures to fall. Ten hours after the impact, giant waves called tsunamis would have approached the eastern coastlines of the Americas and pushed far inland, drowning animals that had survived the initial blast.

WAVE OF EXTINCTIONS

Some scientists claim that within a week of the impact, the most vulnerable animals in North America had become extinct. These included the remaining giant sauropods and top carnivores—species that were already on the endangered list, with relatively few members. Plants may also have started dying off from acid rain and lack of light. But the final extinction of the dinosaurs probably did not come until about 100,000 years after the catastrophe, and the last ammonites (shelled creatures that had been abundant in the seas of the Mesozoic era) survived for a further 200,000 years after that. Global environments, with fully re-established climate, ocean circulation, and normal interactions between animals and plants, probably did not get back to normal for 2.5 million years.

IDENTIFYING THE CRATER

The Chicxulub crater was first discovered in the 1970s but subsequently forgotten, partly because it is hidden under a deep layer of sediments, the result of being underwater for most of its existence. In the 1990s, it was investigated once again and its date of formation was found to correspond very closely to the date of the K-T Boundary. The image of the crater (right) was computer-generated from seismic data and then color-enhanced. The blue area at the bottom represents a furrow that was excavated by the meteorite on approach.

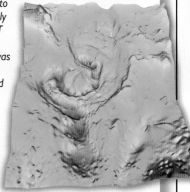

VICTIMS AND SURVIVORS

WITHIN HOURS OF THE CHICXULUB IMPACT, the skies over the immediate region were filled with dust. The situation worsened as forest fires spread, which added smoke and soot to the dust. Within weeks this pollution darkened skies all over the globe, blocking out the Sun and preventing plants in the oceans and on land from photosynthesizing normally.

Plants underpin all life on Earth. They are the food store for herbivores, which in turn constitute food for carnivores. Any major disturbance of the Earth's chemical and physical environments, such as a drastic reduction in light or temperature within the oceans or the atmosphere, immediately affects plant life. The repercussions then cascade throughout the whole of the ecosystem.

After the meteorite impact, the microscopic plants of the oceans were probably the first to die, thereby upsetting the marine ecosystem. The meteorite only accelerated their demise, however, as there is evidence to suggest that they had started to decline before the impact, probably as

SHELLED VICTIMS
Marine animal extinctions were far more numerous at the end of the Cretaceous period than those of the terrestrial animals. Marine animals to die out included the ammonites, which had lived in the oceans for about 300 million years.

EXTINCT HERBIVORE
This plant-eating dinosaur, *Triceratops*, was common in Cretaceous times. By the end of the period, they were still abundant and successful animals. But then, like all the other dinosaurs, they disappeared from the fossil record.

THE "FERN SPIKE"

Fossil evidence shows that, before the K-T extinction, North American landscapes were covered by broad-leaved evergreens and some conifers. In Tertiary strata, the rocks reveal a "fern spike" (sudden preponderance of ferns) immediately after the K-T Boundary. This spike of fossil fern pollen shows that ferns similar to the living fern Stenochlana were tough survivors and unaffected by the impact. Other fossil plants gradually start reappearing in the rock strata over time. When landscapes are devastated by volcanic eruptions today, ferns are the first plants to return, and they dominate the vegetation before other flora grow back. The similarity between this observation and the events of 65 million years ago suggests that plants at the end of the Cretaceous suffered some trauma.

THE END OF THE DINOSAURS

Although the plants recovered, many animal groups did not—most famously, the dinosaurs and the flying pterosaurs. The giant marine reptiles, such as the mosasaurs and plesiosaurs, also died out. There is still much debate over why the dinosaurs became extinct, when many other vertebrates—bony fish (12% extinct), frogs (0%), salamanders (0%), lizards (6%), and placental mammals (14%)—were almost unaffected.

Apart from dinosaurs, the reptiles of the late Cretaceous period, before the mass extinction, included 45 families of turtles, crocodiles, lizards, and snakes. The turtles and crocodiles were most affected, but, like the plants, the survivors adapted rapidly to a new environment. Today, there are still more reptile species than mammals.

The initial decline of the reptiles allowed for the rapid expansion of the mammals, although these also suffered in the mass extinction. About 20 percent of all the early mammal families of the Cretaceous period became extinct. The marsupial mammals were particularly affected.

About 75 percent of all animal species became extinct at the K-T Boundary. Many were rare species and at risk of extinction anyway, but there is no obvious explanation why some species died out and others survived. Some scientists believe that survival was really only a matter of luck.

a result of a major change in ocean circulation. It is speculated that on land, the impact not only blotted out the sunlight but may also have caused widespread fires and acid rain, which would have adversely affected land plants.

The record from the rocks in Hell Creek, Montana, shows that over 75 percent of plant species in the North American interior became extinct. The overall pattern indicates that the newly evolving flowering plants (angiosperms) were among the worst hit, along with some of the common Mesozoic plants, such as the ginkgos and cycads. In the short term, the ferns survived quite well and, in the longer term, the conifers also thrived. Strangely, land plants in the southern hemisphere were barely affected by the extinction event, suggesting that the impact was not as disastrous as some scientists claim.

When global vegetation began to grow back as the effect of the devastating impact receded, the flowering plants were best able to take advantage of the situation. Eventually, they took over most of the landscapes of the world, evolving into an enormous variety of plants, from small weeds and grasses to giant trees.

SHELLED SURVIVOR
Turtles and tortoises belong to the same group of reptiles, the Testudines. Over time they have diversified as both plant- and meat-eaters and have become very successful on land and in water. However, they all retain a similar shelled form, which may have helped them survive the K-T extinction event.

Early Tertiary Age

THIS PERIOD OF RAPID CONTINENTAL MOVEMENT ALSO MARKED THE TIME WHEN MODERN ANIMALS, FROM MAMMALS TO SONGBIRDS, BECAME DOMINANT.

The Tertiary period lasted from 65 million years ago almost to the present day. Its first 30 million years are conventionally divided into two epochs, the Paleocene (65 to 55 million years ago) and the Eocene (55 to 34 million years ago).

The early Tertiary was a time of dramatic mountain building and rearrangement of the global jigsaw of oceans and continents. Africa and India moved relentlessly northward, gradually closing the Tethys Ocean. As these fragments of the old supercontinent of Gondwana crashed into the southern flank of Eurasia, they began to compress sedimentary strata, initiating a process of mountain building along a broad front from the Alps to the Himalayas. Farther west, Iberia (Spain and Portugal) collided with France, pushing up the Pyrenees in the process.

OCEAN FISSURES

The Atlantic Ocean continued to rip open northward during early Tertiary times. The continental crust under the ocean was domed up by a deep-seated mantle "hot spot." As it stretched apart and fractured, great outpourings of lavas emerged from the fissures. A line of huge volcanoes ran from Dingle in southwest Ireland to Skaergaard in eastern Greenland. Iceland was created and Greenland split from Scandinavia.

Sea levels continued to fall from the high point reached during mid-Cretaceous times, but in detail, they fluctuated throughout the Tertiary period. Global climates became increasingly

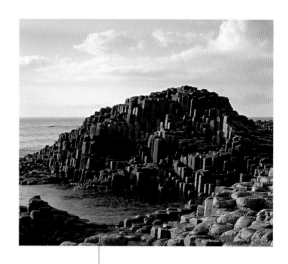

GIANT'S CAUSEWAY
These basalt lavas in Northern Ireland poured out of fissures and volcanoes as the crust rifted with the opening of the North Atlantic in early Tertiary times.

NORTH AMERICA

EUROPE

ATLANTIC OCEAN

TETHYS OCEAN

SOUTH AMERICA

AFRICA

PRISCACARA
This common bony fish is one of two species found in the freshwater Eocene-age deposits of the Green River Formation of Wyoming. It is related to the living perch and grew to 15 inches (38 centimeters). The spiny needles on its back helped protect it from being swallowed whole by larger fish.

MAMMALS DIVERSIFY

The early Tertiary period saw an extraordinarily rapid diversification of mammals. During the entire course of the Tertiary period, which lasted for some 63 million years, nearly 4,000 mammal species evolved. A large proportion of these evolved during the first 10 million years, the Paleocene epoch, including at least 15 new lineages—groups of closely related organisms. The diversification of mammals, many of them plant-eaters, was partly stimulated by the appearance of new angiosperms (flowering plants) at this time. Mammals may also have had the intelligence and adaptability to flourish during a period of rapidly changing environments.

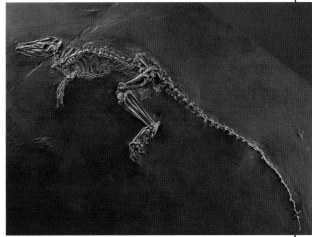

TRIONYX
Growing to 24 inches (60 centimeters) long, this was the largest known Eocene-age freshwater turtle. The shell was covered by a thick skin. The turtle survived dry periods by burrowing into the mud. This example was found in Germany.

humid in early Tertiary times. This allowed tropical and subtropical climates to spread into high latitudes. But from the end of the Eocene epoch, global climates became drier and generally cooler. This had a significant effect on the overall development of marine and terrestrial life.

MODERN LIFE ASSEMBLES
Flora and fauna changed and diversified radically as life recovered from the extinction event at the end of the Cretaceous period. In the marine environment, life rebounded quickly and

creatures began to take on a more present-day appearance. Bony fish (called teleosts) and sharks became dominant, and were joined by the first marine mammals, such as early whales.

However, the most rapid exponential growth was seen on land. Many non-dinosaurian reptiles, such as snakes and lizards, survived from Cretaceous times but failed to capitalize on the demise of the dinosaurs. Instead, the birds, mammals, insects, and flowering plants (angiosperms) quickly came to dominate the land.

KANGAROO RAT
This extinct mammal from Messel in Germany was 30 inches (75 centimeters) long. With its long hind legs and short arms, balanced by a long tail, it looks as if it would have hopped, but the structure of the ankle shows that it actually ran as it preyed on small creatures.

PLANTS AND ANIMALS OF MESSEL

ONE OF THE MOST IMPORTANT fossil sites in the world for early Tertiary life is a quarry in Messel, near Frankfurt in Germany. Some 50 million years ago, the site was a lake that held the remains of plants, vertebrates, and invertebrates. Together, the fossils represent an almost complete ecosystem.

VARIED MAMMALS

Although the mammal fossils form only a small proportion (2 or 3 percent) of the total vertebrate animal life at Messel, 35 different species have nevertheless been found, belonging to 13 orders. These orders all have living representatives, and although the Messel mammals are different in size to modern mammals, they would still look familiar to us today. Marsupial opossums grew to 10 inches (25 centimeters) long, and bats and rodents, such as the 3-foot- (1-meter-) long *Ailuravus*, had started to become very successful. As well as these, tree-climbing, lemurlike primates were found, such as

CONSTRICTORS

Early Tertiary pythons and boas were constrictors, which strangled their prey. The *Palaeopython* grew to 6.5 feet (2 meters) long and fed on small reptiles, birds, and mammals. Poisonous snakes did not evolve until Miocene times.

Europolemur, 20 inches (50 centimeters) long. The primates have fingernails instead of claws and an opposing first finger and thumb that enable them to grip, and later, use tools. Lemurs, monkeys, humans, and other apes are all primates.

The ancestors of horses were then about the size of a large dog, and there were small, rabbit-sized, cud-chewing ancestors of cattle and deer. Other mammals included an anteater, as well as examples of some extinct early mammal groups such as the cat-sized, hooved, meat-eating mammal, *Paroodectes*.

MESSEL POND LIFE

The 65 species of plants that form the basis of the ecosystem were distinctly modern, with now-tropical citrus trees (*Toddalia*), palms (*Phoenicites*), vines (*Vitis*), and laurels (*Laurophyllum*) thriving. Oaks, beeches, and rare conifers, now typical of more temperate environments, also grew. Freshwater ponds and lakes were filled with water

THE MESSEL ECOSYSTEM

The plants of the Messel site are typical of a mixed tropical and temperate climate with tree-sized palms (*Phoenicites*), conifers (*Taxodium*), and grass-like sedges (*Caricoidea*) appearing. These were browsed upon by the primitive horse, *Propalaeotherium*. The vegetation and humid conditions supported a rich insect life and many insect-eating vertebrates such as an anteater (*Eurotamandua*), a primitive hedgehog (*Pholidocercus*), a pangolin (*Eomanis*), and the bat, *Archaeonycteris*. Carnivorous predators included constrictor snakes (*Palaeopython*) and *Asiatosuchus*, a large crocodile.

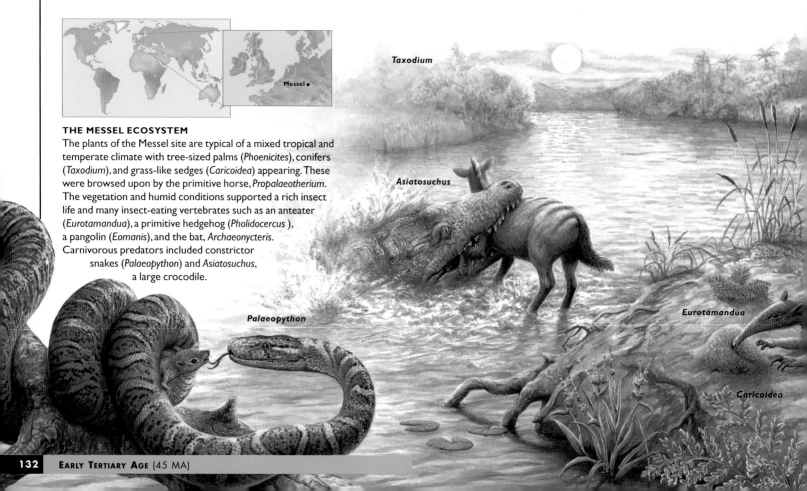

Taxodium

Asiatosuchus

Palaeopython

Eurotamandua

Caricoidea

Messel

lilies and populated with snails and insects, such as waterfleas, skaters, and boatmen.

These insects were preyed upon by frogs, toads, and a salamander (*Chelotriton*). Shoals of predatory fish, aquatic reptiles (such as freshwater turtles), and carnivorous crocodiles up to 9 feet (3 meters) long patrolled the lake.

SNAKES AND LIZARDS

The Messel reptiles include snakes and some large lizards. *Xestops*, an armored lizard, fed on snails alongside a tree-climbing predatory monitor lizard, an iguana, and a snakelike limbless lizard. They all grew to between 8 and 20 inches (20 and 50 centimeters) long.

The first fossil snakes appeared in the late Cretaceous period and although their ancestry is as yet unknown, the group included constrictors, pipe snakes, and digging snakes. The constrictors, over 6 feet (2 meters) long, fed on small animals; one specimen was found with a small alligator in its stomach.

Birds were also very modern in appearance and ranged from the *Aenigmavis*, a flightless bird, to hawks, fowls, ibises, cranes, flamingos, owls, and an ostrichlike bird, *Palaeotis*. This assemblage combines modern European, North American, South American, and southern Asian forms.

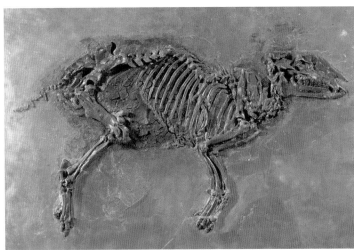

CROSSROADS

The discovery of Eurotamandua, the anteater, and Eomanis, the pangolin, in this European setting is important, since they were thought to be respectively South American and Southeast Asian. Europe may therefore have been a migratory crossroads for Eocene mammals.

PRIMITIVE HORSES

Over 70 fossil horses were found at Messel, including foals and pregnant mares. This *Propalaeotherium* horse, with its four-toed hoof on each front leg and three-toed hoof on each back leg, stood only 24 inches (60 centimeters) high at the shoulder.

Phoenicites

Archaeonycteris

Palaeotis

Eomanis

Propalaeotherium

Pholidocercus

OPENING THE NORTH ATLANTIC

DURING THE EARLY TRIASSIC PERIOD, ABOUT 245 million years ago, the Americas, Europe, and Africa were joined together in the Pangean supercontinent. By 200 million years ago, there were signs of stress, heralding the supercontinent's subsequent break-up. New England and the eastern seaboard developed rifts in the continental crust, through which lava poured out, creating basalt rocks such as the Palisades on the Hudson River in New Jersey. But it was not until mid-Jurassic times, around 180 million years ago, that rift ruptures opened a narrow seaway between the continents and began the formation of the North Atlantic.

TERTIARY VOLCANICS

At first, the widening of the North Atlantic was extremely slow. By the beginning of the Tertiary period, 65 million years ago, Greenland and the British Isles were still joined and Iceland did not exist. But between 63 and 52 million years ago, the region was the site of intense volcanic activity. Vast outpourings of lava, originating from a series of southwest-northeast oriented fissures, inundated the landscape. These eruptions were probably due to the flare-up of a hot spot—an upward flow of hot molten magma from the Earth's interior.

Fracture

Continental crust

Hot magma rising at a hot spot by convection

THE FORMATION OF AN OCEAN

STAGE ONE

A new ocean forms when a continent breaks into smaller pieces. Rifting begins when an upward flow of heat from the Earth's interior stretches the continental crust, causing it to dome and thin. Typically, a three-branched fracture forms. This process first began in Pangea about 200 million years ago.

Active rift arm

Failed arm

Continental crust

STAGE TWO

Two of the fracture branches move farther apart. Molten rock magma wells up between the separating branches. The magma pours out at the surface as lava, through fissures and volcanoes. The third branch becomes inactive and remains as a land depression, known as a failed arm. The Benue Trough in Nigeria is thought to be a failed arm in the opening of the South Atlantic.

COLUMNAR BASALT OF FINGAL'S CAVE

Cooling lava formed the columns that support a sea cave, named for a mythical giant, on the island of Staffa off Scotland's west coast. The lava, part of a 1.2 mile- (2 kilometer-) thick sequence, poured out of a volcano on the nearby island of Mull in Tertiary times, between 60 and 57 million years ago.

STAGES IN THE SPLIT

The opening of the Atlantic over the last 100 million years has been most significant in the separation of Africa from North and South America and Northern Europe from Labrador.

100 MA

50 MA

As the continental crust stretched, Eurasia and Laurentia rifted apart and the new Atlantic ocean floor was created. The main area of seafloor expansion extended to the region between Norway and Greenland. Iceland was formed from magma that welled up through the mid-Atlantic ridge. It still sits on top of a hot spot today.

THE LAVAS

In Northern Ireland and the inner Hebrides of Scotland great masses of basalt lava, with flows 48 feet (15 meters) thick on average, erupted from fissures and volcanoes. The remains of some of the fissures can still be seen. Over 1,500 square miles (3,800 square kilometers) of lava are still preserved in Northern Ireland. The Giant's Causeway, a stepping-stone formation of huge columnar rocks in County Antrim, is one of many visible remnants of the eruptions.

The second phase of igneous activity was the formation of a string of volcanoes from Ireland to the west coast of Scotland. Despite the hardness of the rocks, these now extinct volcanoes were deeply eroded by glaciers during the last ice age (18,000 years ago), making it easier for scientists to study them.

Examination of the region's igneous rocks has provided vital

ICELANDIC FIRE

The hot spot in the Earth's surface that started the rifting of Greenland from the British Isles some 60 million years ago still exists under Iceland. Volcanic eruptions on Iceland give scientists an opportunity to find out how ocean floor rocks are formed.

clues to their formation. The magma from which the rocks were formed underwent cycles of change in composition. Crystals of different minerals sedimenting out of the magma at different times caused some of the rocks to become layered. A layered formation discovered on the island of Rum off Scotland confirms that the rocks created in the Tertiary period were caused by a mantle hot spot. This formation contains abundant platinum group minerals, associated with the high temperatures occurring during mantle plume activity.

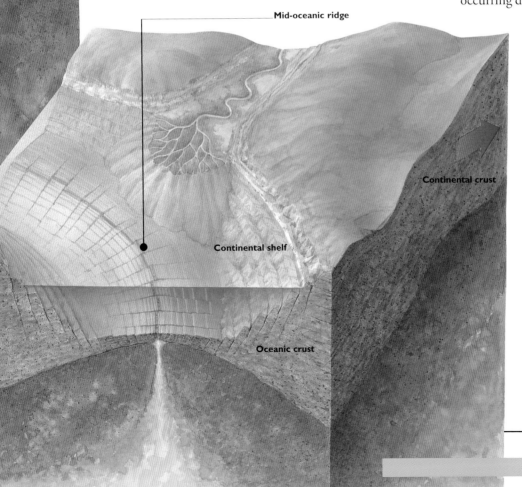

Mid-oceanic ridge

Continental crust

Continental shelf

Oceanic crust

STAGE THREE

Continued rifting separates blocks of continental crust, and the one-time edges become the foundations for continental shelves. The active rift arms develop into a mid-oceanic spreading ridge with the formation of new ocean floor.

FOSSILIZED LAKE

At Ardtun on the Hebridean island of Mull, the first lavas to erupt flowed into a small lake, burying a variety of plants that had been carried into the lake from the surrounding hills and preserving them as fossils. These provide a rare insight into the life of the time. The flora includes trees such as plane, hazel, oak, and the maidenhair tree (ginkgo), all typical of a temperate climate. Insect remains have also been found, including a beetle and a weevil.

THE EVOLUTION OF PLANTS AND FLOWERS

MUCH OF OUR KNOWLEDGE OF THE EARLY evolution of land plants comes from a site at Rhynie in Scotland. The 390-million-year-old Rhynie sediments have fossilized 22 species of plants, including the first primitive plants with veins for circulating water (vascular plants) known as rhyniophytes. These upright plants were bog-dwellers, and grew no more than 8 to 12 inches (20 to 30 centimeters) high.

Some 15 million years later, about 375 million years ago, the first forestlike growth of terrestrial plants appear, as seen from the Gilboa strata in New York's Catskill Mountains. The tree-ferns and clubmosses (lycopsids) were the first plants to grow to 10 feet (3 meters) or more, the size of small modern trees. The evolution of rootlike structures enabled them to grow to this height, and provided access to groundwater. There were also internal structural changes to the stems, which produced the first strengthened, woodlike tissues.

Another major advance was the evolution, from the late Devonian onward, of seed-bearing plants (gymnosperms), which included conifers, ginkgos, palmlike cycads, and pteridosperms (seed-ferns). Through the Mesozoic era, from 248 to 65 million years ago, these plants, together with ferns and horsetails, dominated landscapes worldwide. Many plants reproduced through

EARLY COLONIZERS
Tiny plants called bryophytes, like this living *Marchantia* liverwort from Australia, may have been the first plants to colonize the land in Ordovician times. These plants are incapable, however, of growing far above the ground. Only plants with strengthened stems (vascular plants) can do that. Vascular plants first appeared in Silurian times.

wind-borne seeds; some may even have depended on insects for the fertilization process.

FLOWERING PLANTS

Angiosperms, the flowering plants, first emerged around 140 million years ago. Plant scientists have regarded magnolias as the most primitive living angiosperms, but a new fossil plant from northeast China, called *Archaefructus*, is now considered to be the oldest flowering plant.

By mid-Cretaceous times, the flowering plants had diversified widely and rapidly into the basic

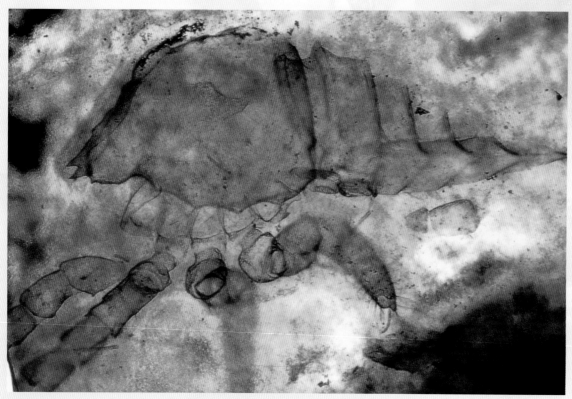

TINY PREDATOR
One of the earliest known land-living predators, *Palaeocharinus*, was found in late Silurian strata in Scotland. It was only 0.02 inches (0.5 millimeters) long, but it preyed on mites that were smaller than itself. These in turn fed on abundant rotting plant vegetation. Their presence shows that simple terrestrial ecosystems already existed 420 million years ago.

FLOWERING PLANT

This 140 million-year-old fossil plant *Archaefructus* comes from early Cretaceous strata in northeast China. It has the critical features of a flowering plant, with fruits enclosed in a female reproductive structure that has developed from a flower. This fossil is the oldest known flowering plant.

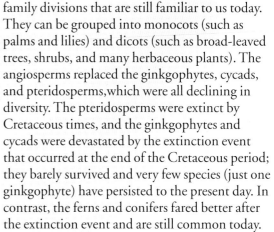

EARLY FLOWER

This flower, *Silvianthemum suecicum*, was found preserved in late Cretaceous strata in Sweden. It is a typical insect-pollinated flower with petals and reproductive parts, both male (the pollen-bearing stamen) and female (the style, which leads to the ovary).

Style

Stamen

Sepal

Petal

Peduncle (stalk)

FOSSIL FLOWERS

Flowers are delicate structures, so the chances of finding a fossilized specimen are small. However, pollen, fruits, and seeds, all part of a flowering plant's reproductive cycle, are much tougher and are often fossilized, although they are usually scattered far and wide. The challenge is to match the pollen, seed, and fruit fossils found in rock strata to a particular plant without the guidance of any flower remains.

family divisions that are still familiar to us today. They can be grouped into monocots (such as palms and lilies) and dicots (such as broad-leaved trees, shrubs, and many herbaceous plants). The angiosperms replaced the ginkgophytes, cycads, and pteridosperms, which were all declining in diversity. The pteridosperms were extinct by Cretaceous times, and the ginkgophytes and cycads were devastated by the extinction event that occurred at the end of the Cretaceous period; they barely survived and very few species (just one ginkgophyte) have persisted to the present day. In contrast, the ferns and conifers fared better after the extinction event and are still common today.

After the mass extinctions at the end of the Cretaceous period, the flowering plants dominated in all their incredible diversity. An increase in global humidity promoted the development of tropical rain forests, which were filled with large-leaved trees. These large leaves had developed distinctive "drip tips" to help shed rainwater. High global temperatures allowed these forests to grow as far north as 60 degrees latitude in some places. In higher latitudes, extensive deciduous woodland replaced the previous broad-leaved evergreens, many of which are now extinct.

All the major groups of flowering plants, including the precursors of the grasses (such as the basic grains—rice, wheat, and corn), had evolved by the beginning of the Tertiary period, which started 65 million years ago. The major types of fruit had also evolved, so that by early Tertiary times there was a wide variety of capsules, nuts, drupes (plumlike fruits), berries, and pods. The world's landscapes have had this familiar modern-looking vegetation ever since.

BEELIKE INSECTS

Although the first true bees appear in mid-Tertiary strata in France, beelike insects are also found in older, late Cretaceous amber from North America.

Mid-Tertiary Period

GLOBAL COOLING, CONTINENTAL COLLISIONS, AND INCREASED ARIDITY ENCOURAGED THE GROWTH OF OPEN GRASSLANDS AND LARGER PLANT-EATERS.

Continents and oceans were close to their present global positions 20 million years ago. There were, however, small, but significant, differences. Australia was still moving north, as were Africa and India, which were heading toward Europe and Asia. The subsequent collisions built the Alps in Europe and the Himalayas in Asia and created the Tibetan plateau, the "roof of the world," 3 miles (5 kilometers) above sea level. The Himalayas are one of Earth's most dramatic features, rising over 4.5 miles (7 kilometers) above sea level to form a 1,800-mile (3,000-kilometer) barrier between India and central Asia.

In North America, terranes (fragments of continental crust) welded onto the west coast, but the connection with South America, broken in mid-Jurassic times, had yet to be re-established. Finally, Greenland separated from Scandinavia.

GLOBAL CLIMATES AND MONSOONS

The global climates of early Tertiary times were still warm and humid. But by about 25 million years ago, the Earth cooled and the Antarctic icecap began to develop. Overall, much drier conditions prevailed. Although there was some fluctuation between colder and warmer phases, the Earth was heading toward the ice ages of the later Quaternary period. The building of the

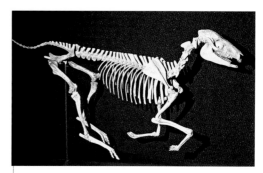

THREE-TOED HORSE
Mesohippus was a primitive horse from North America, the first to have three, rather than four, toes on each foot, making it closer to the single-toed modern horse.

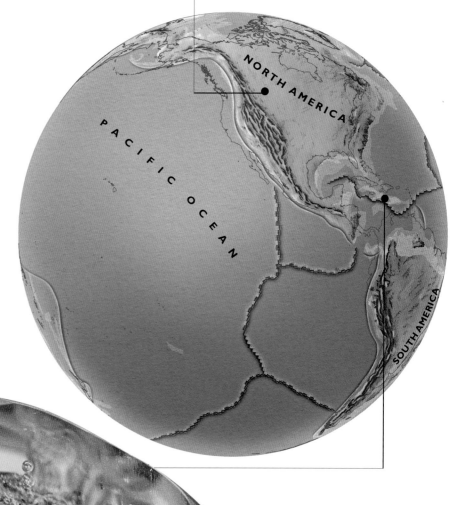

NORTH AMERICA

PACIFIC OCEAN

SOUTH AMERICA

AMBER FROG
Many different kinds of organisms have been trapped in amber resin, but frogs are very rare. Perhaps a bird caught this frog, flew to a resin-producing tree to eat its prey, but dropped it into a patch of sticky resin. This specimen formed in the Dominican Republic at a time of higher sea levels than shown in the maps.

THE SEASONS

A major feature of the cooling of the climate in the mid-Tertiary period is the development of the seasons. These took the form of winter and summer months, and dry and monsoon periods, particularly in Asia. Seasonality requires plants to adopt once- or twice-yearly reproductive phases, with seeds that can survive bad weather while lying in a dormant state. The grasses were particularly successful at doing this, resulting in open savanna grasslands.

BALTIC FLY
The vast majority of creatures trapped in amber are insects, such as this 35-million-year-old fly from the Baltic region of Europe. The almost perfect preservation that amber provides allows creatures to be accurately identified. Despite claims, however, that the genetic blueprint, or DNA, of amber insects can be recovered, modern research shows that this is not yet possible.

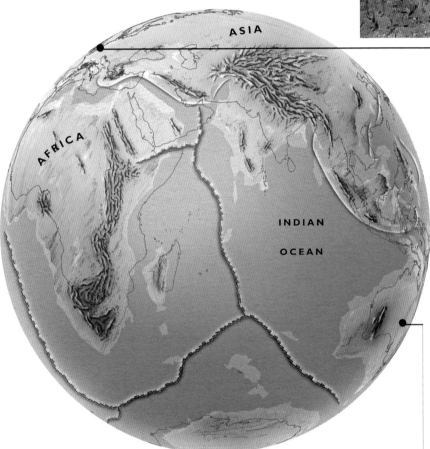

KANGAROO JAW
The Tertiary age rocks of Riversleigh in northwest Queensland, Australia, are rich in fossil remains. Most of the fossils, like this kangaroo jawbone, are well-preserved bones of vertebrates that lived and died in and around the lake. Their corpses sank into the soft mud at the bottom of the lake, which is now hard limestone.

Himalayas and the Tibetan plateau changed the climate of Asia by establishing the monsoon. This occurs because the vast, high Himalayan region is quickly warmed by the summer sun, heating the air and causing it to rise. This draws in moist air from the sea and the moisture falls as rain.

Sea levels fluctuated during Tertiary times but fell overall, putting an end to the continental shelf seas. At the end of the Cretaceous period, about 60 percent of modern North America was under water. By mid-Tertiary times it had fallen to 5 percent, and the seas have not returned since.

FLORA AND FAUNA CHANGES
From early Tertiary times, most plant-eating mammals were small, and many of the flowering plants were large forest trees. Consequently, the plant-eaters were browsers that ate leaves, fallen fruits, and seeds. But as the climate cooled and became drier, the lush forests grew smaller, and were replaced by the open savanna grasslands of North America, Africa, and Asia. These savannas favored grazing plant-eaters and led to a marked increase in the size of the animals. Of the early Tertiary plant-eating mammals, only the horses (which by mid-Tertiary had grown to the size of large modern dogs) and rhinos took full advantage of the change. However, they had to compete with the new cud-chewing plant-eaters such as deer, camels, and later, cowlike bovids and hippos.

Other vertebrate groups promoted by the climate change were the songbirds and primates. The reduction of the forests forced the primates out into the open to obtain food. Movement across large open spaces in turn promoted the use of two legs instead of four, and the use of arms and hands for purposes other than climbing.

RIVERSLEIGH MARSUPIALS

By LATE EOCENE TIMES, AUSTRALIA HAD become isolated from the rest of the world, taking its primitive mammals with it—in particular, the marsupials. These mammals, which give birth to underdeveloped young that are then cared for in a pouch, evolved in mid-Cretaceous times in North America and spread to South America and Australia.

Unlike their South American cousins, which were overthrown by the invasion of more modern placental mammals from North America, the Australian marsupials survived as a dominant group because of their geographic isolation.

RIVERSLEIGH FOSSIL SITE

Evidence for Australian marsupials ranging from 23 million to less than 20,000 years old comes from a remote outback ranch at Riversleigh in northwestern Queensland. Fossil records for the area date from 1900, but the real breakthrough in fossil discovery came in 1983, when a few blocks of weathered Riversleigh limestone were found to be literally bristling with bones. Within an hour or so, the investigating team had found 30 fossil mammals new to science.

THE PLANT-EATING MAMMALS

During Miocene times, the lowland rain forests of Riversleigh were populated by an extraordinary diversity of marsupial mammals. The tree canopies were filled with six or more kinds of possums. The leaf litter on the forest floor was constantly stirred by the rustling feet of tiny wallabies and occasionally by cow-sized, wombat-like diprotodontids as they searched for their favorite plant foods. There were also rodentlike rat kangaroos and a strange beast, *Yalkaparidon*, that is informally described as a "thingodontan." Known only from its skull, its teeth suggest it must have had a very specialized diet, although exactly what it ate is unknown.

THE MEAT-EATERS

Unusual cat-sized marsupial lions (thylacoleonids) were related to the wombats and later, in the Pleistocene period, grew to the size of leopards.

MARSUPIAL "TIGER"

The thylacine Tasmanian "tiger" was a meat-eating marsupial mammal that evolved in Australia. The first fossils of the group were found at Riversleigh. The species survived until 1933, when the last thylacine died in captivity.

RIVERSLEIGH LIFE

Riversleigh was a lowland rain forest teeming with life. Although plant fossils are rare, the remains of plant-eaters, such as the cow-sized *Neohelos*, plant-eating rat kangaroos (*Hypsiprimnodon*), and possums (*Burramys*), show that there was a lot of vegetation. Predators were few but there was a cat-sized marsupial "lion" (*Priscileo*) and a flesh-eating kangaroo (*Ekaltadeta*). The relative lack of predators allowed flightless birds such as *Bullockornis* to develop.

•Riversleigh

Burramys

Hypsiprymnodon

Bullockornis

Priscileo

Flesh-eating kangaroos preyed on a range of small mammals, birds, and invertebrates. Marsupial moles burrowed through the soil and leaf litter after their invertebrate prey. The night skies were filled with a variety of bats competing from their cave homes for the abundant insects. The only other predators were crocodiles that patrolled the lakesides and snakes that slithered along the forest floor, climbed the trees, and swam in the rivers.

THE WATER-DWELLERS

Apart from the large reptilian vertebrates, the freshwaters of the lakes and rivers were inhabited by turtles, frogs, and lungfish, perhaps as much as 13 feet (4 meters) long, eels and catfish, most of which were able to breathe oxygen directly from the atmosphere. The invertebrate prey for these fish included abundant water fleas and snails.

THE BIRDS

By far the most conspicuous of Riversleigh's bird fossils were the so-called thunder birds, a group of large flightless ostrichlike animals that became extinct only some 26,000 years ago and were known to the first aboriginal inhabitants of Australia. They were distantly related to the other bird groups such as the emulike flightless birds. Songbirds (passerines), which comprise more than half of all living species of birds, were also abundant but have yet to be identified.

The only problem with recreating the Riversleigh environment is the lack of plant fossils. In the warm climate of the area, the limestone that forms the rock sediment does not readily preserve plants, which are attacked by microbes and soil-dwelling detritivores such as millipedes, also part of the fossil remains.

BAT BONES

One of the most common fossils found at Riversleigh are bats. Leaf-nosed bats lived in limestone caves in huge numbers. Their bones and droppings accumulated on the floors of the caves and were fossilized.

ROCKY RECORD

Riversleigh holds the record for density of new fossil finds. In 1983, 70 cubic feet (2 cubic meters) of rock from the area yielded 58 new mammals. This is because the area lay in a limestone terrain with plenty of surface water. These were ideal conditions for bone preservation.

Yalkaparidon

Neohelos

Ekaltadeta

Hypsiprymnodon

THE HIMALAYAS AND THE TIBETAN PLATEAU

THE STORY OF HOW THE HIMALAYAS AND THE Tibetan plateau were created begins about 55 million years ago. At the time, India, which was a separate landmass, was crashing into the continent of Asia. The point of collision formed the Himalayas, the highest and youngest mountain range in the world. It also formed the Tibetan plateau, the largest upland region on Earth, which is on average 3 miles (5 kilometers) above sea level. For this reason it is known as the "roof of the world." The rock (called the continental crust) beneath Tibet is an astonishing 46 miles (74 kilometers) thick, about twice the average crustal thickness.

THE FORMATION OF THE HIMALAYAS

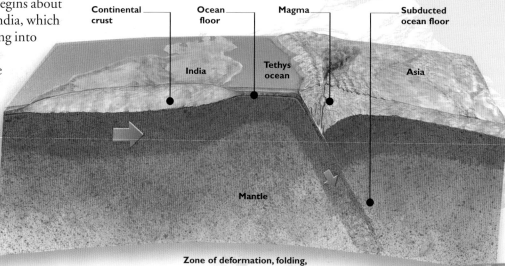

Continental crust · Ocean floor · Magma · Subducted ocean floor · India · Tethys ocean · Asia · Mantle

Zone of deformation, folding, compression, and upthrust

MOUNTAIN-BUILDING MECHANICS

The mechanism by which mountains are formed has long been understood. As two continents collide, enormous forces are exerted on the rock at the point of impact, crumpling, folding, compressing, deforming, and altering its chemical composition. Some of the rock is pushed skyward to form the peaks of the mountains, while other rock is pushed deep down into the Earth's mantle to form the "roots" of the mountains. A mountain range such as the Himalayas is, in effect, the thickening of the crust caused by rocks being pushed both upward and downward.

In addition, the rock of the deep mantle is denser than the rock of the crust above it. As the crust thickens, the mantle effectively buoys up the line of mountains. As the mountains get bigger, this mantle support increases and the entire mountain range is pushed skyward. This elevation

55 MILLION YEARS AGO

The Himalayas were created when India collided with Asia. As India approached Asia, the ocean floor in between the two land-masses was pushed down (subducted) under Asia. The rocks melted, and either cooled to form granite or escaped as magma through volcanoes.

Himalayas · India

Tibetan Plateau

MOUNTAIN PEAKS

Annapurna is just one of many peaks in the Himalayas that rise over 5 miles (8 kilometers) above sea level. These peaks are still being uplifted by some 4 inches (10 centimeters) a century and eroded at the same rate, with the debris carried away by great rivers, such as the Ganges.

DEFYING GRAVITY

The Tibetan plateau covers some 2 million square miles (5 million square kilometers) of Asia, and the remarkable uniformity of its elevation, at about 3 miles (5 kilometers) above sea level, suggests that this may be the maximum possible height at which rocks in the Earth's crust can be supported over such a large surface area. Any further thickening would put such pressure on the rocks deep in the base of the plateau that they would melt and shift.

is counterbalanced, however, by the erosive action of the weather, which continuously strips off the top layer of the mountain peaks.

BUILDING THE TIBETAN PLATEAU

While this model explains the origin of most mountain ranges, it does not explain why the Tibetan plateau, the edge of which is over 190 miles (300 kilometers) away from the Himalayas, is also elevated. It appears that as India approached Asia, the ocean plate in between the two landmasses was pushed under Asia, in a process called subduction. As the two continents collided, part of the landmass of India was also subducted, following the ocean crust down into the mantle. The edge of Asia was pushed over the top of India.

The rock from both continents was folded, deformed, and compressed during the collision, and parts of both continents and the ocean plate were pushed up to form the Himalayas. However, crucially, the Indian crust did not totally subduct. Its rock was less dense than the rock of the Earth's mantle below it, so instead of being pushed downward, it started to move horizontally, effectively pushing a wedge under Asia. The effect was to lift the Tibetan plateau up in one piece, thickening the crust dramatically as it did so.

ROOF OF THE WORLD
A view of the floodplain of the Ganges River (left), the snow-covered Himalayas, and the Tibetan plateau (right), as seen from a NASA Space Shuttle.

25 MILLION YEARS AGO
As India pushed into Asia, the rocks were crumpled together, and pushed down as a deep root or upthrust as a mountain belt. The intervening crust was shortened by some 1,500 miles (2,500 kilometers) and a huge slab, around 180 miles (290 kilometers) wide, was probably pushed under Tibet.

TODAY
In the roots of the mountain chain, the high pressures chemically alter the composition of the rocks. As the mountains are elevated from beneath, their peaks are worn down by erosion. The subduction of India under Asia continues at a rate of 2 inches (5 centimeters) a year.

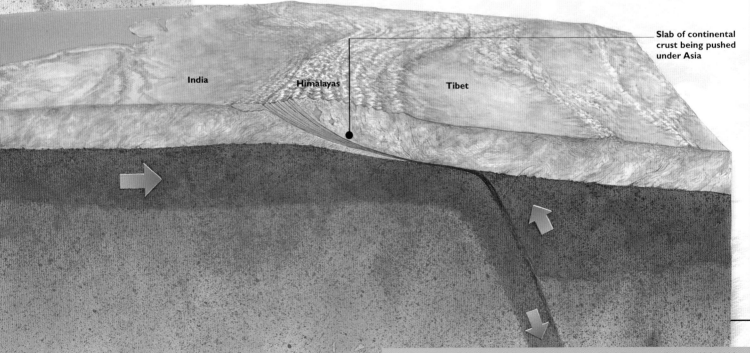

Asia

India   Himalayas   Tibet

Slab of continental crust being pushed under Asia

Late Tertiary Period

THE DIRECT ANCESTORS OF MODERN HUMANS EMERGED IN
AFRICA BETWEEN FIVE AND TWO MILLION YEARS AGO, AS THE
EARTH BEGAN TO COOL TOWARD THE END OF TERTIARY TIMES.

In late Tertiary times (Pliocene), the global distribution of continents and oceans was very similar to that today, and the same inexorable geological forces were at work. At any one time, the outward expansion of ocean floors from mid-ocean ridges averaged about 1 inch (2.5 centimeters) a year. Even at this slow rate some 15½ miles (25 kilometers) of new ocean floor would have been created every million years with the same amount lost by being dragged down into ocean trenches or forced under the landmasses of the continents in areas called subduction zones.

This dynamic activity of the Earth's crust generated constant earthquakes, volcanoes, and plate movement. India continued to push north into Asia, Africa pushed into southern Europe, and East Africa began to break apart. The Red Sea and the Gulf of Aden opened up. The isolation of the two American continents was eventually ended when the Panamanian isthmus reconnected

LENGAI VOLCANO, TANZANIA
A series of volcanoes mark where the crustal rocks of East Africa were rifted some 2 to 5 million years ago. Lava and ashfall blanketed the layers of sediment in the valleys, preserving a treasure trove of fossils for future researchers.

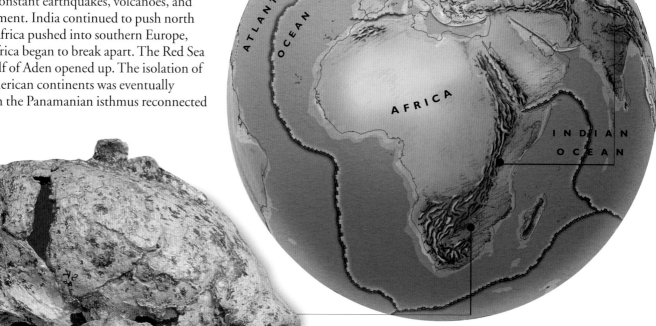

South and North America about 3 million years ago. Subsequently North America and Asia were also connected. These new land bridges allowed the exchange of animals and plants and, eventually, the migration of humans all over the world.

Climate in the late Tertiary period was characterized by fluctuating temperatures and humidity. Sea levels rose and fell several times as water first became locked up, and then released, by the polar icecaps. But these fluctuations were only temporary. Glaciation began in earnest in the northern hemisphere about 2.5 million years ago.

SKULL
Australopithecus robustus lived between 1 and 2.2 million years ago in Africa (this skull was found in South Africa). With a massive muscular jaw and large teeth, it lived mainly on plant food. Adult males grew to 5 feet 4 inches (1.6 meters) tall and were powerfully built.

THE HOMINIDS

Late Tertiary times marked a key stage in the evolution of humankind. This was the period, between 5 and 1.5 million years ago, when the genus Homo evolved from an australopithecine (meaning "southern ape") ancestor in Africa. From the 4.5-million-year-old hominid Ardipithecus ramidus, a succession of southern apes evolved until they became extinct around 1 million years ago. By this time, several different species of Homo had evolved, including two different species of Homo habilis, that belonged to the same group as modern humans, and subsequently, Homo erectus, the first human to migrate from Africa.

FOSSIL FOOTPRINT
About 3.6 million years ago, three of our hominid ancestors, *Australopithecus afarensis,* walked away from a volcanic eruption in the Rift Valley in Tanzania. Their footprints are among the first evidence of hominids walking fully upright. Two of the group walked side by side and the third dogged their steps, treading in the prints of the largest individual.

lake with abundant game. Stone tools from the Afar region, along with cut and hammered bones of bovids and horses, provide some early evidence that hominids killed and butchered large game. This represents a shift from a predominantly vegetarian hominid diet to one that included nutritious meat and bone marrow. The onset of meat-eating seems to coincide with the emergence in East and southern Africa of the genus *Homo* and has major behavioral and social implications since it requires collaborative hunting and the development of skills such as tool-making.

THE EMERGENCE OF HOMINIDS

During the 1990s, it became clear that the 3-million-year-old *Australopithecus afarensis* (first found in the Afar region of northern Ethiopia) is the most likely ancestor of the human lineage, which starts with the 2-million-year-old *Homo habilis,* an inhabitant of East and southern Africa. The vital million-year gap in the fossil record between the two was filled in the late 1990s with the discovery of a new australopithecine, *A. garhi,* also from Afar. These 2.5-million-year-old hominids lived in open grasslands around a

MATTERHORN
The pyramid-shaped horn of this alpine peak in Switzerland has clearly been sculpted by a glacier. Although glaciers are still present in the European Alps, they are only a remnant of the much deeper and more extensive ice sheets that started to develop in late Pliocene times over 2 million years ago.

HOMINIDS AND OTHER MAMMALS

THE LAKESHORE AND RIVER deposits surrounding Lake Turkana in Kenya, East Africa, contain the richest fossil record of early hominids in the world, preserved in strata known as the Koobi Fora Formation.

HUMAN ANCESTORS

The most famous remains from the area are skulls of *Homo habilis*, one of the first representatives of the human genus *Homo* and the ancestor of modern humans. The skulls, dated 1.9 million years old, show the face of *Homo habilis* as having been long, broad, and flat with prominent cheekbones, like that of much older hominids, the australopithecines. But *Homo habilis* was clearly distinguished from its contemporaries, the australopithecines, by the size of its brain case, with a brain capacity of 25 fluid ounces (750 milliliters), compared with less than 17 fluid ounces (500 milliliters) for the australopithecines.

Slightly younger hominid fossils at the same site, dated to 1.8 million years ago, have been distinguished as *Homo erectus*, a species that

RIFT VALLEY LAKE
The region around Lake Turkana has experienced countless volcanic eruptions over the last tens of millions of years. The outpourings of lava and ash have helped bury and preserve sediments containing the fossil remains of our human ancestors.

survived in Africa for more than a million years. It was the most advanced of the Lake Turkana hominids and the first to venture beyond Africa. Indeed, fossils of *Homo erectus*, along with stone tools (Acheulian hand axes), have been discovered throughout Europe and as far afield as China (so-called Peking Man) and Java (Java Man).

One of the most complete *Homo erectus* fossils was found near Lake Turkana in 1984. It is the skeleton of a robustly built boy with long legs and narrow hips. Aged about 11 and standing 5 feet 6 inches (168 centimeters) tall, he had a long, low skull with prominent brow ridges and a slightly more pronounced nose.

The brain size of *Homo erectus* increased over time. By a million years ago, its brain had reached a capacity of about 33 fluid ounces (1,000 milliliters), rising 500,000 years later to about 43 fluid ounces (1,300 milliliters). In comparison, *Homo sapiens* has a brain capacity of 58 fluid ounces (1,750 milliliters).

AFRICAN EDEN

The shores of Lake Turkana supported an abundant wildlife, including some hominids. The savanna grassland fed grazing herds of deer and the three-toed horse *Hipparion*. The woodland foliage was browsed by the giraffid *Sivatherium* and the elephant *Deinotherium*, while hippopotamuses fed on water plants. The burly hominid *Australopithecus boisei* gathered fruit, nuts, and roots. Top predators were big cats such as the saber-tooth *Homotherium* and early human *Homo habilis*. Scavengers included vultures, and hyenas such as *Crocuta*.

Lake Turkana

Ficus, Maytenus, and Cordia

Hipparion

Hippopotamus amphibius

Homo habilis

Sivatherium

Deinotherium

The variety of hominids decreased, so that by 800,000 years ago, *Homo erectus* was one of only two hominids left to carry forward the human lineage. The other is known as *Homo ergaster*.

OTHER TURKANA MAMMALS

There is a wealth of other animal and plant fossils in the surroundings of Lake Turkana, many of them of animals and plants that are familiar to us today. Baboons (*Theropithecus*) and monkeys (*Rhinocolobus*) were as common at this time in the Lake Turkana region as they are today. They generally lived in the riverside forests, although some species preferred more open, drier

woodland. They were hunted by the same large carnivores that live in modern-day savanna communities, such as large lions, pack-hunting hyenas (*Crocuta*), and dogs (canid *Lycaon*).

Elephant-like proboscideans were the largest of the big plant-eaters and lived both on the open savannas and in forested habitats. Early horses (*Hipparion*) were common, but were replaced by the modern savanna-grazing *Equus* around 2.3 million years ago. Camel and giraffe remains have also been found, along with 40 different kinds of bovines. These cowlike creatures eventually inhabited wet grasslands.

Analysis of the plants locked away in the Turkana deposits shows a gradual dominance of grasses over trees and shrubs. Initially, the grasses made up 20 to 40 percent of the vegetation, but over time, this figure increased to 65 percent.

MODERN MEGAHERBIVORES
The African savanna developed in Miocene times (23 to 5 million years ago), as the climate became cooler and drier. Plant-eating mammals emerged from the forests and switched over from browsing foliage to grazing grass.

CONNECTIONS

Twenty-one different types of fossil fish have been found in the Lake Turkana strata, compared to 34 types of fish living in the lake today. These fossils include a freshwater stingray (*Dasyatis africana*) that must have originally migrated into the lake from the Indian Ocean. Other fish include the African lungfish, *Polypterus*, and other species that show an early link with the Nile River in Egypt to the north.

Australopithecus boisei

Homotherium

Crocuta

Mammals of the Americas

For most of the past two hundred million years, South and North America have not been connected. The isolation of South America as an island for long periods of time, combined with migrations of animals both south and north via temporary land bridges, has had a profound effect on the mammal populations of the two continents at different times in the past.

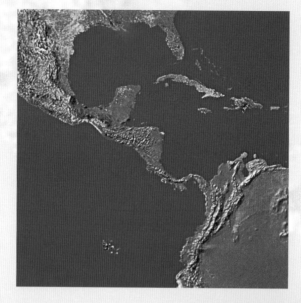

AN INVASION DURING THE CRETACEOUS

During Cretaceous times, a population of small, primitive mammals lived alongside the dinosaurs in South America. In North America, a mammalian group called the therians (made up of placental mammals and marsupials) dominated. Toward the end of the Cretaceous, a connection was temporarily established between North and South as a result of a change in sea levels. Some therians migrated south, where they evolved into some highly unusual and singular forms.

About 15 marsupial families became established in South America during Tertiary times, including a group of saber-toothed marsupial meat-eaters. But the most distinctive animals to develop were a group of placental mammals, the xenarthrans (meaning "strange joints"), including sloths, armadillos, and anteaters. The most spectacular of these were the armadillo-like glyptodonts, which grew to the size of a large automobile. Superficially they resembled ankylosaurs since they had a protective bony shell and a spiked club on the end of the tail. The

BRIDGING THE GAP
The current land bridge between North and South America is a narrow strip of land comprising the countries of Panama and Costa Rica. This bridge was established about 3 million years ago. Before that, occasional falls in sea level may have turned some seabeds into land, allowing animals to migrate across chains of islands in the West Indies and what is now Central America.

ARMORED PLANT-EATER
Doedicurus, a glyptodont, grew to 23 feet (4 meters) in length and lived in Patagonia about 1 to 2 million years ago. It bore a bony club at the end of its tail; the club was covered in spikes and used as a defensive weapon.

tail itself was powerful and flexible, supporting the animal like a tripod when it reared up on its hind legs in defense or for reproduction. The massive skull had powerful jaws and teeth that were used for chewing the tough prairie grasses.

The sloths were also plant-eaters. They first appeared some 30 million years ago and included tree sloths and ground sloths. *Megatherium*, the largest known ground sloth, grew to 19 feet (6 meters) long. Ground sloths were a highly successful group and later

GIANT GROUND SLOTH
Megatherium inhabited an area that now includes Bolivia and Peru. Although as large as a modern elephant, it could rear up on its hind legs, supported by its thick tail. In this position, it browsed near the treetops, hooking down branches with its clawed forefeet.

DIVERGENCE OF

HUMANS ARE MEMBERS OF A LARGE
primates called the catarrhine
includes the apes and the Old W
Africa, Asia, and Europe. The
group can be traced back to
that lived around 28 mil
million years ago, the
diverged on to a se
4.5 million yea
humans dive
The differ
materi
the

spread into North America
across a newly formed land bridge. They survived
until 11,000 years ago when they became extinct
along with many other large plant-eaters.

HOOFED MAMMALS

The hoof-bearing (ungulate) and plant-eating
mammals of Tertiary times are familiar
today. They include pigs, horses,
cows, rhinos, elephants, and
deer. In South America, they
evolved into some
unique rabbit-,
horse-, and camel-
like forms. These included the
10-foot- (3-meter-) long *Macrauchenia*,
which had a long neck, substantial trunk,
and nostrils placed high on the skull between
the eyes. One of the largest hoofed mammals,
Toxodon, had a barrel-shaped body on short,
stocky legs, a broad head, and small 3-toed hoofs.
Charles Darwin, who collected *Toxodon* fossils in
Argentina, described it as "one of the strangest
animals ever discovered."

PAMPAS BRO
Toxodon was a 9-foot- (2.7-
meter-) long rhinoceros-like
plant-eater. A browser and
grazer, it fed on the grasses
and shrubs of the central
Argentinian Pampas region
about 2 million years ago.

extinctions in South America affected the hoofed
animals and xenarthrans but many were already
declining before the northern invaders arrived.

EARLY EQUID
Widespread in North America, Asia, and
Europe 50 million years ago, *Hyracotherium*
(left) was about the size of a labrador dog.
It is thought to be the ancestor of all horses.

MERYCHIPPUS
Herds of *Merychippus*
roamed the North
American prairies 5 to 10
million years ago. It was one
of the first horses to feed
almost entirely on grass.
As an adaptation to this
diet, its teeth were taller
and higher-crowned than
those of its ancestors.

HORSES EXTINCT IN NORTH AMERICA

*Along with many other large mammals, horses
became extinct in North America about 11,000
years ago, possibly as the result of an epidemic
or human activity. But the genus Equus survived
in Europe, Africa, and Asia as zebras, asses, and
wild horses. It is thought that horses were first
domesticated in eastern Asia between 3,000 and
4,000 years ago. The horse was reintroduced to the
Americas in the 16th century by Spanish explorers.*

WILD HORSES
The mustangs of
the 19th-century
American plains
were descended
from domesticated
horses introduced
300 years earlier
by the Spanish.

APES AND HOMINIDS

GROUP OF
, which
rld monkeys of
history of this
a common ancestor
ion years ago. By 22
Old World monkeys had
parate evolutionary path. Only
s ago, the hominid ancestors of
ged from the other African apes.
ence between the DNA (genetic
l) of humans and their closest relatives,
himpanzees, is less than 2 percent.

IN SEARCH OF THE MISSING LINK

Paleontologists have struggled to piece together
the story of human evolution from a fragmentary
fossil record, seeking the "missing link" between
humans and other apes. They have focused on a
range of upright-walking hominids, living in
Africa, that exhibited a mix of traits. Several
species of these "australopithecines" (meaning
"southern apes") have been identified, including
the lightly built *Australopithecus afarensis* and *A.
africanus*, as well as the sturdier
A. robustus and
A. boisei.

DISTANT RELATIVE
The orangutan, a native of
Southeast Asia, was once
thought to be our closest
ape relative. With its large
brain and considerable
intelligence, it was thought
to belong to the same group
of apes as the African
chimpanzee and gorilla. It is
now known, however, that
the African apes are more
closely related to humans.

NEAREST LIVING RELATIVE
Pan paniscus, the pygmy chimp of
Central Africa (also known as the
bonobo), is our nearest living relative.
Its DNA is a few tenths of one
percent closer to ours than that of
the common chimp, *Pan troglodytes*.

THE SKULL OF "MRS. PLES"
This skull of *Australopithecus africanus* was nicknamed "Mrs. Ples" by scientist Robert Broom in 1935. Later, Broom was able to show that this 2.5 to 3.0 million-year-old hominid grew to just over 4 feet (1.4 meters), could stand fully upright, and walk like a human.

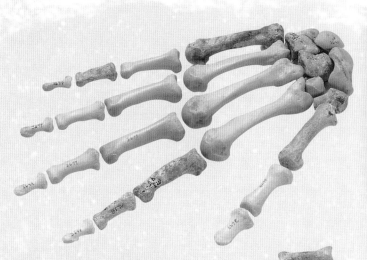

DOWN FROM THE TREES

As more and more research is conducted, the age of these possible human ancestors has been gradually pushed back. In the 1960s, scientists were startled to find that a skull of *A. boisei* from the Olduvai Gorge, Tanzania, was 2 million years old. But in 1994, an australopithecine found in Ethiopia, *Ardipithecus ramidus*, was dated to 4.5 million years ago. The most primitive hominid yet discovered, it bore many similarities to living chimpanzees. However, it did not knuckle-walk like the chimpanzees, but instead walked upright.

A fully grown male *Ardipithecus ramidus* was about 4.5 feet (1.3 meters) tall and weighed around 60 pounds (27 kilograms). Females were considerably smaller and lighter. This species lived in a woodland habitat, sleeping in trees, but active on the ground during the day. Walking upright freed its hands for carrying food and kept the hot sun off its unprotected back. Its dietary habits probably distinguished it from other apes, with the addition of scavenged meat to its staple meals of fruit and plant roots. It may also have banded together to hunt small animals.

It is unlikely that *Ardipithecus ramidus* made tools, since no evidence of these items has been found dating earlier than 2.6 million years ago.

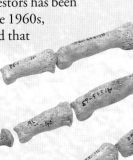

ANCIENT HANDS
The hands of this 3.3 milllion-year-old *Australopithecus afarensis* from Ethiopia are close to, but not the same as, those of modern humans. They show the characteristics of both a tree-climber and a ground-based tool-maker.

However, the early australopithecines probably used sticks, twigs, and bones as tools in the way that chimpanzees do today.

Since the discovery of *Ardipithecus ramidus*, the heritage of the australopithecines has finally been pieced together. *A. anamensis*, found in 1995, is dated at 4.2 to 3.9 million years ago. It has an apelike jaw, but with more advanced teeth. The oldest *A. afarensis* is dated to about 3.8 million years ago. *A. africanus* emerged around 800,000 years later. The latest discovery, *A. garhi*, is around 2.5 million years old, and seems to be the best candidate for direct ancestor of genus *Homo*, while *A. robustus* and *A. boisei* survived alongside *Homo* species for over a million years.

AFRICAN DISCOVERIES

The first evidence for the existence of the man-ape australopithecines was a child's skull found in a cave at Taung, South Africa, in 1924. This "Taung boy" was an *A. africanus*. In 1959, a skull of the larger *A. boisei* was found in the Olduvai Gorge, Tanzania. Dated to 2 million years ago, the skull convinced many researchers that australopithecines were the ancestors of modern humans. "Lucy," a famous example of *A. afarensis*, was found at Hadar, Ethiopia, in 1979.

The Quaternary Age

A VIEW OF THE EARTH 18 THOUSAND YEARS AGO SHOWS A FROZEN WORLD. ICE SHEETS, IN PLACES TWO MILES THICK, COVERED VAST TRACTS OF THE NORTHERN CONTINENTS.

The Quaternary age is the most recent period of geological time, lasting from 1.8 million years ago up to the present day. In geological terms, the Earth 18,000 years ago was almost the same as it is today. Continents, mountains, ocean ridges, and subduction zones were all in nearly identical positions. The face of our planet, however, greatly differed from today, for the Earth was in the grip of an ice age. It was the most recent of many ice ages to have punctuated Earth's history. Huge ice sheets spread southward from the North Pole, and glaciers all over the world were larger than their present sizes.

Despite their name, ice ages are not always unrelentingly cold. During the last ice age, the climate swung between glacials, cold periods when the ice sheets grew, and interglacials, when the ice shrank back. Each glaciation has lasted for about 100,000 years, with periods of warmer interglaciation lasting 10,000 years in between. The Earth is still in the grip of this last ice age, although it is experiencing an interglacial period.

At the peak of the last ice age, ice and frozen ground spread far south of the Arctic circle. So much water became frozen—about 5 percent of all the water on Earth (including 90 percent of the freshwater)—that sea levels fell by 330 feet (100 meters). The drop in sea level meant that shallow

PINGOS
In the Canadian Arctic, the growth of underground ice pushes up mounds called pingos. As the ice core melts, the mound collapses to form a crater. Fossil pingos in Ireland and England show where permafrost once existed during the last ice age.

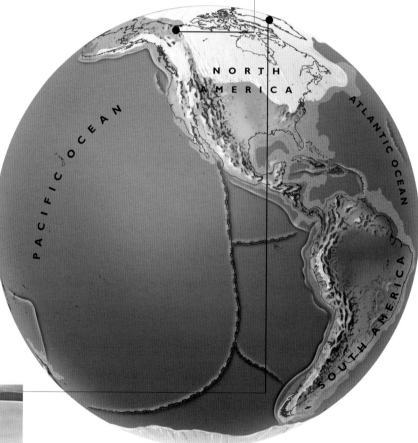

ICE POWER
Ice sheets build up over years. The growing pile of snow compresses the bottom layers into ice. Any slope in the ground makes the pile unstable so that it begins to slide slowly and flow down the hill under its own weight, as if it were a liquid. Here the Greenland ice sheet overflows through a gap in a mountain ridge.

NORTH AND SOUTH

Large-scale glaciation can develop only where there are extensive polar landmasses because land freezes more easily than the sea. During the last glaciation, ice sheets were more widely developed in the northern hemisphere because of the cluster of continents around the Arctic Ocean. The surface waters of the Arctic Ocean did eventually freeze and carry ice as far south as the British Isles.

seas suddenly became dry plains, connecting previously isolated islands and continents. The opening up of these land bridges was to have a dramatic effect on the distribution of animals and plants. Humans also took advantage, passing from Asia into the Americas via the Bering Strait and from Europe into the British Isles.

WHY DID THE ICE ADVANCE?

Fossil records show us that the global climate has been cooling slowly for the past 40 million years. Three million years ago, the cooling quickened and the polar icecaps and mountain glaciers of the northern continents began to grow. These changing

MAMMOTH MOLARS
Woolly mammoths were common across Europe and Asia during the last ice age. Their cheek teeth (above) were massive and heavily ridged to break up the coarse grass and shrubs of the steppe tundra.

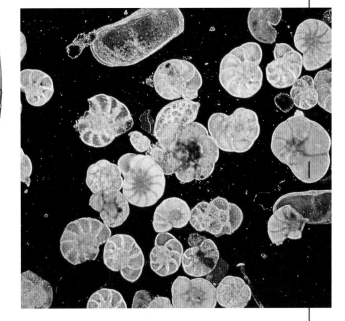

weather patterns were influenced by the configuration of the continents. The gradual rifting of Antarctica from other southern continents led to the formation of a circular current, the Westerly Drift, which cut off the flow of warm air and water, and resulted in the cooling of the South Polar region. A polar icecap formed and sea temperatures dropped, precipitating an overall cooling of the Earth's climate.

About three million years ago, North and South America became joined by a land bridge, the Isthmus of Panama, so warm Atlantic water was no longer able to flow around the equator, but was instead diverted northward. This led to increased precipitation in eastern Canada, Greenland, and Scandinavia—three of the main areas of ice accumulation, where parts of the ice sheets were 10,000 feet (3,000 meters) thick. The warm ocean currents pulled moist air along with them, so that the amount of rain and snow falling on northern lands increased. In turn, the rivers poured more freshwater into the Arctic Ocean. Because freshwater freezes more readily than seawater, the Arctic sea-ice grew quickly.

FOSSIL PROOF
From the shell composition of single-celled creatures (above) trapped in seafloor sediment, geologists can chart past changes in the temperature of seawater. Because sea and air temperatures are closely linked, changes in past climates can also be worked out.

THE RUSSIAN MAMMOTH STEPPE

THE FREEZING CONDITIONS OF A GLACIAL, the coldest phase in an ice age, make it very difficult for plants and animals to survive. For plants, the extreme cold is a very difficult environment to survive in as there is often an absence of water and pollen-carrying insects. Permanently frozen ground also makes it almost impossible for seeds to take root. In turn, animal life cannot be supported, because there is no vegetation for plant-eaters to feed on. To complete the cycle, no meat-eaters can survive, since there are no plant-eaters to prey on.

However, many animals and plants survived the frozen wastelands of the last glacial, in areas beyond the ice. They occupied slightly warmer windswept lands with a summer thaw, deep in the southern parts of the North American and Asian continents. Animals that lived in these areas at the time included the woolly mammoth and rhino, who, like today's polar creatures, were animals that could survive intense cold. Their heavy fur acted as insulation, as did layers of body fat, which also provided a source of energy during the harsh winter months. The cave bear also conserved energy by hibernating.

One of the richest places for fossils of these animals is on the mammoth steppe, what is now

eastern Russia. At the time, the steppe must have resembled a frozen variation on the hot African grasslands of today. Where modern Africa has elephants, rhinos, and lions, the steppe had mammoths, woolly rhinos, and large predatory cats. In effect, the area was home to woollier versions of species that we are familiar with today.

The mammoth steppe was devoid of trees, but during a brief spring and summer, colorful swathes of flowering herbs and grasses burst into

40,000-YEAR-OLD BABY
In June 1977, Dima was discovered in Siberia under 6 feet (2 meters) of frozen silt. Dima was a sickly mammoth, 6 to 12 months old, that had died 40,000 years before when he fell into a pool or bog which froze and preserved his body tissue.

LIFE ON THE MAMMOTH STEPPE
The Russian mammoth steppe was a mostly grassy habitat that stood between the northern ice sheet and wooded habitats farther south. It was home to many large herbivores, including woolly mammoths and rhinos, giant deer, horses, and the ancestors of most domesticated cattle. These were prey to hunters, such as large lion-type cats and humans.

The plants of the mammoth steppe are still seen today. They include a variety of hardy grasses and buttercups, and plants that flower in the Arctic tundra, such as purple and yellow saxifrage.

Mammoth steppe

Woolly mammoth
(*Mammuthus primigenius*)

Woolly rhino
(*Coelodonta antiquitatas*)

Horse
(*Equus*)

life. This annual greening provided food for herds of migratory mammals, which were closely followed by hungry predators. One predator, *Homo sapiens*, humankind, was so successful at exploiting this valuable food resource that many species were soon extinct.

CHANGING GLOBAL CIRCUMSTANCES

As the last glacial period came to an end and the climate warmed, the icecaps started to melt, leading to a radical change in the environment. The amount of habitable land increased as the ice retreated. The rise in temperature suited the growth of trees, so the vast grasslands, which were suited to colder conditions, began to disappear and were replaced by forest. Herds found their migration paths blocked by the new forests and broke up into smaller, more vulnerable groups. The leaves and shrubs that the animals now fed on were much less nutritious than the grasses, and their numbers declined ever more quickly as humans and other predators hunted them. In a few thousand years, the mammoths, woolly rhinos, giant deer, and cave bears were all extinct.

In isolated parts of Eurasia and North America, however, some species survived the most recent ice age, and are still in evidence today. Unfortunately, some, such as the bison, bear, wolf, lynx, arctic fox, and condor, are now endangered. Other survivors fared better, particularly humans.

RECLAIMING THE LAND

At the end of the last glacial phase, the ice sheets began to retreat, and plants were able to colonize the newly exposed land. The first vegetation to become re-established had to be very hardy. The pioneers, like the first plants ever to colonize the land over 450 million years ago, were lichens and mosses. Slowly, enough soil and organic matter gathered to allow other species to thrive. The mosses and lichens were joined by low-lying, tough shrubs and trees such as juniper, dwarf willow, and birch. Sedge grasses, bog cotton, and saxifrages also took root. These species can all be found in today's Arctic tundra.

ARCTIC BLOOM
Blooms of purple saxifrage such as these once colored the mammoth steppe.

CAVE DWELLERS
This stylized image of a mammoth was painted in the cave of La Baume Latrone in France by hunters who lived during the last ice age. The animal's body, 4 feet (1.2 meters) long, is shown in profile, while the tusks are depicted as if seen from the front.

Steppe lion
(*Panthera*)

Glacier

Giant deer
(*Megoloceros giganteus*)

THE HUMAN JOURNEY

THE STORY OF HUMAN EVOLUTION is complex. It can be pieced together only tentatively using fragmentary fossil evidence from around the world. The earliest fossils that we can label *Homo* (human) are roughly 2.4 million years old, come from Eastern and Southern Africa, and belong to *Homo habilis*. Around 1.9 million years ago a type of human more advanced than *Homo habilis* is thought to have evolved in Africa. *Homo erectus*, "upright human," was taller and had a bigger brain than its predecessor and possessed a skeleton similar to that of a modern human. This new type of human was particularly successful and spread relatively rapidly. By 1.8 million years ago humans of this type had reached the Caucasus Mountains in Asia Minor and between one and half a million years ago they had become established in Europe.

By 500,000 years ago, it is now believed that two separate branches of *Homo* were beginning to emerge, one of which eventually gave rise to the Neanderthals, *Homo neanderthalensis*, and the other to modern humans, *Homo sapiens*, meaning wise or knowing human.

ANCIENT ARTS
The culture of Cro-Magnon people was highly developed and even artistic. They left many paintings and sculptures in caves around Europe. This rhinoceros painting was found in a cave in Rouffignac, France.

NEANDERTHALS

The remains of the Neanderthals, *Homo neanderthalensis*, are found only in Europe and the Middle East. Their fossils range in age from 120,000 years to 35,000 years old. Neanderthals have an undeserved reputation for being primitive and stupid when in fact they were culturally advanced. For example they buried their dead and made a variety of tools and weapons.

The remains of the Neanderthals show that they were thicker set and generally stronger than modern people. They also had heavy brow ridges on their skulls and a sloping forehead, and, on average, they actually had larger brains than modern humans. But the Neanderthals all seem to have died out by about 35,000 years ago.

HOMO HEIDELBERGENSIS
This possible immediate ancestor of present-day humans is thought to have first evolved in south and east Africa between 400,000 and 100,000 years ago.

HOMO HABILIS
The first type of human dates back to 2.4 to 1.6 million years ago. *Homo habilis*, meaning "handy man," stood about 5 feet (1.5 meters) tall and weighed approximately 110 pounds (50 kilograms).

HOMO ERECTUS
Homo erectus first appeared in Africa about 1.9 million years ago. This species is considered to be the first hominid to have migrated out of Africa.

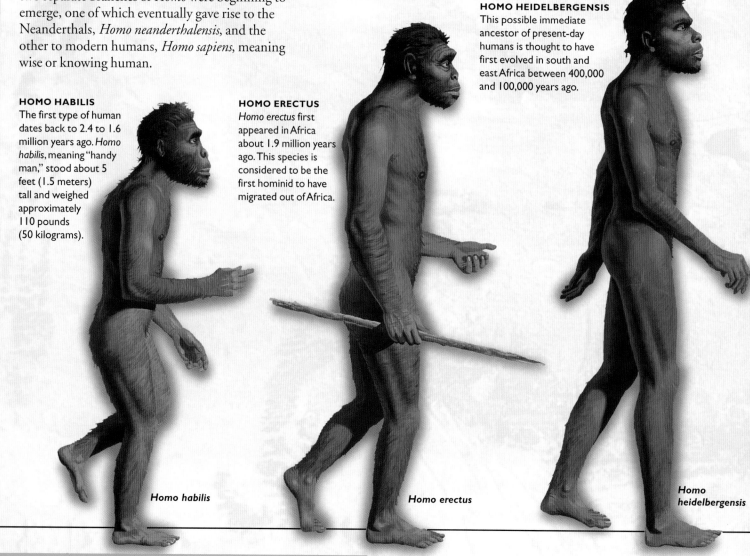

Homo habilis

Homo erectus

Homo heidelbergensis

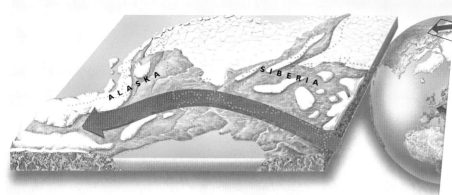

MODERN HUMANS

Homo sapiens probably evolved from an African group descended from the *Homo erectus* lineage; *Homo heidelbergensis* is a possible intermediate form. The earliest definite remains of our species have been found in Africa and are between 100,000 and 120,000 years old. Similar finds in Israel, from around 90,000 years ago, show that modern people reached the region before the Neanderthals. This refutes the theory that modern people are descended from the Neanderthals. It is

currently thought that t...
now-extinct branch of t...
supported by DNA ana...

By 40,000 years ago...
were alive in areas as far apart as...
Europe. Most evidence now suggests that modern humans evolved in Africa and spread to the other continents. They may, however, have interbred with older groups in different areas and have probably evolved locally to a small extent to produce the various peoples of the world today.

600 MA

PRECAMBRIAN

BEYOND TH...

TEN THOUSAND YEA...
cold glacial perio...
most recent ice age...
Global temperatur...
and the great i...
and retreat...
can scar...
creatin...
off...
a...

HOMO NEANDERTHALENSIS
Characterized by short limbs and stocky bodies, Neanderthals were 30 percent heavier than modern humans.

HOMO SAPIENS
The earliest modern humans existed 100,000 years ago. The earliest in Europe, known as Cro-Magnons, lived about 40,000 years ago. Taller and more slender-boned than Neanderthals, they possessed many of the physical features seen in humans today.

Homo neanderthalensis

Homo sapiens

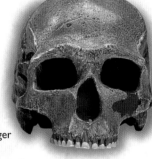

SKULLS
The skull of a Cro-Magnon (top) and a modern human skull (bottom) show only minor differences. Cro-Magnons had more rounded brain cases and slightly larger jaws and noses.

EARLY AMERICAN HUMANS

The Clovis culture, marked by its distinctive style of stone technology, is accepted as the earliest in the Americas, and is about 11,500 years old. The site of Monte Verde, in southern Chile, however, is providing convincing support for much older occupation. Wedged between the Andes and the Pacific Ocean, the site has been dated at 12,500 years old. It is argued that for people to have traveled this far south, some 10,000 miles (16,000 kilometers) from the Bering land bridge, they must have arrived in North America much earlier than 11,500 years ago.

WEAPON MAKERS
The Clovis point is a razor-sharp spearhead made of stone. Many of these points have been found wedged between mammoth bones.

ICE AGE

...S AGO, A ...d in the Earth's ...ame to an end. ...res climbed quickly, ...e sheets began to melt ...just as advancing glaciers ...d sculpt the landscape, ...g deep valleys and smoothed-...ills, so the retreat of an ice sheet ...so leaves its mark.

As the ice melted, great lakes of meltwater began to form. Some lakes were created where rock and ice remnants of the retreating glaciers formed natural dams. When the ice dams finally melted, too, cataclysmic floods followed, such as those that scoured the land to form the remarkable Channeled Scablands in Washington State.

The meltwater also added greatly to ocean volume. Rising seas drowned land bridges such as that joining Alaska to eastern Siberia opening the Bering Strait and isolating the animal and plant life of Northern America from Asia.

In other places, the melting of the ice sheets caused shorelines to be lifted clear of the sea. The ice sheets were extremely heavy and weighed down the continental crust below them, pushing it down into the flexible mantle of the Earth. When the weight of the ice was removed, the land rebounded, inch by inch. Each upward movement created a new coastline and raised the land that was previously on the coast.

THE GOOD TIMES

Temperatures on Earth have been relatively stable for the last 10,000 years, a time during which human civilization has flourished. But this success of humans as a species is having a considerable impact on global

temperatures. Since the beginning of the Industrial Revolution, human activity has had an increasingly damaging effect on the Earth's atmosphere. "Greenhouse" gases released by burning fossil fuels such as coal, gas, and oil trap more of the Sun's energy than is normal, warming the global climate. Some scientists think that the average rise in temperature over the next 50 years may be as much as 9°F (5°C). Ultimately, if this trend continues, the icecaps will melt, and sea levels will rise by about 23 feet (7 meters), enough to flood almost all the world's rivers and coastlines and the cities built on them.

HIGH AND DRY
Raised beaches occur where land that was once pressed down by the weight of an ice sheet "springs back," lifting sections of shoreline, as here on the Isle of Mull, Scotland, clear of the sea (above).

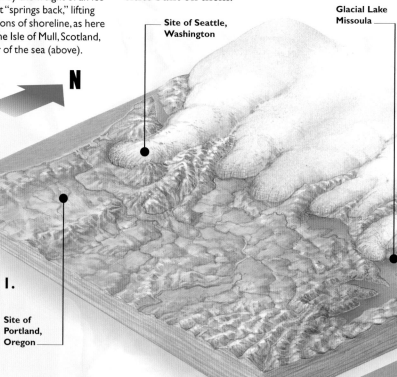

Site of Seattle, Washington

Glacial Lake Missoula

N

I.

Site of Portland, Oregon

ICY RECORDS
Ice sheets build up layer by layer over the years. By drilling deep into them, scientists can extract ice cores that contain ice up to 420,000 years old. Analyzing the ice reveals much about how the Earth's climate has changed. When ice forms, it traps tiny bubbles of air. The varying composition of this air reveals how the atmosphere has changed with time, changes that relate to fluctuations in the temperature of the Earth.

2.

Site of Portland, Oregon

THE POWER OF FLOOD

A sudden flood of meltwater from a glacier can have spectacular consequences. The prehistoric floods that gouged out the Channeled Scablands of eastern Washington State must have also wiped out much of the life in the area as they swept past. Catastrophic floods like this are caused when glacial ice melts rapidly. Often, the heat to melt the ice is supplied by an erupting volcano situated underneath the glacier. Part of the glacier itself can even flow down the slope of the volcano. A dramatic example of this occurred in Iceland in 1996 when a volcano erupted underneath the Vatnajökull glacier. The hot lava and gas quickly melted the glacial ice and precipitated a flood known as a "Jökulhaup." As much as 1.6 million cubic feet (45,000 cubic meters) of water poured down the valley each second, destroying two bridges and sweeping away a six mile section of road.

FIRE AND ICE

As a volcano erupts under the Vatnajökull glacier in Iceland, the ice can be seen cracking as it melts (top left of picture).

UNLIKELY CATCH

Mammoths lived on the dry land between Europe and Britain during the last glacial when sea levels were low. Their fossil teeth and bones are sometimes trawled from what is now the bed of the North Sea.

Site of Seattle, Washington

THE NEXT ICE AGE

Despite global warming, the most recent ice age may not be over. We may be living through a long, warm interglacial period. Evidence shows that previous interglacials have been both longer and warmer. Some scientists think that the present phase of rising temperatures is merely delaying the onset of the next cold period, which could start in 5,000 years' time and last for 15,000 years.

Such predictions are very difficult to make because global warming shows us how small changes in the atmosphere can trigger major effects in the global climate. So far we cannot predict accurately how the warming effect of greenhouse gases will balance other influences that tend to make the climate cooler, and so we cannot be certain when the next ice age will begin.

SCABBING THE LAND

1. Lake Missoula formed when a finger of ice trapped meltwater from the North American ice sheet 13,000 years ago. The lake filled to more than 1,000 feet (300 meters) deep.
2. Eventually, the lake overflowed. More than 720 million cubic feet (20 million cubic meters) of water flooded toward the sea per second, cutting into the bedrock and depositing piles of rock debris as huge sand ripples.

Seattle
Portland

Lake Missoula overflows

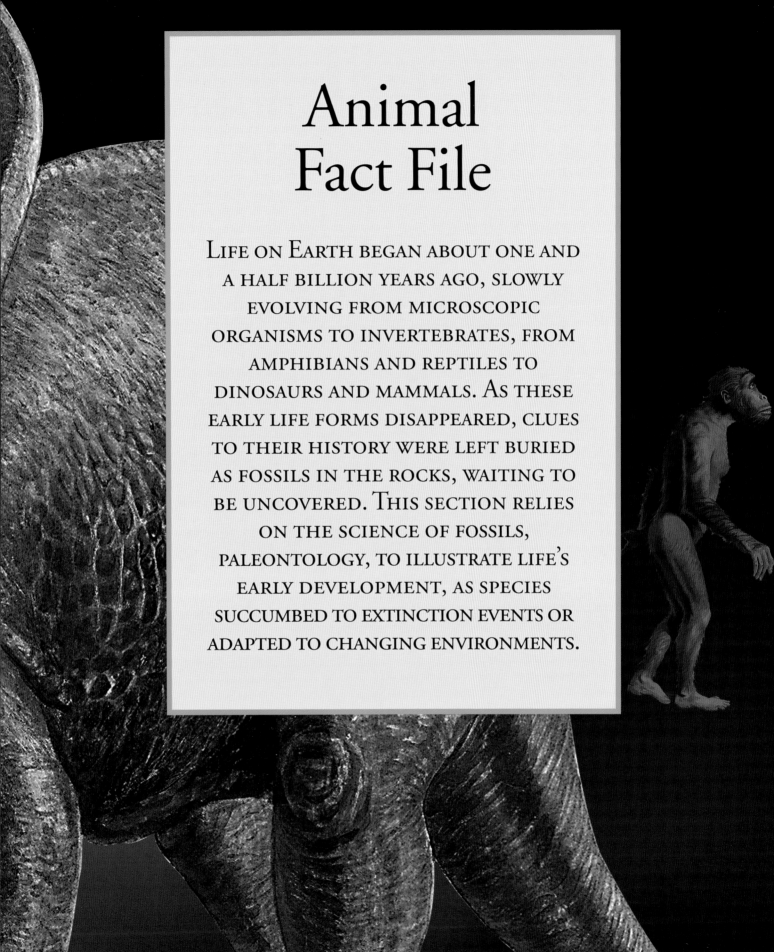

Animal Fact File

LIFE ON EARTH BEGAN ABOUT ONE AND
A HALF BILLION YEARS AGO, SLOWLY
EVOLVING FROM MICROSCOPIC
ORGANISMS TO INVERTEBRATES, FROM
AMPHIBIANS AND REPTILES TO
DINOSAURS AND MAMMALS. AS THESE
EARLY LIFE FORMS DISAPPEARED, CLUES
TO THEIR HISTORY WERE LEFT BURIED
AS FOSSILS IN THE ROCKS, WAITING TO
BE UNCOVERED. THIS SECTION RELIES
ON THE SCIENCE OF FOSSILS,
PALEONTOLOGY, TO ILLUSTRATE LIFE'S
EARLY DEVELOPMENT, AS SPECIES
SUCCUMBED TO EXTINCTION EVENTS OR
ADAPTED TO CHANGING ENVIRONMENTS.

THE FIRST VERTEBRATES

The most primitive backboned animals (or vertebrates as they are technically called) are the fishes, not the familiar kinds of fishes such as sharks and salmon, but somewhat peculiar jawless fishes, the agnathan hagfish (myxinoids) and lampreys (petromyzontiforms).

Despite their lack of familiarity, the agnathans still possess the fundamental characteristics of the vertebrates. These include an articulated stiffening rod running from head to tail with paired blocks of muscles on either side. Contraction of the muscles flexes the body in sinuous waves during swimming. A dorsal nerve cord lies above the backbone and has some enlargement at the front end associated with sense organs. This anterior "brain" is protected within the cranium.

The "backbone" and braincase need not be made of bone. Cartilaginous fishes such as the agnathans and sharks are vertebrates but their "backbones" are stiffened with cartilage. Cartilage is more primitive than bone, although it does not generally fossilize.

Agnathans were much more common in the past. Several groups evolved and occupied ancient seas, then moved into freshwater before dying out at the end of Devonian times. Mostly, these extinct agnathans looked different from the living survivors, which have rather specialized modes of life. Many fossil forms had a leathery covering of bony plates and scales, especially in the head region. But even these extinct forms are probably not the earliest vertebrates.

Conodonts

Evidence strongly suggests that conodonts were the first vertebrates. They were, for a long time, a group of marine animals without a taxonomic home. Their fossil remains consist predominantly of tiny mineralized teeth. Little was known except that they were very common and widely distributed in ancient seas.

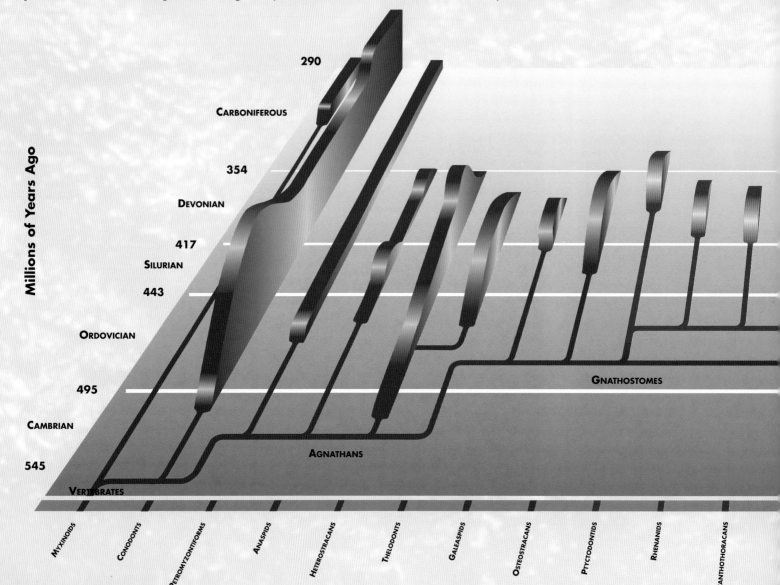

Millions of Years Ago

290

CARBONIFEROUS

354

DEVONIAN

417

SILURIAN

443

ORDOVICIAN

495

CAMBRIAN

545

VERTEBRATES

AGNATHANS

GNATHOSTOMES

MYXINOIDS

CONODONTS

PETROMYZONTIFORMS

ANASPIDS

HETEROSTRACANS

THELODONTS

GALEASPIDS

OSTEOSTRACANS

PTYCTODONTIDS

RHENANIDS

ACANTHOTHORACANS

Discoveries from Scotland have shown that the tiny fossil teeth were part of a feeding apparatus in the mouth of tiny eel-shaped jawless animals. The teeth have detailed structures and a composition that ally them with vertebrate teeth. Conodonts' eyes had vertebrate-type muscles and the body was flexed by paired blocks of muscles called myotomes, just like the vertebrates. The muscles flexed an axial stiffening rod into typically fish-like sinuous waves for swimming.

There is much debate about the relationship of the conodonts to other agnathans and which group of animals they arose from.

The backbone's template

The "template" for the backbone is an axial stiffening rod, called the notochord, which is found in a small group of living marine animals called the cephalochordates. The cephalochordates along with the vertebrates are placed within a larger taxonomic group called the Phylum Chordata. Until recently the cephalochordates had no known fossil record because their unmineralized notochord is

not normally fossilized. However, the Cambrian age Burgess Shale of British Columbia, Canada, fossilized a creature called *Pikaia*, which is almost certainly a fossil cephalochordate.

If the diagnosis of all these extinct ancient fossils is correct then the origin of the vertebrates was much earlier than once suspected.

The jaws that revolutionized life

The development of jawed fish (the gnathostomes) meant that fishes no longer had to rely for sustenance on microscopic organisms. Gnathostomes could actively pursue and seize prey. They could grow larger and specialize in particular lifestyles and diets. Jaws were an evolutionary innovation that led to an explosive radiation and diversification. The chondrichthyans (sharks, skates, rays, and chimaeras), kept the cartilaginous skeleton of their ancestors. Bone replaced cartilage in the others to produce the bony fishes (osteichthyans). Two types of bony fish evolved from a common ancestor— the ray-finned fishes (actinopterygians) and the lobe-finned fishes (sarcopterygians).

Lampreys, and their relatives the hagfishes, are the sole survivors of the first fishes to evolve, the jawless agnathans. One of their members, possibly an osteostracan, gave rise to all the jawed fishes. The Devonian period was the "Age of Fishes," when many of the groups evolved and flourished. The cartilaginous chondrichthyans include the dominant predators of today's seas, the sharks. The bony fishes (osteichthyans) evolved into two groups. The ray-finned actinopterygians include the modern teleosts. And the lobe-finned sarcopterygians were the ancestors of the first land animals.

PLACODERMS

CHONDRICHTHYANS   OSTEICHTHYANS   SARCOPTERYGIANS   TETRAPODS

PETALICHTHYIDS   PHYLLOLEPIDS   ANTIARCHS   ARTHRODIRES   ELASMOBRANCHS   ACANTHODIANS   ACTINOPTERYGIANS   DIPNOANS   ACTINISTIANS   RHIPIDISTIANS   TETRAPODS

The most successful vertebrates

Ray-finned fishes evolved into the most successful group of fishes—the modern teleosts (see pp.182–185). The 21,000 living species make the teleosts the most successful of all living vertebrate groups in terms of abundance. (For comparison, there are about 4000 living species of mammal, 8600 species of bird, 4000 species of reptile, and 2500 species of amphibian.)

In terms of diversity of form and lifestyle, teleosts surpass all other water-dwelling creatures (both freshwater and marine, vertebrate and invertebrate). They range from fast-moving predators, such as barracuda and marlin, to sluggish bottom-dwellers, such as stargazers and flatfish; from typical "fishy" shapes, like mackerel and perch, to weird and wonderful forms like the seahorse, ocean sunfish, and lionfish; from the very surface of the ocean, such as the Atlantic flying fish, to its very depths, such as the deep-sea angler fishes.

Modern teleosts are at the top of an evolutionary ladder that proceeded in a series of steps from one group of ray-finned fishes to another (see pp.178–185). This progression started in the Late Silurian, with the appearance of the paleoniscids. Their heavy scales, inflexible fins, and asymmetrical tails gave way to the thinner scales of the neopterygians, with their flexible jaws and near symmetrical tails. These fishes were replaced in turn by the teleosts, with even thinner scales, symmetrical tails, and highly mobile jaws and fins. Herring-like teleosts were the first to evolve. The group advanced in two major evolutionary bursts. The first occurred in about the middle of the Cretaceous Period, when the salmon/trout group appeared. The second, and final, burst came in the Late Cretaceous/Early Tertiary, when the highly advanced perch-like forms evolved. These make up some 40 percent of the teleosts species of today.

The close of the Mesozoic Era, about 65 million years ago, saw the rise of the teleosts in the waters of the world and also the rise of the mammals on the land. Major changes were occurring at this time in the world's flora and fauna. Fish-eating reptiles, such as the plesiosaurs, ichthyosaurs, and mosasaurs, had become extinct. The dinosaurs disappeared and the pterosaurs vanished from the skies. Many types of small planktonic organisms in the seas disappeared without trace, possibly wiped out by the Cretaceous-Tertiary boundary impact event.

These extinctions seem to have been the signal for the teleosts and the mammals to enter their final explosive phase of evolution, and develop into the creatures that dominate the waters and the land today.

The ancestors of land animals

It may seem strange to describe the evolution of the world's most successful vertebrates—the bony ray-finned teleosts—as an evolutionary sideshow. But this, in fact, is what it was, since in the overall story of the evolution of life the ray-finned fishes were a dead-end. Their bony cousins, the lobe-finned fishes—an unspectacular assemblage by comparison—proved to be in the mainstream of evolution.

One of the members of the lobe-finned group provided the ancestor of the first four-limbed animals, the tetrapods. This transition was accomplished relatively quickly in their evolution; the first lobe-finned fishes appeared in the Early Devonian, and by the end of that period, some 20 million years later, the tetrapods had set foot on dry land.

General trends among fishes

Some general trends can be seen in the evolution of fishes, all of which led to fishes that were better adapted to finding, seizing, and chewing prey, and to detecting and avoiding predators.

The earliest fishes, the ostracoderms, were protected by a heavy bony armor, developed as a plate-like head shield, and thick, square-shaped body scales. Such a covering would have

ANATOMY OF A SHARK

A shark is a typical fish. It has an anal fin and paired pectoral and pelvic fins on the ventral, or under, surface; two dorsal fins on the back; and a caudal or tail fin, in which the upper lobe is often longer than the lower lobe. All the fins are supported by stiff rays. A shark's "backbone" is made of calcium-impregnated cartilage with a thin layer of bone. In bony fishes bone replaces cartilage.

1ST DORSAL FIN

2ND DORSAL FIN

ASYMMETRICAL TAIL

ANAL FIN

PAIRED PECTORAL FINS

PAIRED PELVIC FINS

EVOLUTION OF LUNGS AND SWIM BLADDER

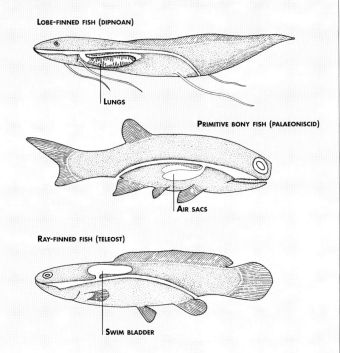

LOBE-FINNED FISH (DIPNOAN)

LUNGS

PRIMITIVE BONY FISH (PALAEONISCID)

AIR SACS

RAY-FINNED FISH (TELEOST)

SWIM BLADDER

The earliest bony fishes (the palaeoniscids), with thick, heavy scales, had paired air sacs connected to the gut. These could be inflated with air to buoy the fish up in the water. As evolution progressed, the bony fishes split into two lines. The lungfish developed air-breathing lungs (while retaining gills), their tissues infolded to increase oxygen uptake. The teleosts, the majority of today's fishes, developed a swim bladder above the throat, to control buoyancy. In the most advanced teleosts, the swim bladder is disconnected from the throat, and is able to secrete and absorb its own gases.

made swimming an energy-expensive process, and many of these fishes lived and fed on the seabed. The upper lobe of their tails was often longer than the lower lobe, which tended to drive the body down in the water, a useful feature for a bottom feeder.

Other ostracoderms developed "fins" in the form of various spines, flaps, and projections, which acted as hydrodynamic aids. These, combined with the enlarged lower lobe of the tail (which tended to drive the fish up in the water) meant that such fishes could swim and feed among the plankton in the surface waters.

The general trend among bony fishes was to develop smaller, thinner scales of a rounded, more hydrodynamic shape. The tail fin became symmetrical, with lobes of equal size, so keeping the fish on a straight course. Paired fins developed at the front of the body (the pectorals) and toward the rear (the pelvics); these not only stabilized the fish, but also worked like built-in oars, allowing it to change direction as it moved.

Accompanying these changes in the shape of the tail and the weight and extent of scales, bony fishes were also developing a more efficient means of controlling their position in the water.

Even the earliest bony fishes possessed paired air sacs on the underside of their bodies. By pumping gases in or out of these sacs, the fish became able to alter its buoyancy and change its level in the water.

In the ray-finned fishes, the air sacs evolved into a single swim bladder, placed above the throat; in most teleosts, it remains connected to the throat, but in the advanced perch-like forms the connection is broken, and the swim bladder functions independently as a sophisticated buoyancy device, secreting and absorbing its own gas.

In the lungfishes, the air sacs evolved into proper air-breathing lungs connected to the blood system, as they are in land-living animals. The walls of the lungs became highly convoluted to increase the uptake of oxygen. Living lungfishes, as well as having gills, can breathe air, and the African species can even exist for long periods out of water, curled up in a burrow in the muddy riverbank.

Feeding and breathing go together in the bony ray-finned fishes. The general trend was for their jaws to become more mobile and flexible, allowing them to be pursed together to form a tube. At the same time, the gill chambers behind the jaws became expandable, so that more water could flow through them. This increased the uptake of oxygen, and so increased the fishes's capability for activity.

Since the tubular jaws acted in conjunction with the expandable gills chambers, this resulted in prey being sucked or drawn toward the fish, rather than the fish having to engulf it at close quarters. Watch a goldfish or any aquarium fish feed, and this method can be seen in action.

EVOLUTION OF JAWS

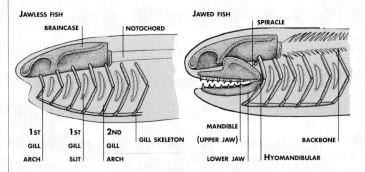

JAWLESS FISH

BRAINCASE · NOTOCHORD

JAWED FISH

SPIRACLE

1ST GILL ARCH · 1ST GILL SLIT · 2ND GILL ARCH · GILL SKELETON

MANDIBLE (UPPER JAW) · BACKBONE

LOWER JAW · HYOMANDIBULAR

The first fishes had neither jaws nor teeth. Their gills, behind the mouth, were supported by a series of arches made of cartilage, between which were the gill slits. Jaws probably evolved from the 1st gill arch on either side, which folded over and joined in the midline to form the upper and lower jaws. Teeth were developed from the skin that lined the mouth. The 2nd gill arch (hyomandibular) moved to support the jaws from behind, and ligaments attached them to the braincase. The 1st gill slits became tiny holes, or spiracles.

JAWLESS FISHES

PHYLUM CHORDATA

The great diversity of backboned animals (vertebrates) and some less familiar animals belong to a larger group—the chordates. They share some primitive features, of which the most obvious include an elongate axial rod, the dorsal notochord that runs from anterior to posterior. In vertebrates, the notochord is ossified to form the backbone. The oldest chordate is the 535-million-year-old cephalochordate, *Pikaia*, from the Middle Cambrian Burgess Shale.

SUBPHYLUM CEPHALOCHORDATA (ACRANIATA)

From the evolutionary point of view, the most important non-vertebrate chordate group is that of the cephalochordates (also known as the acraniates), which includes the remarkable living marine lancelet—*Branchiostoma*. This tiny (2 in/5 cm-long) marine creature is flattened sideways and burrows tail first in the seabed. Its anterior has a perforated pharynx through which seawater is filtered to obtain oxygen and microscopic food. The fossil record of this group is extremely poor.

NAME *Pikaia*

TIME Middle Cambrian

LOCALITY Canada

SIZE 2 in/5 cm long

The quality of preservation of the 535-million-year-old Burgess Shale is so good that fossils of *Pikaia* even show traces of soft tissues. The axial notochord and v-shaped muscle blocks, typical of the pre-vertebrate cephalochordates, can be seen. The notochord is stiff, but flexible, and can be bent into sinuous waves for swimming by pulses of contractions from the muscle blocks on either side of it. *Pikaia* is the oldest known chordate, which means that it, or a similar animal, is our ancestor.

SUBPHYLUM VERTEBRATA (CRANIATA)

Vertebrates as they are commonly known (or craniates) are the main subject of this book. The most important characteristics are the basic chordate ones. But there is the additional feature of "cephalisation" in which the sense organs and their nerve connections are concentrated at the front. This forms the basis of the "brain" (cranium) and part of the developing head region.

CLASS AGNATHA

The first backboned animals (vertebrates) to evolve were agnathans, or "jawless fishes." Fossil traces are found in Late Cambrian rocks, more than 510 million years old. These first fishes had no jaws. Nor did they have paired fins, to stabilize their bodies in the water. Catching prey and eating it presented problems. Consequently, these fishes tended to be small, rarely reaching more than 1 ft/30 cm long. They were restricted to sucking up microscopic food particles from the muddy seabed, or feeding on the plankton that lived in the surface waters.

The internal skeleton was made entirely of gristle or cartilage. This material—unlike bone—decays after death, so paleontologists know that these ancient fishes existed only because their bodies had an "overcoat" of bone, which was preserved. This consisted of bony plates sometimes fused into a large head shield, and small bony scales that covered the body. This armor plating was the only protection against attack from the predatory sea scorpions that inhabited the Paleozoic seas.

The bony armor has been preserved in the rocks, and gives the fossil agnathans their collective name of ostracoderms, meaning "shell-skins." Despite their lack of jaws, ostracoderms dominated the seas and freshwaters of the northern hemisphere for about 130 million years, from Early Ordovician to Late Devonian times.

Two types of agnathan survive today—the worm-like, scavenging hagfishes and the eel-like, parasitic lampreys.

SUBCLASS CONODONTA

The zoological affinities of the extinct conodonts have been a puzzle for over 150 years and were only resolved in 1993 when fossilized soft tissues were found. Before that the conodonts were known as a common group of tiny tooth-like structures found mainly in Paleozoic rocks from the late Cambrian to the end of the Triassic times (540–210 million years ago). The teeth are made of calcium phosphate and were found in bilaterally symmetrical assemblages of several elements with different shapes, clearly forming some kind of small feeding apparatus.

The remarkable discovery of the first conodont animal in Carboniferous rocks in Scotland showed that the feeding apparatus was clearly positioned below a pair of well-developed eyes. The increased cephalisation beyond that seen in the cephalochordates indicates a higher degree of organization, one perhaps closer to the living agnathans the hagfish. The mineralization of the teeth has led to their being placed within the vertebrates, though some experts dispute this.

NAME *Promissum*

TIME Late Ordovician

LOCALITY South Africa

SIZE 16 in / 40 cm

Promissum was an unusually large conodont and is found in the 500 million year old Late Ordovician cold and glacially influenced sea deposits of South Africa. In 1994 specimens of *Promissum* were found with the conodont feeding apparatus preserved below eye capsules and in front of traces of the muscle blocks and notochord. This confirmed the form of the conodont animal, seen from younger Scottish Carboniferous strata.

Order Heterostraci

The heterostracans were the first fishes, and among the earliest of all the vertebrates, to evolve. The oldest undisputed remains date from the Early Ordovician Period, some 500 million years ago. These fishes were the most abundant and diverse of all the agnathans. They reached their peak during Late Silurian and Early Devonian times, when a variety of marine forms evolved, ranging from mud-eating bottom-dwellers to free-swimming plankton-feeders. Later, the heterostracans invaded freshwaters. All had the characteristic bony head shield, which could grow throughout the life of the fish.

NAME *Arandaspis*

TIME Early Ordovician

LOCALITY Australia (Northern Territory)

SIZE possibly 6 in / 15 cm long

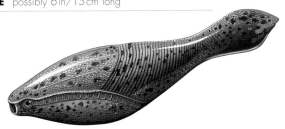

In 1959, the fossilized remains of four distinct types of fish were discovered south of Alice Springs, Australia. The remains were in layers of marine sandstones, laid down in a shallow sea about 500 million years ago. It was not until the late 1960s that the remains were recognized as those of the earliest vertebrates. The name of *Arandaspis* was given to the best-preserved specimens.

Arandaspis had a streamlined, deep-bodied shape. With no fins to stabilize it in the water, it probably would have swum erratically, like a tadpole. Its lower body was covered in oblique rows of small bony scales, each of which was shaped like a cowrie shell, and decorated with pointed tubercles, giving the skin an abrasive texture.

The front of *Arandaspis*' body was encased in a head shield, made from two large plates of thin bone—a deep, rounded ventral (underside) plate and a flatter dorsal (topside) plate. The head shield had openings for the eyes, nostrils, and the single pair of gill apertures on either side. Deep grooves in the shield marked the position of the lateral line canals—the organs that fishes use to sense vibrations.

Arandaspis' jawless mouth was on the underside of its head, a position that suggests that it may have fed on or near the seabed. Like other heterostracans it probably possessed small, movable plates inside its mouth equipped with ridges of dentine. These plates could have formed a pair of flexible "lips," which would have been capable of scooping or sucking up particles of food from the mud of the seabed.

NAME *Pteraspis*

TIME Early Devonian

LOCALITY Europe (UK and Belgium)

SIZE 8 in / 20 cm long

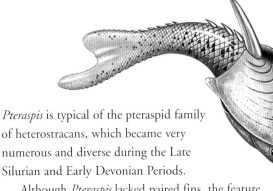

Pteraspis is typical of the pteraspid family of heterostracans, which became very numerous and diverse during the Late Silurian and Early Devonian Periods.

Although *Pteraspis* lacked paired fins, the feature that normally allows for greater stability in the water, it was a powerful swimmer, to judge by several hydrodynamic features of its body. Stability was provided by bony outgrowths from the back of the head shield—a large spine acted as a kind of dorsal fin, while a pair of rigid "wings" or keels functioned as pectoral hydrofoils.

Pteraspis had a long, flexible tail that was also a hydrodynamic shape, with the lower lobe elongated in order to provide lift at the front of the body during swimming. Additional lift in the water was provided by the elongated snout, which was drawn out into a blade-like "rostrum," below which the mouth opened.

Paleontologists think that *Pteraspis* and its relatives probably fed in mid-water or near the surface of the sea, among the shoals of planktonic, shrimp-like crustaceans.

NAME *Doryaspis*

TIME Early Devonian

LOCALITY Spitsbergen

SIZE 6 in/15 cm long

This pteraspid (also called *Lyktaspis*) had a longer snout or rostrum than its relatives. There were bony spines set along its length (like the "saw" of a modern sawfish), and the mouth opened above, rather than below, the rostrum. This strange and impressive appendage must have had some hydrodynamic function, since *Doryaspis'* shape suggests that it was an active swimmer, probably feeding on plankton near the water's surface.

An additional function of the rostrum among pteraspids could have been to stir up the bottom mud or sand, so as to root out crustacean prey.

Doryaspis had unusually long, lateral keels growing from the back of the head shield. The leading edges of the lateral keels were armed with sharp, tooth-like spines. These keels may have acted as gliding planes and, together with the elongated rostrum and downturned tail, would have provided lift at the front of the body while the creature was swimming.

NAME *Drepanaspis*

TIME Early Devonian

LOCALITY Europe (Germany)

SIZE 1 ft/30 cm long

A number of the heterostracans, such as *Drepanaspis*, were well-adapted bottom dwellers, and lived by scavenging in the mud of the seabed for food.

The front of *Drepanspis'* body was broad and flattened, allowing it to hug the seabed as it swam, and on either side of the large, upturned mouth, its small eyes were set wide apart to give it a wide angle of vision.

ORDER THELODONTI

The thelodonts were small jawless fishes, without head shields. Only the tiny bony scales that covered their bodies remain to testify to their existence during Late Silurian and Early Devonian times. Isolated body scales are often found in the ancient sediments that were laid down on sea beds during these periods. The scales can be very useful indicators for scientists seeking to correlate the age of the rocks.

NAME *Thelodus*

TIME Late Silurian

LOCALITY Worldwide

SIZE 7 in/18 cm long

The mouth of this small thelodontid was at the front of the head, suggesting that it fed from the seabed or surface. It could probably swim well. The lower lobe of the tail was elongated, and fins gave stability—a dorsal and anal fin at the rear, and two pectoral flaps at the front.

ORDER OSTEOSTRACI

The osteostracans (also called the cephalaspids, meaning "head shields") appeared in the Late Silurian Period, about 80 million years after the earliest heterostracan fishes. This order evolved in the sea, and then colonized freshwaters.

Osteostracans were flattened bottom-dwelling creatures that sucked up food from the seabed through a rounded mouth on the underside of the head. The head shield was a plate of undivided bone, which did not grow during adult life (unlike the individual head plates of the heterostracan fishes).

Evidently, osteostracans were also good swimmers, since many had a dorsal fin, paired scale-covered flaps where the pectoral fins are normally found, and a strong, upturned tail. The anatomy of osteostracans is well known because of a unique development. Bone was laid down inside the body, in a thin layer over the cartilage of the skeleton. From this fossilized bone, it is possible to trace the structure of the brain, gills, mouth, and even individual nerves and blood vessels.

Concentrated patches of sensory organs on both sides and on top of the head were richly supplied with nerves. They were probably used to detect vibration, or were electric organs.

NAME *Tremataspis*

TIME Late Silurian

LOCALITY Europe (Estonia)

SIZE 4 in/10 cm long

This osteostracan had an unusual extended bony head shield, nearly circular in cross-section. Its eyes and single nostril were on top of the head, near the midline. The shape is probably derived from a more usual flattened head shield and is thought to have been an adaptation to a burrowing mode of life.

Tremataspis' head shield was made of one piece of bone, so it is unlikely that it grew with the animal. Paleontologists think that osteostracans had an unarmored larva, and that the bony shield developed only when the fish was full-grown.

NAME *Dartmuthia*

TIME Late Silurian

LOCALITY Europe (Estonia)

SIZE 4 in/10 cm long

The broad head shield is the only part of *Dartmuthia* that is known. It was a bottom-feeder, with a round, sucking mouth on the underside of the head, like its contemporary *Tremataspis*. There was a small dorsal fin halfway along its back, and the pressure-sensitive organs were well-developed on its head and behind the eyes.

NAME *Hemicyclaspis*

TIME Early Devonian

LOCALITY Europe (England)

SIZE 5 in/13 cm long

This osteostracan was a more powerful swimmer and could maneuver itself better in the water than either of its bottom-dwelling relatives, *Tremataspis* or *Dartmuthia*. Its hydrodynamic features included a dorsal fin, to stabilize the body in the water, and a pair of scale-covered flaps, similar to pectoral fins, which provided uplift and kept the fish on course while swimming.

The corners of *Hemicyclaspis'* head shield were drawn out into keel-like cutwaters. In addition, the upper lobe of the tail was enlarged, producing lift at the rear of the body. This feature would have helped to keep the fish's head down while it sucked up food particles from the seabed.

NAME *Boreaspis*

TIME Early Devonian

LOCALITY Spitsbergen

SIZE 5 in/13 cm long

At least 14 species of *Boreaspis* are known from Early Devonian sandstones in Spitsbergen. They differ in the width of their triangular-shaped head shields, and in the length of the bony spine that grew out from the cheek area on either side. The snout was elongated in all species into a blade-like rostrum. Beside its hydrodynamic function, the rostrum was probably used to probe on the muddy lagoon floor for prey.

ORDER ANASPIDA

The anaspids did not have heavy bony head shields. Their slender, flexible bodies were covered in thin scales and had stabilizing fins. Numerous in the seas of Europe and North America during the Late Silurian Period, they later invaded rivers and lakes during the Devonian, and survived to the end of that period.

NAME *Jamoytius*

TIME Late Silurian

LOCALITY Europe (Scotland)

SIZE 11 in/27 cm long

The *Jamoytius* had a narrow, tubular, eel-like shape, with a long fin on its back, a pair of lateral fins running along its flanks and a small anal fin. Uplift was produced by the strongly downturned tail. *Jamoytius* had a round, sucker-like mouth but it is unlikely to have been a parasite like its living descendant, the marine lamprey. This jawless fish attaches itself to other fishes, rasps away their flesh and then sucks their blood.

NAME *Pharyngolepis*

TIME Late Silurian

LOCALITY Europe (Norway)

SIZE 4 in/10 cm long

Pharyngolepis must have been a poor swimmer because it lacked basic stabilizing fins. A row of crested scales ran along its back, and a pair of bony spines projected from the pectoral area. There was a well-developed anal fin, and the tail was downturned. But none of these features would have stabilized its deep body.

Pharyngolepis probably fed by scooping up tiny food particles from the bottom sediment.

CARTILAGINOUS FISHES

CLASS CHONDRICHTHYES

What could be more evocative of "Jaws" than sharks? In fact, sharks and their relatives—the skates and rays, and the chimaeras or ratfishes—were among the earliest vertebrates to develop jaws and bony teeth (see p.165). The mineralized teeth are normally the only part of these animals to be fossilized.

These jawed fishes also share another feature. All have skeletons made entirely of gristle or cartilage, which unites them as the chondrichthyans, or cartilaginous fishes. (Agnathans also have cartilaginous skeletons, but they have no jaws.) The skeleton is "calcified," or strengthened by prismatic granules of calcium carbonate deposited in the outer layers of the cartilage. These granules are arranged in a mosaic pattern, unique to this group. A thin layer of bone covers the cartilage.

Cartilaginous fishes share other characteristics. For example, their fins are paired, and stiffened by horny rays of cartilage. The pelvic fins in males are modified into penis-like "claspers," to aid in the transfer of sperm during copulation—a feature unique to these fishes. The skin bristles with tiny, teeth-like scales, which give it a rough texture like sandpaper. (In fact, 19th-century cabinet-makers used shark skin, called "shagreen," to give a smooth finish to the wood.) Like the teeth, the body scales are constantly replaced throughout the fish's life.

Two main groups of cartilaginous fishes evolved from a common ancestor during the Early Devonian Period, 400 million years ago (see pp.162–163). Representatives of both groups—the elasmobranchs and the holocephalians—survive today, distinguished by their teeth and different feeding habits.

SUBCLASS ELASMOBRANCHII

The elasmobranchs—sharks, dogfishes, skates, and rays—evolved from a common ancestor during the Early Devonian, some 400 million years ago. Sharks have changed little over this vast span of time. They diversified into many forms during the Carboniferous, and after a period of decline, underwent a second burst of evolution in the Jurassic, when most of the modern groups appeared. Then, as now, sharks were the dominant predators in the seas, ousting other creatures that attempted a marine, fish-eating lifestyle—reptiles such as the ichthyosaurs and plesiosaurs.

The skates, rays, and sawfish evolved in the Early Jurassic, some 200 million years after sharks. They are essentially sharks that have become flattened for a life on the seabed.

NAME	Cladoselache
TIME	Late Devonian
LOCALITY	North America (Ohio)
SIZE	up to 6ft/1.8m

Remains of shark scales are known from the Late Silurian Period and teeth from the Early Devonian. But it is only in the Late Devonian that recognizable specimens are found.

Cladoselache has been remarkably well-fossilized in the Cleveland shales of Ohio, USA. The fleshy outline of its body has been imprinted in the rocks, and even traces of its skin, muscles and kidneys can be seen.

Cladoselache had a streamlined, torpedo-shaped body, with two equal-sized dorsal fins; a pair of large pectoral fins; a pair of smaller pelvic fins; a large tail shaped roughly like a half-moon, with equal-sized lobes, and a pair of horizontal keels at its base. Its head was blunt and its eyes large. Five to seven gill slits opened behind its toothed jaws.

Superficially, the description of this ancient shark that cruised the open seas 400 million years ago is strikingly similar to that of a modern oceanic shark, such as the infamous Great White. The main differences are that the modern shark has a pointed snout, a high first dorsal fin, a tail in which the upper lobe is considerably longer than the lower lobe, and an additional fin—the anal fin.

Like many early sharks, Cladoselache had a spine in front of each dorsal fin. The spines were made of tooth-like dentine and probably skin-covered during life, since they are not coated in the protective layer of enamel seen in later sharks. Another unusual feature of Cladoselache is the lack of scales on its body. The only scales were concentrated round the eyes and along the margins of the fins.

Besides being a powerful swimmer, Cladoselache was obviously a formidable carnivore. Its mouth was filled with sharp, pointed teeth, each with a long central cusp or projection, flanked by several smaller cusps. The seas of the Late Devonian Period teemed with suitable prey—squid, crustaceans, small jawless fishes, and early bony fishes.

NAME *Stethacanthus*

TIME Late Devonian to Late Carboniferous

LOCALITY Europe (Scotland) and North America (Illinois, Iowa, Montana, and Ohio)

SIZE 2 ft 4 in/70 cm long

The remarkable feature of this early shark was the strange adaptation of the first dorsal fin. It was anvil- or T-shaped, and the flat, upper surface bristled with teeth-like denticles. The top of the head was also covered with denticles.

The function of these structures is uncertain. Some paleontologists speculate that they were part of a threat display to others of its kind, maybe giving the impression of an enormous pair of jaws. Another theory suggests that these toothy patches were were connected with sexual display, perhaps forming some sort of mating device.

NAME *Cobelodus*

TIME Middle to Late Carboniferous

LOCALITY North America (Illinois and Iowa)

SIZE up to 6 ft 6 in/2 m long

This strange-looking shark had a bulbous snout and a humpbacked profile, with only one dorsal fin on its back, set far to the rear, above the pelvic fins. It also had remarkably large eyes, which could suggest that it hunted in deep, dark waters for crustaceans and squid.

One of the cartilaginous rays that supported the pectoral fin was drawn out on each side into a whiplash, about 1 ft/30 cm long. These appendages were obviously movable, since they were jointed along their length.

NAME *Xenacanthus*

TIME Late Devonian to Middle Permian

LOCALITY Worldwide

SIZE 2 ft 5 in/75 cm long

Early in their evolution, a group of sharks invaded fresh water, spreading into rivers and lakes all over the world. These xenacanthids were specialized fishes and highly successful, since they existed from Early Devonian times to the end of the Triassic—a span of almost 150 million years.

Xenacanthus was a typical member of the group. A thick spine grew out from the back of its skull. The dorsal fin formed a continuous ribbon along the length of the back, right around the tail, and joined up with the anal fin—like the arrangement seen in the modern Australian lungfish or the conger eel. It probably swam like these modern fishes, with sinuous movements of its long, streamlined body. Paired pectoral and pelvic fins stabilized it from below.

The dentition of these freshwater sharks was unusual; each tooth was V-shaped, and formed of two prominent cusps. Shrimp-like crustaceans were probably the chief prey, as well as the thick-scaled bony fishes, the paleoniscids (see pp.178–180).

NAME *Tristychius*

TIME Early Carboniferous

LOCALITY Europe (Scotland)

SIZE 2 ft/60 cm long

Superficially, *Tristychius* looked like a modern dogfish. It was a hybodontoid shark; this group was to dominate the seas from Carboniferous times to the end of the Cretaceous—a reign of almost 300 million years. Some fine tuning occurred in their structure during this time, but essentially sharks had "got it right" some 40 million years earlier.

Like all its relatives, *Tristychius* had a pair of large spines in front of each dorsal fin. The pectoral and pelvic fins had much narrower bases, and were therefore more flexible swimming appendages than the broad-based, rigid fins of earlier sharks, such as *Cladoselache*. The upper lobe of the tail had developed into the powerful, propulsive, upturned fin seen in modern oceanic sharks.

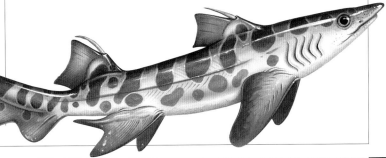

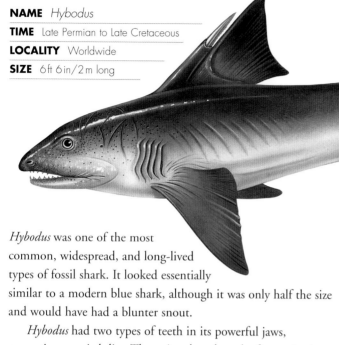

NAME Hybodus

TIME Late Permian to Late Cretaceous

LOCALITY Worldwide

SIZE 6ft 6in/2m long

Hybodus was one of the most common, widespread, and long-lived types of fossil shark. It looked essentially similar to a modern blue shark, although it was only half the size and would have had a blunter snout.

Hybodus had two types of teeth in its powerful jaws, suggesting a varied diet. The pointed teeth at the front seized and pierced its fish prey, while the blunt, low-crowned teeth at the back crushed the fish bones, and also the hard shells of the bottom-dwelling snails, sea urchins, crustaceans, and shellfish that it consumed.

Hybodus and its relatives gained (and their descendants have retained) a reproductive advantage over other fishes. Part of the pelvic fins in the male shark were modified into erectile, penis-like organs called "claspers" (seen in the illustration above). These were inserted into the female during copulation, and sperm was transferred directly into her body—a superior method of fertilizing eggs to the wasteful shedding of sperm into the open sea practiced by most bony fishes.

NAME Scapanorhynchus

TIME Early to Late Cretaceous

LOCALITY Worldwide

SIZE 20in/50cm long

A final burst of evolution among the elasmobranchs in Late Jurassic times led to the development of the modern sharks, skates and rays—known as the neoselachians, or "new sharks."

Several improvements had been made to their skeletons. For example, the cartilaginous "backbone" became strongly impregnated with calcium (calcified) enabling it to resist the powerful forces that were produced by lateral flexure of the body while the animals were swimming.

The bones of the upper jaw became articulated with the braincase by means of a movable joint, which allowed the jaws to be opened wide, and even to be protruded beyond the skull. This modification allowed large chunks of flesh to be gouged from the neoselachians' prey.

Finally, the brain and its sensory areas became larger, especially the olfactory lobes associated with smell.

Scapanorhynchus was an early, but not a typical, neoselachian. It had a greatly elongated snout, and its teeth were all of the biting and tearing kind, suitable for fish-eating.

NAME Spathobathis

TIME Late Jurassic

LOCALITY Europe (France and Germany)

SIZE 20in/50cm long

Of the elasmobranch skates, rays, and sawfishes, the rays were the first to evolve. *Spathobathis* is the earliest known ray, and it is strikingly similar to the modern-day Guitar or Banjo fish which occurs in the Atlantic waters off North America.

Spathobathis' body was essentially similar to that of a shark, but it was broad and flattened to suit a life on the seabed. The eyes and spiracles (for water intake) were repositioned on top of

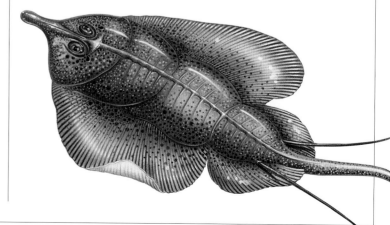

the ray's head, and the mouth and gill slits were on the underside of the body. The pair of pectoral fins were expanded into great "wings" for swimming.

The teeth of this ancient ray were also broad and flattened, and formed effective shellfish-crushers. Its elongated snout was used to probe the seabed in search of its prey.

NAME *Sclerorhynchus*

TIME Late Cretaceous

LOCALITY Africa (Morocco), Asia (Lebanon), and North America (Texas)

SIZE 3 ft 3 in/1 m long

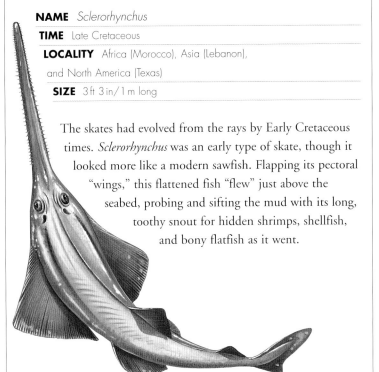

The skates had evolved from the rays by Early Cretaceous times. *Sclerorhynchus* was an early type of skate, though it looked more like a modern sawfish. Flapping its pectoral "wings," this flattened fish "flew" just above the seabed, probing and sifting the mud with its long, toothy snout for hidden shrimps, shellfish, and bony flatfish as it went.

SUBCLASS HOLOCEPHALI

The second major group of cartilaginous fishes are the holocephalians, or chimaeras—which are commonly known as rabbit-fishes or ratfishes. The Holocephali appeared in the Early Carboniferous when a few forms, such as *Deltoptychius,* acquired the so-called rat-like appearance and had long, thin tails. But it was not until the Jurassic, and fish such as *Ischyodus,* that the modern chimaera form became common. The males of the subclass have penis-like claspers.

Today, 25 species of this subclass inhabit the oceans of the world, usually swimming in deep water and feeding on the seabed.

NAME *Deltoptychius*

TIME Early to Late Carboniferous

LOCALITY Europe (Ireland and Scotland)

SIZE 18 in/45 cm long

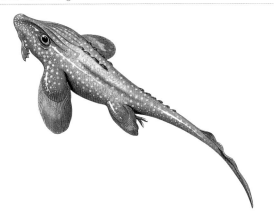

This early ratfish had practically all of the features that distinguish its modern descendants. *Deltoptychius* swam by flexing its long body and whiplash tail from side to side, and gliding along on its outstretched, wing-like pectoral fins.

The large eyes of *Deltoptychius* enabled it to see better in the gloomy ocean depths, and its large dental plates (rather than individual teeth) were used to crush its shellfish prey.

NAME *Ischyodus*

TIME Middle Jurassic to Paleocene

LOCALITY Europe (England, France and Germany) and New Zealand

SIZE 5 ft/1.5 m long

Ischyodus, which lived more than 150 million years ago, was practically identical in size and shape to *Chimaera monstrosa*—the modern ratfish which is found today inhabiting the depths of the Atlantic and Mediterranean oceans. *Ischyodus* had the same large eyes, pursed lips, tall dorsal fin, fan-like pectorals, and whiplash tail of its living relative. It even had a similar spine in front of the dorsal fin, which in the living species is connected to a venom gland, and is used by the creature to defend itself against predators.

SPINY SHARKS AND ARMORED FISHES

CLASS ACANTHODII

The acanthodians—commonly known as the "spiny sharks"— are the earliest known vertebrates with jaws. These structures are presumed to have evolved from the first gill arch of some ancestral jawless fish which had a gill skeleton made of pieces of jointed cartilage (see p.165).

The popular name "spiny sharks" is really a misnomer for these early jawed fishes. The name was coined because they were generally shark-shaped, with a streamlined body, paired fins, and a strongly upturned tail; stout bony spines supported all the fins except the tail—hence, "spiny sharks." Fossilized spines are often all that remains of these fishes in ancient sedimentary rocks.

In fact, acanthodians were a much earlier group of fishes than sharks. They evolved in the sea at the beginning of the Silurian Period, some 50 million years before the first sharks appeared. Later the acanthodians colonized freshwaters, and thrived in the rivers and lakes during the Devonian and in the coal swamps of the Carboniferous. But the first bony fishes were already showing their potential to dominate the waters of the world, and their competition proved too much for the spiny sharks, which died out in Permian times.

Many paleontologists consider that the acanthodians were close to the ancestors of the bony fishes. Although their internal skeletons were made of cartilage, a bone-like material had developed in the skins of these fishes, in the form of closely fitting scales. Some scales were greatly enlarged, and formed a bony covering on top of the head and over the lower shoulder girdle. Others formed a bony flap over the gill openings (the operculum in later bony fishes).

NAME *Climatius*

TIME Late Silurian to Early Devonian

LOCALITY Europe (UK) and North America (Canada)

SIZE 3 in/7.5 cm long

The name "spiny shark" seems particularly appropriate for this fish. Its tiny body was crowded with spines and fins. Two large dorsal fins rose from the back, each supported in front by a stout

bony spine, superficially embedded in the skin. There was a large anal fin and spine at the back, and a pair of large pectoral fins with spines at the front.

The underside of *Climatius'* body bristled with spines, but had no fins. There was also a pair of pelvic spines and four pairs of sharp belly spines.

Climatius was obviously an active swimmer, to judge by its stabilizing fins and the powerful, shark-like tail, with its large, upturned upper lobe. Like many other acanthodians, it had no teeth in its upper jaw, but there were whorls of small teeth in the lower jaw, continually replaced as they were being worn— another shark-like feature. Its large eyes suggest that sight was the chief sense used for locating prey, and it probably fed on crustaceans and fish fry in mid-water and at the surface.

Its swimming agility and the tight-fitting armor of bony scales must have protected *Climatius* from attack by larger fish and predatory invertebrates, such as squid. The 15 fin spines that arrayed its body were its chief defence, making it extremely awkward to swallow.

NAME *Acanthodes*

TIME Early Carboniferous to Early Permian

LOCALITY Australia (Victoria), Europe (Czechoslovakia, England, Germany, Scotland, and Spain), and North America (Illinois, Kansas, Pennsylvania, and West Virginia)

SIZE 1 ft/30 cm long

Acanthodes was a member of the last group of spiny sharks to evolve. They had no teeth in their jaws, but the gills were equipped with long bony "rakers" made of tooth-like spikes. *Acanthodes* and its relatives were probably filter-feeders, sieving tiny, planktonic animals through their gills.

Like all later acanthodians, *Acanthodes* was larger than its earlier relatives; some members of its group reached lengths of over 6 ft 6 in/2 m. *Acanthodes* was also less spiny than earlier forms. Its paired pectoral fins still had stout spines, as did the large anal fin. But there was only one spiny dorsal fin, set far back near the tail, and the pair of ribbon-like pelvic fins that ran along the belly each had a single spine. Thus, *Acanthodes* only had six fin spines on its body, compared with the 15 spines of its prickly relative, *Climatius*.

CLASS PLACODERMI

The placoderms, or "flat-plated skins," were a strange assemblage of heavily armored jawed fishes. Several large interlocking plates formed a bony head shield, while another series of plates encased the front part of the body in a trunk shield. The rest of the body was usually naked, with no scaly covering.

The placoderms represent a specialized offshoot from the main evolutionary line leading to the bony fishes (see pp.178–189). It was a comparatively short-lived group, which first appeared in the Early Devonian Period and had died out by the Early Carboniferous.

Many placoderms spent their lives foraging for food on the seabed, with their flattened bodies weighed down by their heavy bony armor. Others had less armor and became swimmers in the open sea. The jaws of all of these fishes were equipped with broad dental plates (rather than individual teeth), which were used for crushing hard-shelled prey.

Representatives from each of the four main groups of placoderm (rhenanids, ptyctodontids, arthrodires, and antiarchs) are described.

NAME *Gemuendina*

TIME Early Devonian

LOCALITY Europe (Germany)

SIZE 1 ft/30 cm long

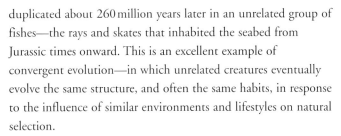

The rounded and flattened body of this early bottom-dwelling placoderm (of the rhenanid order) was remarkably similar to that of a modern ray. The pectoral fins of *Gemuendina* were drawn out into wing-like lobes on either side of the body, and the eyes and nostrils were repositioned on top of the head. These features were

duplicated about 260 million years later in an unrelated group of fishes—the rays and skates that inhabited the seabed from Jurassic times onward. This is an excellent example of convergent evolution—in which unrelated creatures eventually evolve the same structure, and often the same habits, in response to the influence of similar environments and lifestyles on natural selection.

Gemuendina was not equipped with the heavy armor of its later relatives, however. Instead a mosaic of small bony plates covered its body, decorated with sharp, defensive denticles; a few large plates were developed above and below the head.

This placoderm also lacked the characteristic tooth plates of its later relatives. Instead, the jaws were equipped with star shaped tubercles, which acted like teeth. The jaws could be protruded out of the mouth in order to pick up sea urchins and shellfish from the seabed. The creatures were then crushed between the *Gemuendina's* teeth-like tubercles.

NAME *Ctenurella*

TIME Late Devonian

LOCALITY Australia (Western Australia), and Europe (Germany)

SIZE 5 in/13 cm long

Ctenurella was a small, naked placoderm (one of the ptyctodontids). Its only protective armor was developed on top of its head and in a band around the shoulder girdle. It had two dorsal fins, one upright and the other long and low. Large, paired pectoral and pelvic fins stabilized it from below, and the tail tapered to a whiplash.

This small placoderm was equipped with crushing tooth plates in its jaws, the upper bones of which were firmly fused to the braincase. It fed on the seabed, grinding up shellfish and sea urchins with its strong jaws. It could obviously swim, to judge by its hydrodynamic shape and paired fins.

Here again, as with *Gemuendina* (left), is an excellent example of convergent evolution. As in the case of the ray-like rhenanids, *Ctenurella* and its relatives had evolved a body design that was to appear again in a later group of cartilaginous fishes— the chimaeras or ratfishes (see p.173). These placoderms even had similar penis-like claspers to those developed in the males of the cartilaginous group of fishes.

NAME *Groenlandaspis*

TIME Late Devonian

LOCALITY Antarctica (South Victoria Land), Australia (New South Wales), Europe (England, Ireland, and Turkey), and Greenland

SIZE 3 in/7.5 cm long

This tiny armored fish, found in sites literally poles apart, was a member of the most abundant and diverse group of placoderms—the arthrodires, or "jointed-necked" fishes. The arthrodires account for 60 percent of all known placoderms.

Groenlandaspis was a flattened bottom-dweller, crushing molluscs and crustaceans between its tooth plates. Since the lower jaw could not be dropped while the fish was lying flat on the seabed, this fish, like most of its relatives, evolved an ingenious hinge system to allow it to open its jaws wide to engulf large prey. The head shield was hinged to the trunk shield by a pair of ball-and-socket joints set high up on either side of the body. These hinges allowed the head to be tilted up and back, while the lower jaw dropped and the gaping mouth moved forward to seize the prey.

NAME *Coccosteus*

TIME Middle to Late Devonian

LOCALITY Europe (Scotland and former USSR) and North America (Ohio)

SIZE 16 in/40 cm long

Coccosteus was a fast-moving hunter and scavenger of the seabed. Its smooth, streamlined body (devoid of scales), whose hydrodynamic features included paired fins, upturned tail, and a stabilizing dorsal fin, made it a powerful swimmer.

It must also have been an aggressive carnivore, due to improvements in the jointing system of its neck. Not only were the head and trunk shields hinged externally, as in

Groenlandaspis (above); an internal joint had also developed between the neck vertebrae and the back of the skull, enabling *Coccosteus* to tilt its head back farther. Thus, it could attain an even wider gape than its relative. Its jaws were also longer than those of *Groenlandaspis*, so extending its predatory range.

Another advantage of the jointed-neck system was that the up-and-down movement of the head would have helped to pump water through the gills, which expanded when the mouth was opened; more water flowing through the gills meant a greater uptake of oxygen and increased activity. *Coccosteus* probably supplemented its diet by swallowing mouthfuls of mud and digesting the organic matter contained in it.

NAME *Dunkleosteus*

TIME Late Devonian

LOCALITY Africa (Morocco), Europe (Belgium and Poland), and North America (California, Ohio, Pennsylvania, and Tennessee)

SIZE 11 ft 6 in/3.5 m long

Some arthrodires grew to an enormous size, and these large fish may even have competed for prey with contemporary sharks such as *Cladoselache* (see p.170). *Dunkleosteus* was the giant of the group, with a skull over 2 ft/65 cm long. Some of its relatives, such as *Dinichthys* and *Titanichthys*, rivalled it in size, at 7 ft/2.1 m and 11 ft/3.4 m respectively.

The bony trunk shield in *Dunkleosteus* stopped short of the pectoral fins, so freeing them for better control of steering and braking maneuvers. Sinuous movements of the smooth, scaleless body and the long, eel-like tail would have swept this great creature through the sea in search of its fish prey.

The jointed neck and hinged body shields endowed *Dunkleosteus* with a slow, powerful bite. Once the victim had been caught, the great dental plates got to work, with the fang-like picks at the front of the jaws holding and piercing the prey, while the sharp-edged, cutting pavements at the back broke it up.

NAME *Bothriolepis*

TIME Late Devonian

LOCALITY Worldwide

SIZE 1 ft/30 cm long

Bothriolepis was a member of the most heavily armored group of placoderms, the antiarchs. These fishes shared a common ancestor with the arthrodires, and like many of them, were flattened bottom-dwellers—although antiarchs lived in freshwaters. The head was protected by a short bony shield, which hinged onto a long trunk shield.

The pectoral fins of *Bothriolepis* and its relatives were reduced to a pair of bony-plated spines, which could have played no role in swimming. They articulated with the front edge of the trunk shield via a complex hinge. A joint halfway along their length suggests that they could have been bent, and used like stilts to carry their heavy owner over the river bed. The upturned tail would have produced lift at the rear of the body, keeping the fish's head down while it scavenged in the mud or sand of the seabed for food particles.

NAME *Palaeospondylus*

TIME Middle Devonian

LOCALITY Europe (Scotland)

SIZE 2 in/6 cm long

This tiny creature has vexed paleontologists ever since its discovery in 1890. Hundreds of specimens have been found at the one Scottish locality. All consisted of a long "backbone" with spines at one end, presumably supporting a tail fin, and a strangely shaped skull at the other end. This creature had no obvious jaws and no paired fins.

Over the years, *Palaeospondylus* has variously been interpreted as a jawless agnathan, a naked placoderm, a type of ratfish, or even a lungfish. Some have even suggested that it represents the tadpole larva of an amphibian. To add to the enigma, paleontologists have not been able to determine whether the skeleton is made of calcified cartilage or of bone.

PRIMITIVE RAY-FINNED FISHES

CLASS OSTEICHTHYES

In terms of abundance and diversity, the "bony fishes," or osteichthyans, are the success story of vertebrate evolution: there are more than 20,000 modern species, accounting for half of all living vertebrates. In a sense, the bony fishes are also the most successful group of vertebrates, since their descendants inherited the lands of the world in the form of the tetrapods: amphibians, reptiles, birds, and mammals.

All osteichthyans, ancient and modern, are characterized by an internal skeleton which is completely "ossified," or made of bone. The replacement of cartilage by bone happened suddenly in their evolution. It was preceded by the laying down of a thin film of bone over the skull and "backbone" in the agnathans and cartilaginous fishes. The bony skeletons of these fishes increases their preservation potential considerably, so that their fossil record is much bettter than that of the cartilaginous fishes.

Two major groups (or subclasses) of bony fishes evolved some 400 million years ago. They are distinguished by the arrangement of the skeleton that supports their fins. The "ray-finned" fishes, or actinopterygians, include the majority of today's bony fishes, the teleosts (see pp.182–185). The "lobe-finned" fishes, or sarcopterygians (see pp.186–189), provided the ancestors of the first land animals.

SUBCLASS ACTINOPTERYGII

The ray-finned actinopterygians were the earliest bony fishes to appear. A great diversity, first of marine and then of freshwater types, evolved some 400 million years ago. Today, this ancient group lives on in the vast and varied assemblage of modern teleosts, as well as in the much rarer representatives—the sturgeons, paddlefishes, bowfin, garpike, and birchirs.

The characteristic feature of the actinopterygians, both fossil and modern, is the skeleton of parallel bony rays that supports and stiffens each fin—hence the name, "ray-finned" fishes. In early actinopterygians the fins were quite immovable; in later, more advanced, forms they became more flexible, culminating in the highly mobile fins of modern bony fishes.

Other improvements were made as the actinopterygians evolved toward modern teleosts. A swim bladder developed from the paired air sacs of earlier fishes, enabling the fish to control its buoyancy (see p.165). Heavy scales were replaced by a lighter, more flexible scaly covering. And the tail became symmetrical, with equal-sized lobes to provide an even, propulsive thrust.

The classification of bony fishes is extremely complex, with several dozen orders involved; five of these have been selected here to illustrate the evolution of the group (see pp.162–163).

The palaeoniscids were the earliest ray-finned fishes to appear, more than 400 million years ago. They evolved rapidly, and many groups invaded freshwaters. Toward the end of the Paleozoic, these early fishes (sometimes grouped as the chondrosteans) gave rise to many new types (the neopterygians, see p.181), from which arose the teleosts.

The typical features of the early ray-finned fishes were thick bony scales which articulated with each other; a single dorsal fin to the rear of the body; and an asymmetric, shark-like tail.

NAME	Cheirolepis
TIME	Middle to Late Devonian
LOCALITY	Europe (Scotland) and North America (Canada)
SIZE	up to 22 in/55 cm long

Cheirolepis was a fast-moving freshwater predator and one of the largest of the palaeoniscids. Its streamlined body was encased in a heavy coat of small, rectangular scales, arranged in diagonal rows—just like those of the spiny sharks. (The scales were covered with a unique type of enamel called ganoine, which gives the palaeoniscids their collective name of "ganoid" fishes.) A row of large scales stiffened the top side of the tail's elongated upper lobe, enhancing its powerful flexing movements during swimming. These scales were a unique feature of all early ray-finned fishes. While the upturned tail tended to drive the fish downward in the water, paired pectoral and pelvic fins on the underside counteracted this, elevating the body at the front. Stability was provided by the large dorsal and anal fins.

Like all palaeoniscids, *Cheirolepis* had large eyes, and probably hunted by sight. Its jaws were equipped with many sharp teeth, and could be opened sufficiently wide to engulf prey two-thirds its own length.

NAME *Moythomasia*

TIME Middle to Late Devonian

LOCALITY Australia (Western Australia) and Europe (Germany)

SIZE 3.5 in/9 cm long

The palaeoniscids evolved into a great variety of forms during the Devonian, and became the most abundant and diverse of freshwater fishes in the Late Paleozoic.

A contemporary of *Cheirolepis*, *Moythomasia* had evolved a new type of ganoid scale, unique to the early ray-finned fishes. A peg on the top edge of each scale fitted into a socket on the bottom edge of the scale above. Thus all the body scales articulated with each other, to form a flexible and protective coat of armor.

NAME *Canobius*

TIME Early Carboniferous

LOCALITY Europe (Scotland)

SIZE 3 in/7 cm long

A new development had occurred in the skull of this tiny fish. The cheek bones and the hyomandibular bones, which attached the upper jaws to the braincase (see p.165), both became upright. This meant that *Canobius'* jaws were suspended vertically beneath the braincase (rather than obliquely as in other palaeoniscids). The new arrangement allowed the mouth to be opened wider, while at the same time the gill chambers behind the jaws were greatly expanded.

This innovation affected both respiration and feeding. Respiration was improved because, as the mouth was opened wide, a greater volume of water passed over the gills. More oxygen could therefore be absorbed from the water, which in turn permitted increased activity. As for feeding, *Canobius*

could now exploit a rich source of food. Tiny planktonic creatures were carried into its gaping mouth in the surge of incoming water, and were caught on the minute teeth that lined its jaws and gills.

NAME *Platysomus*

TIME Early Carboniferous to Late Permian

LOCALITY Worldwide

SIZE 7 in/18 cm long

One family of palaeoniscids became disc-shaped—rather like such modern teleosts as the reef-dwelling blue tang or the Amazon discus fish. *Platysomus*, which lived in both freshwater and the sea, is one example of this.

Its deep body was fringed toward the rear by the elongated dorsal and anal fins. The pectoral and pelvic fins were tiny. *Platysomus* must have sculled along, bending its body from side to side in a slow swimming action. A fairly straight course could have been maintained, since the tail was deeply forked and symmetrical, although the main propulsive force still came from the tail's upper lobe which, as in all the early ray-finned fishes, was stiffened by rows of stout scales.

Like *Canobius*, the jaws of *Platysomus* were suspended vertically from its braincase, giving it the advantage of a wide gape and bulging gill chambers when the mouth was open. *Platysomus* probably also ate plankton.

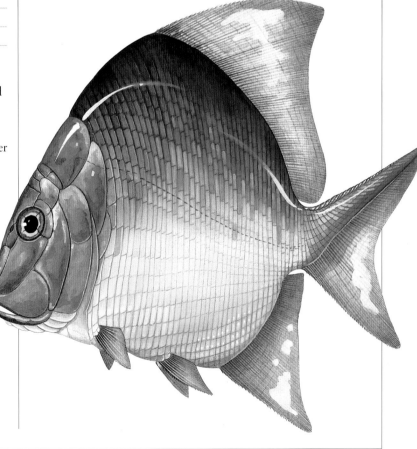

NAME *Palaeoniscum*

TIME Late Permian

LOCALITY Europe (England and Germany), Greenland, and North America (USA)

SIZE up to 1 ft/30 cm long

With its torpedo-shaped body, high dorsal fin and powerful, deeply forked tail, *Palaeoniscum* was built for speed. It must have been a ferocious predator of other freshwater bony fishes. Its jaws were set with numerous sharp teeth, which were constantly being replaced throughout its lifetime.

Like all early ray-finned fishes, *Palaeoniscum* had a pair of air sacs connected to the throat, which could be inflated to act as a primitive buoyancy device (see p.165).

NAME *Saurichthys*

TIME Early to Middle Triassic

LOCALITY Worldwide

SIZE up to 3 ft 3 in/1 m long

The long, narrow body of this freshwater palaeoniscid is reminiscent of that of the modern pike, as is the positioning of its dorsal and anal fins, which were placed well back on the body, near the symmetrical equal-lobed tail.

It is likely that *Saurichthys* also behaved rather like a modern pike. It may have ambushed its prey, lurking among the water weeds or lying still on the river bed, and seizing passing fishes in its toothed jaws.

Saurichthys' jaws were elongated into a long beak-like stucture, almost a third of the total body length, which—as well as contributing to its distinctive appearance—greatly extended the fish's predatory range. The symmetrical placing of *Saurichthys*' fins, together with its long streamlined shape and a great reduction in its bony coat of scales, would have made it a powerful swimmer.

NAME *Perleidus*

TIME Early to Middle Triassic

LOCALITY Worldwide

SIZE 6 in/15 cm long

Perleidus and its relatives evolved from the palaeoniscids, and survived throughout the 35 million years of the Triassic Period. They were all freshwater predators with strong, toothed jaws, which could be opened wide due to their vertical suspension from the braincase, a feature first developed in their predecessor, *Canobius* (see p.179).

A notable feature of this group was the flexibility of their dorsal and anal fins. This improvement was made possible by a reduction in the number of bony rays within each fin, a thickening of the bases of those rays that remained, and an alignment with their bony supports within the body. Such mobile fins, combined with an almost symmetrical tail, allowed greater swimming maneuverability.

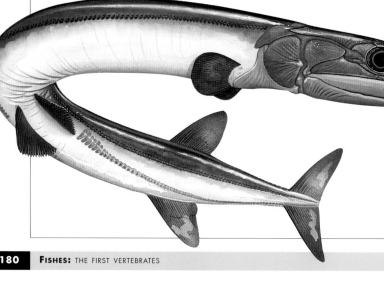

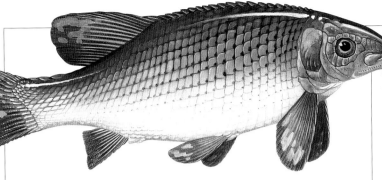

NAME *Lepidotes*

TIME Late Triassic to Early Cretaceous

LOCALITY Worldwide

SIZE 1 ft/30 cm long

Toward the end of the Paleozoic Era, many new types of ray-finned fishes evolved from the marine palaeoniscids. Grouped together as the neopterygians, these fishes display many of the features that were later developed in the modern bony fishes, which descended from this group.

Lepidotes, a member of the semionotids, had evolved one such feature, a new jaw mechanism that allowed it to feed differently from earlier fishes. Its upper jaw bones were shortened and freed of their connection to the cheek bones, to which they had formerly been fused. This new mobility allowed the mouth to be formed into a tube, and prey could be sucked from a distance toward the fish, rather than engulfed at close quarters as early fishes had done.

NAME *Dapedium*

TIME Late Triassic to Early Jurassic

LOCALITY Asia (India) and Europe (England)

SIZE 14 in/35 cm long

The deep, round body of *Dapedium* (like *Lepidotes*, a member of the semionotids) was stabilized by long dorsal and anal fins at the rear. Its body was covered in heavy, protective scales with a thick outer layer of enamel.

Dapedium had long, peg-like teeth in its jaws and crushing teeth on its palate. These, combined with its body shape, suggest that it was a mollusc-eater, weaving slowly through the coral reefs of the Early Mesozoic seas.

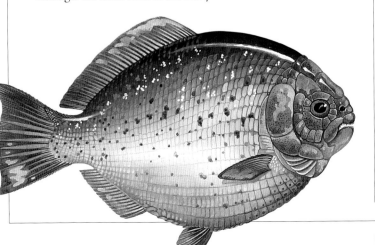

NAME *Pycnodus*

TIME Middle Cretaceous to Middle Eocene

LOCALITY Asia (India) and Europe (Belgium, England, and Italy)

SIZE 5 in/12 cm long

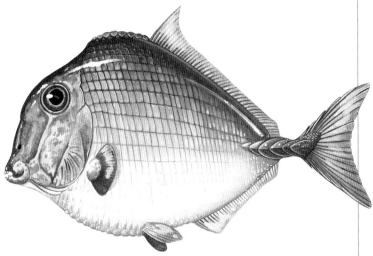

Although belonging to a later group (the pycnodontids), *Pycnodus* had evolved the same deep-bodied shape and grinding teeth as *Dapedium*, probably in response to living in the same type of environment—calm reef waters—and eating similar food —hard-shelled molluscs, corals, and sea urchins.

NAME *Aspidorhynchus*

TIME Middle Jurassic to Late Cretaceous

LOCALITY Antarctica and Europe (England, France, and Germany)

SIZE 2 ft/60 cm long

Superficially, *Aspidorhynchus* looked like the modern gar, or garpike (*Lepisosteus*) of North America, although there is no evolutionary relationship between them. Like it, *Aspidorhynchus* must have been a ferocious predator. Its elongated body, protected by thick scales, was perfectly adapted for fast swimming. The symmetrical tail propelled it, the dorsal and anal fins stabilized it, and the paired pectoral and pelvic fins kept it on course. The jaws were studded with sharp, pointed teeth and the upper jaw was elongated into a toothless guard.

Aspidorhynchus and its relatives, the aspidorhynchids, are closely related to the modern teleosts (see pp.182–185), and most probably shared a common ancestry with them. Only a single species of aspidorhynchid survives today—the bowfin, *Amia calva*, of North American freshwaters.

MODERN RAY-FINNED FISHES

ORDER TELEOSTEI

By the close of the Mesozoic Era, some 65 million years ago, the teleosts were well-established as the dominant bony fishes in the seas, lakes, and rivers of the world.

The teleosts had evolved more than 150 million years before the end of the Mesozoic. They first appeared in the seas of the Late Triassic Period, some 220 million years ago. Initially, they were small herring-type fishes, with symmetrical tails and flexible jaws, rather like advanced neopterygians such as *Aspidorhynchus* (see p.181). But in the middle of the Cretaceous Period, the teleosts underwent an explosive phase in their evolution, which resulted in more advanced fishes like the modern salmon and trout. These diversified rapidly, and by Late Cretaceous/Early Tertiary times, a second evolutionary burst gave rise to the highly advanced teleosts of today—the spiny-rayed, perch-like fishes (see p.185).

rectangular (rhomboid) scales. But the scales were comparatively smaller and allowed greater flexibility during swimming.

Its tail was symmetrical and halfmoon-shaped, superficially like that of a modern mackerel, although there were many more bony fin rays supporting the tail lobes than in modern teleosts.

Its fins, too, were arranged differently. Besides the long anal fin, there was only one dorsal fin. The extra large pectoral fins were low on either side (rather than high up on the flanks, behind the gills, as in more advanced bony fishes). The pelvic fins were unusually small and placed halfway down the belly.

Hypsocormus did, however, have fairly advanced jaws. They were flexible and mobile, and well-equipped with muscle attachment points to ensure a powerful bite. The upper and lower jaw bones were long, and had teeth along their length.

NAME *Hypsocormus*

TIME Middle to Late Jurassic

LOCALITY Europe (England and Germany)

SIZE up to 3 ft 3 in/1 m long

The dividing line between the advanced neopterygians (see p.181) and the primitive teleosts is unclear. *Hypsocormus* was a fast-swimming, fish-eating predator, which could have belonged to either group since it had both primitive and advanced features. For example, it had the heavy, "old-fashioned" body armor of its palaeoniscid ancestors—thick, enamel-covered,

NAME *Pholidophorus*

TIME Middle Triassic to Late Jurassic

LOCALITY Africa (Kenya and Tanzania), Europe (England, Germany, Italy, and former USSR), and South America (Argentina)

SIZE 16 in/40 cm long

Pholidophorus is one of the earliest known undisputed teleosts to appear in the sea. Superficially, it looked like a modern herring, with a symmetrical tail, a single dorsal fin placed halfway along its back, paired pectoral and pelvic fins on the underside, and an anal fin toward the tail. With large

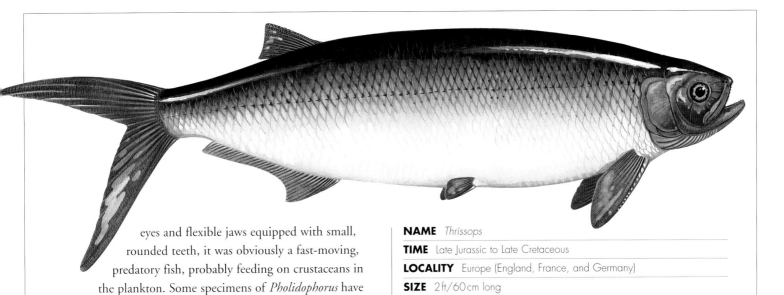

eyes and flexible jaws equipped with small, rounded teeth, it was obviously a fast-moving, predatory fish, probably feeding on crustaceans in the plankton. Some specimens of *Pholidophorus* have also been found with the remains of other bony fishes in their stomachs.

Despite their "modern" appearance, *Pholidophorus* and its relatives were primitive bony fishes, as betrayed by two main features. Their bodies were encased in the heavy, enamelled scales of the earlier "ganoid" fishes, the palaeoniscids (see pp.178–180). And their "backbones" were only made of bone in places. Their successors, the leptolepids, were the first teleosts to have a backbone made entirely of bone.

NAME *Leptolepis*

TIME Middle Triassic to Early Cretaceous

LOCALITY Africa (Tanzania), Australia (New South Wales), Europe (Austria, England, France, and Germany), and North America (Nevada)

SIZE 1 ft/30 cm long

Leptolepis and its relatives were herring-type fishes, like the pholidophorids. But unlike them, the leptolepids lived and moved in shoals, gaining safety in numbers as they fed on plankton in the surface waters.

This gregarious lifestyle can be deduced from the many fossil finds in which hundreds of these fishes have been preserved in the same slab of rock.

The leptolepids were also more advanced than the pholidophorids in two important respects. First, their skeletons were made entirely of bone, and second, their bodies were covered in thin, rounded scales with no enamel coat. Both these developments made the leptolepids better swimmers. The backbone formed a strong, yet flexible, rod to resist the pressures created by the S-shaped bending of the body during swimming. The thin scales reduced the fishes' weight, and their rounded shape made the body more hydrodynamic.

NAME *Thrissops*

TIME Late Jurassic to Late Cretaceous

LOCALITY Europe (England, France, and Germany)

SIZE 2 ft/60 cm long

Thrissops (above) was a streamlined predator that hunted others of its own kind in the warm, shallow seas of the Late Mesozoic, some 140 million years ago. Its tail was deeply cleft into two equal lobes, which may have increased its speed. The pelvic fins were tiny, and could have played little part in stabilizing the fish's deep body in the water. Perhaps to compensate for this, the anal fin formed a long fringe on the fish's underside.

Thrissops was small in comparison with some of its relatives, such as *Xiphactinus* (formerly called *Portheus*). This fossil fish grew to a length of 13 ft/4 m—as large as any shark that cruised Cretaceous seas. One specimen is preserved with a 6 ft/1.8 m bony fish intact within its stomach.

A modern group of freshwater fishes may be the sole survivors of *Thrissops* and its relatives. These modern fishes are called the "bony tongues" (grouped together as the Osteoglossoformes) because of the tooth plates embedded in their stout tongues. The tongue shears against the teeth on the palate, so holding and crushing prey.

A member of this modern group, the huge bony-tongued pirarucu (*Arapaima gigas*) of the South American rivers, is the world's largest known freshwater fish. It reaches a length of 13 ft/4 m and a weight of some 440 lbs/200 kg.

NAME *Protobrama*

TIME Late Cretaceous

LOCALITY Asia (Lebanon)

SIZE 6 in/15 cm long

This small relative of *Thrissops* had lost its pelvic fins. Its deep body was fringed toward the rear by a long dorsal and anal fin, in front of the deeply forked tail. The pectoral fins were placed high on the flanks, greatly improving its maneuverability.

The size of *Protobrama* and its body shape suggest that it may have been a reef-dweller, nipping in and out of the coral formations in pursuit of its prey.

NAME *Enchodus*

TIME Late Cretaceous to Paleocene

LOCALITY Worldwide

SIZE 7 in/18 cm long

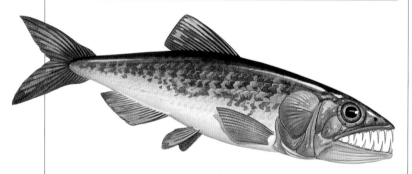

At the very end of the Cretaceous and during the Early Tertiary, a second burst of evolution led to the advanced bony fishes. Salmon and trout are survivors of this evolutionary phase, and from their ancestors descended all the modern types of teleost.

Enchodus was one of these early, salmon-like teleosts. Its large head and big eyes, together with the lightweight, streamlined body, suggests an agile predator of the open seas. The scales were reduced to a band along each flank; the pelvic fins were set well back on the belly, directly beneath the large, stabilizing dorsal fin; and the pectoral fins were mounted higher on the flanks, giving greater control of steering and braking.

The most remarkable feature of *Enchodus*, however, was its mouthful of greatly elongated teeth. The teeth were slightly recurved and interlocked when the jaws were closed, thus forming an effective trap. *Enchodus* probably preyed on plankton-eating fishes in the surface waters.

NAME *Hypsidoris*

TIME Eocene

LOCALITY North America (Wyoming)

SIZE 8 in/20 cm long

Early in the Tertiary, a group of fishes (called the Ostariophysi) diverged from the main teleost line, and became specialized for freshwater life, though some groups later returned to the sea. More than 6000 species survive, including the carp, minnow, goldfish, loach, piranha, and catfish.

With its whiskery feelers, *Hypsidoris* was strikingly similar to a modern catfish. It lived in the subtropical rivers and lakes of western North America some 50 million years ago. Many excellent specimens have been preserved in the Green River deposits of Wyoming, laid down in the Eocene.

The structure of *Hypsidoris'* backbone indicates that it had the acute hearing (especially of high-frequency sounds) characteristic of all living ostariophysid fishes.

This sensitivity to sound is due to a unique specialization of the vertebrae at the front of the backbone in these fishes. The vertebrae are modified into a chain of small, movable bones, which can transmit vibrations picked up by the swim bladder (which acts as a hydrophone and resonator) to the inner ear. There, the vibrations are interpreted by the brain as either potential prey or approaching predator.

These sound-transmitting bones in fishes are called the Weberian ossicles, and serve a similar function to the hammer-anvil-stirrup chain in the middle ear of mammals (see p.328).

Like its modern relatives, *Hypsidoris* had a stout spine at the front edge of each pectoral fin. These spines were defensive, and could be erected by powerful muscles in times of need. Prey was located, or danger sensed, by its acute hearing—a valuable asset in the often dark and murky waters of the sediment-laden rivers in which it lived.

Having homed in on the potential prey, its edibility was assessed at closer quarters by the long, sensory filaments surrounding the catfish's mouth. These "feelers" were sensitive to touch and to chemical substances in the water. Fish were *Hypsidoris'* chief prey, but crayfish and other bottom-dwellers were also detected by the trailing feelers.

NAME *Sphenocephalus*

TIME Late Cretaceous

LOCALITY Europe (England and Italy)

SIZE 8 in/20 cm long

Two groups of advanced teleosts arose from the ancestral salmon/trout group. These were the cod/haddock-type fishes (the paracanthopterygians) and the spiny-rayed, perch-like fishes (the acanthopterygians).

Sphenocephalus seems to have been intermediate in structure between the two groups. In fact, it is remarkably similar in appearance to the living freshwater "trout-perch" of North America, so called because it has both primitive-trout and advanced-perch characteristics.

Besides its rather large head, the distinctive feature of *Sphenocephalus* was that its pelvic fins had moved forward to lie beneath the pectoral fins, which were placed high on the sides of its body. The arrangement of these paired fins greatly enhanced the fish's maneuverability. In the modern cod group, the pelvic fins are actually in front of the pectorals.

NAME *Berycopsis*

TIME Late Cretaceous

LOCALITY Europe (England)

SIZE 14 in/35 cm long

Berycopsis was one of the earliest spiny-rayed teleosts (the acanthopterygians) to appear. Today, this group, with an evolutionary history of some 70 million years, is the most successful and varied of all the bony fishes, accounting for 40 percent of living species. Modern members of the group range from barracuda and swordfish, to perch, tropical reef fish, flatfish, and seahorses.

Berycopsis had all the typical features of the group. The first fin ray in the dorsal and anal fin was enlarged into a stout spine, which could be erected for defence (hence the name of the group, "spiny-rayed" fishes). Its pectoral fins were placed high on the side of the body, to better control steering and braking; the pelvic fins had moved forward, to counterbalance the pectorals. *Berycopsis'* body had a lightweight coat of thin, rounded scales, their surfaces made abrasive by tiny, comb-like teeth. Its swim bladder was no longer connected to the throat, and the fish relied on the bladder's own gas-secreting and absorbing glands to make it neutrally buoyant.

NAME *Eobothus*

TIME Middle Eocene

LOCALITY Asia (China) and Europe (England and France)

SIZE 4 in/10 cm long

As evolutionary "late-comers," the flatfishes, such as *Eobothus*, filled one of the few remaining niches left among the spiny-rayed fish group. They became specialized for living and feeding on the seabed. Unlike the rays and skates, which became flattened from top to bottom, the flatfish became compressed from side to side during development. Young fish look like other ray-finned fish and swim normally, but as they grow the eye, on what is to be the underside, migrates onto the top side. This is accompanied by other complex structural modifications of the skeleton, nerves, and muscles.

As in all flatfish, *Eobothus'* dorsal and anal fins formed an almost-continuous fringe around its oval-shaped body. The fish glided over the seabed with an undulating motion of these fins. The success of this peculiar fish form is shown by the 570 species of flatfish, most of which are marine but three of which live in freshwater. Plaice, sole, turbot, halibut, and flounder are living relatives of *Eobothus*.

LOBE-FINNED FISHES

SUBCLASS SARCOPTERYGII

In the Early Devonian, about 390 million years ago, the first lobe-finned fishes (sarcopterygians) appeared in the sea. Only seven species survive today—a single species of coelacanth and six species of lungfish (see p.189). Some 10 million years before this, the first ray-finned fishes (actinopterygians, see pp.178–185) had evolved, and their fate was very different, with 21,000 species alive today to testify to their success.

Both these types of fishes are bony fishes (osteichthyans); both have an internal skeleton of bone and an external skeleton of bony scales. But their fins differ fundamentally.

The fins of actinopterygians are supported by numerous stiff, parallel bony rays (hence the common name for the group, "ray-finned" fishes). There are no muscles within the fins; they are moved by muscles within the body.

In contrast, the paired pectoral and pelvic fins of sarcopterygians consist of long, fleshy, muscular lobes (hence the common name for the group, "lobe-finned" fishes). Each lobe is supported by a central core of individual bones, which articulate with each other. The first bone of the series articulates with a sturdy shoulder (pectoral) or a hip (pelvic) girdle. Most of the bones can be directly related to the bones that make up the limbs of land animals (see p.193).

The rounded tip of each lobed fin is stiffened by bony rays, which fan out from the bony skeleton above. Muscles within each lobe can move the fin rays independently of one another.

The structure of these muscular, lobed fins was of great evolutionary importance, because some member of the lobe-finned group of fishes (and paleontologists still hotly debate which member, see pp.191, 193) was to evolve into the first tetrapod (see pp.192, 194); tetrapods, in turn, gave rise to the first amphibians.

The lobe-finned fishes are grouped into two major types, both with living, though exceedingly rare, representatives. First, there are the extinct rhipidistians (the Porolepiformes and the Osteolepiformes, see pp.186–188) and the related coelacanths, or actinistians, today represented by a single marine species. These two groups are classed as the crossopterygians. The second major group of lobe-finned fishes are the lungfishes, or dipnoans.

ORDER ONYCHODONTIFORMES

The onychodontiforms were an odd group of Devonian rhipidistians. They were undoubtedly lobe-finned fishes, possibly the most primitive of the group, and yet they did not have the characteristic muscular, lobed fins.

NAME	*Strunius*
TIME	Late Devonian
LOCALITY	Europe (Germany)
SIZE	4 in/10 cm long

Strunius had a short body, compressed from side to side, and covered in large, rounded, bony scales. It had the characteristic jointed skull that is unique to both the rhipidistians and the coelacanths (but not the lungfishes). This design evolved as an adaptation to increase the bite-power of the jaws. This was necessary if they were to feed successfully on the chief prey of the day, the palaeoniscid ray-finned fishes, which were covered in thick bony scales (see p.178).

The bones on the roof of *Strunius'* skull were divided across the midline by a deep joint, which separated the bony skull into front and back portions. The braincase, fused to the skull roof, was presumably similarly jointed, and a large muscle probably connected both halves. (This is the arrangement seen in *Eusthenopteron* and coelacanths.) When this muscle contracted, it pulled the front half of the skull downward, and the teeth were sunk into the prey.

The arrangement of the fins on *Strunius'* body was like that of all other rhipidistians, in fact of all other lobe-finned fishes. There were two dorsal fins on its back, set near the tail, and paired pectoral and pelvic fins, plus a single anal fin, on its underside. The tail was three-pronged, with two equal lobes on either side of a central axis. The fins were not the usual muscular lobes: they were stiffened by numerous bony rays, like those of the ray-finned fishes.

ORDER POROLEPIFORMES

The porolepiforms, like the onychodontiforms, were rhipidistians that existed only during the Devonian Period. But, unlike their contemporaries, the porolepiforms had developed the muscular, lobed fins typical of the sarcopterygians. They also had the unique jointed skull, as described for *Strunius*.

NAME *Gyroptychius*

TIME Middle Devonian

LOCALITY Europe (Scotland)

SIZE 1 ft/30 cm long

Gyroptychius was a fast-moving, long-bodied predator found in Devonian rivers, with small eyes and a keen sense of smell. Like other porolepiforms, it had short jaws. This actually enhanced the bite-power of the jaws.

Gyroptychius had fleshy, muscular fins, all of which, except for the pectorals were concentrated at the rear of the body. This increased the propulsive force of the arrow-shaped tail.

NAME *Holoptychius*

TIME Late Devonian

LOCALITY Worldwide

SIZE 20 in/50 cm long

Holoptychius was a deep-bodied, streamlined fish, with a lightweight covering of thin, rounded scales which promoted fast swimming. It was a voracious predator of other bony fishes. Like all its rhipidistian relatives, it had fang-like teeth arranged around the margin of its palate, and numerous smaller, pointed teeth lined both jaws. Its victims would have been held fast between the teeth, then swallowed whole.

Holoptychius had an asymmetrical tail. The powerful thrust produced by its upper lobe during swimming would have tended to drive *Holoptychius* down in the water. To compensate for this, the muscular pectoral fins were extra-long and mounted high on the flanks. They acted as hydrofoils; their slightest movement out to the sides would have elevated the front of the body, and counteracted the down-thrust produced by the tail. The pectoral fins also stabilized the fish and steered a course by their concerted movements.

ORDER OSTEOLEPIFORMES

The osteolepiforms were the longest-lived group of rhipidistian fishes. They appeared in the Early Devonian and died out during the Early Permian, a span of some 130 million years. Many paleontologists are convinced that these rhipidistians were the ancestors of the tetrapods (see pp.191, 193).

NAME *Osteolepis*

TIME Middle Devonian

LOCALITY Antarctica, Asia (India and Iran), and Europe (Latvia and Scotland)

SIZE 8 in/20 cm long

This early member of the osteolepiforms was encased in thick, square scales, which must have weighted its body in freshwater. A thin layer of bony and spongy tissue (called cosmine) covered the scales and the bones of the head. This outer coat of cosmine was a vitally important feature in *Osteolepis* and other early lobe-finned fishes, since through it ran tiny canals that were connected to sensory cells deeper in the skin. These canals opened on the surface as tiny pores. Thus, the whole surface of the body was alive with sensory receptors. These probably detected vibrations in the water, warning *Osteolepis* of the approach of potential prey or predators, and perhaps also detected chemical substances.

NAME *Eusthenopteron*

TIME Late Devonian

LOCALITY Europe (Scotland and former USSR) and North America (Canada)

SIZE up to 4 ft / 1.2 m long

NAME *Macropoma*

TIME Late Cretaceous

LOCALITY Europe (Czechoslovakia and England)

SIZE 22 in / 55 cm long

Large rhipidistian fish like *Eusthenopteron* are considered by many paleontologists to be closely linked to the early tetrapods on the basis of several features. The pyramidal arrangement of the bones in its paired fins is strikingly similar to the arrangement of the limb bones in land animals (see pp.193). In addition, the structure of its backbone, the pattern of the skull bones and the complex, labyrinthine folding of the enamel inside each tooth all bear a remarkable resemblance to these features in the first tetrapods (see pp.194–197).

Eusthenopteron was a long-bodied, predatory fish with a powerful three-pronged tail, consisting of two equal-sized lobes on either side of the bony axis of the vertebral column. Its pectoral fins were placed well forward on the body, and articulated with the shoulder girdle, which in turn articulated with the back of the skull. The pelvic fins were well to the rear, as were the two dorsal and anal fins.

INFRACLASS ACTINISTIA

The actinistians, or coelacanths, have a long evolutionary history. They arose in the Middle Devonian, and the last fossils found are from the Late Cretaceous, some 70 million years ago.

In 1938 a living coelacanth was caught in the deep waters that separate Madagascar from southern Africa. The people of the Comoro Islands had known of this fish for generations, but it was new to science. In 1998 a new population of coelacanths was found on the other side of the Indian Ocean near Sulawesi, Indonesia. The term "living fossil" was awarded to *Latimeria chalumnae*, which has proved to be the only surviving species of a group that first evolved over 380 million years ago.

Although *Macropoma* was only about one-sixth the length of its living relative, *Latimeria*, in all other respects these two fishes, which are separated in time by almost 70 million years, are remarkably similar.

Macropoma had a short, deep body and a bulbous, three-lobed tail—a design characteristic of coelacanths. The only teeth in its mouth were concentrated at the front, but the hinge joint in the skull (the same arrangement as in the rhipidistians) ensured that the jaws could be opened wide and closed forcefully on prey. Its pectoral fins were set high on the flanks, to aid maneuvrability, and the pelvic fins were placed midway along the belly. The first of the dorsal fins was sail-like and supported internally by long bony rays; the other fins were fleshy, muscular lobes.

The living coelacanth is one of the few bony fishes that give birth to live young. Whether this was also the case among its ancient relatives is not known, but discoveries of fossil coelacanths in Niger and Brazil may shed light on their breeding habits.

ORDER DIPNOI

The dipnoans, or lungfishes, arose in Early Devonian times and survive to this day in the form of three genera of highly specialized freshwater fishes—the Australian lungfish (*Neoceratodus*), the African lungfish (*Protopterus*) and the South American lungfish (*Lepidosiren*). The African and South American fishes live in tropical areas subject to drought. When the waters get low or become stagnant, the fish can change from its normal gill-breathing method to breathing air at the surface. Air is taken in through external nostrils, which are placed low on either side of the mouth; it then passes directly to the internal nostrils on the roof of the mouth and into the two lungs (only one in the Australian species) connected to the throat on the underside. Fossil lungfishes also had internal nostrils, so they too could breathe air in times of necessity.

Fossil lungfishes, like some modern species, could survive out of water during the dry season by "hibernating" in watertight burrows in the mud, which were linked by tiny air vents to the surface.

NAME *Dipnorhynchus*

TIME Early to Middle Devonian

LOCALITY Australia (Western Australia) and Europe (Germany)

SIZE 3 ft/90 cm long

Even the earliest lungfishes were quite different to other lobe-finned fishes. For example, *Dipnorhynchus'* skull and braincase did not have the hinge joint that divided the skulls of coelacanths and rhipidistians into two parts. Its skull was a solid bony box, like that of the first tetrapod land animals. This early lungfish had also lost its cheek teeth; these were replaced by a crushing surface of tooth-like "blisters" on the palate and lower jaw. Another advanced feature was that the palate was fused to the braincase (as in land animals).

NAME *Dipterus*

TIME Middle to Late Devonian

LOCALITY Europe (Germany and Scotland)

SIZE 14 in/35 cm long

The surface of raised blisters that acted as teeth in *Dipnorhynchus* had been replaced by a pair of large, fan-shaped tooth plates on the palate and on the lower jaws of *Dipterus* (above). This type of dentition was to remain practically unchanged over the next 380 million years.

The arrangement of the fins, however, has changed. The two dorsal fins of *Dipterus*, together with the tail fin and anal fin, have merged in modern species.

NAME *Griphognathus*

TIME Late Devonian

LOCALITY Australia (Western Australia) and Europe (Germany)

SIZE 2 ft/60 cm long

By the end of the Devonian Period, various specialized types of lungfish had evolved. *Griphognathus* had an elongated snout, and small, teeth-like denticles, capped with enamel, studded its palate and lower jaws. Like all the other members of the order, this lungfish was covered in large, overlapping, rounded scales, and the tail was asymmetrical.

INVADERS OF THE LAND

The modern newts and salamanders (urodeles), and frogs and toads (anurans) are the amphibian survivors of the tetrapods that first ventured out of the water and began to take advantage of the evolutionary opportunity presented by land, some 370 million years ago. Their pioneering land effort was not a total success, however, since amphibians must still return to water to breed. It was their descendants, the reptiles, that truly conquered the land.

The very word *amphibia* defines the essential quality of these animals, for it means "both lives." It refers to their ability to live in two radically different worlds—the world of water, which their fish ancestors still inhabit, and the world of land, which their descendants, the reptiles, eventually inherited.

The young amphibian larva that emerges from the egg is adapted to life in water—it has gills and a swimming tail. Later, there is a fairly rapid change in structure (a metamorphosis), encapsulating in a few short weeks the evolutionary development of their ancestors, when the larva loses these aquatic features and replaces them with lungs and

stronger limbs to adapt it to life on land.

There are several reasons for believing that the fossil amphibians of the Paleozoic Era passed through a similar aquatic larval stage of development. In some cases, juvenile specimens have been found in which traces of the gills have been preserved, and a series of progressively larger forms link them to an adult which retains no trace of gills and must have breathed through lungs.

In other cases, such as *Seymouria* (see p.197), the head of young fossil specimens still shows traces of canals in which were located the sensory, lateral-line organs (inherited from their fish ancestors). Such organs could only have served their purpose in the aquatic environment of a larval stage.

Finally, some living amphibians, such as the mudpuppy of North America, have returned to a wholly aquatic lifestyle, retaining into adulthood the gills that previously only the larva had possessed. This is true also of some of the Paleozoic amphibians, such as *Gerrothorax*, with its three pairs of feathery gills (see p.197).

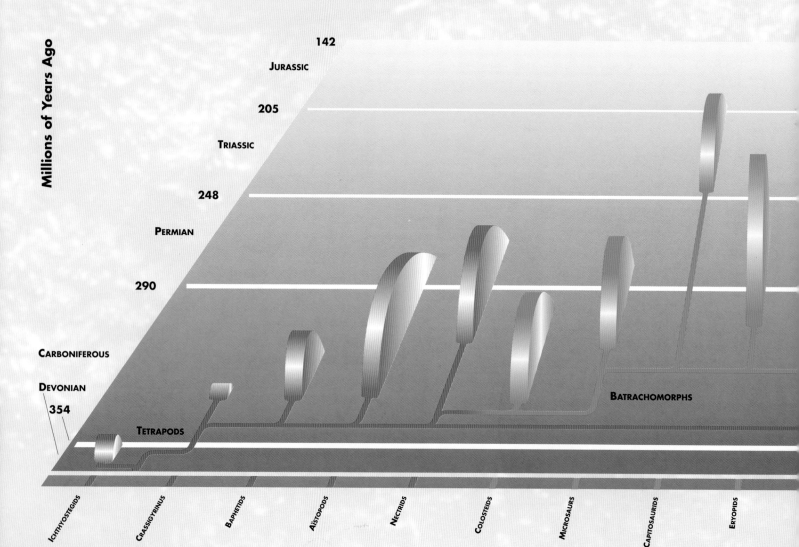

The problems of breathing on land

Amphibians' characteristic moist skin is one of the ways in which they differ most markedly from their Paleozoic ancestors. Modern amphibians supplement their normal respiratory exchange through the lungs by breathing through their moist skins. But this, in turn, limits their size and way of life. Many Paleozoic amphibious tetrapods had scales or armor covering their bodies, and many of them grew to a great size. Both these facts suggest that the early tetrapods had not evolved the skin respiration system of their living descendants. Those ancient tetrapods that did emerge from the water to live on land must, therefore, have had an impermeable, leathery, or scaly skin, to prevent water loss. Such a covering would have made them rather slow and cumbersome.

Living amphibians are grouped together as the lissamphibians and their fossil record as recognizable groups only extends back as far as Triassic times. Their evolutionary relationships with the older extinct groups of early tetrapods have not been well-established. This is one of the reasons that the first land-going vertebrates are no longer regarded as amphibians but instead are given the less definite assignation of tetrapods.

A controversial lineage

Paleontologists agree that the first tetrapods must have evolved from one of the three groups of lobe-finned fishes. These are the living lungfish or dipnoans; the coelacanths or actinistians, also living; or the extinct rhipidistians (the porolepiforms/osteolepiforms).

The muscles and bony axis of the paired fleshy fins of these fishes provide a structure that could have evolved into the limbs of an early tetrapod (see p.193). Similarly, there seems little doubt that these fishes possessed lungs like those of amphibians. Living lungfish, for example, have them, and a similar structure (though single) is present in the living coelacanths (see p.188). It is, therefore, considered likely that the extinct rhipidistians also had lungs. Support for this belief comes from the fact that lungfish and the rhipidistians have openings in the palate of their mouths that are similar to the internal nostrils of amphibians.

Most paleontologists consider that the first tetrapods evolved from the rhipidistian fishes, based on the remarkable similarity in the pattern of bones in their skulls and fins/limbs. Other paleontologists, however, believe that the lungfish were ancestral to the tetrapods, since the development of the lungs, nostrils, and limbs of living lungfish is strikingly similar to those of living amphibians.

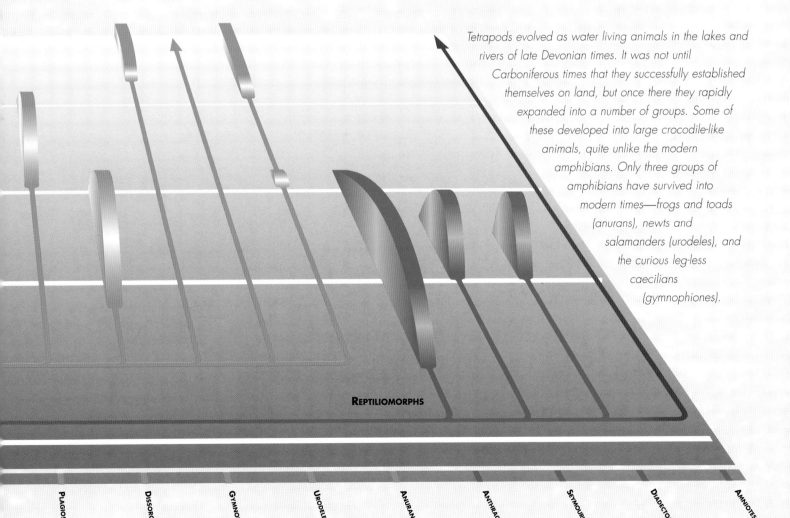

Tetrapods evolved as water living animals in the lakes and rivers of late Devonian times. It was not until Carboniferous times that they successfully established themselves on land, but once there they rapidly expanded into a number of groups. Some of these developed into large crocodile-like animals, quite unlike the modern amphibians. Only three groups of amphibians have survived into modern times—frogs and toads (anurans), newts and salamanders (urodeles), and the curious leg-less caecilians (gymnophiones).

REPTILIOMORPHS

PLAGIOSAURIDS DISSOROPHIDS GYMNOPHIONES URODELES ANURANS ANTHRACOSAURS SEYMOURIAMORPHS DIADECTOMORPHS AMNIOTES

Acanthostega (above) and Ichthyostega are the most important early tetrapods known. They combine typically "fishy" features, such as a laterally flattened tail, gills, and lateral line sensory system with characteristic tetrapod features such as four limbs and a deep ribcage. They would seem to fill the evolutionary "gap" between the fishes and land going tetrapods. However, it is now realised that the limbs were better adapted for life in shallow fast-flowing streams than for walking on land. The limbs were probably used for swimming, especially the hind ones, which point backwards. The forelimbs could have held onto submerged plant roots and grubbed in the stream sediment for food. The recent discoveries of Acanthostega and Tulerpeton have greatly increased our knowledge of early tetrapod evolution. It used to be thought that these animals established the basic five-fingered plan for tetrapods, but this is not the case. Acanthostega had eight fingers and toes, Ichthyostega at least seven toes and an unknown number of fingers, while Tulerpeton had six fingers and toes. The so-called five-digit limb plan was not established until Carboniferous times.

An evolutionary opportunity

Whatever may have been the group from which the first tetrapods evolved, the interesting question is why did they leave their ancestral waters to brave the land, with its greater range of temperature and the dangers of desiccation? At one time, it was thought that this evolutionary change had taken place in an environment liable to seasonal drought. In such an environment, there would have been considerable advantage for any fish that was capable of leaving its drying-up pond or stream, and traveling overland in search of another home that might still contain water.

The current theory suggests that it was more likely the pressure of predation in the waters themselves that drove the first tetrapods ashore. With their lungs and stout, muscular limbs, the early tetrapods might well have moved out of the water and up the river bank, to escape larger, predatory fishes. Once on land, they would have found a rich source of food in the numerous insects, worms, snails, and other invertebrates that lived in the mud and moist vegetation. Here lay the opportunity that evoked the crucial evolutionary changes that eventually produced the first land-going tetrapods.

From Carboniferous through to Triassic times, a period of more than 150 million years, the early tetrapods diversified into very many different groups and more than 70 families have been named. The fossil remains of their skeletons furnish evidence that some of the early tetrapods evolved as true amphibians; these are generally referred to as batrachomorphs. Others evolved in the direction of the amniote reptiles, and these are generally referred to as reptiliomorphs.

Radiation of the early tetrapods

The earliest tetrapods, such as *Ichthyostega*, have been found in rocks of Late Devonian age in Greenland. At that time – some 370 million years ago—Greenland was part of a Euramerican continent that lay near the equator, and stretched from today's western North America to eastern Europe.

A remarkable feature of the distribution of these early tetrapods, and of their relatives, the reptiles, is that until the middle of the Permian Period (about 100 million years later), nearly every one of them has been found only on this former Euramerican continent. This strongly suggests that this continent was the homebase in which they first evolved and diversified. Only after the middle of the Permian—when Asia and the southern landmass of Gondwanaland had become attached to Euramerica to form the supercontinent of Pangaea—did the amphibians and reptiles spread throughout the world.

In the Early Carboniferous (Mississippian) times that followed the Devonian, there was an increase in diversity of the

Paleozoic amphibians. Nearly all of these amphibians were aquatic or semi-aquatic.

In the Late Carboniferous (Pennsylvanian), much of the Euramerican continent was covered by low-lying, tropical swamplands. From these swamps rose tall coniferous trees, 49–130 ft/15–40 m tall, and tree ferns up to 25 ft/7.5 m tall. Seed ferns and other smaller plants abounded.

A variety of insects, spiders, millipedes, and centipedes lived in the rich leaf litter that covered the forest floor. A giant dragonfly-like insect, *Meganeura*, with a wingspan of up to 2 ft 5 in/76 cm, flew among the trees, while a giant centipede-like arthropod, *Arthropleura*, up to 6 ft 6 in/2 m long, fed on the leaf litter. The thick accumulations of leaves eventually formed the rich coal deposits that have long been mined in eastern North America, Britain, and central Europe.

The fresh waters of this landscape abounded with fishes, providing the amphibians with a rich food source. The total known amphibian fauna of the Late Carboniferous comprises over 70 genera in 34 families, representing all of the Paleozoic orders.

In the succeeding Permian Period, the Paleozoic amphibians reached their greatest diversity, with nearly 100 genera known in 40 families. However, an interesting change occurred in the amphibian fauna during the 40-odd million years of the Permian.

The amphibians of the Early Permian are known best from the Red Beds of Texas. These seem to have been laid down in a flood-plain or delta environment, similar to that around the Mississippi River today. The amphibians shared this environment with the pelycosaurs, early types of mammal-like reptile (see pp.330–332).

At this time, the amphibians made a decisive shift to the land. About 60 percent were terrestrial, another 15 percent were semi-terrestrial, and only 25 percent were exclusively aquatic.

This, however, was to be the peak of achievement for the amphibians in their conquest of the land. The Late Permian Karroo Beds of southern Africa reveal an amphibian fauna in which terrestrial and aquatic types are now equal in diversity, and most of the terrestrial forms have a protective body armor. This change was due to the rise of the therapsids, the mammal-like reptiles (see pp.332–337), which ousted amphibians from most of their recently acquired, land-based niches.

Demise of the ancient amphibians

The Triassic Period saw the final exclusion of the ancient amphibians from the land. Although over 80 genera are known, these belong to only 15 families, and all are temnospondyls. Almost without exception, they were aquatic, but some were of considerable size. The largest known amphibian, *Parotosuchus*, from southern Africa, was probably over 13 ft/4 m long.

The long existence of the fossil amphibian groups was now almost over. Only two genera are known in the Jurassic, one in Australia and the other in China. By this time, the ancestors of today's moist-skinned amphibians had already appeared. The first frog, *Triadobatrachus*, is known from the Early Triassic of Madagascar; bones of the first urodele (the group to which modern newts and salamanders belong) are found in Jurassic rocks. The other order of modern amphibians, the caecilians (Gymnophiona), are almost unknown in the fossil record.

FROM FLESHY-LOBED FIN TO FORELEG

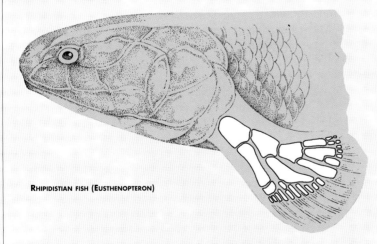

RHIPIDISTIAN FISH (EUSTHENOPTERON)

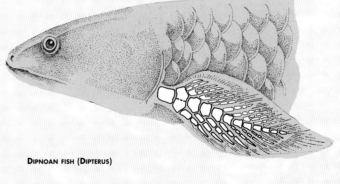

DIPNOAN FISH (DIPTERUS)

The ancestor of the land animals was one of the lobe-finned fishes. It may have been one of the rhipidistians, such as Eusthenopteron, or it may have been one of the dipnoans, represented today by the lungfish. The internal skeleton of the pectoral fin of both types of fish is shown here.

EARLY TETRAPODS

The first tetrapods to colonize dry land most probably evolved from the first aquatic tetrapods. By Carboniferous times, the existence of new terrestrial habitats with well-established vegetation, inhabited by numerous arthropods, opened up new possibilities for land-going amphibian tetrapods.

Classically, these animals were subdivided into the labyrinthodonts, which had large bodies and conical teeth with infolded (labyrinthine) enamel; small lepospondyls which had simple teeth; and the modern lissamphibians, such as the frogs and salamanders of today. But research has made it clear that the labyrinthodonts and lepospondyls contain unrelated groups with different origins. The classification has been modified.

Family Acanthostegidae

So far there is but a single genus in this family—*Acanthostega*. Hovewer, the characters of this primiative tetrapod are sufficiently different from those of *Ichthyostega* to be placed in a separate family. The presence of two pairs of well-developed limbs denotes that tetrapod status had evolved in these animals, but analysis of the articulation of the limbs and the presence of internal gills showed that they were still fundamentally aquatic.

NAME	*Acanthostega*
TIME	Late Devonian
LOCALITY	Greenland
SIZE	2ft/60cm long

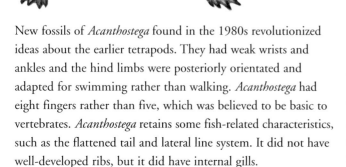

New fossils of *Acanthostega* found in the 1980s revolutionized ideas about the earlier tetrapods. They had weak wrists and ankles and the hind limbs were posteriorly orientated and adapted for swimming rather than walking. *Acanthostega* had eight fingers rather than five, which was believed to be basic to vertebrates. *Acanthostega* retains some fish-related characteristics, such as the flattened tail and lateral line system. It did not have well-developed ribs, but it did have internal gills.

The jaws had an array of sharply-pointed teeth which imply that *Acanthostega* was an active predator that fed on fish.

Family Ichthyostegidae

The fossil remains of early tetrapods are so rare that at the moment most species are placed in their own families. Additionally, their inter-relationships are unknown so there is no higher classification. Fossil remains of ichthyostegids have only been found in rocks of Late Devonian age in Greenland so far.

NAME	*Ichthyostega*
TIME	Late Devonian
LOCALITY	Greenland
SIZE	3ft 3in/1m long

Ichthyostega is one of the earliest tetrapods. It was a large, aquatic animal, bigger than any of its fish ancestors, with a long deep body and a heavy skull of solid bone. Its four limbs were well-developed but not suitable for movement on land, as previously thought. The hind limbs were directed backwards, like those of a seal, and were better adapted for a paddling mode of swimming than for walking. The feet had seven toes. It is not known how many digits were on the forelimbs. If they were like those of the contemporary tetrapod *Acanthostega*, they would have had more than five digits and would have been adapted for holding onto submerged vegetation in fast-flowing rivers and grubbing around in sediment for arthropod and molluscan food.

The fish-like tail of this creature was laterally flattened and had a delicate fin more suited for swimming than moving around on land. The ribs were flattened, giving the body a deep profile. There was a lateral line system, which is a sensory system similar to that used by fish for detection of vibration, but effective only in water.

Ichthyostega's skull is dorsally flattened, with the eyes placed high on the skull roof, giving a field of view similar to that of living aquatic crocodiles. Its wide mouth was full of small, sharp, conical teeth. The palate was also studded with teeth, some of them long and fang-like, similar to the teeth of the rhipidistian fishes, and well-adapted for a mode of life as an active predator.

The new understanding of *Ichthyostega* and the other early tetrapods suggests that they were not land-going as previously thought, but well-adapted for aquatic life in the shallow, fast-flowing rivers of the late Devonian continents.

Family Baphetidae

An early Carboniferous family of tetrapods are characterized by key-hole shaped eye sockets with unusual pointed openings at the front that may have housed a special gland.

NAME	*Eucritta*
TIME	Lower Carboniferous
LOCALITY	Scotland
SIZE	10 in /25cm

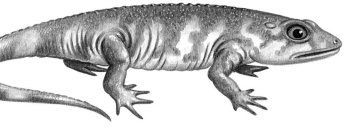

This newly-described (1998) fossil from 334 million-year-old Scottish rocks combines features usually associated with different groups of tetrapods. The skull is amphibian-like, the palate is reptile-like and the eye socket baphetid-like. It supports the view that the separation of living amphibians and reptiles was not present when the early tetrapods arose.

Eucritta melanolimnites ("creature from the black lagoon"), inhabited a shallow lake surrounded by active volcanoes.

ORDER UNCERTAIN

The remains of about five genera of Carboniferous tetrapods have been found in Europe and North America. They can be grouped in families, but do not fit any of the known orders.

NAME	*Crassigyrinus*
TIME	Early Carboniferous
LOCALITY	Europe (Scotland)
SIZE	6 ft 6 in/2 m long

Crassigyrinus had a fish-like body tapering into a long tail, with tiny fin-like limbs. Its head was about 1 ft/30 cm long, and the teeth-filled jaws could probably open wide. Its close-set eyes were particularly large. These unusual features suggest that *Crassigyrinus* had lost the use of its limbs, and reverted to an aquatic life. Its teeth are those of a fish-eater, and the streamlined body indicates a fast-moving predator. The large eyes may suggest that it hunted in the dark, murky Carboniferous swamps.

NAME	*Greererpeton*
TIME	Early Carboniferous
LOCALITY	North America (West Virginia)
SIZE	5 ft/1.5 m long

Although *Greererpeton* evolved amongst the first land-living temnospondyls it soon reverted to a fully aquatic life. Its slim body shape would have been ideal for moving through water with sinuous undulations. The low flat head was about 7 in/18 cm long. The elongated body (which had 40 vertebrae, about twice the usual number) ended in a long tail. The legs were short, each with five toes for steering and braking.

Open grooves along the sides of *Greererpeton*'s skull are a sign of its fish ancestry. They mark the position of sensory lateral line canals, which was used to detect water-borne vibrations. *Greererpeton*'s ear structure was poorly developed, unlike that of land-living amphibians.

Colosteids have been placed with the temnospondyls in some classifications and with the anthracosaurs in the others, though the skull is different from most members of that group.

ORDER TEMNOSPONDYLI

The temnospondyls are undoubted amphibians which evolved at the end of the Early Carboniferous Period (Late Mississippian), about 330 million years ago.

Over the following 120 million years, they developed into many varied, often very large, terrestrial forms. With the rise of the terrestrial mammal-like reptiles (see pp.326–337) in the early Permian Period, however, competition for resources on land increased and the temnospondyls were forced back to the damp places from whence they came. The temnospondyls had become extinct by the Early Jurassic times, but not before some of their members had given rise to the proanurans, the ancestors of the modern frogs and toads (see p.200). Representatives of the main temnospondyl families are described.

NAME *Eryops*

TIME Late Carboniferous to Early Permian

LOCALITY North America (New Mexico, Oklahoma, and Texas)

SIZE 6 ft 6 in/2 m long

This large, semi-aquatic creature was a member of the eryopid family which thrived in North America from Late Carboniferous (Pennsylvanian) times through to the end of the Permian Period.

Eryops' thick-set body and large head were supported by sturdy, short limbs. Bony plates covered its back, perhaps to help support *Eryops'* body when it came out of the water onto land.

The size of the head and the position of the jaw hinge suggest that *Eryops* probably fed in water. The physiology indicates that the large mouth could probably not have been opened on land without lifting its head clear of the ground.

Eryops was one of the top carnivores in its biota. It was truly amphibious and it fed on smaller tetrapods and fish.

NAME *Cacops*

TIME Early Permian

LOCALITY North America (Texas)

SIZE 16 in/40 cm long

Cacops was a member of the dissorophids. This diverse family of temnospondyls arose slightly later than the eryopids, and became extinct in the Early Triassic. Many dissorophids were fully-adapted land-living amphibians.

Cacops and its relatives, along with some of the eryopids, were quick to adapt to the drier Carboniferous climate. *Cacops* was well-adapted to life on land. Bony plates covered its body, and a row of thick armor ran down the backbone. Its legs were well-adapted for walking, and were almost reptile-like in structure. A broad opening (the otic notch) behind each eye was covered by a taut membrane which acted as an eardrum.

NAME *Platyhystrix*

TIME Early Permian

LOCALITY North America (Texas)

SIZE 3 ft 3 in/1 m long

Platyhystrix was more heavily armored than its close relative, *Cacops*. It had a more pronounced covering of armor plates on its back to protect itself against predators. Certain carnivorous pelycosaurs, such as the sphenacodont *Dimetrodon* (see p.331), lived in the same area and would have preyed on *Platyhystrix* and its terrestrial relatives.

Platyhystrix's most arresting feature was the spectacular "sail" on its back, made of tall spines that grew up from the vertebrae. Blood-rich skin may have covered the whole structure. Contemporary pelycosaurs, *Dimetrodon* and *Edaphosaurus*, also had great sails. It is thought that the sails served as a device to help these cold-blooded reptiles regulate their body temperature.

NAME *Peltobatrachus*

TIME Late Permian

LOCALITY Africa (Tanzania)

SIZE 2 ft 3 in/70 cm long

Peltobatrachus was a slow-moving, fully terrestrial amphibian. Its body was enclosed in heavy armor like that of an armadillo, which served as protection against the dominant carnivores of the day—the gorgonopsian therapsids with their enormous canine teeth (see p.333).

Peltobatrachus' bony armor-plating was arranged in broad shields over the shoulders and behind the hips, and in close-fitting bands across the body. The teeth of this amphibian have not been found, but it probably ate insects, worms, and snails, just as armadillos do today.

NAME *Paracyclotosaurus*

TIME Late Triassic

LOCALITY Australia (Queensland)

SIZE 7 ft 5 in/2.3 m long

By Triassic times, two groups of mammal-like reptiles, the dicynodonts and cynodonts, dominated the land. *Paracyclotosaurus*, and other amphibians of the capitosaur family, had been forced to return to the water. A general adaptation among these Triassic water-dwellers was toward a general flattening of the body. The head of the bulky *Paracyclotosaurus* was flat-topped and almost 2 ft/60 cm long. The point of articulation with the neck was almost on the same plane as the jaw hinge. As a result, the mouth could be opened easily by raising the head.

NAME *Gerrothorax*

TIME Late Triassic

LOCALITY Europe (Sweden)

SIZE 3 ft 3 in/1 m long

The general trend toward flattening the body reached its climax among the plagiosaurs, such as *Gerrothorax*. This large amphibian probably lay quite still on the stream or lake bed, camouflaged among the sand and pebbles, watching for fish with its upwardly directed eyes. It may even have attracted prey with a fleshy, brightly coloured lure dangling inside its open mouth. Once the prey was within easy reach, *Gerrothorax* would have swiftly closed its gaping jaws, trapping the victim.

Gerrothorax could live permanently in water because it still retained the three pairs of feathery gills that it possessed as a larva. So, this ancient creature clearly proves that fossil amphibians, like their modern counterparts, went through an aquatic, gill-breathing, larval stage before developing into a four-legged, lung-breathing adult.

ORDER ANTHRACOSAURIA

The anthracosaurs (also known as batrachosaurs) were amphibian tetrapods that arose during the Carboniferous and survived until the middle of the Permian. They were not so numerous or diverse as the temnospondyls. Among their members were the ancestors of the reptiles, and they are generally referred to as reptiliomorphs.

NAME *Eogyrinus*

TIME Late Carboniferous

LOCALITY Europe (England)

SIZE 15 ft/4.6 m long

Eogyrinus was a long-bodied aquatic predator which probably lived an alligator-type life in the deltas and swamps of the Carboniferous coal forests. It swam after its fish prey using powerful strokes of the long tail, its body stabilized by the tall, fish-like dorsal fin on its back.

NAME *Seymouria*

TIME Early Permian

LOCALITY North America (Texas)

SIZE 2 ft/60 cm long

Specimens of this seymouriamorph were found in the Red Beds of Texas. It was a well-adapted land-dweller, with many reptilian features (such as the structure of its hip and shoulder girdles).

In fact, *Seymouria* was originally thought to be an early reptile, until fossilized juveniles were found. Their skulls clearly showed the marks of fish-like, lateral line canals, whose only function is to detect water-borne vibrations.

LEPOSPONDYLS

Contemporary with the large, bulky temnospondyls (see pp.195–197) and reptiliomorphs (see pp.201, 206) were a group of smaller, insectivorous amphibians, classically grouped together as the "lepospondyls." It is now known that these include at least two unrelated groups: the extinct batrachomorphs and the living lissamphibians. These amphibians evolved in the Carboniferous Period and survived until the end of the Permian.

During this span of some 100 million years, a variety of small batrachomorphs evolved, which tended to look like salamanders or snakes. They can be grouped into three major orders—the aïstopods, nectrideans, and microsaurs.

ORDER AÏSTOPODA

The earliest group of batrachomorphs, the aïstopods, were the most specialized of all amphibians. They first appeared in the Early Carboniferous (Mississippian)—about 20 million years after the first tetrapods, the ichthyostegids (see p.194), had set foot on land. Presumably the aïstopods evolved from a four-legged ancestor, but almost immediately they lost their legs, and became snake-like, burrowing amphibians.

Obviously, this specialized way of life had its advantages, since the aïstopods were a long-lived group, surviving for almost 80 million years, until the middle of the Permian Period.

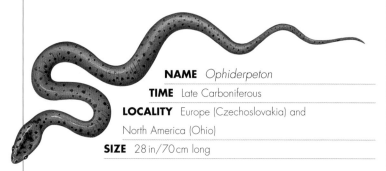

NAME *Ophiderpeton*

TIME Late Carboniferous

LOCALITY Europe (Czechoslovakia) and North America (Ohio)

SIZE 28 in/70 cm long

About 230 vertebrae made up the body of this snake-like aïstopod. There is no trace of limbs within the skeleton. The eyes were large, and placed forward on the skull, which was about 6 in/15 cm long and similar in structure to that of a primitive tetrapod, although no definite connection has been found between the two groups.

Ophiderpeton must have led the life of a burrower. Such a lifestyle would have paid dividends during the Late Carboniferous, when vast amounts of rotting vegetation were accumulating on the forest floor and in the swamps—the coal beds of today. Insects, worms, centipedes, snails, and other invertebrates lived and fed on this debris, providing *Ophiderpeton* with a rich source of food.

NAME *Phlegethontia*

TIME Late Carboniferous to Early Permian

LOCALITY Europe (Czechoslovakia) and North America (Ohio)

SIZE 3 ft 3 in/1 m long

Although *Phlegethontia* had the same snake-like body as that of *Ophiderpeton* (left), and presumably led a similar burrowing life, its skull was quite different in structure. Large openings, separated by narrow bones, made it a lightweight structure (fenestrated like that of a modern snake).

ORDER NECTRIDEA

The nectrideans were four-legged amphibians. They were newt-like in appearance and with long, flattened tails to provide the propulsion when swimming. Exclusively aquatic in lifestyle, they evolved during the Late Carboniferous, and survived until the end of the Permian Period.

Early nectrideans had a skull structure very like that of an early tetrapod. Their limbs were well-developed, with five toes on each. The later members of the group tended to have small forelimbs, and a toe had been lost from each. The snout also became greatly elongated in some of the later nectrideans.

NAME *Keraterpeton*

TIME Late Carboniferous

LOCALITY Europe (Czechoslovakia) and North America (Ohio)

SIZE 1 ft/30 cm long

The tail of *Keraterpeton* was more than twice the length of the animal's body and head combined. It was flattened sideways, and would have provided the propulsive force that pushed the animal through the murky waters of the coal swamps in which it

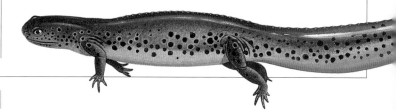

lived. The five-toed hind legs were longer than the four-toed forelegs. The short and rounded skull had eyes set far forward.

Despite its long, slender body, *Keraterpeton* had no more trunk vertebrae than usual (15–26 on average), unlike other long-bodied amphibians, such as the anthracosaur *Eogyrinus* which had 40 vertebrae in front of the hips (see p.197).

NAME *Diplocaulus*

TIME Early to Late Permian

LOCALITY North America (Texas)

SIZE 3 ft 3 in/1 m long

Diplocaulus had a distinctive flattened, triangular-shaped head, rather like a boomerang. Two of the bones at the back of the skull had become greatly elongated on each side to form the points of the triangle.

The body was short, and the limbs weak. *Diplocaulus'* tail, too, was quite short, unlike the tails of other nectrideans, a physical feature that has led some paleontologists to think that this amphibian probably moved through the water by undulating its flattened body in an up-and-down motion rather than using its tail in the usual manner.

Diplocaulus may have lived on the bottom of ponds and streams. The triangular "wings" on either side of the creature's head may have acted like hydrofoils, allowing the animal to swim above the river bed facing into the current. Alternatively, perhaps the odd shape of the creature's head made *Diplocaulus* an awkward mouthful to swallow, and so acted as a deterrent to such local predators as the thick-set, semi-aquatic temnospondyl *Eryops* (see p.196).

ORDER MICROSAURIA

The microsaurs, or "small lizards," were the most varied group of "lepospondyls," with terrestrial types that lived like lizards, burrowing types with legs, and aquatic types that kept their larval gills into adult life. Notwithstanding this diversity, all microsaurs had small legs and short tails.

The group evolved late in the Carboniferous Period, and survived into the Early Permian. They may have been the ancestors of the newts and salamanders.

NAME *Microbrachis*

TIME Late Carboniferous

LOCALITY Europe (Czechoslovakia)

SIZE 6 in/15 cm long

This tiny microsaur had the typical elongated body of an aquatic animal, made up of more than 40 vertebrae. Its legs were tiny, and played no part in swimming, which was achieved instead by sideways undulations of the body and slender tail. This amphibian probably fed on small shrimp-like invertebrates among the freshwater plankton.

Microbrachis was a Peter Pan among the batrachomorphs, since the adult retained the three pairs of feathery gills it had as a larva. This phenomenon is called paedomorphosis, and is seen in several modern salamanders, such as the cave-dwelling olm of Europe and the North American mudpuppy. The Mexican axolotl also retains the tadpole tail of its youth.

NAME *Pantylus*

TIME Early Permian

LOCALITY North America (Texas)

SIZE 10 in/25 cm long

A great head on a small, scaly body characterized this microsaur. It was a well-adapted land animal, moving about on short, sturdy limbs. It probably lived like a modern lizard, scuttling about after insects and other small invertebrates, which were crushed by the numerous large, blunt teeth.

ORDER ANURA

As adults, the anurans—frogs and toads—are the most specialized of all vertebrates, with the shortest backbones in the animal kingdom and powerful jumping legs. Anurans undergo a profound transformation from limbless, herbivorous, swimming tadpole with a long tail, to jumping, insectivorous, tailless adult.

Paleontologists are fairly certain that today's frogs and toads arose from among the land-living temnospondyls, possibly from eryopid-types (see p.196). The first amphibian to resemble a modern frog dates from Early Triassic times (below).

NAME *Vieraella*

TIME Early Jurassic

LOCALITY South America (Argentina)

SIZE Just over 1 in/3 cm long

After *Triadobatrachus*, there is a frustrating gap of about 30 million years in the fossil record of the anurans. Then, the first true frogs appear in the Early Jurassic.

Vieraella is the oldest-known frog. In all respects its anatomy is essentially the same as that of a modern frog, with the characteristic lattice-work skull, long hip girdle (which is shaped rather like a three-pronged fork) and long jumping legs.

NAME
Triadobatrachus

TIME Early Triassic

LOCALITY
Madagascar

SIZE 4 in/10 cm long

This tiny creature lived about 240 million years ago. Its hip structure suggests that it swam by kicking out with its short hind legs. This vigorous motion may have evolved over millions of years into the jumping action of modern frogs.

Triadobatrachus' skull is strikingly similar to that of a modern frog. It would have been able to hear well on land, because the bony parts of the ear were well-developed, and there was a broad eardrum on either side to pick up air-borne sounds.

Triadobatrachus had a relatively short body, with 14 back vertebrae as opposed to the usual 24 vertebrae of primitive amphibians, but a long one relative to the five to nine back vertebrae of the modern frog. It also had a short tail, which has been lost in modern anurans.

Triadobatrachus represents an intermediate stage in the evolution of the anurans, sufficiently different from its descendants to be placed in a distinct order (Proanura) and family of its own.

NAME *Palaeobatrachus*

TIME Eocene to Miocene

LOCALITY Europe (Belgium and France) and North America (Montana and Wyoming)

SIZE 4 in/10 cm long

An offshoot from the main line of frog evolution, *Palaeobatrachus'* remains have been preserved in large numbers within the freshwater sedimentary deposits of Early Tertiary Europe. Even fossilized specimens of *Palaeobatrachus'* tadpoles have been discovered.

Palaeobatrachus probably looked and behaved like a modern African clawed toad (*Xenopus laevis*). It would have been an adept swimmer, as fast as any fish, with a streamlined body and powerful, webbed feet.

ORDER URODELA

Newts and salamanders, which are grouped together as urodeles, first appeared in Late Jurassic times. Their modern descendants are the least specialized of living amphibians—they do not have the shortened backbone or powerful jumping legs of the anurans. Unlike frogs and toads, they do not undergo a complicated metamorphosis, because the larvae and adults live similar lives: both are long-tailed, swimming insectivores.

The ancestors of the urodeles remain a mystery. They may have had a common ancestor with the anurans (which are suspected to have descended from the temnospondyls, see pp.195–197). Or they may have arisen from among the microsaurs (see p.199). No linking fossils have yet been found, however.

NAME *Karaurus*

TIME Late Jurassic

LOCALITY Asia (Kazakhstan)

SIZE 8 in/20 cm long

Salamanders seem to have changed little over the known 150 million years of their evolution. The structure of the oldest-known salamander, *Karaurus*, is practically the same as that of modern forms. Its lifestyle was presumably similar too—it would have been a good swimmer and a voracious predator of snails, worms, crustaceans, and insects.

ORDER UNCERTAIN

Some of the Late Carboniferous and Early Permian land-living tetrapods were very close in evolutionary terms to the origin of the amniote reptiles. They are generally referred to as reptiliomorphs and are characterized by a mobile braincase which can rotate against the bones of the palate.

NAME *Diadectes*

TIME Early Permian

LOCALITY North America (Texas)

SIZE 10 ft/3 m long

This creature was one of the bulkiest land animals alive in Early Permian times. Its skeleton was like that of a reptile, and well-adapted to life on land. But certain features of the skull prove that it was not a member of that group.

Diadectes had a specialized skull, with a secondary bony palate (a feature found in advanced reptiles which allowed them to chew and breathe at the same time, see p.329), though this was only partially developed. It had stout grinding teeth in its short, strong jaws.

It is possible that *Diadectes* ate shellfish, but its bulky body suggests that it ate plants. If so, it was the first amphibian herbivore, and lived at the same time as the first reptilian herbivore, *Edaphosaurus* (see p.332).

CONQUERORS OF THE LAND

Within the unfolding history of the vertebrates, each new group has been hallmarked by some new feature, or number of features, that allowed it either to survive more efficiently in the environment of its ancestors, and thus to replace them, or to move on and conquer new environments.

The egg that revolutionized life

Below a certain size, a vertebrate would find life on land impossible. Its weight would be too great for its frail limbs to bear or propel, and it would rapidly lose its body moisture and dry out. Amphibians solve this problem by dividing growth into two phases. The egg first develops into an aquatic larva; this feeds and grows into a miniature adult, which then leaves the water and emerges onto land. Reptiles, have found another solution. The evolution of a shelled egg was the innovation that allowed the reptiles to quit the water, and to step out on land, equipped for terrestrial life. They could dispense with the aquatic larval phase that was, and still is, obligatory for amphibians.

A reptile's egg is similar to that of a bird, except that the shell is usually leathery and not hard, and the egg contains less-watery albumen. The shell protects the developing embryo from drying out, and from predators. Safe within its egg, the developing reptile can sustain a longer period of growth; it emerges only when it has reached a size at which it is already competent to survive on land.

The egg's shell inevitably cuts off the developing reptile from the surrounding world. The embryo must, therefore, be self-sufficient throughout its term of development. This is achieved by a food source, the yolk, and a series of ingenious membranes—the amnion, allantois, and chorion—that transform the egg into an independent, life-support unit.

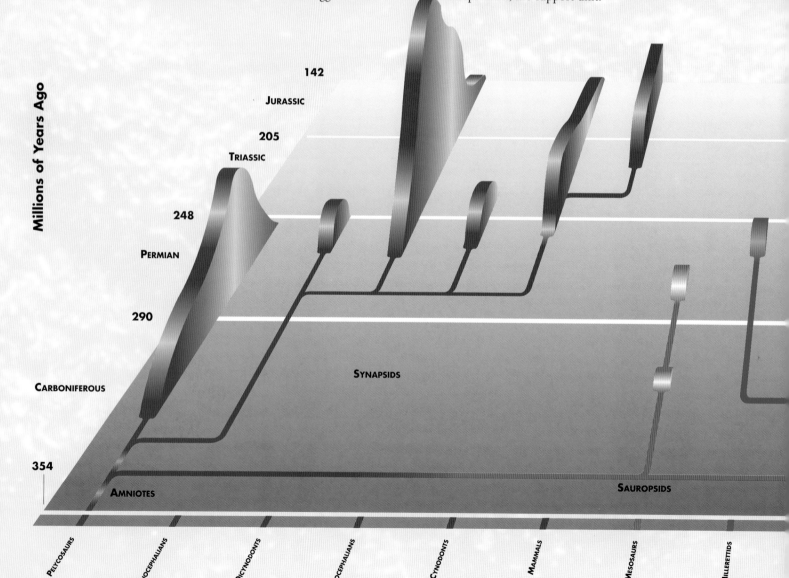

The eggs of modern reptiles show the same pattern of membranes, and biologists are confident that a single, ancestral group of original reptiles possessed this new, complicated type of "amniotic" egg, and that all later groups of vertebrates evolved from this basal stock.

Land adaptations for adult reptiles

Although protection of the developing embryo from drying out was a great step forward in the conquest of the land, two other innovations were necessary before that conquest was complete. First, reptiles had to be protected from desiccation after they emerged from the egg. This was achieved by evolving a horny layer that covered their scales or armor, making them impermeable to water loss.

Second, in order to remain active, reptiles had to develop a more efficient breathing method than that of their amphibian ancestors. Amphibians ventilate their lungs by means of a throat pump, which forces air into the lungs. Reptiles developed a new system, in which the rib cage was expanded and contracted, resulting in air being sucked into the lungs, and then expelled. The capacity of this system was limited only by the volume of the lungs, not merely by the volume of the mouth.

However, even with all these adaptations, living reptiles are still, like amphibians, limited in one respect. They are "cold-blooded"— that is, they obtain nearly all of their energy from the heat of the sun. When the weather or climate becomes cooler, their body temperature is lowered, and they become inactive. The physiology of reptiles is, therefore, geared to a low and varying body temperature, and they cannot sustain prolonged periods of activity.

In contrast, "warm-blooded" birds and mammals obtain their energy from their food, and have a high, constant body temperature, independent of their surroundings, which allows them to sustain a high rate of activity for longer periods. Paleontologists are currently debating whether dinosaurs were cold- or warm-blooded.

Like their amphibian ancestors, and the fish before them, reptiles move by lateral flexure of their bodies. The upper parts of a reptile's limbs project laterally from the body, since the length of each stride depends on the distance across the body from one knee or elbow joint to the other. The feet are also angled somewhat to the side, to resist

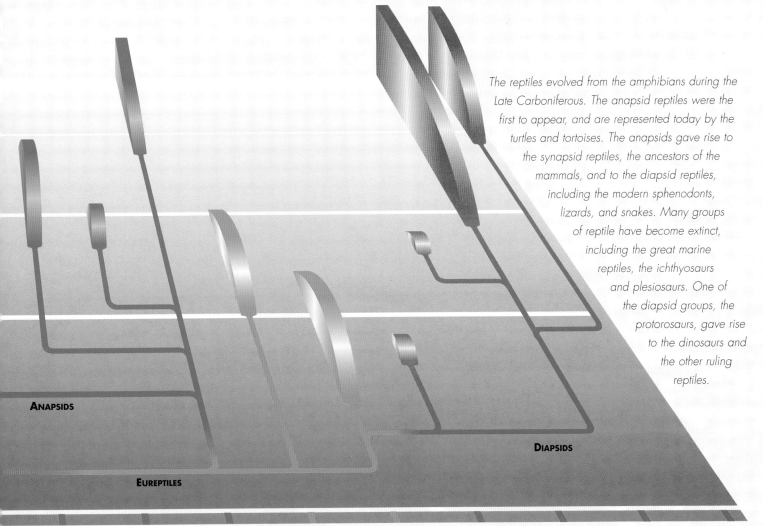

The reptiles evolved from the amphibians during the Late Carboniferous. The anapsid reptiles were the first to appear, and are represented today by the turtles and tortoises. The anapsids gave rise to the synapsid reptiles, the ancestors of the mammals, and to the diapsid reptiles, including the modern sphenodonts, lizards, and snakes. Many groups of reptile have become extinct, including the great marine reptiles, the ichthyosaurs and plesiosaurs. One of the diapsid groups, the protorosaurs, gave rise to the dinosaurs and the other ruling reptiles.

ANAPSIDS

EUREPTILES

DIAPSIDS

PROCOLOPHONIDS

PAREIASAURS

TESTUDINES

CAPTORHINIDS

PROTOROTHYRIDIDS

PETROLACOSAURUS

PROTOROSAURUS

ARCHOSAURS

LEPIDOSAURS

the lateral forces produced by this type of movement. Toes have to be different lengths if they are to leave the ground at the same time, so that they share weight of the body evenly.

As a result of all these adaptations, both structural and physiological, reptiles were able to colonize the land to the full, living even in the hottest deserts. The peak of their evolutionary development was reached in the form of the great dinosaurs, which grew to sizes that even their successors, the mammals, were unable to rival.

Radiation of the reptiles

The reptiles evolved from the early tetrapods some time in the Late Carboniferous (Pennsylvanian) period. The earliest-known reptile is *Hylonomus* (see p.206), preserved in the Late Carboniferous rocks of Nova Scotia. These rocks are about 300 million years old—60 million years after the early tetrapods started the invasion of the land.

From *Hylonomus*, many different types of reptile evolved. Like the early amphibians, all of the early reptiles seem to have been confined to the ancient continent of Euramerica. Most of these different lineages of reptile can be distinguished by the pattern of openings in the skull.

REPTILIAN BEGINNINGS

The reptiles are one of the most successful groups of vertebrates on Earth. Despite the loss of all the dinosaurs and their numerous distant relatives in the K/T extinction, reptiles (over 6500 living species) are still more numerous than mammals (some 4000 living species). Today most reptiles are relatively small lizards and it is perhaps ironical that the whole group began its extraordinary success from an apparently unpromising beginning, a small lizard-like creature.

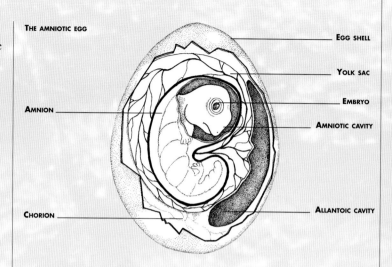

THE AMNIOTIC EGG

EGG SHELL

YOLK SAC

EMBRYO

AMNION

AMNIOTIC CAVITY

CHORION

ALLANTOIC CAVITY

There are four membranes inside the shelled egg of a reptile—the amnion, chorion, allantois, and yolk sac. Each plays a particular role to enable the embryo—in this case a turtle—to develop to maturity within its protective egg, independent of its surroundings. The developing embryo is suspended in a fluid-filled cavity surrounded by the amnion. It receives nourishment from the surrounding yolk sac through blood vessels connected to its gut. Waste products are excreted into the allantoic cavity. Oxygen enters the egg via the chorion, which lies just beneath the egg's porous shell.

Evidence shows that Hylonomus (below), from the late Carboniferous strata of Nova Scotia, is the earliest known true reptile. Older reptile-like forms such as Westlothiana, from Scotland show a mixture of early tetrapod and reptilian characters and are regarded as "reptiliomorphs."

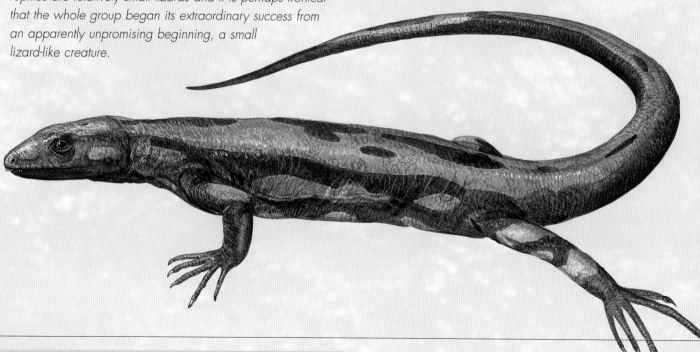

In addition to skull structure, evidence for the interrelationships of reptiles can be seen in the structure of their ankles and major blood vessels. In some reptiles, one of the ankle bones is hooked, and provides extra leverage for one of the foot muscles (just as our projecting heel bone provides leverage for the Achilles tendon). This type of ankle is found in all lizards and chelonians (including modern turtles and tortoises), as well as in the "ruling reptile" lineage—the crocodiles, dinosaurs, and their relatives.

The living representatives of all these groups also have an unusual arrangement of the major blood vessels near the heart. These twist around one another in a spiral fashion.

For all these reasons—skulls, ankles, and blood vessels—paleontologists are confident that these groups of reptile are closely related to each other.

Skull patterns

In the earliest reptiles, as in their amphibian ancestors, the skull was a box of bone, without any openings except for those of the eyes and nostrils. The muscles of the jaws were attached to the underside of the bony roof of the skull.

In most of the later reptiles, the weight of the animal's skull was reduced by the development of areas in which the bone was replaced by a sheet of lighter, elastic, tendon-like material. This material decays and does not fossilize, but the areas in which it was located appear in a fossilized skull as holes (called temporal openings) between the bones. These openings not only serve to lighten the skull, but also provide additional attachment points to which the jaw muscles can attach, thereby increasing the bite-power of the jaws.

The presence or absence of these temporal openings in the skull form the basis for grouping reptiles into major groups, but recently doubts have been cast on their validity. The earliest reptiles (such as *Hylonomus* and other protorothyridids) had no temporal openings, and their skulls are called anapsid.

The ruling reptiles—including the dinosaurs, pterosaurs, and crocodiles—have diapsid skulls, with two pairs of openings behind the eyes on each side. The primitive lizards, the sphenodonts (which today are represented by the sole surviving member, the tuatara), also have a diapsid skull. Later lizards have made the skull even lighter and more flexible, by losing the bar of bone below the lower opening on each side. Snakes have taken this evolutionary tendency even further, by dispensing with the bar of bone between the upper and lower openings.

Other groups of reptiles are not so easily defined. The extinct marine reptiles, the nothosaurs and plesiosaurs, for example, developed a skull pattern (sometimes called euryapsid) similar to that of most lizards. These groups would also seem to have evolved from diapsid ancestors. Two other groups of extinct marine reptiles, the ichthyosaurs and placodonts, also have a euryapsid type of skull. But these animals are very different from one another and also from the plesiosaurs. Each reptile group may have evolved from diapsids, but there is no evidence to detail their precise lines of ancestry. A similar uncertainty surrounds the origin of the diapsid, herbivorous rhynchosaurs, which are also extinct.

HOW A REPTILE MOVES

The legs of a typical reptile, such as a lizard, are splayed out to the side of its body. This results in a sprawling gait, with the whole body being twisted from side to side at each step. Here the backbone and limb girdles are emphasized to illustrate this bending of the body.

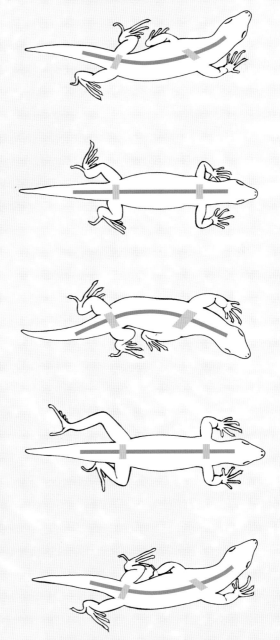

EARLY REPTILES

REPTILIOMORPHS

Reptiliomorphs are those vertebrates which have an incomplete number of reptilian characteristics. They are not fully developed reptiles. They may be a transitionary form between the early tetrapods and true reptiles.

NAME *Westlothiana*

TIME Lower Carboniferous

LOCALITY Scotland

TIME 11 in/30cm

Westlothiana was first found in 1984, and was nick-named "Lizzie the lizard." It hit the headlines as the oldest known reptile or amniote, capable of laying shelled eggs and therefore being independent of water for breeding like amphibians. "Lizzie" is about 26 million years older than the previously "oldest" reptile *Hylonomus* from Joggins, Nova Scotia. Detailed analysis of the skull and post-cranial skeleton of *Westlothiana* shows a mixture of reptilian features with primitive tetrapod ones so that it is now considered to be a "stem amniote" or reptiliomorph.

SUBCLASS ANAPSIDA

The most primitive reptiles, the anapsids, all shared a common characteristic—the skull was a heavy, solid box of bone, with no openings apart from the sockets to accommodate the animals' eyes and nostrils (see p.205). The muscles that controlled the jaws were confined within this strong, bony box; a position which limited their size and length, and meant that the mouth could not be opened very wide or closed with any force.

In more advanced reptiles, openings developed in the skull that allowed for more efficient jaws. Such "diapsid" reptiles and their descendants had much greater bite-power, and could open their jaws wider which enabled them to tackle larger prey (see p.226).

Only one order of anapsid reptiles has survived— the chelonians (the turtles and tortoises, see pp.210–213).

The other two orders of primitive reptiles, the captorhinids and the mesosaurs, became extinct over 250 million years ago.

ORDER CAPTORHINIDA

The captorhinids (which are also sometimes called the cotylosaurs) are the earliest and most primitive of all reptiles. They evolved from the amphibians during the Late Carboniferous Period, 300 million years ago but had become extinct by the end of the Triassic, about 90 million years later.

Two major evolutionary lines arose from the captorhinid order: one led to the evolution of mammals, and the second to the ruling reptiles (see pp.232–313).

Family Protorothyridae

The Protorothyridae family contains the earliest known reptiles.

The family first appeared in the Late Carboniferous Period, and survived into Mid-Permian times, a span of 50 million years. Protorothyridids were the basal stock from which many specialized groups may have evolved. Their descendants included the ruling reptiles (see pp.232–313).

NAME *Hylonomus*

TIME Late Carboniferous

LOCALITY North America (Nova Scotia)

SIZE 8 in/20cm long

Hylonomus is the earliest-known, fully adapted terrestrial vertebrate. It closely resembled a modern lizard and probably ate insects and other invertebrates, crushing them with its conical teeth. The teeth were simple and unspecialized, but some of the front ones were longer than the rest—a feature usually found in the more advanced reptiles.

Hylonomus was preserved in the coal beds of Nova Scotia, perishing in the holes left by rotted giant club mosses, where they had ventured in search of invertebrate food.

Family Captorhinidae

The Captorhinidae family of primitive reptiles lived through the Permian Period, surviving for almost 40 million years before their extinction. They lived in Africa, Asia, India, and North America.

Although the captorhinids were primitive creatures, they were more advanced than their protorothyridid ancestors. Their skulls were much stronger, with the braincase now firmly attached to the skull roof and cheeks, and the multiple rows of teeth in their jaws were capable of dealing with tough plants or hard-shelled animals.

NAME *Labidosaurus*

TIME Early Permian

LOCALITY North America (Texas)

SIZE 2 ft 5 in/75 cm long

This primitive, heavily built reptile was squat with a large head and a short tail. Its shape suggests that it was at home on land.

A typical captorhinid, *Labidosaurus* had several rows of teeth in the jaws, all of which would have been functional at the same time. The rows in *Labidosaurus'* mouth provided a broad surface on which shelled invertebrates, such as insects and snails could be crushed, or tough plant material ground down.

Family Procolophonidae

This family ranged throughout the world from Late Permian times to the end of the Triassic. Early members were small and lightly built. The members of the family were probably quite agile creatures, which chased, caught and crushed insects and other invertebrates with the many small, peg-like teeth.

Later members, however, from the Mid-Triassic onward, were larger creatures with a very different dentition. Their broad cheek teeth suggest that they probably ate plants.

Strange bony spikes grew outward from the sides of their skulls, presumably as a means of defense for these heavy, slow-moving herbivores.

NAME *Hypsognathus*

TIME Late Triassic

LOCALITY North America (New Jersey)

SIZE 13 in/33 cm long

One of the later members of the family, *Hypsognathus* had many features that indicate it was a plant-eater. Its wide, squat body suggests that it was not agile and its broad cheek teeth were suitable for grinding up tough plant material. Spikes around its head were probably for defense.

Family Pareiasauridae

The pareiasaurs were the largest of the early, primitive reptiles, reaching lengths of up to 10 ft/3 m. These massive herbivores had sturdy limbs, which in later members tended to be placed beneath the body allowing them to walk in a more upright way.

Pareiasaurs appeared in southern Africa during the Mid-Permian, and spread to Europe and Asia in large numbers. At the end of that period they became extinct.

NAME *Pareiasaurus*

TIME Middle Permian

LOCALITY Southern and eastern Africa, and eastern Europe

SIZE 8 ft/2.5 m long

This animal was a typical member of the family. *Pareiasaurus'* back was protected by bony plates embedded in its skin. Its thick and strong legs splayed out in typical reptilian fashion, supporting the animal's huge body. The skull was heavy and solid and studded with spikes and warty lumps.

The teeth were small and leaf-shaped, with serrated edges in order to deal with the tough plants that the animal ate. Even its palate had teeth to grind its food.

EARLY REPTILES CONTINUED

NAME *Scutosaurus*

TIME Late Permian

LOCALITY Eastern Europe

SIZE 8 ft/2.5 m long

The typical features of the pareiasaur family—a massive body, a heavy, spiked head, and bony armor—had become developed to an extreme extent in *Scutosaurus*.

This later member of the pareiasaur family had also developed a more upright gait than its relatives. Its legs were drawn in, and held more directly beneath the animal's body in order to support its great weight. This evolutionary trend was to be perfected later among the later ruling reptiles, the dinosaurs (see pp.232–313).

The presence of such large plant-eaters as *Pareiasaurus* and *Scutosaurus* throughout eastern Europe during Permian times could suggest that the climate in that region was quite warm and stable at the time, because such heavy, slow-moving reptiles as these would not have been able to migrate in order to avoid cold conditions, nor would they have been able to hibernate through the winter months.

NAME *Elginia*

TIME Late Permian

LOCALITY Europe (Scotland)

SIZE 2 ft/60 cm long

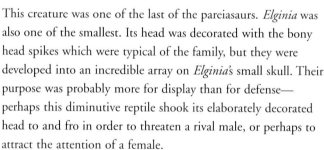

This creature was one of the last of the pareiasaurs. *Elginia* was also one of the smallest. Its head was decorated with the bony head spikes which were typical of the family, but they were developed into an incredible array on *Elginia*'s small skull. Their purpose was probably more for display than for defense—perhaps this diminutive reptile shook its elaborately decorated head to and fro in order to threaten a rival male, or perhaps to attract the attention of a female.

Family Millerettidae

The millerettids were a family of anapsid reptiles with a pair of openings in the skull behind the eyes. This characteristic is unusual in the anapsid order, which were the group of reptiles characterized generally by an absence of openings in their skulls, apart from the eyes and nostrils.

Despite this contradictory evidence, the other features of their skulls place the millerettids firmly within the anapsid group. It is most likely that this family represented a specialized side branch of the main reptilian family tree, and evolved these skull openings independently.

The millerettids were all small insectivores that lived from the Middle to Late Permian Period in southern Africa and so far, their remains have not been discovered elsewhere.

NAME	Milleretta
TIME	Late Permian
LOCALITY	South Africa
SIZE	2 ft/60 cm long

The *Milleretta* was a small, lizard-like creature which was quick and agile enough to chase after fast-moving insects.

Because of the pair of openings in its skull, some paleontologists used to hold the theory, which has now been disproved, that *Milleretta*, or a closely related member of its family, may have been ancestral to the more advanced group of reptiles, the diapsids, which had two pairs of openings on either side of the skull (see p.209). The diapsid group includes nearly all the modern reptiles and the extinct dinosaurs and pterosaurs.

However, the remains of the earliest-known diapsid, the araeoscelid *Petrolacosaurus* (see p.226), date from the Late Carboniferous Period—more than 40 million years before the evolution of the millerettids.

ORDER MESOSAURIA

The mesosaurs were early aquatic reptiles, the first group to return to the water since their ancestors had adopted a land-living existence. They appeared at the beginning of the Permian Period, and died out relatively soon after. Their remains have only been found in the southern hemisphere.

Family Mesosauridae

This is the only family of mesosaurs. Its members were all fully aquatic, swimming by means of a long, broad tail and long hind legs, and steering with the forelimbs. The mesosaurs probably sieved plankton from the water through the fine, pointed teeth in their elongated jaws.

NAME	Mesosaurus
TIME	Early Permian
LOCALITY	Southern Africa and South America (Brazil)
SIZE	up to 3 ft 3 in/1 m long

This creature was one of the first reptiles to revert to a water-dwelling existence. It had many adaptations to an aquatic life. Its long tail was flattened from side to side, possibly with a fin running along its length, top and bottom. Its hind legs were long, and the elongated foot-bones were splayed and probably webbed. The shorter forelegs also had broad, webbed feet. The tail and hind legs propelled the animal, and the forelegs steered it.

Mesosaurus could bend easily from side to side, as seen in the flexible structure of the backbone, though it could not twist its body. The ribs were greatly thickened—an aquatic adaptation also seen in the modern sirenians, or sea cows.

Mesosaurus' head was long and narrow, with the nostrils high on its snout near the eyes. It had only to break the surface of the water to breathe and see. An array of long, delicate teeth armed the elongated jaws. Each tooth fitted into its own socket—a feature of meat-eating animals. Yet the teeth would have been too fine for capturing prey. Instead, they probably formed a kind of sieve through which small shrimp-like animals were filtered from the water—similar to how a modern flamingo feeds with its comb-like bill.

The evolutionary importance of *Mesosaurus* does not derive from its aquatic adaptations, but from its geographical distribution. Remains have been found in southern Africa and eastern South America. This distribution was one of the earliest pieces of evidence for continental drift. The animal could not have swum across the South Atlantic; the only explanation, for its peculiar distribution is that these two continents had not yet split apart when *Mesosaurus* was alive.

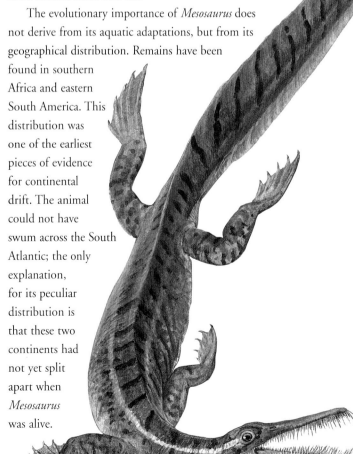

TURTLES, TORTOISES, AND TERRAPINS

ORDER TESTUDINES (CHELONIA)

Turtles, tortoises, and terrapins are the only surviving members of this ancient group of reptiles, the testudins or chelonians. They differ from all other reptiles in having their bodies, except for the head, tail and legs, enclosed within a shell, above and below. Many of them can pull their heads and legs into the shell for total protection.

Even the earliest chelonians, dating from the Late Triassic, had a shell; in fact, today's turtles and tortoises have hardly changed since those times, over 200 million years ago.

Like other anapsids (see pp.206–213), chelonians have solidly roofed skulls, with no openings in them save for the eyes and nostrils. They are classified for convenience in the anapsid subclass, but some paleontologists believe that their anatomy is so specialized, and their lifestyle so different from other reptiles', that they should be put in an order (Testudines) of their own.

There are two distinct suborders of chelonian, which include the 230 species of living turtles, tortoises, and terrapins. They are distinguished from each other by the way in which the animal retracts its head into its shell—either by bending the neck sideways (*Pleurodira*) or by bending it back vertically (*Cryptodira*). The members of a third suborder (*Proganochelydia*) are all now extinct, but they were the ancestors of the chelonian group (below).

SUBORDER PROGANOCHELYDIA

The proganochelids were land-living, tortoise-like reptiles with shells encasing their bodies. They began to evolve in Late Triassic times, some 215 million years ago, and were most probably the stock from which today's land tortoises and aquatic turtles arose. But the ancestry of the proganochelids themselves is not known. Most paleontologists believe it to lie among one of the early groups of anapsid reptiles, perhaps the pareaisaurs or procolophonids (see pp.207–208).

Family Proganochelidae

Most of the early tortoises belong to this family, and date from the Late Triassic Period. The best-preserved skeletons have been found in Germany although others have come from Southeast Asia, North America, and southern Africa. Many of the characteristic features seen in modern tortoises were developed at this early stage in their evolution.

NAME	*Proganochelys*
TIME	Late Triassic
LOCALITY	Europe (Germany)
SIZE	3 ft 3 in / 1 m long

This is the most primitive chelonian known, but the typical tortoise shape and structure were already well-established. In fact, *Proganochelys* was remarkably similar to a modern land-living tortoise, except that it could not retract its head or legs into its shell.

The body of this ancient tortoise was short and broad, with only ten elongated vertebrae making up the backbone. This is also a feature of modern chelonians and, except for frogs, gives them the shortest backbones among vertebrate animals. *Proganochelys*' short neck (made up of only eight vertebrae) and head were armed with bony knobs.

Proganochelys had a broad, domed shell (known as the carapace) covering its back, and flat, bony plates (the plastron) protected its underside. About 60 plates of various sizes made up the shell, and they were solidly fused to the underlying vertebrae and ribs. Their arrangement was essentially the same as that found in the shells of modern turtles and tortoises. Unlike its

modern relatives, however, *Proganochelys* had a number of extra plates around the margin of its shell. These projected outward, and gave the legs some protection.

In life, the shell would have been completely scaled over with plates of smooth horn—the beautiful "tortoise shell" from which combs and other ornaments are made. (The horn itself does not fossilize, but marks on the bones indicate its presence.)

The only teeth in *Proganochelys'* mouth were on its palate. Otherwise, it had the typical toothless, horny beak characteristic of modern tortoises. Like them, *Proganochelys* probably spent most its time cropping low-growing vegetation.

SUBORDER PLEURODIRA

A few members of this group of aquatic chelonians survive today, and are known as the "side-neck" turtles, because of their peculiar method of retracting their head inside their shells. This is done with a sideways-flexing of the short neck, and is made possible by the jointing system between the vertebrae.

Pleurodires date from Jurassic times and were once abundant in the rivers and lakes of the world. Today, only 49 species survive, grouped in two families—the Pelomedusidae (below) and the Chelidae. All are restricted to the fresh waters of the southern continents.

Family Pelomedusidae

These aquatic turtles were the most prolific of all the pleurodires during Late Cretaceous and Early Tertiary times. There are only 19 living species—in the rivers and lakes of tropical Africa, Madagascar, and South America.

NAME *Stupendemys*

TIME Early Pliocene

LOCALITY South America (Venezuela)

SIZE 6 ft 6 in/2 m long

This turtle (left), extinct for some three million years, was a giant among the pleurodires; in fact, it was the largest fresh-water turtle that has ever existed. None of its modern relatives come close to it in size—the largest living species is the Arrau Turtle of the Orinoco and Amazon rivers of South America (*Podocnemis expansa*), and it only grows up to 2 ft 6 in/75 cm in length.

The heavy shell that covered *Stupendemys'* back was immensely broad and over 6 ft/1.8 m long. Its weight would have allowed the animal to stay submerged for fairly long periods, while it cropped the prodigious quantities of weeds needed to fuel its body.

SUBORDER CRYPTODIRA

The cryptodires were the most successful group of chelonians, and survive to this day—most modern turtles and tortoises belong to this group. Many of them can retract their heads into the shell by lowering the neck and pulling it back vertically.

As a group, the cryptodires evolved along with their pleurodire cousins during Jurassic times. But by the end of that period they had become enormously diverse, and replaced the pleurodires in the seas, rivers, and lakes of the world. New forms developed on land.

Family Meiolaniidae

The land tortoises of this family appeared in the Late Cretaceous Period, and only became extinct relatively recently in the Pleistocene, less than two million years ago. Although unable to retract their heads into their shells, they were well-protected in other ways.

NAME *Meiolania*

TIME Pleistocene

LOCALITY Australia (Queensland, New Caledonia, and Lord Howe Island)

SIZE 8 ft/2.5 m long

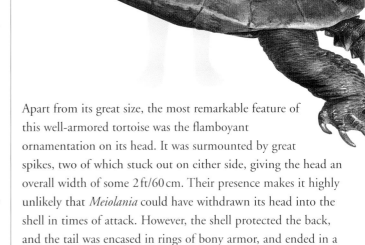

Apart from its great size, the most remarkable feature of this well-armored tortoise was the flamboyant ornamentation on its head. It was surmounted by great spikes, two of which stuck out on either side, giving the head an overall width of some 2 ft/60 cm. Their presence makes it highly unlikely that *Meiolania* could have withdrawn its head into the shell in times of attack. However, the shell protected the back, and the tail was encased in rings of bony armor, and ended in a spiked club.

Family Testudinidae

Modern land tortoises belong to the Testudinidae family, the most successful of the cryptodires. They appeared in modern form during Eocene times some 50 million years ago, and have remained practically unchanged since.

All tortoises have high, domed shells in order to accommodate the capacious gut which is needed to digest their plant food. The shell also offers protection from attack since the animal can withdraw its head and elephantine legs inside.

NAME	Testudo atlas
TIME	Pleistocene
LOCALITY	Asia (India)
SIZE	up to 8 ft/2.5 m long

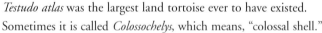

Testudo atlas was the largest land tortoise ever to have existed. Sometimes it is called *Colossochelys*, which means, "colossal shell."

This mighty creature weighed about 4½ US tons/4 tonnes. Its elephantine legs sprawled out at the sides of its body in the typical reptilian fashion, and supported the massive protective shell which was carried on its back. Cushioned pads on the soles of *Testudo atlas'* compact feet spread the animal's considerable weight evenly over the five, heavy-nailed toes of each foot—an arrangement similar to that seen in modern elephants.

Testudo atlas probably fed exclusively on plants, as do most of its modern relatives (though some are known to eat slugs and worms). It would have spent its time browsing and cropping leaves with its sharp, toothless beak, without fear of being attacked. Because if a predator, such as one of the saber-toothed cats, did try to attack, *T. atlas* would have pulled its head and legs back into its shell, and presented a solid, bony box, which would have been almost impossible to move or turn over.

The modern counterpart of this extinct tortoise, in terms of size and weight, is the Galápagos giant tortoise, *Geochelone elephantopus,* found on the Galápagos Islands, off the coast of Ecuador. But even this large animal is only 4 ft/1.2 m long—half the length of *T. atlas*—and weighs a mere 500 lb/225 kg.

Family Protostegidae

The protostegids numbered among their members some of the most spectacular sea turtles that ever lived. All species are now extinct, but they thrived during the Late Cretaceous Period. By the Late Cretaceous the protostegids had developed the two main features that distinguish all sea turtles from their land and river-based relatives.

First, since there were fewer predators in the sea than on land, the sea turtles did not need to carry such heavy armor on their backs, and so the shell was reduced to a much lighter structure, which also made the turtles more maneuverable than their land-living relatives. Second, the toes of the front and back limbs were greatly elongated, and modified into broad flippers which gave greater propulsion when swimming.

Today, only seven species of sea turtle survive, grouped in two families. All of the species are endangered due to man's interference with their habitats, especially their nesting beaches. The green turtle and the great leatherback turtle, both of which inhabit warm seas, are the most familiar members of the families. No sea turtle, either extinct or modern, has the ability to retract its head or legs into the shell.

NAME *Archelon*

TIME Late Cretaceous

LOCALITY North America (Kansas and South Dakota)

SIZE 12 ft/3.7 m long

This giant turtle which inhabited the seas of the Cretaceous Period did not have the heavy, many-plated shell that was characteristic of its land and freshwater relatives. Instead, the shell of *Archelon* was reduced to a framework of transverse struts, made from the bony ribs that grew out from its backbone. Most probably, the ribs were covered by a thick coat of rubbery skin (as seen in the modern leatherback turtle), rather than by the usual plates of horn.

The limbs of this ancient sea turtle were transformed into massive paddles that would have cleaved the water in powerful, vertical strokes—the method is comparable to the underwater flight of penguins, which propel themselves along by flapping their wings. The front flippers of *Archelon* were well-developed, and would have provided the main propulsive force.

Like the modern leatherback turtle, *Archelon* probably fed on a diet of jellyfish, whose soft bodies were easily dealt with by the reptile's weak jaws and toothless beak.

Family Trionychidae

This family of soft-shelled turtles first appeared, along with the sea turtles, in the Late Jurassic Period. They were an early group of specialized cryptodires, and a relatively successful one, since over 30 species survive today, in the freshwaters of North America, Africa, and Asia.

The shells of trionychids are low and rounded, and have lost the horny covering that usually protects the underlying bony plates. Instead, a layer of soft, leathery skin covers the shell, hence the name of the family.

NAME *Palaeotrionyx*

TIME Paleocene

LOCALITY Western North America

SIZE 18 in/45 cm long

This extinct, freshwater turtle was a specialized cryptodire. Unlike most of its relatives, it had a long, mobile neck, only three toes on each foot, and a skin-covered shell, rather than the usual coat of horny plates.

Palaeotrionyx was probably similar in appearance and lifestyle to its living cousins, the soft-shelled turtles (*Trionyx* species) of North America and Africa. Like them, it was probably omnivorous, using its sharp beak to crop water weeds and snap up insects, molluscs, crayfish, and even small fish.

SEMI-AQUATIC AND MARINE REPTILES

During the Mesozoic Era, several groups of reptiles returned to the sea, and became adapted to a marine life. The ichthyosaurs, or "fish lizards," and the long-necked plesiosaurs were the most successful of these groups, and they dominated the seas of the world for more than 100 million years.

The relationship of these marine reptiles to other reptilian orders, and even to each other, is still unclear. But they are sufficiently alike in one respect to be grouped together conveniently: their common feature is a pair of openings in the skull, behind the eyes and below the cheekbones.

There are four distinct types of marine reptile, each of which shows a different degree of adaptation to life in the marine environment. The least specialized were the placodonts of the Triassic Period (below). The nothosaurs, also of the Triassic, were more adapted to aquatic life (see p.216), and their relatives, the plesiosaurs (see pp.218–221), ranged the open seas throughout Jurassic and Cretaceous times (see pp.222–225). The ichthyosaurs shared the Jurassic seas with the plesiosaurs, and were the most specialized group of marine reptiles.

ORDER PLACODONTIA

The placodonts were the least specialized swimmers among the marine reptiles. They appeared and disappeared in the Triassic Period, and during this span of some 35 million years, many types evolved. But they never became fully adapted to life in the open seas. Placodonts were confined to the shallow, coastal waters of the Tethys Sea, which existed at the time between the northern landmass of Laurasia and the southern landmass of Gondwanaland. Many placodonts had turtle-like shells protecting their backs and undersides from predators.

Family Placodontidae

This group of semi-aquatic reptiles was equally at home walking along the seashore or swimming in the coastal shallows. Both areas provided them with rich feeding grounds for their preferred diet of shellfish, which were crushed between the placodont's broad teeth.

NAME	*Placodus*
TIME	Early to Middle Triassic
LOCALITY	Europe (Alps)
SIZE	6 ft 6 in/2 m long

The skull of *Placodus* shows that this reptile was a specialized feeder. Its teeth were fully adapted to a shellfish diet. An array of blunt teeth protruded at the front of the jaws, and were used to pluck shellfish—bivalves and brachiopods—off the rocks. The back teeth were broad and flat, for crushing the shells (hence the name of the family, Placodontidae, meaning "flat-plate tooth.") Even the palate was covered with large, crushing teeth.

This formidable battery of teeth was powered by massive jaw muscles, which could extend through the pair of openings on each side of the creature's skull to provide the jaws with great bite-power.

Some modern sharks (such as the Port Jackson shark, *Heterodontus portusjacksoni*) that eat such hard-shelled animals as molluscs, crustaceans, and sea urchins have the same kind of specialized teeth. So similar are they that when the teeth of *Placodus* were originally found, paleontologists thought that they belonged to ancient sharks.

Placodus was hardly modified at all for its aquatic lifestyle and it was anything but streamlined. Its body was stocky, its neck short, and its limbs sprawled out to the sides of its body like those of early, land-living reptiles. Its only swimming aids were the webs of skin between the five toes of each foot, and the long, slender tail, which was flattened from side to side and may have had a fin running along its length.

Like all placodonts, the underside of *Placodus'* body was protected by a strong armor of belly ribs. A row of bony knobs was raised above the backbone, and provided some protection for this otherwise defenseless animal. Body armor was developed to a much greater extent in later placodonts.

Family Cyamodontidae

This group of placodonts had developed turtle-like shells on their backs. They evolved in the Mid-Triassic and survived to the end of that period.

These shelled placodonts assumed a more completely aquatic lifestyle than *Placodus* (left), and began to look and behave more like modern turtles, although they were unrelated. The phenomenon of unrelated animals evolving similar characteristics is known as convergent evolution.

NAME *Placochelys*

TIME Middle to Late Triassic

LOCALITY Europe (Germany)

SIZE 3 ft/90 cm long

This small reptile was well-adapted to an aquatic lifestyle in the seas of the Middle to Late Triassic Period. The slender body of *Placodus* had been replaced by a broad, flat, turtle-like body in *Placochelys* and a tight mosaic of tough knobby plates covered the creature's back, forming a protective body armor. *Placochelys*' tail was short, and its limbs had evolved into elongated paddles which provided the animal with propulsion in the water.

Placochelys' head, however, was that of a specialized shellfish-eater. It had lost the protruding front teeth seen in *Placodus* and in their place was a horny, toothless beak. However, this was still strong enough to enable it to pluck shellfish from the rocks. Like *Placodus*, strong muscles provided the jaws with great bite power. The jaws were equipped with broad, crushing teeth along the sides and on the palate to cope with the shells of its prey.

Family Henodontidae

These armored placodonts evolved in the Late Triassic Period. The similarity to modern turtles, which was first developed among the cyamodonts, was developed to an extreme in members of the Henodontidae family. The henodontids had developed a great, bony shell that covered their backs and undersides, and they had lost most of their teeth, which had been replaced with a horny beak similar to those of modern turtle species.

NAME *Henodus*

TIME Late Triassic

LOCALITY Europe (Germany)

SIZE 3 ft 3 in/1 m long

The body of *Henodus* was as broad as it was long—the same shape as that of a modern turtle. Its back and belly were covered in an irregular mosaic of many-sided, bony plates. These formed a defensive shell to protect it from attack by other marine reptiles, such as the ichthyosaurs, in the Triassic seas.

Many more plates made up the shell of *Henodus* than are present in the shell of a modern-day turtle. But as in a modern turtle, the shell was completely covered by plates of horn.

Henodus' head was peculiarly square and box-like. There were no teeth in its jaws; instead, there was probably a horny beak, similar to that of a modern turtle, which could be used effectively to both dislodge and crush the shellfish on which it lived.

SEMI-AQUATIC AND MARINE REPTILES CONTINUED

ORDER UNCERTAIN

The claudiosaurs were marine reptiles that evolved in the Late Permian Period. Their classification is uncertain as yet, but they may represent a transition group between the land-living eosuchian reptiles (see p.228–229) and the later, more advanced aquatic reptiles, the nothosaurs and their relatives, the plesiosaurs.

Only one genus of claudiosaur has been found to date—a semi-aquatic, lizard-like animal named *Claudiosaurus,* which is placed in its own family, the Claudiosauridae.

NAME *Claudiosaurus*

TIME Late Permian

LOCALITY Madagascar

SIZE 2 ft/60 cm long

Claudiosaurus was a long-necked, lizard-like animal, whose lifestyle could be compared to that of the modern marine iguana. *Claudiosaurus,* probably spent much of its time resting on rocky beaches, warming up its body so that it could go foraging. It would have fed underwater, poking its long, flexible neck and small head in among the seaweed to find edible plants and animals. When it swam, its legs would have been folded against the body to give a more streamlined shape, and offer less resistance to the water. The main propulsive force came from sideways undulations of the rear body and long, narrow tail.

There was quite a lot of cartilage in the skeleton of *Claudiosaurus.* This suggests that the animal relied on the buoyancy of the water to give it support. Also, the breastbone, or sternum, was neither well-developed nor ossified, as it is in true terrestrial animals, where it braces the ribs apart on the underside of the body as an adaptation to walking. The sternum in *Claudiosaurus* suggests that its limbs were not well-adapted for moving on land.

ORDER NOTHOSAURIA

Nothosaurs were streamlined, fish-eating marine reptiles. Their necks, bodies, and tails were long, their feet were webbed, and they had many sharp teeth in the narrow jaws. Their forelegs were much sturdier than their hind legs, which suggests that they were more actively used for propulsion.

Like the placodonts, nothosaurs evolved and died out during the Triassic Period. Some paleontologists believe that they may be a halfway stage between the land-living reptiles and the aquatic plesiosaurs. However, certain features in the palate and shoulder girdles show that the nothosaurs were not the direct ancestors of the plesiosaurs, rather an offshoot of their ancestors.

Family Nothosauridae

There are several families of nothosaurs, but the best-known representatives belong to the family Nothosauridae. They have been found in the marine sediments of Europe and Asia.

NAME *Nothosaurus*

TIME Early to Late Triassic

LOCALITY Asia (China, Israel, and Russia), Europe (Germany, Netherlands, and Switzerland), and North Africa

SIZE 10 ft/3 m long

This typical nothosaur probably lived as modern seals do, fishing at sea and resting on land. It had few adaptations to aquatic life. The feet had five long toes, and several well-preserved specimens show that these were webbed. The body, neck, and tail were long and flexible. The length of the spines on the vertebrae of the tail suggest that it probably had a fin. The jaws of *Nothosaurus* presented a formidable fish trap— long and slim, with sharp, interlocking teeth.

NAME *Lariosaurus*

TIME Middle Triassic

LOCALITY Europe (Spain)

SIZE 2 ft/60 cm long

Lariosaurus was one of the smaller nothosaurs, though not the smallest—some of them were only 8 in/20 cm long. It possessed a number of primitive features, including a short neck and short toes. The webs of skin between the toes would therefore have been small in area, and not much use for swimming. This reptile probably spent much of its time walking about on the seashore or paddling around in the coastal shallows, feeding on small fishes and shrimps.

NAME *Ceresiosaurus*

TIME Middle Triassic

LOCALITY Europe

SIZE 13 ft/4 m long

The toes of *Ceresiosaurus* were much longer than those of most other nothosaurs. In fact, the animal exhibited the phenomenon of hyperphalangy, in which the number of bones (phalanges) in each toe is increased. Longer toes mean longer feet, and *Ceresiosaurus* had two pairs of paddle-like flippers. These would have been efficient swimming organs, and anticipated the great, oar-like limbs of the advanced swimmers of the Jurassic Period, the plesiosaurs (see pp.218–221).

Ceresiosaurus swam by undulating its long, sinuous body and tail from side to side. The bones of the forelegs were more massive than those of the hind legs, suggesting that the front flippers played more of a role in swimming, maybe for effective steering and braking.

Family Pistosauridae

The close relationship between the nothosaurs and plesiosaurs is revealed in the characteristics of the sole member of the Pistosauridae family. Most of the skeleton of *Pistosaurus* is similar to that of a typical nothosaur (particularly the body), but the creature's skull also displays many plesiosaur features, as does its backbone.

NAME *Pistosaurus*

TIME Middle Triassic

LOCALITY Europe (France and Germany)

SIZE 10 ft/3 m long

This marine reptile may represent an intermediate stage between the nothosaurs and the plesiosaurs, since it possessed features from both of these groups. Its plesiosaur-type head still had the palate of a nothosaur. And its nothosaur-type body still had the stiff backbone typical of the plesiosaurs, which meant that most of the propulsion came from the creature's paddle-like limbs. This was in contrast to the swimming method of the nothosaurs and other earlier marine reptiles, which used lateral undulations of the body and tail as the chief propulsive force to move them through the water.

Pistosaurus had a mouthful of sharp, pointed teeth. It would have been an efficient fish-eater—a way of life shared by both the nothosaurs and the plesiosaurs.

ORDER PLESIOSAURIA

The great ocean-going reptiles of the Mesozoic Era were the plesiosaurs. Some of these marine creatures were huge—reaching lengths of up to 46ft/14m. The plesiosaurs had become adapted for life in the sea by evolving their limbs into long, narrow flippers which made swimming through the water more efficient. Instead of there being only five or fewer bones in each finger or toe, there were up to ten in each. The plesiosaurs had sturdy, deep bodies and relatively short tails.

At one time, paleontologists believed that the plesiosaurians had used their flippers like enormous oars—moving their limbs backward and forward in order to "row" themselves through the water. However, a more recent theory suggests that the plesiosaurs' flippers were moved in great vertical strokes, rather like the wings of a bird, and that plesiosaurs in fact "flew" along in the water, beating their limbs in slow, steady rhythm.

The flippers were hydrofoil shaped, like aeroplane wings—with rounded leading edges and tapering rear ends. Their shape is comparable to the wings of modern penguins or the flippers of sea turtles, both of which swim in a kind of "subaqueous flight."

These specialized limbs of the plesiosaurs required modifications in the animals' limb girdles, and their structure was unique to this group of marine reptiles. The collar bones and two of the three hip bones were massive, and formed broad plates on the underside of the animal's body. The powerful muscles that operated the limbs were attached to these great, bony plates.

A dense series of belly ribs connected the bones of the shoulder and hip girdles on the animal's underside. This made the short body more rigid, and provided a strong, solid arrangement against which the great flippers could work. The belly ribs would also have protected the animal when it had to leave the water in order to lay its eggs. Just as modern sea turtles have a belly armor of bony plates, so the belly ribs of plesiosaurs would have protected their undersides as they dragged themselves ashore and crawled laboriously up the beach, pushing their bodies along with their powerful flippers.

There is no evidence to show that the plesiosaurs gave birth to live young, as the ichthyosaurs did (see pp.222–225). It is likely that they came ashore and laid their eggs in nests dug out of the sand, just as sea turtles do today. However, the plesiosaurs would probably have been even more clumsy when they came onto land than turtles because of their unwieldy long necks. They would have been highly vulnerable to attack by predators at such times. Like modern baby turtles, the newly-hatched young would have faced a dangerous trek down the beach to the sea.

The ancestry of the plesiosaurs is not known. Paleontologists used to think that they had probably evolved directly from one of the well-known nothosaurs, but they now recognize a more likely candidate in the Mid-Triassic reptile *Pistosaurus* (see p.217), whose physical structure seems to be intermediate between the two groups—*Pistosaurus* had the body of a nothosaur and the skull of a plesiosaur.

There were two major groups (or superfamilies) of plesiosaurian. The main differences between the members of the two groups was in the lengths of their necks and the nature of their feeding habits. The plesiosaurs had long necks and short heads, and fed on smaller sea creatures. The pliosaurs had short necks and large heads which enabled them to bite and swallow larger prey. Because of these different characteristics the two groups probably did not compete with one another or with their cousins the ichthyosaurs or "fish lizards" (see pp.222–225) for food although they shared the same seas for many millions of years. Both the plesiosaurs and the pliosaurs survived to the end of the Cretaceous Period.

SUPERFAMILY PLESIOSAUROIDEA

The early members of this group of long-necked marine reptiles were the basal stock from which all other plesiosaurs later developed. The Plesiosauroidea superfamily first appeared in Early Jurassic times, and flourished throughout that period. One family, the elasmosaurs (right), continued to the very end of the Cretaceous Period, and were the last of the group to survive.

The general evolutionary trend among the various families of plesiosaur was toward the development of longer necks and limbs. This reached an extreme in later members of the group, some of which had necks as long as their bodies and tails combined. They also had huge, paddle-like flippers that would have swept them inexorably through the water.

The forelimbs of these plesiosaurs were always somewhat larger than the hind limbs.

The plesiosauroids fed on modest-sized fishes and squid. Their long necks enabled these great creatures to raise their heads high above the surface of the sea and scan the waves in search of potential prey.

Family Plesiosauridae

This group has small skulls and moderately long necks. They are mainly known from fossils found in Europe dating from the Early Jurasssic Period.

NAME	Plesiosaurus
TIME	Early Jurassic
LOCALITY	Europe (England and Germany)
SIZE	7ft 6in/2.3m long

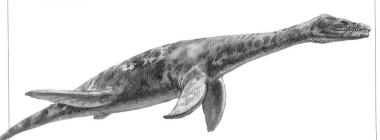

Plesiosaurs seem to have changed little during their 135 million years of evolution. The earliest member of the group, *Plesiosaurus*, had already developed all the main structural features that characterize these marine reptiles.

There were several species of the genus *Plesiosaurus*. *Plesiosaurus macrocephalus*, for example, had a larger head than most species, but in other respects its structure sets the pattern for all its relatives.

A plesiosaur was built for maneuverability, rather than speed. Its fish-hunting habits would have required quite precise movements. For example, a forward stroke by the flippers on one side of the body, coupled with a backward stroke by the flippers on the other side, would have turned the animal's short body almost on the spot. Its long neck could then dart out swiftly to catch fast-swimming prey.

Family Cryptoclididae

The cryptoclidids tended to have long necks made up of some 30 vertebrae. The skull had a long snout with the nostrils set back from the tip. Their geological range extended from the Late Jurassic to the Late Cretaceous.

NAME	Cryptoclidus
TIME	Late Jurassic
LOCALITY	Europe (England)
SIZE	13ft/4m long

Cryptoclidus and other members of its family retained the same moderately long neck proportions as *Plesiosaurus*. But they evolved a large number of very sharply-pointed curved teeth which intermeshed when the jaws were closed. This arrangement formed a fine trap for holding very small fishes or shrimps.

Like other Late Jurassic plesiosaurs, *Cryptoclidus* had perfected the transformation of the limbs into flippers by greatly increasing the number of bones in each of the five digits to produce a long, flexible paddle.

Family Elasmosauridae

A long-ranging group which arose in the Early Jurassic and increased in diversity during the late Jurassic and Cretaceous. Some of the Late Cretaceous forms had extremely long necks with up to 76 vertebrae.

NAME	Muraenosaurus
TIME	Late Jurassic
LOCALITY	Europe (England and France)
SIZE	20ft/6m long

The most successful family of plesiosaurs were the elasmosaurs, of which *Muraenosaurus* is an early member. They evolved in the middle of the Jurassic Period and survived to the end of the Cretaceous. Elasmosaurs had the longest necks of all plesiosaurs.

The neck of *Muraenosaurus* was as long as its body and tail combined and was supported by 44 vertebrae. The head, perched at the end of this crane-like neck, was tiny—only about one-sixteenth of the total body length.

The typically short, stiff plesiosaur body had become quite stout and inflexible in *Muraenosaurus*. This rigidity would have helped to make the flippers more effective propulsion organs.

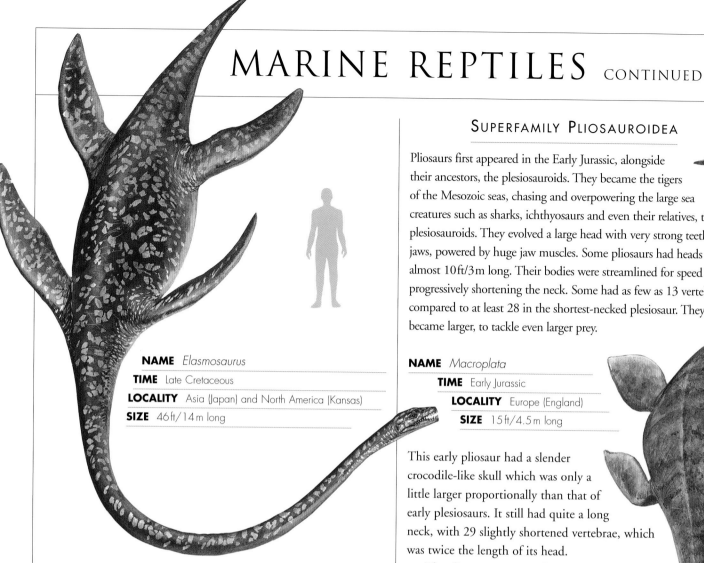

SUPERFAMILY PLIOSAUROIDEA

Pliosaurs first appeared in the Early Jurassic, alongside their ancestors, the plesiosauroids. They became the tigers of the Mesozoic seas, chasing and overpowering the large sea creatures such as sharks, ichthyosaurs and even their relatives, the plesiosauroids. They evolved a large head with very strong teeth and jaws, powered by huge jaw muscles. Some pliosaurs had heads almost 10ft/3m long. Their bodies were streamlined for speed by progressively shortening the neck. Some had as few as 13 vertebrae, compared to at least 28 in the shortest-necked plesiosaur. They also became larger, to tackle even larger prey.

NAME *Elasmosaurus*

TIME Late Cretaceous

LOCALITY Asia (Japan) and North America (Kansas)

SIZE 46ft/14m long

NAME *Macroplata*

TIME Early Jurassic

LOCALITY Europe (England)

SIZE 15ft/4.5m long

This early pliosaur had a slender crocodile-like skull which was only a little larger proportionally than that of early plesiosaurs. It still had quite a long neck, with 29 slightly shortened vertebrae, which was twice the length of its head.

The pliosaurs progressively improved the limbs into powerful paddles, with a great increase in the number of bones in the digits. But the hind limb, not the forelimb, became the larger, implying a difference in the use of the limbs in the two groups.

NAME *Peloneustes*

TIME Late Jurassic

LOCALITY Europe (England and the former USSR)

SIZE 10ft/3m long

"Snakes threaded through the bodies of turtles"—was the description of the plesiosaurs coined by Dean Conybeare, a nineteenth-century English paleontologist who did much of the initial work on these reptiles. *Elasmosaurus*, was the longest known plesiosaur. More than half of its total length was neck—26ft/5m out of a total of 46ft/14m.

Elasmosaurus had 71 vertebrae—more than the earliest plesiosaurs, which had about 28 neck vertebrae. The structure would have enabled *Elasmosaurus* to curl its neck around sideways, making almost two full circles on each side of its body. It would have been only half as flexible in the vertical plane. However, had *Elasmosaurus* swung its neck around underwater while swimming, it would have met great water resistance.

Some paleontologists suggest, therefore, that the habit of such long-necked reptiles was to paddle along on the surface, their necks held clear of the water. When fish or other prey were spotted from this vantage point, the long neck was plunged into the sea, and the prey snapped up. The modern anhinga, or snake bird, has a long neck, and hunts in much the same way.

Although smaller than *Macroplata*, this pliosaur (below) shows an advance in the trend to a larger head and shorter neck. It had only about 20 neck vertebrae and its head and neck were of almost equal length. *Peloneustes'* more streamlined shape enabled it to swim rapidly after its fast-moving prey and its long head gave it the reach that its short neck did not allow. Its teeth were adapted to its diet, being fewer and less sharp than those of the fish-eating plesiosaurs, and better for catching soft-bodied squid and crushing the hard shells of ammonites.

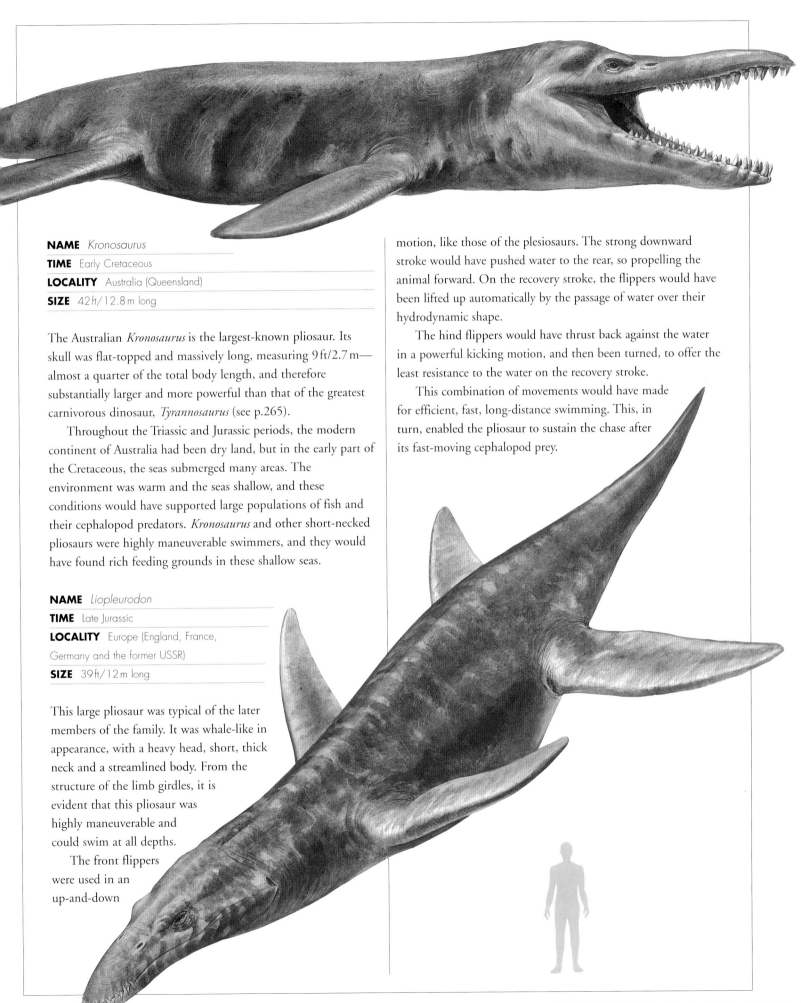

NAME *Kronosaurus*

TIME Early Cretaceous

LOCALITY Australia (Queensland)

SIZE 42 ft/12.8 m long

The Australian *Kronosaurus* is the largest-known pliosaur. Its skull was flat-topped and massively long, measuring 9 ft/2.7 m— almost a quarter of the total body length, and therefore substantially larger and more powerful than that of the greatest carnivorous dinosaur, *Tyrannosaurus* (see p.265).

Throughout the Triassic and Jurassic periods, the modern continent of Australia had been dry land, but in the early part of the Cretaceous, the seas submerged many areas. The environment was warm and the seas shallow, and these conditions would have supported large populations of fish and their cephalopod predators. *Kronosaurus* and other short-necked pliosaurs were highly maneuverable swimmers, and they would have found rich feeding grounds in these shallow seas.

NAME *Liopleurodon*

TIME Late Jurassic

LOCALITY Europe (England, France, Germany and the former USSR)

SIZE 39 ft/12 m long

This large pliosaur was typical of the later members of the family. It was whale-like in appearance, with a heavy head, short, thick neck and a streamlined body. From the structure of the limb girdles, it is evident that this pliosaur was highly maneuverable and could swim at all depths.

The front flippers were used in an up-and-down motion, like those of the plesiosaurs. The strong downward stroke would have pushed water to the rear, so propelling the animal forward. On the recovery stroke, the flippers would have been lifted up automatically by the passage of water over their hydrodynamic shape.

The hind flippers would have thrust back against the water in a powerful kicking motion, and then been turned, to offer the least resistance to the water on the recovery stroke.

This combination of movements would have made for efficient, fast, long-distance swimming. This, in turn, enabled the pliosaur to sustain the chase after its fast-moving cephalopod prey.

ORDER ICHTHYOSAURIA

The ichthyosaurs were the most specialized of marine reptiles. Their name means "fish lizards," and describes them well, since they ate fish, and were shaped like fish (though, of course, they were air-breathing reptiles). In fact, their overall body shape was like that of a modern mackerel or tuna— a highly streamlined form that allowed these living fish to reach swimming speeds of over 25 mph/40 kmph.

Unlike their contemporaries, the plesiosaurs (see pp.218–221), ichthyosaurs did not rely on their paddle-like flippers for swimming. Instead, they developed a fish-like tail, the lateral movements of which provided the animal's main propulsive force, just like the tail of a modern shark or tuna.

So fully adapted were the ichthyosaurs to a marine life that they could no longer come ashore to lay eggs, in the same way as the sea turtles and plesiosaurs. Instead, ichthyosaurs gave birth to live young at sea. In fact, some of the most remarkable of fossil finds show adult female ichthyosaurs with young babies just emerging from their bodies—preserved forever in the process of birth.

As a group, the ichthyosaurs occupied the same ecological niche as today's dolphins. They were wide-ranging and highly successful for about 100 million years. These aquatic creatures cruised the open seas of the world from Early Triassic times, and reached their peak of diversity in the Jurassic Period. Thereafter, they declined until, by the mid-Cretaceous, they were all but extinct. The demise of this group could be related to competition from the advanced sharks, which had evolved into their modern form by this time, and were the dominant carnivores of the Late Mesozoic seas (see pp.170–172).

The origin of the ichthyosaurs is not known. The only certainty is the fact that they descended from some terrestrial group of reptiles, rather than evolving from one of the known types of aquatic reptile.

Family Shastasauridae

The shastasaurs were among the earliest ichthyosaurs to appear, in Mid-Triassic deposits, mainly in those from North America. (Older types are known from Japan and China, dating from the Early Triassic Period.) At this early stage of their evolution the shastasaurs moved in an eel-like fashion. However, by the end of the Triassic Period, they had evolved the fish shape characteristic of the ichthyosaur group and swam in a manner more like modern fishes.

NAME	*Cymbospondylus*
TIME	Middle Triassic
LOCALITY	North America (Nevada)
SIZE	33 ft/10 m long

This large ichthyosaur was one of the least fish-like of the group. The body and tail made up most of its length. There was no fin on its back nor on its tail, features that were to develop in later ichthyosaurs. However, it did have the typical long, beak-like jaws, armed with pointed teeth—the sign of a fish-eater.

The limbs of *Cymbospondylus* were short, and looked more like the fins of fish than the paddles of later ichthyosaurs. They would not have been effective for swimming, so they were probably used to control steering and braking. The main propulsive force in swimming must, therefore, have been provided by lateral undulations of the animal's long body.

NAME	*Shonisaurus*
TIME	Late Triassic
LOCALITY	North America (Nevada)
SIZE	49 ft/15 m long

Shonisaurus is the largest-known ichthyosaur, and the only almost-complete skeleton known from Late Triassic rocks. It had developed the fish-like shape characteristic of the group and its enormous length was divided approximately into equal thirds—the head and neck, the body, and the tail.

The backbone of *Shonisaurus*, too, had started to include a typical feature of later ichthyosaurs—it bent downward into the lower lobe of the tail.

It seems likely that *Shonisaurus* was an independent, specialized offshoot from the main line of ichthyosaurs. It had a number of structural peculiarities. For example, its jaws were greatly elongated, and had teeth only at the front.

Its limbs were also extended into extra-long, narrow paddles. This was not a typical feature of the ichthyosaurs. Not only were the paddles unusually long, but the fact that they were of equal size was also unusual—the front pair of limbs in most ichthyosaurs were generally longer than the hind pair.

Family Mixosauridae

The mixosaurs had developed a stabilizing fin on the back (like the dorsal fin of a fish)—a swimming aid which was present in all later ichthyosaurs. But the mixosaurids did not have the typical fish-like tail, with two equal lobes, that made their later relatives such powerful swimmers.

In mixosaurs, the end of the backbone was not bent sharply down into the tail, as it was in later ichthyosaurs; instead, the vertebrae were extended upward, probably to support a low fin on top of the tail.

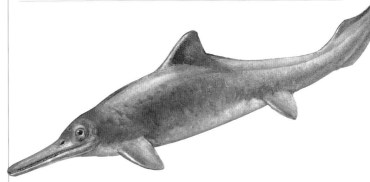

NAME	*Mixosaurus*
TIME	Middle Triassic
LOCALITY	Asia (China and Timor, Indonesia), Europe (Alps), North America (Alaska, Canadian Arctic, and Nevada), and Spitsbergen
SIZE	3 ft 3 in / 1 m long

Mixosaurus seems to have been intermediate in appearance between the early, primitive ichthyosaurs, as exemplified by *Cymbospondylus* (left), and the later, more advanced types. For example, *Mixosaurus* had a fish-like body with a dorsal fin on its back, and probably also the beginnings of a fin on the top of its tail. Its limbs had become transformed by the evolutionary process into short paddles, the front pair being longer than the hind pair. Each paddle consisted of five toes, which were greatly elongated by the addition of many small bones (hyperphalangy). The long, narrow jaws were equipped with sharp teeth, adapted for catching and eating fish.

Family Ichthyosauridae

The most typical fish lizards belong to this large family, which flourished throughout the Jurassic Period and into the Cretaceous. The Ichthyosauridae family are known from some remarkably well-preserved fossil specimens, which show them to have been highly specialized marine-living animals.

The ichthyosaurs had developed a streamlined body, torpedo-shaped, with a stabilizing dorsal fin on the back; short, paired paddles which were used for steering; and a strong, fish-like tail with two equal lobes which produced the propulsion for swimming. Ball-and-socket joints between the tail vertebrae allowed for powerful sweeping strokes from side to side. The powerful tail, together with the great flexibility of the backbone, propelled the animal rapidly through the water—the swimming method which is also used by modern-day, fast-moving fishes.

Fossil ichthyosaurids were first found at the beginning of the 19th century by the Anning family in the Jurassic limestones of Lyme Regis, on the southern coast of England.

NAME Ichthyosaurus

TIME Early Jurassic to Early Cretaceous

LOCALITY Europe (England and Germany), Greenland, and North America (Alberta)

SIZE up to 6 ft 6 in/2 m long

Ichthyosaurus is one of the best-known prehistoric animals, since a graphic record of its remains are preserved in the shales of southern Germany, near Holzmaden. These rocks were laid down in shallow waters during the Early Jurassic. Several hundred complete skeletons of *Ichthyosaurus* have been found, their bones still articulating with each other. The tiny bones of their young were also found inside the bodies of several adults. This—combined with some specimens where the young is preserved actually emerging from the body of the adult (tail-first, as in modern whales)—shows without a doubt that these marine reptiles gave birth to live young at sea.

The find in Germany also yielded a unique picture of how the animals looked in life. A thin film of carbon had been laid down around many of the specimens, outlining the exact shape of their bodies when the flesh was still on the bones. The characteristic features of a typical ichthyosaur can be clearly seen —the high dorsal fin on the back; the half-moon shape of the tail (caudal) fin, with the backbone angled down sharply into its lower lobe; and the short, hydrofoil-shaped paddles that enclosed the elongated toes of the limbs, the front pair longer than the hind pair.

The nostrils of *Ichthyosaurus* were set far back on its snout near the eyes, so the animal only had to break the surface of the water to breathe. The bones of the ear were massive, and probably transmitted mined vibrations from the water to the inner ear, so that the direction of potential prey could be judged. But *Ichthyosaurus'* main sense for locating its prey would have been sight—its eyes were large and, most probably, extremely sensitive.

Even fossil droppings (called coprolites) and stomach contents of these marine reptiles have been preserved in the rocks. They confirm that fish was the bulk of the diet, but that cephalopods were also eaten.

The remains of pigment cells have also been preserved, and analysis of these suggests that the smooth, thick skin of *Ichthyosaurus* was a dark reddish-brown.

NAME Ophthalmosaurus

TIME Late Jurassic

LOCALITY Europe (England and France), North America (Western USA and Canadian Arctic), and South America (Argentina)

SIZE 11 ft 6 in/3.5 m long

Ophthalmosaurus was even more streamlined than its contemporary, *Ichthyosaurus*. Its body was shaped almost like a teardrop—massive and rounded at the front, and tapering toward the rear to culminate in the great, halfmoon-shaped caudal fin. Its front limbs were much more developed than the hind limbs, indicating that the front paddles did most of the steering and stabilizing work, with the tail propelling the body from the rear.

The most remarkable feature of *Ophthalmosaurus* was its huge eyes. Their sockets are about 4 in/10 cm in diameter, and occupy almost the whole depth of the skull on each side. A ring of bony plates (sclerotic ring) surrounded each eyeball, to prevent the soft tissues from collapsing under the external water pressure, and to help with focusing. (The eyes of all ichthyosaurs had these sclerotic rings, but they are particularly noticeable in *Ophthalmosaurus*.)

The super-large eyes of this ichthyosaur suggest that it was a night-feeder. It probably hunted close to the surface, feeding on squid, which in turn were feeding on the plankton-eating fish.

Family Stenopterygiidae

During the Jurassic Period, two distinct types of ichthyosaur evolved, differing in the shape of their paddle-like limbs. *Ichthyosaurus* and members of its family had short, broad paddles, with more toes than the normal five—sometimes up to nine toes in each limb. The stenopterygiids, in contrast, had longer, narrow paddles, each made up of five toes but with an increased number of bones in each toe.

NAME *Stenopterygius*
TIME Early to Middle Jurassic
LOCALITY Europe (England and Germany)
SIZE 10 ft/3 m long

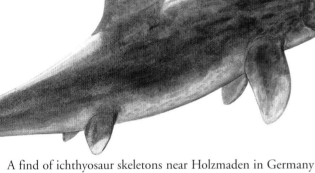

A find of ichthyosaur skeletons near Holzmaden in Germany includes well-preserved specimens of *Stenopterygius*. *Stenopterygius* was similar in build to *Ichthyosaurus*, but had a smaller head and the narrow paddles characteristic of its family. Five toes made up each paddle, many more bones gave them their narrow shape.

Family Leptopterygiidae

This family contains the last surviving members of the ichthyosaurs before they became extinct at the base of the Late Cretaceous. Like the earlier stenopterygiids (above), the leptopterygiids had narrow paddles, with a great number of bones in each of the five toes.

NAME *Eurhinosaurus*
TIME Early Jurassic
LOCALITY Europe (Germany)
SIZE 6 ft 6 in/2 m long

This extraordinary-looking ichthyosaur, was unlike any other known member of the group. Its upper jaw was twice the length of its lower jaw, giving it the appearance of a modern sawfish. Teeth stuck out sideways along the length of the blade-like projection. The function of this strange structure is not known for certain, just as the purpose of the saw of the modern sawfish also remains somewhat mysterious. *Eurhinosaurus* could have used it to probe around in the sand or mud of the seabed, or among seaweeds and rocks, to flush out flatfish, shrimps, or octopus. Perhaps it was also swung rapidly from side to side as *Eurhinosaurus* swam through a shoal of fish, stunning and wounding them as it passed.

NAME *Temnodontosaurus*
TIME Early Jurassic
LOCALITY Europe (England and Germany)
SIZE 30 ft/9 m long

This large creature (sometimes known as *Leptopterygius*) must have cruised the warm waters of the shallow Jurassic seas looking for food, its movements finely controlled by the long, narrow paddles at the front of its body. Propelled through the water by its great tail, *Temnodontosaurus* would have preyed upon large squid and ammonites.

EARLY DIAPSIDS

SUBCLASS DIAPSIDA

Most modern reptiles belong to the diapsids, an ancient group that first appeared in Late Carboniferous times, more than 300 million years ago. The skulls of these animals are distinctive because they have a pair of openings on either side of the skull behind the eye (see p.205).

The muscles of the jaws are attached to ligaments that stretch across these holes, and endow their owners with stronger jaws, which can be opened wide and closed forcefully to deal with large prey.

The diapsids are not only an ancient group. They are also an important group in evolutionary terms, because from them came the ancestors of most modern reptiles (lizards, snakes, and tuataras), and the ancestors of the ruling reptiles (the extinct dinosaurs and pterosaurs, and the modern crocodiles).

ORDER ARAEOSCELIDIA

The earliest and most primitive of the diapsid reptiles were the small, lizard-like araeoscelids, with long necks and slim running legs. Only about four genera are known, classed in two families. They date from the Late Carboniferous Period to the middle of the Permian—a span of less than 40 million years.

NAME	Petrolacosaurus
TIME	Late Carboniferous
LOCALITY	North America (Kansas)
SIZE	16 in/40 cm long

The earliest-known diapsid reptile, with the characteristic pair of openings on either side of its skull, looked much like a modern lizard, but with longer legs and a tail as long as its body and head combined. *Petrolacosaurus* probably also behaved like a modern lizard. It would have been an active hunter, chasing

around after insects and other small invertebrates. Its home was the dry, upland areas of what is now Kansas, above the swampy marshes where coal was forming during the Late Carboniferous (Pennsylvanian) Period.

The jaws of this early reptile were equipped with many sharp, pointed teeth, including an upper pair of canines. This arrangement is reminiscent of that of *Hylonomus*, the most primitive reptile known (see p.206).

Despite the newly evolved openings in its diapsid skull, the jaws of *Petrolacosaurus* were not very strong. The openings probably served to lighten the skull, rather than to provide attachment points for the jaw muscles—which was their function in later diapsids.

NAME	Araeoscelis
TIME	Early Permian
LOCALITY	North America (Texas)
SIZE	2 ft/60 cm long

Araeoscelis was the closest relative of *Petrolacosaurus* (left), although it lived several million years later. Both animals were similar in appearance—they were lizard-like creatures, with long running legs, long necks, and small heads.

The teeth of *Araeoscelis*, however, were different to those of its earlier relative, and indicate that this creature may have been a more specialized feeder. Instead of the sharp, pointed teeth of *Petrolacosaurus*, *Araeoscelis* had fairly massive, blunt, conical teeth which would have been ideal for crushing the tough chitinous covering of insects such as beetles.

Associated with this specialized diet there was a structural change in the skull of *Araeoscelis*. One of the two pairs of openings in its otherwise-typical diapsid skull had been closed over with bone. This feature was probably an adaptation to strengthen the skull, so that the animal could develop a more powerful bite, which would enable it to deal with its tougher food source.

Order Uncertain

There is no fossil record of diapsid reptiles during the Mid-Permian Period. So far, no traces have been found to indicate the course of their evolution during this time. However, in the Late Permian a number of specialized groups appear, which cannot be related to each other with any certainty.

The weigeltisaurid family is one such specialized group, with only a few members known from Madagascar and Europe.

Family Weigeltisauridae

NAME	Coelurosauravus
TIME	Late Permian
LOCALITY	Madagascar
SIZE	16 in/40 cm long

This early reptile was highly adapted for gliding through the air, and probably looked similar to the modern lizard known as the flying dragon, *Draco volans*, of Southeast Asia.

The ribs of *Coelurosauravus* were greatly elongated on each side of its short body. Flaps of skin would have connected the ribs, to form a pair of "wings" with a total span of about 1 ft/30 cm. This reptile probably lived in forests, like the modern flying dragon, and glided from tree to tree, feeding on insects. Its legs would have been held out from its body as it glided, its feet spread wide to offer resistance to the air, and hence slow its descent.

The skull of *Coelurosauravus* was lighter than that of other early diapsids. The openings for the eyes were huge, and there was a wide frill developed from the bones at the back of its head, presumably to make it more aerodynamic.

Order Thalattosauria

The thalattosaurs were another specialized group of early diapsid reptiles that lived during the Triassic Period. They were adapted to a marine way of life, probably spending most of their time at sea, and only coming ashore to lay their eggs.

The few thalattosaurs known from Europe and western North America are classed in three families, of which the Askeptosauridae is the best known.

NAME	Askeptosaurus
TIME	Middle Triassic
LOCALITY	Europe (Switzerland)
SIZE	6 ft 6 in/2 m long

As with many animals adapted to an aquatic way of life, the neck and body of *Askeptosaurus* were long and slim. Its tail was greatly elongated and almost ribbon-like, and accounted for about half the body length. Sinuous movements of the body and tail would have propelled the animal, eel-style, through the water. Its feet, too, would have helped in swimming—they were broad and webbed, and were probably used to control direction and speed by steering and braking.

Askeptosaurus had long jaws, armed with many sharp teeth. It probably dived deep after its fish prey. This is deduced from two features: its eyes were large, for seeing in the ocean's twilight zone, and they were strengthened by a ring of bony plates, in order to prevent the eyeballs collapsing under the great water pressure at depth.

EARLY DIAPSIDS CONTINUED

ORDER CHORISTODERA

A strange assemblage of crocodile-like reptiles diverged from the main diapsid line during the Early Cretaceous Period, some 140 million years ago. The Choristodera lived in the freshwaters of North America, Europe and eastern Asia until well into the Tertiary—becoming extinct during the Eocene Epoch, some 50 million years ago.

NAME *Champsosaurus*

TIME Late Cretaceous to Eocene

LOCALITY Europe (Belgium and France) and North America (Alberta, Montana, New Mexico, and Wyoming)

SIZE 5 ft/1.5 m long

Champsosaurus lived in the rivers and swamps of Europe and western North America throughout Late Cretaceous and Early Tertiary times. With its long, narrow jaws, which were filled with fine, pointed teeth, *Champsosaurus* could easily have been mistaken for a close relative of the crocodile—the modern gavial of India. However, although both animals are diapsid reptiles, they are not closely related to each other. Their similarity can be explained instead by the phenomenon of convergent evolution, in which adaptation to life in a particular environment leads unrelated animals to adopt the same body shape, and often the same behavior.

Champsosaurus probably swam using lateral undulations of its sinuous body and tail to propel itself while holding its legs tight against the flanks to give itself a more streamlined shape—the same swimming method can be seen in modern crocodiles and marine iguanas.

This reptile was a fish-eater with extremely powerful jaws. The great width of the *Champsosaurus'* skull behind the eyes would have provided a large surface area to which jaw muscles could have been attached, to give great bite-power.

ORDER EOSUCHIA

The lizard-like eosuchians are thought to be close to the ancestry of the later, advanced diapsid reptiles, many of which survive today in the form of snakes and lizards (see pp.230–231).

Eosuchians first appeared in Late Permian times, and continued until the middle of the Triassic. They are grouped into four families, all of whose members were apparently confined to southern and eastern Africa, and Madagascar. The family Tangasauridae contains two representative members (below).

NAME *Thadeosaurus*

TIME Late Permian

LOCALITY Madagascar

SIZE 2 ft/60 cm long

The tremendously long tail of the land-living *Thadeosaurus* measured about 16 in/40 cm—making up two-thirds of the animal's total length. The five clawed toes of each foot were greatly elongated, and so arranged that the longer toes were on the outside. This characteristic had the advantage of allowing most of the animal's toes to remain in contact with the ground as the foot was lifted, giving a strong push off the surface with each step taken and facilitating a more powerful stride. The sternum, or breastbone, was massively developed, a feature which helped to increase the stride of the forelegs.

NAME *Hovasaurus*

TIME Late Permian

LOCALITY Madagascar

SIZE 20 in/50 cm long

The most striking feature of this aquatic lizard-like reptile was its tail. Not only was it twice the length of the rest of the animal's body; it was also deep and flattened from side to side. Each of the tail vertebrae was extended above and below the midline. The result was a tail that formed a broad, stiff paddle, allowing *Hovasaurus* to swim efficiently.

Another unusual feature of *Hovasaurus* is the mass of pebbles found in the abdominal cavities of most of the specimens recovered. Evidently, these reptiles swallowed stones as ballast, to help them sink quickly in the water when diving for their fish prey, or to keep them submerged when feeding.

SUPERORDER LEPIDOSAURIA

The evolutionary line leading to the surviving lepidosaurs—the 6000 species of modern snakes and lizards—arose from an eosuchian-type ancestor some time during the Late Permian Period. A third group of lepidosaurs, the sphenodonts, did not meet with such success (below).

ORDER SPHENODONTIDA

The sphenodonts (also called rhynchocephalids) are an ancient group of lepidosaurs. They are an offshoot from the main evolutionary line of diapsids leading to true lizards and snakes.

Once a diverse group, sphenodonts appeared in the Late Triassic, over 200 million years ago, and many families evolved during the subsequent Jurassic Period. Thereafter, their members began to decline, perhaps due to competition from the true lizards, which were well-established at that stage.

The sole surviving member of the whole sphenodont order is the tuatara, *Sphenodon punctatus*, found only in New Zealand.

NAME *Planocephalosaurus*

TIME Late Triassic

LOCALITY Europe (England)

SIZE 8 in/20 cm long

This lizard-like animal was among the earliest of the sphenodonts to evolve. Its skeleton is almost identical to that of the modern tuatara of New Zealand. But its skull is primitive—its teeth are fused to the jaw, rather than attached to grooves in the jaw bones as in advanced lizards.

The teeth of *Planocephalosaurus* were strong, and its jaws could have delivered a powerful bite. It would have crushed insects between its teeth, supplementing its diet with worms and snails, and probably the occasional small lizard.

NAME *Pleurosaurus*

TIME Late Jurassic to Early Cretaceous

LOCALITY Europe (Germany)

SIZE 2 ft/60 cm long

Pleurosaurus was a member of the pleurosaur family—a group of specialized sphenodonts that evolved on land, but returned to the water during Early Jurassic times. The only specific aquatic adaptation among the pleurosaurs seems to have been a great elongation of the body—up to 57 vertebrae in some types, about twice the typical sphenodont number.

Snake-like movements of the long, sinuous body and tail moved *Pleurosaurus* rapidly through the water. Its nostrils were set far back on its snout, near to the eyes. Its legs were much shorter than those of land-living sphenodonts, and played no role in swimming.

SNAKES AND LIZARDS

ORDER SQUAMATA

The most successful group of reptiles today comprises the lizards and snakes. There are some 6000 species of walkers, gliders, crawlers, swimmers, climbers, and burrowers, living in every continent of the world except Antarctica. They are descended from an ancient lineage of diapsid reptiles, most probably the lizard-like eosuchians, stretching back over 250 million years, to Late Permian times (see pp.228–229). The other living reptiles—the turtles, tortoises and crocodiles—evolved along quite different lines (see pp.210–213, 242–245).

The chief feature that distinguishes the lizards and snakes from all other diapsid reptiles (including their closest relatives, the sphenodonts, see p.229), is the great flexibility and power of their jaws. Two structural changes brought this about. First was the loss of the lower arch of bone that enclosed the lower pair of openings in the skull. This gave more room for larger muscles to develop to operate the jaws. Second, a movable hinge joint developed within the skull, which provided even more flexibility in the movements of the jaws.

SUBORDER LACERTILIA

Lizards are a much more ancient group than snakes. The earliest known lizard-like reptiles were small insectivores that inhabited southern Africa during the Late Permian Period. Few fossils remain to trace the course of their evolution during the first half of the Mesozoic Era. However, at the end of the Jurassic Period the group seems to have undergone a burst of evolutionary development, and primitive members of all the major modern groups had suddenly appeared—including geckos, skinks, iguanas, slow worms, and monitors.

Besides the changes in the skull that produced more efficient jaws, other structural changes gave lizards better hearing and better articulating surfaces in the joints of their limbs for improved walking. All these features combined to make lizards fast, efficient hunters, able to deal with comparatively large prey, such as other reptiles.

Family Kuehneosauridae

Members of this family are among the earliest-known lizard-like reptiles. They are often placed in the lepidosauromorphs because their relationships may be closer to the sphenodonts than the lacertilians. Early though they were, they had a specialized lifestyle—that of gliding through the air on outstretched, wing-like membranes.

NAME	*Kuehneosaurus*
TIME	Late Triassic
LOCALITY	Europe (England)
SIZE	26 in/65 cm long

This long-legged lizard could glide through the air on a pair of membranous "wings" which spanned more than 1 ft/30 cm and projected out from each side of its body between the front and hind limbs.

Greatly elongated ribs formed the framework for the skin-covered gliding membranes—the same arrangement developed by the gliding *Coelurosauravus* (see p.227) and the living flying dragon *Draco volans*, of Southeast Asia.

Family Ardeosauridae

The Gekkota or geckos were among the earliest of the modern groups of lizard to appear, in the Late Jurassic Period. The only surviving family, the Gekkonidae, evolved relatively recently—in the Late Eocene, some 40 million years ago. It contains more than 670 species, which have spread throughout the warm tropical zones of the world.

NAME	*Ardeosaurus*
TIME	Late Jurassic
LOCALITY	Europe (Germany)
SIZE	8 in/20 cm long

This early gecko had the flattened head and large eyes typical of its modern relatives. Like them, it was probably a night-hunter, agile enough to snap up insects, spiders, and smaller lizards with its powerful jaws. Whether it had the "friction pads" of today's geckos is not known; these are specialized scales under the toes which enable the animal to climb up smooth, vertical surfaces.

Family Varanidae

The anguimorphs or monitors are the largest of all land lizards. They appeared in the Late Cretaceous Period, more than 80 million years ago, and have changed little since. They were large, heavy, active hunters. The forked tongue acts as an organ of smell. Modern representatives include the Komodo dragon.

NAME	Megalania
TIME	Pleistocene
LOCALITY	Australia (Queensland)
SIZE	up to 26 ft/8 m long

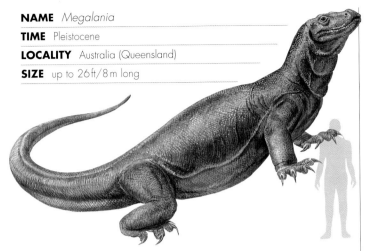

This relative of the Komodo dragon, *Varanus komodensis*, of Indonesia, hunted on the plains of Australia less than 2 million years ago, ambushing large marsupials, such as kangaroos, grazing there. It would have torn off chunks of flesh with its powerful jaws and long, sharp teeth, serrated along their edges.

Family Mosasauridae

This successful, though short-lived, offshoot from the monitor lizard group was fully adapted to a marine life, during the Late Cretaceous Period.

NAME	Platecarpus
TIME	Late Cretaceous
LOCALITY	Europe (Belgium) and North America (Alabama, Colorado, Kansas, and Mississippi)
SIZE	14 ft/4.3 m long

Platecarpus swam in the seas some 75 million years ago. Its tail was as long as its body, and was probably flattened from side to side, with a broad, vertical fin running along its length, above and below. Snake-like undulations of the long, sinuous body, combined with the finned tail, would have propelled *Platecarpus* forward, while the short legs and broad, webbed feet were used to steer.

This marine lizard would have eaten fish and soft-bodied cephalopods, snapping them up in its long, pointed jaws, which were equipped with many sharp, conical teeth. *Platecarpus* would also have tackled the ammonites, whose soft bodies were enclosed within a hard, coiled shell.

NAME	Plotosaurus
TIME	Late Cretaceous
LOCALITY	North America (Kansas)
SIZE	33 ft/10 m long

Plotosaurus was a giant among mosasaurs. About 50 vertebrae made up its body and neck, with at least the same number again making up the long tail. The rear of its tail was expanded into a vertical fin.

Its limbs were developed into short flippers, with the front pair longer than the hind pair due to a greater number of bones in each toe. Impressions preserved in the chalk near the bones of the limbs suggest that *Plotosaurus* was covered in a scaly skin, like a modern snake.

SUBORDER SERPENTES

Modern snakes developed during Miocene times some 20 million years ago. But the oldest-known snake is over 100 million years old, and comes from Early Cretaceous rocks in North Africa. It has many of features of the modern groups— elongation of the body; loss of limbs, bony arches above the two lower openings in the skull; and flexibility of the jaw hinges. Snakes are believed to have evolved from a type of burrowing lizard, or from an aquatic, monitor-type lizard.

NAME	Pachyrhachis
TIME	Early Cretaceous
LOCALITY	Asia (Israel)
SIZE	3 ft 3 in/1 m long

The aquatic reptile *Pachyrhachis* had the long body of a snake and the large head of a monitor lizard. The limbs and shoulder girdles had disappeared, but there were still traces of the hip bones. The ribs were broad and evidently *Pachyrhachis* swam by snake-like undulations.

DINOSAURS AND THEIR KIN

The dinosaurs and their kin—the crocodiles and flying pterosaurs —dominated the air, land, and waters of the Earth during the Mesozoic Era. This "Age of the Ruling Reptiles" began more than 200 million years ago, and ended some 65 million years ago. During this time, some of nature's most awesome beasts evolved. The carnivorous dinosaurs stood 20 ft/6 m tall, the plant-eating dinosaurs were some 85 ft/26 m long, and pterosaurs had a wingspan of some 40 ft/12.2 m. The sole surviving members of this great assemblage of "ruling reptiles" (the archosaurs) are today's crocodiles.

The first step in the evolution of the ruling reptiles was taken in the Late Permian Period, some 250 million years ago. A new line of small, diapsid reptiles evolved, and from them radiated a variety of reptiles, which have been called the thecodontians, but are now known to include several unrelated groups. Now generally referred to as the basal archosaurs, they thrived during the subsequent Triassic Period, and some of their members became progressively more skilled at walking upright on two legs. The dinosaurs (see pp.250–313), the crocodiles (see pp.242–245), and probably also the flying pterosaurs (see pp.246–249) evolved from these basal archosaurs of the Triassic.

Past masters of the world

The first-recorded dinosaur bones were found in England. They belonged to the giant carnivore *Megalosaurus* (see p.260) and the giant herbivore *Iguanodon* (see p.287) and were described to the scientific community in 1824 and 1825. Over a decade passed before Sir Richard Owen, the English anatomist, realised that they were representatives of an extinct group of reptiles. It was he who, in 1842, coined the name *Dinosauria* for them, meaning "terrible lizards."

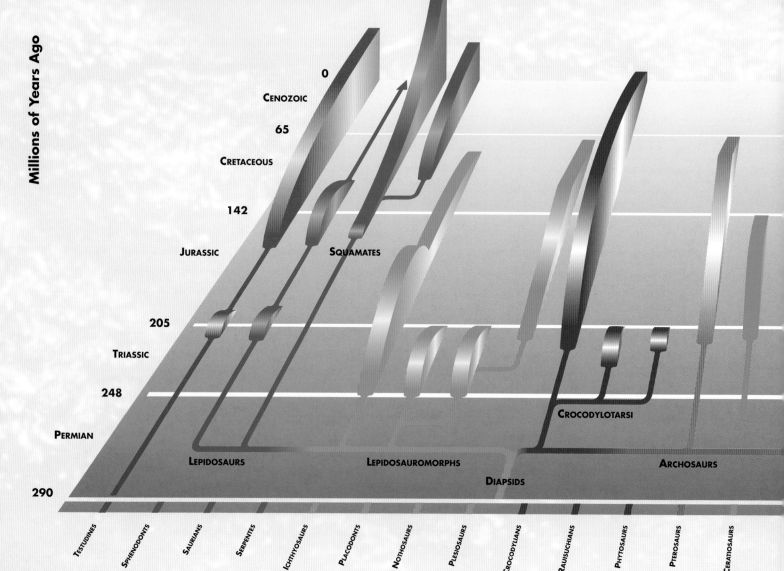

Over the next 50 years, many dinosaurs were discovered in Europe and North America. Various systems of classification were proposed, but it was not until 1887 that another English anatomist, Harry Seeley, recognized that there were two distinct types of hip girdle or pelvis (see p.234). In some dinosaurs, the pelvis was of a normal reptilian build; Seeley called this group the Saurischia, or "lizard-hipped" dinosaurs. In others, the pelvis resembled that of modern birds; he called these the Ornithischia, or "bird-hipped" dinosaurs.

Both groups may have evolved independently from the thecodontians, but it is also possible that the "bird-hipped" species evolved from an early "lizard-hipped" dinosaur.

Dinosaur finds

The first traces of dinosaurs in North America were found in the Triassic rocks of the Connecticut Valley in 1835. They were footprints, recording the passage of great, two-legged creatures 220 million years ago. Edward Hitchcock, Professor of Theology and Geology, and later President, in Amherst College in Massachusetts, described the footprints in 1848; concluding that enormous birds had made them. The first description of dinosaur bones from North America was made by Dr. Joseph Leidy of the Academy of Natural Science in Philadelphia in 1856. He described dinosaur teeth from Montana and two years later the first skeleton of a North American dinosaur (*Hadrosaurus* see p.291).

An immense wealth of dinosaurs was soon to be revealed in the American Mid-West, among the great Jurassic and Cretaceous deposits laid down over 65 million years ago. The driving force for their discovery lay in the rivalry between two leading paleontologists, both wealthy men: Othniel Charles Marsh, of Yale University, and Edward Drinker Cope, of the Academy of Natural Science in Philadelphia.

The first bones of dinosaurs that lived in the Late Jurassic, 150 million years ago, were discovered in 1877 in the Morrison Formation of Colorado, and later in Wyoming. Samples found their way to both Marsh and Cope, and the "dinosaur wars" began. Rival teams of fossil hunters went west. Marsh financed six years of excavation at Como Bluff in Wyoming, where many bones were collected. Cope, too, sent parties to that region, as well as to Colorado.

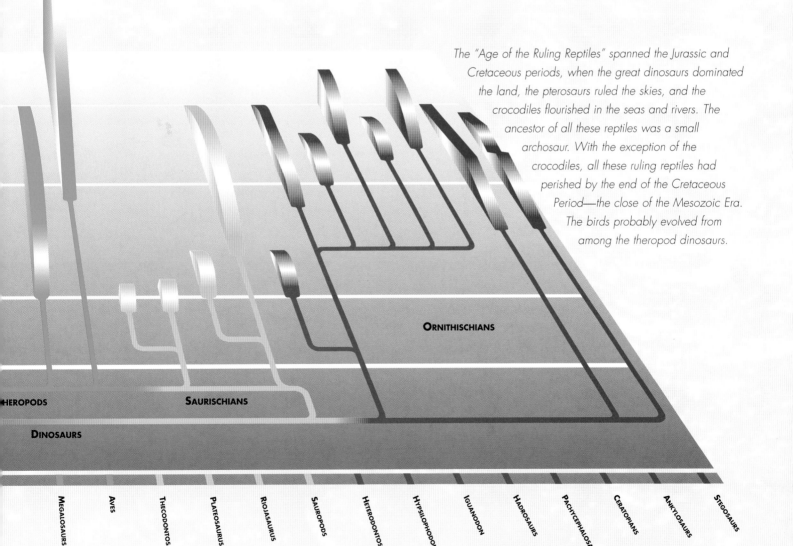

The "Age of the Ruling Reptiles" spanned the Jurassic and Cretaceous periods, when the great dinosaurs dominated the land, the pterosaurs ruled the skies, and the crocodiles flourished in the seas and rivers. The ancestor of all these reptiles was a small archosaur. With the exception of the crocodiles, all these ruling reptiles had perished by the end of the Cretaceous Period—the close of the Mesozoic Era. The birds probably evolved from among the theropod dinosaurs.

ORNITHISCHIANS

THEROPODS

SAURISCHIANS

DINOSAURS

MEGALOSAURS · AVES · THECODONTOSAURUS · PLATEOSAURUS · RIOJASAURUS · SAUROPODS · HETERODONTOSAURIDS · HYPSILOPHODONTIDS · IGUANODON · HADROSAURS · PACHYCEPHALOSAURS · CERATOPIANS · ANKYLOSAURS · STEGOSAURS

From these Late Jurassic sites, many now-famous dinosaurs were described by both men, including *Allosaurus* (see p.261), *Ceratosaurus* (see p.250), *Camarasaurus* (see p.272), *Diplodocus* and *Apatosaurus* (popularly known as *Brontosaurus,* see pp.274–275), *Camptosaurus* (see p.286) and *Stegosaurus* (see p.298).

The richest treasure house of dinosaurs was found in the Late Cretaceous rocks of Montana and Colorado, laid down toward the end of the Mesozoic Era, between 100 and 65 million years ago. Due to the rivalry between Marsh and Cope many creatures were discovered, among them *Ornithomimus* (see p.253), *Nodosaurus* (see p.302), and *Triceratops* (see p.310).

Canada, too, has contributed its share of dinosaurs to the world's museums. The Late Cretaceous deposits of Red Deer River Valley, Alberta, were discovered and explored cooperatively by parties from both the American Museum of Natural History in New York, and the National Museum of Canada, and the Royal Ontario Museum. The valley yielded a rich variety of dinosaurs, especially during the years 1910 to 1917, among them the tyrannosaur *Albertosaurus* (see p.263), the duckbilled dinosaur *Corythosaurus* (see p.295), and the horned ceratopian *Styracosaurus* (see p.319).

The Gobi Desert of Outer Mongolia, central Asia, was first explored by expeditions from the American Museum of Natural History during the years 1922 to 1925. Ironically, it was the search for fossil humans, rather than fossil reptiles, that led to the exploration of the region, which yielded an array of Late Cretaceous beasts, including *Protoceratops* together with its nests and eggs (see p.308), and the saurischian dinosaurs *Oviraptor* (one specimen preserved with a clutch of *Protoceratops'* eggs, see p.244), *Velociraptor,* and *Saurornithoides* (see p.255).

Dinosaurs have been found in South America, Africa, Australia, New Zealand, and Antarctica. The dinosaur localities of the southern hemisphere are increasingly important, with remarkable new finds being made in Argentina.

Perhaps the most famous African locality is Tendaguru in Tanzania, East Africa, where a wealth of Late Jurassic dinosaurs was found, similar to those of the Morrison Formation in the western USA.

Another African site, discovered in 1987 in Niger, south of the Sahara, promises to be a rich source of dinosaur remains. Initial work has unearthed the bones of *Camarasaurus,* one of the giant, plant-eating sauropods, and a giant tyrannosaur *Carcharodontosaurus.*

A worldwide distribution

Although the dinosaurs of the southern hemisphere are less well-known than those of the north, there is little doubt that, in reality, they were just as diverse. Both "lizard-" and "bird-hipped" dinosaurs evolved in the Triassic, when all the continents of the world were still joined together in one super-landmass called Pangaea. Any land animal, including dinosaurs, could have spread throughout the world.

The continents were still joined throughout the Jurassic, and it was not until the Late Cretaceous that there is evidence of different, isolated dinosaur faunas. By then, there were two separate areas of land in the northern hemisphere—Euramerica

DINOSAUR HIPS

When dinosaurs evolved an upright, two-legged posture, they had to evolve a new attachment site for the muscles that swung the powerful hindlimbs forward. Lizard-hipped dinosaurs evolved a downward and forward extension of the pubic bone to which the muscles attach. In bird-hipped dinosaurs, the muscles were attached to either a forward extension of the ilium, or, in later types, to a new "pre-pubic" extension of the pubis.

LIZARD-HIPPED DINOSAUR
(*MASSOPONDYLUS*)

BIRD-HIPPED DINOSAUR
(*MONTANOCERATOPS*)

and Asiamerica. For some reason, many new types of Late Cretaceous dinosaur evolved in Asiamerica, including the hadrosaurs, ornithomimids, troodontids, tyrannosaurs, and protoceratopsids. As a result, older types of dinosaur, such as the iguanodonts, persisted for longer in Euramerica, safe from the competition of their new relatives.

About 300 genera of dinosaur have so far been described, of which about 55 percent are "lizard-hipped" saurischians, and the rest are "bird-hipped" ornithischians. Only 7 percent of known dinosaurs come from Triassic rocks (nearly all saurischians), and 28 percent from Jurassic rocks. The remaining 65 percent come from Cretaceous rocks, and three-quarters of these have been found only in the Late Cretaceous. It is significant that at the end of the Cretaceous, the flowering plants underwent an explosive evolution, diversifying into many new types which adapted to niches all over the world. This new food source may well have led to the evolution of new dinosaur types.

Warm-blooded dinosaurs?

Biologists have long assumed that dinosaurs, like the living reptiles and the ancestral amphibians, were cold-blooded (ectothermal). But recently it has been suggested that they may have been warm-blooded (endothermal), like modern birds and mammals.

Cold-blooded animals rely mainly on the sun for heat and energy. Warm-blooded animals, in contrast, rely on energy from food. There are a number of lines of evidence which are claimed to support the argument for dinosaurs being warm-blooded (ectotherms). Measurements from their trackways has suggested that some were very active predators. Estimated running speeds of up to 40 km/h (30mph) suggest high metabolic rates. Dinosaur remains have been found within the Alaskan Arctic Circle of Cretaceous times and normally only warm blooded animals can tolerate such conditions. The detailed internal structure of dinosaur bones is in many ways more like that of mammals than reptiles. But, this may reflect a fast rate of growth.

It is possible that dinosaurs were intermediate—neither typically cold- nor warm-blooded. Some may have been warm-blooded, but the ratio of body volume to surface area of some of the larger ones would have kept them at fairly constant temperatures anyway.

Mass-extinction of the dinosaurs

The disappearance of the dinosaurs worldwide at the end of the Mesozoic Era is the best-known mass-extinction event of the prehistoric world. But other extinctions took place at or about the same time. The flying pterosaurs, and also the marine ichthyosaurs, plesiosaurs, and mosasaurs, all disappeared at or near the end of the Cretaceous. And several marine invertebrate groups suffered the same fate—ammonites, certain bivalves, and many tiny organisms of the plankton.

Since modern methods of dating rocks are accurate only to within a few hundreds of thousands of years, it is difficult to be certain whether the terrestrial and marine extinctions of the Cretaceous took place at the same time. It seems that the vertebrate extinctions happened gradually. For example, the ichthyosaurs became extinct before the end of the Cretaceous, while the plesiosaurs, pterosaurs, and dinosaurs may have been becoming less common toward the end of that period. These facts suggest some gradual change in the environment taking place worldwide, rather than the popular notion of a cataclysmic event that wiped out huge numbers of creatures.

Sea levels dropped comparatively rapidly during the Late Cretaceous. As a result, the average air temperature dropped, and the climate became more variable worldwide. This could have been the cause of the gradual decline of the pterosaurs and dinosaurs, especially if the dinosaurs depended on an equable environment to maintain their body temperature.

In contrast, the extinction of many types of microscopic marine invertebrates seems to have happened suddenly and simultaneously, at the end of the Cretaceous. They disappeared at precisely the time that the rocks show abnormally high concentrations of several normally rare metals, such as iridium, osmium, and rhodium. This enriched layer has been found in some 50 localities, ranging from North America and Europe to New Zealand, and in deep-sea sediments of the Pacific.

The American scientists Luis and Walter Alvarez pointed out that these metals are present in the same proportions as in meteorites. In 1980 they suggested that a great meteorite, some 6 ml/10 km in diameter, hit Earth at the end of the Cretaceous Period, some 65 million years ago. An intense search for the impact crater ensued, and in 1991 a crater of the right order of size and age was located, buried under nearly half a mile (1 km) of younger sediments at Chicxulub in the Yucatan Peninsula, Mexico. Establishing the size of the crater and how much rock had been excavated by the impact proved difficult, but was eventually achieved by geophysical measurement in 1998.

The Chicxulub meteorite made a hole 5 ml/12 km deep and 60 ml/100 km wide and blasted some 38,400 cu ml/50,000 cu km of pulverized rock into the atmosphere. The rock dust, CO_2 and SO_2 released would have had a considerable impact on global weather; it may have produced an initial cooling followed by marked warming, and caused a breakdown in the food chain. This could well have finally driven vulnerable species, including dinosaurs, to extinction. The regional effect was devastating to the Americas. A tidal wave over half a mile (1 km) high swept all life from coastal areas and wildfire burned the forests further inland and all that lived in them. It probably took more than a million years for conditions to return to normal.

EARLY RULING REPTILES

INFRACLASS ARCHOSAUROMORPHA

Cladistic analysis has suggested that the amniotes can be divided into three groups—the diapsids and anapsids, which form the Eureptilia, and the synapsids. In the Late Permian, around 250 million years ago, diapsid reptiles divided into two groups that subsequently became of particular importance. The archosauromorphs (a name which means "ruling reptile forms") gave rise to the dinosaurs, crocodilians, and birds, and the lepidosauromorphs, which in turn led to the snakes and lizards.

The archosauromorphs include the rhynchosaurs, prolacertiformes, and archosaurs. Of these, the prolacertiformes arose during mid Permian times, the archosaurs at the end of the Permian and the other two groups arose during the Triassic Period.

Most archosauromorphs were well-adapted land-living animals. The long legs of these creatures tended to be placed more directly under the body than is common in other reptiles, which made them more stable and faster moving. Associated with this evolutionary change were improvements in the feet, particularly the articulation of the ankle joints and flexibility of the first digit ("big toe") of the archosaur foot which improved their locomotion.

The Prolacertiformes include the carnivorous protosaurs (the earliest-known members of this infraclass), such as *Protosaurus* of late Permian times, and the plant-eating rhynchosaurs are represented by *Hyperodapedon* from the late Triassic Period.

The most important of the early archosauromorph groups were the Archosauria. The Triassic evolution of the Archosaurs was to change the history of life on land for nearly 200 million years. From the Archosauria radiated the dinosaurs, crocodiles, the flying pterosaurs, and birds.

NAME	*Hyperodapedon*
TIME	Late Triassic
LOCALITY	Asia (India) and Europe (Scotland)
SIZE	4ft/1.3m long

Hyperodapedon (below) was a member of the rhynchosaur group of early reptiles and was especially common in South America and Africa. These creatures were all heavy, barrel-shaped plant-eaters, which thrived from the Middle to Late Triassic. They were the most abundant reptiles of the day.

The success, though short-lived, of *Hyperodapedon* and its rhynchosaur relatives can be attributed to their teeth. There were two broad tooth plates on each side of the upper jaw. Each tooth plate was well-equipped with several rows of teeth, and a groove ran down the middle. The two single tooth rows of the animal's lower jaws fitted into this groove when the mouth was closed, to give a strong chopping action which was well-suited to the animal's vegetarian diet.

Rhynchosaurs would have feasted on seed ferns, which were abundant everywhere during the Triassic Period. But these plants died out at the end of that period, and were replaced by conifers. Rhynchosaurs died out too, and their herbivorous ecological niche was taken by the newly evolved, plant-eating dinosaurs. The "Age of Ruling Reptiles" had begun.

ORDER PROLACERTIFORMES

Prolacertifomes appeared during the Mid Permian Period, but became abundant in the Triassic. Initially they looked like large lizards with long necks, but some developed this tendency to an extreme. They shared many characteristics with archosaurs, such as a long snout and narrow skull and backward curving teeth.

NAME *Protorosaurus*

TIME Late Permian

LOCALITY Europe (Germany)

SIZE up to 6ft 6in/2m long

This lizard-type reptile is the earliest known archosauromorph. *Protosaurus* inhabited the deserts of Europe toward the end of the Permian Period, about 250 million years ago.

Protosaurus would have been an agile, speedy animal. Its long legs were tucked in under its body, allowing it to chase after fast-moving prey—mainly insects. Its neck was made up of seven large and greatly elongated vertebrae.

NAME *Tanystropheus*

TIME Middle Triassic

LOCALITY Asia (Israel) and Europe (Germany and Switzerland)

SIZE 10ft/3m long

The long necks which are characteristic of the protorosaurs reached an extreme in this member of the group. *Tanystropheus'* neck was longer than its body and tail combined. Yet, only 10 vertebrae made up the neck—only three more than in *Protorosaurus*—but each bone was greatly elongated. In fact, when these neck bones were first discovered, they were initially thought to be leg bones.

The shape of *Tanystropheus'* shape is so bizarre and unlikely that some paleontologists believe that this creature would have been unable to support its extremely long neck on land and must have lived in water. But *Tanystropheus* shows no specific adaptations to an aquatic life. Perhaps it lived on the shoreline, dipping its head into the water after fish or shellfish, and crushing them with its peg-like teeth.

SUPERORDER ARCHOSAURIA

The archosaurs were the most spectacular group of "ruling reptiles." They dominated life on Earth during the Mesozoic Era, reigning for more than 180 million years. Flying reptiles, the pterosaurs, ruled the skies (see pp.246–249); dinosaurs ruled the lands (see pp.250–313); and crocodiles—the only surviving archosaurs—invaded the seas and freshwaters (see pp.242–245).

These diverse creatures all shared a common feature—a diapsid skull, with two openings behind each eye (see p.205).

The earliest archosaurs appeared in the Late Permian, more than 250 million years ago. They evolved rapidly into many diverse forms through the Triassic and became extinct by the end of that period. Their evolutionary history was brief (less than 40 million years) but successful and from them arose the ancestors of the ruling reptiles. There were some short lived forms in the Early and Mid Triassic before a major split occurred. One line led to the crccodiles and the other to the dinosaurs and birds.

The remaining Triassic archosaurs that do not belong to either of these groups were previously grouped as the thecodontians but they are now known to be a paraphyletic group from different origins. These basal archosaurs include Early Triassic forms such as the proterosuchids, which took over carnivorous niches which had been occupied in the Permian by animals such as the gorgonopsids. *Euparkeria*, the little archosaur from the Mid Triassic of South Africa is sometimes placed in the orhithosuchids or regarded separately, but it marks the beginning of the first major development of the archosaurs. The rauisuchids, phytosaurs, and stagenolepidids have been recently characterized as basal crutotarsans and grouped with the crocodylomorphs.

These early archosaurs show a general evolutionary trend toward a more upright stance, with the hind limbs in particular being progressively brought in from their former, sprawling position at the side of the body to be oriented more directly beneath the body. This trend was eventually perfected in the ornithosuchians, which could walk upright on two legs.

Family Proterosuchidae

The proterosuchians were the earliest of the archosaurs to appear, and they are known from Late Permian times in Russia (about 250 million years ago). Some proterosuchians were aquatic, crocodile-like animals, while other members of the family were fully adapted land-dwellers. They spread throughout the world during the Triassic Period and died out at the end of that period (about 210 million years ago).

NAME   *Chasmatosaurus*

TIME   Early Triassic

LOCALITY   Africa (South Africa) and Asia (China)

SIZE   6 ft 6 in/2 m long

NAME   *Erythrosuchus*

TIME   Early Triassic

LOCALITY   Africa (South Africa)

SIZE   15 ft/4.5 m long

Chasmatosaurus (formerly named *Proterosuchus*) is the earliest well known archosaur. It looked rather like a modern crocodile, and probably behaved in much the same way. Its robust limbs, each with five toes, were angled out horizontally from the body, resulting in a sprawling, lizard-like gait.

Although *Chasmatosaurus* could walk on land, it probably spent most of its time in rivers, swimming after its fish prey using sinuous movements of the long tail and body. Its jaws were well-equipped with sharp, backwardly curved teeth, each set in a shallow socket, the upper jaw turned down sharply at its tip. There were also teeth on the palate—a primitive feature, lost in later archosaurs.

Erythrosuchus and other members of its family were the largest, land-living predators during the Early and Middle Triassic Period (about 250–230 million years ago). Some of them reached a length of 16 ft/5 m. They must have exerted a profound, selective pressure on the evolution of other terrestrial reptiles. For example, several new types of thecodontian with protective body armor appeared around this time, such as the aetosaurs (Family Stagenolepididae) and phytosaurs.

Erythrosuchus had a large head, up to 3 ft 3 in/1 m long, and its powerful jaws were filled with sharp, conical teeth. It was a top predator which probably preyed on the large herbivorous dicynodonts of the time.

Its legs were held rather more directly beneath its bulky body than those of the sprawling *Chasmatosaurus*, suggesting that this active predator could move more effectively on land.

Family Rauisuchidae

This group of crocodile-like archosaurs were the major carnivorous land-dwellers of the time, some of them growing up to 20 ft/6 m long. They evolved in the Mid-Triassic and survived to the end of that period. They are known from the Americas, East Africa and western Europe.

Not only were the hind limbs of rauisuchids held more directly beneath the body, but an effective ankle joint had been developed, together with a heel that enhanced the leverage and flexure of the feet during walking.

NAME	*Ticinosuchus*
TIME	Middle Triassic
LOCALITY	Europe (Switzerland)
SIZE	10 ft/3 m long

The back of this medium-sized rauisuchiad was lightly armored, with a double row of small, bony plates; the long tail was also armored, above and below. From the structure of the hips, and the ball-and-socket joints with which the thigh bones (femurs) connect, paleontologists can tell that the hind legs of *Ticinosuchus* were held almost directly beneath its body, unlike the sprawl position in earlier archosaurs.

In addition, the ankle joints of *Ticinosuchus* and other rauisuchids had become adapted for walking on land, and part of one of the foot bones had developed into a heel. This was an important innovation, since a strong tendon (the equivalent of our Achilles tendon) could attach to the heel, and serve as a lever to flex the foot.

Until the development of the heel, it had been the fifth, or outer, foot bone (metatarsal), together with the long fifth toe, that helped to lever the foot off the ground. Animals with heels could afford to reduce the length of the fifth toe. In some, it was lost completely; in others, it was shortened so that it did not reach the ground at all.

Family Phytosauridae

The phytosaurs were aquatic carnivores that are known only from the Late Triassic Period (about 210 million years ago).

With their heavily armored, crocodile-like bodies, up to 16 ft/5 m long, it is likely that the phytosaur family were the dominant predators in the rivers of the northern hemisphere during this period.

Family Phytosauridae represents a classic case of parallel evolution with the true crocodiles; both types of reptile are descended from the same ancestral archosaur stock, and each assumed independently the same general structure in response to the same way of life and environmental factors. They differed from the crocodiles in having nostrils above the eyes instead of at the tip of the snout.

NAME	*Rutiodon*
TIME	Late Triassic
LOCALITY	Europe (Germany and Switzerland) and North America (Arizona, New Mexico, North Carolina, and Texas)
SIZE	10 ft/3 m long

Rutiodon (below) was a typical member of the phytosaur family. Its back, flanks, and tail were heavily armored with bony plates. It had a long snout like a modern gavial (a modern crocodile found only in Indian rivers), and its jaws were filled with sharp teeth, which would have been ideal tools for catching and eating fish. *Rutiodon* probably also ate other reptiles, since their remains have been found preserved in the body cavities of some fossilized phytosaurs.

Rutiodon and its relatives bore a striking resemblance to modern-day crocodiles. However, the immediate feature that distinguishes the *Rutiodon* from modern crocodiles is the position of the nostrils. In phytosaurs, the nostrils were elevated on a bony bump set far back on the animals' snout, near the eyes. However, in modern crocodiles the nostrils are positioned at the tip of the snout.

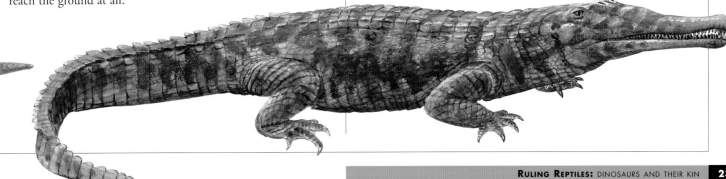

Family Stagenolepididae

Unlike all their archosaur relatives, the stagenolepidids, or aetosaurs, as they are more commonly known, were plant-eating archosaurs. They had small, leaf-shaped teeth, and their deep, bulky bodies were encased in a heavy, bony armor. Looking like short-snouted crocodiles, aetosaurs were an offshoot from the main archosaur line, and are known only from the Late Triassic of Europe and North and South America.

NAME *Stagonolepis*
TIME Late Triassic
LOCALITY Europe (Scotland)
SIZE 10 ft/3 m long

The deep body of *Stagonolepis* is typical of the herbivorous aetosaurs, and was developed to accommodate the longer intestines needed to digest plant food. A slow-moving browser, *Stagonolepis* also needed its heavy body armor to protect itself from attack by its agile, carnivorous, thecodontian relatives.

Stagonolepis had a small head for its size, only 10 in/25 cm out of a total length of 10 ft/3 m. It had no teeth at the front of its foreshortened jaws, but the peg-like teeth at the back would have dealt effectively with tough plants such as horsetails, ferns, and the newly evolved cycads. The snout was flattened and almost pig-like, a good shape for rooting in the undergrowth.

NAME *Desmatosuchus*
TIME Late Triassic
LOCALITY North America (Texas)
SIZE 16 ft/5 m long

This large North American aetosaur had particularly heavy body armor. Quadrangular plates covered its back and tail and part of its belly, while long spines, up to 18 in/45 cm long, projected from its shoulders. It had a small head, pig-like snout, and weak, peg-like teeth suited to plant-eating.

Family Ornithosuchidae

Paleontologists are undecided about the relation of ornithosuchids to dinosaurs. They share some characteristics of the limbs, but in other ways are closer to crocodiles and are therefore placed with them in the Crurotarsi. They are known from the Late Triassic in Scotland and South America.

NAME *Euparkeria*
TIME Early Triassic
LOCALITY Africa (South Africa)
SIZE up to 2 ft/60 cm long

The powerful hind legs and long tail that had evolved in the ancestral archosaurs gave rise to a new stance in their descendants, the ornithosuchians. *Euparkeria* was an early member of this group. It was a small, slimly built creature, with light bony plates down the center of its back and tail. The hind legs were longer than the forelegs by about one-third.

Although it spent most of its time on all-fours, this ornithosuchid was capable of rising up on its hind legs to run away from danger. Its long tail, which made up about half of the total body length, would have been stretched out behind to balance it at the hips as it ran. This two-legged (bipedal) stance was to become the norm among the carnivorous dinosaurs that made their first appearance at the end of the Triassic (see pp.250–253).

Euparkeria's skull was large, but its weight was reduced by several wide openings between the bones. Its teeth were well-suited to a carnivorous diet—long and sharp, curved slightly backward and serrated along the edges.

NAME	*Ornithosuchus*
TIME	Late Triassic
LOCALITY	Europe (Scotland)
SIZE	13 ft/4 m long

At one time, *Ornithosuchus* was regarded by some paleontologists as a primitive dinosaur. However, it is now thought to be more closely related to the crocodiles.

One feature of *Ornithosuchus* that led to its misidentification as an early dinosaur was its stance. This was certainly dinosaur-like—its hind legs were held vertically beneath its body, a position that allowed it to walk upright. Moving about on all-fours was probably its more usual method of locomotion, however; the faster upright stance would have been reserved for a speedy escape in case of emergency, as with *Euparkeria*.

The primitive features of *Ornithosuchus* include a double row of bony plates down its back; a short, broad pelvis, which was attached to the backbone by a weak arrangement of only three vertebrae; and five toes on each hind foot. However, its skull is advanced, and strikingly similar in structure to that of the large theropods, such as *Tyrannosaurus*.

NAME	*Lagosuchus*
TIME	Middle Triassic
LOCALITY	South America (Argentina)
SIZE	1 ft/30 cm long

The diminutive *Lagosuchus* and its relatives are the most dinosaur-like of all the known ornithosuchids. The resemblance is based mainly on the structure of its hip bones and ankle joints and on the long, slim hind legs, in which the shin bones are almost twice the length of the thigh bones.

This structure of the leg bones is a feature of fast-running animals, which can be particularly well-seen in the bipedal dinosaurs. Like the other ornithosuchids, *Lagosuchus* would have been capable of rising up on its hind legs. It is no longer believed, however, as it once was, that *Lagosuchus* is the most likely ancestor of the dinosaurs.

Family Uncertain

The single species *Longisquama insignis*, first described in 1970, has some unusual features, which distinguish it from any named family. Paleontologists are reluctant to name a new family for a single species and would rather wait for further information and specimens before making a taxonomic judgement.

NAME	*Longisquama*
TIME	Early Triassic
LOCALITY	Asia (Turkestan)
SIZE	6 in/15 cm long

A curious, lizard-like creature, *Longisquama* was a tiny ornithosuchid. It cannot be placed in any of the known suborders or families of the group. Its body was covered in overlapping, keeled scales. A remarkable row of tall scales, stiff and V-shaped in cross-section, rose from the back. Their function is unknown. They could have been display structures, used either for attracting a mate or for warning away rivals. Other suggestions are that they could have been used for gliding through the air, or as heat-exchange devices; they may even have been an early stage in the evolution of feathers.

CROCODILES

SUPERORDER CROCODYLOMORPHA

The crocodiles and their close relatives are the only representatives of the archosaurs, or ruling reptiles, alive today. Remarkably consistent in structure throughout their evolution, crocodiles have changed little since they first appeared in Mid-Triassic times, some 230 million years ago.

The crocodiles probably evolved from an ornithosuchian type of archosaur (see pp.240–241). Although modern crocodiles are more at home in water than on land, they evolved as small, terrestrial carnivores, capable of running upright on their long, slim hind legs, unlike the short limbs of their modern relatives.

Crocodiles have long, low, massive skulls, to resist the pressure created by the powerful snapping of their jaws. The muscles attach far back on the skull, allowing the jaws to open wide. A secondary palate of bone separates the mouth from the nasal passages, allowing the animal to breathe while eating.

Family Sphenosuchidae

The sphenosuchians are the earliest known crocodiles, making their appearance in the middle of the Triassic Period. So similar are they to the lightly built ornithosuchians (see pp.240–241) that they were long regarded as belonging to that group. These early crocodiles were built for a life on land.

NAME *Gracilisuchus*

TIME Middle Triassic

LOCALITY South America (Argentina)

SIZE 1 ft/30 cm long

This tiny creature was classified with the ornithosuchians until the early 1980s. Like them, it had a lightly built body and a disproportionately large head, and it could run erect on its slim hind legs. However, the structure of its skull, neck vertebrae and ankle joints place it firmly among the crocodiles.

Gracilisuchus was a well-adapted land animal, protected by a double row of bony plates that interlocked down the length of its backbone, to the tip of the tail. It probably chased after small lizards on its long hind legs, despatching them in its powerful jaws, armed with sharp, recurved teeth.

Family Saltoposuchidae

Although true crocodiles did not appear until the early Jurassic, there were some close relatives in the Late Triassic Period, all of which are now placed in the Superorder Crocodylomorpha. Some of these close relatives, such as the saltoposuchids, appear at first to be most unlike crocodiles. However, they do have in common some important features which are considered to be diagnostically crocodilian.

NAME *Terrestrisuchus*

TIME Late Triassic

LOCALITY Europe (Wales)

SIZE 10 in/50 cm long

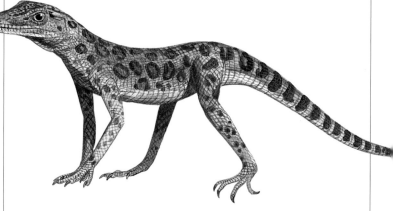

Terrestrisuchus was smaller and much more delicately built than *Gracilisuchus* (left). Its body was also shorter, with extremely long, slim limbs and greatly elongated foot bones in the hind legs. The tail was almost twice the length of the body and head combined. Its head was more crocodile-like—longer and lower—than that of its earlier relative.

From its light build—almost like that of a greyhound, although it was completely unrelated to that mammal— it seems that *Terrestrisuchus* must have sprinted over the dry landscape of Late Triassic Europe, snapping up insects and small lizards in its elongated jaws. It probably ran mostly on four legs, but could easily have risen upright to move even faster, using its long tail to help it keep its balance.

ORDER CROCODYLIA

Today, crocodiles are a small group of eight genera, comprising crocodiles, alligators, and gavials, all found in the tropics—a tiny vestige of a once abundant and highly successful group. Marine forms were particularly successful in the Jurassic when they competed with other marine reptiles. In the Tertiary, some became fully terrestrial, competing with mammals and giant birds for the top carnivore niches in South America.

Family Protosuchidae

Although their skulls were slightly more crocodile-like in appearance, the protosuchians were long-legged land-dwellers like the sphenosuchians. Some may have developed a secondary palate separating the mouth and nasal passages, but made of a fleshy membrane, not the bony palate of later crocodiles.

NAME	Protosuchus
TIME	Early Jurassic
LOCALITY	North America (Arizona)
SIZE	3 ft 3 in/1 m long

This terrestrial crocodile's skull was more crocodile-like than that of the earlier sphenosuchids. The short jaws broadened out at the base of the snout into a fairly wide area at the back of the skull, providing a large surface to which the jaw muscles could attach. This increased the gape and the force with which the jaws could be closed. A pair of canine-like teeth at the front of the lower jaw fitted into notches on either side of the upper jaw when the mouth was closed—as seen in modern crocodiles.

DIVISION MESOEUCROCODYLIA

Most of the fossil crocodiles belong to this group, though they include some that are not closely related, which is recognized by their being placed in this division along with the eusuchians.

They evolved in the Early Jurassic, most probably from the protosuchids (left); the last known member of the division dates from the relatively recent Miocene Epoch, 15 million years ago. Most of them were either fully adapted land-dwellers, like their predecessors, or semi-aquatic in their habits.

One terrestrial family, the sebecids, inhabited South America during Early Tertiary times. Their teeth were saw-edged and compressed into long blades, like those of large carnosaur dinosaurs. This has led some paleontologists to speculate that they were the dominant predators of the day, since no large, carnivorous mammal had reached South America at the time.

Only four families had a fully aquatic lifestyle, of which the teleosaurs and metriorhynchs are probably the best known.

NAME	Teleosaurus
TIME	Early Jurassic
LOCALITY	Europe (France)
SIZE	10 ft/3 m long

Teleosaurus was a member of one of the four families of Mesozoic crocodiles that adopted the sea as their home and shared the seas of the world with the ichthyosaurs and plesiosaurs throughout the Jurassic Period and into the Cretaceous. It probably looked similar to the modern gavial of India's northern rivers.

The body of this ancient marine crocodile was long and slim, its back heavily armored like that of a modern crocodile. Its powerful jaws were tremendously narrow and elongated, in comparison with those of its land-living relatives, and lined with numerous sharp teeth. These interlocked when the mouth was closed, to form an ideal trap for catching slippery fish or squid.

Teleosaurus' forelegs were particularly short—only half the length of the hind legs—and were probably held flat against the flanks during swimming to give a more hydrodynamic shape. Sinuous movements of the body and long, narrow tail would have moved *Teleosaurus* rapidly through water, like a modern aquatic lizard.

NAME *Metriorhynchus*

TIME Middle to Late Jurassic

LOCALITY Europe (England and France) and South America (Chile)

SIZE 10 ft/3 m long

Metriorhynchus and other members of the metriorhynch family were the most specialized of all the aquatic crocodiles. They had dispensed with the heavy back armor of their relatives, because such protection was unnecessary in their aquatic environment. The loss of the armor had the additional advantage of making them more maneuverable, allowing the sinuous movements of the body which were necessary for swimming. *Metriorhynchus'* limbs were transformed into paddle-like flippers, the hind pair longer than the front pair. And their tails had developed a large, fish-like fin which could be moved from side to side in order to propel the animal smoothly through the water. This fin was supported by the sharply downturned tip of the animal's backbone. Exactly the same adaptations were developed independently by the ichthyosaurs (see pp.222–225), a group of fish-like reptiles.

Geosaurus was another member of the metriorhynch family, found in Late Jurassic and Early Cretaceous sediments in South America and Europe. It was about the same length as its relative *Metriorhynchus*, but even more streamlined in shape. One excellent fossil specimen of *Geosaurus* from southern Germany was outlined by a fine film of carbon. This provided invaluable information for paleontologists, showing the shape of the fleshy limbs in life. The front flippers were considerably shorter than the hind pair, and the tail fin was particularly large. The tip of the backbone bent even more sharply into the lower lobe than did the backbone of *Metriorhynchus*.

NAME *Bernissartia*

TIME Early Cretaceous

LOCALITY Europe (Belgium and England)

SIZE 2 ft/60 cm long

This crocodile was tiny in comparison with its relatives. It lived along the shores of the shallow Wealden Lake that stretched from southeast England into Belgium during Early Cretaceous times, some 130 million years ago.

Bernissartia led a semi-aquatic life, judging by the two types of teeth in its jaws. Those at the front were long and pointed, as if for catching fish, while those at the back were broad and flat, as if for crushing shellfish, or even the bones of dead animals.

SUBORDER EUSUCHIA

This group of true crocodiles includes the 21 living species of modern crocodile, the seven species of alligator and caiman, and the single species of gavial. Crocodiles and alligators appeared in their modern forms in the Late Cretaceous. But their ancestors evolved at least 80 million years before that, in the Late Jurassic. They probably descended from among the semi-aquatic mesoeucrocodylians.

The eusuchians were once a much more abundant and widespread group than they are today. They lived in the swamps, rivers and lakes of the late Mesozoic Era. They were contemporaries of the great dinosaurs, and most probably preyed on them when they strayed too close to the water's edge.

Sturdy, well-armored bodies, massive heads, powerful jaws, and meat-shearing teeth—these weapons of the crocodile would have been used to overpower even a large dinosaur. Once it had been dragged into the water, the crocodile could have held it under in a vice-like grip; the secondary bony palate allowed the crocodile to open its mouth without inhaling water.

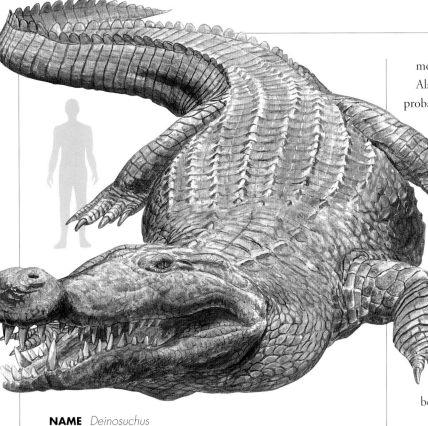

mouths underwater to seize prey without swallowing water. Also in common with its modern counterparts, *Deinosuchus* probably swallowed stones. These would have remained in the stomach to act as stabilizing ballast in the water.

Some paleontologists, however, dispute this account of *Deinosuchus'* lifestyle. They suggest that *Deinosuchus* was smaller than the measurements of its skull seem to suggest and was in fact a short-bodied, long-legged predator that lived on land. Until more fossil remains of the skeleton are found, the way of life of this gargantuan crocodile will remain uncertain.

Gigantic crocodiles were not confined to the Mesozoic Era. *Rhamphosuchus* was a gavial known from the Pliocene deposits of India. Only part of its jawbone has been found, but on the basis of this find it is estimated that this creature may have been the same size as *Deinosuchus*.

NAME	*Deinosuchus*
TIME	Late Cretaceous
LOCALITY	North America (Texas)
SIZE	possibly 49 ft/15 m long

Only the skull of this immense crocodile (above) has been found, and this alone measured more than 6 ft 6 in/2 m in length. Assuming *Deinosuchus* had the same body proportions as those of other crocodiles, its overall length is judged to be just under 50 ft/15.2 m—several times bigger than most of its relatives. The name *Deinosuchus* reflects this imposing size: it means "terrible crocodile." It is also sometimes known as *Phobosuchus*, meaning "horror crocodile."

Deinosuchus lived in the swamps of Texas toward the end of the Cretaceous Period. For food it probably ambushed passing dinosaurs, lying very still and grabbing its prey in the same way that the modern Nile crocodile seizes mammals and birds that come to the water's edge to drink. Unlike earlier crocodilians, all eusuchians such as *Deinosuchus* had a secondary bony roof (palate) to the mouth. This advanced feature is clearly advantageous to aquatic predators because it allows them to open their

NAME	*Pristichampsus*
TIME	Eocene
LOCALITY	Europe (Germany) and North America (Wyoming)
SIZE	10 ft/3 m long

A number of heavily armored eusuchians lived on land during Tertiary times. *Pristichampsus* (below) was typical of these terrestrial crocodiles. It had long legs well-suited to running and its feet had hooves instead of claws—an additional adaptation to its terrestrial lifestyle. It would have fed on the abundant mammals that had recently evolved, and that had replaced the dinosaurs throughout the world.

Pristichampsus' fearsome teeth were well-suited to its carnivorous diet: they were sharp and flattened from side to side with saw-edges, rather like steak knives. Such teeth were almost identical to those of the largest carnivorous dinosaurs, such as *Tyrannosaurus* or *Albertosaurus*. When isolated teeth of *Pristichampsus* were found in Tertiary deposits, paleontologists at first thought they belonged to such theropod dinosaurs, and mistakenly took them as evidence that these great creatures had survived into Tertiary times.

FLYING REPTILES

ORDER PTEROSAURIA

The first group of vertebrates to take to the air as a way of life were the pterosaurs. These flying reptiles flew on "wings" made of skin, which were attached along the length of the greatly elongated, fourth fingers of each hand, and rejoined the body at thigh-level.

These flying reptiles evolved in Late Triassic times, some 70 million years before the first-known bird, *Archaeopteryx*, appeared (see p.318). They thrived throughout the Jurassic and early part of the Cretaceous, diversifying into many forms, among them the largest flying creatures of all time. Then the group began to decline, its last members becoming extinct at the end of the Mesozoic Era. Pterosaur remains have been found all over the world, except in Antarctica, mostly in marine deposits.

There are two suborders of pterosaur (below). The earliest and most primitive types are the rhamphorhynchs; the later types include the more familiar flying reptiles—the pterodactyls.

SUBORDER RHAMPHORHYNCHOIDEA

The earliest-known pterosaurs were already advanced flyers by the Late Triassic Period, 190 million years ago. They flourished worldwide until their extinction at the end of the Jurassic.

NAME *Eudimorphodon*
TIME Late Triassic
LOCALITY Europe (Italy)
SIZE 2 ft 5 in/75 cm wingspan

Eudimorphodon is well-known from remains preserved in marine rocks of northern Italy. It was a typical rhamphorhynch, with a short neck and a bony tail, which made up about half the animal's length of 2 ft 4 in/70 cm. The head was large, but lightweight, owing to the two pairs of openings in its diapsid skull.

The membranous flaps of skin that made up *Eudimorphodon*'s wings were attached to the enormously elongated fourth finger of each hand. This finger was composed of four extra-long finger bones (phalanges), and was attached to the wrist by an elongated hand bone (metacarpal). The wings joined the body on each side at the thighs. Another small flying membrane also ran from the bones of each wrist to the base of the animal's neck.

Eudimorphodon was evidently an active flyer, capable of flapping its wings like a modern bird. The sternum, or breastbone, was developed into a broad, flattened plate, to which the powerful flight muscles attached, although the keel was low in comparison to the great keel of modern flying birds.

The long tail would have been held out rigidly during flight, its vertebrae lashed together by bony tendons into an inflexible rod, which counterbalanced the animal's comparatively heavy forequarters. As in many other rhamphorhynchs, there was a vertical, diamond-shaped flap at the tip of the tail, which most probably functioned as a rudder during flight.

The short jaws of *Eudimorphodon* were armed with two kinds of teeth. There were long, peg-like teeth at the front of the mouth, and short, broad teeth at the back. This pterosaur probably flew low over the sea, its large eyes trained on the surface to spot its fish prey.

NAME *Dimorphodon*
TIME Early Jurassic
LOCALITY Europe (England)
SIZE 4 ft/1.2 m wingspan

Dimorphodon had the disproportionately large head typical of the rhamphorhynchs. It measured about 8 in/20 cm long, about a quarter of the total body length. But it had a remarkable puffin-like shape, deep and narrow, unlike that of its relatives. There seems to be no structural reason for this, since the teeth show that the jaws were simple. Perhaps the shape of the head represents some type of display structure for territorial or courtship behavior, like the showy heads of modern hornbills or toucans.

The walking method of pterosaurs has long been debated. Based on studies of *Dimorphodon*'s hips and legs, some paleontologists believe that they had an erect, bird-like stance, with the legs directly under the body, so that they could run on their toes quite quickly.

But finds of other types of pterosaur in 1986 indicate that perhaps *Dimorphodon* was an exception. These recent finds show that the upper leg bones splayed out sideways from the hips, which could only have resulted in a clumsy, sprawling, bat-like gait. It has been suggested that pterosaurs spent much of their time hanging from cliffs and branches, using their clawed fingers and toes to reach these vantage points, from which they could then launch themselves.

NAME *Rhamphorhynchus*

TIME Late Jurassic

LOCALITY Europe (Germany) and Africa (Tanzania)

SIZE 3 ft 3 in / 1 m wingspan

This pterosaur is particularly well known because it was preserved in the fine-grained limestones of Solnhofen in southern Germany which also yielded specimens of the earliest known bird, *Archaeopteryx*, complete with impressions of its feathers (see p.318).

Similarly, the fine structure of *Rhamphorhynchus'* wings, made of membranous skin, has been preserved in these limestones. Microscopic study reveals that thin fibers ran from the front to the back of the wings, strengthening them—a comparable structure to the radiating fingers that support the wings of a modern bat.

Rhamphorhynchus had long, narrow jaws filled with sharp teeth that pointed outward, like the barbs on a fishing spear. Fish remains have been found in the crop and stomach of some specimens; its habit was probably to skim over the water, its long tail held out for stability, snapping up fish in its jaws.

NAME *Scaphognathus*

TIME Late Jurassic

LOCALITY Europe (England)

SIZE 3 ft 3 in / 1 m wingspan

Scaphognathus, although similar to *Rhamphorhynchus* has a shorter head, long teeth and a blunter tip to its jaws. It is not clear whether it was an insect feeder or a fish catcher.

The skull of one specimen of this typical rhamphorhynch is sufficiently well-preserved for the brain cavity to be studied by scientists. The size of the brain cavity revealed that *Scaphognathus* had a much larger brain in comparison to that of other similar-sized reptiles. Its brain was almost as large as that of a modern bird.

Paleontologists have studied the relative sizes of the areas of the brain that controlled various senses. They conclude that *Scaphognathus*, and presumably all its relatives, had excellent eyesight, but a poor sense of smell.

The cerebellum and associated lobes in the brain were highly developed, indicating agility of movement, which supports the theory that small pterosaurs made active flapping movements, like small modern birds.

NAME *Sordes*

TIME Late Jurassic

LOCALITY Asia (Kazakhstan)

SIZE 1 ft 6 in / 50 cm wingspan

For a long time paleontologists have argued about whether carnivorous dinosaurs and pterosaurs were endothermic or warm-blooded. The active, predatory life of both these types of ruling reptile would suggest that they had a high metabolic rate, and could control their body temperature.

To support this theory, some paleontologists have suggested that both dinosaurs and pterosaurs were covered in an insulating layer of down or hair, as an aid to regulating their body temperature. In the case of dinosaurs, no such evidence has ever been found. However, a find in 1971 seemed to confirm the theory for the pterosaurs. A specimen of *Sordes pilosus* was discovered, southeast of the Ural Mountains. The creature's body appeared, from the impressions in the fine-grained deposits, to be covered in a pelt of dense fur while the tail and wings were naked.

Although the exact nature of the hair that covered *Sordes pilosus* has not yet been confirmed, presumably it is different from mammalian hair in detail, but performed a similar function—to act as an insulation and keep the body warm. Like bird feathers, the pterosaur hair probably evolved from reptile body scales.

NAME *Anurognathus*

TIME Late Jurassic

LOCALITY Europe (Germany)

SIZE 1 ft/30 cm wingspan

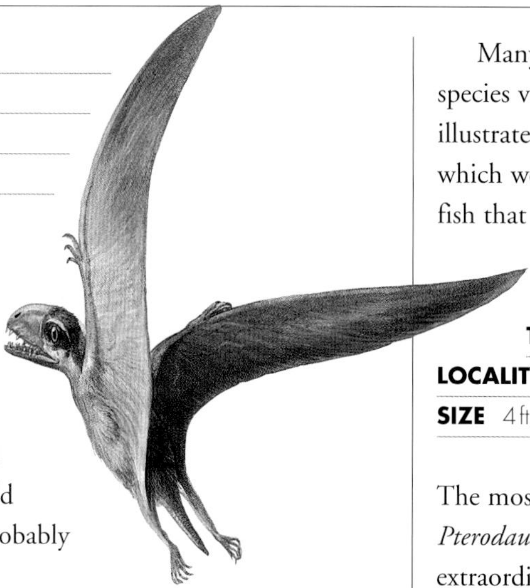

This comparatively small rhamphorhynch had a deep, narrow head with short jaws, which were filled with strong, peg-like teeth, suited to crushing and grinding. This structure could suggest that *Anurognathus* probably lived on a diet of insects.

Unlike other rhamphorhynchs, *Anurognathus* had a short tail, and this feature, combined with the small body size, would have made it highly maneuverable when in flight chasing after its fast-moving prey.

SUBORDER PTERODACTYLOIDEA

The pterodactyls are the most familiar of the flying reptiles. They were already established in Late Jurassic times, when their relatives, the rhamphorhynchs, became extinct. The pterodactyls continued through the Cretaceous, although only a few types survived to the end of that period.

These pterosaurs had the same general structure as the earlier rhamphorhynchs, but the tail was shorter, the neck longer and the skull more elongate.

The suborder Pterodactyloidea ranged from some of the smallest known pterosaurs to some of the largest flying vertebrates that ever lived.

NAME *Pterodactylus*

TIME Late Jurassic

LOCALITY Africa (Tanzania) and Europe (England, France, and Germany)

SIZE up to 2 ft 5 in/75 cm wingspan

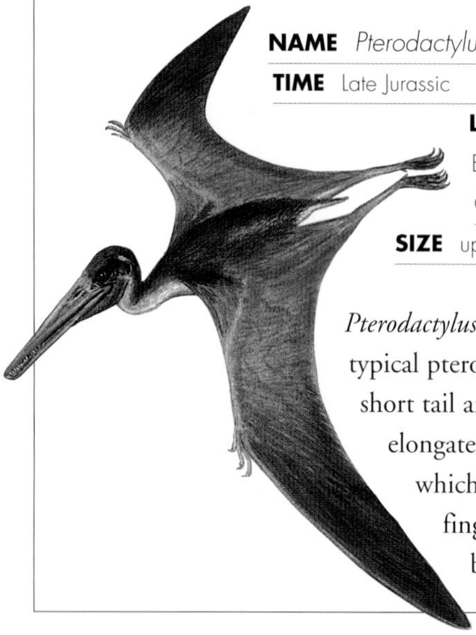

Pterodactylus demonstrates all of the typical pterodactyl features. It had a short tail and a long neck, and greatly elongated hand bones (metacarpals), which, with the long fourth fingers, supported the creature's broad wings.

Many species of *Pterodactylus* have been discovered, each species varying in the size and shape of the head. The species illustrated here, *Pterodactylus kochi*, had long, narrow jaws, which were lined with sharp teeth with which it devoured the fish that were its habitual prey.

NAME *Pterodaustro*

TIME Late Jurassic

LOCALITY South America (Argentina)

SIZE 4 ft/1.2 m wingspan

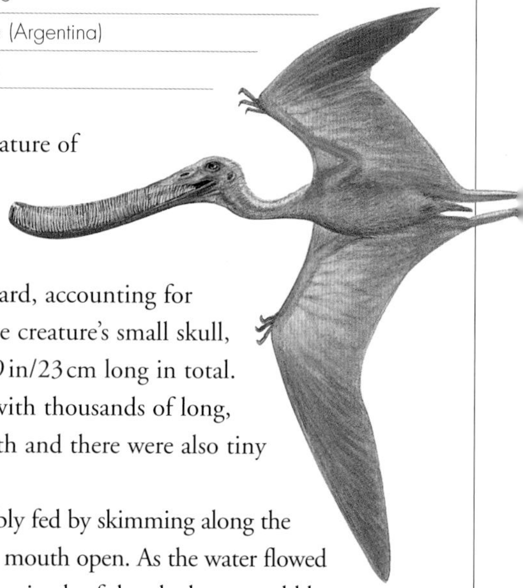

The most remarkable feature of *Pterodaustro* was its extraordinary jaws. They were elongated, slender and curved upward, accounting for most of the length of the creature's small skull, which measured about 9 in/23 cm long in total. The lower jaw bristled with thousands of long, fine, densely packed teeth and there were also tiny teeth in the upper jaw.

This pterosaur probably fed by skimming along the surface of the sea with its mouth open. As the water flowed through its jaws, the tiny animals of the plankton would have been enmeshed on the sieve-like teeth—a feeding method which can be compared with that of a modern baleen whale.

NAME *Cearadactylus*

TIME Early Cretaceous

LOCALITY South America (Brazil)

SIZE 13 ft/4 m wingspan

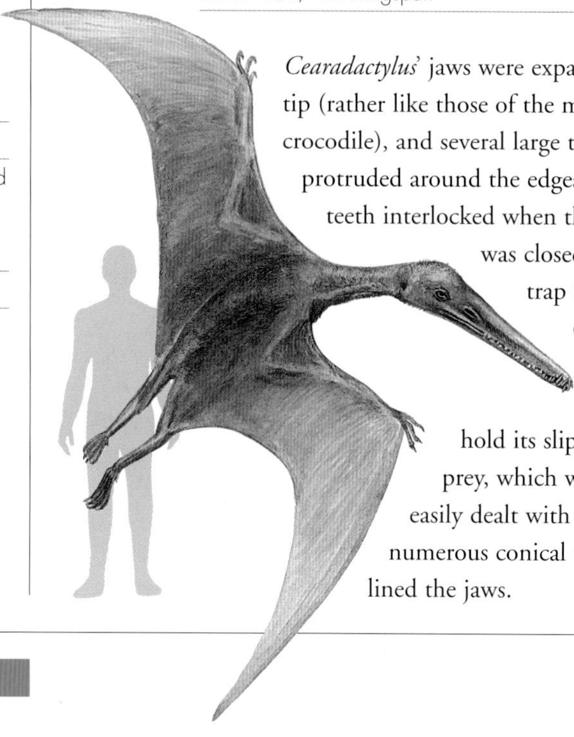

Cearadactylus' jaws were expanded at the tip (rather like those of the modern gavial crocodile), and several large teeth protruded around the edges. These teeth interlocked when the mouth was closed, forming a trap in which *Cearadactylus* could tightly hold its slippery fish prey, which was then easily dealt with by the numerous conical teeth that lined the jaws.

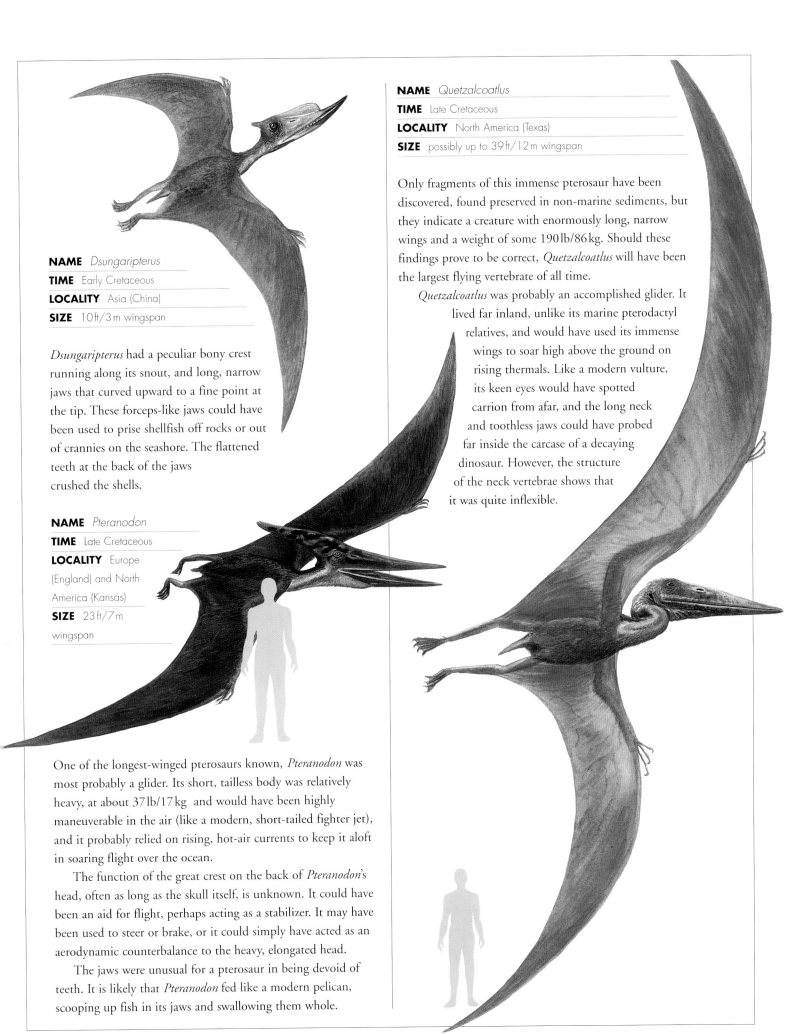

NAME *Dsungaripterus*
TIME Early Cretaceous
LOCALITY Asia (China)
SIZE 10 ft/3 m wingspan

Dsungaripterus had a peculiar bony crest running along its snout, and long, narrow jaws that curved upward to a fine point at the tip. These forceps-like jaws could have been used to prise shellfish off rocks or out of crannies on the seashore. The flattened teeth at the back of the jaws crushed the shells.

NAME *Pteranodon*
TIME Late Cretaceous
LOCALITY Europe (England) and North America (Kansas)
SIZE 23 ft/7 m wingspan

One of the longest-winged pterosaurs known, *Pteranodon* was most probably a glider. Its short, tailless body was relatively heavy, at about 37 lb/17 kg and would have been highly maneuverable in the air (like a modern, short-tailed fighter jet), and it probably relied on rising, hot-air currents to keep it aloft in soaring flight over the ocean.

The function of the great crest on the back of *Pteranodon*'s head, often as long as the skull itself, is unknown. It could have been an aid for flight, perhaps acting as a stabilizer. It may have been used to steer or brake, or it could simply have acted as an aerodynamic counterbalance to the heavy, elongated head.

The jaws were unusual for a pterosaur in being devoid of teeth. It is likely that *Pteranodon* fed like a modern pelican, scooping up fish in its jaws and swallowing them whole.

NAME *Quetzalcoatlus*
TIME Late Cretaceous
LOCALITY North America (Texas)
SIZE possibly up to 39 ft/12 m wingspan

Only fragments of this immense pterosaur have been discovered, found preserved in non-marine sediments, but they indicate a creature with enormously long, narrow wings and a weight of some 190 lb/86 kg. Should these findings prove to be correct, *Quetzalcoatlus* will have been the largest flying vertebrate of all time.

Quetzalcoatlus was probably an accomplished glider. It lived far inland, unlike its marine pterodactyl relatives, and would have used its immense wings to soar high above the ground on rising thermals. Like a modern vulture, its keen eyes would have spotted carrion from afar, and the long neck and toothless jaws could have probed far inside the carcase of a decaying dinosaur. However, the structure of the neck vertebrae shows that it was quite inflexible.

CARNIVOROUS DINOSAURS

SUBORDER THEROPODA

The great reptilian order of "lizard-hipped" dinosaurs, the Saurischia, can be divided into two distinct groups (suborders) on the basis of what they ate. The plant-eaters belong to the Sauropodomorpha (see pp.266–277) and the flesh-eaters belong to the Theropoda.

INFRAORDER CERATOSAURIA

Traditionally, carnivorous theropods were subdivided (into infraorders) according to size: large, massively-built predators (see pp.258–265); medium-sized carnivores with a killing claw on each foot (see pp.254–257); and small, lightweight hunters, the ceratosaurs, with thin-walled, hollow bones that made up not only their tails, but most of their delicately built bodies. Their inter-relationships, however, are not at all clear, and different classifications have been produced.

Family Ceratosauridae

A small horn on the snout characterizes this family. They lived in North America and East Africa in Late Jurassic times. Similarities to megalosaurs have led to debate about their classification. They are sometimes included with the carnosaurs.

NAME	Ceratosaurus
TIME	Late Jurassic
LOCALITY	North America (Colorado and Wyoming)
SIZE	20 ft/6 m long

The function of the horn on the snout is unclear. It may have been for defense or sexual display. *Ceratosaurus* was an active predator. Its massive jaws had sharp, curved teeth. The short arms had four clawed fingers. Each foot had three clawed toes. A row of bony plates forming a serrated crest down its back may have been a temperature control device.

Footprints of *Ceratosaurus* in the rocks of the Morrison Formation in the western USA suggest that they moved in groups, and may have cooperated to kill large prey.

Family Podokesauridae

The earliest and most primitive of the small carnivorous theropods were the podokesaurids, which were around for some 50 million years—from the Late Triassic to the Early Jurassic.

They were little different from their immediate ancestors, the early archosaur reptiles (see p.237). They were fast, active predators (possibly hunting in packs) and ran on long legs, with necks and long tails outstretched for balance. Arms were shorter than the legs. The head was wedge-shaped, with many sharp, pointed teeth in the jaws.

NAME	Procompsognathus
TIME	Late Triassic
LOCALITY	Europe (Germany)
SIZE	4 ft/1.2 m long

This rapacious little beast was one of the earliest dinosaurs. It lived in the deserts of northern Europe during Triassic times. It would have chased its prey, which was small lizards and insects, on its long legs, running with only three of its four toes touching the ground.

Each hand had five fingers, which is a primitive feature, since the trend was toward fewer fingers and toes.

NAME	Saltopus
TIME	Late Triassic
LOCALITY	Europe (Scotland)
SIZE	2 ft/60 cm long

Saltopus is one of the smallest and lightest dinosaurs discovered. It was similar to its relative *Procompsognathus*, but was much smaller and lighter. It was shorter than a domestic cat, and probably weighed as little as 2 lb/1 kg.

Saltopus still had the primitive feature of five fingers on each hand, although the fourth and fifth digits were tiny. But it was more advanced than *Procompsognathus* in its hip/backbone arrangement. Four of the spine's sacral vertebrae were fused to its hips (rather than only the three of its relative), and this formed a fairly solid anchor for its long, agile legs.

NAME Coelophysis

TIME Late Triassic

LOCALITY North America (Connecticut and New Mexico)

SIZE 8–10 ft/2.4–3 m long

The appearance of this comparatively large ceratosaur is well known from a find made in 1947 at Ghost Ranch in New Mexico. A number of skeletons of different sizes were massed together, about a dozen of them complete. There were very young individuals (maybe just hatched) and adults, ranging in length from 3–10 ft/1–3 m. The find suggests that they lived as a group, and must have all died at the same time.

This dinosaur must have been a ferocious hunter—it was built for speed. Its slender, hollow-boned body probably weighed less than 50 lb/23 kg. The neck, tail, and legs were long and slim, the tail making up about half the body length. The long, narrow head was armed with many sharp teeth, each with a cutting, serrated edge. The bird-like feet had three walking toes with sharp claws. There were four fingers on each hand, though only three were strong enough to grasp prey.

Coelophysis probably roamed the upland forests, hunting in packs close to streams and lakes. Their prey would have included small, shrew-like mammals.

Two of the adult skeletons found in New Mexico contained the bones of tiny *Coelophysis* in their body cavities. Initially, paleontologists thought that this meant *Coelophysis* gave birth to live young, rather than laying eggs like most other reptiles. But the hip bones proved too narrow for this to be the case. The conclusion seems to be that this dinosaur was cannibalistic.

DIVISION MANIRAPTORA

This group of theropods shares a number of characteristics with the birds, especially, as the name suggests, in the hand. Indeed, in some modern classifications, the division includes the birds. Other features are also shared, such as modified tail vertebrae and a downwardly directed pubis.

Family not named

NAME Protarchaeopteryx

TIME Late Jurassic/Early Cretaceous

LOCALITY China

SIZE 3 ft 3 in/1 m long

One of the most remarkable recent discoveries has been the Chinese find of small bipedal theropods that were feathered but could not fly. In skeletal structure *Protarchaeopteryx* is a typical coelurid dinosaur, but it is similar in form to the earliest true bird *Archaeopteryx*. *Protarchaeopteryx* has a short skull and teeth that retain primitive serrations. The skeleton has light hollow bird-like bones, a "wishbone" and shorter forelimbs than hind limbs. The hand is elongate with sharp curved claws and the tail had 28 vertebrae. Most important, is the remarkable preservation of small down feathers (about 1 inch/2–3 cm long) on the chest, tail and upper legs. Clusters of large symmetrical feathers (6 in/10 cm long) are attached to the end of the tail and the arms.

Family Coeluridae

Coelurids flourished worldwide from the Late Jurassic to the Early Cretaceous. They were lightweight, active predators, running about on long legs, and grasping prey with their three strong, clawed fingers on each hand.

NAME Coelurus

TIME Late Jurassic

LOCALITY North America (Wyoming)

SIZE 6 ft 6 in/2 m long

Coelurus had a small, low head (only about 8 in/20 cm long), and the hollow, bird-like bones that characterized early dinosaurs. This active predator lived in the forests and swamps of North America. Its hands, with their three clawed fingers, were long and strong, to grasp the flesh of its small animal prey.

CARNIVOROUS DINOSAURS

Family Compsognathidae

There is only one known member of this family. It was a
contemporary of the coelurids, and closely resembled them.

NAME *Compsognathus*

TIME Late Jurassic

LOCALITY
(Germany
and France)

SIZE 2 ft/60 cm long

This tiny, chicken sized, two-legged creature probably weighed
up to 8 lb/3.6 kg. *Compsognathus* must have been a swift hunter.
It was designed for speed with hollow bones; a long neck; a long
tail for balance; short arms with two pincer-like fingers; slender,
long-shinned legs; and bird-like feet with three clawed toes. (A
tiny fourth toe pointed backwards.)

Compsognathus is similar to *Archaeopteryx* (see p.318). Both
inhabited the Late Jurassic wooded islands and
lagoons of southern Germany.

NAME *Sinosauropteryx*

TIME Late Jurassic/Early Cretaceous

LOCALITY China

SIZE 4 ft/1.2 m long

First discovered in the same region of China as the
Protarchaeopteryx and *Caudipteryx* in 1996, *Sinosauropteryx*
was the first of the feathered dinosaurs. This chicken sized
theropod had a long tail, short and stout forelimbs with a very
specialized hand. It was an effective predator; fossilized stomach
remains include a lizard and a small mammal. For the first time,
eggs have been found in the body cavity of a female dinosaur.
The distribution of the fossil eggs suggests the presence of
typically reptilian paired oviducts rather
than a single avian-type oviduct.

A hair-like feathery fringe or crest
some 2 in (4 cm) high

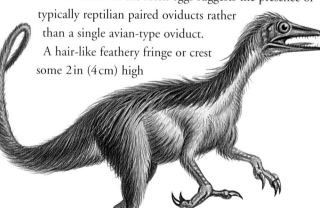

probably ran from the top of the skull to the tail. These
protofeathers were nothing to do with flight and may have had a
role in camouflage, display or species recognition.

Sinosauropteryx is closely related to and similar in
appearance to the coelurid theropod *Compsognathus*.

Family Ornithomimidae

The so-called "bird mimics" were a specialized offshoot of the
coelurosaurs. About the same height and proportions as an ostrich,
except with long arms with three powerful fingers, they seem to
have had a similar lifestyle to that bird, hence the popular
name of the group: "ostrich dinosaurs." They were widespread in
North America and East Asia in Mid Cretaceous times, but seem
to have died out before the end of that period.

All were large, long-legged sprinters. It has been estimated that
some of them could run at speeds of 22–37 mph/35–60 kmph.
They probably traveled the plains in groups, looking after their
young while on the move.

Unlike other dinosaurs, instead of teeth the ornithomimids had
a horny, bird-like beak, which was used to snap up small animals
and insects. Other special features were exceptionally large eyes
and big brains. Both features would have made them
well-coordinated, efficient, and intelligent hunters.

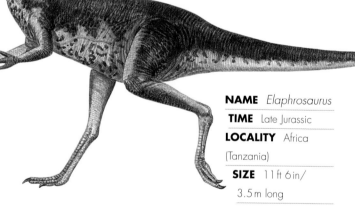

NAME *Elaphrosaurus*

TIME Late Jurassic

LOCALITY Africa
(Tanzania)

SIZE 11 ft 6 in/
3.5 m long

Only one skeleton of *Elaphrosaurus* has been found and,
unfortunately, the skull was missing. Since the characteristic
feature of the ornithomimids was that they had no teeth, it is
impossible to say whether *Elaphrosaurus* belonged to this family.
Loose teeth have been found in the same sediments, and these
may belong to this dinosaur.

The rest of the creature's skeleton, however, seems to be
intermediate in structure between the Jurassic coelurids and the
later, Cretaceous ornithomimids. It may be that *Elaphrosaurus*,
or a close relative, was the ancestor of the ostrich dinosaurs.

NAME *Dromiceiomimus*

TIME Late Cretaceous

LOCALITY North America (Alberta)

SIZE 11 ft 6 in/3.5 m long

Ornithomimids had long, slender legs. The shin bone (tibia) was about 20 percent longer than the thigh bone (femur) —a sure sign of a sprinter. *Dromiceiomimus'* particularly long shins indicate that it was a very fast runner indeed.

Dromiceiomimus' brain cavity and eye sockets indicate that it had an exceptionally large brain, and huge eyes (proportionally larger than those of any modern land animal). *Dromiceiomimus* most probably hunted after dark, chasing small mammals and lizards through the deciduous woods in which it lived.

NAME *Ornithomimus*

TIME Late Cretaceous

LOCALITY North America (Colorado and Montana) and Asia (Tibet)

SIZE 11 ft 6 in/3.5 m long

This ostrich dinosaur was the typical ornithomimid. It had a small, thin-boned head with a large brain cavity, no teeth and beak-like jaws.

Ornithomimus would have sprinted along with its body parallel to the ground, balanced by its extra-long, outstretched tail. This was kept stiff by strong ligaments that lashed the vertebrae together to form a rigid structure. Its neck would have curved upward in an S-bend, holding the head high allowing the best use of its large eyes. The arms dangled above the ground, with the dextrous, clawed fingers ready to grasp potential food.

Like other ornithomimids, *Ornithomimus* was probably omnivorous, eating leaves, fruit, insects, and small animals, such as lizards and mammals. It may even have raided the nests of other dinosaurs and eaten their eggs. If caught by a parent, it would have employed its only means of defense—running away at a speed, it is estimated, of up to 30 mph/50 kmph.

NAME *Struthiomimus*

TIME Late Cretaceous

LOCALITY North America (Alberta and New Jersey)

SIZE 11 ft 6 in/3.5 m long

For years after its discovery in 1914, *Struthiomimus* (below) was thought to be the same animal as *Ornithomimus*. More research in 1972 showed that they were different, albeit in small ways.

Struthiomimus had longer arms than its relative, and stronger, curved claws on its fingers. It also existed slightly earlier than *Ornithomimus*, in the Late Cretaceous, and individuals probably hunted along riverbanks in more open country, in contrast to the dense cypress swamps and forests inhabited by *Ornithomimus*.

NAME *Gallimimus*

TIME Late Cretaceous

LOCALITY Asia (Mongolia)

SIZE 13 ft/4 m long

This is the largest known ostrich dinosaur (below). It had a long snout ending in a broad, flat-tipped beak, and its spade-like hands seem poorly designed for grasping. Perhaps it was a specialist feeder, using its hands to unearth other dinosaurs' eggs.

In 1965, the remains of much larger bird-like dinosaurs were found in Late Cretaceous deposits in the Gobi Desert. The find, named *Deinocheirus*, consisted of a pair of shoulder bones and arms. Each arm measured 8 ft/2.5 m from the shoulder to the tip of the three powerful, clawed fingers. Each claw bone was about 10 in/25 cm long, and would have had an even longer nail. No other parts of the skeleton have been found, so it is impossible to say whether this animal was in a family of its own until it can be classified with more certainty.

Family Oviraptoridae

This small family of toothless theropods lived in Late Cretaceous times in eastern Asia, and were named the "egg thieves" because of their suspected eating habits. They had large heads and short, deep beaks—quite unlike the long, narrow skulls and pointed beaks of their relatives, the ornithomimids, known as the "ostrich dinosaurs" (see pp.252–253).

NAME *Oviraptor*

TIME Late Cretaceous

LOCALITY Asia (Mongolia)

SIZE 6 ft / 1.8 m long

This "egg thief," after whom the family is named, had a distinctive skull, different from that of any other dinosaur. The head was almost parrot-like—short and deep, with a stumpy beak and no teeth. Powerful muscles operated the curved jaws, and gave the beak enough power to crush objects as hard as bones. There was also a small, horn-like crest above the snout.

Oviraptor's body, however, was typical of the small, flesh-eating maniraptorans (see pp.251–257). There were three grasping fingers on each hand, with strongly curved nails (each about 3 in/8 cm long). The animal walked upright on long, slender legs, each with three clawed toes. The body was balanced by the long, outstretched tail.

When the first specimen of *Oviraptor* was found in 1924, it was preserved with a clutch of eggs, which were thought to have been laid by the herbivorous dinosaur *Protoceratops* (see p.308). The inference was that the "egg thief" had been caught in the act of raiding a nest and overcome by a sandstorm which entombed it. Now that an *Oviraptor* embryo has been found in one of the eggs, however, it appears that this dinosaur was completely misnamed. Seemingly it died while refusing to abandon its nest and unhatched eggs.

Family Dromaeosauridae

Members of this family must have been among the most fearsome predators of the Cretaceous Period in North America and Asia. They had the light, speedy body of a coelurosaur, and the large head of a carnosaur. Although they were no larger than many of the other meat-eaters around at the time, dromaeosaurs were formidable predators. They had a lethal weapon in the form of a large, sickle-shaped claw on the second toe of each foot. They were also armed with sharp, pointed teeth and clawed, grasping hands. They had large brains, and were intelligent enough to have hunted in packs. They shared these characteristics with the maniraptorans and birds.

NAME *Deinonychus*

TIME Early Cretaceous

LOCALITY North America (Montana)

SIZE 10–13 ft / 3–4 m long

The discovery of *Deinonychus* in 1964 in the claystones of Montana is one of the most exciting finds in the recent history of paleontology. Well-preserved skeletons revealed a dinosaur built for the chase and the kill—a fast, agile, intelligent predator.

Deinonychus had the lightweight body characteristic of the coelurosaurs, from which it probably evolved. It was, on average, 10 ft/3 m long, stood about 6 ft/1.8 m tall, and weighed some 150 lb/68 kg. The large head was equipped with many meat-shearing teeth, which were curved backward to allow great chunks of flesh to be torn from the prey. The arms were quite long for a theropod (though still much shorter than the legs), and hung from sturdy shoulder girdles. Each hand had three grasping fingers with long, strongly curved claws.

The legs were slender, with long shin bones and four clawed toes on each foot. The first toe was residual, as in most of the later theropods; the third and fourth toes carried the whole weight of the body.

But it was the remarkable adaptation of the second toe that gave *Deinonychus* its most offensive weapon—and its name, which means "terrible claw." The second toe on each foot had a large, sickle-shaped claw, 5 in/13 cm long. This would have been used like a dagger, to slash through a victim's flesh as *Deinonychus* stood on one leg and lashed out with the other.

NAME	*Dromaeosaurus*
TIME	Late Cretaceous
LOCALITY	North America (Alberta)
SIZE	6ft/1.8m long

This dromaeosaur was the first of the sickle-clawed dinosaurs to be discovered, in Canada in 1914, and gave its name to the whole family. However, it was not until *Deinonychus* was unearthed in 1964 that the true nature and significance of *Dromaeosaurus* was assessed. Up until then, it was regarded as either a large coelurosaur or a small carnosaur. The new find made it apparent that the creature belonged to an intermediate group, and shared features with both types of theropod.

Dromaeosaurus is only known from its skull and some odd bones. But from such meagre finds, paleontologists can piece together a picture of a dinosaur smaller than *Deinonychus*, intelligent and agile, a rapacious predator with large, killing claws on its toes, though not as large as those of *Deinonychus*.

When *Deinonychus* ran, the sickle-clawed toes were flicked back and held clear of the ground. The body was held horizontally and balanced by the long, outstretched tail. This was kept rigid by bundles of bony rods that grew out from the vertebrae, and formed a supporting framework to stiffen the tail along most of its length. When *Deinonychus* was standing on one foot and attacking with the other, balance was essential and a tail like a ramrod would have made the pose easier to hold. The big brain (evident from the size of the skull's brain cavity) would have coordinated a finely-tuned nervous system to control such complex movements.

One of the finds in Montana revealed five complete skeletons of *Deinonychus* lying by the body of a large, plant-eating dinosaur called *Tenontosaurus*, which measured some 24ft/7.3m long (see p.284). This assemblage of bodies was most probably brought together by chance after death, washed down by a flood into a hollow or river basin.

But one could, perhaps, reconstruct the scene that may have taken place some 140 million years ago. A small pack of *Deinonychus* surrounded the plant-eater. Some may have leapt on its back, and held on with their clawed hands, while slashing

NAME	*Velociraptor*
TIME	Late Cretaceous
LOCALITY	Asia (Mongolia and China)
SIZE	6ft/1.8m long

through its thick hide by repeated kicks of the dagger-like killing claws on their feet. The plant-eater may have wounded or even killed some of its attackers by lashing out with its long, heavy tail or rearing up on its hind legs to crash down on their bodies. But, perhaps in the end, it succumbed and bled to death, while the pack of carnivores waited nearby.

The active, predatory lifestyle suggested by the anatomy of *Deinonychus* is seen by some paleontologists as strong evidence that it was an endothermic ("warm-blooded") creature, and could control its body temperature, as do modern birds and mammals (see p.235).

A dramatic find in Mongolia in 1971 revealed two fossilized skeletons—*Velociraptor* locked in combat with the horned dinosaur *Protoceratops* (see p.308). A great struggle had obviously taken place, since *Velociraptor* had died grasping the head shield of *Protoceratops* with its hands, while ripping into the belly with its sickle-clawed feet. *Protoceratops* had caved in the chest of *Velociraptor*, possibly with its horny beak, before it, too, died. The scene was indicative of the ferocious lifestyle of the dromaeosaurs in general, and *Velociraptor* in particular.

The long, low, flat-snouted head of *Velociraptor* is the main feature that distinguishes it from other dromaeosaurs, which typically had short, deep heads. In other respects, it was similar to them, although its sickle claws were relatively small.

NAME *Saurornitholestes*

TIME Late Cretaceous

LOCALITY North America (Alberta)

SIZE 6 ft/1.8 m long

In 1978, the skull and some arm bones and teeth of this dinosaur were found. It is not clear whether it was a dromaeosaur or one of the "bird-lizards," the saurornithoidids (below).

The scanty remains suggest that *Saurornitholestes* had a larger brain than was usual among the dromaeosaurs (but not among the saurornithoidids), and that it possessed powerful hands adapted for grasping. The restoration shown above is based on the evidence available, but remains highly speculative.

Family Saurornithoididae

Like the dromaeosaurs, these "bird-lizards" were fast, intelligent, rapacious predators, though smaller and lighter in build. They also had a sickle-shaped, killer claw on each foot.

But the skull of these saurornithoidids shows the greatest development. The brain cavity was large. Relative to body weight, it was about seven times the volume of the brain cavity of their modern relative, the crocodile. In addition to this well-developed nervous system, these dinosaurs had large eyes and it seems very likely that they had binocular vision.

Thus, the saurornithoidids of Late Cretaceous times—living in North America, southern Europe, and Mongolia—were among the most efficient hunters of the carnivorous dinosaurs.

NAME *Saurornithoides*

TIME Late Cretaceous

LOCALITY Asia (Mongolia)

SIZE 6 ft 6 in/2 m long

Although the skull was bird-like—long, low, and light—it housed a large brain, giving its owner an intelligence far superior to that of most other dinosaurs around at the time. The eyes must have been huge relative to the head, judging from the size of their sockets. Moreover, their position suggests that these dinosaurs used binocular vision, allowing them to judge distances between objects.

Such large eyes suggest nocturnal habits. *Saurornithoides*, together with other members of its family, was probably active after twilight, dodging through the woods to hunt down small mammals and reptiles.

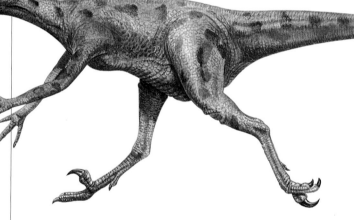

NAME *Stenonychosaurus*

TIME Late Cretaceous

LOCALITY North America (Alberta)

SIZE 6 ft 6 in/2 m long

This was the "brainiest" dinosaur of them all—the brain cavity in the skull is, relative to its body size, the largest so far discovered. Its brain was larger than that of a modern emu. Comparing its brain size to that of a modern mammal, scientists think *Stenonychosaurus* was about as intelligent as an opossum.

Only incomplete skeletons of this saurornithoidid have been found. It seems to differ little in structure from *Saurornithoides* (left), leading some paleontologists to think that it is actually the same animal. However, the clawed fingers of the *Stenonychosaurus* specimens seem longer and slimmer than those of *Saurornithoides*. Also, *Stenonychosaurus* was probably of a lighter overall build; it is estimated that its live weight would have been 60–100 lb/27–45 kg.

Like other members of its family, *Stenonychosaurus* possessed large eyes—each eye was about 2 in/52 mm across, the same size as that of a modern ostrich. The combination of large brain, large eyes, and slim build indicate that it was an agile night hunter, with fast reflexes and well-developed senses.

Family Baryonychidae

This family was created in 1986 to cover one member—*Baryonyx*, which has a narrow, crocodile-like skull, adapted for fish-eating. New spinosaurid remains from Africa show similar adaptations, and the two families may be closely related.

NAME	*Baryonyx*
TIME	Early Cretaceous
LOCALITY	Europe (England)
SIZE	20 ft/6 m long

Two unusual features made this large, theropod dinosaur quite distinct from any other. Its first singular characteristic was a huge, curved claw, about 1 ft/30 cm long—hence its scientific name *Baryonyx*, meaning "heavy claw," and its popular nickname of "Claws." However, the claw was not attached to the animal's skeleton, so it is not known whether it was part of the forefeet or hind feet.

Paleontologists assume that the claw belonged to one of the forefeet, since the forelimbs of this dinosaur were unusually thick and powerful compared to those of other theropods, and would therefore have been able to carry such a large weapon. In addition, the great size of the *Baryonyx* would have made the large claw difficult to wield if it had been located on one of the animal's hind feet.

The second peculiar feature of *Baryonyx* was its skull, which was long and narrow, rather like that of a crocodile. The jaws were armed with a great number of small, pointed teeth, twice as many as a theropod usually possessed. There was also a bony crest on top of the head. The neck was not as flexible as that of other theropods, and could not have been carried in their characteristic S-shaped curve.

The habits of this mysterious beast may be surmised from these two distinctive features and some fish remain that were found with the skeleton. It is possible that *Baryonyx* hunted on all-fours along riverbanks, hooking fish out of the water with its long, gaff-like claws on the front legs—a hunting technique that grizzly bears can be seen employing on riverbanks today.

INFRAORDER CARNOSAURIA

Some of the largest terrestrial carnivores that have ever existed belong to this group of theropod dinosaurs—the carnosaurs or "flesh lizards." The taxonomic basis of this group has been questioned recently since many of the characteristics may well be size-related convergences. *Tyrannosaurus* is the most familiar member of the group. They were massively built animals, and dominated life in Jurassic and Cretaceous times.

Their efficiency as predators is, however, debatable. In reality, the largest of them, such as *Tyrannosaurus* and *Tarbosaurus*, could have been part-time scavengers. They may have been the "hyenas" of the dinosaur world rather than the "lions." It is likely that their sheer bulk would have precluded any sustained chase. But they could have ambushed prey, attacking in short bursts of speed, like a modern tiger.

There were also other smaller carnosaurs that were lighter and more agile than their giant contemporaries.

Family Megalosauridae

The earliest and most familiar carnosaurs belong to this family of "great lizards." Their remains have been found in North America, Africa, and Europe, and as a group they span a period of 140 million years—from the Early Jurassic Period to the end of the Cretaceous.

All were enormous, big-boned creatures. The large head was high and narrow, equipped with powerful jaws and many sharp, saw-edged teeth. The arms were short but strong. The legs were long and massive enough to support the great body weight on the three spreading, clawed toes of each foot (a tiny fourth toe was also present), yet light enough to allow the creature to amble along quite quickly.

NAME *Teratosaurus*

TIME Late Triassic

LOCALITY Europe (Germany)

SIZE 20 ft/6 m long

This is a puzzling beast among the dinosaurs. From fragments of its skeleton, mostly teeth, paleontologists have tentatively constructed a picture of *Teratosaurus* as a primitive carnosaur.

It was a large, two-legged creature, with a heavy head and many sharp, curved teeth. Its body was also heavy, with a short neck and long, stiffened tail. Sturdy legs ended in three

powerful, clawed toes, for walking and ripping flesh. (A fourth toe was present, but it was tiny.) The short, strong arms had grasping fingers with curved claws.

From the remains of *Teratosaurus*, and fragments of related beasts found in southern Africa, some paleontologists postulate that a group of large, meat-eating theropods may have existed some 60 million years before the main stock of carnosaurs appeared, in Early Jurassic times. *Teratosaurus* may, therefore, be the earliest-known relative of the megalosaur family.

However, other paleontologists are of the opinion that *Teratosaurus* may be an early member of the prosauropod group of dinosaurs (see pp.266–269) or even a large representative of the thecodontians, from which group arose the ancient ancestors of the dinosaurs (see p.267).

NAME *Proceratosaurus*

TIME Middle Jurassic

LOCALITY Europe (England)

SIZE 16 ft/5 m long

This early carnosaur is known only from a single skull. Although longer than average, the skull shows the same general features as other primitive carnosaurs. But there is one atypical feature—a small horn above the snout. This suggests that this creature may have been an ancestor, or even an early member, of the ceratosaurs, those theropods characterized by a nose horn (see pp.250–251). The restoration shows *Proceratosaurus* as a typical carnosaur—large head, short neck, heavy body, long tail, short arms with clawed fingers, and long legs for running, each foot bearing three toes.

NAME *Dilophosaurus*

TIME Early Jurassic

LOCALITY North America (Arizona)

SIZE 20 ft/6 m long

Found in Early Jurassic strata, *Dilophosaurus* is the earliest known large carnivorous dinosaur. The broad range of animal remains found in the strata indicates that these carnosaurs were part of quite cosmopolitan communities, including sauropods and theropods of various sizes. First discovered in 1942 by an expedition from the University of California, *Dilophosaurus* seems to have been a lightly built carnosaur. This sounds like a contradiction, but it was intermediate in structure between the carnosaurs and the coelurosaurs. Its head was large (a typical carnosaur feature) but light-boned, while its neck, tail, and arms were long and slender (typical coelurosaur features, see pp.250–257).

The skull of *Dilophosaurus* was unusual for any group. A pair of semicircular bony crests rose vertically on either side of the skull. Although the crests were wafer-thin in places, they were strengthened by vertical struts of bone. At the back of the head, the tip of each crest narrowed into a spike.

The function of these head crests remains a mystery. Some paleontologists think that they could have been used for sexual display, and that only the males had them—a theory supported by the fact that not all specimens found had the crests. Indeed, there were none on the first few skeletons unearthed, and the animals were thought to have been a species of *Megalosaurus* (see p.260). The crests have never been found actually attached to the skull, but lying nearby, so there is a certain amount of guesswork about their position in life, and there is even the possibility that they belonged to another dinosaur.

The jaws of *Dilophosaurus* give a clue to its lifestyle. The lower jaw was strong and full of long, sharp, thin teeth. The upper jaw, however, had a cluster of teeth at the front, separate from the rest of the teeth—similar to the arrangement in the jaws of a modern crocodile.

Although *Dilophosaurus* had a large head and strong jaws, it probably did not kill its victims by biting them: the thin teeth and delicate head crests would have been too vulnerable. It is more likely that it caught and ripped its prey apart with the clawed feet and hands. Or, like many of its relatives, it could have been a scavenger, feeding on the kills of stronger carnosaurs.

NAME *Eustreptospondylus*

TIME Middle Jurassic to Late Cretaceous

LOCALITY Europe (England)

SIZE 23 ft/7 m long

Until the discovery of a nearly complete skeleton of this early megalosaur in southern England, and its description in 1964, *Eustreptospondylus* remains were identified as *Megalosaurus*. The skeleton which revealed that this was in fact a separate animal, despite its similar build to *Megalosaurus,* is now mounted in the University Museum of Oxford, and although parts of its skull are missing, it remains the best-preserved specimen of any European carnosaur.

NAME *Megalosaurus*

TIME Early Jurassic to Late Jurassic

LOCALITY Europe (England and France) and Africa (Morocco)

SIZE 30 ft/9 m long

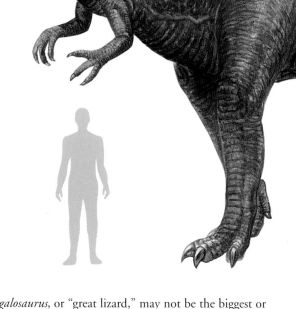

Megalosaurus, or "great lizard," may not be the biggest or heaviest dinosaur, but it can claim a number of "firsts." The first dinosaur bone on record, discovered in England in 1676, probably belonged to *Megalosaurus*. It was the first dinosaur to be scientifically named and described in the 1820s, and it was one of the three fossils that prompted the English paleontologist Richard Owen in 1842 to coin the name for the whole group: he chose "Dinosauria," meaning "terrible lizards."

With an overall length of 30 ft/9 in, a height of 10 ft/3 m, and an estimated weight in life of 1 US ton/900 kg, *Megalosaurus* was a massive creature. A short, muscular neck carried the large head, with its powerful, hinged jaws armed with curved, saw-edged fangs. Its fingers and toes were strong and clawed. With such weapons, *Megalosaurus* was well-equipped to attack and kill large, long-necked, plant-eating dinosaurs (see pp.270–277).

Trackways of *Megalosaurus* footprints are seen in the limestone rocks of southern England, and show how these bulky bipeds walked upright on two legs, their toes pointing slightly inward, and their long tails probably swinging from side to side at each step acting as a counterbalances to their heavy bodies.

Family Allosauridae

Allosaurs were similar in build to megalosaurs, but even larger. They were the largest carnosaurs around during Late Jurassic times, and lumbered through every continent in the world. But they were soon to be rivalled by even bigger creatures—the tyrannosaurs of the Cretaceous Period (see pp.263–265).

NAME *Yangchuanosaurus*

TIME Late Jurassic

LOCALITY Asia (China)

SIZE up to 33 ft/10 m long

The skeleton of this large carnosaur was discovered in Sichuan (Szechuan) Province of eastern China, and described in 1978. It is now on display in the Natural History Museum in Beijing (Peking).

It was a typical allosaur, with a huge head and powerful jaws, equipped with sharp fangs that curved backward and were serrated along their edges like steak knives. The neck was short and thick but flexible. The long tail made up about half the total body length. It was flattened from side to side and held out stiffly to balance the deep, narrow body of the animal as it strode along on its huge, pillar-like legs. Three great, clawed toes bore the whole weight of the body. (As usual, there was a small first toe that pointed backwards.) Short arms ended in three powerful, clawed fingers.

The skull of *Yangchuanosaurus* differs from that of other allosaurs in having more teeth at the front of the jaws, and a bony hump above the snout.

NAME *Allosaurus*

TIME Late Jurassic to Early Cretaceous

LOCALITY North America (Colorado, Utah, and Wyoming), Africa (Tanzania), and Australia

SIZE up to 39 ft/12 m long

This enormous carnosaur, the largest member of the family Allosauridae, would probably have been the most fearsome predator of the Late Jurassic Period. *Allosaurus* would have weighed between 1–2 US tons/1–2 tonnes, and must have stood some 15 ft/4.6 m tall.

In appearance, *Allosaurus* was a bigger version of its close relative and contemporary *Megalosaurus* (opposite), although it had a few peculiarities of its own. The head, for example, had two bony bumps above the eyes, and a narrow bony ridge running from between the eyes down to the tip of the snout, giving it a distinctive shape. An opening in the side of the skull around the snout area is thought to have housed a salt gland. *Allosaurus* had five pairs of teeth in the upper jaw, compared to four in *Megalosaurus*.

The skull was massive in size, but not in weight. This was due to several large openings ("windows" or fenestrae) between various bones of the skull that reduced its solid structure to an intricate network of bony struts, so lessening its weight. The bones themselves were only loosely articulated with one another (a feature also seen in the skulls of other large carnosaurs, such as *Ceratosaurus*, see p.250). This resulted in a degree of flexibility, which added to the strength of the lightly built skull.

Allosaurus' efficiency as a hunter is a matter of debate among experts. Some paleontologists believe that it was too heavy and clumsy to have run down prey, and therefore probably fed on carrion. Others believe that it was quite an agile creature for its size, and may even have hunted in packs to bring down the giant, plant-eating dinosaurs of the day, such as *Apatosaurus* (*Brontosaurus*) and *Diplodocus*. Bones of *Apatosaurus* have, in fact, been found in western North America bearing the marks of teeth resembling those of *Allosaurus*. Similar broken teeth have also been found scattered around other specimens of this plant-eater.

A single site in Utah discovered in 1927, the Cleveland-Lloyd Dinosaur Quarry, has revealed thousands of dinosaur bones including the remains of 44 individual *Allosaurus*. The remains include individuals which range in size from 10ft (3m) long juveniles to fully grown adults. the accompanying remains give a reasonable insight into the diversity of dinosaurs at the time and include ornithopods, stegosaurs, ankylosaurs, sauropods, and another theropod, *Ceratosaurus*.

Family Spinosauridae

The spinosaurids were a specialized group of large Cretaceous theropods. Some had backbones elongated into a tall crest or "sail," like that of the "fin-backed" pelycosaurs and perhaps with a similar thermo-regulatory purpose.

The discovery of a new spinosaurid from Africa (*Suchomimus*) with a long crocodile-like snout suggests a close relationship between the spinosaurids and *Baryonyx*. If this surmise is correct, it also suggests a connection across the seaway from Africa to Europe in Early Cretaceous times.

NAME	*Acrocanthosaurus*
TIME	Early Cretaceous
LOCALITY	North America (Oklahoma)
SIZE	43 ft / 13 m long

In 1950, several skeletons of this enormous, flesh-eating dinosaur were found in North America. The name *Acrocanthosaurus* means "top spiny lizard," and refers to the elongated spines (up to 1 ft/30 cm long) that grew up from the animal's backbone. These spines would have been covered by a web of skin, to form a pronounced ridge or crest running down the length of the back.

The crest of *Acrocanthosaurus* was low in comparison to that of some of its relatives living in other parts of the world. For example, *Altispinax* of western Europe had spines that were about four times the length of the vertebrae from which they grew, while *Spinosaurus* of Africa had a "sail" over 6 ft/1.8 m high on its back (right).

NAME	*Spinosaurus*
TIME	Late Cretaceous
LOCALITY	Africa (Egypt and Niger)
SIZE	39 ft / 12 m long

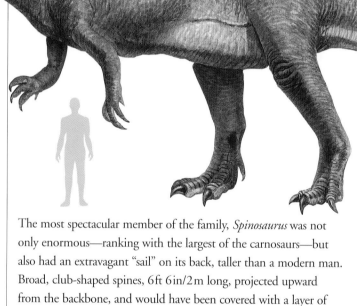

The most spectacular member of the family, *Spinosaurus* was not only enormous—ranking with the largest of the carnosaurs—but also had an extravagant "sail" on its back, taller than a modern man. Broad, club-shaped spines, 6 ft 6 in/2 m long, projected upward from the backbone, and would have been covered with a layer of skin. The whole arrangement was reminiscent of the tall fin on the back of the pelycosaur *Dimetrodon* (see p.331).

The function of this strange, and highly vulnerable, structure is not known for certain. One theory is that the sail acted as a crude device to regulate body temperature. When the animal stood with the sail turned sideways, towards the sun's rays, its large surface area, which was amply supplied with blood vessels, would absorb heat rapidly.

The warmed-up blood would then be carried all over the body. To lower its body temperature, the animal would angle its sail into the wind, so dissipating heat.

The advantage to *Spinosaurus* would be that it could warm up quickly in the early morning, and be prepared for hunting well in advance of its cold, sluggish prey, which was mostly composed of other reptiles.

An alternative theory is that the sail was brightly coloured, and was used for sexual display by the males to attract the attention of the females. Males could also have used their sails to threaten each other during the ritualistic fights engaged in to establish dominance.

There is no reason why both theories cannot apply, with the sail being used as a heat exchanger and as a sexual ploy.

At about the same time that *Spinosaurus* inhabited western Africa, a large, two-legged, plant-eating dinosaur, *Ouranosaurus* also lived in the region. It, too, had a high sail on its back (see pp.288–289). There is therefore good reason to believe that some environmental or climatic factor influenced the development of these structures.

The bony sail would have increased *Spinosaurus'* weight considerably. The total body weight is estimated to have been some 7 US tons/6 tonnes—close to that of *Tyrannosaurus*, the largest carnosaur of them all (see p.265).

The arms of *Spinosaurus* were larger than is usual among large theropods, and it is possible that it spent some of its time on all-fours, which was an unusual posture among the two-legged carnosaurs. Its teeth were also different from those of other carnosaurs: they were straight rather than curved.

Family Tyrannosauridae

The largest terrestrial carnivores that ever lived belonged to this family of "tyrant lizards." It was a small, specialized group, with less than a dozen types (genera) identified to date. Yet its members have inspired the popular notion of what flesh-eating dinosaurs looked like and how they behaved.

The evolutionary relationships and taxonomic position of the tyrannosaurids have been questioned by some dinosaur experts recently. On the basis of certain specialized structures in the ankle, it is suggested that they are more closely related to the ornithomimids (see pp.252–253) and troodontids, and should therefore be placed with them within the Subdivision Arctrometatarsalia.

The remains of tyrannosaurs have been found in Asia and western North America. As a group they were short-lived, appearing in Late Cretaceous times and disappearing at the end of that period in the mysterious mass extinction of all the dinosaurs. Their existence, spanning less than 15 million years, was only a "moment" in terms of the evolution of life.

Tyrannosaurs had a well-developed second set of ribs on the underside of the body. A possible explanation for these extra ribs and the short arms could be that when a tyrannosaur rested it lay on its belly, the innards would have been supported by the extra ribs, and not crushed by the great weight of the body. When the animal got up, its tiny arms stopped the bulky frame from sliding forward, and steadied it as it rose to its feet.

There is also a suggestion that the tiny arms were used by the males to hold on to the females while mating.

NAME	*Albertosaurus*
TIME	Late Cretaceous
LOCALITY	North America (Alberta)
SIZE	26 ft/8 m long

This "small" tyrannosaur shows all the features common to the family. It was massively built, with a big head and short body, balanced at the hips by a long, strong tail. Pillar-like legs, with three-toed, spreading, feet supported the great body weight.

Albertosaurus and other members of its family were specialized theropods. Their arms were puny in comparison to the size of the body—they were so short that they could not have reached up to the mouth. There were only two fingers on each hand, which would not have been very effective for grasping prey. And although the jaws could be opened wide, the bones of the skull were rigidly fixed, without the same degree of flexibility as seen in the skulls of the allosaurs (see pp.260–261).

NAME *Alioramus*

TIME Late Cretaceous

LOCALITY Asia (Mongolia)

SIZE 20ft/6m long

NAME *Tarbosaurus*

TIME Late Cretaceous

LOCALITY Asia (Mongolia)

SIZE up to 46ft/14m long

This giant carnosaur lumbered around the lands of central Asia, eating anything it came across, whether dead or alive. Its skills as a hunter are suspect, because of its sheer bulk. It could have preyed on the herbivorous duckbilled and armored dinosaurs that lived in its environment. It could also have supplemented its diet with the kills of other carnosaurs. It was probably big enough to scare off even the most tenacious predator.

Many *Tarbosaurus* skeletons have been unearthed in Mongolia, some complete. Its structure was almost identical to *Tyrannosaurus*, but it was more lightly built with a longer skull. It has been possible to analyze the upright posture of this tyrannosaur. The back would have been held almost horizontal, with the body balanced at the hips. The long, flexible neck curved abruptly upward from the body, with the heavy head held almost at right angles to it in a bird-like pose. In the fossil finds, *Tarbosaurus'* head was pulled right back, toward its shoulders. This often happens when an animal dies, because the ligaments of the neck dry out and shrink, pulling the head backward into an unnatural position.

A group of Asiatic tyrannosaurs, represented by *Alioramus*, differed from "typical" tyrannosaurs in the shape of their skulls. Whereas most members of the family had deep skulls with short snouts, *Alioramus* and its relatives had shallow skulls with long snouts. There were also some bony knobs or spikes on the face between the eyes and the tip of the snout. These may have been display features that distinguished the sexes—perhaps with the males having larger structures than the females for use in courting displays or to threaten other males.

Alioramus and its tyrannosaur relatives lived in Asia and western North America during the Late Cretaceous Period. At that time, the modern continents of Asia and North America were joined into one enormous landmass; the Bering Strait that separates them today was then dry land. But the North American part was divided in two by a shallow sea that ran north to south, with "Asiamerica" to the west, and "Euramerica" to the east.

Animals, including the great tyrannosaurs, would have been able to migrate freely between Asia and western North America, but relatively few seem to have managed to cross the great divide over to the eastern half of the landmass. However, the remains of one tyrannosaur, similar to *Albertosaurus* (see p.263), have been found in the eastern USA.

NAME
Daspletosaurus

TIME Late
Cretaceous

LOCALITY North
America (Alberta)

SIZE 28 ft/8.5 m long

The short, deep jaws of this
massive meat-eater held
even larger teeth
than other
tyrannosaurs, though they were fewer
in number. Each tooth was dagger-sharp, curved and saw-edged.
Formidable jaws, clawed feet and sheer bulk (a body weight of
up to 4 US tons/3.6 tonnes) were the weapons used by
Daspletosaurus. It was capable of killing the large, horned,
dinosaurs that browsed the forests of northern North America.

NAME *Tyrannosaurus*

TIME Late Cretaceous

LOCALITY North America (Alberta, Montana, Saskatchewan, Texas, and
Wyoming) and Asia (Mongolia)

SIZE up to 49 ft/15 m long

This awesome theropod was the largest of the carnosaur dinosaurs
—the largest known terrestrial carnivore.

On average, *Tyrannosaurus* was 39 ft/12 m long, up to 20 ft/6 m
tall, and weighed about 8 US tons/7 tonnes (heavier than a
modern, adult African bull elephant). Its head alone was over

4 ft/1.25 m long, and was armed with fangs, each some
6 in/15 cm in length.

No complete skeleton has yet been
found, although
many bones and
teeth have surfaced since it was first discovered in the USA in
1902. Early reconstructions were often inaccurate; mounted
skeletons often show the animal propped up on a whip-like tail,
its body sloping backward at an angle of 45°. But since the
skeletons of other tyrannosaurids have been unearthed, such as
Tarbosaurus in Mongolia, we now have a more accurate idea of the
stance of these dinosaurs.

Investigations of *Tyrannosaurus'* structure have triggered some
debate over whether it really was a fearsome predator. The
animal's hips and legs seemed to indicate that *Tyrannosaurus* may
have been no more than a slow-moving scavenger, only able to
take small, clumsy steps.

Calculations have also suggested that the animal's weight and
height were so great that if it fell while running, the impact would
have been enough to break its skull. The tiny forearms would not
have broken the force of the impact.

However, some paleontologists believe that the purpose of the
unusually wide area of the skull behind the eyes was to anchor
extremely powerful jaw muscles. Taken together with other
features—such as the robust, saw-edged teeth; the strong, flexible
neck; the large areas of the brain associated with sight and smell;
and the possibility of binocular vision—the findings argue in
favor of an active, predatory lifestyle.

It is surmised that *Tyrannosaurus'* diet could have consisted
primarily of the duckbilled dinosaurs, or hadrosaurs, that browsed
the hardwood forests of North America (see pp.290–297). These
animals lived in herds, and sprinted away on two legs when
danger threatened. So it is likely that *Tyrannosaurus* hid among
the trees, ambushing its prey with a short burst of speed as it held
its mouth open wide. The force of any impact would have been
absorbed by its strong teeth, sturdy skull, and powerful neck.

EARLY HERBIVOROUS DINOSAURS

SUBORDER SAUROPODOMORPHA

The lifestyle of the sauropodomorph dinosaurs was completely different from that of their contemporaries, the theropods. Although both were saurischians, or "lizard-hipped" dinosaurs, the theropods were two-legged carnivores (see pp.250–265), whereas the sauropodomorphs were, in the main, four-legged herbivores. The differences in gait are reflected in the bones of the feet. Yet their lives were inextricably linked, since the sauropodomorphs were probably the chief prey of the larger predatory theropods.

INFRAORDER PROSAUROPODA

Like the theropods, the sauropodomorphs can be grouped according to their size. There were gigantic types, with long necks and tails, placed in the Infraorder Sauropoda (see pp.270–277). *Apatosaurus* (previously known as *Brontosaurus*) is the most famous sauropod (see p.275).

There were also smaller sauropodomorphs (though some were still fairly large, at over 30 ft/9 m), which are grouped in the Infraorder Prosauropoda. As their name implies, they were "before the sauropods," and lived during Late Triassic times. Current theory rejects the once-held notion that the prosauropods were the direct ancestors of the sauropods. They are now generally regarded as a side branch of the sauropod family tree—a branch that got fatally pruned in the Early Jurassic Period.

Prosauropods themselves are thought to have evolved from theropod-type ancestors. The remains of two likely candidates have been found, both from South America. *Staurikosaurus* is the only known dinosaur from the Mid-Triassic Period, and was about 6 ft 6 in/2 m long; *Herrerasaurus*, from the Late Triassic, was 10 ft/3 m long. Both seem to have been active, two-legged flesh-eaters, with large heads and long tails.

Family Anchisauridae

This family comprises most of the earliest prosauropods, which were among the first dinosaurs to appear. Members of the family were all fairly small creatures (reaching less than 10 ft/3 m in length), with long, lightly-built bodies, slim limbs, small heads and long necks and tails.

Anchisaurs seem to represent an early experiment in plant-eating among dinosaurs. Their teeth were cylindrical and blunt, with file-like serrations along the edges – like the teeth of some modern herbivorous lizards such as the land iguanas of South America. The serrations would have helped shred plant material and thereby aid digestion. The arms were only slightly shorter than the legs, which suggests that the animal probably spent much of its time on all-fours. This stance would have made it easier to reach plants growing at ground level. But the ankle joint was strong and well-developed too, indicating that the animal could also stand up on its hind legs, and use its hands to pluck off higher vegetation.

Some paleontologists believe that anchisaur-type prosauropods may have been the ancestors of the bird-hipped dinosaurs, the ornithischians (see pp.278–313). Certain features of *Anchisaurus* (below), in particular, seem similar. Its long, slender neck, the structure of its shoulders and forelimbs, and details of its hip bones and ankle joints – all these structures are similar to those of some of the early ornithopods, such as *Heterodontosaurus* (see p.279).

NAME *Anchisaurus*

TIME Early Jurassic

LOCALITY North America (Connecticut) and southern Africa

SIZE 7 ft/2.1 m long

This early dinosaur was probably typical of the small prosauropods. It had a small head, tall, flexible neck and long, slim body. The arms were shorter than the legs, by about a third. Each hand had five fingers, though the two outer ones were quite short. The first finger, or "thumb," was equipped with a large claw, which may have been used for rooting up plants or perhaps for fighting.

The round, blunt teeth suggest that *Anchisaurus* ate plants.

Ferns and horsetails flourished in damp places at the time, and conifers and palm-like cycads grew in drier, upland areas. But all plant-eaters, including modern ones, need a larger digestive system than meat-eaters, since tough, fibrous plant material takes longer to break down than flesh. So, a capacious stomach and long intestines would have been found in *Anchisaurus'* long body, accommodated in front of the hips. This mass of innards would have unbalanced a two-legged animal so, it is argued, *Anchisaurus* and its relatives had to take up a four-legged stance most of the time for stability.

All the continents of today's world were fused together into one great landmass in Jurassic times, some 200 million years ago, when *Anchisaurus* was alive. To find its remains in such divergent places as the eastern seaboard of North America and in southern Africa is therefore not surprising, and is further evidence for the theory of plate tectonics.

near the entrance to the limestone caves; when it died, it was covered over by later, Triassic deposits. Alternatively, its bones could have been washed into the caves and gullies by torrents during the rainy seasons.

Thecodontosaurus has many features of a basic sauropodomorph and is sometimes placed with other genera in a separate family of thecodontosaurids.

NAME	*Efraasia*
TIME	Late Triassic
LOCALITY	Europe (Germany)
SIZE	8 ft/2.4 m long

NAME	*Thecodontosaurus*
TIME	Late Triassic to Early Jurassic
LOCALITY	Europe (England) and southern Africa
SIZE	7 ft/2.1 m long

Thecodontosaurus was similar in build to *Anchisaurus*, but with a shorter neck and more teeth. It was first named in 1843 from remains discovered near Bristol in southwest England. The bones were found in Triassic deposits that had been laid down in gullies and caves eroded out of limestones that had been formed in earlier, Carboniferous times. During the desert-like climate that prevailed in Europe during Late Triassic times, when *Thecodontosaurus* was living, these limestones would have formed high, parched plateaus.

Piecing together such climatic and rock evidence suggests that *Thecodontosaurus* lived in dry, upland areas, possibly in or

Discovered in 1909 by E. Fraas and named after him, *Efraasia* was slightly larger than its prosauropod relatives, but otherwise similar in build. Like them, it had multipurpose hands. Its long fingers could have grasped small plants and bundles of leaves, with the help of its mobile "thumbs." The wrist joint was also well-developed, so the palm of the hand could be pressed to the ground easily, enabling the animal to walk on all-fours.

Efraasia had a primitive feature, however; only two sacral vertebrae joined the hips to the backbone, which made for a rather weak arrangement of the hindquarters. All the other "lizard-hipped" dinosaurs had at least three vertebrae linking the hips to the spine.

Efraasia was just one of several prosauropods which appear in abundance in the Late Triassic of Germany. Others include *Plateosaurus*, *Sellosaurus*, and *Thecodontosaurus* and they are accompanied by theropods, phytosaurs, rauisuchids, and aetosaurs. It is thought that they migrated into the area from elsewhere as yet unknown.

EARLY HERBIVOROUS DINOSAURS CONTINUED

Family Plateosauridae

These heavy, large, stout-limbed prosauropods were bigger versions of their contemporaries, the anchisaurs. The proportions of their bodies are reminiscent of the giant sauropods, such as *Apatosaurus* (*Brontosaurus*) that thrived later, in the Late Jurassic and Cretaceous periods (see p.275).

NAME *Massospondylus*

TIME Late Triassic

LOCALITY Africa (South Africa and Zimbabwe) and North America (Arizona)

SIZE 13 ft/4 m long

This was the most common prosauropod in southern Africa. It was named in 1854 by the English paleontologist Richard Owen from a few large vertebrae found in South Africa. On the basis of these bones, he called the dinosaur *Massospondylus*, which means "massive vertebra."

Massospondylus had a tiny head perched on a particularly long and flexible neck. Its five-fingered hands were massive and had a great span; they could have been used for walking or for grasping hold of food. Each "thumb" had a large, curved claw.

Polished stones have been found in the stomach cavities of some skeletons. When *Massospondylus* swallowed these stones they would have had rough edges and would have helped the dinosaur to grind up the tough plant material that it ate. Many modern birds retain stones in their gizzards for just the same purpose. Since *Massospondylus* probably spent most of its time eating, in order to maintain its great body mass, the surface of these stones would have been polished smooth in a short time, and been of no further use. Then they would have been regurgitated and replaced with fresh, rough-edged stones.

NAME *Plateosaurus*

TIME Late Triassic

LOCALITY Europe (England, France, Germany, and Switzerland)

SIZE up to 23 ft/7 m long

Plateosaurus is the best known of the prosauropods. Dozens of well-preserved skeletons have been unearthed in Triassic sandstones all over western Europe. In some locations, groups of complete individual fossils have been found. Mass burials of this kind suggest that the *Plateosaurus* was a gregarious creature. Herds traveled together through the Triassic desert landscape of Europe, searching for new feeding grounds. An alternative explanation for the groups of fossils, however, is that solitary individuals inhabited dry, upland areas. When they died, their bodies would have been washed away in the periodic flash floods that are typical of desert environments even today. Many individual corpses could have piled up at the end of well-worn flood channels formed at the edge of desert basins.

Plateosaurus was a large animal, its tail making up about half its length. It had a stronger, deeper head than most prosauropods. Its many small, leaf-shaped teeth, and the low-slung hinge of its lower jaw (to give the muscles greater leverage) suggest that it fed exclusively on plants.

Plateosaurus would have moved about on all-fours most of the time, occasionally rearing up and stretching out its long neck to browse at higher levels. The foliage of trees such as cycads and various conifers, which flourished in Late Triassic Europe, would have featured in its diet.

Similar herbivorous dinosaurs to *Plateosaurus* lived in other parts of the world. In southern China there was the 20 ft/6 m-long *Lufengosaurus*, and in South America there was the smaller, 13 ft/4 m-long *Coloradia*. The presence of these animals, with similar builds and lifestyles, in such widely-spaced parts of the globe is further evidence to support the theory that all continents were fused together into one gigantic landmass (Gondwanaland) in those days.

NAME *Mussaurus*

TIME Late Triassic to Early Jurassic

LOCALITY South America (Argentina)

SIZE possibly 10 ft/3 m long

When paleontologists unearthed a group of tiny, perfectly-formed dinosaurs in southern Argentina in 1979, it seemed as though they had discovered the smallest ever type of dinosaur and they promptly called it "mouse lizard." However, the skeletons had been found in a nest alongside two small, almost intact eggs, each measuring only 1 in/25 mm on the longest axis. The largest skeleton was only 8 in/20 cm long. It had a large head, with big eyes, and a short neck—features you would expect to find in a young animal, not yet fully developed. Paleontologists now think that the adult *Mussaurus* could have grown up to 10 ft/3 m in length, with the body proportions of a typical prosauropod.

Family Melanorosauridae

This family contains the largest prosauropods. Some experts think that they may even have been early representatives of the giant, plant-eating sauropods.

Melanorosaurs walked exclusively on four legs, unlike their smaller, more lightweight contemporaries, the anchisaurs (see pp.266–267), which could also walk on two.

NAME *Riojasaurus*

TIME Late Triassic to Early Jurassic

LOCALITY South America (Argentina)

SIZE up to 33 ft/10 m long

The limb bones, and the shoulder and hip girdles of this large prosauropod, were more massive than those of its relatives, the plateosaurs (opposite). This indicates that it had to walk on four legs to support its weight. The skeleton was modified accordingly. The limb bones were thick and solid, and held vertically under the body. The hips were fused to the backbone by three vertebrae, giving a solid attachment for the legs. The vertebrae had extra articulating surfaces to keep the backbone rigid.

Riojasaurus was named after the northwestern Argentinian province of La Rioja where it was found along with another basal prosauropod, the plateosaur *Coloradisaurus*. *Mussaurus* was another South American prosauropod from Patagonia.. Together, they show that there was a rapid and considerable increase in abundance and body size (at least for some of them) in Late Triassic prosauropods. Other large prosauropods, similar in build and structure, lived in southern Africa at about the same time—*Roccosaurus* and *Thotobolosaurus* of the Late Triassic, and *Vulcanodon* of the Early Jurassic. This last animal exhibits a mixture of features.

Some of them were "primitive" prosauropod characteristics, while others were "advanced" sauropod traits. *Vulcanodon* may, therefore, have been closely related to the giant, long-necked browsers of the Mesozoic Era, the sauropods.

LONG-NECKED BROWSING DINOSAURS

INFRAORDER SAUROPODA

Between 65 and 200 million years ago, the largest herbivores —in fact, the largest land animals ever to have lived—were the giant, long-necked, four-legged sauropods. As a group, they survived for some 50 million years. They evolved in the Late Triassic or Early Jurassic, reached their peak in the Late Jurassic, and became extinct by the end of the Cretaceous. Even in the early stages of their evolution, most sauropods were huge—well over 50 ft/15.2 m long.

The body plan of all sauropods was structurally similar. There was a small head on top of an extra-long neck; a long, deep body to accommodate an enormous gut; thick, pillar-like legs with five-toed, spreading feet; and a long, thick tail that tapered gradually to a whiplash.

Two special adaptations of the skeleton were evident, even in the earliest sauropods. First, great cavities were hollowed out of the vertebrae: this helped to lighten the load of the animal considerably, while still retaining the structural strength of its skeleton. This hollowing-out became more extreme as the sauropods evolved, so that bone was developed only along the lines of stress (comparable to the steel struts in a crane jib).

The second special skeletal feature was that the massive hip girdle was firmly fused to the backbone by four (and in later types, five) sacral vertebrae, which formed a solid support for the heavy body and tail.

Family Cetiosauridae

The earliest sauropods lived worldwide during the Jurassic Period and into the Cretaceous. Their name means "whale lizards," referring to their great size.

Two primitive features remained in members of the cetiosaur family. First, their vertebrae were only partially hollowed out. And second, the hips were attached to the backbone by four sacral vertebrae, a weaker arrangement than in later sauropods. They may be close to the origins of the giant sauropods of the Late Jurassic. Nevertheless, this is still a poorly defined group.

NAME	
Barapasaurus	
TIME	Early Jurassic
LOCALITY	Asia (India)
SIZE	49 ft/15 m long

A field in central India yielded the only sauropod to be found on that subcontinent to date, and also the world's oldest known sauropod. *Barapasaurus* probably lived alongside the later prosauropods.

In build, *Barapasaurus* followed the general sauropod plan, like *Vulcanodon*, its contemporary from Southern Africa and the only other Triassic sauropod known. Only the neck and some of the back vertebrae were hollowed out, as a weight-saving adaptation. Its teeth were spoon-shaped and saw-edged, ideal for eating plants.

NAME	*Cetiosaurus*
TIME	Middle Jurassic to Late Jurassic
LOCALITY	Europe (England) and Africa (Morocco)
SIZE	up to 60 ft/18.3 m long

Bones of this huge sauropod were discovered in 1809 in Oxfordshire in southern England, 32 years before anyone had heard of "dinosaurs." People thought the bones belonged to some great marine animal, hence the name *Cetiosaurus*, or "whale lizard." Others thought the bones came from some huge crocodile. It was not until the remains of a similar sauropod, *Haplocanthosaurus*, were found in the Late Jurassic rocks of Colorado in western North America, that the true nature of the beast was appreciated.

Cetiosaurus was massively built, but with a shorter neck and tail than usual among sauropods. It may have weighed over 10 US tons/ 9 tonnes. The backbone was a solid mass, since the vertebrae were hardly hollowed out at all.

A skeleton of *Cetiosaurus* that was unearthed in Morocco in 1979 revealed the size of the animal. The animal's thigh bone alone measured over 6 ft/1.8 m long, and one of the shoulder blades measured over 5 ft/1.5 m in length. The amount of plant food needed to power such great limbs must have been enormous.

Family Brachiosauridae

Members of this family were the giants of the sauropod group. They ranged through North America, Europe, and eastern Africa during Mid-Jurassic to Early Cretaceous times. All had a similar structure—small heads perched on extra-long necks, deep bodies, and shortish tails. They differed from all other sauropods in that their front legs were longer than their hind legs, so that the body sloped down from the shoulders, like that of a modern giraffe.

Until recently, brachiosaurs could claim to have included not only the most massive dinosaur ever to have lived, but also the largest creature ever to have walked on land. This was *Brachiosaurus* (right). But recent finds in North America show that there were even larger sauropods. In the 1970s, massive bones from two sauropods were found in Colorado, and unofficially called *Supersaurus* and *Ultrasaurus*. In 1986, even larger bones were unearthed in New Mexico, and provisionally named *Seismosaurus*. Some of the remains are enormous, and suggest creatures more than 100 ft/30 m long. There is a shoulder blade 8 ft/2.4 m long, and individual vertebrae 5 ft/1.5 m long.

NAME	*Brachiosaurus*
TIME	Late Jurassic
LOCALITY	North America (Colorado) and Africa (Tanzania and Algeria)
SIZE	75 ft/23 m long

Of all the land animals for which a complete skeleton exists, *Brachiosaurus* is the largest and most massive. A complete specimen of *Brachiosaurus* is displayed in the Paleontological Museum at Humboldt University in East Berlin. It is the largest mounted skeleton in existence. Its bones were found in Tanzania, East Africa, by a university expedition in 1908–12.

Brachiosaurus was, on average, 75 ft/23 m long, and 41 ft/12.6 m tall. Its shoulders were 21 ft/6.4 m off the ground: the upper arm bone, or humerus, alone accounted for 7 ft/2.1 m of this height. It weighed 89 US tons/80 tonnes—almost three times the weight of that other well-known giant sauropod *Apatosaurus* (*Brontosaurus*), or the equivalent of 12 modern, adult African bull elephants.

The secret of supporting such a massive body lay in the construction of *Brachiosaurus'* backbone. Great chunks of bone were hollowed out from the sides of each vertebra, to leave a structure, anchor-shaped in cross-section, made of thin sheets and struts of bone. The resulting skeleton was a masterpiece of engineering—a lightweight framework, made of immensely strong, yet flexible, vertebrae, each articulated to provide maximum strength along the lines of stress.

Brachiosaurus had a deep, domed head, with a broad, flat snout. The head was tiny in comparison with the creature's body, and the brain cavity was equally small.

LONG-NECKED BROWSING DINOSAURS CONTINUED

Pointed, peg-like teeth lined the jaws. Two great nasal openings (external "nostrils") were on top of the head above the eyes, as in all other sauropods.

The position of the nasal openings originally led paleontologists to think that *Brachiosaurus* and its other massive relatives spent most of their time submerged in water, browsing on soft weeds, with their nostrils above the surface, breathing in air. But it is now recognized that the pressure exerted by the great depth of water needed to cover the animals would have made breathing difficult, if not impossible. Footprints and trackways left by these giant sauropods confirm that they were not aquatic but terrestrial plant-eaters.

An animal's fleshy nostrils may not necessarily be close to its external nasal openings. Modern elephants, for example, have nasal openings on the upper part of the skull, but they breathe through the fleshy nostrils at the tip of their trunks. This raises the question, did some sauropods have trunks?

Another possible function of the large nasal openings of sauropods involves heat regulation; the openings may have been lined with moist, blood-rich skin that helped to keep the animal's brain cool in hot weather.

Brachiosaurus' neck was extremely long, making up about half of its height. There were no more neck vertebrae than usual among sauropods (between 12 and 19), but each was elongated to three times the length of the vertebrae of the back.

An unusual feature among sauropods—but a characteristic of the brachiosaur family—was that the front legs were longer than the back legs. So, the whole body sloped down from its highest point at the shoulders, as in a modern giraffe, giving the animal's long neck an even greater reach to tree-top foliage that was beyond the reach of other dinosaurs.

Family Camarasauridae

Members of this family were much smaller than their contemporaries, the brachiosaurs and diplodocids. Their necks and tails were shorter, and their skulls were higher, with blunter snouts. The teeth, too, were quite different from those of other sauropods; they were long, spoon-shaped, and forward-pointing. All these features suggest that the camarasaurs ate different plants from the larger sauropods in the locality, and so did not compete with them for food.

NAME	*Camarasaurus*
TIME	Late Jurassic
LOCALITY	North America (Colorado, Oklahoma, Utah, and Wyoming)
SIZE	up to 59 ft/18 m long

This ubiquitous sauropod probably roamed in herds over the moist, tropical plains that covered western North America during the Jurassic Period. Its heavy, spoon-shaped teeth could have dealt with fibrous plants, such as ferns and horsetails, and it could have reached up to the lower branches of conifer trees, tearing away great mouthfuls of tough, needle-like leaves.

Camarasaurus had enormous nasal openings on top of its skull. Their size, together with the animal's short face, has led some paleontologists to speculate that this sauropod had a trunk, like that of a modern elephant, which it used in the same way. However, other scientists think that the large nasal openings acted as a cooling device for the brain (see *Brachiosaurus*, pp.271–272).

The remains of juveniles have been found with adult *Camarasaurus* in the same sequence of rocks (known as the Morrison Formation) in the western USA. This suggests that the young traveled with the herd, maybe on long migrations in search of food. Periodic droughts typical of this tropical Jurassic land could have made such migrations necessary.

Another clue to lifestyle is found in the isolated heaps of polished pebbles preserved in the same rocks. These could be the regurgitated stomach stones. Many sauropods, including *Camarasaurus*, swallowed rough-edged stones as an aid to grinding up their tough plant food. (Many modern birds also swallow stones for the same reason.) When the stones became so worn as to be of little use as digestive aids, they were regurgitated and replaced with new rough-edged stones.

NAME *Euhelopus*

TIME Late Jurassic or Early Cretaceous

LOCALITY Asia (China)

SIZE 49 ft / 15 m long

Although *Euhelopus* and *Camarasaurus* lived on opposite sides of the world, the two sauropods were closely related and of similar build. There were some differences, however. For example, *Euhelopus* had a much longer neck, made up of 17–19 elongated vertebrae (*Camarasaurus* had a short neck, with only about 12 vertebrae). In addition, *Euhelopus* did not have the "pug nose" of its relative; its head was longer, with a more pointed snout. But like *Camarasaurus*, it possessed the same heavy, spoon-shaped teeth, and large nasal openings on top of its head.

NAME *Opisthocoelicaudia*

TIME Late Cretaceous

LOCALITY Asia (Mongolia)

SIZE possibly 40 ft / 12.2 m long

The exact size and appearance of this sauropod can only be guessed at, since the one skeleton unearthed in the Gobi Desert of Mongolia was missing its neck and head. However, the rest of the body was well-preserved, and seems to be that of a typical, though relatively small and streamlined, camarasaur.

It is the way in which the tail vertebrae lock together that sets *Opisthocoelicaudia* apart from all other known sauropods. Usually, a sauropod's vertebrae are hollowed out on their front ends (i.e. concave toward the animal's head), and they lock together in a forward-pointing arrangement. The tail vertebrae of *Opisthocoelicaudia*, however, are concave on their rear faces, and lock together in a backward-pointing direction, towards the tip of the tail. This feature gives the animal its name, which means "tail bones hollow at the back."

The peculiar articulation of *Opisthocoelicaudia*'s tail formed a powerful and rigid arrangement. Some paleontologists have suggested that the tail was used as a prop to steady the animal when it reared up on hind legs to feed on the topmost branches of trees. Other sauropod dinosaurs, such as the diplodocids (see pp.274–276) and the titanosaurs (see p.277), seem to have used their tails to prop themselves up in the same way.

LONG-NECKED BROWSING
DINOSAURS CONTINUED

Family Diplodocidae

Diplodocids were sauropod dinosaurs with enormously long necks and even longer tails. Their bodies and limbs were slender, and their heads tiny. But despite their great length, these giant plant-eaters were lightweights in comparison to their relatives, the bulky brachiosaurs (see pp.271–272). This was because the vertebrae of diplodocids had been reduced to a complex latticework of bony struts, designed to save weight, and yet be able to take maximum stress.

The diplodocid family thrived worldwide during the Late Jurassic Period and into the Cretaceous. But toward the end of that period, the group seems to have gone into decline, with only a few representatives restricted to eastern Asia.

NAME Diplodocus

TIME Late Jurassic

LOCALITY North America (Colorado, Montana, Utah, and Wyoming)

SIZE 85 ft/26 m long

Diplodocus was a huge animal, some specimens reaching lengths of 100 ft/30 m, although the average individual was 85 ft/26 m long. Most of its length was accounted for by the long neck (about 24 ft/7.3 m), and the extra-long tail (about 46 ft, 14 m). The high, narrow body was only about 13 ft/4 m long, and the tiny head measured just over 2 ft/60 cm in length.

Despite its great size, Diplodocus weighed only 11 US tons/10 tonnes—about one-eighth the weight of Brachiosaurus (see pp.271–272), and one-third that of Apatosaurus (also known as Brontosaurus, opposite), neither of which were as long as Diplodocus. The

reason for this was in the lightweight structure of the animal's vertebrae, which were so hollowed out as to be almost cavernous. But the bony struts that remained were strong enough to support the animal's great frame.

The name Diplodocus means "double beam," and refers to a pair of anvil-shaped bones, or skids, that grew from the underside of each vertebra of the tail. These would have protected the delicate blood vessels and tissues on the underside of the tail as it was dragged over the rough ground.

A well-preserved skeleton of Diplodocus was found in Wyoming at the turn of the century by an expedition financed by the American steel millionaire, Andrew Carnegie. Several casts were made of this skeleton and distributed to eight museums throughout the world. Unfortunately, the original Wyoming specimen was incomplete—the bones of the front feet were never found. But in order to complete the casts, the feet were modeled—inaccurately, as it turned out—on the feet of Camarasaurus (see pp.272–273), a sauropod that lived in Wyoming at the same time as Diplodocus. The mistake can be seen in the front feet—Diplodocus had only one clawed toe on each foot, not three as portrayed.

The hind legs of Diplodocus were longer than the front legs—as was usual among the sauropods (except for the brachiosaur family). The animal's body sloped downward from the high hips. The vertebrae of the lower back, hips, and upper tail had developed tall, vertical spines, and these would have formed attachment points for strong muscles to operate the enormous neck and tail.

It was probably Diplodocus' habit to rear up on its hind legs, bending the tail around to form a "third leg" for balance. Stretching up with its long neck, the animal could browse on the uppermost cones and leaves of the coniferous trees that dotted the Jurassic landscape. Just like today in parts of Africa where herds of giraffes gather, the trees of 150 million years ago would have had a distinctive "browsing line," below which level most of the leaves would have been stripped away. But instead of the modern-day browsing line at a height of about 20 ft/6 m, the Jurassic line would have been 49 ft/15 m above the ground.

The only predators big enough to attack *Diplodocus* would have been members of the allosaur family, such as *Allosaurus*, which weighed up to 2 US tons/2 tonnes (see p.261). *Diplodocus'* only weapons against such powerful carnivores were its tail and forelegs, combined with its bulk. The long, flexible tail, powered by great back muscles, could have swept clear a large area around the animal, and the whip-like tip could have stunned a predator. Another ploy could have been to rear up on hind legs and bring the stout forelegs crashing down on its attacker.

NAME *Apatosaurus* (Brontosaurus)

TIME Late Jurassic

LOCALITY North America (Colorado, Oklahoma, Utah, and Wyoming)

SIZE up to 70 ft/ 21.3 m long

The giant, plant-eating dinosaur *Apatosaurus* was once known by the more familiar and evocative name of *Brontosaurus*. This means "thunder lizard," and could be a reference to the noise its 33 US ton/30 tonne bulk must have made as it walked through its homeland in today's western USA. But *Brontosaurus* was the second name allocated to remains of the beast. So, according to strict scientific convention, it is more properly called by the first name given to it—*Apatosaurus*.

Up until 1975, the skull of *Apatosaurus* was unknown, although the rest of its skeleton had been discovered about 100 years before. The head of this giant sauropod was

tiny in comparison with its body—a mere 22 in/55 cm long out of a total body length of over 65 ft/20 m. Although it was not as long as *Diplodocus*, *Apatosaurus* was simply a bulkier version of it. Both animals had long, slender peg-like teeth that grew only at the front of their jaws. The teeth were clearly not very strong and were replaced by new ones as they became worn. There are gaps between them and strange outward facing wear marks on the cutting ends. Such large bulky animals are always herbivores and have to spend much of their lives eating to get enough low-energy plant material to survive. Until recently the feeding habits of peg-toothed sauropods has been something of a mystery. Now research shows that the wear was produced by the action of stripping foliage from branches, using the "gappy" teeth as rakes.

Both animals could rear up on their hind legs to crop the highest vegetation—though this would have been much more of an effort for *Apatosaurus* since it weighed three times as much as *Diplodocus*. However, *Apatosaurus'* great weight could have been used effectively against a predator such as *Allosaurus*. The plant-eater could have reared up and then brought its heavy forelegs down to crush its enemy. It seems that this ploy did not always work, since many bones of *Apatosaurus* have been found scored with tooth marks similar to those of *Allosaurus* (see p.261). But it could be that the carnivore did not overcome *Apatosaurus*, but came across dead specimens and fed off their corpses.

Apatosaurus had a longer tail than *Diplodocus*, made up of no less than 82 interlocking vertebrae (as compared with 73 in *Diplodocus*). Like *Diplodocus*, it had pairs of bony skids on the underside of the tail vertebrae, which would have helped to protect the soft tissues of the tail.

Apatosaurus could have used its heavy tail as a great whiplash to deter attackers. The tail was powered by strong back muscles, which were anchored to tall spines projecting from the vertebrae of the lower body.

Like *Diplodocus*, *Apatosaurus* had five short toes on each foot, with one claw on the "big toe" of each front foot, and three claws on each back foot. There were thick wedges of weight-bearing cartilage in the ankle joints (as in those of modern elephants), for flexibility and to spread its weight.

NAME *Dicraeosaurus*

TIME Late Jurassic

LOCALITY Africa (Tanzania)

SIZE 41 ft/12.6 m long

NAME *Mamenchisaurus*

TIME Late Jurassic

LOCALITY Asia (Mongolia)

SIZE 72 ft/22 m long

Not all diplodocids were giants. *Dicraeosaurus* (right) was a relatively small member of the family. It was different in other ways, too—its neck was shorter, its head larger and its tail lacked the whiplash end.

The tall spines that projected from the vertebrae, and provided muscle-attachment points, were not straight as in *Diplodocus* and *Apatosaurus*. Each spine was forked at the top, like a "Y," and this feature gives *Dicraeosaurus* its name—"forked lizard." These tall spines were not confined to the lower back and upper tail as they were in other diplodocids. They ranged along the whole length of the back and even up into the neck. Perhaps they carried strong ligaments, which linked several vertebrae at a time to give extra strength to the backbone.

The remains of *Dicraeosaurus* were found in the fossil-rich rocks of Tendaguru Hill, in modern Tanzania. These Late Jurassic rocks yielded many other dinosaurs, including the giant sauropod *Brachiosaurus* (see pp.271–272) and the plated dinosaur *Kentrosaurus* (see p.300), a relative of *Stegosaurus* (see pp.298–299). All these plant-eaters lived together peacefully on the tropical river plains of eastern Africa, browsing on different plants that grew at different levels, thereby avoiding competition with each other.

This animal (below) had the longest neck of any known dinosaur— of any known animal, in fact. Its neck is so unusual in structure that many paleontologists place *Mamenchisaurus* in a family of its own.

The neck accounted for almost half the animal's total length. It consisted of 19 vertebrae, each elongated to over twice the length of the 12 back vertebrae. Slender, bony struts grew out from each neck vertebra and overlapped the one behind, to provide greater strength and support.

As the animal walked, its stiff neck must have been held out almost horizontally from the body. All movement would have been restricted to the flexible joint between the neck and head, plus a swinging motion from the shoulders. Presumably, this super-long neck gave *Mamenchisaurus* an advantage over other long-necked sauropods in the locality. When it reared up on hind legs, it was able to reach a new food source—the fresh growth at the very tips of the uppermost branches of conifers.

In 1986, the bones of a mighty sauropod were unearthed in Late Jurassic deposits in New Mexico. These have yet to be studied and formally described, but their owner has been tentatively given the name *Seismosaurus* ("earthquake lizard") to reflect its possible size. Initial calculations put this beast at 130 ft/40 m long. Its proportions seem to be like those of *Diplodocus*, but the forelegs were longer. If the early findings prove correct, *Seismosaurus* will hold the record for the world's largest-ever land animal.

Family Titanosauridae

This was the latest family of sauropods, surviving right to the end of the Cretaceous Period. The group was widespread, ranging all over the world, especially in the southern continents, and survived for about 80 million years. Not all members of this family were "titans" (the mythical giants of Greek legend), as their name implies. Most averaged 40–50 ft/12.2–15.2 m long, which was small in comparison to some of the brachiosaurs and diplodocids.

To date, only fragmentary remains of titanosaurs have been found, not complete skeletons. They seem to have been like *Diplodocus* in structure, but with a shorter neck and a high skull that sloped steeply down to the snout. But unlike *Diplodocus* and other large sauropods, titanosaurs had solid vertebrae; their bones were not hollowed out as a weight-saving adaptation. In addition to this solid skeleton, some animals also had bony armor covering their backs—a unique feature in sauropods.

NAME *Saltasaurus*

TIME Late Cretaceous

LOCALITY South America (Argentina)

SIZE 39 ft/12 m long

The remains of this medium-sized sauropod came as a surprise to paleontologists when discovered in Salta Province of northwest Argentina in 1970. Lying around a group of skeletons were thousands of bony plates. Most of these were tiny, about ¼ in/5 mm across; others were larger, about 4½ in/11 cm across, and may have borne horny spikes.

Dinosaur skin is not normally preserved, so we have little or no evidence of its nature, beyond an expectation that it was scaly because they were reptiles. But here there is good evidence that in life, these bony plates would have studded the thick skin of the animal's broad back and sides, forming a protective armor for the otherwise defenseless plant-eater against the flesh-eating carnosaurs of the day (see pp.258–265). The tail was flexible and could have supported the body when the animal reared up to reach high vegetation.

The fact that these unique armored sauropods were confined largely to South America indicates that the continent could have been separate, in Mid Cretaceous times, from the great northern landmass that included North America and Eurasia. Present-day Central America was under water in the Mid Cretaceous. So the South American fauna would have developed in isolation, removed from evolutionary changes.

NAME *Alamosaurus*

TIME Late Cretaceous

LOCALITY North America (Montana, New Mexico, Texas, and Utah)

SIZE 69 ft/21 m long

Alamosaurus was among the last sauropods to live before the mass extinction of the dinosaurs at the end of the Cretaceous Period, 65 million years ago. During Late Cretaceous times, there had been a dramatic climatic change in many parts of the world. Much of lowland North America had turned into moist, swampy jungle, which was the domain of the ornithopod dinosaurs—two-legged sprinters with bird-like feet (see pp.278–297). But there were still some high, dry places where the sauropods could live.

It is appropriate that this section on the great saurischian dinosaurs should end with *Alamosaurus*. It was one of the last dinosaurs to survive, and, perhaps coincidentally, is named after the Alamo, that famous fortress in San Antonio where the Texans made their last stand in 1836 against the Mexicans.

FABROSAURS, HETERODONTOSAURS, AND PACHYCEPHALOSAURS

INFRAORDER ORNITHOPODA

Members of the great reptilian order of "bird-hipped" dinosaurs, the Ornithischia, were all plant-eaters. The cheek teeth of most ornithischian dinosaurs were set slightly in from the edges of the jaws. The space lateral to the teeth was probably enclosed by fleshy cheeks which prevented food from falling out of the sides of the mouth during the lengthy process of chewing. These cheeks may have been the reason for the great success of the small to medium-sized (up to 33 ft/10 m long) plant-eating dinosaurs of the Jurassic and Cretaceous periods. Linked to this success was the extinction of their early, cheekless rivals, the prosauropod saurischians of the Triassic (see pp.266–269).

Ornithischian dinosaurs fall into several groups, some of which consist of four-legged creatures that were armed in various ways. The stegosaurs had bony plates down their backs (see pp.298–300). The ankylosaurs had armor-plated skins and "clubs" at the end of their tails (see pp.291–305). The ceratopsids had horns on their heads and bony neck frills (see pp.306–313).

The ornithopods, or "bird feet," walked on two legs, and may have been the ancestral group from which the other ornithischian dinosaurs evolved. They varied in size, habits, and distribution, but structurally they were all similar. A highly successful group, they survived for 148 million years, spanning the whole of the Jurassic and Cretaceous periods.

Family Fabrosauridae

The earliest-known ornithopods belong to this family and date from the Early Jurassic Period, some 200 million years ago. This was the heyday of the fabrosaurs, and they spread throughout the world. In appearance, they were small and lizard-like, but they ran upright on long, slender legs. Superficially, they looked like small, carnivorous theropod dinosaurs (see pp.250–265). In some classifications they are placed apart from the ornithopods but still within the ornithischians.

NAME *Lesothosaurus*

TIME Early Jurassic

LOCALITY Africa (Lesotho)

SIZE 3 ft 3 in/1 m long

This small animal was lightly built and fleet of foot, well-suited to sprinting over the hot, dry plains of southern Africa. Its long legs, short arms, flexible neck and slender tail set the general pattern for all subsequent ornithopods. Its skull was small, short and flat-faced, rather like that of a modern iguana. The pointed teeth had grooved edges: during chewing, its upper teeth fitted alternately between the lower ones, producing a chopping motion which would have dealt with tough plants.

A pair of *Lesothosaurus* skeletons found together in southern Africa were curled up and surrounded by worn, discarded teeth, although the skulls of both animals contained a full set of teeth. On the basis of this find, some paleontologists think that they may have slept through the hottest, driest months of the year underground, as do many modern desert creatures. The worn teeth could have been shed during sleep, while new ones grew.

Another find in Lesotho consisted of a jawbone and some teeth. These scanty remains were called *Fabrosaurus*. It is possible that this animal and *Lesothosaurus* were the same creature.

NAME *Scutellosaurus*

TIME Early Jurassic

LOCALITY North America (Arizona)

SIZE 4 ft/1.2 m long

Scutellosaurus was an armored fabrosaur—the only one known. Rows of bony studs covered its back and flanks, forming a kind of skin armor. Perhaps to compensate for this extra weight,

Scutellosaurus' tail was particularly long, about half the total body length. It would have been held out stiffly behind the body to help the animal balance on its hind legs when it needed to run away from an attacker.

The arms, too, were longer than those of other fabrosaurs, suggesting that *Scutellosaurus* probably browsed and rested on all-fours, relying on its armor as its first means of defense.

NAME *Echinodon*

TIME Late Jurassic or Early Cretaceous

LOCALITY Europe (England)

SIZE 2 ft/60 cm long

Only the jaw bones of this small fabrosaur have been found. But they provide enough evidence to tell paleontologists that *Echinodon* had a shorter head than *Lesothosaurus*, and that it also possessed unusual teeth. Most reptiles have teeth all of the same size and shape, but *Echinodon* had paired canine-type teeth at the front of its jaws, long and sharp, like the "eye teeth" of modern cats and dogs. Such teeth were also a feature of a group of contemporary ornithopods—the heterodontosaurs.

Family Heterodontosauridae

Members of the heterodontosaur family looked very much like fabrosaurs and lived at the same time, but they are distinguished from members of that family by their teeth, which were quite different. In fact, the dental arrangement of the Heterodontosauridae family was unique among dinosaurs, and indeed among most other reptiles as well.

Heterodontosaurs were among the first dinosaurs to have developed cheeks, to retain food within the mouth during chewing. They also had three kinds of teeth in their jaws, each of which performed a different function (see *Heterodontosaurus*, right). The family's name reflects this distinctive feature—"varied-toothed lizards."

NAME *Heterodontosaurus*

TIME Early Jurassic

LOCALITY Africa (South Africa)

SIZE 3 ft/90 cm long

The rabbit-sized skull of *Heterodontosaurus* was discovered in 1962 in South Africa's Cape Province, and a complete skeleton has since been found. In build it was like a fabrosaur—a small lightweight, two-legged plant-eater.

Heterodontosaurus was, however, remarkable because of its teeth. Usually, a reptile's teeth are all the same size and shape. But *Heterodontosaurus* had three kinds of teeth—a dental pattern that is reminiscent of a mammal's, although *Heterodontosaurus* had no connection with the mammalian line of evolution.

At the front of the upper jaw there were some small, pointed teeth (like a mammal's incisors). There were no opposing teeth at the front of the lower jaw; instead, the chin bone carried a horny beak. This bone (known as the predentary) was unique to the ornithischian dinosaurs. No other reptile, or indeed any backboned animal, has this bone: usually, the two dentary bones that make up the lower jaw meet in the center to form the chin.

Behind the upper teeth and lower beak, *Heterodontosaurus* had two pairs of large, canine-type teeth (like the canines of a mammal). The lower pair fitted into a socket in the upper jaw. Behind these canines were the back teeth—tall, chisel-like teeth with cutting edges (comparable to a mammal's molars).

Each type of tooth performed a different job. The pointed ones at the front combined with the beak to nip off leaves; the back teeth cut the leaves up with a scissor-like motion and ground them into small pieces.

Nobody knows the function of this animal's canine teeth. Carnivorous mammals have canines for tearing apart flesh, but *Heterodontosaurus* was a plant-eater. Some skulls have been found that had no canines, or even sockets that would have contained them. This has led some paleontologists to suggest that only the males had canines, and that they used them for fighting each other. According to this theory, skulls without canines would have belonged to females.

FABROSAURS, HETERODONTOSAURS, AND PACHYCEPHALOSAURS CONTINUED

NAME *Pisanosaurus*

TIME Late Triassic

LOCALITY South America (Argentina)

SIZE 3 ft/90 cm long

Pisanosaurus has the distinction of being the oldest-known of the successful and long-lived order of ornithischian dinosaurs. It lived during Late Triassic times, several million years before any other "bird-hipped" dinosaur appeared.

Although its fossil remains are scanty, paleontologists think that *Pisanosaurus* belongs to the heterodontosaur family. The fact that all members of this family discovered to date lived in southern Africa or South America is taken as strong evidence that these southern continents were still joined together during Late Triassic times.

INFRAORDER PACHYCEPHALOSAURIA

The skulls of the so-called "thick-headed lizards," or boneheads, were dome-shaped, giving their owners a bizarre appearance. The pachycephalosaurs had high foreheads and thick skull caps, made up of enormously thickened bones. Some species also had bony frills, knobs, and spikes on the back and sides of their heads, and sometimes on their snouts.

Most paleontologists believe that these boneheaded dinosaurs had a lifestyle similar to that of modern mountain goats. Like these mammals, they would have lived together in herds, and the males would most likely have engaged in competitive, head-butting fights to establish a pecking order.

In other respects, pachycephalosaurs were like ornithopods— two-legged plant-eaters, with five-fingered hands, three-toed feet (with a tiny first toe), and a long, heavy tail. As a group they

were rare, known mainly from Late Cretaceous times in North America and central Asia. But one bonehead, called *Yaverlandia*, has been found earlier than this—dating from Early Cretaceous rocks in southern England.

Family Pachycephalosauridae

The pachycephalosaurid family have the characteristic thick, high-domed skulls of this infraorder, which probably denotes a competitive head-butting habit.

NAME *Stegoceras*

TIME Late Cretaceous

LOCALITY North America (Alberta)

SIZE 6 ft 6 in/2 m long

The whole body of this boneheaded dinosaur seems designed to provide the power behind the ramming head. When an animal charged a rival, its head would have been lowered at right angles, and its neck, body, and tail held out stiffly in a horizontal line, balanced at the hips. The skull cap was thickened into a high dome of solid bone, and the small brain was well-protected inside. This domed area would have absorbed the main impact of the blow as the animal crashed head-on against its opponent. A full-grown *Stegoceras* could have weighed 120 lb/54.4 kg.

The "grain" of the bone in the dome was angled perpendicularly to the surface, and this orientation would have made it capable of withstanding great impact.

Stegoceras, like other pachycephalosaurs, had small, slightly curved and serrated teeth that were highly effective for shredding plant material. Their life habits were probably similar to those of modern wild sheep and goats.

NAME *Prenocephale*

TIME Late Cretaceous

LOCALITY Asia (Mongolia)

SIZE 8 ft/2.4 m long

A truly bulbous dome surmounted the head of *Prenocephale*, and a row of bony spikes and bumps surrounded back and sides of the solid skull. It is probable that the females had smaller, thinner skulls than the males, just as the females of the modern big-horned sheep of the Rocky Mountains in the USA have smaller horns than the males.

Like other boneheaded dinosaurs, *Prenocephale* probably had large eyes and a keen sense of smell. It lived in upland forests, browsing on leaves and fruits.

NAME *Pachycephalosaurus*

TIME Late Cretaceous

LOCALITY North America (Alberta)

SIZE 15 ft/4.6 m long

Pachycephalosaurus was a giant among boneheads. Although it is known only from its skull, this measured 2 ft/60 cm in length. The enormous dome on top of the head was made of solid bone, some 10 in/25 cm thick. Like a great crash helmet, the thick skull could have absorbed tremendous impact as rival males butted each other, head-on.

Pachycephalosaurus was not only the biggest member of the bonehead family, it was also the last member to exist before all its plant-eating relatives and its carnivorous cousins became extinct at the end of the Cretaceous Period.

Family Homalocephalidae

This family of pachycephalosaurs have low, domed skulls. Paleontologists believe that the homalocephalids used their skulls for for a head-pushing, rather than butting, habit.

NAME *Homalocephale*

TIME Late Cretaceous

LOCALITY Asia (Mongolia)

SIZE 10 ft/3 m long

Homalocephale means "even head," and refers to the fact that this pachycephalosaur did not have a dome on top of its skull. It had a rather flat, wedge-shaped head, although the bones of the skull cap were greatly thickened. There were numerous pits and bony knobs scattered all over the head. This has led some paleontologists to think that rival male *Homalocephale* fought the same kinds of ritualistic, head-butting battles as do the modern marine iguanas of the Galápagos Islands.

Homalocephale had broad hips, and paleontologists interpret this in different ways. Some suggest that the hips could have absorbed the impact when rival males fought. Others postulate that the hips indicate this bonehead gave birth to live young.

HYPSILOPHODONTS

FAMILY HYPSILOPHODONTIDAE

Hypsilophodonts were the "gazelles" of the dinosaur world. They probably lived in social herds, like modern deer, and would have been continually alert. When danger threatened, they sprinted off at high speed, their lightweight bodies and long, running legs facilitating a fast retreat.

Hypsilophodonts were among the most successful of the dinosaurs. As a group they flourished for about 100 million years, from the Late Jurassic to the end of the Cretaceous, and spread to every continent in the world except Asia.

They are also an important group in the evolution of the dinosaurs. Paleontologists believe that the hypsilophodonts gave rise to two other major groups of ornithopods—the familiar iguanodonts (see pp.286–289) and the abundant "duckbills" or hadrosaurs (see pp.290–297).

The herbivorous lifestyle of hypsilophodonts was similar to that of the fabrosaurs (see pp.278–279), the group of earlier Jurassic ornithopods that became extinct at about the same time the hypsilophodonts began their rise. In fact, the chronological evidence combined with several similarities has led some paleontologists to believe that the fabrosaurs were the direct ancestors of the hypsilophodonts.

Structurally, the fabrosaurs and hypsilophodonts were similar. But the hypsilophodonts had several anatomical modifications. For example, they had developed the retaining cheeks that prevented food from falling out of the sides of the mouth. And their upper and lower teeth met, or occluded, as regular rows, rather than interlocking alternately as those of fabrosaurs. This would have given a better chewing and grinding surface.

The hips of hypsilophodonts were also more advanced than those of the fabrosaurs. Part of the pubis bone (known as the pre-pubic process) projected forward, and provided an extra area to which the muscles of the hind legs could attach (see p.234). This resulted in greater running power. But this extra bone was still small enough to leave room for the plant-eater's capacious gut, which was accommodated, in the usual arrangement, in front of its hips.

From the Late Cretaceous rocks of Montana comes possible evidence of how hypsilophodonts lived. Ten dinosaur nests were unearthed there in 1979. Each nest contained about 24 small, ellipsoidal eggs, arranged in a circular pattern, all with the pointed ends downward. The remains of young hypsilophodonts were also discovered in the same area. From this indirect evidence, paleontologists have surmised that the young left the nest immediately on hatching, but remained in the same area for a time, being cared for by their parent or parents. The fact that the eggs were so precisely arranged in the nests suggests that there was certainly some parental care, at least before birth. Modern turtles and alligators also lay their eggs carefully in well-concealed nests in a similar manner, though turtles then vacate the nesting site, leaving their young to take their chances alone.

In contrast, when the eggs of sauropod dinosaurs have been found, they are always laid out in lines, as though the female dropped them while on the move rather than collecting them together in a nest. This suggests that the sauropod eggs were probably left unguarded or cared for and that the offspring were on their own after they hatched out.

NAME *Dryosaurus*

TIME Late Jurassic to Early Cretaceous

LOCALITY North America (Colorado, Utah, and Wyoming), Africa (Tanzania). Possibly Australia and Europe (England and Romania)

SIZE up to 10 ft/3 m long

Dryosaurus (also known as *Dysalotosaurus*) was one of the largest of the hypsilophodonts. Although it was also one of the earliest members of the family, its anatomy was advanced in several ways. For example, each of its long, slender legs had only three toes. And there were no teeth in the front part of the upper jaw. Instead, the horny beak at the front of the lower jaw met with a tough, toothless pad opposite on the upper jaw—an efficient arrangement for cropping vegetation.

Like other members of this family of long-legged sprinters, *Dryosaurus'* shin bones were much longer than its thigh bones. The animal's running power came from the heavy leg muscles, which were concentrated around the short thigh bones, and the lower leg. The creature's long feet were operated by light but powerful tendons.

With these characteristics the leg works somewhat like a long pendulum which has a great deal of length but only a small weight on the end. As a consequence of these proportions it has a short swing-time or "period." When the animal is running the hind leg moves backwards and forwards very quickly—an obvious advantage for a creature that needs to be able to move at great speed.

A further and very necessary aid to speed is a tail to counterbalance the forward weight of *Dryosaurus'* large gut and body. The effectiveness of the tail as a counterbalance is increased by its stiffness. This is achieved by ossified ligaments which link the vertebrae of the tail together. This arrangement gave *Dryosaurus* extra speed and it is exactly the same as the pattern possessed by modern deer and gazelle.

Dryosaurus was obviously a wide-ranging ornithopod, with remains occuring as far apart as western North America and East Africa. In Jurassic times, these continents had begun to separate, but only the initial stretch of the North Atlantic Ocean separated them from each other, and it would still have been possible for animals to migrate across land by way of Europe (where remains of what may be dryosaurs have also been found) and via Siberia and Alaska, which were still linked. This migration explains why the dinosaur remains found in the fossil-rich beds of the Morrison Formation in the western USA are so similar to those that have been discovered in Tendaguru Hill of Tanzania.

Dryosaurus would, therefore, have shared its world with giant plant-eating dinosaurs such as *Apatosaurus* (=*Brontosaurus*), *Diplodocus* and *Brachiosaurus*; small, rapacious carnivores such as the coelurosaurs *Coelurus* and *Elaphrosaurus*; and large carnosaurs such as *Allosaurus* and the horned *Ceratosaurus*.

NAME	*Hypsilophodon*
TIME	Early Cretaceous
LOCALITY	Europe (England and Portugal) and North America (South Dakota)
SIZE	5 ft/1.5 m long

About 20 perfect skeletons of this small hypsilophodont were found in one particular bed of Lower Cretaceous rocks in the Isle of Wight, just off the coast of southern England. This find probably represents a herd of animals that lived and died together, perhaps overwhelmed by the rising tide of the shallow seas that lay over northern Europe some 120 million years ago.

Hypsilophodon is the classic representative of the family, and has given its name to the whole group. Its name means "high ridge tooth," and refers to the tall, grooved cheek teeth. The upper and lower teeth met to form a flat surface ideally suited to chewing and grinding up tough plant food. These teeth are are typical feature of all hypsilophodonts.

Oddly enough, in comparison with its earlier relatives of the Late Jurassic (see *Dryosaurus*, pp.282–283), *Hypsilophodon* had certain primitive features. For example, it had four toes on each foot, and there were incisor-type teeth at the front of the upper jaw. When these were closed on the toothless, horny beak of the lower jaw, they formed an effective device for cropping vegetation (compare *Heterodontosaurus*, p.279).

Hypsilophodon may also have been armored, with two rows of thin, bony scales running down either side of its back. But paleontologists are uncertain about this feature.

The study of *Hypsilophodon* since its discovery in the 19th century is a classic story of paleontological research and shows how, even with perfect fossil remains, paleontologists also have to rely on analogies with living creatures to infer the lifestyles of new discoveries. When *Hypsilophodon* was first described by Thomas H. Huxley in 1870, paleontologists of the day were struck by the similarity of its build to that of a modern tree kangaroo. For almost a century, classic illustrations of *Hypsilophodon* showed it perched, bird-like, in a tree, with three of its four toes gripping the branch, and the fourth toe directed backward. This reconstruction neatly filled an ecological niche not yet occupied by any dinosaur and so, the idea of a tree-dwelling, plant-eating ornithopod was conceived.

It was not until 1974 that the skeleton of *Hypsilophodon* was reassessed. Paleontologists concluded that there was no evidence to show that it lived in trees. In fact, it was a perfectly-adapted terrestrial animal, capable of running rapidly on two legs.

NAME *Othnielia*

TIME Late Jurassic

LOCALITY North America (Utah and Wyoming)

SIZE 4 ft 6 in/1.4 m long

This dinosaur is named after the famous 19th-century American fossil-hunter and professor at Yale University, Othniel Charles Marsh (see pp.233–234). He had originally given it the name *Nanosaurus* in 1877, but it was renamed exactly 100 years later, in 1977, to commemorate his prolific and pioneering fieldwork in the study of dinosaurs.

Othnielia was a typical hypsilophodont, with long legs and tail, a lightweight body, and short arms with five-fingered hands. Only its teeth differed. They were proportionally smaller than those of other hypsilophodonts, and were completely covered in enamel, not just on their grinding faces.

It is possible that *Othnielia* ate tougher plants than usual, which would explain the presence of the protective tooth enamel to avoid excessive wear. A tough, fibrous diet would also have meant that *Othnielia* had to grind its food down more finely before it could be digested. As an aid to this, *Othnielia*, like all its relatives, had cheeks that retained the food in the mouth while it was being chewed.

NAME *Tenontosaurus*

TIME Early Cretaceous

LOCALITY North America (Arizona, Montana, Oklahoma, and Texas)

SIZE 24 ft/7.3 m long

This dinosaur is so uncharacteristically large compared with other hypsilophodonts that some paleontologists class it with the iguanodonts (see pp.286–289). Indeed, its skull is very similar in shape to that of an iguanodont, but its teeth and their arrangement in the jaws place it firmly in the hypsilophodont family.

Over half the total length of *Tenontosaurus* was made up of the tail, which was enormously thick and heavy. The animal is estimated to have weighed about 1 US ton/900 kg, and probably spent much of its time on all-fours. Its arms were much longer and stouter than those of other hypsilophodonts.

A remarkable find in the rocks of Montana consisted of a skeleton of *Tenontosaurus* surrounded by five complete specimens of *Deinonychus*, a ferocious predator of the day (see pp.254–255). Although these bodies were most likely brought together by chance after death, perhaps in a flash flood, it is interesting to speculate that this mass-burial could have been the outcome of an encounter between the bulky plant-eater and a pack of predators.

Although *Deinonychus* was only about 10 ft/3 m long, it had sharp, meat-shearing fangs, and great, dagger-like claws on its feet. The bulky *Tenontosaurus* could have put up a good fight, kicking out with its heavy-clawed feet or using its great tail as a whiplash. But these were paltry defenses when compared with the lethal weapons of the agile carnivores.

NAME *Thescelosaurus*

TIME Late Cretaceous

LOCALITY North America (Alberta, Montana, Saskatchewan and Wyoming)

SIZE 11 ft 6 in/3.5 m long

NAME *Parksosaurus*

TIME Late Cretaceous

LOCALITY North America (Alberta)

SIZE 8 ft/2.4 m long

Thescelosaurus was discovered in the topmost rocks of the Late Cretaceous Period in western North America. It was bulkier and bigger-boned than its closest relatives, the typically small, lightweight hypsilophodonts. It is possible that *Thescelosaurus* is not a hypsilophodont, but a member of the iguanodont family.

Several features distinguish *Thescelosaurus* from other hypsilophodonts. It had teeth in the front of its upper jaw. It had five toes on each foot (hypsilophodonts had three or four). And its thigh bones were as long as its shin bones (the shins of the hypsilophodonts were longer than the thighs).

The structure of the legs strongly suggests that *Thescelosaurus* was not a gazelle-type sprinter but a slower-moving creature. Although it was not built for speedy escape, rows of bony studs set in the skin of its back would have offered it some protection.

Parksosaurus was one of the last of the long-lived hypsilophodont family still surviving at the time of the mass-extinction of the dinosaurs at the end of the Cretaceous Period. It was similar in build to all other hypsilophodonts with short arms, long shins and feet for sprinting and a stiffened counterbalancing tail. It also has a relatively small head with ridged cheek teeth and a horny beak replacing the front teeth, but there were minor differences in the skull, notably its large eyes. *Hypsilophodon* (see p.283) from the Early Cretaceous appears to be most closely related to *Parksosaurus*.

Parksosaurus probably foraged close to the ground, snuffling about among the low-growing undergrowth, and selectively nipping off its preferred food with its narrow, beaked jaws.

IGUANODONTS

FAMILY IGUANODONTIDAE

The iguanodonts evolved in the Mid Jurassic, about 170 million years ago, and spread throughout the world. *Iguanodon* is the most popular and familiar member of this family of large, plant-eating, ornithopod dinosaurs. They have even been found within what is now the Arctic Circle, although these lands would have been ice-free all those millennia ago. Iguanodonts reached their peak of diversity and abundance by the end of the Early Cretaceous. Thereafter they declined, and finally died out at the end of that period.

Unlike their ancestors—the gazelle-like hypsilophodonts (see pp.282–285)—iguanodonts did not evolve as running animals. Their bodies were bulky and big-boned; the thigh bones were longer than the shin bones (the relative lengths are reversed in sprinting animals); and both the fore- and hind feet had heavy, hoof-like nails. Iguanodonts, therefore, were probably fairly slow-moving animals that spent most of their time on all-fours, browsing on low-growing plants such as horsetails. The beak-like jaws would nip off the leaves, and the rows of high, ridged cheek-teeth would then grind them down to a pulp. These dinosaurs could also rear up on their hind legs to reach higher vegetation and to escape from predators.

The stance of these reptiles has undergone several stages of reinterpretation since they were first found in the early 19th century. To begin with, they were seen as quadrupeds, based on an assumed similarity to living reptiles such as the iguana. However, when more complete specimens were found at the end of the century, it was realized that there was a considerable disparity in size between the forelimbs and hind limbs. This, plus the large tail, was compared with the anatomy and habits of the mammalian kangaroo. It was imagined that the iguanadonts used their large muscular tails for support when reaching to browse in high canopy vegetation. More recently, it was discovered that the tail vertebrae have ossified ligaments interconnecting and stiffening them. It now appears that the tail was used more as a counterbalance to the heavy body and that the iguanodonts probably had a semi-quadrupedal gait—like, indeed, some kangaroos. They could have moved either quadrupedally or bipedally.

NAME	*Callovosaurus*
TIME	Middle Jurassic
LOCALITY	Europe (England)
SIZE	11 ft 6 in / 3.5 m long

Known only from a single thigh bone, *Callovosaurus* was unlike its contemporary relatives, the hypsilophodonts. It was, in fact, the earliest-known member of the iguanodonts, and presumably was similar in structure and appearance to the later *Camptosaurus* (below).

NAME	*Camptosaurus*
TIME	Late Jurassic
LOCALITY	Europe (England and Portugal) and North America (Colorado, South Dakota, Utah, and Wyoming)
SIZE	20 ft / 6 m long

Like *Callovosaurus*, *Camptosaurus* was a primitive member of the iguanodont family. The many skeletons found—particularly in the dinosaur-rich beds of the Morrison Formation in the western USA—suggest that it was an abundant dinosaur.

The skull of *Camptosaurus* was very different from that of its hypsilophodont ancestors. It was long, low and broad; it was also heavy, since some of the gaps between the bones had been closed up. The snout was elongated, and the jaws formed a toothless beak at the tip. A bony palate separated the breathing passages from the eating area of the mouth. This allowed the animal to breathe and chew at the same time – an important development for all herbivores, since they had to spend most of their time eating in order to fuel their massive bodies. *Camptosaurus'* legs were long and powerful, each with three hoofed toes. The thigh bones were massive and slightly curved. The arms were much shorter than the legs, but also equipped with small hoof-like nails, so that the animal could use its hands as feet.

NAME	*Iguanodon*
TIME	Early Cretaceous
LOCALITY	Europe (eg England, Belgium and Germany), North America (Utah), Africa (Tunisia), and Asia (Mongolia)
SIZE	30 ft/9 m long

Iguanodon deserves its place in dinosaur lore. It was the second dinosaur to be discovered, although the word "dinosaur" had yet to be invented (see p.232). Part of its great shin bone was found in southern England in 1809, and then some teeth and other bones were discovered in 1819. Scientists of the day regarded the teeth as belonging to some giant mammal. But Gideon Mantell, a geologist and keen fossil collector, saw that the teeth were reptilian, and that they resembled those of the modern iguana of Central and South America. He named the animal *Iguanodon*, and described it in 1825 to the scientific community. Mantell attempted a restoration, but with the sparse information available, it was speculative. He reconstructed *Iguanodon* as a dragon-like beast, with a heavy tail and small, lizard-like head. He placed a short horn—actually one of the animal's "thumbs"—on the snout.

It was not until 1877 that the true nature of *Iguanodon* became apparent. During that year, in the small town of Bernissart in Belgium, the massive bones of what turned out to be 31 *Iguanodon* were found by workers tunnelling through coal deposits. These spectacular skeletons are now on display in the Royal National Institute of Natural Sciences in Brussels.

Iguanodon stood 16 ft/5 m tall, measured 30 ft/9 m in length, and probably weighed about 5 US tons/4.5 tonnes. Herds of *Iguanodon* would have roamed the tropical Cretaceous landscape, browsing on ferns and horsetails near rivers. Although usually on all-fours, they could also walk upright, using their long outstretched tails to balance.

The head of this great dinosaur ended in a prominent snout and powerful, beak-like jaws. The cheek teeth would have provided a strong, grinding action, because the bones of the upper jaw could move apart when the lower jaw was raised up between them. The banks of cheek teeth then moved past each other, pulverizing the plant food.

The legs were long and pillar-like, each with three stout toes, ending in heavy, hoof-like nails. Each short arm had a five-fingered hand, which could be splayed wide, and used for walking when the animal was on all-fours. Three of the fingers had hoof-like nails. The fifth, or "little," finger was flexible enough to have been used for grasping or hooking down leaves to the mouth. The first finger, or "thumb," was developed into a prominent spike, which stuck out sideways from the hand. In 1825, Mantell had found only one of these thumb spikes and, not knowing which part of the animal it came from, placed it, incorrectly, on the snout as a horn.

The function of these thumb spikes is not known. They could have been used to tear down foliage, as defense against attacks from contemporary predators like *Megalosaurus* (see p.260). Or, perhaps, the spikes were sexual display structures used in courtship and mating.

Like *Megalosaurus*, *Iguanodon* has left its footprints in the rocks of southern England. Great trackways suggest that the animals were walking upright at the time they passed, and were traveling in a herd. Similar footprints, though no actual bones, have also been found in South America and in Spitzbergen, north of today's Arctic Circle, which shows how widespread *Iguanodon* must have been 100 million years ago.

NAME *Vectisaurus*

TIME Early Cretaceous

LOCALITY Europe (England)

SIZE 13 ft/4 m long

Vectisaurus was a close relative of *Iguanodon*, living in the same place at the same time. Indeed, some paleontologists think it was simply a species of *Iguanodon*.

Unlike its famous relative, only scanty remains have been found of *Vectisaurus*, on the Isle of Wight, off the southern English coast. The only difference between it and *Iguanodon* was the height of the spines that grew upward from its backbone. These spines were long enough in *Vectisaurus* to have formed a prominent ridge down the animal's back. This feature has led some paleontologists to think that *Vectisaurus* may represent an early stage in the evolution of the "fin-backed" ornithischian dinosaurs, such as *Ouranosaurus* (right).

Vectisaurus belongs to the Wealden fauna of southern England, which is the most varied Early Cretaceous dinosaur assemblage in Europe. The animals include several other ornithopods such as *Hypsilophodon* and *Valdosaurus*; several species of *Iguanodon*; the nodosaurids *Hylaeosaurus* and *Polacanthus*; the early pachycephalosaurid *Yaverlandia*; several sauropods (including a brachiosaurid, titanosaurid, and possibly a diplodocid); and finally several theropods.

NAME *Ouranosaurus*

TIME Early Cretaceous

LOCALITY Africa (Niger)

SIZE 23 ft/7 m long

Two complete skeletons of *Ouranosaurus* were found in 1965, in the southern Sahara of northeastern Niger. Although the remains were identified as belonging to an iguanodont, it was an unusual-looking member of the family. It had a tall wall of spines running down the center of its back, from the shoulders to halfway along the tail. These spines were outgrowths from the vertebrae of the back, and would have been covered with skin to form a prominent "fin" or "sail."

Another group of dinosaurs, the saurischian spinosaurs, also sported such a fin on the back (see pp.262–263). In fact, one of their members, the large, carnivorous *Spinosaurus*, lived in Niger at about the same time as *Ouranosaurus*.

The function of the fin in the saurischian and ornithischian dinosaurs is not known for certain, but many researchers believe that it was used by these dinosaurs as a mechanism to regulate their body temperature. Such large, bulky animals as *Spinosaurus* and *Ouranosaurus* could easily have become overheated in the hot conditions that prevailed in West Africa during the Cretaceous Period. When the fin was turned toward the sun's rays, its large surface area would have absorbed heat. When it was turned away from the sun, it would have lost heat. Such tall, vertebral spines would have made the body and tail of *Ouranosaurus* quite rigid. But this rigidity was compensated for by the extreme flexibility of the neck. Some paleontologists have proposed that the tall spines actually supported a muscular hump on the back of *Ouranosaurus*, rather like that of a modern American bison. *Ouranosaurus'* skull was also unlike that of other iguanodonts. It was long and low, and sloped gently down to a wide, flat, snout.

The overall appearance of *Ouranosaurus'* skull is reminiscent of a later group of ornithischian dinosaurs, the "duckbills" or hadrosaurs, that evolved in Late Cretaceous times (see pp.290–297). A pair of bony bumps on the skull increased *Ouranosaurus'* likeness to those hadrosaurs with low crests on their heads.

In other respects, *Ouranosaurus* was like *Iguanodon*. It had five-fingered hands, although they were much smaller and the fingers much shorter than those of *Iguanodon*, and only the second and third fingers had "walking hooves." The three-toed feet had heavy, hoof-like nails, as in *Iguanodon*, and the neck was short but flexible.

All in all, *Ouranosaurus* lived like other members of its family. It was probably a slow-moving browser that spent most of its time on all-fours, cropping leaves, fruits, and seeds with its horny, duck-like beak.

NAME *Muttaburrasaurus*

TIME Early Cretaceous

LOCALITY Australia (Queensland)

SIZE 24 ft/7.3 m long

Although Australia reputedly has few dinosaur fossils, the last few years have seen a considerable increase in the rate of discovery especially in Queensland. Two kinds of sauropod are known from the Cretaceous deposits of the region but the most common dinosaurs appear to have been the ankylosaurs (*Minmi*) and large ornithopods—*Muttaburrasaurus*. Both of the latter are quite distinct and probably represent endemic lineages, suggesting that during the Early Cretaceous, the continent of Australia was isolated.

Muttaburrasaurus was unearthed in 1981 from what are now the grasslands of central Queensland. In structure, this creature was similar to *Iguanodon*. Only the skull exhibited minor differences. There was a bony bump on the snout in front of the eyes. It is thought by paleontologists that this could have been a sexual display structure, and it was similar in appearance to the crests possessed by some of the later hadrosaurs, such as *Kritosaurus* (see p.291).

Also, there is evidence that the external nostrils were greatly enlarged, indicating that the sense of smell was extremely important to these creatures.

NAME *Probactrosaurus*

TIME Early Cretaceous

LOCALITY Asia (China)

SIZE 20 ft/6 m long

By the end of the Early Cretaceous Period, about 100 million years ago, iguanodonts had reached their peak both in terms of abundance and diversity, and they had spread all over the world. They began to decline from the Mid-Cretaceous Period onward, and very few remains are found in the Late Cretaceous. *Probactrosaurus* of eastern Asia and *Muttaburrasaurus* of Australia were among the few iguanodonts to survive to the end of the Mesozoic Era.

The demise of the iguanodonts was probably linked with the rise of a most successful group of plant-eating ornithopods. These were the duckbilled dinosaurs, or hadrosaurs, that were already common by Late Cretaceous times (see pp.290–297). Like the West African *Ouranosaurus* (opposite), the anatomy of *Probactrosaurus* has several features akin to the hadrosaurs, but the skull is only incompletely known. It could, therefore, have been close to the ancestry of that group, or it may even have been an early member of it.

DUCKBILLED DINOSAURS

FAMILY HADROSAURIDAE

The hadrosaurs were the most common, varied and well-adapted group of ornithopod dinosaurs. Theirs is a real success story in the history of the ruling reptiles. The group probably evolved in central Asia, and by Late Cretaceous times it had spread all over the lands of the northern hemisphere—migrating eastward into North America across the land bridge that existed at the time. From there the group moved eastward again, into Europe.

The spread of the hadrosaurs however was inhibited somewhat by the fact that the southern landmass of Gondwanaland had broken up by Late Cretaceous times and the continents were drifting apart. No hadrosaurs have been found in Africa, India, or Australia. But some obviously managed to reach South America, because the remains of a primitive, flat-headed hadrosaur, called *Secernosaurus*, were discovered in Late Cretaceous rocks in southern Argentina. These animals probably crossed over into South America from North America via the chain of volcanic islands that existed where Central America now lies.

Superficially, hadrosaurs looked quite different from each other—with many variations of crests and bumps on their heads. Structurally, however, they were all the same. The most obvious feature that united them as a group was the way the front of the face was elongated into a broad, flattened snout with a toothless beak. This beak looked rather like the bill of a modern duck, and it is this feature that has given the group its popular name of "duckbilled" dinosaurs.

Although there were no teeth in the front of a hadrosaur's mouth, there were batteries of cheek teeth arranged in rows in the upper and lower jaws. New teeth continually grew to replace old, worn ones (see *Edmontosaurus*, p.293) which had been worn down or damaged due to the hadrosaurs' tough plant diet. This was a unique development among dinosaurs, and was probably a major factor in the success of the group.

Another likely reason for the hadrosaurs' success was that the flowering plants (angiosperms) had evolved during the Cretaceous Period, and toward the end of that period had multiplied over all the surface of the earth. So, as well as plant foods such as ferns, horsetails, cycads and conifers, hadrosaurs were now able to add a profusion of flowering plants to their diet. Competition from the successful hadrosaurs could well have been an important factor in the decline of the other types of plant-eating dinosaurs—the iguanodonts and giant sauropods—which were not able to compete for resources with these versatile newcomers.

All hadrosaurs had long hind legs and shorter forelegs, both equipped with hoof-like nails for walking. It is likely that they spent most of their time browsing on all fours, but when they had to escape from predators, they would have been able to rear up on their hind legs and sprint away, using their long tails to maintain their balance as they ran.

The hadrosaur family is divided into two distinct groups (subfamilies), categorized according to the type of crest. The first group of animals had flat heads surmounted with solid, bony crests—some even had no crests at all. This flat-headed group is called the hadrosaurine duckbills. They were the most successful, long-lived and wide-ranging members of the family, being among the last dinosaurs to survive.

The second group of hadrosaurs had high, domed heads, surmounted by flamboyant, hollow crests. This second group are called the lambeosaurine duckbills (see pp.295–297). They seem to have evolved in North America, and been largely confined to that continent.

NAME *Bactrosaurus*

TIME Late Cretaceous

LOCALITY Asia (Mongolia and China)

SIZE 13 ft/4 m long

The earliest-known hadrosaur and one of the smallest members of the family, *Bactrosaurus* seems to have been intermediate in structure between the two types of duckbills. It had a low, flat head with no crest, and a narrow bill (both features of the hadrosaurine duckbills), but in build it was like a lambeosaurine duckbill. It had the characteristic dentition of the hadrosaurs, with batteries of cheek teeth; these were set well back in the mouth and were capable of grinding tough plant material. *Bactrosaurus* most probably represents an ancestral stage in the development of the group. It could have evolved from one of the iguanodont family, such as *Probactrosaurus* of China (see p.289).

NAME *Kritosaurus*

TIME Late Cretaceous

LOCALITY North America
(Alberta, Montana, and New Mexico)

SIZE 30 ft/9 m long

NAME *Hadrosaurus*

TIME Late Cretaceous

LOCALITY North America (Montana, New Jersey, New Mexico, and South Dakota)

SIZE 30 ft/9 m long

Hadrosaurus, meaning "big lizard," has the distinction of being the first dinosaur to be discovered in North America. Its bones were found in New Jersey, and it was reconstructed and named in 1858 by the American professor of anatomy, Joseph Leidy, of the University of Pennsylvania. Joseph Leidy recognized that *Hadrosaurus* was structurally related to *Iguanodon,* the remains of which had first been discovered in southern England, and described in 1825 (see p.287).

Leidy was able to avoid the errors of Mantell who made the early, inaccurate reconstructions of *Iguanodon* as a four-legged, dragon-like creature. Leidy had the benefit of more complete skeletal material to work with and was an anatomist by training. By comparison, Mantell's fossils were very incomplete and, although a medical doctor, Mantell had no special training in vertebrate anatomy.

Leidy was able to infer from the structure of *Hadrosaurus* that it could rise up on its hind legs. He showed it in a running pose as a bipedal animal—standing upright on two legs, its short arms dangling and its body bent horizontal to the ground, balanced by the long, outstretched tail.

Hadrosaurus was the typical member of the duckbill family. Like *Kritosaurus,* it did not have a crest on its long, low head, but there was a large hump on its snout, which was formed from solid bone, and was probably covered with thick, hard skin. *Hadrosaurus'* bill, at the front of the jaws, had no teeth, but there were hundreds of teeth at the back of the jaws, and these would have been in a continual state of replacement with new teeth growing to replace those worn down by the animal's tough vegetarian diet.

Hadrosaurs could move their upper and lower jaws against each other in both a vertical and horizontal direction. This range of movement would have produced strong chewing and grinding actions, which would have thoroughly pulverized the food before it was swallowed, making it easier to digest.

Kritosaurus was a typical member of the flat-headed group of duckbilled dinosaurs. Although this creature did not have a crest on its head, the structure of its skull does reveal the beginnings of one—developed as a large, bony hump on the snout in front of the eyes.

The function of this hump of solid bone is not known. It could have been a sexual display structure, perhaps possessed by the males of the species only, and used in courtship and mating. Alternatively, it is possible that the bony hump had the same purpose as the thickened skull caps of the pachycephalosaurs (see pp.280–281). In these creatures the strengthened skull caps served to absorb the impact when rival males crashed head-on in their ritualistic, head-butting battles. These battles probably took place at the beginning of each season to decide leadership of the herd, and control of the harem.

Like most hadrosaurs, *Kritosaurus* had five or six paired rows of grinding cheek teeth, in both the upper and lower jaws. The rows of teeth grew from inside the jaws progressively towards the wear surfaces. Only the uppermost rows of teeth were in use at any one time.

Some paleontologists believe that *Kritosaurus* and *Hadrosaurus* were not in fact separate genera, but merely different species of the same animal.

NAME *Maiasaura*

TIME Late Cretaceous

LOCALITY North America (Montana)

SIZE 30 ft/9 m long

NAME *Shantungosaurus*

TIME Late Cretaceous

LOCALITY Asia (China)

SIZE 43 ft/13 m long

This massive, flat-headed duckbill was among the biggest of the hadrosaurs. An almost complete specimen was discovered in Shandong (formerly Shantung) Province of eastern China during the 1970s, and its reconstructed skeleton is now on display in Beijing's (Peking's) Natural History Museum.

Shantungosaurus had an extra-long tail, accounting for almost half its total body length. This was needed to counterbalance the animal's great weight—probably over 5 US tons/4.5 tonnes. When *Shantungosaurus* walked upright, the tail was held out behind, balancing the body at the hips.

This duckbill's tail was deep, and flattened from side to side—rather like the tail of a crocodile. Because of this structure, paleontologists originally thought that duckbills spent most of their time in water, and used their tails for swimming. However, the vertebrae of the tail were lashed together by bony tendons, making it much too inflexible to have acted as a paddle. In addition, the spines above and below the tail vertebrae sloped backward. In true aquatic animals, these spines are vertical, to provide attachment points for strong swimming muscles.

Shantungosaurus and its relatives most likely ventured into water only to escape predators.

The discovery of *Maiasaura* in 1978 gave paleontologists a new insight into the family life of dinosaurs. In that year, a complete nesting site was found in Montana—the remains of an ancient nursery, some 75 million years old, where duckbills laid their eggs, and the young could develop in a safe and nurturing environment, protected from predators.

This exciting find consisted of the skeleton of an adult (the mother, presumably); several youngsters (each about 3 ft 3 in/1 m long); a group of hatchlings (each about 20 in/50 cm long) together in a fossilized nest; and several other nests complete with intact eggs, and pieces of broken shell lying around.

The nests themselves had been made of heaped-up mounds of mud—long since turned to solid rock—each about 10 ft/3 m in diameter and 5 ft/1.5 m high. In the center of each mound was a crater-like depression, about 6 ft 6 in/2 m in diameter and 2 ft 6 in/0.75 m deep. The spacing between the nests was about 23 ft/7 m, indicating that the mothers nested fairly close to each other, since the average length of *Maiasaura* was some 26 ft/8 m.

The fossilized eggs found in the nests were obviously placed with care. They were arranged in circles within the crater, layer upon layer. The mother probably covered over each layer with earth or sand as she went, and then covered the whole nest with earth when she was finished. This would have kept the eggs warm while they hatched, and well-concealed from predators.

These duckbilled hadrosaurs were obviously social animals, as seen by this nursery site. The females nested in groups, probably even returning to the same site each year, as do some modern animals—seabirds, turtles, and fish. The youngsters stayed with their mothers until they were mature enough to fend for themselves—also seen in many modern groups.

NAME *Anatosaurus*

TIME Late Cretaceous

LOCALITY North America (Alberta)

SIZE 33 ft/10 m long

The popular name for this group of dinosaurs, the "duckbills," was coined after the discovery of the broad, flat skull of this hadrosaur in western North

NAME *Edmontosaurus*

TIME Late Cretaceous

LOCALITY North America (Alberta and Montana)

SIZE 43 ft/13 m long

America. The name *Anatosaurus*, in fact, means "duck lizard," and refers to the animal's horny, toothless bill or beak. The fossil evidence for *Anatosaurus* is good, with several well-preserved skeletons of *Anatosaurus* having been found. From these specimens, paleontologists can tell that this duckbill was over 30 ft/9 m long, stood some 13 ft/4 m tall, and probably weighed about 4 US tons/3.6 tonnes. Two "mummified" specimens were also found—a rare and highly informative discovery—with dried-up tendons and the contents of their stomachs intact. Analysis of the stomach contents revealed that the last meal eaten by these two individuals consisted of pine needles, twigs, seeds, and fruits.

Impressions of the animals' skin were also preserved, stamped into the surrounding rocks. Though all the skin had long since rotted, these impressions show that *Anatosaurus* was covered in a thick, leathery hide.

The same mummified specimens appeared to have had webs of skin between the three main fingers of each hand. At first, this was taken as support for the theory that duckbills were aquatic animals, using their webbed hands and flattened tails for swimming. Closer examination, however, indicated that the hands could not be stretched widely, and it seems more likely that the webs of skin were the shrivelled remains of weight-bearing walking pads, calloused with wear like those on the feet of modern camels. Taken in conjunction with the presence of hoof-like nails on two of the main fingers of each hand, this interpretation of the "webs" supports the current theory that duckbills were true land-dwellers that walked on all-fours.

Many skulls of this large, flat-headed duckbill have been found. The teeth are particularly well-preserved, and show the typical hadrosaur pattern of dentition. Behind the toothless beak, banks of tightly-packed teeth formed a veritable grinding pavement in both jaws. As those at the top were worn down and discarded, new teeth would have grown to replace them from beneath. At any one time, there may have been over 1000 teeth in *Edmontosaurus'* mouth.

The outer edge of each tooth was coated with hard enamel, which wore away more slowly than the dentine that made up the rest of the tooth. The result was that each tooth had a cutting ridge of hard, upstanding enamel. Packed so closely together in each jaw, the batteries of teeth presented a coarse, abrasive surface for pulverizing plant food.

The jaw structure of this creature was rather like that of *Iguanodon* (see p.287) in that the upper jaw could move over the lower jaw, so that the teeth ground against each other when the mouth was closed. This feature produced a shearing, grinding action between the tooth rows, capable of shredding the toughest of plant material. Indeed, *Edmontosaurus* and its relatives lived on coarse food, as the fossilized stomach contents of *Anatosaurus* showed.

Like other hadrosaurs, *Edmontosaurus* had a long tail that counterbalanced the weight of the front end of the animal's body when it rose up on its hind legs in order to run. The tail was also deep—like that of *Shantungosaurus* (opposite)—with long spines extending below the vertebrae, and could have been of some use in swimming when *Edmontosaurus* occasionally ventured into water.

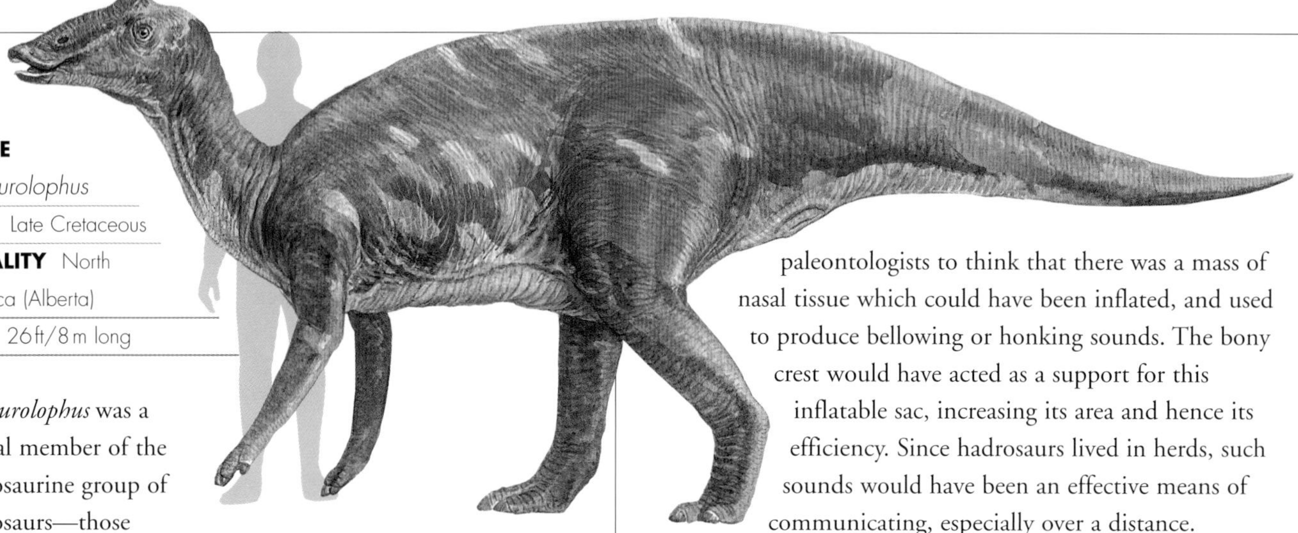

NAME
Prosaurolophus

TIME Late Cretaceous

LOCALITY North America (Alberta)

SIZE 26ft/8m long

Prosaurolophus was a typical member of the hadrosaurine group of hadrosaurs—those duckbills with solid, bony crests on their heads. Its skull was similar to that of one of the flat-headed duckbills, such as *Anatosaurus* (see pp.292–293), but the nasal bones were extended into a low crest of bone that ran from the tip of the broad snout to the top of the head, where it was developed into a small, bony knob. Since this crest became more pronounced in relatives of *Prosaurolophus*, this duckbill may have been ancestral to later members of the family, such as *Saurolophus*.

NAME *Saurolophus*

TIME Late Cretaceous

LOCALITY North America (Alberta and California) and Asia (Mongolia)

SIZE 30ft/9m long

The face of this large duckbill swept upward in a curve, from the broad, flattened snout to the tip of a solid, bony crest that sloped backward from the top of its head. The Asian species had a larger crest than its North American relative and a correspondingly larger body, about 39ft/12m long.

The crest was an extension of the nasal bones, and the nasal passages would have run through it. This has led some paleontologists to think that there was a mass of nasal tissue which could have been inflated, and used to produce bellowing or honking sounds. The bony crest would have acted as a support for this inflatable sac, increasing its area and hence its efficiency. Since hadrosaurs lived in herds, such sounds would have been an effective means of communicating, especially over a distance.

NAME *Tsintaosaurus*

TIME Late Cretaceous

LOCALITY Asia (China)

SIZE 33ft/10m long

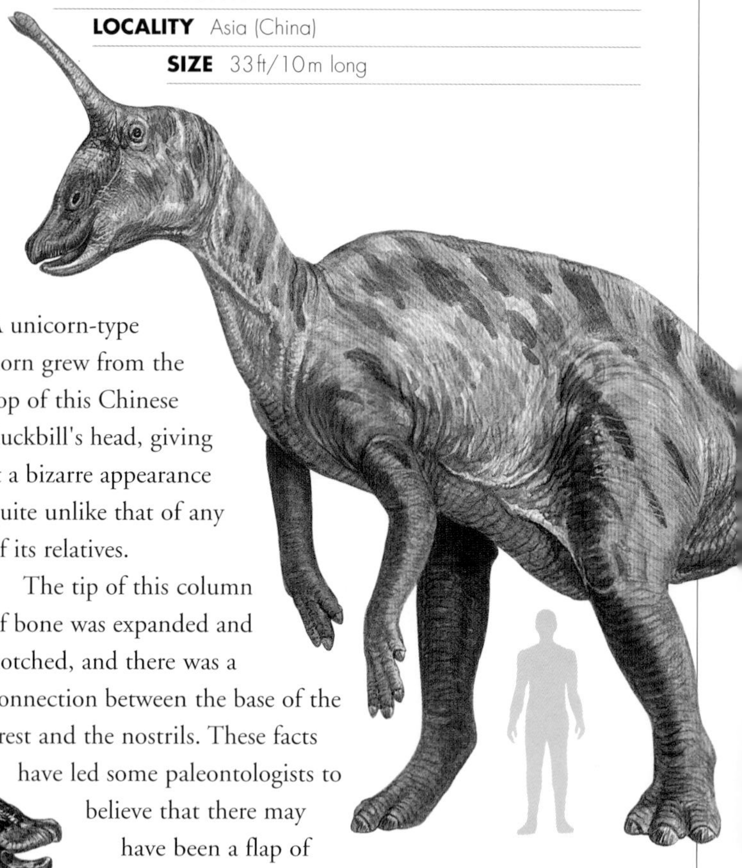

A unicorn-type horn grew from the top of this Chinese duckbill's head, giving it a bizarre appearance quite unlike that of any of its relatives.

The tip of this column of bone was expanded and notched, and there was a connection between the base of the crest and the nostrils. These facts have led some paleontologists to believe that there may have been a flap of skin attached to the horn, or stretched between the tip of the horn and the beak. This flap could have been inflated like a balloon, and used as a signalling device, either for courtship or for threatening rivals. It may have been brightly colored, and would have made a spectacular display.

Other paleontologists, however, think that the horn was wrongly mounted in the reconstruction of the original specimen of *Tsintaosaurus* and should point backward, as in *Saurolophus*.

NAME	*Corythosaurus*
TIME	Late Cretaceous
LOCALITY	North America (Alberta and Montana)
SIZE	30 ft/9 m long

A spectacular semicircular crest decorated the head of this large, North American duckbill, which weighed almost 5 US tons/4.5 tonnes. The crest rose steeply from just in front of the animal's eyes into a tall, narrow fan shape (about 1 ft/30 cm high) that curved down to the back of the head.

Several sizes of crest have been found in different specimens of *Corythosaurus*. This could reflect different species of this duckbill or, more likely, the specimens may simply represent different growth stages of the same species, with juvenile specimens having much smaller crests than adults. There may even have been a size difference between the sexes, with full-grown males having the largest crests.

Corythosaurus was a typical member of the lambeosaurine group of hadrosaurs—those duckbills with hollow crests on their heads. (Solid head crests characterized the hadrosaurine duckbills, see pp.290–294) As a group, the hollow-crested types seem to have evolved in North America, and been largely confined to the western part of that continent. Some species have also been found in eastern Asia. These widely separated finds lend support to the theory that western North America and eastern Asia were joined together in Late Cretaceous times as one landmass, "Asiamerica," which was surrounded by shallow continental seas.

The domed crest was made up of the greatly expanded nasal bones. The hollows inside the crest were the actual nasal passages, which ran up into the crest and looped back down into the snout. Several theories have been proposed for such an arrangement, some of them more likely than others. The old notion, for example, that hadrosaurs were aquatic animals, led to the belief that the crest, with its series of hollow tubes, was some kind of snorkel, which allowed the animal to breathe air while its mouth and nostrils were submerged. Another theory proposed that the crest acted as an air reservoir, so that the duckbill could draw on its supply while swimming or feeding underwater.

It is now known that the duckbills were well-adapted land animals. They were also gregarious and lived in herds, browsing in the forests on tough pine needles, magnolia leaves, seeds, and fruits of all kinds. When threatened by predators such as *Tyrannosaurus*, they could sprint away on two legs. They may even have taken to water to escape.

Several more likely explanations exist for the hollow crest, and it is quite possible that it served some or all of the proposed functions. First, the hollow crest with its convoluted tube system could have been used as a vocal resonator—like the pipe of a trombone—to produce sounds that allowed communication with the rest of the herd. These sounds could have been made for a variety of purposes—to warn other members in the herd of danger, to win a mate or discourage a rival, and to facilitate species-recognition between groups.

The results of recent American research seem to support this theory. An exact model of a lambeosaur's crest was constructed, and experiments show that these duckbills could have produced a kind of foghorn sound from such a structure. These booming, resonant notes would have been heard over wide distances, and provided these forest-dwellers with an effective means of communicating both within and between herds. The postulated inflatable nasal sacs on the faces of the flat-headed, solid-crested duckbills (in the hadrosaurine subfamily) probably served the same purpose.

Another theory proposes that the long air passage within the hollow crest could have served as a cooling system. Its surface may have been lined with a moist membrane, evaporation from which would have reduced the temperature of the surrounding tissue. This would have helped to cool down the animal when it was browsing in the open under the hot sun, or after a strenuous flight from a predator.

A third theory suggests that the hollow crest enhanced *Corythosaurus'* sense of smell, helping it to find food, detect the approach of danger and keep with the herd.

A primitive-looking crested duckbill was found in Montana after the discovery of *Corythosaurus*, and named *Procheneosaurus*. Its crest was much smaller than that of *Corythosaurus*, but it contained the same, typical S-shaped air passage. Some paleontologists think that this creature is possibly the most primitive of the hollow-crested duckbills. Others, however, believe it to be simply a juvenile specimen of *Corythosaurus* itself.

DUCKBILLED DINOSAURS CONTINUED

NAME *Hypacrosaurus*

TIME Late Cretaceous

LOCALITY North America
(Alberta and Montana)

SIZE 30 ft/9 m long

Another duckbill with a
prominent semicircular crest on
its head was *Hypacrosaurus*. The crest was
similar to that of *Corythosaurus*,
but not so tall or narrow. Nor did it rise so
steeply from the animal's face as that of
Corythosaurus, but rather sloped upward in a
gentle curve. Since *Hypacrosaurus* is found in
slightly later rock deposits than
Corythosaurus, it is possible that it evolved
from the earlier duckbill.

Another difference between these two similar-sized duckbills
was that the back vertebrae of *Hypacrosaurus* were extended
upward into tall spines, which would have formed a prominent
skin-covered ridge down the animal's back. The function of this
ridge may have been to regulate the body temperature, operating
in the same way as that proposed for other reptiles, such as the
fin-backed pelycosaurs (see pp.330–332) or the carnivorous
spinosaurs (see pp.262–263).

There is evidence from trackways which suggests that these
large hadrosaurids were quadrupedal for most of the time

ungainly, mounted as it was on the long, flexible neck.

Like all members of the duckbill family, *Lambeosaurus*
moved about on all-fours while browsing on low-growing
vegetation. The animal's flexible neck seems to have been an
adaptation that allowed it to reach around its body easily and
gather low-growing plants from a wide area without having to
shift its position.

The Californian specimen of *Lambeosaurus* seems to have
been a giant among duckbills. Although the remains are
fragmentary, the size and weight of the bones found indicate
that their owner may well have reached a length of 54 ft/16.5 m,
making it the largest hadrosaur known.

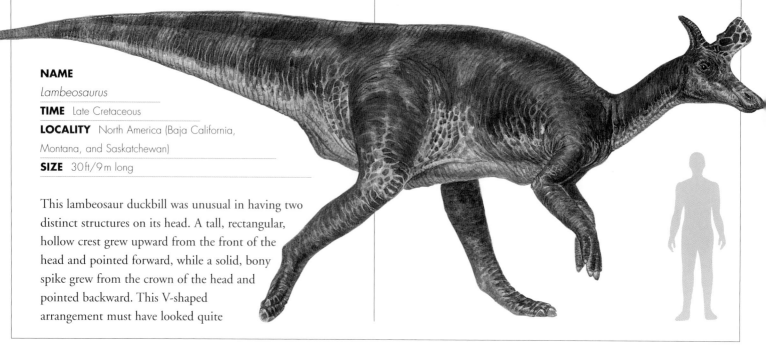

NAME

Lambeosaurus

TIME Late Cretaceous

LOCALITY North America (Baja California,
Montana, and Saskatchewan)

SIZE 30 ft/9 m long

This lambeosaur duckbill was unusual in having two
distinct structures on its head. A tall, rectangular,
hollow crest grew upward from the front of the
head and pointed forward, while a solid, bony
spike grew from the crown of the head and
pointed backward. This V-shaped
arrangement must have looked quite

NAME *Parasaurolophus*

TIME Late Cretaceous

LOCALITY North America (Alberta, New Mexico, and Utah)

SIZE 33 ft/10 m long

Like *Saurolophus* (see p.294), this duckbill had a shorter snout than other hadrosaurs, and a single backward-pointing, horn-like crest mounted on the top of its head. But there the resemblance ends, since the crest of the lambeosaurine *Parasaurolophus* was not solid like that of its hadrosaurine relative. Instead, it was constructed like a hollow tube, and was many times longer than that of *Saurolophus*. In fact, the great crest was up to 6 ft/1.8 m long. Inside, in an arrangement similar to that of *Corythosaurus*, the paired nasal passages ran from the nostrils right up to the tip of the crest, and then curved back down to the snout.

A skull with a much shorter crest and more tightly curved nasal passages was originally identified as a separate species of *Parasaurolophus*. But it is now regarded as belonging to a female of the long-crested type, in accordance with the theory that the sexes had crests of different sizes.

A unique feature of *Parasaurolophus* was a notch in its backbone which occurs behind the shoulders, just at the point where the tip of the crest would abut the back when the duckbill's neck was held in its natural, S-shaped pose. Some paleontologists have suggested that the crest fitted into this notch while the animal was running through dense undergrowth. Then, the crest would have acted like a deflector, sweeping low-hanging branches upward and away from the body. The head crest of the modern cassowary is often used to break a path in the same way.

The tail of *Parasaurolophus* was also unusual, in that it was particularly deep. This has led some researchers to think that it

may have been brightly patterned, and was used as a signaling device, perhaps during courtship or maybe to help the herd stay together as it moved through the forest. In addition, it has been suggested that there could have been a frill of skin at the back of the head, loosely connecting the crest with the neck. This frill could also have been brightly coloured, and may have served a similar display function.

If the theory is correct that the hollow crest was used as a vocal resonating chamber (see *Corythosaurus*, p.295) then one might suppose that the sounds produced through the long crest of *Parasaurolophus* were different from those produced, for example, by the high, semicircular crest of *Corythosaurus*. Indeed, the head-dresses of the lambeosaurine duckbills show such a variety in size and shape that it seems likely that different species had quite different calls.

The forests of North America in Late Cretaceous times must have reverberated with sounds—from the foghorn bellowings of the hollow-crested duckbills, to the honking and trumpeting that came from the nasal sacs of their neighbours, the solid-crested duckbills.

The skeleton is quite heavily built, especially in the shoulder region, hips, and front legs. The increased musculature and robustness of the front end suggests that *Parasaurolophus* made a great deal of use of its front legs for walking. Likewise, the hip region has enlarged pelvic bones for increased muscle attachment and strength required to rear up on the hind legs.

The bulk of these hadrosaurids originate in the Middle Cretaceous and are well-distributed across the northern continents but are less well known from the southern continents. They were remarkably diverse and evolved rapidly into the Upper Cretaceous. Although there was some turnover in genera, within the dinosaurs as a whole, the group were one of the main victims of the end Cretaceous extinction.

ARMORED DINOSAURS

SUBORDER THYREOPHORA

Recently the great order of ornithischian ("bird-hipped") dinosaurs has been divided into two suborders, the cerapodans and the thyreophorans. The latter suborder includes the stegosaurids and ankylosaurids as well as the more primitive scelidosaurids and are characterized by parallel rows of keeled bony scutes down the back and sides.

Family Scelidosauridae

The position of the scelidosaurs in the dinosaur array is controversial. Some paleontologists maintain that they were the ancestors of the stegosaurs, while others believe them to be ancestral ankylosaurs. Here, they are placed with both of those groups as a family of the Suborder Thyreophora.

NAME *Scelidosaurus*

TIME Early Jurassic

LOCALITY Europe (England)

SIZE 13 ft/4 m long

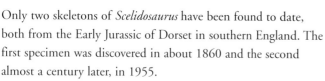

Only two skeletons of *Scelidosaurus* have been found to date, both from the Early Jurassic of Dorset in southern England. The first specimen was discovered in about 1860 and the second almost a century later, in 1955.

Scelidosaurus seems to be one of the earliest and most primitive of the ornithischian dinosaurs. It had a small head (only about 8 in/20 cm long), a toothless beak and small, leaf-shaped teeth in its weak jaws. The body, however, was massive and stoutly armored: the back was covered in bony plates, which were studded with parallel rows of spikes running from the neck to the tip of the tail and over the upper flanks. It is this arrangement of the armor that leads some paleontologists to believe that *Scelidosaurus* was a primitive type of ankylosaur, but this relationship is not universally accepted.

INFRAORDER STEGOSAURIA

The stegosaurs were a distinctive group of ornithischian, or "bird-hipped," dinosaurs. Their small-headed, massive bodies were characterized by double rows of great, bony plates that extended down either side of the backbone. Their heavy tails were armed with pairs of long, sharp spikes.

Like their ornithopod relatives, such as the iguanodonts (see pp.286–289) and the duckbills (see pp.290–297), the stegosaurs were plant-eaters, and probably lived in herds. But unlike the more agile ornithopods, stegosaurs moved about exclusively on four legs, and were not capable of running on two legs to escape predators. Their body armor made up for this deficiency. When attacked, they would most likely have stood their ground, lashing out with the spiked tail, and protected to a certain extent by the bony plates on the back.

Family Stegosauridae

All the familiar stegosaurs belong to this family, including *Stegosaurus* itself. They evolved in Mid-Jurassic times, some 170 million years ago, and reached their peak of diversity by the end of that period. A wide-ranging group, they spread through western North America, western Europe, East Asia, and East Africa. By Early Cretaceous times, the stegosaurs had started to decline, although it is quite possible that some species survived in isolated pockets until the end of the Cretaceous.

NAME *Stegosaurus*

TIME Late Jurassic

LOCALITY North America (Colorado, Oklahoma, Utah, and Wyoming)

SIZE up to 30 ft/9 m long

This armored dinosaur is the state fossil of Colorado and the largest and most familiar of the stegosaurs. A double row of broad, bony plates, shaped like huge arrowheads, ran down either side of the backbone, from just behind its head to halfway along its tail. Some of the plates were over 2 ft/60 cm high.

The heavy tail was armed with pairs of vicious spikes, each about 3 ft 3 in/1 m long. The number of spikes varied between species: *Stegosaurus ungulatus* had four pairs, *S. stenops* had two.

No-one is certain exactly how the bony plates were arranged on the back of *Stegosaurus*. Although many well-preserved specimens have been found—one of the best is mounted in Colorado's Denver Museum of Natural History—the plates have never been found actually attached to the skeleton. Some paleontologists maintain that they lay flat in or on the skin, and formed a defensive armor over the back and upper flanks.

Most paleontologists, however, believe that the plates stood up almost vertically, and were arranged either in a zigzag pattern or opposite each other in pairs. They would have formed a spiky fence, protecting *Stegosaurus* from attack by such predators as the contemporary carnosaur *Allosaurus* (see p.261). They were probably covered in tough horn, like the horns of modern cattle.

Alternatively, a thin layer of blood-rich skin could have covered the plates. This theory has led some paleontologists to propose an entirely different function for the plates—that of heat exchangers, a crude but effective means of regulating body temperature. The near-vertical plates could have been arranged alternately down the back. Their large surface area and rich supply of blood would have enabled them to absorb heat rapidly when oriented toward the sun (thus raising the body's internal temperature), and to lose heat when turned away.

The long, sturdy spikes on the tail of *Stegosaurus* were probably covered in horn, and were undoubtedly used for defense. *Stegosaurus* could have swung its long, heavy tail from side to side, and inflicted great damage on an attacker.

On average, *Stegosaurus* was 20 ft/6 m long, and weighed up to 2 US tons/2 tonnes. The massive hind legs, with their heavy hooves, were over twice the length of the forelegs—a striking feature in this four-legged animal, since it meant that the body sloped forward from its highest point at the hips.

Tall spines projected upward from the vertebrae of the hips and base of the tail, probably acting as anchor points for strong back muscles. This arrangement suggests that *Stegosaurus* could have lifted its forelegs off the ground without much effort, allowing it to feed off the lower branches of trees.

The skull of this huge dinosaur was only about 16 in/40 cm long. The brain was correspondingly small, about the size of a walnut. *Stegosaurus* was not particularly well-equipped for chewing plant food: it had a toothless beak at the front of the jaws, and the cheek teeth were small and weak. In order to digest its food, it is likely that *Stegosaurus* swallowed stones (as did many of the herbivorous dinosaurs), and held them in its stomach, where they helped to grind down tough plant material.

An intriguing cavity in the hip vertebrae of *Stegosaurus*, above the hind legs and just at the point where the spinal cord would have passed in life, has led paleontologists to speculate that this site housed a "second brain" that controlled the movements of the animal's hindquarters. This "brain" would really have been a conglomeration of nervous tissue, situated where the nerves of the hips and hind legs met. In fact, all backboned animals have this extra "brain," but its size is related to the size of the hips: in big-hipped animals, such as many of the dinosaurs, the hip's "brain" was larger than that of the skull.

An alternative theory proposes that the cavity housed a gland that produced glycogen. Doses of this sugary substance could have been released to provide the animal's hindquarters with an extra boost of energy in times of stress.

NAME *Kentrosaurus*

TIME Late Jurassic

LOCALITY Africa (Tanzania)

SIZE 16 ft/5 m long

Well-preserved remains of this East African stegosaur—a contemporary of the *Stegosaurus*—have been found in modern Tanzania among the fossil-rich deposits of Tendaguru Hill.

Kentrosaurus was not as large as its North American relative, but it was at least as well armored. A double row of narrow, triangular, bony plates rose on either side of the backbone, grouped in pairs along the neck, shoulders, and front part of the back. Halfway along the back, the plates gave way to pairs of sharp spikes (some of them about 2 ft/60 cm long) that ran along the remainder of the backbone right to the tip of the tail. In addition, a pair of extra-long spikes stuck out at hip-level on each side, affording good protection should a predator attack from the side.

NAME *Tuojiangosaurus*

TIME Late Jurassic

LOCALITY Asia (China)

SIZE 23 ft/7 m long

Tuojiangosaurus is one of several armored dinosaurs found in China. It was the first stegosaur to be discovered in Asia, and is known from an almost complete specimen. Structurally similar to *Stegosaurus*, it had a small, narrow head with low teeth and a heavily built body. Fifteen pairs of bony plates surmounted its back, becoming taller and more spike-like over the hips and down the tail. As in *Stegosaurus stenops*, there were two pairs of long spikes on the tail.

It seems that *Tuojiangosaurus* was not able to rear up on its hind legs, as was *Stegosaurus*. This is deduced from the fact that the tall spines that projected upward from the back vertebrae of *Stegosaurus* (to provide muscle-attachment points) are not present in either *Tuojiangosaurus* or *Kentrosaurus*. This suggests that they were ground-feeding animals.

NAME *Wuerhosaurus*

TIME Early Cretaceous

LOCALITY Asia (China)

SIZE 20 ft/6 m long

This Chinese stegosaur is known only from a few fragmentary remains of bones and scattered plates. The restoration here is therefore tentative. *Wuerhosaurus* is one of the few to have survived into Early Cretaceous times. However, another possible stegosaur, *Dravidosaurus*, has been found in India in Late Cretaceous beds. It is possible that India was an island continent at that time, isolated from the other landmasses, and a few species may have survived there, while the rest died out.

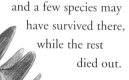

Infraorder Ankylosauria

The decline of the stegosaurs toward the end of the Jurassic Period may be linked to the rise of another group of armored dinosaurs, the ankylosaurs. They spread throughout the northern continents during Cretaceous times, and were particularly abundant in Asiamerica toward the end of that period.

Like the stegosaurs, ankylosaurs were heavily-built, four-legged plant-eaters. They were also armored, but with a different, and more effective, kind of defensive plating than that of the stegosaurs. The neck, back, flanks, and tail were entirely covered in a mosaic of flat, bony plates, which were embedded in the thick, leathery skin, and covered in horn. Spikes and knobs of various sizes studded the bony armor.

There were two distinct families of ankylosaur. The nodosaurs had narrow skulls, armored backs and rows of long spikes projecting from their flanks. The ankylosaurs themselves had broad skulls and a heavy "club" of solid bone at the end of their tails (see pp.304–305).

Family Nodosauridae

The nodosaurids were the earlier and more primitive of the two families of ankylosaur, and ranged throughout the northern hemisphere during the Cretaceous Period. Some paleontologists think that they may have evolved in Europe during the Late Jurassic, and then spread to the other northern continents. Some types at least also reached the southern hemisphere—*Minmi* is a recent discovery from Australia.

The nodosaurids had narrow skulls, longer than they were wide. Solid, bony plates covered the body from neck to tail, and long spikes guarded the flanks.

There is considerable uncertainty about nodosaurid inter-relationships and future finds will doubtless necessitate reassessment of the classification of the group.

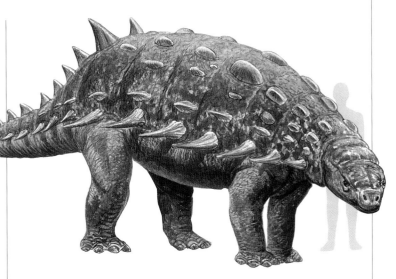

NAME	*Hylaeosaurus*
TIME	Early Cretaceous
LOCALITY	Europe (England)
SIZE	20 ft/6 m long

Hylaeosaurus is the earliest creature that can definitely be identified as a nodosaur. Its remains were first found in Sussex in southern England in the late 1820s, and named by that English pioneer of paleontology, Gideon Mantell, in 1832. To this day, its bones are still imprisoned in the slab of rock in which they were fossilized, but there are now plans to extract the skeleton with the use of acetic acid. This dissolves away the mineral calcite, which cements together the particles of rock, and will therefore release the fossilized bones.

Until new evidence is available, the restoration of *Hylaeosaurus* shown here must remain speculative. The narrow head, armor-plated body and tail, and the outwardly projecting spikes on the flanks were typical nodosaur features.

NAME	*Polacanthus*
TIME	Early Cretaceous
LOCALITY	Europe (England)
SIZE	13 ft/4 m long

This "many-spined" nodosaur was a contemporary of *Hylaeosaurus*. Indeed, some paleontologists are of the opinion that the two animals are the same. The remains of *Polacanthus* consist of the bones of the sturdy hind legs and some solid armor plates and spines.

Because of the incomplete nature of the remains, it is not known exactly how the armor was arranged on the body. The restoration shown here is the traditional view of the animal. Pairs of heavy, vertical spines protected the shoulders and upper back; a shield of fused bone covered the hips; and two lines of small, vertical spines ran down to the tip of the deep, heavy tail.

NAME *Sauropelta*

TIME Early Cretaceous

LOCALITY North America (Montana)

SIZE 25 ft/7.6 m long

Sauropelta, from the western USA, is the largest known member of the nodosaur family of ankylosaurs, the armored dinosaurs of Cretaceous times. It is estimated to have weighed over 3 US tons/3 tonnes.

Its massive body was encased in a bony armor. Bands of horn-covered plates with raised keels ran transversely over the body from the neck to the end of the long, tapering tail. The plates were embedded in the skin to form a strong flexible covering all over the back. Attacks from the side were deterred by a row of sharp spikes along each flank. This slow-moving herbivore would have needed such protection against the attacks of the carnivorous dinosaurs of the day.

NAME *Silvisaurus*

TIME Early Cretaceous

LOCALITY North America (Kansas)

SIZE 11 ft/3.4 m long

Silvisaurus was covered in the heavy bony armor characteristic of the nodosaurs. Thick plates encased the animal's neck, a more open arrangement of plates lay across the back and tail, and heavy spikes flanked the body. *Silvisaurus* is, however, considered to be a primitive member of the family. Most nodosaurs had toothless beaks at the front of their jaws, but *Silvisaurus* retained teeth in its upper jaw. Some paleontologists therefore believe that it may be ancestral to some of the later nodosaurs.

As in most of the nodosaurs and later ankylosaurs, the amount of bone in the skull of *Silvisaurus* was much reduced, so that it was lightweight and full of cavities and air passages. These could have been used to produce sounds for communicating with other members of the species. Such vocalization was not unknown among dinosaurs: for example, the gregarious duckbills had inflatable nasal sacs or hollow crests on their heads, through which the animals probably produced sounds for social communications among the herd (see pp.290–297).

NAME *Nodosaurus*

TIME Late Cretaceous

LOCALITY North America (Kansas and Wyoming)

SIZE 18 ft/5.5 m long

Nodosaurus is the typical nodosaur, and has given its name to the whole family). Its body armor was arranged from neck to tail in transverse bands: narrow, rectangular plates covered the ribs, alternating with broad plates that occupied the spaces in between. Hundreds of bony nodes studded the broad plates, hence the animal's name— *Nodosaurus*, meaning "node lizard." The skull of *Nodosaurus* was small, long, and narrow, and the teeth were weak—typical features of the family. The shoulders and hips were powerfully developed to carry the great weight of the body armor, as were the strong, stout legs, which had broad, hoofed feet. The bones of the hips were so modified as weight-bearing structures that they no longer resembled the typical ornithischian, or "bird-hipped," pattern (see pp.278–313).

The skeletons of several nodosaurs, all lying on their backs, were found in Kansas in marine sediments of Late Cretaceous age. They may represent a small herd of animals that were overcome and washed down to the sea; alternatively, these individuals could have come together after death by chance.

In either case, as they were swept along in the river, the decaying organs would have generated gases that bloated the body. This, combined with the weight of the armor on the back, would have made them top-heavy, and so they would have flipped over and floated downstream on their backs. Eventually, they would have sunk into the mud of the seabed, belly-side up, in which position they were preserved.

NAME *Struthiosaurus*

TIME Late Cretaceous

LOCALITY Europe (Austria, France, Hungary, and Romania)

SIZE 6 ft 6 in/2 m long

Struthiosaurus is the smallest known member of the nodosaur family, and of the whole ankylosaur group. This has led to the suggestion that it may have evolved on islands. Many large animals develop dwarf species when confined to isolated habitats—an adaptation to limited food resources. In Tertiary times, for example, species of dwarf elephant and hippopotamus evolved on the Mediterranean islands. A modern example is provided by the ponies of the Shetland Islands off northern Scotland.

In Late Cretaceous times, some 80 million years ago, most of modern Europe was covered by shallow seas. Islands were the only dry land. Perhaps groups of *Struthiosaurus* got marooned on various of these islands, and evolved as smaller species just as the fauna of today's Galápagos Islands is thought to have developed.

Whatever the circumstances of its development, *Struthiosaurus* retained its body armor. A variety of armor covered its back. There were plates around the neck; small bony studs covered the back and tail; and spikes guarded each flank.

Struthiosaurus fossils are still poorly understood and various different names have been given to fragmentary specimens.

NAME *Panoplosaurus*

TIME Late Cretaceous

LOCALITY North America (Alberta, Montana, South Dakota, and Texas)

SIZE 15 ft/4.4 m long

The latest of the nodosaurs to arise, and the last known, *Panoplosaurus* was a medium-sized animal in comparison to some of its relatives. But it was massively built, and encased in a heavy body armor. It is estimated that it could have weighed as much as 4 US tons/3.6 tonnes.

Panoplosaurus' body armor consisted of broad, square plates with keels, arranged in wide bands across the neck and shoulders. The rest of the back was covered in smaller, bony studs. Massive spikes, angled to the side and front, guarded each flank, especially on the shoulders.

Even *Panoplosaurus'* head was protected with thick, bony plates. These are fused so solidly to the underlying skull bones that their boundaries cannot be seen. But on the inside, this solid, bony box was full of cavities and air passages, with a bony palate separating the nasal system from the mouth. This would have enabled the animal to eat and breathe at the same time. The snout was narrow, which could suggest that *Panoplosaurus* rooted about among the ground vegetation to find the plants that it preferred as food.

It is likely that *Panoplosaurus* actively defended itself against attack, unlike many of its relatives, which would probably have squatted down on the ground and relied on their armor plating to protect them. *Panoplosaurus* could have charged, directing one of its spiked shoulders toward the attacker. Its forelegs were strongly built, and especially well-endowed with muscles in the elbow area. This suggests that the animal was quite maneuverable, and could move its forequarters nimbly in reaction to its enemy's tactics. A charging rhinoceros is the most apt, modern comparison.

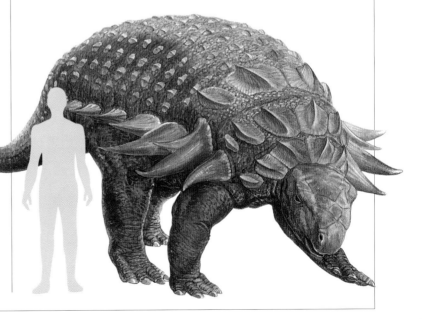

Family Ankylosauridae

This family of armored dinosaurs became abundant toward the end of the Cretaceous Period, and largely replaced their relatives, the nodosaurs, in western North America and East Asia. Like the nodosaurs, they were heavily armored on the back with thick plates and spikes. But the head armor was more extensively developed, and there was a unique weapon at the tip of their tails: a large ball of fused bone, which could be swung like a club with potentially lethal effect on an attacker.

These ankylosaurs were built like military tanks, and some species were about the same size. They were shorter and stockier than the nodosaurs, with massive-boned hips and hind legs to support the heavy, clubbed tail. The hips were fused to the backbone by at least eight sacral vertebrae, forming a super-strong anchor for the hindquarters. The hip bones themselves had degenerated into a shapeless mass, with no obvious trace of the bird-like arrangement so characteristic of the ornithischian dinosaurs.

NAME	Talarurus
TIME	Late Cretaceous
LOCALITY	Asia (Mongolia)
SIZE	16ft/5m long

Talarurus shows the typical features of the family. The armored skull broadened out at the back into a pair of bony spikes, which gave this dinosaur the appearance of having ears. Another pair of spikes projected from the cheeks. There was a toothless beak at the front of the jaws and small weak teeth in the back.

The barrel-shaped body was armored with thick plates, and fringed with spikes on the flanks. The club at the end of the tail was formed from three masses of fused bone, and welded to the tail vertebrae. Bony tendons lashed the vertebrae together, so that when the animal walked, its tail was held off the ground. The base of the tail was supple and well-muscled.

When *Talarurus* was threatened by, for example, a contemporary tyrannosaur like *Tarbosaurus* (see p.264), it would have swung its clubbed tail at the attacker. The ramrod stiffness of the tail would have increased the force of the mass at its tip.

NAME	Euoplocephalus
TIME	Late Cretaceous
LOCALITY	North America (Alberta)
SIZE	18ft/5.5m long

Most of our knowledge of ankylosaurs is based on studies of this animal, carried out in the 1970s and 1980s. Bands of armor were embedded in the skin of the back, and dotted with huge bony studs. Heavy plates covered the neck, and large, triangular spines protected the shoulders and base of the tail.

Externally, the head was a heavy box of bone, covered in plates that were fused to the skull bones. Inside was the complex of chambers and air passages that characterized both the ankylosaurs and nodosaurs. Thick spines protected the sides of the face. Even the eyelids were armored, forming shutters that could descend to guard the eyes when danger threatened. These bony eyelids were only accessory structures: the real eyelids would have consisted of the usual delicate membranes. There was a horny, toothless beak at the front of the broad face.

It may be that *Euoplocephalus* was an indiscriminate eater, cropping any vegetation that presented itself. Its nodosaur relatives had narrow snouts, and probably were more selective in what they ate.

NAME *Saichania*

TIME Late Cretaceous

LOCALITY Asia (Mongolia)

SIZE 23 ft/7 m long

The massive head of *Saichania* was armored with great bony nodules that stuck out in high relief. Spikes swept outward from each flank, and the whole of the back and tail were protected by rows of knobbly plates.

Inside the skull, the air passages were more complex than those of other ankylosaurs, and were probably more effective in cooling and moistening inhaled air before it reached the lungs. The bony palate, separating the nasal tubes from the mouth, was also stronger than in other ankylosaurs, perhaps allowing the animal to eat tougher plants. And there is some evidence to show that there may have been a salt gland associated with *Saichania's* nostrils.

Taken together, all these features could suggest that *Saichania* lived in a hot, arid environment, unlike the cold climate that prevails in modern Mongolia's Gobi Desert where the remains of this ankylosaur were found.

NAME *Ankylosaurus*

TIME Late Cretaceous

LOCALITY North America (Alberta and Montana)

SIZE up to 33 ft/10 m long

Ankylosaurus was one of the last of the armored dinosaurs to survive, right to the end of the Cretaceous Period. The largest of the ankylosaurs, it gives its name to the family. It was a massively built animal, and probably weighed a good 4 US tons/3.6 tonnes. *Ankylosaurus'* skull was about 2 ft 5 in/ 76 cm long and its body was broad (16 ft/5 m at the widest point) and squat. It was supported on strong, stumpy legs set directly beneath the body.

Thick bands of heavy armor ran across *Ankylosaurus'* back, from the top of the head to near the tip of the tail. The tail ended in the great, bony club that is the distinguishing feature of this dinosaur family. The creature's armor consisted of hundreds of oval-shaped plates set close together, and embedded in the leathery hide. This open arrangement would have given great flexibility to the armor plating, combining strength with maneuverability.

Ankylosaurus had a blunt snout, a broad face and a toothless beak. A pair of spikes stuck out on either side at the back of the head, and two more spikes projected from the cheeks.

When attacked, *Ankylosaurus* would probably have stood its ground, well-protected by its body armor. When the predator got within range, the heavy, clubbed tail would have been swung sideways with great force and if it hit its target, the attacker would have been severely wounded.

HORNED DINOSAURS

INFRAORDER CERATOPSIA

This infraorder is now placed under the Suborder Cerapoda—along with the pachycephalosaurs and ornithopods—on the basis of a number of shared characteristics. All of its members have five or fewer premaxillary teeth and a gap between the premaxilla and maxilla teeth.

The horned ceratopians were the last group of ornithischian, or "bird-hipped," dinosaurs to evolve before the whole assemblage of these ruling reptiles suffered mass extinction at the end of the Mesozoic Era.

The ceratopians (also sometimes called ceratopsians) evolved late in the Cretaceous Period. As a group, they existed for a mere 20 million years before becoming extinct, but in that short time, geologically speaking, they established themselves all over western North America and central Asia.

They were well-armored dinosaurs, although their weaponry was confined to the head, unlike the heavy armor plating that covered the backs of the ankylosaurs (see pp.301–305). The advanced ceratopians had massive heads, armed with a sharp, parrot-like beak at the front; long, pointed horns on the brow or snout, sometimes both; and a great sheet of bone, the "frill," which grew from the back of the skull and curved upward, to protect the neck and often the shoulders too.

The success of the ceratopians can be related to their efficient chopping teeth and powerful jaws. These dinosaurs could eat even the toughest of plant foods, including a relatively new source—the shrubby flowering plants, similar to magnolia, that had begun to thrive worldwide in Late Cretaceous times. Ceratopians probably lived in herds in the upland forests, browsing on low-growing trees and ground vegetation.

Family Psittacosauridae

The "parrot" dinosaurs were a rare group of ornithischian dinosaurs, found only in the Early Cretaceous rocks of East Asia. Their skulls show many features that suggest that they were the ancestors of the horned dinosaurs, or ceratopians. Their long-tailed and relatively lightly-built bodies, however, were similar to those of the gazelle-like hypsilophodonts, from which stock they probably arose (see pp.283–285).

Like the hypsilophodonts, the parrot dinosaurs could rise up on two legs to run away from predators. The suggestion, therefore, is that the early ceratopians, descended from the parrot dinosaurs, were also bipedal, and only reverted to a four-legged stance later in their evolution.

NAME	*Psittacosaurus*	
TIME	Early Cretaceous	
	LOCALITY	Asia (China, Mongolia, and Siberia)
	SIZE	up to 8 ft/2.5 m long

A square skull and a horny, toothless curved beak are the features that have given this Asian dinosaur its name— *Psittacosaurus*, meaning "parrot lizard."

A thick ridge of bone on the top of the skull squared off the head at the back. This ridge served as an anchor point for the muscles of the powerful lower jaws. Over millions of years, it was to develop into the characteristic great, bony neck frill of the later ceratopians. The cheek bones of *Psittacosaurus* were drawn out into a pair of horn-like projections—the forerunners of the horny spikes that grew out from each side of the head shield of later ceratopians. *Psittacosaurus* had a long flexible neck, four blunt claws on each hand, long hind limbs and short forelimbs. Its long tail helped it to maintain its bipedal stance.

The ancestor of the ceratopian group is believed to be among the parrot dinosaurs. However, it is unlikely to have been *Psittacosaurus* itself, since this animal had only four fingers on each hand, while the ceratopians had five. Also, *Psittacosaurus* had no teeth in its beak, while the early ceratopians, the protoceratopids, had teeth in the upper beak.

Several juvenile *Psittacosaurus* have been found, one of which at only 24 cm/12 in long is the smallest dinosaurs known.

Family Protoceratopsidae

The protoceratopids constitute the early, primitive horned dinosaurs, although only some had horns. They evolved in Asia, in the same region as the parrot dinosaurs (from which stock they probably evolved), but lived there many millions of years later, in the Late Cretaceous. They also spread to western North America.

Like the earlier parrot dinosaurs, the protoceratopids could walk upright, although it is likely that they spent most of their time browsing on all-fours, and only rose up on two legs when they had to run away from predators.

The protoceratopids were much smaller than their later relatives, the ceratopids. They shared the characteristic parrot-like beak of the psittacosaurs, but unlike them they had teeth in the upper beak: this is considered a primitive feature, lost in the more advanced ceratopids.

The protoceratopids had no horns on their heads, or else only rudimentary ones. However, they did have the beginnings of the neck frill that was to become so prominent in the later ceratopids.

NAME *Microceratops*

TIME Late Cretaceous

LOCALITY Asia (China and Mongolia)

SIZE 2 ft/60 cm long

This creature is the smallest horned dinosaur known. It was probably not a direct ancestor of the later ceratopids, but rather an early, specialized offshoot of the main group.

Microceratops was a lightly-built, two-legged runner, as evidenced by the length of its shin bones—almost twice as long as the thigh bones, the sign of a sprinting animal. Its front legs, however, were also quite long in comparison to other bipedal dinosaurs, so it probably moved about mainly on four legs, only rising upright to escape from danger. Its lifestyle would have been similar to that of such ornithopods as the gazelle-like hypsilophodonts of North America.

NAME *Leptoceratops*

TIME Late Cretaceous

LOCALITY North America (Alberta and Wyoming) and Asia (Mongolia)

SIZE 7 ft/2.1 m long

Leptoceratops is one of the few protoceratopids known from North America: most of the family lived in Asia. In appearance, it was intermediate between the lightly-built parrot dinosaurs and the heavier, early

horned dinosaurs. It could probably walk on two legs as easily as on four. *Leptoceratops'* hind legs were built for running, as evidenced by the long shin bones. The five clawed fingers of each hand could be used to grasp bundles of leaves, and pass them to the mouth.

The bones at the back of *Leptoceratops'* skull were expanded upward into a tall peak. This was an intermediate stage in development between the muscle-attachment ridge of the parrot dinosaurs and the neck frill of the horned dinosaurs.

NAME *Bagaceratops*

TIME Late Cretaceous

LOCALITY Asia (Mongolia)

SIZE 3 ft 3 in/1 m long

This small protoceratopid represents another specialized offshoot from the main evolutionary branch of the horned dinosaurs. It had a squat, heavy body and long tail, supported on solid legs, five-toed at the front and four-toed at the back.

Bagaceratops possessed several of the features that were to be developed in the later horned dinosaurs. There was a prominent bony ridge at the back of its skull (the precursor of the ceratopids' neck frill); a pair of leaf-shaped projections on either cheek (part of the ceratopids' head shield); and a definite, though short, horn halfway along its snout (anticipating the great horns of the ceratopids). In addition, it had lost its teeth in the upper beak; other members of its family retained these teeth, which is considered a primitive feature. But despite these advanced characteristics, *Bagaceratops* was probably not the direct ancestor of the horned dinosaurs.

NAME *Protoceratops*

TIME Late Cretaceous

LOCALITY Asia (Mongolia)

SIZE up to 9 ft/2.7 m long

The average adult of this early horned dinosaur (right) measured about 6 ft 6 in/2 m long, and weighed almost 400 lbs/180 kg. It had a well-developed broad neck frill at the back of its large, heavy skull. This would have provided anchoring points for the powerful muscles of the toothed, beaked jaws.

Although *Protoceratops* had no horns, it did have a prominent bump midway along its snout—more of a crest than a horn. This bump seems to have been larger in older male specimens, suggesting that it may have been used for ritual head-butting fights between rival males.

Protoceratops almost certainly spent most of its time on all-fours. However, the hind legs were still long in comparison to the forelegs, so it seems probable that this animal could also run upright, as did its likely ancestors, the parrot dinosaurs.

In the 1920s, the first dinosaur eggs and nests were discovered in Mongolia. They belonged to *Protoceratops*. The nests, dug in the sand over 70 million years ago, contained clutches of eggs, as many as 18 in some nests. Each egg was sausage-shaped, about 8 in/20 cm long, with a thin, wrinkled shell, only a fraction of an inch thick. The eggs were carefully laid in three-tiered spirals. Astonishingly, some of the eggs were still intact, and inside were found fragments of fossilized bones from tiny *Protoceratops* embryos.

Plant-eating dinosaurs, such as *Leptoceratops* and *Triceratops,* were thought to have muscular cheeks to keep food in their mouths while chewing. However, no evidence for such cheeks has been found. They probably had stiff horny coverings to the jaws, which would have been less efficient. It may be necessary to remodel the way we think these dinosaurs fed.

the ceratopids. However, *Montanoceratops* had the typical primitive features of the protoceratopid family—teeth in the upper beak, and claws on its feet, rather than hooves.

The tail of this medium-sized ceratopian was unusually deep due to the presence of tall spines that jutted upward from the vertebrae along its length. The fossil evidence also suggests that the tail was also extremely flexible, and could be moved easily and rapidly from side to side. A possible explanation for these features could be that the tail—which may have been brightly colored—was used as a sexual signal during the mating season, or for recognition of its own species.

Family Ceratopsidae

The most abundant large herbivores of the Late Cretaceous period in western North America were the great horned dinosaurs of this family. Their fossil remains have been found nowhere else in the world.

Exclusively four-legged, these herbivores were well-protected from attack by contemporary, bipedal carnosaurs, such as *Tyrannosaurus* (see p.266) and *Albertosaurus* (see p.263). Long, sharp horns grew from their massive heads, and a large bony frill,

NAME *Montanoceratops*

TIME Late Cretaceous

LOCALITY North America (Montana)

SIZE 10 ft/3 m long

This North American dinosaur (right) was similar in appearance to *Protoceratops* (above), with the notable exception of having a definite horn on its snout. This has led some paleontologists to regard it as an early member of the more advanced family of horned dinosaurs, developed from the rear skull bones, guarded their necks. The head was relatively large and heavy in proportion to the body size. Pillar-like legs, with their heavy, hoofed feet, supported a stocky body that was covered in thick hide. There was also safety in numbers, and the horned dinosaurs moved in great herds through the upland forests, foraging for plant food and chopping off vegetation with their sharp, toothless beaks.

The family of horned dinosaurs is divided into two evolutionary lines. Some members of the family had short neck frills and great horns on the snout, while others had long neck frills and great horns on the brow.

NAME	*Centrosaurus*
TIME	Late Cretaceous
LOCALITY	North America (Alberta and Montana)
SIZE	20 ft/6 m long

This horned dinosaur was a typical member of the short-frilled group. (It used to be known by the name *Monoclonius*.) A long horn surmounted the snout of *Centrosaurus,* giving it an appearance somewhat like that of the modern rhinoceros, (in some species, this horn curved forward), and two short horns rose above its eyes from the brow.

The neck frill stood up from behind the head, and its wavy edge was fringed with spines. There were two large openings on either side of the frill, which in life were covered over with skin, as was the rest of the frill. These holes reduced the weight of the bony structure, and their edges provided additional attachment points for the powerful jaw muscles. A strong ball-and-socket joint connected the head to the neck. This

was placed well forward in the skull, about under the eye region, so that the weight of the heavy frill at the back of the head was balanced by the great horn on the front. This mobile joint ensured that *Centrosaurus* could turn its massive head easily and quickly. This was important for such a slow-moving animal, since its head weapons were its only defense. Some of the neck vertebrae were fused together, to increase its strength, and the muscles of the forequarters were powerfully developed.

As with all of the ceratopids, *Centrosaurus'* tail was relatively short in comparison to those of the protoceratopids, with only its tip resting on the ground. Unlike their protoceratopid relatives, these four-legged animals did not rise up on their hind legs and so did not need a long tail to balance their body weight.

NAME	*Pachyrhinosaurus*
TIME	Late Cretaceous
LOCALITY	North America (Alberta)
SIZE	18 ft/5.5 m long

So far only two skulls of *Pachyrhinosaurus* have been found, and it seems to have been an unusual "horned dinosaur" because it apparently had no horns. Instead, there was a large, thick pad of bone above the eyes where the brow horns were usually found.

There are two theories to account for this strange bony pad. Some paleontologists equate its function with the thickened skull caps of the boneheaded dinosaurs—for in-fighting among male members of the herd. Other paleontologists, however, believe that the bony pad simply represents scar tissue where the brow horns had fallen off. Supporters of this theory expect that eventually specimens will be discovered with their brow horns intact, settling the argument once and for all.

NAME *Styracosaurus*

TIME Late Cretaceous

LOCALITY North America (Alberta and Montana)

SIZE 17 ft/5.2 m long

One of the most spectacular of the short-frilled family of horned dinosaurs was the well-armed *Styracosaurus*. It had an enormous, straight horn on its snout, directed upward and forward. Two smaller horns grew above the eyes. The remarkable neck frill, like an oriental dancer's head-dress, had six main spikes arrayed around its top, some as large as the nose horn. A number of smaller spikes made up a defensive fringe.

As in other short-frilled ceratopids, there were two large, skin-covered openings in the frill, which reduced the weight of this great bony structure considerably.

Styracosaurus could certainly have defended itself well. Charging head-down, rhinoceros-style, at an attacking *Tyrannosaurus*, for example, the herbivore's great nose horn could have ripped open the carnivore's soft belly, and the bony frill would have presented a formidable array of spikes to protect its neck from the carnivore's powerful jaws.

The spikes on the frill probably also provided a highly effective defensive display. If *Styracosaurus* stood head-on to an enemy, or even a rival male in its own herd, the spikes would have stood out from around its face, making the animal look sufficiently fearsome to deter most attackers. Modern African elephants hold their great ears out at the sides of the head to intimidate others in the same way.

NAME *Triceratops*

TIME Late Cretaceous

LOCALITY North America (Alberta, Colorado, Montana, South Dakota, Saskatchewan, and Wyoming)

SIZE 30 ft/9 m long

Triceratops is the most familiar of the horned dinosaurs. It was also the most abundant of the group, as well as the largest and the heaviest. It is thought to have weighed up to 11 US tons/10 tonnes—heavier than a modern, adult African bull elephant. Its skull alone, with the short neck frill, was over 6 ft 6 in/2 m long.

Great herds of these imposing horned dinosaurs lived throughout western North America toward the very end of the Late Cretaceous Period, some 70 to 65 million years ago. They were the most common of the ceratopids, and the last member of the short-frilled group to survive.

The name *Triceratops* means "three-horned face." Although this dinosaur belonged to the short-frilled group—in which the nose horn was typically longer than the brow horns—the arrangement of horns on the face of *Triceratops* was more like that of the long-frilled types (see *Chasmosaurus*, right) for

example). It had a short, thick nose horn and two long brow horns, each over 3ft 3in/1m long. In some species, the brow horns could have been even longer, reaching beyond the snout.

Also unlike other members of its group, *Triceratops'* neck frill was a solid sheet of bone. The fact that there were no openings in it suggests that its main function was to act as a defensive shield, rather than as an anchoring plate for the jaw muscles. In some species, there were pointed knobs, like great barnacles, set all around the edge of the frill, offering further protection.

Because of the massive, solid structure of *Triceratops'* skull, it was more likely to survive through fossilization than other, less robust, dinosaur skulls. Hundreds of well-preserved specimens have been found over the years in the western states of North America. Othniel C. Marsh, the famous American fossil-hunter, first named the beast in 1889. By the turn of the century, another American fossil-hunter, Barnum Brown, is supposed to have discovered over 500 skulls.

Today, more than 15 species of *Triceratops* are recognized, all distinguished by differences in the structure of the skull. However, some of these may in fact represent different sexes and growth stages in individuals of a much smaller number of species.

Many of the skulls, horns, and neck frills have been found to be damaged and scarred. This suggests that individual *Triceratops* often sparred with one another, possibly by locking horns and shoving with the head shield, rather than doing any actual damage with the sharp horns. The full potential of these weapons was probably reserved to inflict damage on a real enemy, such as one of the large, contemporary tyrannosaurs—*Tyrannosaurus* or *Albertosaurus*.

NAME	*Chasmosaurus*
TIME	Late Cretaceous
LOCALITY	North America (Alberta)
SIZE	17ft/5.2m long

Chasmosaurus was a typical long-frilled type of horned dinosaur. Its skull was quite long and narrow, with a pair of long, upwardly curved horns on the brow and a single, shorter horn on the snout. The bony frill, however, was enormous, stretching from the back of the skull to cover the neck and upper shoulders. Its margin was elaborated with bony spikes and knobs. The two openings on either side of the frill were so large that the frill itself provided a mere framework surrounding these great holes. So, although the bony frill was a vast size, it was lightweight, and allowed the head to be moved easily.

This spectacular frill was undoubtedly a display structure and may have been brightly colored. The great head area that it presented would have acted as a warning to attackers, whether predators or rival males, or as a sexual signal to females, especially when the head was moved about. It is possible that all the males in a herd would cooperate in a display of threat, forming a ring around the young in times of danger, and shaking their great heads and neck frills at the enemy.

Some paleontologists think that these horned dinosaurs could run quite quickly when necessary. This is suggested by certain features of their anatomy. The shoulder blades, for example, were not firmly fixed to the rest of the skeleton, and there were no collar bones to keep them in place. So, the whole shoulder girdle would have moved back and forth with the forelegs, helping the animal to run quickly.

In contrast, the hips were firmly fixed in position, attached to the backbone by eight sacral vertebrae, which provided a strong, solid anchor for the heavy hindquarters.

NAME *Arrhinoceratops*

TIME Late Cretaceous

LOCALITY North America (Alberta and Utah)

SIZE 18ft/5.5m long

The name *Arrhinoceratops* means "no nose-horned face" and was given to the animal by its discoverer William Parks (who excavated it from the Red Deer River, Alberta in 1925) because he thought that it lacked a nose horn. Parks believed that there should be a separate bone to support a nose-horn, but this is now known to be incorrect. *Arrhinoceratops* has a distinct bony knob where the horn should be and modern interpretation regards this as sufficient evidence for the presence of a horn. However, because the internationally recognised laws of biological nomenclature are based on historical priority, this dinosaur has to keep its completely inappropriate name.

Arrhinoceratops was a close relative of the long-frilled dinosaur *Chasmosaurus* (see previous page). But it resembled the short-frilled *Triceratops* in having a short face, and well-developed brow horns that curved forward over the snout. There was also a modest-sized nose horn.

Round openings cut through the bone of *Arrhinoceratops'* neck frill, thereby reducing its weight. The frill itself was a large one, as in *Chasmosaurus*, and had a deeply scalloped margin, which was set with great bony knobs at wide intervals.

The remains of this North American horned dinosaur are not as common as many others of its family. This may be due to the fact that the animal itself was not abundant, or to its favored habitats: perhaps it inhabited dry, upland areas where it was less likely to become fossilized.

NAME *Anchiceratops*

TIME Late Cretaceous

LOCALITY North America (Alberta)

SIZE 20ft/6m long

The long-frilled *Anchiceratops* lived near the very end of the Late Cretaceous Period, later than its relative *Chasmosaurus*. In fact, it has been suggested by some paleontologists that *Anchiceratops* could have been a descendant of that dinosaur.

Although it was somewhat larger than its relative *Chasmosaurus*, *Anchiceratops* was more streamlined in build. Its bulky body was longer, with a shorter tail, and the tall neck frill was considerably narrower. Two long, narrow horns curved forward from the creature's heavy brow, and a shorter nose horn pointed directly ahead.

Anchiceratops' frill was divided along the midline by a strong ridge. On either side of the ridge there were medium-sized openings in the bone. A pair of horn-like protuberances pointed forward at the top-rear edge of the frill.

The remains of *Anchiceratops* have been unearthed from deposits laid down in deltas, mixed with beds of coal, and dating from the topmost rocks of the Late Cretaceous Period. The location of the fossil finds of *Anchiceratops* suggests that this dinosaur may have inhabited swamps or the surrounding areas. It would probably have fed, using its sharp beak and shearing cheek teeth, on the abundant vegetation that grew in this waterlogged environment—such plants as swamp cypresses, ferns, giant redwoods, and cycads.

NAME	Pentaceratops
TIME	Late Cretaceous
LOCALITY	North America (New Mexico)
SIZE	20 ft/6 m long

Like *Anchiceratops*, *Pentaceratops* may well have been a descendant of *Chasmosaurus*, which lived earlier in Late Cretaceous times. It, too, had a huge neck frill, its margin fringed with small spines. In some species, the frill stretched halfway along the back, and as many as four large openings punctured the bony surface, reducing its weight.

When *Pentaceratops* was discovered, the scientists reckoned that they had found an unusual dinosaur with five horns on its face, hence its name. In fact, *Pentaceratops* had the usual three-horned face: there was a short, stout horn on its snout and a pair of long horns that curved forward from the brow. The two remaining "horns" were merely outgrowths of the cheek bones, and were not unusual features among the long-frilled ceratopids.

NAME	Torosaurus
TIME	Late Cretaceous
LOCALITY	North America (Montana, South Dakota, Texas, Utah, and Wyoming)
SIZE	25 ft/7.6 m long

This horned dinosaur, whose name means "bull lizard," is found in the topmost beds of the Late Cretaceous. It was the largest, and the last, of the long-frilled group and a contemporary of the short-frilled *Triceratops*, the largest of all the horned dinosaurs. Herds of both types of horned dinosaur would probably have roamed together through the North American landscape some 70 million years ago.

The skull of *Torosaurus* is the largest known from any land-living animal, either modern or extinct, with a length of 8 ft 5 in/2.6 m. The enormous neck frill extended along half this length, rising from the back of the head in a hollowed-out sheet, with the usual pair of large openings. The margin was smooth, lacking the usual array of bony knobs.

Two great horns surmounted the brow of *Torosaurus*, and a shorter horn grew from its snout, above the massive, sharp beak. All three horns were straight and pointed forward.

Few predators would have risked attacking such a formidable animal as *Torosaurus*. Weighing some 9 US tons/8 tonnes and moving at a fair pace on its stout legs, its head armed, its neck and upper back protected by the great frill and the rest of its body covered in thick hide—this horned dinosaur could have done battle with the largest of carnivorous dinosaurs. However, by the end of the Cretaceous Period the days of the dinosaurs were numbered. The "Age of Dinosaurs" ended some 65 million years ago, with a worldwide mass-extinction. Several other major groups disappeared at about the same time—the plesiosaurs, ichthyosaurs, and ammonites in the sea, and the pterosaurs in the air. No trace of any of these groups has been found in the rocks of the subsequent Tertiary Period.

Dozens of theories have been put forward in the past to account for this mass extinction. Hypotheses, such as virus attack from outer space, temperature change, producing juveniles of one sex only and egg shells too thick for the embryos to break out of, range from the peculiar to the plainly eccentric. It is now generally accepted that there was a major impact event and a major change in sea-level at the end of the Cretaceous, both of which would have had a severe effect on the global food chain (see p.235). However, there are still many unanswered questions about why some organisms should have survived and others have become extinct.

MASTERS OF THE AIR

The conquest of the air was the last great opportunity for the vertebrates, demanding dramatic modifications of both structure and physiology. Such modifications have evolved independently within mammals and reptiles who have evolved powered flight. Arguably, the most successful of the reptilian fliers were the birds.

Flight engineering

The birds are the acknowledged masters of the air. Their abundance and diversity, both past and present (with some 166 families of living birds), exceeds that of any other flying creature. Their success lies in the development of a structure unique in the animal world—feathers. These aerodynamic structures developed from reptilian scales. They are lightweight and easily replaced if damaged, in contrast to the vulnerable skin-wings of pterosaurs and bats.

By evolving feathered wings, birds acquired the enlarged surface area needed to support the body in the air. Their modified forelimbs were wholly devoted to flight, folding away on land. The hind limbs became adapted for walking upright.

The power for flapping flight comes from large muscles that make up 15 to 30 percent of a bird's body weight. They stretch down from the wings and attach to the pectoral, or shoulder, girdle.

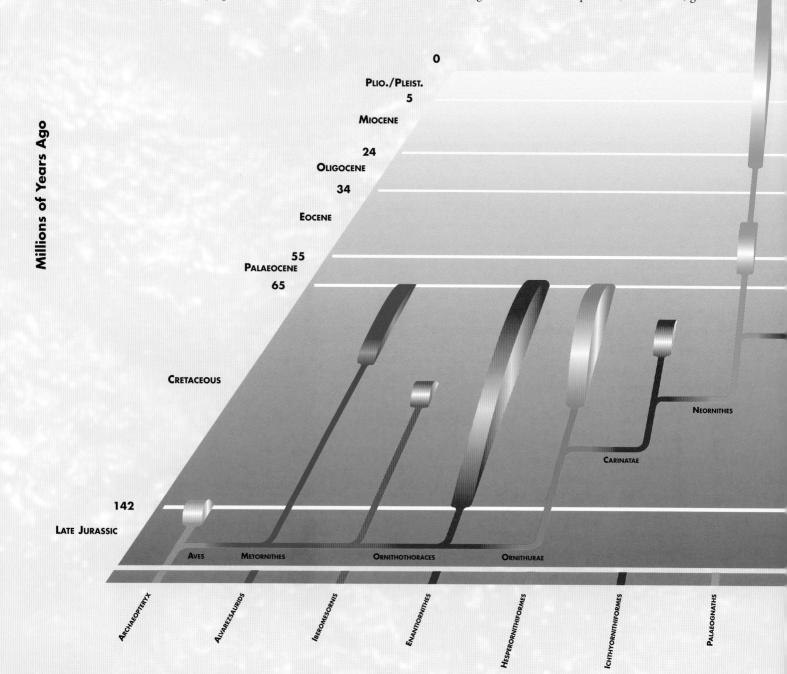

Millions of Years Ago

PLIO./PLEIST. 5
MIOCENE
24
OLIGOCENE
34
EOCENE
55
PALAEOCENE
65
CRETACEOUS
142
LATE JURASSIC

NEORNITHES
CARINATAE
AVES   METORNITHES   ORNITHOTHORACES   ORNITHURAE

ARCHAEOPTERYX   ALVAREZSAURIDS   IBEROMESORNIS   ENANTIORNITHES   HESPERORNITHIFORMES   ICHTHYORNITHIFORMES   PALAEOGNATHS

The sternum (breast bone) is greatly enlarged, and bears a prominent keel (carina) down the middle; both surfaces provide a large area to which wing muscles attach. They also attach to the fused clavicles (collar bones), which form the wishbone (furcula), and to a membrane connecting the wishbone and sternum.

To provide length and space for these muscles, the shoulder joints have moved upward, to a position level with the backbone. And to resist the powerful forces produced when the flight muscles contract, the sternum is braced away from the shoulder joints and backbone.

For a bird to launch itself, the hind legs must be long and powerful, so the bones of the lower leg and some of the bones of the ankle, to add a new section (the tarso-metatarsus), are elongated. The powerful muscles needed to swing the legs forward and backward are attached to the modified pelvic, or hip, girdle, whose bones have become elongated. The ilium projects far forward from the hip joint, and is strongly attached to the backbone by between 11 and 23 vertebrae (compared with only two or three in most reptiles). The pubis and ischium both project backward from the hip joint.

A bird's body is short to balance it while walking and it has moved back between the legs to bring the center of gravity to a point above the feet. The enlarged sternum lies between the knees.

The wings propel and guide the bird, so a long tail is not needed for stability and has been reduced to a short "pygostyle." The tail feathers can be erected to form a fan that acts as a brake.

Archaeopteryx, *the earliest-known bird, appeared in the Late Jurassic. The Cretaceous Period saw an explosive evolution of the birds, with many new groups, and most modern groups had appeared by the end of that period or by the Eocene.*

Since the fragile bones of birds are rarely fossilized, this evolution chart is based on recent studies, carried out in the USA by Sibley and his colleagues, on the genetic material of modern birds.

Only a proportion of the 27 or so orders of modern birds are shown here. Relatively few groups have become extinct over their 140 million years of evolution.

NEOGNATHAE

DUCKS, CHICKENS

GREBES, PENGUINS, PELICANS

CRANES, SHOREBIRDS, PIGEONS

STORKS

FALCONS, OWLS

NIGHTJARS, SWIFTS

KINGFISHERS, WOODPECKERS, SONGBIRDS

Fuelling the changes

A bird's physiology had to change in order to cope with the energy demands of flight. The respiratory system became more efficient. A unique arrangement of numerous air sacs off the main respiratory passage ensures that air passes through a bird's lungs in a continual stream. Birds are warm-blooded, so their levels of energy do not vary with the environmental temperature. Insulation is provided by the feathers.

Archaeopteryx: the first bird

A modern bird's skeleton is so different from that of any reptile, so the origins of birds could not be deduced with certainty until *Archaeopteryx* was discovered in Late Jurassic limestones. It is an intermediate, in time and structure, between reptiles and birds.

Archaeopteryx was fossilized in such fine-grained sediments that the clear impression of its feathers can be seen around the skeleton. The feathers and the shape of the wings, are exactly like those of living, flying birds. It also had a wishbone, which forms an attachment site for flight muscles. The wing feathers of *Archaeopteryx* are remarkably modern, fully developed with asymmetrical flight feathers with downy elements near the base.

Archaeopteryx had small, sharp teeth in its jaws, replaced in later birds by a horny, toothless beak. It had three clawed fingers on each forelimb, each distinct from the others (unlike their partly fused arrangement in modern birds). And it had a long, bony tail, fringed on either side by long feathers to provide uplift.

Archaeopteryx probably lived in trees, eating the insects there, and using both flapping and gliding flight to get from tree to tree. From time to time, it would have landed on the ground, and used its sharp, clawed fingers to climb back into the trees.

Apart from the proportions of its wings, the skeleton of *Archaeopteryx* is strikingly similar to that of a small, bipedal dinosaur, such as the coelurosaur *Compsognathus*. Most paleontologists believe that it evolved from just such a dinosaur.

The problem of the evolution of feathers has intrigued scientists for many years since the first fossil feather was found in the late Jurassic strata of Solenhofen in Bavaria in 1861. There are two main kinds of feathers: the long tough flight feathers and the smaller fluffy body and down feathers. Flight feathers are characteristically asymmetric. However, feathers must have initially evolved for some other purpose—organisms cannot develop a structure before its use.

The main possibility seemed to be body insulation, which is of particular importance for small animals, without much in the way of defense

mechanisms, which need to be constantly active and alert to predators. Birds are warm blooded and the feathers both conserve heat and shield the animal from high temperatures.

Until recently, feathers have also been thought to be unique to birds. But the discovery of feathered dinosaurs in China has shown that they are not. The Chinese dinosaurs (see p.252) also raise interesting questions about the pre-adaptive role of feathers. These dinosaurs were not capable of flight since the feathers are restricted to bunches of long symmetric feathers on their hands and long bony tail. Some have a crest of feather-like structures running from the head down the neck and along the back. The body was also covered with small down feathers.

There is clearly a function as insulation, but the hand and crest feathers must have had other uses. The most obvious is for sexual display and perhaps species recognition.

Further new finds from Las Hoyas in central Spain are also helping to fill in some of the large gaps in the fossil record. The Las Hoyas site was an ancient lake and filled with very fine-grained calcareous mud deposits in the early to mid Cretaceous, which preserve very detailed structures. The Spanish deposits promise to give insights into the early evolution of the birds. One new form, called *Iberomesornis*, seems to help bridge the gap between *Archaeopteryx* and the first of the Enantiornithes.

The "missing link" controversy

As a link between reptiles and birds, *Archaeopteryx* is a major piece of evidence for Darwin's theory of evolution. Its importance was recognized when it was discovered in 1861. *Archaeopteryx* has, therefore, always been a target of attack for those who question the theory of gradual evolutionary change. In 1985, the British astronomers Fred Hoyle and N.C. Wickramasinghe suggested that many evolutionary innovations were the result of a shower of extra-terrestrial viruses, which infected organisms with new characteristics. They suggested that birds and mammals evolved, and the dinosaurs became extinct due to such a virus shower, at the end of the Cretaceous.

Archaeopteryx, one of the most important fossils ever found, has features that link it incontrovertibly with reptiles and birds.

Archaeopteryx, dating from over 80 million years before the Late Cretaceous, is a fatal weakness in this virus-shower theory. So Hoyle and Wickramasinghe suggested that the specimens of *Archaeopteryx* were fakes. However, the *Archaeopteryx* fossils have been shown to be genuine.

The evolution of birds

Between *Archaeopteryx* and the diverse fossil record of living bird groups there is a time gap representing most of the Cretaceous (some 70 million years). It is partly filled with a sporadic record of archaic toothed birds which have little or no known relationship with modern birds. Two unusual groups (subclasses) existed in the Cretaceous Period. One group, the Enantiornithes, were discovered in Argentina, and described in 1981. Still only poorly known, certain features of their legs, upper arm bones, and shoulder girdles distinguish them from all other birds.

Another Cretaceous group, the Odontornithes, provides the next major window on bird evolution. These early seabirds had teeth in their jaws. Some had lost the power of flight; others still had wings, and were probably more like modern terns.

Several types of birds have lost the ability to fly. This seems to happen when there are no active predators, as at the end of the Cretaceous, when the dinosaurs disappeared, and mammalian carnivores had not yet appeared. Flightless birds evolved in the relative safety of, for example, South America.

Modern flightless birds (the ostrich, emu, kiwi, cassowary, and rhea), and the extinct moas and elephant birds, are grouped as Ratites. They all have the bony palate and shoulder girdle, which may suggest that they descended from flying birds.

Living birds and their fossil representatives are grouped in the subclass Neornithes. They share a common, complicated structure of the bony palate, and this fact leads paleontologists to believe that they have descended from a common ancestor.

There is considerable argument about the origin of the modern birds. Some experts claim that a few pre-Tertiary fossil birds belong to modern groups such as the charadriiforms (shorebirds) and gaviiforms (ducks). Others say that few bird lineages survived the Cretaceous extinction.

There is a lack of abundant bird fossils. Birds are not easily preserved. In the next decade or so, more and better-preserved fossil birds will probably be found.

Birds have retained essentially the same skeletal structure. The fossil record reveals little about the interrelationships of the modern birds. Since the record is so patchy, and impressions of feathers are rarely fossilized, no-one can be certain what prehistoric birds looked like. The reconstructions here are mainly the traditional view of these birds, based on the known fossil names and a degree of guesswork from studies of modern, related species.

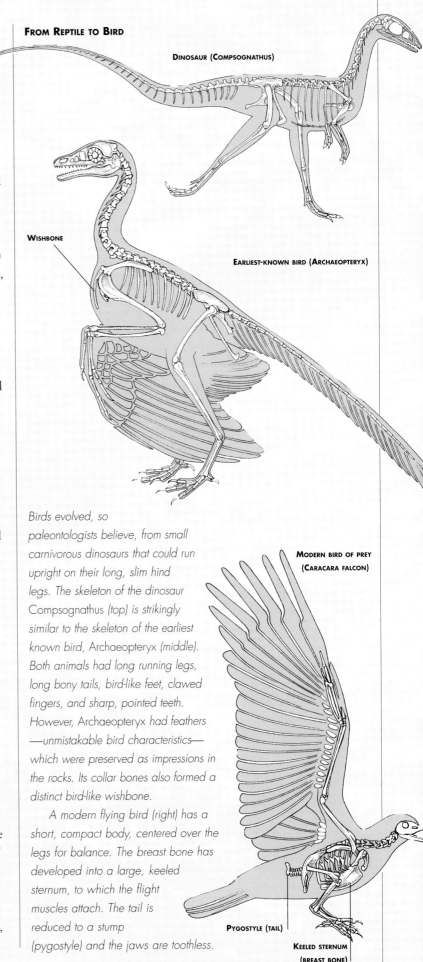

FROM REPTILE TO BIRD

DINOSAUR (COMPSOGNATHUS)

WISHBONE

EARLIEST-KNOWN BIRD (ARCHAEOPTERYX)

MODERN BIRD OF PREY (CARACARA FALCON)

PYGOSTYLE (TAIL)

KEELED STERNUM (BREAST BONE)

Birds evolved, so paleontologists believe, from small carnivorous dinosaurs that could run upright on their long, slim hind legs. The skeleton of the dinosaur Compsognathus (top) is strikingly similar to the skeleton of the earliest known bird, Archaeopteryx (middle). Both animals had long running legs, long bony tails, bird-like feet, clawed fingers, and sharp, pointed teeth. However, Archaeopteryx had feathers —unmistakable bird characteristics— which were preserved as impressions in the rocks. Its collar bones also formed a distinct bird-like wishbone.

A modern flying bird (right) has a short, compact body, centered over the legs for balance. The breast bone has developed into a large, keeled sternum, to which the flight muscles attach. The tail is reduced to a stump (pygostyle) and the jaws are toothless.

EARLY AND FLIGHTLESS BIRDS

CLASS AVES

This large group of highly successful flying vertebrates contains nearly 9000 living species arranged in some 160 families, of which 134 have fossil representatives. There are a further 77 extinct families. Despite significant advances in recent years, major difficulties remain in understanding bird phylogeny, with molecular and morphological evidence indicating very different relationships.

Family Archaeopterygidae

This group of "ancient birds" currently contains one genus—*Archaeopteryx*—and perhaps only one species. This is the earliest-known bird, and it occupies a special place in evolutionary history, since it shows in its structure the link between two major groups—the reptiles and the birds.

NAME *Archaeopteryx lithographica*

TIME Late Jurassic

LOCALITY Europe (Germany)

SIZE 14 in/35 cm long

The discovery of *Archaeopteryx* is a classic in the history of paleontology. In 1861, blocks of fine-grained limestone were being cut in a quarry at Solnhofen, southern Germany. These rocks are of Late Jurassic age, some 150 million years old: one split slab revealed the almost perfect skeleton of *Archaeopteryx*, the first-known bird. Not only were most of its delicate bones intact, but the impression of its feathers was stamped in the rocks, preserved in their natural positions on the wings and tail. A glass-fiber cast of this specimen is displayed in London's Natural History Museum.

A second, more complete specimen was discovered from the same site in 1877, and this slab of rock, together with its priceless occupant, is now housed in Berlin's Humboldt University Museum. Four more specimens are now known.

These fossil finds reveal a creature about the size of a modern pigeon, with a small head and large eyes, pointed teeth in its jaws and a long bony tail. Its limbs were long and slender, with three clawed digits on each elongated hand, and it had typical bird feet. *Archaeopteryx* lower-leg bones were long, and indicate a running animal.

This description does not wholly fit in with the picture of most modern birds, but *Archaeopteryx* had two unmistakable bird features. It had a well-developed wishbone (formed by the union of the two collar bones) and the typical feathers of a bird, attached to its long arms and tail.

Were it not for these bird-like characteristics, *Archaeopteryx* could easily be mistaken for one of the coelurosaurs small, two-legged, carnivorous dinosaurs (see pp.250–253). Indeed, one of the most recent *Archaeopteryx* specimens, discovered in Germany in 1951, was attributed to the coelurosaur *Compsognathus* until the early 1970s, when impressions of its feathers were noticed.

Most paleontologists believe that *Archaeopteryx* was an insectivorous creature that inhabited open forests, and could fly or glide from tree to tree. It may have caught insects on the wing as it flew, or perhaps it swooped down in surprise attacks on ground-living invertebrates. Its clawed hands and feet could have been used to haul it up the trunks of trees and to clamber among the branches, in order to launch itself on the next flight.

The sternum, or breastbone, of *Archaeopteryx* appears to have been tiny, unlike the great, keeled sternum of modern birds, which provides the main site for the attachment of powerful wing muscles. Some paleontologists have suggested that the feathers of *Archaeopteryx* were merely for insulation, rather than for flight. This ancestral bird was almost certainly warm-blooded, like its modern relatives. By controlling its body temperature, it could have led a more active, predatory life.

However, *Archaeopteryx's* feathers are so similar in structure and arrangement on the wings to those of modern birds that it is almost certain they were used for flying, even if this was less powerful than the flight of modern birds.

SUBCLASS ODONTORNITHES

This group of "toothed birds" lived throughout the Cretaceous Period. The Odontornithes subclass were similar to modern birds, except that they possessed small, pointed teeth set in sockets in their jaws.

They had developed (though some had already lost) the main structural feature necessary for sustained flight: a broad, keeled sternum to which the powerful wing muscles could attach. They had lost the long bony tail of their ancestors.

ORDER ICHTHYORNITHIFORMES

Members of this group of primitive, probably fish-eating, seabirds are common in marine deposits of Late Cretaceous age in North America. They were good flyers, to judge from the strong, keeled sternum.

NAME *Ichthyornis dispar*
TIME Late Cretaceous
LOCALITY North America (Kansas and Texas)
SIZE 8 in/20 cm tall

First discovered in the 1870s, the toothed jaws of this ancient bird were originally thought to belong to a mosasaur—a contemporary, fish-eating marine lizard (see p.231). This reptile was preserved in the same rocks, and had similar jaws and teeth to those of *Ichthyornis*.

Ichthyornis dispar and others of its genus had a general structure like that of a large, modern sea tern, but with a proportionally bigger head and bill. The large sternum suggests strong flight.

ORDER HESPERORNITHIFORMES

This Cretaceous group of toothed birds were specialized diving seabirds that had lost the power of flight. Although they had a well-developed sternum, the keel was reduced, and the wings had degenerated. These birds seem to have fished the shallow waters that covered much of central North America during Cretaceous times, and would have nested on low shores.

NAME *Hesperornis regalis*
TIME Late Cretaceous
LOCALITY North America (Kansas)
SIZE 6 ft/1.8 m tall

This large, flightless bird differed from other toothed seabirds in having lost its wings almost completely. It swam with powerful kicks of its large, webbed feet, set well back on the body, propelling itself along in the manner of a modern loon or grebe.

Hesperornis regalis could have chased fast-moving fish and squid underwater, holding such slippery prey in its long bill, equipped with sharp, pointed teeth. It probably nested at the water's edge, like a modern loon, and it would have been clumsy and vulnerable while on land.

SUBCLASS NEORNITHES

This group of "new birds" encompasses all recent species. They began to adapt to varied environments in the Early Cretaceous, and representatives of most of the modern groups had appeared by the Early Eocene, some 50 million years ago.

A number of extinct groups and species are known, of which the following are some of the more striking.

ORDER STRUTHIORNITHIFORMES

The typically large, long-legged flightless birds, collectively known as the Ratites, belong to this order. All have small or tiny wings, and the sternum has lost the keel that provides the attachment site for the wing muscles of flying birds.

Ratites first appeared during the Cretaceous or Early Tertiary, and different types evolved on the separating continents. Today, the only survivors of the group are the emus and cassowaries of Australia and New Guinea, the kiwis of New Zealand, the rheas of South America, and the ostriches of Africa (which were formerly also in Eurasia).

Two spectacular groups have become extinct only recently—the elephant birds of Madagascar and the moas of New Zealand.

EARLY AND FLIGHTLESS BIRDS CONTINUED

NAME *Aepyornis titan*

TIME Pleistocene to Recent

LOCALITY Madagascar

SIZE up to 10 ft/3 m tall

NAME *Dinornis maximus*

TIME Pleistocene to Recent

LOCALITY New Zealand

SIZE up to 11 ft 6 in/3.5 m tall

Dinornis maximus was the tallest bird that ever existed—taller than the great elephant bird of Madagascar, but of a much lighter build. It was one of about a dozen types of flightless moa that survived in New Zealand until recent times.

Man came to the New Zealand islands in about the 10th century, and over the next 800 years destroyed most of the forests by burning them for agriculture, and hunted the moas relentlessly, causing their extinction by the year 1800.

All moas were bulky, heavy-legged, long-necked birds. In the absence of large carnivores and herbivores, these slow-moving birds had taken the place usually occupied by browsing mammals, feeding off the rich supplies of seeds and fruits.

This species is the largest of the extinct genus *Aepyornis* and weighed up to 500 lb/500 kg. The common name— elephant birds —stems from Arabian tales of the "rukhkh," that could carry off an elephant. *Aepyornis'* legs ended in three widely spread, stumpy toes. The elongated, thick thigh bones are evidence that it was not a runner.

Aepyornis eggs were over 1 ft/30 cm long, could hold 19 pints/9 liters and may have weighed 20 lb/10 kg.

Aepyornis bird had no special defenses—no teeth, no talons, and no wings. Size and strength were protection against predators. When man arrived in Madagascar, less than 1500 years ago, species of *Aepyornis* were still alive. It may have become extinct in the 17th century.

NAME *Emeus crassus*

TIME Pleistocene to Recent

LOCALITY New Zealand

SIZE 5 ft/1.5 m tall

This moa, only half the height of *Dinornis*, was peculiar in having massive lower legs, which were out of all proportion to its body size. Its feet were also enormously broad. It must have been a painfully slow-moving animal, providing easy prey for the moa-hunters.

The modern kiwi, the bird which is the emblem of New Zealand, is regarded by some paleontologists as a highly specialized moa. The three living species are tiny in comparison to their extinct relatives, being less than 2 ft/60 cm tall.

ORDER COLUMBIFORMES

Modern pigeons have changed little since their first appearance in the Late Cretaceous or Early Tertiary. Larger types of Columbiformes evolved on warm islands, which were free of predators, especially during Pleistocene times when several large, and often flightless, forms inhabited the Mascarene Islands of the Indian Ocean.

NAME *Raphus cucullatus*

TIME Pleistocene to Recent

LOCALITY Mauritius

SIZE 3 ft 3 in / 1 m tall

Raphus cucullatus, commonly known as the dodo, was a giant, terrestrial pigeon that became another casualty of man's habit of destruction. Flightless and slow-moving, it was easy prey to sailors who stopped off on islands in the Indian Ocean to restock their larders.

The dodo was about the size of a modern turkey, and was covered in soft, downy feathers. It had a fat body (weighing some 50 lb / 23 kg), a large head and a bald face. It had a massively strong, hooked bill and a curly, tufted tail. Its wings were tiny and useless, and it had a ponderous gait, waddling about on stout, toed feet, feeding on low-growing plants, seeds, and fallen fruits.

There were no natural predators on the island of Mauritius to disturb the dodo's slow progress or to endanger it which left the dodo so ill-equipped to defend itself against large predators that it did not even flee the hungry sailors. *Raphus cucullatus* was not only easy prey for the people landing on the island, but also for the animals (pigs and dogs, for example) which were introduced to the island. This had caused the extermination of the dodo by the 17th century—less than 200 years after it had first been discovered.

ORDER CICONIIFORMES

This large order includes the modern shorebirds—the wading water birds (other than waterfowl, see p.325), the seabirds and the typical birds of prey. Most of the Ciconiiformes evolved and diverged to occupy different habitats toward the end of the Cretaceous Period. Birds of prey, such as the eagles, were widespread from Eocene times onwards.

NAME *Harpagornis moorei*

TIME Pleistocene to Recent

LOCALITY New Zealand

SIZE possibly 3 ft 6 in / 1 m tall

This eagle may not have been much larger than many of its modern relatives, the eagles and Old World vultures, but it was stronger and more heavily built. The legs of *Harpagornis moorei* were stout and equipped with heavy talons, the beak was deep and sharply hooked, and the bird's powerful and impressive wings spanned some 7 ft / 2.1 m.

Harpagornis moorei coexisted with moas in New Zealand, and became extinct at about the same time—perhaps as recently as the 17th century. Since there were no other large predators on the New Zealand islands, this bird may have fed on the smaller moas, *Emeus crassus* for example, and on other birds which have also since become extinct, such as the flightless goose.

Moas would have been bulky prey to attack, but their probable slowness of movement, together with their relatively small heads and their long necks, could have made them vulnerable to aerial attack. Certainly, the moa chicks would have provided easy prey for these powerful raptors.

WATER AND LAND BIRDS

NAME *Palaelodus ambiguus*

TIME Late to Early Oligocene

LOCALITY Europe (France)

SIZE 2ft/60cm tall

This medium-sized, long-legged shorebird is related to the modern wading and water birds, seabirds and birds of prey (grouped in the Order Ciconiiformes, see p.321).

It is often suggested by paleontologists that *Palaelodus* and its relatives represented early flamingos. But recent assessment instead suggests that they were more likely to be of shorebird origin and that they branched off fairly late from the main shorebird assemblage, and lived from the Late Oligocene to the Early Pliocene in Europe, North Africa, and North America.

Paleontologists really know very little about what the head and bill of *Palaelodus* would have looked like; the reconstruction (above) is the traditional view of the bird. However, the structure of its legs suggests that rather than wading in shallow water it may have dived and swum underwater to feed, behaving in a way similar to a modern diving duck.

NAME *Pinguinus impennis*

TIME Pleistocene to Recent

LOCALITY Small islands off western Europe (British Isles), Greenland, Iceland, and North America (Maine to Labrador)

SIZE 20in/50cm tall

Another member of the ciconiiformes, the great auk, *Pinguinus impennis*, lost its final battle against extinction on a small island off Iceland in 1844. For years, it had been relentlessly hunted by sailors for its flesh, its eggs, and the layer of insulating fat beneath its skin, which was used to provide oil for lamps.

Despite its name, the great auk was not a large bird, being only about half as tall again as the razorbill, the modern auk that it most resembled. It differed only in that it had become flightless. *Pinguinus impennis* was a well-adapted seabird, like all modern auks, propelled by its webbed feet when on the surface, and using its small wings for propulsion when swimming underwater after its fish prey.

The legs of the great auk were set well back on its body, allowing it to walk upright on land, although it would have moved in a slow and awkward way.

It nested in colonies on islands where it could get ashore easily, and incubated its single egg on bare ground. These nesting colonies, however, were highly vulnerable, and the birds were either killed on the spot by sailors or herded live into boats, like sheep.

The great auk evolved in the Pleistocene epoch, some 2 million years ago. Other members of the auk family, however, date back to Miocene times, and probably even earlier. During the ice ages of the Pleistocene, great auks swam southward, and they are known from the Mediterranean and Florida.

Although unrelated to the modern penguins of the southern hemisphere, the great auk was their northern counterpart in lifestyle and appearance. In fact, *Pinguinus impennis* was the original "penguin," being given this name by early mariners. Today's penguins are named after it.

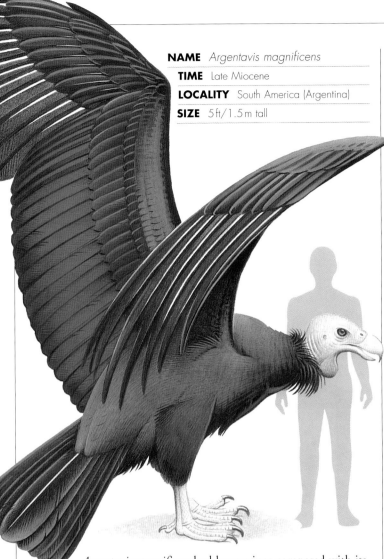

NAME *Argentavis magnificens*

TIME Late Miocene

LOCALITY South America (Argentina)

SIZE 5 ft / 1.5 m tall

NAME *Limnofregata azygosternum*

TIME Early Eocene

LOCALITY North America (Wyoming)

SIZE up to 1 ft / 30 cm tall

Limnofregata azygosternum appears to have been an ancestral form of the modern frigatebirds. Today, these are specialized marine birds, related to pelicans, and almost wholly adapted to an aerial existence over the sea. But 50 million years ago, they were only just evolving, and *Limnofregata* may be a halfway stage in their development.

Limnofregata's general structure was similar (although a less extreme adaptation to its lifestyle) to that of modern frigatebirds. Its legs and feet, although reduced in size, were larger and longer than those of modern species. Its wings, too, were proportionally shorter, with a span of about 3 ft 3 in/1 m (compared with the long wings of the modern frigatebirds, which can reach up to 8 ft/2.5 m wingspan in the largest species). Its bill was shorter, more tapering and less hooked than that of living species.

However, unlike the modern frigatebirds, *Limnofregata azygosternum* did not glide on thermals over the ocean. Instead, it flew by flapping its wings, and its habitat was large, freshwater lakes, far inland. It was probably more like a gull in appearance and feeding method, than frigatebirds and it was more likely to land on water than its modern relatives, which snatch up fish and squid without alighting on the water surface.

Argentavis magnificens had huge wings compared with its body size. Although only some of its bones have been found, estimates place its wingspan at about 24 ft/7.3 m—twice the wingspan of the longest-winged living bird, the wandering albatross.

A bird of this size did not fly by flapping its wings. It would have conserved its energy by gliding from one food source to another, using as few wingbeats as possible. Launching itself from high places, it used the rising thermal currents of warm air during the day to keep it aloft. As with the modern albatross, its initial take-off technique was probably awkward.

Argentavis was most probably a scavenger, like its modern relatives; the New World vultures. Its deep, hooked beak would have been used to tear through the tough hide of dead animals, rather than used to attack live prey. The large, herbivorous mammals that grazed the open plains of Argentina during the Miocene provided a rich food source. But such a large bird was vulnerable to changes in food supply or climate. *Argentavis'* fate would have been closely linked to that of the early mammals of South America (see pp.390–397).

Argentavis was more closely related to storks than to other birds of prey; in fact, they share a common origin with the storks, diverging from them very early in the Tertiary Period.

NAME *Osteodontornis orri*

TIME Late Miocene

LOCALITY North America (California)

SIZE 4 ft / 1.2 m tall

Osteodontornis orri is one of the "bony-toothed" gliding seabirds. They combine pelican and petrel/albatross characteristics. They probably arose from a common ancestor in the Late Cretaceous and by the Late Paleocene, they were highly developed. They were the largest seabirds during the Tertiary, perhaps preventing the evolution of larger albatrosses.

Osteodontornis' body was heavily built, with legs and feet like a huge petrel. The long, narrow wings, designed for constant gliding flight, had a wingspan in some of the larger species of up to 20 ft / 6 m, and would have been held out stiffly. They were probably not much use for strong or rapid maneuvers.

The head, with its heavy, long, pelican-like bill, probably rested back on the shoulders in flight, like a modern heron or pelican. Its bill was as long as that of a modern pelican, but stouter and more rounded, with a hook at its tip. Large and small tooth-like outgrowths projected along the edges of both jaw bones. When the bill was closed, those of the lower jaw fitted into deep grooves on the palate inside the upper jaw.

The wing structure suggests that it may have snatched prey from at, or just below, the water surface. The bony spikes on the bill would have been ideal for gripping slippery fish or squid. The slanting roof of the throat suggests that there was an elastic pouch along the neck, used as a temporary fish larder.

Nothing is known of the nesting habits of these birds. They probably chose level-topped islands, which would have provided a good runway for easy take-off. Constant, but not violent, breezes were essential for their gliding flight. Perhaps stormier, more varied weather during the Pleistocene caused the demise of these birds, some 2 million years ago.

ORDER GRUIFORMES

The Gruiformes evolved in Late Cretaceous times, 90 million years ago, and rapidly diversified into a great assemblage, ranging from small, strong flyers to giant, flightless forms. Most of today's Gruiformes are aquatic birds, such as the long-legged cranes and rails, moorhens, and coots. There are also some ground-living species, such as the bustards and trumpeters.

NAME *Phorusrhacus inflatus*

TIME Early to Middle Miocene

LOCALITY South America (Patagonia)

SIZE 5 ft / 1.5 m tall

Phorusrhacus inflatus was a medium-sized member of a family of flightless birds that became the dominant predators in South America during the Tertiary Period. All the phorusrhacids had strong running legs; small, useless wings; and large heads, equipped with great, eagle-like beaks. Some species were giants, and stood 10 ft / 3 m tall: the head of one species was over 1 ft 6 in / 50 cm long.

In the Early Tertiary, South America had become an island continent. The dinosaurs had died out, and no large carnivores had evolved to take their place. *Phorusrhacus* and its relatives filled this vacant niche. Some paleontologists have suggested that phorusrhacids were also carrion-eaters, using their deep, hooked beaks for tearing at the flesh of dead animals, as well as for seizing prey.

These formidable birds were extinct by the Early Pleistocene. But their nearest modern relatives may be the two species of seriema that live in the grasslands of South America today. These small, ground-living birds can fly, but prefer to run.

NAME *Neocathartes grallator*

TIME Late Eocene to Early Miocene

LOCALITY North America (Wyoming)

SIZE 18 in/45 cm tall

Originally thought to be a New World vulture modified for running, *Neocathartes* appears to be a flesh-eating member of another group of gruiform ground birds, the bathornithids. It was slimly built and capable of flight, although from its structure it is likely that it spent most of its time hunting on the ground.

Chasing after prey on its long legs, in the manner of a modern secretary bird, *Neocathartes'* clawed feet and hawk-like beak would have coped easily with small rodents and reptiles.

NAME *Diatryma gigantea*

TIME Early Eocene

LOCALITY Europe (Belgium, England, and France) and North America (New Jersey, New Mexico, and Wyoming)

SIZE 7 ft/2.1 m tall

Diatryma gigantea was a giant flightless bird that lived in North America and western Europe during the Paleocene and Eocene when the continents were joined together.

Like other members of its family, it was heavily built with tiny wings, incapable of flight. Its stout legs were armed with strong, clawed feet. The bird's large head (with its massive, hooked beak) was almost the size of that of a modern horse.

Some paleontologists suggest that the diatrymids became the dominant carnivores in the northern hemisphere because there were no other large predators around at the time. So, like the later phorusrhacids in South America, the diatrymids may have been the dominant predators.

Other paleontologists, however, have suggested that the diatrymids were actually herbivorous creatures that used their heavy, sharp-edged beaks to shear through tough vegetation, such as tussocks of grass or rush-like growth.

ORDER ANSERIFORMES

The ancestors of today's waterfowl—the ducks, geese, and swans— belong to this order. They diverged from other birds early in the Cretaceous Period.

NAME *Presbyornis pervetus*

TIME Late Cretaceous to Early Eocene

LOCALITY Europe (England), North America (Utah and Wyoming), and South America (Patagonia)

SIZE 3 ft 3 in/1 m tall

Presbyornis was a typical member of its family—a long-legged, long-necked bird, so slenderly built that paleontologists first thought it was a flamingo, until it was discovered that its head and bill were similar to those of modern ducks.

From the abundant remains of both bones and eggs, it seems that *Presbyornis pervetus* flocked together on the shallow margins of lakes. They nested in great, open colonies, and would have waded in the shallows, sifting the water with their broad, flattened bills to remove tiny animals and plants—a method used by modern dabbling ducks.

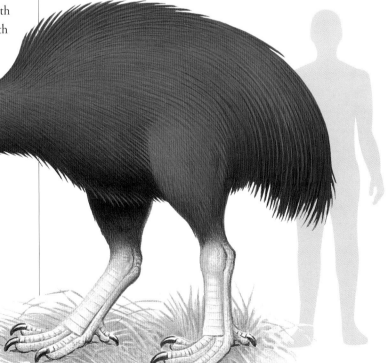

ANCESTORS OF THE MAMMALS

In the warm, moist, tropical forests that covered Nova Scotia in the Late Carboniferous Period, more than 300 million years ago, there lived two types of reptile. Both looked much the same—small and lizard-like, with legs and feet that sprawled out to the sides of their bodies. One, *Hylonomus*, scuttled about after insects, and tried to avoid being eaten by the other—the larger, predatory *Archaeothyris*, with its powerful, snapping jaws and sharp, pointed teeth.

While *Hylonomus* (see p.206) was the earliest known reptile, *Archaeothyris*, an ophiacodontid, was the first of a long line of reptiles that were to dominate the land for the next 80 million years, throughout the Permian and much of the Triassic. These were the mammal-like reptiles, so-called because their evolutionary history culminated in the mammals—the most varied and successful group of vertebrates alive today (see pp.338–441).

At first, the mammal-like reptiles gave no hint of any unusual potential. Only a feature of their skulls betrays their ultimate affinities with the mammals. A pair of openings, set low behind each eye socket, distinguishes them from all other reptiles. The same structure—known as "synapsid"—is seen in mammals, although the design is modified with much larger openings. Other reptiles fit into the anapsid group (no skull opening) or diapsid group (two skull openings), their living descendants being, respectively, the turtles and tortoises, and the lizards, snakes, and crocodiles.

The development of stronger jaws among the mammal-like reptiles and their descendants, the mammals, is believed to have been the direct result of the evolution of the synapsid type of skull. Related to this was the development of a new type of dentition—the typical mammalian pattern, with teeth of different sizes and shapes for different purposes: sharp-edged incisors for cutting, pointed canines for tearing, and cheek teeth with a crushing surface for chewing.

Rise of the mammal-like reptiles

The earliest synapsid reptiles to evolve were the pelycosaurs (see pp.330–332). From such little creatures as *Archaeothyris* a great variety of large reptiles evolved, both carnivorous and herbivorous. Their heyday was during the early part of the Permian Period, when they constituted some 70 percent of the terrestrial fauna. Their remains are particularly common in Texas. Some 280 million years ago, the warm, tropical humid, delta floodplains of this region would have swarmed with a variety of early amphibians and fishes, all of them prey to the powerful jaws of the dominant predators of the day, the land-living pelycosaurs.

Toward the middle of the Permian Period, a more advanced group of mammal-like reptiles arose from the pelycosaurs, and ultimately replaced them. These were the therapsids, the direct ancestors of the mammals. Their fossil remains are first found in rocks of European

Russia at the base of the Late Permian; their sudden appearance in the fossil record suggests that they may have evolved earlier in more upland areas (where fossilization is less likely).

During the Late Permian Period, these therapsids spread to the great southern landmass of Gondwanaland. Many types are found in the Karroo rocks, laid down in the lowland basin of southern Africa. Others are found in European Russia, in the sediments eroded from the newly formed Ural Mountains. Later still, in the Early Triassic Period, the therapsids spread to Asia, South America, India, and even Antarctica, all of which were joined together at the time into the supercontinent Pangaea.

The therapsids enjoyed domination of the land until the middle of the Triassic Period, and successfully adopted the diverse lifestyles of carnivores, herbivores, and insectivores. At that point, however, two new groups of terrestrial reptiles surged into their ecological niches—the early, carnivorous ruling reptiles (see pp.250–265) and the herbivorous rhynchosaurs (see p.236).

Thereafter, the therapsids began their slow decline; 55 million years later, by Mid-Jurassic times, the last group (the tritylodont cynodonts, see p.337) finally became extinct. But not before its members had given rise to the first mammals—tiny, shrew-like creatures that were to wait for more than 150 million years before they entered the limelight of vertebrate history.

Through these insignificant little creatures, the synapsid reptiles had the last laugh over their dinosaur usurpers, when those great creatures lay dead at the end of the Cretaceous Period, their reign over, and the mammal-like reptiles survived to inherit the earth in the form of their mammalian descendants.

Vital steps toward warm-bloodedness

The main advance of mammals over reptiles is their ability to regulate their body temperature. Mammals are warm-blooded, or endotherms; reptiles are cold-blooded, or ectotherms (see p.235). But there is little doubt that the early mammals, like reptiles, were still cold-blooded creatures, relying on the sun as their prime source of body heat. Strong evidence for this is provided by the remains of the early synapsids, such as the sphenacodont pelycosaurs. Some of these animals had great skin-covered sails on their backs, the function of which must have been to control body temperature—to absorb heat when cold, and radiate it when warm (see *Dimetrodon*, p.331).

Pelycosaurs without such obvious regulatory devices, and early therapsids such as the dinocephalians, probably controlled their body temperature simply by virtue of their greater body size. A larger, bulkier body retains a greater amount of heat than a small one, providing a thermal reservoir that reduces the effects of fluctuations in the environmental temperature.

However, the later therapsid reptiles developed other features that would finally end their dependence on the sun as a source of energy. By eating more food more frequently, and by digesting and metabolizing it more quickly and efficiently, they could now rely on food as a major energy source.

This new method of controlling body temperature required many changes, including better jaws and teeth, better locomotion, better breathing control, and better external insulation to maintain the body's internal temperature.

Dental developments

An innovation among the mammal-like reptiles was the evolution of teeth of different sizes and shapes (called a "heterodont" dentition). Even the earliest pelycosaurs had three distinct kinds of teeth in their jaws. The food-grasping incisors at the front were separated from the biting cheek teeth at the back by several long, stabbing canines.

In normal reptilian fashion, all of these teeth were renewed periodically by waves of replacement along each jaw and the old, worn teeth discarded; the even-numbered teeth were replaced in one wave,

and the odd-numbered teeth in the next. The more advanced therapsids, however, had departed from this reptilian "all-change" method of tooth replacement. Instead, the teeth were replaced only a few times during the animal's life.

This new pattern of tooth replacement was a major development, because it meant that each tooth could remain in the jaws for a longer period. As a result, the opposing crowns of the upper and lower teeth could develop a complex pattern of crests and valleys. These could then meet in a precision bite, and presented a rough surface on which

The mammal-like reptiles appeared during the Late Carboniferous Period in the form of the pelycosaurs, all of which were well-adapted land animals. It is believed that some of them, including the edaphosaurs, could control their body temperature by means of a large, heat-regulating "sail" on their backs.

The sphenacodonts were the ancestors of the advanced mammal-like reptiles, the therapsids. Many of these were ferocious carnivores, which dominated land life during the Late Permian. Others, such as the dicynodonts, were large plant-eaters.

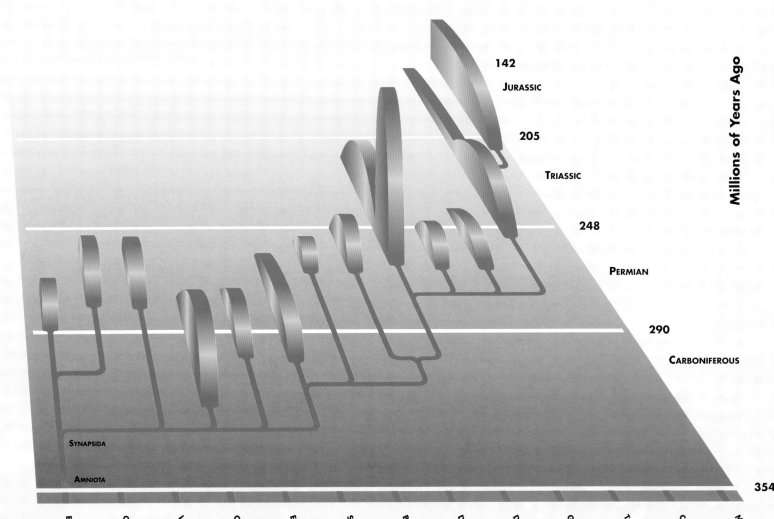

Millions of Years Ago

142
JURASSIC

205
TRIASSIC

248
PERMIAN

290
CARBONIFEROUS

354

SYNAPSIDA

AMNIOTA

EOTHYRIDIDS · CASEIDS · VARANOPSEIDS · OPHIACODONTIDS · EDAPHOSAURIDS · SPHENACODONTIDS · BIARMOSUCHIANS · DINOCEPHALIANS · DICYNODONTS · GORGONOPSIANS · THEROCEPHALIANS · CYNODONTS · MAMMALS

food could be cut, crushed, and ground to a pulp before being swallowed. The well-chewed food could then be digested more quickly and easily, which resulted in a more rapid release of the vital nutrients needed to fuel the body.

The jaws and skull of the mammal-like reptiles also changed. First, the size of the synapsid openings in the skull increased, allowing longer jaw muscles to develop. Second, the back of the skull became longer, and the sides bowed out, to produce more space for the jaw muscles. Both of these developments allowed for stronger jaw muscles resulting in a more powerful bite.

Third, there was an improvement in the structure of the lower jaw. Previously, some of the jaw muscles were attached to the large dentary bone at the front of the jaw, while others were attached to a number of smaller bones at the back. These smaller bones were progressively reduced in size among the therapsids (and finally lost completely from the jaws of mammals, so removing a potential weakness in the junction between the bones of the lower jaws. The dentary bone itself also developed a high flange (the coronoid process) at the back, and this provided an additional attachment point for larger, more powerful jaw muscles.

Another small change in connection with the jaw bones of mammal-like reptiles had the spectacularly important result of providing better hearing in mammals. The two bones that had formed the joint between the skull and the lower jaw in the mammal-like reptiles gradually retreated into the middle ear of mammals. Here, they linked up with the already present stapes ("stirrup") bone, to form a chain of three bones (called the hammer, anvil, and stirrup because of their shapes). Sound is transmitted along this chain from the outer eardrum to the fluid-filled canals of the inner ear.

The progressive integration of these three small bones into the ear can be traced in the remains of therapsids from the Triassic Period. In fact, these changes can still be observed,

dramatically telescoped in time, during the development *in utero* of a modern mammal embryo. They provide as good a proof of evolutionary change as that provided by *Archaeopteryx* for the link between reptiles and birds (see p.318).

Mammals also developed a pair of fleshy ear-flaps on either side of their heads. It is not certain precisely when these external ears evolved, but they have been shown on some of the later therapsids illustrated on p.337.

Limb improvements

While all these changes were occurring in the jaws and teeth of the mammal-like reptiles, other changes in the skeleton were taking place that made the limbs of these creatures more efficient. The primitive pelycosaurs of the Late Carboniferous Period, such as *Archaeothyris*, still moved in the old reptilian fashion—bending the body from side to side, with the limbs sprawled out horizontally.

By the Early Permian, sphenacodonts, such as *Dimetrodon*, had evolved a new and better type of locomotion. The shape of the bones in the hips and hind limbs, and of the joints between the vertebrae, show that the stride of the hind limbs was accompanied by an up-and-down flexure of the backbone.

From *Dimetrodon* onward, the evolutionary story of the mammal-like reptiles is of a steady and rapid increase in this flexing of the limbs and body in the vertical, rather than the "old-fashioned" horizontal plane.

In addition, the feet changed position relative to the legs, from projecting to the sides to pointing forward, and the toes became shorter and of similar lengths.

This whole system of locomotion had far more potential for fast movement, since a longer stride and a faster swing of the legs could now be achieved simply by elongating various bones of the limbs and feet.

AN ADVANCED MAMMAL-LIKE REPTILE (*THRINAXODON*)

Thrinaxodon *walked like a mammal, with its legs directly beneath its body. Its teeth and jaws were powerful, with a high coronoid process on the lower jaw for strong muscle attachment. The rib cage was probably closed off by a muscular diaphragm, which allowed the lungs to expand and contract for efficient breathing.*

Better breathing

Other features of the advanced therapsid reptiles strongly suggest that they were warm-blooded, like their descendants, the mammals. For example, the abrupt reduction in the extent of the ribs in such cynodonts as *Thrinaxodon* suggests that the whole front part of the body cavity, which houses the vital organs, the lungs and heart, had been closed off by a muscular sheet of tissue, the diaphragm. This development set off a chain of events. It allowed larger lungs to be filled and emptied more rapidly and more frequently, which, in turn, resulted in more oxygen entering the bloodstream. This permitted the tissues to use oxygen faster—to speed up digestion or to increase muscular exertion, when, for example, chasing prey or avoiding predators.

Because the tissues of a warm-blooded animal require a constant supply of oxygen, it cannot stop breathing for more than a short time. This need conflicts with the need to keep food in the mouth while it is being chewed up. This problem was solved in some of the advanced therapsids (the therocephalians and the cynodonts) by the development of a secondary palate—a shelf of bone that separated the air passage from the mouth, allowing them to breathe and chew at the same time. The existence of such a structure provides further support for the theory that these mammal-like reptiles were already warm-blooded.

Insulation for survival

There is no way of knowing whether the mammal-like reptiles were covered in hair or fur. Such insulation is not necessary in larger animals (and many of the therapsids were large), since they have a proportionately smaller surface area through which to lose heat. It is significant, however, that the final transition between the mammal-like reptiles and the mammals, at the end of the Triassic, was accompanied by a marked reduction in size.

The first mammals, such as *Megazostrodon* (see p.342) were tiny, shrew-like creatures. It is likely that they were hairy and fully endothermic (warm-blooded), and possessed mammary glands—that is, they possessed those features that characterize true mammals. It is also likely that they were nocturnal burrowers, but there is no direct fossil evidence for any of this. What is known is that they had enlargements of the brain associated with hearing and smell, both of which are particularly useful for nocturnal animals. Their teeth indicate that they were insect-eaters and it would have been advantageous for them to be nocturnal to avoid having to compete with insect-eating birds and lizards. A nocturnal burrowing habit would also have helped them keep out of the way of the abundant reptilian predators and may well have helped them survive the extinction at the end of the Cretaceous.

FROM MAMMAL-LIKE REPTILE TO MAMMAL

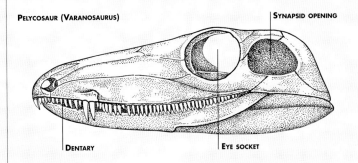

PELYCOSAUR (VARANOSAURUS) — SYNAPSID OPENING — DENTARY — EYE SOCKET

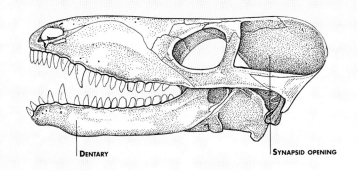

PRIMITIVE THERAPSID (PROCYNOSUCHUS) — DENTARY — SYNAPSID OPENING

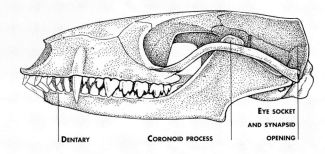

EARLIEST MAMMAL (MORGANUCODON) — DENTARY — CORONOID PROCESS — EYE SOCKET AND SYNAPSID OPENING

A mammal's strong, biting jaws resulted from progressive changes in the skull and lower jaws of their ancestors. In the earliest mammal-like reptiles, the pelycosaurs, the lower jaw was made of several bones, the dentary being the largest. In the more advanced therapsids, the skull was higher and the synapsid opening larger, for longer jaw muscles. The dentary bone was also larger. In the mammals, the eye socket and synapsid opening merged, and the lower jaw was formed entirely of the dentary. this had a high coronoid process which formed an extra site for muscle attachment. The small bones at the rear of the therapsid's lower jaw had moved into the mammal's middle ear, to form part of a chain along which sound was transmitted.

PELYCOSAURS AND THERAPSIDS

SUBCLASS SYNAPSIDA

The reptilian ancestors of the mammals—the pelycosaurs and therapsids—and the mammals themselves all share the same type of synapsid skull (see p.205). The single, large opening behind each eye socket allowed the development of longer jaw muscles, which resulted in stronger jaws that could be opened wide and closed forcefully, to deal with large prey.

ORDER PELYCOSAURIA

Pelycosaurs were the earliest of the synapsid (mammal-like) reptiles to evolve. They first appeared during the Late Carboniferous Period, some 300 million years ago when reptiles were first colonizing the land. Like the early reptiles, the pelycosaurs started as small, lizard-like creatures. But they evolved into many different types, of a much heavier build and with strong jaws and teeth of different sizes and shapes.

The ophiacodont family were the earliest and the most primitive pelycosaurs, and were the ancestors of the other three families. Carnivorous sphenacodonts were the most important group in evolutionary terms because they were the direct ancestors of the therapsid reptiles and, indirectly, of mammals.

The edaphosaurs were large plant-eaters, related to the sphenacodonts, but with a very different skull and dentition. The caseids were also herbivorous, and the latest, and last, of the pelycosaurs to evolve.

Family Ophiacodontidae

This group of six or seven genera ranging from the Late Carboniferous to the Mid Permian includes the earliest and most primitive known of the pelycosaurs.

NAME *Archaeothyris*
TIME Late Carboniferous
LOCALITY North America (Nova Scotia)
SIZE 20 in/50 cm long

This small, lizard-like ophiacodont is the earliest-known pelycosaur. Its remains were found in the same Late Carboniferous (Pennsylvanian) locality as those of

the first-known reptile, the anapsid *Hylonomus*. These rocks indicate a warm, tropical, humid climate, with great forests of conifers and a rich undergrowth of ferns and club mosses. In the lowland swamps, masses of decaying vegetation would have accumulated (giving rise to the coal beds of today), providing food and breeding grounds for insects and other invertebrates. They, in turn, attracted insectivorous reptiles, such as *Hylonomus*, which were probably preyed upon by the larger, newly evolved synapsid reptiles, such as *Archaeothyris*.

Archaeothyris was already more advanced than the other early anapsid reptiles. Its jaws were strong, and could be opened wide and snapped shut. Although its teeth were all the same shape—sharp and pointed—they were of different sizes, including a large pair of canines at the front of the jaws. Such teeth suggest a varied, carnivorous diet.

NAME *Ophiacodon*
TIME Early Permian
LOCALITY North America (Texas)
SIZE up to 12 ft/3.6 m long

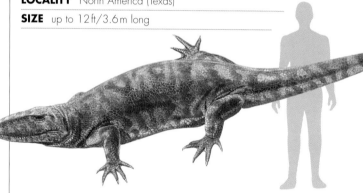

Ophiacodon shows the rapid evolution of features within the pelycosaur group. Its skull had changed from the small, low shape of its earlier relative *Archaeothyris* (left) to a deep, narrow shape. This allowed more space for longer jaw muscles to develop. Its hind limbs were longer than the forelimbs, and set somewhat more directly beneath the body. So, although it still sprawled like a typical reptile, *Ophiacodon* was probably a better runner than *Archaeothyris*.

Ophiacodon was considerably larger than the earlier pelycosaurs, and this factor may have helped it to control its body temperature. It is estimated to have weighed between 66 lb and 110 lb/30 kg and 50 kg. To support this considerable weight, it is likely that it spent some of its time in water, scuttling about floodplains or swamps, catching fish and amphibians in its elongated jaws, and despatching them with its sharp teeth.

Family Varanopseidae

This group includes four or five small pelycosaurs, all early Permian and all found in North America. With long limbs and light skeletons, they have been interpreted as active carnivores.

NAME *Varanosaurus*

TIME Early Permian

LOCALITY North America (Texas)

SIZE 5 ft / 1.5 m long

Varanosaurus lived in the same place at the same time as *Ophiacodon* (left), and probably competed with it for fish in the same swamps. Its skull was also deep and narrow, the jaws somewhat elongated and armed with small, spiky teeth. It had the build of a modern monitor lizard.

Family Sphenacodontidae

The largest group of bigger pelycosaurs, this family comprises eight carnivorous genera including *Dimetrodon*, one of the best known of the "sail-finned" pelycosaurs.

NAME *Sphenacodon*

TIME Early Permian

LOCALITY North America (New Mexico)

SIZE 10 ft / 3 m long

This large sphenacodont is typical of the family, with a deep, narrow skull, massive jaws and varied teeth: long canines, dagger-like incisors and small, cutting cheek teeth. The sphenacodonts were the first animals to develop such specialized teeth, and were the first large terrestrial carnivores.

The vertebral spines of *Sphenacodon*'s backbone were long, and acted as attachment points for massive back muscles, allowing it to lunge powerfully at its prey. In other members of the family, these spines were elongated, and supported a huge fin or "sail," probably for regulating body temperature.

NAME *Dimetrodon*

TIME Early Permian

LOCALITY North America (Oklahoma and Texas)

SIZE 10 ft / 3 m long

The spectacular "sail" on the back of *Dimetrodon* has earned it the popular name of the "finback," and is believed to be an early method of controlling body temperature.

The framework for the sail was provided by the elongated spines of the animal's back vertebrae, which were up to 3 ft 3 in / 1 m long in the center. In life, a sheet of skin covered the spines, and this was probably richly supplied with blood vessels.

Dimetrodon's likely routine would have been to stand with its sail oriented toward the sun in the early morning. Like a solar heater, the sail would have absorbed heat and warmed the blood, which then coursed through the body, raising the reptile's temperature so it could begin its daily hunt for food. To cool down, after a strenuous chase, for example, *Dimetrodon* angled its sail away from the sun and into the wind, dissipating heat.

An interesting example of convergent evolution is seen between these synapsid sphenacodonts and the unrelated diapsid reptiles, the dinosaurs. Two dinosaurs, *Spinosaurus* (see pp.262–263) and *Ouranosaurus* (see pp.288–289)—both living in West Africa during the Cretaceous—had also developed solar-heating sails on their backs.

According to calculations, a *Dimetrodon* weighing about 440 lb / 200 kg would have taken about an hour and a half to raise its body temperature from 79°F to 90°F (26°C to 32°C). Without the sail, the same animal would have needed to bask in the sun for more than three and a half hours to achieve the same rise in temperature.

The massive canines and well-developed shearing teeth of *Dimetrodon* confirm that it was a formidable predator: its name means "two kinds of teeth." Its prey would have included other pelycosaurs, which without the advantage of a sail would have remained slow and sluggish until the sun warmed them sufficiently to allow activity.

Family Edaphosauridae

This group of "sail-finned" pelycosaurs ranged from Late Carboniferous to Mid Permian in age. They show several adaptations for a herbivorous habit, such as palatal teeth forming a broad crushing area.

NAME *Edaphosaurus*

TIME Late Carboniferous to Early Permian

LOCALITY Europe (Czechoslovakia) and North America (Texas)

SIZE 10 ft/3 m long

Edaphosaurus had a large sail on its back, similar to that of *Dimetrodon*. It differed in that the extended vertebral spines of *Edaphosaurus* had cross-pieces of bone along their length. As well as serving to regulate body temperature, it is possible that the sail could also have served for display purposes—either of courtship or of threat—and it may have been brightly colored.

This bulky pelycosaur was not an active creature, nor was it built for speed. Its body was long and barrel-shaped to accommodate the large gut, its limbs were short and stocky, and it had a sprawling gait not suited to running. Its teeth were those of a plant-eater. As well as the closely packed, peg-like teeth which lined the jaws, there were also teeth on the palate, which formed a broad, chewing pavement, ideal for chopping and grinding plant material.

Family Caseidae

These Mid Permian pelycosaurs included both large and small forms, which have been found in North America and Europe. Their teeth show adaptations for a herbivorous diet, and such a lifestyle is also suggested by the barrel-shaped ribcage, which would have contained the enlarged stomach necessary for a massive plant-digesting gut.

NAME *Casea*

TIME Early Permian

LOCALITY Europe (France) and North America (Texas)

SIZE 4 ft/1.2 m long

The caseids, represented by *Casea*, were the last family of pelycosaurs to evolve, in Early Permian times. They became the most abundant of the plant-eating pelycosaurs, and thrived almost to the end of the Permian.

Casea was one of the smaller members of the family; some of its more imposing relatives reached lengths of 10 ft/3 m and weights of more than 1320 lb/600 kg. All of the caseids had deep, bulky bodies, in which the rib cage was enormously expanded in order to accommodate the long, plant-digesting gut. Their square-shaped heads were tiny, with enormous synapsid openings at the back and large nasal openings at the front.

The caseids were unique among pelycosaurs in having no teeth in the lower jaw. Those in the upper jaw were thick, blunt pegs with wavy edges, like those of modern herbivorous lizards. Numerous small teeth studded the palate. This dentition suggests that they lived in a diet of tough plants, such as ferns and horsetails, which would have needed grinding and chewing.

ORDER THERAPSIDA

The therapsids were advanced synapsid reptiles, descendants of the carnivorous sphenacodonts and the direct ancestors of the mammals. Although the remains of the first therapsids are found at the base of the Late Permian, they had diverged from the sphenacodont pelycosaurs more than 20 million years before, probably during the Early Permian. They spread rapidly to all parts of the world, including Antarctica.

The therapsids are grouped into several suborders (see p.482), only one of which, the cynodonts (see pp.336–337), survived into the Jurassic Period.

NAME *Phthinosuchus*

TIME Base of Late Permian

LOCALITY Europe (USSR)

SIZE 5 ft/1.5 m long

Only the skull of this primitive therapsid is known. It is strikingly similar to that of a sphenacodont, but with larger synapsid openings behind the eyes and more prominent canine teeth. Paleontologists believe it to be intermediate in structure between the pelycosaurs and the therapsids.

NAME *Titanosuchus*

TIME Late Permian

LOCALITY Africa (South Africa)

SIZE 8 ft/2.5 m long

Titanosuchus was a member of the large-skulled dinocephalians or "terrible heads." It was carnivorous, with sharp incisors and fang-like canines at the front of the jaws, and meat-shearing teeth at the back. Its main prey would have been its herbivorous relatives.

NAME *Moschops*

TIME Late Permian

LOCALITY Africa (South Africa)

SIZE 16 ft/5 m long

The Karroo Beds of South Africa have yielded many therapsids, among them this plant-eating dinocephalian (right), with a massive skull and deep body. The bones of its forehead were greatly thickened, suggesting that it engaged in head-butting battles for dominance—as did the boneheaded dinosaurs or pachycephalosaurs (see pp.280–281).

    Moschops had sturdy, sprawling forelegs; the longer hind legs were placed directly under the hips. Its short jaws had numerous chisel-edged teeth for cropping vegetation.

NAME *Lycaenops*

TIME Late Permian

LOCALITY Africa (South Africa)

SIZE 3 ft 3 in/1 m long

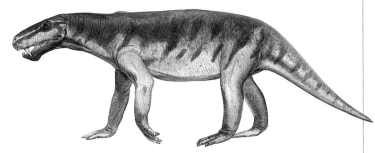

Lycaenops, or "wolf face," was a small, lightly-built carnivore, with long running legs. It was a member of the gorgonopsians, the dominant predators of the Late Permian in southern Africa and European Russia. It may have hunted in packs, and probably preyed on large, plant-eating therapsids, such as *Moschops*. The canines were particularly long, and the front part of the skull was deeper than normal to accommodate their roots.

NAME *Galechirus*

TIME Late Permian

LOCALITY Africa (South Africa)

SIZE 1 ft/30 cm long

This tiny lizard-like reptile is thought to be an early member of the dicynodonts (see pp.334–335)—the most abundant and successful group of the plant-eating therapsids. However, *Galechirus'* teeth suggest that it was actually an insectivore. Many paleontologists think that *Galechirus* simply represents the juvenile form of an adult therapsid.

THERAPSIDS

SUBORDER DICYNODONTIA

The dicynodonts were the most successful and wide-ranging group of plant-eating therapsids, or mammal-like reptiles. They evolved during the Late Permian Period, and survived to the end of the Triassic Period—a span of almost 50 million years. The only group of therapsids that outlived the dicynodonts were the cynodonts (see pp.336–337), which were the direct ancestors of the mammals (see pp.338–441).

The advanced development of the dicynodonts' skulls and jaws was the main factor in the animals' success. The synapsid openings at the back of the skull (see p.205) were greatly enlarged in dicynodonts, so as to allow for longer, stronger muscles to operate the creatures' jaws. The hinge between the lower jaw and the skull also permitted the jaws to move forward and backward with a strong, shearing action, ideal for grinding up vegetation. And the dentition of these reptiles was unique. These adaptations equipped the dicynodonts to cope with all kinds of tough plant material.

NAME *Robertia*

TIME Late Permian

LOCALITY Africa (South Africa)

SIZE 18 in / 45 cm long

Although *Robertia* was among the first dicynodonts to evolve, it had already evolved the specialized dentition characteristic of its later relatives. There was a horny, turtle-like beak at the front of its jaws, and the only teeth that remained were a pair of tusk-like canines in the upper jaw (an arrangement reflected by the name dicynodont, which means "two dog teeth").

In the case of *Robertia*, there was a notch in the jaw immediately in front of the canine teeth, into which tough stems, twigs and roots could presumably be inserted, then severed by the sharp beak.

NAME *Cistecephalus*

TIME Late Permian

LOCALITY Africa (South Africa)

SIZE 13 in / 33 cm long

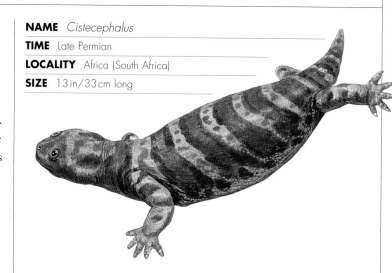

Dicynodonts adapted to many lifestyles. Some were semi-aquatic, while others browsed in the coniferous forests. Some, such as *Cistecephalus*, lived underground.

This creature had a wedge-shaped, flattened head, a short body and strong, stumpy forelimbs with broad toes, like those of a modern mole. It probably used its powerful limbs to dig into the soil to find worms, snails, and insects.

NAME *Dicynodon*

TIME Late Permian

LOCALITY Africa (South Africa and Tanzania)

SIZE 4 ft / 1.2 m long

Dicynodon had the characteristic pair of canine tusks in its upper jaw, which gives the dicynodont group its name, "two dog teeth." It may have used these strong tusks to root up plants.

Another group of herbivorous reptiles, the pareiasaurs, were contemporaries of *Dicynodon*. Some of these were elephantine beasts, heavily armored and with a full set of leaf-shaped teeth in their jaws. This was quite a different dentition to that of the horny-beaked, virtually toothless dicynodonts. These two types of unrelated reptile avoided competition with each other by eating different plants.

NAME *Lystrosaurus*

TIME Early Triassic

LOCALITY Africa (South Africa), Antarctica, Asia (China and India), and Europe (former USSR)

SIZE 3 ft 3 in/1 m long

The remains of *Lystrosaurus* were found in Antarctica in the late 1960s. The wide distribution of this sturdy, herbivore provides further evidence that, during Late Permian and Triassic times, India and all the southern continents were united as one landmass, Gondwanaland.

Lystrosaurus used to be regarded as a kind of reptilian "hippopotamus" which wallowed in shallows, browsing on water weeds. New analysis shows that it probably fed on more resistant vegetation and may have burrowed Both habits are more likely for an animal adapting to an increasingly semi-arid climate.

NAME *Kannemeyeria*

TIME Early Triassic

LOCALITY Africa (South Africa), Asia (India), and South America (Argentina)

SIZE up to 10 ft/3 m long

A skull bone of the ox-sized *Kannemeyeria*, or a close relative, was found in Australia in 1985, adding to the mass of biological evidence for Gondwanaland. This dicynodont was a well-adapted land-living herbivore. Its limb girdles formed massive plates of bone, to support the heavy, bulky body.

Kannemeyeria's massive head was lightweight, due to the great size of the openings for the eyes, nostrils, and jaw muscles. Mouthfuls of leaves and roots would have been torn up by the powerful, horny beak and ground down by the shearing action of the toothless jaws.

SUBORDER THEROCEPHALIA

The Late Permian rocks of European Russia and southern Africa reveal the remains of advanced mammal-like reptiles, the therocephalians. They are also known from eastern Asia and southern and eastern Africa. They survived until the middle of the Triassic Period.

NAME *Ericiolacerta*

TIME Early Triassic

LOCALITY Africa (South Africa)

SIZE 8 in/20 cm long

This lizard-like creature was an active insectivore, judging from its small teeth and long, slim limbs.

The abundant plant life of early Triassic Africa—horsetails, ferns, conifers, and early cycads—that supported the great populations of dicynodonts also provided home and food for many insects and other invertebrates. These, in turn, were a source of suitable prey for small therocephalians such as *Ericiolacerta*.

SUBORDER CYNODONTIA

The cynodonts, or "dog teeth," were the most successful group of therapsid reptiles. Not only were they the longest-lived group, surviving for some 80 million years, from Late Permian times to about the middle of the Jurassic. They were also the direct ancestors of the world's most successful modern group of animals—the mammals.

The first fossil cynodonts are found in the Late Permian rocks of European Russia and southern Africa. They show many advanced mammalian characteristics. For example, they had fewer bones in the lower jaw, a secondary bony palate and a complex pattern on the crowns of their cheek teeth.

Such advanced features suggest that these reptiles had evolved much earlier, probably during the early part of the Permian. Their ancestors were most probably among the carnivorous sphenacodont pelycosaurs (see p.331), which had already evolved a crude method of temperature control.

Although there is no trace in the fossil record, the cynodonts may well have been covered with hair, which would have insulated them and helped to maintain a high body temperature.

NAME	*Procynosuchus*
TIME	Late Permian
LOCALITY	Africa (South Africa)
SIZE	2 ft/60 cm long

Although not a typical cynodont, *Procynosuchus* is interesting because, although it is one of the earliest and most primitive members of the group, it was specialized for living in water.

The rear of its body and tail were more flexible than was usual among cynodonts, and could obviously be flexed from side to side, in a crocodile-style swimming motion. The tail vertebrae were flattened, to increase the surface area, making the tail a more efficient swimming organ. And the limbs were paddle-like, similar to those of a modern otter.

Despite these specialized features, *Procynosuchus* is thought to be close to the ancestor of all the cynodonts.

NAME	*Thrinaxodon*
TIME	Early Triassic
LOCALITY	Africa (South Africa) and Antarctica
SIZE	20 in/50 cm long

Thrinaxodon was much more mammal-like than its earlier relative, *Procynosuchus*. It was a small, solidly-built carnivore, probably capable of running quite fast due to the erect posture of its strong hind legs. The body was long and distinctly divided (for the first time among vertebrates) into a chest (thoracic) and lower back (lumbar) region. The division was marked by the extent of the ribs: only the thoracic vertebrae bore ribs, and these formed a distinct cage, which housed the vital organs.

As in living mammals, there was probably a sheet of muscular tissue, the diaphragm, that closed off the rib cage in *Thrinaxodon*. As the animal breathed, the movement of the diaphragm would have filled and emptied its lungs efficiently—an essential development in the evolution of body temperature control (see p.326–327). Another indication that *Thrinaxodon* could control its body temperature is the presence of a secondary bony palate, which completely separated the breathing passage from the mouth. This development allowed the animal to breathe at the same time as retaining food in its mouth for longer periods, chewing it up into small pieces for quicker digestion.

Many other structural changes had occurred in *Thrinaxodon*'s skeleton. For example, one of the foot bones had developed a heel which, with the help of strong tendons, would have levered the foot clear of the ground. The toes were of equal length, allowing the body weight to be evenly distributed.

Another mammalian trend is seen in the lower jaw of *Thrinaxodon*. The teeth on either side were set into a single bone, the dentary, which had become larger at the expense of the smaller bones at the back of the jaw. The effect of this trend among cynodonts, toward a single lower jaw bone, was to make the jaws stronger.

function as in living rodents and rabbits. These animals can nip in their cheeks to keep the food in the back of the mouth while it is being chewed.

The precise matching of the cheek teeth, and the advantage of concentrating chewing in the back of the mouth, would have made *Massetognathus* and its relatives efficient plant processors.

NAME *Oligokyphus*

TIME Early Jurassic

LOCALITY Europe (England)

SIZE 20 in/50 cm long

NAME *Cynognathus*

TIME Early Triassic

LOCALITY Africa (South Africa) and South America (Argentina)

SIZE 3 ft 3 in/1 m long

The jaws of *Cynognathus* show without doubt that it was a ferocious predator. It was one of the largest cynodonts, strongly built, with its hind limbs placed directly beneath its body. Its head was more than 1 ft/30 cm long.

Practically the whole of the lower jaw on each side was made up of a single bone, the dentary, into which the teeth were set—cutting incisors, stabbing canines, and shearing cheek teeth. A great bony flange (the coronoid process) at the back of the dentary articulated with the skull, and enabling the jaws to open wide. It also provided an area to which extra jaw muscles could attach, giving the jaws tremendous bite-power.

NAME *Massetognathus*

TIME Middle Triassic

LOCALITY South America (Argentina)

SIZE 19 in/48 cm long

Of the dozen or so cynodont families, only three included herbivores. The traversodonts, represented by *Massetognathus*, were plant-eaters, with a distinctive dentition. The cheek teeth were greatly expanded and the crowns were patterned with a series of crests and valleys.

The teeth of the lower jaw fitted into those of the upper jaw. There was also a gap between the cheek teeth and the small canines toward the front of the jaws which probably had the same

Oligokyphus and other members of its herbivorous family, the tritylodonts, were the last group of cynodonts to appear, in the Late Triassic. They were the longest-lived group of all therapsids, and the only mammal-like reptiles to endure into the Jurassic.

Oligokyphus was like a modern weasel in appearance, with a long, slim body and tail. Its forelegs, as well as its hind legs, were placed directly beneath the body, as they are in mammals. This little cynodont had achieved a fully upright, four-legged posture, unlike all other therapsids, which had sprawling forelimbs.

The dentition of the plant-eating *Oligokyphus* was also significantly different from that of other cynodonts. It had no canines, and the front pair of incisors were greatly enlarged, like those of a gnawing mammal such as a beaver. Like *Massetognathus*, a large gap separated the incisors from the square-shaped cheek teeth.

The cheek teeth in the top jaw had three rows of cusps running along its length, with grooves between: the lower teeth had two rows of cusps which fitted into the grooves, allowing the teeth to meet in a precision bite.

Oligokyphus is so like a mammal that paleontologists believed it to be a member of that group for years. But the small bones at the back of the lower jaw betray its reptilian affinities.

THE EVOLUTION OF VERSATILITY

The word mammal comes from the most important and unique characteristic of all species in this class of vertebrates, including humans: the presence in females of mammary glands, which produce milk to feed the young. Even the egg-laying mammals—the echidnas and platypus—have mammary glands.

The evolutionary implications of this milk-feeding strategy are enormous. The mother can leave her offspring in a den or nest while she goes foraging or hunting; she is then able to produce milk and so provide her young with a regular supply of this highly nutritious food. With nothing to do but sleep and suckle, the infants can grow fast.

The second most important mammalian characteristic is the presence of hairs, which usually form a dense fur coat. The prime purpose of the fur is to retain body heat, for mammals are warm-blooded. Most mammals keep their bodies at a constant temperature,

which is usually well above that of the environment. Humans, for example, have a body temperature of about 98.6°F/37°C; if the air temperature is lower, then we shiver and must put on clothes to keep warm; if it is higher, then we sweat to lose heat.

By maintaining this regular temperature, mammals can be very active for long periods, regardless of external conditions. But they pay a high price for this benefit; mammals must eat a great deal of food to produce the energy needed for such a high level of activity.

The earliest known mammals appeared in Late Triassic times, about 220 million years ago. Throughout the Jurassic and Cretaceous, mammals remained only minor elements in the world land faunas, which were dominated by reptiles, and in particular by dinosaurs.

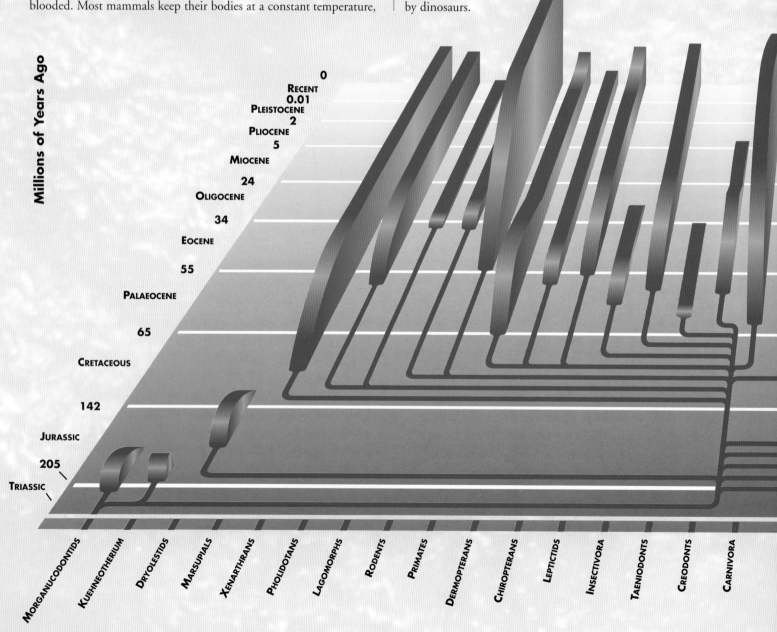

Mesozoic mammals were all small shrew- or vole-sized creatures. They lived by scavenging small animals. Other early mammals, such as multituberculates, probably ate plant matter, as do the voles today.

With the close of the Mesozoic Era, the world changed. On land, the major development was the disappearance of the dinosaurs. The succeeding Cenozoic Era began 65 million years ago, and the dominant forms of life on land since then have been flowering plants, insects, birds, and mammals.

The rise of the mammals

The emergence of tropical rainforests, temperate woodlands, savannah, and prairie grasslands, provided new habitats for mammals to exploit. Mammals have inhabited all continents, most large islands and the oceans worldwide. Today, Antarctica is the only large landmass without resident mammals, save for the sealions on its shores. However, back in Eocene times, 50 million years ago, Antarctica had a wooded landscape in which lived marsupial mammals.

Mammals enjoyed their maximum diversity about 15 million years ago, during the Miocene. Since then, world climates have deteriorated, culminating in the Great Ice Age of the Pleistocene, which began about 2 million years ago. Diversity is always greatest in the tropics, and the shrinkage of tropical habitats is largely responsible for the decline in the number of mammal species. But alternate cold and warm periods of the Ice Age encouraged the evolution of remarkable large mammals, such as the woolly mammoth, giant deer, and ground sloths—all of which disappeared within the last 12,000 years.

An active lifestyle calls for a high degree of control over the nervous system, so mammals have a large and complex brain capable of rapidly processing information fed to it from the eyes, nose, and ears.

Limb adaptations

As the small, shrew-like early mammals evolved into large forms, they extended their range from the undergrowth up into the trees and out into the scrublands; some took to the water and others took to the air.

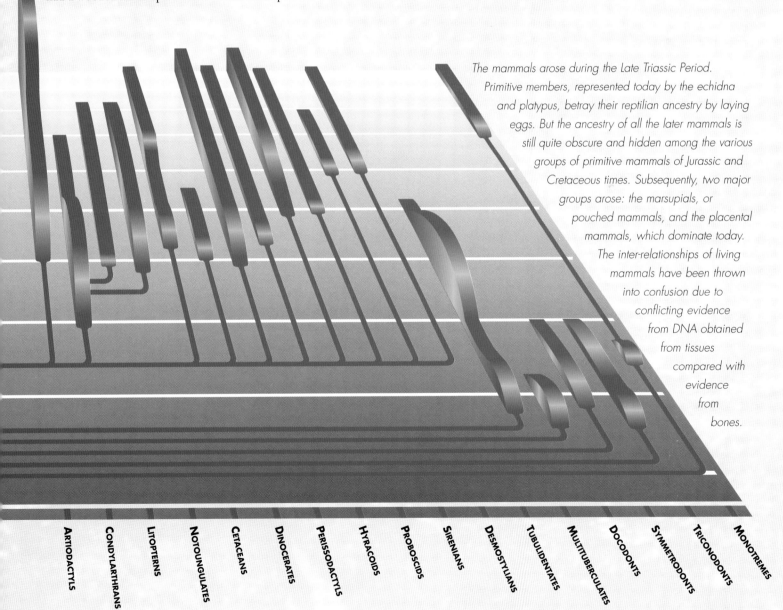

The mammals arose during the Late Triassic Period. Primitive members, represented today by the echidna and platypus, betray their reptilian ancestry by laying eggs. But the ancestry of all the later mammals is still quite obscure and hidden among the various groups of primitive mammals of Jurassic and Cretaceous times. Subsequently, two major groups arose: the marsupials, or pouched mammals, and the placental mammals, which dominate today. The inter-relationships of living mammals have been thrown into confusion due to conflicting evidence from DNA obtained from tissues compared with evidence from bones.

ARTIODACTYLS CONDYLARTHRANS LITOPTERNS NOTOUNGULATES CETACEANS DINOCERATES PERISSODACTYLS HYRACOIDS PROBOSCIDS SIRENIANS DESMOSTYLIANS TUBULIDENTATES MULTITUBERCULATES DOCODONTS SYMMETRODONTS TRICONODONTS MONOTREMES

All these exploitations of different environments required the evolving mammals to develop adaptations in their limbs. Shrews have basically primitive five-toed, or pentadactyl, feet. Those of fast-running predators, such as domestic cats, are essentially large-scale versions of this plan, with the loss of the inner toe. Mammals that climb and brachiate (swing from branch to branch) evolved elongated arms and legs with long fingers.

Mammals that graze the prairies and tropical savannahs have long slender legs with hoofed feet; in these "ungulate" mammals, the legs have only one purpose—to move the animal. The ability to turn the feet sideways is lost, and the lateral digits also disappear until only two toes (as in cattle) or a single toe (as in horses) remain. Carnivores cannot pursue this economical course, since they must use their limbs for various purposes— walking, running, crawling, digging, climbing, and swimming, as well as for seizing, holding, and tearing into their prey. Their limbs retain the primitive structure for a multipurpose life.

Seals and sealions swim using highly modified limbs; the upper part of the limb is short, and the foot elongated and webbed to form a paddle. In whales, by contrast, the main power is provided by up-and-down movements of the tail fin. The forelimbs, modified into fins, are used mainly to control direction, and the hind limbs are totally absent.

Bats make use of another sort of modification of their forelimbs as "wings," by elongating three fingers which radiate out like the spokes of an umbrella to provide support for the flight membrane, or patagium, made of a thin layer of skin.

Mammals basically have three different types of horny outgrowths at the end of their digits: nails, claws, and hooves. Nails are found in primates, elephants, and rhinoceroses. Claws are best developed in carnivores, but also occur in digging animals such as anteaters. Hooves characterize mammals, such as horses and antelopes, which live on grass-covered plains and scrub. They are also found in mountain goats and desert camels.

So, by elongating or shortening parts of the primitive pentadactyl limb, and sometimes by losing bones and digits, the basic cat-like leg has become modified to enable mammals to move in virtually all types of environments.

Mammal teeth

The ability to move efficiently through a great range of different habitats enables mammals to exploit a wide range of food. This, in turn, requires a dentition adapted for obtaining the food in the first place, and then reducing it to an easily swallowed mass. A mammal also needs an efficient digestive system, which can process the food to extract the maximum amount of nutrients.

Mammals are classified primarily on the basis of the structure and arrangement of their teeth and their limbs: that is, on how they feed and how they move. Since they have to move to obtain their food, these two functions are intimately related.

Teeth are made of tough calcium phosphate, so they fossilize well and outlast every other part of a mammal's body. After death it is teeth which are most likely to endure the centuries and even millennia.

During its lifetime, a mammal has two sets of teeth: the first dentition erupts after weaning and lasts only a short time, allowing the animal to feed while growing rapidly. The second, permanent set erupts to replace this. In an unspecialized, primitive mammal it comprises 44 teeth. These teeth are arranged in a distinct series, with different shapes and functions: three incisors, one canine, four premolars, and three molars make up a total of 11 teeth in each half of each jaw. Few mammals exhibit this "primitive" pattern without modification; some teeth have been lost, and those that remain are further specialized.

The incisors are sited at the front of the jaws; they usually have a chisel edge, and are used for holding and tearing. Specializations include the loss of two incisors, with the remaining one becoming a tusk or a cutting tool.

The canine (or dogtooth) is a small tusk-like tooth used by carnivores to pierce and hold their prey; in some it becomes greatly enlarged to form a sabre-tooth. In most herbivores, such as rabbits, cattle, and horses, the canine is lost or is at most vestigial.

The incisors and canines are often separated, especially in herbivores, by a gap (the diastema) from the premolars and molars—the "cheek teeth." This allows their different functions to proceed simultaneously.

Like the incisors and canines, the premolars are often simple in shape, with only a single "cusp" (projection) on their biting surface, but they have two roots instead of one. The premolars are often reduced in number, and may be specialized. In the hyenas, for example, premolars are thick, low cones used to crush bones, while they have become "molarized" in many herbivores, taking on the form and grinding function of the molar teeth.

The molars are usually the most complex of the teeth. They have no precursors in the milk dentition, and erupt last. The molars are usually multicusped and multirooted. The cusp patterns are constant for each mammal family and genus, and are of enormous value in identification and classification.

In primitive mammals, the cusps on the molar teeth are arranged in reverse triangles. These interlocked as the jaws closed to give a series of zigzag cutting edges to pierce soft food, such as worms or insects. Full closure of the jaw cut up the food fully.

Carnivores have refined the cutting action, and evolved scissor-like blades—"carnassial teeth" for slicing meat. In herbivores, the addition of a fourth cusp changed the triangle into a square. This provides a solid platform, so that when the upper and lower teeth meet as the jaws close, the food is crushed. Sideways, front-to-back, or circular movements can then break up the food ready for swallowing.

Mammal teeth and feet are well-adapted for particular lifestyles. Most mammals have four kinds of teeth—incisors, canines, premolars, and molars—whose functions vary with diet.

In a carnivore, such as a dog, prey is killed with the canines and skinned with the incisor teeth. Molars and premolars cut flesh. A herbivore such as a horse crops grass with strong incisors and grinds it with molars and premolars. The canines have been lost or are reduced. The gap (diastema) between the front and back teeth separates the cropping and grinding actions of the jaws. An insectivore such as a hedgehog seizes prey with its incisors; molars pierce and cut soft food.

Carnivores use their limbs for capturing prey and for locomotion. They are essentially primitive and unspecialized. Herbivore feet are, by contrast, specialized for movement over the ground, with the lateral toes reduced as in Parahippus (above). Insectivores have five-toed, lightly built unspecialized feet which perform a variety of functions digging, grasping, climbing, swimming, and running.

Reproduction and classification

Mammals are reproductively highly sophisticated. This has traditionally been the basis for their classification into the major groups, the egg-laying Prototheria and the live-bearing Theria.

The Prototheria represent a more primitive group and are thought to include extinct groups such as the multituberculates as well as the living monotremes. However, there is no direct proof that the extinct groups were egg-laying. Indeed, there are good arguments that some of them may not have been. Many are very small animals with pelvic openings smaller than any living egg-laying animals. It may be that such morphological constraints may have promoted the development and bearing of live though very immature young, similar to those of marsupials today. Monotremes survive today only in Australasia as the echidnas (spiny anteaters) and a single species of platypus. There is a considerable problem in identifying fossil monotremes, and the relationships of the few known extinct forms with the living monotremes is highly problematic.

Marsupials, or pouched mammals, have little or no placenta and are grouped as the Metatheria. The young are born in a far less advanced state than Eutherian mammals (also called the Placentalia), and continue their development after birth by crawling into their mother's pouch and attaching themselves to a nipple. Molecular data suggest that the marsupials are more primitive than the placentals and are more closely related to the monotremes. Their fossil record through the Tertiary into the Cretaceous is well-established, but the origin of the group is not.

In the advanced Eutherian mammals, the fetus develops within a uterus, or womb, where it is nourished through the placenta by its mother's bloodstream. Again, there is a vast fossil record throughout the Tertiary, with the majority of groups still having at least some living representatives. However, there are a number of extinct groups, such as the condylarthrans and creodonts. Their inter-relationships and origins are largely unresolved. The problems of classification have been exacerbated by contradictions between the molecular and morphological evidence for affinity. And, of course, the biomolecule markers—the DNA proteins that are analysed for evidence of genetic make-up—are unknown for most of the extinct groups, except for those that have only recently become extinct, such as the quagga and the mammoth. (Frozen mammoth and bison tissue from the Siberian and Alaskan permafrost is sufficiently well-preserved to yield molecular evidence.)

PRIMITIVE MAMMALS

SUBCLASS PROTOTHERIA

The most primitive mammals belong to this group of "first mammals." Some modern classifications make a greater separation between the living mammal groups (the therians) and the extinct groups. Most of the latter are placed in the Subclass Mammaliaformes, which is nearly equivalent to the prototherians. However, recent discoveries of fragmentary fossil remains from the Late Triassic rocks of Texas (*Adelobasileus*) and Early Jurassic of China (*Sinocodon*) cannot yet be fitted into even this classification. Furthermore, the inter-relationships between the primitive mammal groups are far from clear, largely because so much of the fossil material just consists of teeth remains. Nevertheless, it is still thought that they all evolved from the cynodonts (see pp.336–337), a group of synapsid reptiles, during the late Triassic Period, some 220 million years ago.

The only surviving "prototherians" are the monotremes—the echidnas, or spiny anteaters, and the duckbilled platypus, all of which are found only in Australasia. The reproductive method of the monotremes still reflects their reptilian ancestry— they all lay eggs. However, the newly-hatched young then suckle milk from their mothers, as all other mammals do.

Family Morganucodontidae

As an extinct group, the morganucodonts—thought to represent the earliest true or modern mammals—are not accessible to molecular assessment. For the time being, they are probably best placed along with the other extinct primitive groups, such as the kuehneotheriids and dryolestids, outside the associations of living mammal groups.

These earliest well-known mammals inhabited the desert environments during the Late Triassic Period. They were very small furry creatures, only about 5 in/12 cm long—as tiny as some of the smallest living mammals. They looked similar to modern shrews, but in many respects they still resembled the ancestral group of advanced mammal-like reptiles, the therapsids (see pp.332–337).

Their mode of locomotion was mammalian and possibly quite rapid, but may not have been able to sustain running for any great length of time. Well-developed and pointed cutting teeth suggest a carnivorous diet of insects. They were capable of a fairly complex chewing motion, in which the jaws could move sideways to a limited extent. This means that food could be digested quickly in order to release the vital energy needed to maintain both the high rate of metabolism which is typical of warm-blooded mammals and a predatory lifestyle. Like small modern mammals, the morganucodonts would have had to spend most of their waking hours eating and they were probably nocturnal.

Fossils of the morganucodonts have been discovered in Europe, southern Africa, and eastern Asia.

NAME	*Megazostrodon*
TIME	Late Triassic to Early Jurassic
LOCALITY	Africa (Lesotho)
SIZE	5 in/12 cm long

The morganucodont *Megazostrodon* looked similar to a modern shrew, and may have behaved in a similar way too. However, its limbs stuck out from its body to some extent, which implies that it probably had a more sprawling and less efficient gait than modern shrews.

Megazostrodon probably hunted for insects and other small invertebrates among the leaf litter and undergrowth, probably during the night, when it was less likely to fall prey to carnivorous dinosaurs.

Its body shape is well known from an almost complete skeleton found in Lesotho, while remains of closely-related animals have been found in China and Britain. The skeleton is very similar to that of primitive mammals.

Family Haramiyidae

This little-known group of primitive mammals with broad cheek teeth originated in the Late Triassic and extended through into the Mid Jurassic Period. The Haramiyidae family may be related to the ancestors of the multituberculates.

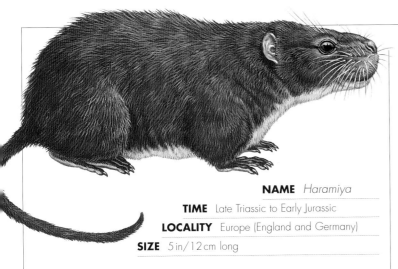

NAME *Haramiya*

TIME Late Triassic to Early Jurassic

LOCALITY Europe (England and Germany)

SIZE 5 in / 12 cm long

Haramiya is known from only a few isolated teeth. This fragmentary evidence suggests that it was somewhat like a miniature vole, and crushed its food with its broad cheek teeth. It may have lived on low-growing vegetation, possibly on the fruits of cycad-like plants.

ORDER MULTITUBERCULATA

The multituberculates were the earliest of the plant-eating mammals, evolving during the Late Jurassic and Early Cretaceous, with some groups surviving into the Oligocene. They were the largest group of Mesozoic mammals and ranged from mouse-sized creatures to animals the size of a modern beaver (very large for a primitive mammal). They were distinctly rodent-like in appearance, although they were in no way related to these animals. The similarity, especially of the tooth arrangement, is simply an adaptation to the same lifestyle and feeding habits.

Like rodents, the multituberculates had gnawing incisor teeth at the front of their jaws and grinding premolar and molar teeth at the back. The two types of teeth were separated by a gap called a diastema, which enabled them to be used independently. The array of grinding cheek teeth had many cusps (projections) to break up tough vegetation, as in many rodents.

The jaws worked with an up-and-down action, without the sideways movement of the early insectivorous mammals, such as

Megazostrodon (opposite). The multituberculates show no close affinity with any of the other mammal groups, and it is possible that they evolved independently from the mammal-like reptiles.

New discoveries from the Late Cretaceous of Mongolia of virtually complete skeletons promise to increase our understanding of this group and its relationships to the other primitive mammals.

Family Ptilodontidae

The Ptilodontidae family consists of animals with long tails. The tails were prehensile, serving as a fifth limb which could be used for grasping branches of the trees in which they probably lived. Their feet also show adaptations for climbing: like squirrels, ptilodonts could point their toes backward, due to a highly mobile ankle joint, an adaptation which enabled them to run down a tree trunk headfirst. They could also spread their big toes wide, to give a sure grip, aided by sharp claws. Their remains have been found mainly in North America.

NAME *Ptilodus*

TIME Early to Late Paleocene

LOCALITY North America (the Rockies, New Mexico to Saskatchewan)

SIZE 20 in / 50 cm long

Apart from its long, prehensile tail, *Ptilodus* was similar to a modern squirrel in appearance, and may have lived in a similar way—scampering about in the branches of trees.

The lower premolar teeth were very large and blade-like, and *Ptilodus* may have used them to strip the husks from tough nuts and seeds.

Family Dryolestidae

The dryolestids probably represent an offshoot of the evolutionary line that eventually led to the modern mammals. The family members are known only from the remains of a few teeth and jaw bones. The remains show that the mammalian jaw hinge had fully evolved in this group. Three bones that had been part of the jaw in their reptiless were now incorporated into the middle ear, as the hammer, anvil, and stirrup bones. These tiny bones form part of a chain of communication along which sound is transmitted to the inner ear.

NAME	Crusafontia
TIME	Early Cretaceous
LOCALITY	Europe (Portugal)
SIZE	4 in/10 cm long

The dryolestid *Crusafontia* is known only from a few teeth. The reconstruction (above) is based on a relatively complete skeleton of another member of the family from the Late Jurassic Period of Portugal.

Paleontologists believe that *Crusafontia* probably resembled a tiny squirrel, living in trees and feeding on fruit, nuts, and seeds. The creature's long tail may have been prehensile.

The bones of *Crusafontia*'s hip girdle suggest that it may have reproduced the way a marsupial does— giving birth to very immature young then suckling them in a pouch for the first few weeks of their lives.

SUBCLASS THERIA

This great group includes the majority of fossil mammals and their living relatives. The subclass is subdivided into three major orders—the pantotheres, which were restricted to the Mesozoic Era; the marsupials, or pouched mammals, which still survive in Australasia and America; and the eutherians, or placental mammals, which include all other living mammals and many extinct ones, too.

INFRACLASS METATHERIA

The two major subgroups of the subclass Theria—the Metatheria and Eutheria— diverged from a common ancestor early in the Cretaceous Period. The Metatheria contains only one order, the Marsupialia, or pouched mammals. This group is dealt with in detail on pp.346–349, but a primitive member is described here as a comparison with other primitive mammals.

NAME	Alphadon
TIME	Late Cretaceous
LOCALITY	North America (Alberta to New Mexico)
SIZE	1 ft/30 cm long

Primitive marsupials such as *Alphadon* were probably very similar to modern opossums. They were omnivores, and ate a wide range of foods, including insects, small vertebrates, and fruit. They were probably also tree-dwellers, able to climb well, using feet equipped with opposable toes, which could be brought together to give a good grip, and prehensile tails. Their small size and tree-dwelling habits would have meant that they did not compete directly for food with the Late Cretaceous dinosaurs, and so were able to survive alongside them.

INFRACLASS EUTHERIA (PLACENTALIA)

The placental mammals, or eutherians, give birth to well-developed young after nurturing them for some time inside a womb. They make up the vast majority of modern mammals, and are grouped into about 24 orders (see pp.482–483).

One of the earliest families known, the *Zalambdalestidae* (below), may represent a side-branch from the main evolutionary line rather than a direct stage in the evolution of later placentals.

NAME *Zalambdalestes*

TIME Late Cretaceous

LOCALITY Asia (Mongolia)

SIZE 8 in/20 cm long

Zalambdalestes looked very much like the modern elephant shrew. It had a long upturned snout and powerful little legs, the back pair being longer than the front. The legs had greatly elongated foot bones. The fingers could not be brought to meet each other (they were not opposable), which is a development that is essential for giving a good grip, so *Zalambdalestes* is unlikely to have been a tree climber.

The animal's brain was quite small and the eyes large. *Zalambdalestes* may well have behaved in a similar way to the modern elephant shrews, running and jumping through the undergrowth after insects, and catching them with its long incisor teeth.

ORDER PRIMATES

It is possible that the primates are the most ancient order of placental mammals and date back as far as Late Cretaceous times—some 70 million years ago. The more advanced members of the primate group are dealt with on pp.430–441, but a primitive form, which provides the basis for the claimed longevity of the order, is described here in order to give a comparison with contemporary mammals.

The Family Paromomyidae consisted of small creatures quite similar in many ways to modern tree shrews, which may have been the ancestors of the later lemurs, monkeys, and apes.

However, some paleontologists do not regard the Family Paromomyidae as members of the Primate order at all, but place them instead in a group of their own called the Primatomorpha.

NAME *Purgatorius*

TIME Late Cretaceous and Early Paleocene

LOCALITY North America (Montana)

SIZE possibly 4 in/10 cm long

Little is known about this small animal except for what can be deduced by paleontologists from the single molar tooth which was discovered in Late Cretaceous rocks in Montana. However, even such a tiny piece of evidence as this single tooth is important because it belonged to the earliest-known primate. The tooth resembles the molars of a modern lemur. More complete sets of teeth from a slightly later, but related, creature from the Early Paleocene Period indicate that *Purgatorius* may have been omnivorous. However, the creature's diminutive size—it probably weighed no more than about ¾ oz/20 g—suggests that it was most probably an insect-eater first and foremost.

MARSUPIALS

ORDER MARSUPIALIA

The marsupials—including the familiar kangaroos and koalas of Australia, and the opossums of America—are among the most ancient of all of the orders of mammals. They evolved during the Late Cretaceous, between 100 and 75 million years ago.

The unique feature of marsupials is their method of reproduction. Placentals (the vast majority of mammals, including humans) nurture their young via a placenta within a womb, and do not give birth until the young have reached a relatively advanced stage. But marsupials give birth to very small and immature young—little more than embryos. These are then suckled, usually in a pouch on the belly, and grow to maturity outside the mother's body.

Recent molecular data puts greater weight on the differences between the marsupials and the placentals than traditional morphological methods. The marsupials are more closely associated with the primitive egg-laying monotremes.

The marsupials seem to have evolved in North or South America, and one group migrated via Antarctica (then much warmer than it is today) to Australia. A further group of marsupials moved via North America into Europe. The closeness of the drifting continents to one another in Late Cretaceous times enabled them to do this. The marsupials flourished in isolation in South America during the Tertiary, where they developed before the placental mammals, and in Australia, where they have their stronghold today.

Another group of marsupials moved into Europe via North America during the Early Eocene, and in the Oligocene reached North Africa and central Asia. These were the didelphids, represented today by the opossums. They are thought of as the most primitive of the marsupials and are the group to which the earliest-known marsupials belong.

By the Early Miocene, didelphid marsupials had become extinct in North America, and they disappeared from Europe, too, by Middle Miocene times. Although they never returned to Europe, the modern genus *Didelphis* (the Virginia opossum) re-entered North America from South America some 3 million years ago, via the newly formed Panama land bridge.

However, the South American marsupials are nearly all gone, wiped out by invasions of placental mammals from North America. This happened when, during the Pliocene, a Central American land bridge was formed between these two great continents. This bridge was a tenuous one, however, and was not "permanent" until the Panama connection was created.

The Australian marsupials still flourish today, despite competition from placentals. The reason may be that Australia had been moving northward by the slow process of continental drift during the Tertiary. This drift was relatively rapid, and the Australian climate changed from temperate conditions to tropical rainforest in a few tens of millions of years. The marsupials there had to evolve to keep up with this change, resulting in genetically strong stock. However, some have been much reduced in numbers (such as koala bears) or have become extinct (such as the Tasmanian "wolf," or thylacine) as a result of human activities.

In contrast, South America has remained stationary during the same period. The animals did not need to evolve so much, so placental invaders found a relatively primitive and genetically weak fauna population there, which was easy to replace.

Family Borhyaenidae

This family evolved from didelphid ancestors and consists entirely of extinct carnivorous South American marsupials. Although completely unrelated to placental mammals of other continents, the borhyaenids have short limbs and rather doglike skulls. Thus they evolved body shapes and lifestyles similar to those of cats, dogs, bears, and other placental carnivores. This is a superb example of convergent evolution.

NAME	*Cladosictis*
TIME	Late Oligocene to Early Miocene
LOCALITY	South America (Patagonia)
SIZE	2 ft 6 in/80 cm long

Cladosictis was a primitive carnivorous marsupial that may have resembled an otter in shape and size, with a long body and tail and short limbs. It probably scampered through the undergrowth, seeking out, chasing, and catching small mammals and reptiles, and swam in rivers after fish. It may even have eaten reptiles' or birds' eggs and insects. The tooth pattern was similar to that of carnivorous placental mammals. The teeth consisted of incisors at the front for holding prey, followed by pointed canines for killing it, and meat-shearing (carnassial) premolars and molars at the back.

NAME	Borhyaena
TIME	Late Oligocene to Early Miocene
LOCALITY	South America (Patagonial)
SIZE	5 ft / 1.5 m long

Some borhyaenids were rather bearlike, with heavy bodies and flat feet. The wolf-sized *Borhyaena* was typical of this group, but other closely related types ranged from fox-sized creatures to animals as big as bears.

These were the main predators of the day. Their prey would have included the plant-eating hoofed mammals (see pp.390–397) that were restricted to South America. The short limbs suggest that *Borhyaena* itself was not much of a runner, but probably ambushed its prey. It may also have been a scavenger.

Family Thylacosmilidae

In this group of large predatory marsupials, the skull became very similar to that of the placental saber-tooth cats. The incisor teeth were lost, and very long upper canine teeth developcd, which grew continually. These were formidable weapons.

NAME	Thylocosmilus
TIME	Late Miocene to Early Pliocene
LOCALITY	South America (Argentina)
SIZE	4 ft / 1.2 m long

Thylacosmilus, like the saber-tooth cats of North America and Europe (see pp.366–368), sported a pair of upper canine teeth that had evolved into long, stabbing sabers projecting down well below the creature's mouth-line. In both of these unrelated creatures, the musculature of the neck and jaws allowed the saber teeth to be driven downward with a tremendous killing force. The powerful jaws were capable of a gape that would leave the teeth clear to do their work.

Unlike the saber-tooth cats, *Thylacosmilus* had no incisor teeth or scabbardlike rooth-guards on its lower jaw. Also the saber teeth grew continuously throughout life, rather like the incisors of rodents.

The victims of *Thylacosmilus* may have been large, slow-moving hoofed mammals that could not be killed rapidly with a quick bite to the neck. The saber teeth would have inflicted deep wounds, and the prey presumably bled to death.

Family Argyrolagidae

The Argyrolagidae family consists of animals very similar to the kangaroo rats and jerboas of today, bur they are completely unrelated to them. Like such rodents, they may have lived in arid desert environments and been mostly nocturnal animals. They would have moved swiftly over the open ground by a series of prodigious leaps, and fed on the shoots and roots of desert plants.

NAME	Argyrolagus
TIME	Late Miocene to Late Pliocene
LOCALITY	South America (Patagonial)
SIZE	16 in / 40 cm long

Just like modern kangaroo rats and other desert rodents (to which it is no relation); *Argyrolagus* moved quickly over open country on its slim, two-toed hind legs, balanced by its long heavy tail. The head was somewhat rodentlike, but it had a pointed snout. Enormous eye sockets, which suggest that the animal foraged only at night, were situated far back in the skull. The teeth suggest that it ate desert plants.

Family Necrolestidae

This family has a single member, the extinct *Necrolestes* (below), so specialized that it can be classed with no other animal. However, its jaws and teeth do show some resemblance to those of the living golden moles of Africa. However, the golden moles are themselves a highly problematic group which are currently placed in the Insectivora.

NAME *Necrolestes*

TIME Early Miocene

LOCALITY South America (Patagonia)

SIZE possibly 6 in/15 cm long

All that is known of this little creature is a single specimen of the tip of the jaws with an oddly upturned snout. This may have ended in fleshy folds, possibly serving as sensitive organs of touch that helped the animal to find its food, like the complex fringe of tentacles surrounding the nostrils of the living star-nosed mole.

From its many fine teeth, paleontologists think that *Necrolestes* ate insects or worms. It may have lived as a burrower —hence its ghoulish name, which means "grave-robber."

Family Thylacoleonidae

This family of lionlike marsupials lived in Australia in Pliocene and Pleistocene times. They probably hunted on the Australian grasslands. Research suggests that they may be related to living phalangeroid possums and kangaroos.

NAME *Thylacoleo*

TIME Pleistocene

LOCALITY Australia (New South Wales, Queensland, Western and South Australia)

SIZE 5 ft 6 in/1.7 m long

This "marsupial lion" had a short, catlike face. Projecting front incisors were modified into killing teeth and looked rather like the canines in the placental carnivores—the canines themselves

wete insignificant. The back teeth formed powerful meat-shearing blades.

Thylacoleo was once believed to have used its unusual front teeth to break open nuts and fruit. However, recent studies have shown that wear on the teeth is consistent with a meat-eating diet, and the animal probably preyed on the giant kangaroos and wombats of rhe time.

Family Diprotodontidae

This major group of Australian marsupials includes mostly herbivorous animals. Diprotodonts have a single pair of lower incisors, which point forward. They have between one and three pairs of upper incisors, no canines, and a long gap (diastema) between their incisors and cheek teeth, as in rodents. The second and third toes of their hind feet are greatly reduced in size and are bound within a single sheath of tissue—a specialization used for grooming.

The diprotodontids evolved during the Mid Miocene and survived through into the Holocene, and it is possible that they were hunted to extinction by the early Australian aborigines. At present the group is thought to be related to the living wombats (vombatoids).

NAME *Diprotodon*

TIME Pleistocene

LOCALITY Australia (South Australia)

SIZE 10 ft/3 m long

The grazing marsupials attained their greatest size in *Diprotodon* and its relatives. In appearance *Diprotodon* was rather like a rhinoceros-sized wombat.

This impressive creature probably fed on a particular species of salt-bush, which it could scrape out of the ground with its paws. Remains of this bush have been found in the stomach cavities of several fossil specimens.

The body, head, and neck of *Diprotodon* were massive, and the animal's limbs were strong. The feet were plantigrade, or flat-footed, so that the considerable weight was borne on the palms and the soles, in the same way as in a bear, rather than on the toes. Unlike the feet of other mammals, the outer ("little") toe of this animal was the longest—a peculiar feature with no apparent function.

Complete *Diprotodon* skeletons have been found preserved in lake muds. In the dry climates in which these animals lived, salt crusts may have formed over the local lakes of the open landscape. The heavy *Diprotodon* would easily have fallen through and become entombed in the mud beneath.

Family Palorchestidae

This family of large herbivores inhabited Australia from Miocene to Pleistocene times. The Family Palorchestidae may have been the marsupial equivalents of the placental ground sloths (see pp.350–351).

NAME *Palorchestes*

TIME Miocene to Pleistocene

LOCALITY Australia

SIZE 8 ft/2.5 m long

The arrangement of the nasal bones in the skull of this animal suggests that it probably had some sort of trunk. In that case *Palorchestes* would have looked like a giant marsupial tapir.

Palorchestes' front legs were strong, and each had five toes equipped with huge claws. This characteristic has led experts to believe that this creature may have fed by pulling down branches in order to reach the leaves.

Family Macropodidae

The most familiar of the modern marsupials, eleven genera of kangaroos and wallabies, are included in the family Macropodidae, which is distributed throughout Australia and New Guinea.

The kangaroos arose in early Miocene times and developed larger forms in the Pliocene. They became adapted to a wide range of habitats: plains, mountainsides, and forests (even developing some arboreal species).

Even though the Pleistocene extinction greatly reduced the overall diversity of this family, the macropodid kangaroos still represent the largest radiation of marsupials, with 14 living species of *Macropus*.

NAME *Procoptodon*

TIME Pleistocene

LOCALITY Australia

SIZE 10 ft/3 m long

Extinct kangaroos tended to be generally larger than the modern forms and had some different features. *Procoptodon* was the largest of these kangaroos and was distinctive because of the short face. It was also set apart from the modern kangaroos by the fact that each hind foot had only a single long, functional toe (the fourth), with mere nailless stumps on each side. However, *Procoptodon* was probably just as capable of fast hopping as modern kangaroos, which can reach up to 30 mph/50 kmph over short distances.

Procoptodon was a grazing kangaroo, which fed on grass and low-growing vegetation, like most modern forms. Other extinct kangaroos, however, were browsers, using their great height to reach up into trees to feed on leaves.

GLYPTODONTS, SLOTHS, ARMADILLOS, AND ANTEATERS

COHORT EDENTATA

The edentates are represented today by the anteaters, tree sloths, and armadillos. The name of the cohort (a grouping of many orders) means "without teeth," but in fact only the anteaters are completely toothless. The other members of the Edentata cohort have teeth, although these have become reduced to just a few rudimentary pegs, often without roots or a protective enamel covering.

The edentates comprise some of the world's most bizarre mammals. In addition to the living anteaters with their greatly elongated snouts, the armadillos with their flexible suits of armor, and the proverbially slow sloths, the edentates include several strange, extinct groups. There were the tanklike glyptodonts with solid, immovable body armor, and the giant ground sloths, up to 6 ft/1.8 m high. Both these prehistoric animals ranged widely throughout North and South America during Pleistocene times.

The anteaters and armadillos became highly adapted for feeding on ants and termites. Glyptodonts, ground sloths, and tree sloths are vegetarian.

The edentates first appear in the Early Tertiary, but their evolutionary origins are obscure. Molecular data from living forms is not as complete as for many other mammals, but it does seem to indicate a surprising closeness to the carnivores, whales, and even-toed ungulates. The group has had a remarkable history which is not in the least evident from the few remaining living forms.

Family Metacheiromyidae

These earliest and most primitive of the edentates, have uncertain relationships with other edentate groups. The Metacheiromyidae family may be the ancestors of the scaly anteaters or pangolins.

NAME *Metacheiromys*

TIME Middle Eocene

LOCALITY North America (Wyoming)

SIZE 18 in/45 cm long

With its short legs, sharp claws, and long, heavy tail, *Metacheiromys* may have resembled a modern mongoose. However, it had a long, narrow head, more like that of an armadillo. It had strong canines, but had lost almost all of its cheek teeth. Horny pads grew in their place, which the animal doubtless used to crush its prey.

Metacheiromys' habitat was the dense subtropical forests that covered parts of the western United States during the Eocene. The claws on its forefeet were much larger than those on its hind feet, so *Metacheiromys* probably dug for its food, rooting out ants, beetles, and grubs buried in the soil.

ORDER XENARTHRA

The name Xenarthra refers to the extra joints between the vertebrae which are a characteristic of this group. Their presence may have allowed animals as diverse as glyptodonts and armadillos to support the weight of a heavy suit of armor, or the giant ground sloths to haul their huge bodies into a near, vertical position in order to feed on leaves from branches at considerable heights.

The xenarthrans evolved in South America during the Paleocene, some 60 million years ago. They flourished on their island continent, isolated from predators and evolutionary changes. Then, in the Early Pliocene, about 5 million years ago, the land bridge that had once connected the two Americas during Early Tertiary times was re-established; and glyptodonts, ground sloths, and armadillos lumbered across it, heading north.

Families Mylodontidae, Megatheriidae, and Megalonychidae

Today's tree sloths of Central and South America look and behave quite differently from their ancestors, the extinct ground sloths. Many of these creatures were so large that they could never have hauled their bulk up into the trees, and so were permanently grounded. One of the largest, *Megatherium*, was some 10 times bigger than its living relatives.

Ground sloths were slow-moving creatures and strict vegetarians. They appeared in Early Oligocene times, some 35 million years ago, and survived up to recent times.

NAME *Hapalops*

TIME Early to Middle Miocene

LOCALITY South America (Patagonia)

SIZE 30 cm/1 m long

By Miocene times, some 20 million years ago, ground sloths had become well-established in South America. *Hapalops* was an early Miocene member of the group, and it was small in comparison with its later relatives.

Its short head, stout body, and long tail were supported on long, slender forelegs and even longer, heavier hind legs. The long, curved claws on its toes must have forced this sloth to walk on the knuckles of its front feet, rather like a modern gorilla.

Being of fairly light build, *Hapalops* could have spent some of its time in trees, clinging on with its sharp-clawed feet and using its long legs to hook down succulent leaves and fruit.

Like all the edentates, *Hapalops* had very few teeth, only four or five pairs of cheek teeth remaining in its jaws.

NAME *Megatherium*

TIME Pleistocene

LOCALITY South America (Patagonia, Bolivia, and Peru)

SIZE 20 ft/6 m long

This gigantic creature is the largest-known ground sloth. It probably weighed as much as 3 tons/3 tonnes. Its head was deep and bearlike, and its jaws were equipped with strong muscles for grinding up its plant food between the few remaining, peg-shaped cheek teeth.

Although this giant ground sloth was as large as a modern elephant, it would have been able to rear up on its sturdy hind legs, supported on its thick tail. (Such a two-legged pose is reminiscent of the great herbivorous dinosaurs, such as *Apatosaurus,* see p.275.) In this position, *Megatherium* could browse near the treetops, hooking down branches with its three-clawed forefeet.

NAME *Glossotherium*

TIME Pliocene to Pleistocene

LOCALITY North America (California)

SIZE 13 ft/4 m long

The Rancho La Brea tar pits in Los Angeles have yielded excellent specimens of this great ground sloth, which traveled up from South America, some 3 million years ago, over the newly reformed land bridge. There it met its fate in the sticky pools of crude oil that had seeped up to the surface and lay covered by water.

Glossotherium was a bulky creature, with a large head and heavy tail. Its long, clawed feet were turned inward, as they are in its relatives, so it walked on its knuckles, gorilla-style. *Glossotherium* could rear up on its hind legs and used the long claws to bring food to its mouth. It seems to have lived on desert shrubs, to judge by the plant remains found preserved in its fossil droppings.

The giant ground sloths died out only 11,000 years ago. It is still not clear whether humans were responsible for their demise.

Family Glyptodontidae

The glyptodonts were gigantic, armadillolike creatures, which can be thought of as the mammalian equivalent of the heavily armored dinosaurs called ankylosaurs (see pp.301–305). Some 50 genera evolved from the Early Miocene, about 20 million years ago, reaching their peak of success on the grasslands of South America and southern North America during the Pliocene and Pleistocene Epochs, between about 5 million and 3 million years ago. The glyptodonts survived until historical times and feature in the legends of Patagonian Indians.

Glyptodonts were grazing animals, lacking teeth in the front of their mouths, but equipped with powerful grinding teeth at the back of the mouth. They had massive, deep jaws with downward-pointing projections of their cheekbones, which provided a site for the attachment of the powerful muscles that the animals needed in order to chew up the grasses and other tough vegetation on which they lived.

Some glyptodonts became very large: one of the biggest, *Glyptodon*, which lived in Argentina during the Pleistocene, between 2 million and 15,000 years ago, was the size of a small car and as formidably armored as a military tank (5 ft/1.5 m tall and 10 ft 6 in/3.3 m long). The glyptodonts evolved from armadillolike animals with armor arranged in rings.

By the end of the Pliocene, about 2 million years ago, the armor had become fused to form a rigid bony dome-shaped "shell" made up of a mosaic of polygonal bony plates that enclosed the animal's back, a helmet above its skull, and a series of rings or a solid tube of bone around the tail. This armor accounted for 20 percent of the animal's weight (the tusks of an elephant account for only 3 percent).

NAME *Doedicurus*

TIME Pleislocene

LOCALITY South America (Patagonia)

SIZE 13 ft/4 m long

In addition to being protected by an armored suit, *Doedicurus* possessed a powerful defensive weapon at the end of its tail—a bony club covered in spikes and borne at the end of a stiff shaft. This

remarkable structure bore a striking resemblance to the maces carried by medieval knights and, like them, was probably used by its owner to flail out at enemies—such as the carnivorous borhyenids (see pp.346–347).

Family Dasypodidae

The armadillos first appeared in Argentina in Late Paleocene times, about 60 million years ago. By the Late Oligocene, some 30 million years ago, several forms had evolved the characteristic jointed armor seen in the living armadillos, which are essentially very similar and are included in the same family. Armadillos have always remained restricted to the Americas: the 20 modern species are almost all found in South and Central America, though one has recently extended its range into the southern part of the United States.

NAME *Peltephilus*

TIME Oligocene to Miocene

LOCALITY South America (Patagonia)

SIZE 20 ft/6 m long

The armor of *Peltephilus*, like that of other armadillos, developed from its skin and consisted of tough bony plates, or "scutes," covered with horn. These were arranged in bands around the armadillo's body and were connected to the underlying skin, making a flexible protective "shell."

On the snout of *Peltephilus* a pair of long scutes was modified into a pair of horn cores, covered in life with horn. Unlike the true horns of cattle, sheep, or antelope, the bony core was not an outgrowth of the skull bones. *Peltephilus* may also have borne a second, smaller pair of horns farther forward on its snout. Because it is peculiar among the edentates in having large caninelike teeth, *Peltephilus* may possibly have been a carnivore or carrion-eater.

Family Myrmecophagidae

The myrmecophagids, or "true anteaters" (to distinguish them from the completely unrelated marsupial anteaters such as the modern numbat *Myrmecobius*) are highly specialized for exploiting a diet of ants and termites. They have a very poor fossil record, and as a result their evolution is little known. An early form, *Protamandua,* from the Early Miocene about 20 million years ago, was already a typical anteater.

NAME *Eurotamandua*

TIME Middle Eocene

LOCALITY Europe (Germany)

SIZE 3 ft/90 cm long

Until recently, when a fossil anteater was discovered in deposits of oil shale near Frankfurt in Germany and named *Eurotamandua*, paleontologists thought that anteaters were confined to South America. With its long tubular snout, weak toothless jaws, and powerful forelimbs armed with huge claws, this was undoubtedly an anteater and seems to have been very similar to the modern collared anteater *Tamandua*.

The fossil record of anteaters is poor, so it is not known how this exciting European find fits into the overall evolutionary history of the group. Evidence of *Eurotamandua's* typical anteater diet is provided by the fossilized ants found at the German site. It has been claimed that *Eurotamandua* is not a myrmecophagid, but an unrelated ant-eating placental mammal that has evolved and adapted to a similar lifestyle (a phenomenon known as convergent morphology).

Family Manidae

Manidae is the sole family in the Order Pholidota. The members of the family are the pangolins—curious mammals which are covered in protective horny, overlapping scales made up of densely fused hairs. This peculiar armor gives them the appearance of giant, animated pine cones. When the animal curls up in a ball, it forms an almost impenetrable shield. Pangolins have sturdy limbs, which are well-adapted for unearthing their insect prey, and which are used in some cases for digging out burrows to sleep in.

Pangolins have often been grouped together with the anteaters and armadillos because of their very similar lifestyles: they all feed largely on ants and termites, which they pick up with their narrow, sticky tongues. However, this grouping is probably an arrangement of convenience rather than a reflection of any close relationship.

The extreme specializations of all of these creatures make it difficult to determine their true relationships. However, molecular data suggests, somewhat surprisingly, that like the other edentates, pangolins are closely associated with the Carnivora. All seven living species of pangolins are placed in the single genus *Manis*. They are found in tropical Africa and Southeast Asia.

NAME *Eomanis*

TIME Middle Eocene

LOCALITY Europe (Germany)

SIZE 20 in/50 cm long

The earliest known pangolin, *Eomanis* is represented by a well-preserved fossil from the same oil shale deposits that yielded the skeleton of *Eurotamandua*. Even the scales were preserved, and it is quite obvious that *Eomanis* looked very much like the pangolins of today. The animal may have been able to close its eyes, ears, and nostrils as a protection against ant stings, as the modern species is able to do. From the fossilised remains of *Eomanis'* stomach, it is clear that its diet consisted of both plant matter and insects.

INSECTIVORES
AND CREODONTS

A wide range of orders of both living and fossil animals have traditionally been placed within the superorder Insectivora. The group was based on an understanding of the morphology of the living hedgehogs, shrews, and moles. The extinct anagalids are an example of a group which was thought to be within the insectivores but is now associated with the elephant shrews. Likewise, the dermopterans (including the extant flying lemurs) and chiropterans (including the extant bats) are grouped together outside the insectivores.

Molecular data shows that the relationships of the Insectivora with the Carnivora and other living groups are problematic. Consequently the status of the Insectivora as a natural unit is in doubt, and it is now considered to be something of a taxonomic "wastebasket." Nevertheless, it is still regarded as a primitive group and placed at the base of the placental mammals, with the hedgehog as the oldest of living placental groups.

ORDER ANAGALIDA

The anagalids were rabbitlike, digging mammals, known from the Early Tertiary rocks of eastern Asia. Once believed to be related to the elephant shrews, anagalids are now considered to have more in common with the rodents and rabbits.

NAME *Anagale*

TIME Early Oligocene

LOCALITY Asia (Mongolia)

SIZE 1 ft/30 cm long

Anagale may have looked similar to a modern rabbit in some respects, but it had a long tail and, probably, short ears. It also ran about, rather than jumping rabbit-style. This pattern of behavior and movement is conjectured from the proportions of the bones in the animal's hind legs.

Anagale's hind legs were a little longer than the forelegs, and they were equipped with spade-like claws on the feet. *Anagale* probably searched through the soil for beetles, grubs, worms, and the like. The fact that the teeth in many specimens found are thoroughly worn down suggests that it also ate the soil—perhaps the easiest way of extracting food from it.

ORDER DERMOPTERA

The dermopterans constitute the group of "flying lemurs"—a somewhat confusing name since the dermopterans are neither lemurs, nor are they capable of flight. Only two species have managed to survive until today—the Malayan and Philippine colugos (*Cynocephalus variegatus* and *C. volans*) of Southeast Asia. Both creatures are strict vegetarians.

These modern animals, less than 1 ft/30 cm long, can glide as far as 450 ft/137 m from tree to tree on outstretched skin membranes. It is assumed, though there is no direct evidence for this, that Mid-Paleocene and Early Eocene dermopterans could do likewise.

There is a gap in the colugo's fossil record from the Miocene to the living forms. There is some evidence that dermopterans are closely related to bats, tree shrews, and primates, and that they all share a common ancestry with insectivores. However, this relationship is by no means certain: the similarities displayed may simply be a result of convergent evolution of unrelated groups. The molecular evidence supports the association with the tree shrews and bats.

NAME *Planetetherium*

TIME Late Paleocene

LOCALITY North America (Montana)

SIZE 10 in/25 cm long

Planetetherium's remains have been found in beds of coal formed over many millions of years from dense lakeside forests of cypress trees.

As in the colugos, each incisor was divided to make a forward-pointing comb, with about five "teeth" arising from each root. Their function is unknown—they may have been used for grooming, or for scraping and straining food.

ORDER CHIROPTERA

These are the bats—the only mammals to have evolved true, powered flight. The order Chiroptera have achieved this feat by modifying their forelimbs into flapping wings, made of a thin membrane (the patagium) and supported by four greatly elongated fingers.

Most modern bats use echolocation to detect obstacles, prey, and predators in the darkness of night and the gloom of their roosting haunts. The bat emits high-frequency sounds that bounce off objects in its path and are picked up by the sensitive ears of the bat. The bat then analyzes and acts on the information it receives.

The development of this extraordinary natural radar system involved extensive modification of the bat's larynx, nose, ears, and brain. However, it is impossible to trace the course of this evolution because the parts of the body which are concerned do not fossilize.

There are two distinct suborders of living bats. The Microchiroptera (or microbats) are by far the most numerous, with some 780 species alive today. They are found the world over, except for the Arctic and Antarctic regions and on the highest mountains. Most microbats are small nocturnal animals with tiny eyes and large, often complex, extremely sensitive ears. Many microbats also have specialized outgrowths of the nose that are used for echolocation.

The nature and arrangement of their teeth depends largely on their diet, but the great majority catch insects on the wing and have shearing ridges on their upper molars arranged in a W-shaped pattern. A few species are carnivorous.

The second suborder is the Megachiroptera (or megabats), with about 170 species alive today. These are the fruit bats and are restricted to the Old World tropics. They are large animals with foxlike faces, hence their alternative name of flying foxes. The megabats lack the large, complex ears and elaborate noses characteristic of the microbats.

Traditionally the bats are grouped with the "flying lemurs" (dermopterans) and tree shrews (scandentians), but recent molecular data from a microbat has placed them closer to the carnivores.

NAME *Icaronycteris*

TIME Early Eocene

LOCALITY North America (Wyoming)

SIZE 5 1/2 in/14 cm long, 14 in/37 cm Wingspon

Icaronycteris must have been almost identical to a modern microbat, but still had a few very primitive features. Its wings were relatively short and broad, and its mouth contained a large number of teeth, arranged like those of an insectivore. The body was not quite as rigid as that of a modern bat, and the tail was long and not connected to the hind legs by a web of skin. The thumb and first finger each bore a claw—modern bats have a claw only on the thumb—for hanging vertically from cave walls or other supports. Even at this early stage in their evolution, bats roosted upside down.

Icaronycteris undoubtedly lived like the modern microbats, catching insects on the wing, probably while flying low over water in the evening when there were few birds around.

Some remarkably well-preserved bats are known from the Middle Eocene oil shale deposits of Messel near Frankfurt-am-Main in Germany. Even the wing membranes are still visible, and remains found in the area of the bat's stomach confirm that it was an insect-eater.

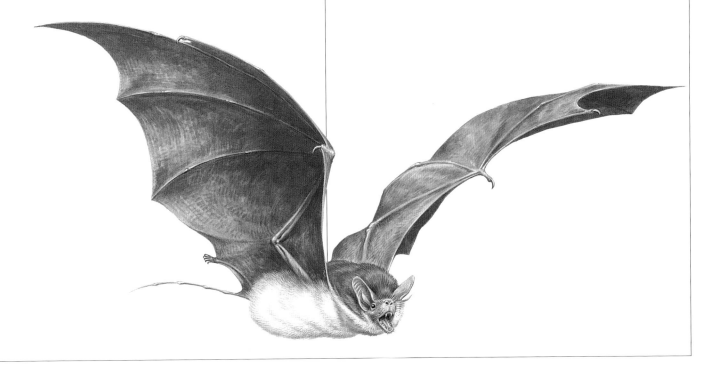

INSECTIVORES AND CREODONTS CONTINUED

SUPERORDER INSECTIVORA

Fossil forms of the Insectivora are known from the Mid-Cretaceous, about 100 million years ago, which makes them the earliest known placental mammals. Although patchy, the fossil record includes about 150 genera throughout the northern hemisphere, in Africa, Southeast Asia, and Central America. There is a single species of living shrew in South America.

Almost all insectivores are small, and nocturnal or crepuscular (active at dusk or dawn). They usually have poor vision but good senses of smell and hearing. Many species of shrews use echolocation. Because of their small size and high metabolic rate, they must feed more or less constantly.

Insectivores are a successful group of animals: they have colonized an impressive range of habitats and adopted a variety of lifestyles, from burrowing underground to a semi-aquatic existence. Their diet is equally varied: as well as insects, they eat worms, mollusks, and other invertebrates, small fish, amphibians, reptiles, birds, mammals, and small amounts of plant matter. To deal with this varied diet, the dentition in both fossil and living forms is usually quite complete.

The skeleton is generally little modified from the basic mammalian plan, with five digits on each foot and platigrade locomotion (palms and soles touching the ground). Moles and golden moles, however, have shortened and strengthened forelimbs for digging.

ORDER LEPTICTIDA

The leptictids were one of many primitive groups of shrewlike mammals known from the Late Cretaceous, about 70 million years ago. They became prolific in the early part of the Tertiary and appeared in North America, Asia, Africa, and Europe.

NAME *Leptictidium*
TIME Middle Eocene
LOCALITY Europe (Germany)
SIZE 2 ft 6 in/75 cm long

Leptictidium probably resembled the modern elephant shrew, except for its longer hind legs and tail. It was a bipedal runner, like humans and some of the smaller flesh-eating dinosaurs. The hind legs were long, light, and birdlike,

with most of the muscles concentrated around the thigh. The forelimbs were less than half the length of the hind limbs and were adapted for holding food. The body was very short, and the long tail served as a balancing organ.

Leptictidium ate more than insects: some skeletons show the remains of small mammal bones, lizard bones, and plant matter.

ORDER LIPOTYPHLA

The Lipotyphla includes five fossil and seven living families. The latter include hedgehogs, shrews, and moles, as well as solenodons of the West Indies, golden moles of Africa, tenrecs of Madagascar, and otter shrews of Central Africa.

NAME *Palaeorycles*
TIME Early Paleocene to Early Eocene
LOCALITY North America (New Mexico)
SIZE 5 in/12.5 cm long

A well-preserved skull shows *Palaeoryctes* must have closely resembled a modern shrew in appearance, with a small sleek body and a pointed snout armed with little insect-crushing teeth. Although it ate mostly insects, probably beetles and caterpillars, it may have taken a wide range of foods, including small vertebrates. Such a generalized feeder would have been in a good position to evolve into more specialized types, and *Palaeoryctes* or a close relative may have evolved into the great flesh-eating mammals of the Early Tertiary—the creodonts.

ORDER CREODONTA

The creodonts were the dominant flesh-eating mammals worldwide throughout the early part of the Tertiary, between about 60 and 30 million years ago, except in South America and Australia. Yet they had all disappeared by the Late Miocene, some 7 million years ago. Before doing so, they evolved a great number of forms ranging from stoat- to bear-sized, anticipating the members of the order Carnivora.

Main differences between the creodonts and the carnivores proper are the smaller brains of the creodonts, the lack of a bone enclosing the middle ear, their different foot bones (the wrist bones are not fused and the claw bones have a groove in them), and differences in the teeth, especially in those teeth that perform a carnassial function (the pairs of teeth, which are formed like scissor-blades to shear meat).

The 50 or so genera of creodonts are classified in two families —the Oxyaenidae and Hyaenodontidae. It used to be thought that the creodonts were ancestors of the modern carnivores. But recent analyses suggest that the creodonts are probably not a natural group but are derived from different origins.

NAME	*Sarkastodon*
TIME	Late Eocene
LOCALITY	Asia (Mongolia)
SIZE	10 ft / 3 m long

Around 35 million years ago, during the Late Eocene, Central Asia boasted some huge mammals, notably brontotheres, chalicotheres, and rhinoceroses (see pp.402–409). To exploit such massive prey, the creodonts grew to a great size, too. *Sarkastodon* was one of the largest, bigger than the biggest bear. The teeth were large and heavy, and thick like those of a modern grizzly bear. *Sarkastodon* probably ate a wide range of foods.

Other oxyenids living in the northern hemisphere during Paleocene and Eocene times, between about 55 million and 40 million years ago, included animals that resembled wolverines and cats.

NAME	*Hyaenodon*
TIME	Late Eocene to Early Miocene
LOCALITY	Widespread over North America, Europe (France), Asia (China), and Africa (Kenya)
SIZE	up to 4 ft / 1.2 m long

The hyenodonts, the later family of creodonts, were a larger group than the oxyenids. They evolved in the Eocene and persisted to the Late Miocene, ranging from North America to Asia, Europe, and Africa.

Hyaenodon was a widespread and long-lived genus including many species, from animals the size of a stoat to species as large as a hyena. Its long, slim legs and digitigrade feet (only the toes touched the ground) indicate that *Hyaenodon* could run, though its spreading toes suggest that it would not have been very fast. *Hyaenodon* may have been hyenalike in habits, actively hunting down other animals, but also scavenging dead ones.

MUSTELIDS AND BEARS

ORDER CARNIVORA

Cats, civets and mongooses, dogs, bears and pandas, stoats, weasels and otters, seals, sea lions, and walruses—all these mammals belong to the large order Carnivora. All of the animals in the order Carnivora are carnivores, meaning "meat-eaters," and they all share a common feature relating to their teeth. Living carnivores have (and their ancestors also had) a pair of meat-shearing teeth, called carnassial teeth, which have become specialized for slicing up flesh. However, some members of the Carnivora order, such as seals, have lost these teeth, since they have developed and evolved to feed mainly on fish and therefore no longer need them.

However, not all animals that eat meat are members of the order Carnivora. The toothed whales, for example, are not "true carnivores," although one species which is part of the group, the orca, is a formidable predator and will eat other whales and seals and sea birds.

An extinct group of ferocious carnivores, the creodonts (see p.357) were not members of the order Carnivora, nor were the insatiable carnivorous dinosaurs. Conversely, not all members of the Carnivora only eat meat. Bears and badgers, for example, are omnivores, and consume a wide range of animal and plant food.

Besides the meat-shearing blades of the carnassial teeth, true carnivores are also distinguished by having small, sharp incisor teeth at the front of their jaws for holding prey and large, pointed canine teeth for delivering the killing bite (see p.340)

The order Carnivora has traditionally been divided into two major groups, the fissipeds (meaning "split feet") and the pinnipeds (meaning "fin feet"). However, it is now thought that the relationships within the order are more complicated was previously believed, and this is reflected in more modern classifications. The extinct miacids are treated separately, and the feliforms (cats and hyenas) are distinguished from the caniforms (dogs, weasels, civets, and bears). The pinnipeds, made up of the seals, sea lions, and walruses, are still grouped together. Molecular analysis now groups the Carnivora with the whales and even-toed ungulates.

Carnivores appeared during Late Cretaceous or Early Paleocene times, about 70–65 million years ago. The carnivores evolved from the same ancestors as did the insectivores (see pp.354, 356), but the carnivores remained relatively insignificant until Oligocene times, some 35 million years ago. At this time they began to replace the creodonts, which had been the dominant carnivorous land mammals up to that time.

Family Mesonychidae

The miacids were the earliest true carnivores to appear, during the Paleocene, 60 million years ago. This is an "artificial" group, since it contains animals that were not closely related. However, it is a convenient classification that distinguishes these early carnivores from the more modern types. Miacids were mostly small mammals that lived in woodlands. The scant remains they have left indicate that they resembled the creodonts in many ways, although they were possibly more intelligent and had better-developed meat-shearing teeth.

NAME	*Miacis*
TIME	Paleocene to Middle Eocene
LOCALITY	Europe (Germany)
SIZE	8 in/20 cm long

Scampering through the branches, this animal must have looked like a modern pine marten (*Martes martes*). The shape of its limbs and its flexible shoulder and elbow joints indicate that it was well-adapted for moving through the trees of its native tropical swamp forest.

Miacis probably also lived in much the same way as a pine marten, hunting small mammals and birds on the ground and in the trees. It may also have eaten insects, birds' eggs, and fruit. A primitive feature of *Miacis* was its full set of 44 teeth. This is the basic number of mammalian teeth, but the more advanced carnivores lost many of them during their evolution into more specialized forms.

Family Mustelidae

Mustelids probably evolved from the miacids in the Early Tertiary. Modern members of the family include weasels, stoats, badgers and otters, civets, genets, and mongooses—all slim, long-bodied hunters.

NAME *Potamotherium*

TIME Early Miocene

LOCALITY Europe (France)

SIZE 5 ft / 1.5 m long

Potamotherium is the earliest-known otter, and like its modern counterpart it had a long, sinuous body and short legs. It probably ran through the riverside undergrowth in a series of leaps, with its back arched and its head close to the ground. *Potamotherium*'s sense of smell was not well developed, but its senses of hearing and sight seem to have been acute, helping it to hunt down its fish prey in the water.

Potamotherium was without a doubt an excellent swimmer. The creature's sleek, streamlined shape would have cut through the water, and its flexible backbone meant it could dive and dart about easily underwater.

The otters are the only mustelids that are well represented in the fossil record. This is probably because they lived near water, and so were more likely to become buried in sediments and subsequently fossilized. Paleontologists believe that the true seals, or phocids (see p.370), evolved from a mustelid ancestor.

Family Procyonidae

The procyonids, including the modern raccoons, pandas, and coatis, first appeared in the Early Oligocene, about 35 million years ago. They had the typical meat-shearing blades on their premolar and molar teeth, the characteristic feature of the true carnivores. But this design has been lost in modern members of the family, and their premolars and molars have reverted to a purely grinding and crushing function.

This dentition suits the omnivorous diet of most modern procyonids. However, the diet of the giant panda, *Ailuropoda melanoleura*, consists almost exclusively of bamboo shoots, and it is probable that this animal is more closely related to the bears than to the raccoons.

NAME *Plesictis*

TIME Early Oligocene to Early Miocene

LOCALITY Asia (China), Europe (France), and North America (USA)

SIZE 2 ft 5 in / 75 cm long

This tree-living hunter had big eyes, perhaps for nocturnal hunting, and a long tail for balance. It was similar to the modern cacomistle (*Bassaricus sumichrasti*) and may have been its direct ancestor. It probably led much the same lifestyle, scampering through the trees.

Like other procyonids, the cusps of its teeth were blunt and the molars were square in cross-section, indicating that it was probably omnivorous, eating eggs, insects, and plant matter, as well as hunting for small mammals and birds.

NAME *Chapalmalania*

TIME Late Pliocene

LOCALITY South America (Argentina)

SIZE 5 ft / 1.5 m long

The procyonids traveled south from North America via the Central American land bridge. Once in South America, they evolved into a number of specialized forms. *Chapalmalania* was a gigantic raccoon that must have looked rather like the modern giant panda. It was so large that its remains were at first thought to be those of a bear. Like the panda, it probably had a specialized diet, relying on some local plant on the mountainsides for much of its food.

Family Amphicyonidae

The amphicyonids were a family of "bear-dogs" that existed from the Eocene Epoch 50 million years ago to Miocene times, about 5 million years ago.

Amphicyonids were a varied and successful group of large hunting animals. They spread throughout Europe, Asia, and North America. When the creodonts declined, the amphicyonids replaced them in the ecosystems and were then themselves replaced by the "true dogs" during Pliocene times (some 5 million years ago).

The amphicyonids' common name "bear-dogs" refers to their similarity to both of these creatures. The amphicyonid's body was bearlike in shape and bulk. They walked with the whole foot placed on the ground (known as plantigrade locomotion, and the same method that is used by bears and humans), rather than just the toes (known as digitigrade locomotion, the method used by the fleet-footed cats and dogs). The shape of the head and the arrangement of the teeth, however, were more doglike.

NAME	*Amphicyon*
TIME	Middle Oligocene to Early Miocene
LOCALITY	Europe (France and Germany) and North America (Nebraska)
SIZE	6ft 6in/2m long

Amphicyon was a typical "bear-dog." It probably looked like a large bear with the strong, sharp teeth of a wolf. It had a thick neck, strong legs, and a heavy tail. It may have led a similar life to that of a modern brown or grizzly bear, eating a wide range of plant and animal foods, and killing its prey with powerful blows from its strong forefeet.

Amphicyon must have been a fearsome adversary for any other creature living on the plains of the northern hemisphere in Mid Tertiary times, about 30 million years ago. One fossil species, *Amphicyon giganteus*, from the Miocene of Europe, was about the same size as a modern tiger.

Family Ursidae

The Ursidae family comprises the bears. Taxonomically, the bears are associated with the dogs (canids), raccoons (procyonids), and weasels (mustelids) as caniforms.

The ursids occur later in the fossil record than many other carnivores, having first appeared in Europe during Oligocene times. Since their first appearance, they have spread throughout most of the world.

Although there are no bears native to Africa today, there are two separate records of bears having inhabited that continent in the past. The primitive *Agriotherium* (below) lived in southwestern Africa during the Pliocene, some 5 million years ago, and brown bears are known to have lived in the Atlas Mountains of northern Africa during the Pleistocene Epoch, even surviving into recent times.

Bears are omnivorous creatures, consuming anything that they can catch, from small mammals to fish and insects. They also forage for fruit, eggs, nuts, and, of course, honey. They generally search for food by day, and their eyesight and hearing are quite poor, though their sense of smell is very acute.

Their pattern of dentition reflects their catholic diet. Bears have unspecialized incisors, long canines, reduced or absent premolars (with no meat-shearing blades), and broad, flat molars with rounded cusps. The molars are probably the most used of this animal's teeth, being used to crush up the tough plant food that makes up the major part of a bear's diet.

The modern Kodiak bear (*Ursus arctos middendorffi*) which is found in the forests of Kodiak, Afognak, and Shuyak islands on the northwestern coast of the United States, is the world's largest living land carnivore.

NAME *Agriotherium*

TIME Late Miocene to Pleistocene

LOCALITY Africa (Namibia), Asia (China), and Europe (France)

SIZE 6ft 6in/2m long

Although bears are no longer found in Africa, they were in the past. *Agriotherium* lived in southwestern Africa. *Agriotherium* was a very large bear, even larger than the Kodiak bear. It was also very primitive and looked like a dog in some ways. However, its teeth had developed the typical bear pattern, so it is safe to assume that it was omnivorous.

NAME *Hemicyon*

TIME Early to Late Miocene

LOCALITY Asia (Mongolia), Europe (France and Spain), and North America (USA)

SIZE 5ft/1.5m long

Despite its great size, *Hemicyon* was lightly built for a bear. Indeed, it was more like a heavy dog, and its name means "half-dog." It was probably more carnivorous than most other bears, so it was likely to have been an active

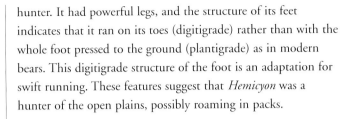

hunter. It had powerful legs, and the structure of its feet indicates that it ran on its toes (digitigrade) rather than with the whole foot pressed to the ground (plantigrade) as in modern bears. This digitigrade structure of the foot is an adaptation for swift running. These features suggest that *Hemicyon* was a hunter of the open plains, possibly roaming in packs.

NAME *Ursus spelaeus*

TIME Pleistocene to Recent

LOCALITY Europe (Austria, Germany, Netherlands, Spain, UK, and former USSR)

SIZE 6ft 6in/2m long

The genus *Ursus* is represented today by the brown, or grizzly, bear, the polar bear, and the American black bear. But in Pleistocene times, the cave bear, *Ursus spelaeus*, was a particularly numerous and impressive species.

Ursus spelaeus lived in Europe during the height of the last Ice Age and often escaped the worst of the winters by hibernating in alpine caves. Many bears seem to have congregated together for this long, annual sleep, to judge from the heaps of fossil bones that have been found together.

One cave, the Drachenhohle, or "Dragon's Cave," in Austria for example, contains the remains of more than 30,000 cave bears. And many of them seem to have died in their sleep, possibly during their period of hibernation.

Despite its great size and fearsome appearance, the cave bear was probably a vegetarian. It was hunted by Neanderthal people (see p.441), and its bones were important in their rituals.

DOGS AND HYENAS

FAMILY CANIDAE

The canids—including the modern foxes, jackals, coyotes, wolves, and dogs—are a successful group of "all-rounders." With an evolutionary history of some 40 million years, they have become adapted to an enormous range of habitats and a wide variety of diets. As members of the order Carnivora (see p.358), the Canidae family are related to the otters and weasels, cats and mongooses, and to the seals, sea lions, and walruses.

First known from Late Eocene times, about 40 million years ago, the earliest canids were relatively short-legged animals that resembled mongooses and civets more than modern dogs. They were almost entirely restricted to North America, the center of canid evolution; the family did not colonize other continents until the end of the Miocene, as recently as 6 million years ago.

From a mere five genera in the Early Oligocene (35 million years ago), the canids had evolved and diversified to 42 genera by the Late Miocene (10 to 6 million years ago). This was their heyday, and they have since declined to the 12 modern genera alive today, which includes the domesticated dog.

The teeth of canids have contributed much to their versatility of habitat and diet. In addition to the large, pointed canine teeth (the word canine simply means "doglike") and well-developed meat-shearing (carnassial) teeth, they also possess powerful crushing molars at the back of the jaws. So they are omnivorous—eating anything from bones and flesh, to insects and fruit.

Canids have also evolved a superb sense of smell, good vision, and acute hearing. Their long limbs and great stamina, combined with their style of running on the tips of their toes (called digitigrade locomotion), allow them to chase swift-moving prey for considerable distances, until they succumb through exhaustion.

Intelligence and social living, as seen today in hyenas and wolves, also enhance their ability to catch prey, avoid predators, rear young successfully, and colonize new habitats.

NAME	*Phlaocyon*
TIME	Early Miocene
LOCALITY	North America (Nebraska)
SIZE	2 ft 6 in/80 cm long

Just as *Hesperocyon* superficially resembled a member of the cat family (felids), so *Phlaocyon* looked more like a member of the raccoon family (procyonids, see p.359). However, several features of its skull suggest it did belong to the dog family (canids), though it was a very primitive member.

Phlaocyon probably lived much like a modern raccoon. Although its feet were distinctly doglike, its limbs were adapted for climbing trees rather than for running. It had a short, broad head with the eyes set well forward.

The lower jaw of *Phlaocyon* was curved, similar to the lower jaw of a raccoon, and the premolars and molars were all grinding teeth. The creature's dentition did not include the meat-cutting blades that are so typical of dogs. The pattern and type of teeth suggest that *Phlaocyon* was probably omnivorous, feeding on a mixed diet of seeds, fruit, insects, and birds' eggs, as well as small mammals and birds.

NAME	*Hesperocyon*
TIME	Early Oligocene to Early Miocene
LOCALITY	North America (Nebraska)
SIZE	2 ft 6 in/80 cm long

An active little animal, looking like a mongoose or civet, *Hesperocyon* was one of the earliest members of the canid family to appear. With its long flexible body and tail, and its short, weak legs and spreading five-toed feet, it may not have looked much like a dog. However, the structure of its ear bones and the arrangement of its teeth show without a doubt that it was a primitive canid.

Fossils of the creature's skull show that parts of the inner ear were enclosed in bone rather than in cartilage (gristle)—a dog-like feature that distinguishes *Hesperocyon* from more primitive carnivores, such as *Miacis* (see p.358).

The teeth of *Hesperocyon* show that the last molar tooth was missing from each side of the upper jaw, giving a set of 42 teeth rather than the usual complement of 44. The last upper premolar tooth and the first lower molar tooth on each side were modified into meat-cutting (carnassial) blades, typical of dogs and most other true carnivores (that is, those grouped in the order Carnivora).

NAME *Cynodesmus*

TIME Late Oligocene to Early Miocene

LOCALITY North America (Nebraska)

SIZE 3 ft 3 in/1 m long

Cynodesmus was one of the first canids that actually looked like a modern dog. It was roughly the size and shape of the coyote, *Canis latrans*, of today's North and Central America. Its face, however, was shorter (the long snout of typical dogs was to develop much later in their evolution), and its body was still long, with a heavy tail.

Cynodesmus' legs were fairly doglike, but they were not yet as efficient for running as those of modern dogs. The open grasslands of North America had not formed at this time; their development encouraged the evolution of fast-moving grazing

mammals, which in turn led to the rapid evolution of swift-footed hunters such as dogs.

There were still five toes on each of *Cynodesmus'* feet, although the first toes were smaller than the rest. Its claws were narrow and partially retractable, like those of a cat, rather than the thick, blunt, weight-bearing structures that developed in later dogs. It was probably *Cynodesmus'* habit to ambush its prey, cat-style, rather than running it down, dog-style.

NAME *Cerdocyon*

TIME Pleistocene

LOCALITY South America (Argentina)

SIZE 2 ft 6 in/80 cm long

The dog family evolved in North America throughout the Tertiary Period. The animals that belonged to this group could not reach South America because the two continents were separated by a sea.

Then, toward the end of the Tertiary, in Pliocene times (about 5 million years ago), the Central American land bridge was re-established, and animals could migrate southward. The dogs crossed into South America in the Early Pleistocene, some 2 million years ago, and the early fox *Cerdocyon* was among the invaders in this trek southward.

Two million years later, *Cerdocyon* lives on in the form of the common zorro or crab-eating fox, *Cerdocyon thous,* which is found from Colombia to northern Argentina.

Crabs are only part of the diet of this omnivorous night-hunter. Depending upon seasonal availability, it also eats rats, mice, frogs, and insects using its keen sense of hearing when hunting in the dark, and employing both stealthy and "dash and grab" hunting techniques to catch its quarry. The crab-eating fox will also consume fruit and carrion, and any creature's eggs that it can find. Its Pleistocene relative probably pursued much the same opportunistic lifestyle.

NAME *Osteoborus*

TIME Late Miocene to Early Pleistocene

LOCALITY North America (Nebraska)

SIZE 2 ft 6 in/80 cm long

Osteoborus' was a member of the borophagines, a group of scavenging dogs that first appeared in late Miocene times, about 8 million years ago.

Osteoborus' heavy build and rather bulbous, swollen forehead gave it a somewhat bearlike appearance; however, this creature's scavenging hyenalike habits were partly reflected by the huge, bone-crushing premolar teeth that lined its jaws. *Osteoborus'* skull had also developed a shortened form in order to accommodate the massive muscles that were needed to work the animal's powerful jaws. This rugged combination of strong jaws and crushing teeth enabled *Osteoborus* to chew and splinter the bones of carcasses in order to reach the soft and nutritious bone marrow inside.

Osteoborus was a widespread inhabitant of North America, where it probably occupied the same ecological niche as the contemporary hyenas in Europe, Asia, and Africa, scavenging what it could from dead animals or robbing other predators of their kills. *Osteoborus'* scavenging role in the ecosystem was eventually taken over in North America by more typical dogs, such as *Canis dirus*.

NAME *Canis dirus*

TIME Pleistocene to Recent

LOCALITY North America (California)

SIZE 4 ft 6 in/1.5 m long

The genus of dogs called *Canis* includes the nine living species of wolves, coyotes, jackals, and dogs—both wild dogs and every domestic breed, from Great Dane to Chihuahua. Many more species existed in the past, one of the best known being *C. dirus*, the dire wolf. In appearance, this prehistoric wolf was much like its modern counterpart, but it was more heavily built. It was probably a scavenger rather than a hunter, filling the niche of borophagines, such as *Osteoborus*, after their extinction in the Early Pleistocene.

The remains of more than 2,000 dire wolves have been excavated from the tar pits of Rancho La Brea, where the city of Los Angeles stands today. About 25,000 years ago, crude oil seeped to the surface here and evaporated away, leaving behind pools of sticky tar. These pools trapped unwary animals, such as ground sloths and elephants. The dying animals attracted carnivores, such as the dire wolf, which also became stuck.

Their fossilization has left a detailed record of life in Pleistocene times. The dire wolves and saber-tooths fought, since their bones are often covered with scars from each other's formidable teeth.

More intelligent, active hunters, such as the contemporary lions and dogs, were rarely trapped. It seems that they could more readily appreciate the danger of the pools.

Family Hyaenidae

The hyenas, also members of the order Carnivora, appeared only relatively recently, in Mid-Miocene times, about 15 million years ago. They probably evolved on the African continent and then spread throughout the Old World. Nowadays, the hyenids are grouped with the feliforms and are thought to have originated from the viverrids (civets and relatives).

The only hyena known from the New World is *Chamaporthetes,* which lived in North America during the Pleistocene. It also lived throughout Africa, Asia, and Europe. It was a fast-running hunter rather than a scavenger, and its legs and teeth were similar to those of the modern cheetah. Indeed, in Africa it had to compete with the true cheetahs, which also lived there during Pleistocene times.

The role of mammalian scavenger in North America was played chiefly by the heavy-toothed borophagine dogs, such as *Osteoborus.* Their diet and lifestyle mirrored that of the hyenas elsewhere in the world.

Today, hyenas are restricted to the warmer areas of Africa and Asia. Although they are chiefly scavengers, they are also agile and intelligent hunters, running in packs to bring down swift-footed grazing mammals such as gazelle. They have heavy bone-crushing teeth, and their remarkably tough digestive system allows them to absorb the organic matter in bone, while indigestible bone fragments, hooves, horns, ligaments, and hair are regurgitated as pellets.

NAME *Ictitherium*

TIME Middle Miocene to Early Pliocene

LOCALITY Africa (Morocco) and Europe (Greece)

SIZE 4 ft/1.2 m

Ictitherium was one of the earliest hyenas and probably looked more like a civet (a relative of the mongooses and genets, see p.369) in build and appearance. It also had teeth similar to those of a civet, which were well suited to an insectivorous diet, rather than the formidable bone-crunching teeth of hyenas.

Along with its primitive relatives, *Ictitherium* was among the most widespread hunters of its time. Indeed, at one stage during the Pliocene, its fossil remains outnumber those of all other carnivores put together.

Groups of animals are often found fossilized together, which suggests that a flood may have swept them all away at the same time. It is likely that this early hyena had already evolved a relatively advanced social order and hunted down their prey in packs, as hyenas do today.

NAME *Percocruta*

TIME Middle to Late Miocene

LOCALITY Widespread in Africa, Asia, and Europe

SIZE 5 ft/1.5 m long

Hyenas of the genus *Percocruta* were the largest hyenas that ever lived. One species, *P. gigantea* which was unearthed in China, was as large as a modern-day lion.

Despite its great size, *Percocruta* was very similar to the present-day spotted hyena, *Crocuta crocuta,* of the African grasslands. This creature was much more widespread in Pleistocene times than it is today; fossilized remains have been found throughout Africa, Europe, and Asia.

Like its modern relative, *Percocruta* had a large head and thickset muzzle with extraordinarily powerful jaws, armed with great bone-crushing teeth that would have suited a scavenging lifestyle. It also had the typical sloping stance of its modern relatives, with power forequarters and shorter hind legs. It probably moved with a similar loping gait.

CATS AND MONGOOSES

FAMILY NIMRAVIDAE

The nimravids were the earliest cats to evolve, in the Early Oligocene Epoch, about 35 million years ago. They survived until Late Miocene times, about 8 million years ago. The members of the family Nimravidae are sometimes called false saber-tooths to distinguish them from the true saber-tooths, grouped in the family Felidae (below).

Nimravids had long, low bodies and long tails. Their prominent upper canine teeth (the "sabers") were longer than those of modern cats, but shorter than those of the true saber-tooths, whereas their lower canines were proportionally longer.

NAME *Nimravus*

TIME Early Oligocene to Early Miocene

RANGE Europe (France) and North America (Colorado, Nebraska, North and South Dakota, and Wyoming)

SIZE 4 ft/1.2 m long

Even as long ago as the Early Oligocene, this false saber-tooth was a contemporary of other saber-tooths in Europe and North America, such as *Eusmilus*, and competed with them for food and habitat.

Nimravus, with its sleek body, was probably not unlike the modern caracal (*Felis caracal*) which occurs in Africa and Asia, although it had a longer back and more dog-like feet. The creature's head was short and the eyes were positioned so that they could be directed forward. This is an important development for a hunting animal because it provides stereoscopic vision which allows the animal to accurately judge the distance between itself and its quarry.

Nimravus' claws were thin and very sharp, and they could be partially retracted in order to prevent them from becoming damaged while the animal was running.

Nimravus probably hunted small mammals and birds; these it caught by ambush, like most cats, rather than by swift pursuit, the typical method used by dogs.

Family Felidae

The modern cat family contains such familiar creatures as the lion, tiger, leopard, cheetah, and domestic cat.

Felids are the most highly specialized of all mammalian hunters. When the grassland environments developed during the Mid Tertiary Period, some 15 million years ago, the cats and dogs evolved in response. They developed to hunt down the herbivores grazing on the great plains. In these open landscapes, any prey animal could see danger approaching from a long way off, and a successful predator had to be either a skilled stalker or a very fast runner. Cats have adopted the first approach, hunting by stealth. Dogs, however, employ the second hunting method, chasing down prey.

Some cats, such as tigers, evolved as solitary hunters that caught and killed their prey by stalking and ambushing it. However, other cats, such as lions, developed a social, cooperative lifestyle and stalked their prey in well-coordinated groups, called prides.

Cats also developed two chief methods of killing their prey once it had been caught. The first method was employed by the "biting cats," including all the modern types. These species killed their victims by breaking their necks with one swift, powerful bite from their sharp canine teeth. The second method was specific to the saber-tooth cats, all of which are now extinct. These species used their greatly developed canine teeth to inflict deep wounds on their quarry and would then simply have waited for it to bleed to death.

In addition to the true saber-tooths, another group of felids also developed saber-like teeth, just as the primitive nimravid cats had done. Saber-tooth cats are often misnamed "saber-tooth tigers," but they are not closely related to those big cats.

The felids originated in the Early Oligocene Epoch having evolved from the viverrids.

NAME *Eusmilus*

TIME Oligocene

LOCALITY Europe (France) and North America (Colorado, Nebraska, North and South Dakota, and Wyoming)

SIZE 8 ft/2.5 m

NAME *Megantereon*

TIME Late Miocene to Early Pleistocene

LOCALITY Africa (South Africa), Asia (India), Europe (France), and North America (Texas)

SIZE 4 ft/1.2 m long

This leopard-sized cat was rather long-bodied and short-legged compared with a modern big cat. *Eusmilus* first appeared in Europe toward the very end of Eocene times, about 40 million years ago, and then spread eastwards across the Bering land bridge, which was in existence at the time, into North America during the Oligocene.

Eusmilus was typical of the group of false saber-tooth felids. The animal's pair of upper canine teeth had become enlarged into well-developed, stabbing "sabers." The lower canines, however, were insignificant, and many of the other teeth had been lost. *Eusmilus* had only 26 teeth in its jaws, a relatively small number compared with the maximum of 44 found in some carnivores.

The jaw hinge was modified to open to an angle of 90°, which allowed the great saber teeth to do their work. The lower jaw had bony guards that lay along the length of the sabers, protecting them from damage when the animal's mouth was closed. In this respect *Eusmilus* resembled the marsupial saber-tooth *Thylacosmilus* (see p.347), although these mammals were not related. Their similarity is an example of similar environmental conditions resulting in the evolution of similar characteristics in unrelated animals (a phenomenon known as convergent evolution).

Eusmilus and other false saber-tooth cats inhabited the same parts of the world at the same time, and there is fossil evidence that their paths crossed. A skull of *Nimravus* found in North America is pierced in the forehead region, the hole exactly matching the dimensions of *Eusmilus*' saber tooth. The wound was not fatal, however, for *Nimravus* survived the fight long enough to allow its wound to heal.

Megantereon was an early true saber-tooth cat, and it was probably ancestral to other forms of saber-tooths. Its teeth were not quite long enough to be really saber-like; they were more like daggers in size and shape, so *Megantereon* and its immediate relatives are often known as the dirk-tooth cats (from the Scottish word for dagger, "dirk").

The development of long canine teeth enabled these powerful predators to hunt and kill the large, thick-skinned grazing mammals that shared their habitat. From stalking the prey, a short dash and leap would bring the animal down. Then neck bites would cause blood loss and shock, and a strangulation hold would soon kill the victim.

Megantereon flourished in the Mediterranean region during the Late Pliocene and Early Pleistocene, between about 3 and 2 million years ago. The genera also spread across Africa and North America from its center of origin in northern India during Late Miocene times.

TIME Late Pleistocene

LOCALITY North America (California) and South America (Argentina)

SIZE 4 ft/1.2 m long

NAME *Homotherium*

TIME Early to Late Pleistocene

LOCALITY Africa (Ethiopia), Asia (China and Java), Europe (UK), and North America (Tennessee and Texas)

SIZE 4 ft/1.2 m

Besides saber-tooth and dirk-tooth cats, there were also scimitar-tooth cats, so called because their death-dealing canines were shorter and flatter than those of the saber-tooths. They also curved backward, like a scimitar's blade. The back teeth consisted of powerful, meat-shearing (carnassial) blades for slicing up flesh.

In profile, *Homotherium* must have had the sloping look of a hyena, since its forelegs were longer than its hind legs. When it walked, the whole foot was placed firmly on the ground, as in a bear or a human. This is called "plantigrade" locomotion, and contrasts with most other cats, which walk on their toes (called "digitigrade" locomotion).

Homotherium survived until the end of the advance of the ice in the Pleistocene, about 14,000 years ago. Scimitar-tooth cats probably preyed on mammoths, since in Texas the remains of young mammoths have been preserved alongside the bones of a family group of scimitar-tooths. *Homotherium* may have become extinct when its prey died out in the northern continents at the end of the Pleistocene ice age.

Smilodon was the classic saber-tooth cat. Unlike most other cats, it had a short tail, like that of a modern bobcat. Its whole body was powerfully built, with the muscles of its shoulders and neck so arranged as to produce a powerful downward lunge of its massive head. The jaw opened to an angle of over 120°, to allow the huge pair of saber teeth in its upper jaws to be driven into the victim.

The sabers were oval in cross-section to retain strength, but also to ensure minimum resistance as they were sunk into the prey. They were also serrated like steak-knives along their rear edges, so they pierced the victim's flesh more easily.

Smilodon probably preyed on large, slow-moving, thick-skinned animals, such as mammoths and bison. Unable to kill its prey with a quick bite to the neck, this saber-tooth cat probably inflicted deep wounds in the victim's flanks or hindquarters, and then simply waited for it to bleed to death.

More than 2000 skeletons of *Smilodon* have been recovered from the Pleistocene tar pits of Rancho La Brea in Los Angeles, along with similar numbers of other carnivores, such as the dire wolf, *Canis dirus* (see p.363). These animals had not yet developed the cunning of modern carnivores, and were lured into the tar by large animals already trapped there. The species of *Smilodon* found is *S. californicus*, and it has been adopted as the state fossil of California.

Another species of *Smilodon*, *S. neogaeus*, has been found in Argentina. It migrated from North America in Pleistocene times, once the land bridge between the two continents had been re-established at the beginning of the Pliocene Epoch, about 5 million years ago.

NAME *Dinofelis*

TIME Late Pliocene to Middle Pleistocene

LOCALITY Africa (South Africa), Asia (China and India), Europe (France), and North America (Texas)

SIZE 4 ft/1.2 m long

Dinofelis was a panther-sized cat, with flattened, canines that were short compared with the saber-tooths, scimitar-tooths or dirk-tooths, but longer than those of the biting cats. It is a matter of debate among paleontologists as to which subfamily of the felids *Dinofelis* belongs.

    Dinofelis became extinct in Eurasia and North America during the Early Pleistocene, but survived in Africa until Mid-Pleistocene times. The Chinese species, *D. abeli*, (named in honor of an Austrian paleontologist, Professor Abel) is the largest-known form.

NAME *Panthera*

TIME Pleistocene to Recent

LOCALITY Africa (South Africa), Asia (India), Europe (England), and North America (California)

SIZE up to 11 ft 6 in/3.5 m long

Panthera leo, the modern lion, is found today in parts of Africa and in the Gir Forest of western India. A typical biting cat, its canine teeth (which are short compared with most extinct cats) are used to kill prey by biting through the neck and throttling it. The long, sharp claws can be fully retracted and tucked away beneath a sheath of skin, to prevent them becoming blunt.

    There are two notable extinct subspecies of lion. *Panthera leo spelaea* was the cave lion of Europe. It was probably the largest cat that ever lived, being about 25 percent larger than the modern lion, and even bigger than the largest living cat, the Siberian subspecies of the tiger, *Panthera tigris altaica*. Cave paintings and other archeological discoveries indicate that the cave lion existed until historical times in southeastern Europe; its last stronghold seems to have been in the Balkans, up to about 2000 years ago.

    The other subspecies of extinct lion was *Panthera leo atrox*, which ranged throughout North America and was also found in northern South America. This subspecies evidently crossed to North America by way of the Bering Strait during the last ice age, about 35,000 to 20,000 years ago.

    Remains of this lion have been found in Alaska. But the most famous fossils come from the tar pits of Rancho La Brea in Los Angeles. They are scarcer than the remains of other carnivores, perhaps because the lion was intelligent enough to avoid the pits.

Family Viverridae

This family of small carnivores contains the modern civets, genets, and mongooses. Viverrids are among the oldest of the carnivores, with ancestry dating back as far as the Middle Paleocene, about 60 million years ago. They are also among the most adaptable and least specialized of all carnivores. Early viverrids gave rise to the hyaenas in the Miocene and the cats (felids) in the early Oligocene.

    Viverrids are mostly long-bodied, short-legged animals. Many are opportunistic omnivores, eating a great variety of food—from earthworms, molluscs, fish, birds, and reptiles (including snakes in the case of mongooses), to eggs, carrion, and fruit.

    Despite the wide range of the group today—they are found throughout much of the Old World tropics (viverrids are the only group of carnivores in Madagascar)—the fossil record is poor.

NAME *Kanuites*

TIME Miocene

LOCALITY Africa (Kenya)

SIZE 3 ft/90 cm long

The viverrids have changed remarkably little during their evolution, and *Kanuites* probably looked similar to the existing genets (*Genetta*). It had a long tail and perhaps retractable claws like those of a cat. It was probably omnivorous and may have lived in trees as well as on the ground.

SEALS, SEALIONS, AND WALRUSES

SUBORDER PINNIPEDIA

The order Carnivora includes not only the dominant carnivores of the land, the cats, dogs, and bears, but also a successful group of marine carnivores, grouped together as the pinnipeds. They include the modern sealions and fur seals (Otariidae), walruses (Odobenidae), and the true seals (Phocidae). All have feet modified into flippers or pinnae.

The pinnipeds probably evolved in the northern hemisphere during the Late Oligocene, about 30 million years ago. They do not seem to have spread south of the equator until the Miocene, some 10 million years later. Although sealions and walruses were thought to have evolved from bear-like ancestors, and the true seals from otter-like carnivores, current opinion favours a single origin for the whole group from an ancestor among the mustelids (weasels, otters, and their relatives, see pp.358–359).

Family Phocidae

Seals may not look much like dogs or cats, but they are nonetheless members of the order Carnivora. Grouped as phocids, they probably evolved from an otter-like mustelid, such as *Potamotherium* (see p.359), in the Late Oligocene, some 30 million years ago. They appeared in European waters, and then spread north and south to the Arctic and Antarctic Oceans, and west to the Pacific, adapting to a marine, fish-eating life. However, they still leave the sea to breed on land.

The phocids are often called the "true seals," to distinguish them from the otariids, or "eared seals" (the sealions and fur seals). They are more abundant and varied today than the sealions, fur seals, and walruses, but their fossil record is sparse.

NAME *Acrophoca*
TIME Early Pliocene
LOCALITY South America (Peru)
SIZE 5 ft/1.5 m long

Acrophoca may have been the ancestor of the modern leopard seal, *Hydrurga leptonyx*. It was a fish-eater, but it seems to have been less adapted to an aquatic life, and spent much of its time on or near the shore. Its flippers were not so well-developed, its neck was longer and less streamlined than that of a modern seal (more like that of its otter-like ancestor). Its snout was quite pointed.

Family Enliarctidae

The enaliarctids were the earliest members of the otariids to evolve, and were the ancestors of the modern sealions, fur seals and walruses. They lived during the Early Miocene, about 23 million years ago, and like the phocids, probably evolved from among the mustelids.

Later in the Miocene, about 18 million years ago, enaliarctids gave rise to another extinct family of early seals, the desmatophocids. Later still, about 15 million years ago, some of the enaliarctids evolved into the odobenids, or walruses. Another branch, which evolved in the Middle Miocene about 13 million years ago, led to the otariids, the sealions, and fur seals.

NAME *Enaliarctos*
TIME Early Miocene
LOCALITY North America (Pacific coast)
SIZE 5 ft/1.5 m long

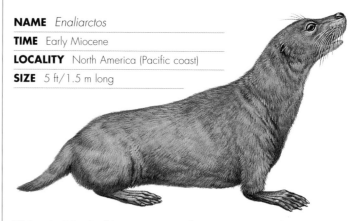

This primitive-looking sea mammal represents an early stage in the adaptation of a land-dwelling carnivore to a marine lifestyle. *Enaliarctos* is almost halfway between an otter and a sealion. Its cheek teeth still bore meat-shearing (carnassial) blades like those of a land-living dog. Its body was streamlined and rather otter-like, with distinct legs and a tail, although the feet were already modified into paddles.

Like the modern sea otter, *Enaliarctos* probably spent time on land as well as in the water, and eating a variety of marine animals, including fish and shellfish. Some sealion characteristics had already evolved, such as the large eyes, sophisticated senses associated with the whiskers, and the specialization of the inner ears for detecting the direction of sound underwater. These senses helped *Enaliarctos* to find its prey. Smell probably played a minor role in hunting, as in living pinnipeds.

Family Desmatophocidae

The desmatophocids were a family of primitive sealions. These carnivores are superficially similar to the seals of the family Phocidae, and they display the same adaptations to the same way of life.

The most obvious difference between the two groups is in the structure of their hind limbs. Sealions, fur seals, and walruses can turn the hind flippers forward to help them move on land—something the true seals cannot do.

NAME *Desmatophoca*

TIME Middle Miocene

LOCALITY Asia (Japan) and North America (California and Oregon)

SIZE 5 ft 6 in/1.7 m long

The typical streamlined shape of the modern sealion had begun to appear with *Desmatophoca*. As in its living relatives, its forelimbs were stronger than the hind limbs, and the feet were modified to form paddles, with the fingers elongated, splayed out, and held together by webs of skin to produce a large surface area for swimming. All the bones in the limbs were shortened to make them stronger.

Although *Desmatophoca* still had a tail, in contrast to the sealions, this was greatly reduced, being only about the length of the animal's skull. Like its ancestor *Enaliarctos*, its eyes were enormous, which suggests that sight was its most important sense for hunting. Its hearing may not have been fully adapted for detecting underwater sounds, but it no doubt served the animal well on land.

Family Odobenidae

The walruses, or odobenids, differ from the sealions and fur seals in that they are adapted to feed on shellfish rather than on fish. Their upper canine teeth are enlarged into a pair of heavy tusks, in both sexes, and used to prise and probe their mollusc prey from the seabed.

By the Early Pliocene, about 5 million years ago, at least five genera of walrus, many of them looking rather like sealions, lived on the North Pacific coast. Some of the early walruses swam across the seaway that separated North America from South America in the Late Miocene, about 8 million years ago. By the Early Pliocene, about 3 million years later, they had moved northward to American and European North Atlantic coastal waters.

Later in the Pliocene, walruses became extinct in the Pacific, where they had originated. The North Atlantic populations flourished in the meantime, and groups eventually made their way back to the North Pacific by way of the Arctic Ocean about 1 million years ago.

The one remaining member of the genus—*Odobenus rosmarus*—inhabits the Arctic seas from East Canada and Greenland to Northern Eurasia and West Alaska. The walrus has long been a valuable source of food for the eskimo populations of the Arctic regions.

NAME *Imagotaria*

TIME Late Miocene

LOCALITY North America (Pacific coast)

SIZE 6 ft/1.8 m long

Imagotaria is classed as a walrus, but it probably looked and behaved like a sealion. It may represent a transitional stage in the evolution of the walruses. The canine teeth, used by sealions to catch fish, had begun to enlarge, but had not yet formed the tusks used by walruses to dig up shellfish. The back teeth had not yet evolved into the broad shell-crushers of modern walruses so it probably ate fish and shellfish.

ORDER DESMOSTYLA

The desmostylians were a group of strange aquatic mammals that have been aptly described as "seahorses." Members of this order were about the size of a pony, and superficially similar in appearance: they lived along the coasts of the North Pacific in Miocene times, between about 25 and 5 million years ago.

The single record of a fossil from coastal Florida suggests that desmostylians found their way from the Pacific into the Atlantic via the narrow seaway that separated North and South America until the Pliocene, about 5 million years ago. However, the origin, relationships and diet of the desmostylians remain a mystery. Paleontologists generally believe that they are associated with the proboscids along with the sirenians.

NAME	*Desmostylus*
TIME	Miocene
LOCALITY	Asia (Japan) and North America (Pacific coast)
SIZE	6 ft/1.8 m long

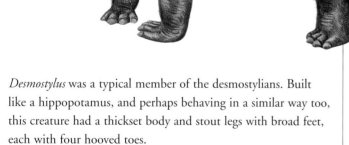

Desmostylus was a typical member of the desmostylians. Built like a hippopotamus, and perhaps behaving in a similar way too, this creature had a thickset body and stout legs with broad feet, each with four hooved toes.

The bones of the lower foreleg were fused into a solid pillar, which meant that the foot could not be turned without turning the whole limb. Underwater, the animal probably poled itself along, in the same manner as a modern hippo "walks" over the riverbed. However, on land, this construction would have meant that *Desmostylus* was quite clumsy.

The front parts of both the upper and lower jaws were elongated and carried an array of forward-pointing tusks, formed by the elongated incisors and canines. The animal's head must have looked similar to that of some of the shovel-tusked elephants that were in existence at the same time (see pp.383–386). *Desmostylus's* unusual back teeth formed clusters of upright cylinders.

Desmostylus must have had an amphibious lifestyle, paddling around in the coastal shallows and using its strong front tusks to prise shellfish from the rocks. It may also have sunk down to the seabed in search of food. Some paleontologists have also suggested that it grazed on the seaweeds that were left exposed between the tides.

ORDER SIRENIA

The sirenians, or sea cows, are the only group of mammals to have become fully adapted, aquatic herbivores. Today, they are represented by three species of manatee (*Trichechus*) and a single species of dugong (*Dugong dugon*). A fifth species in the order, Steller's sea cow, which had adapted to cold temperatures and fed on the kelp beds in the northern Pacific ocean, became extinct as recently as 1768.

All animals in the order are characterised by bulbous bodies, forelimbs modified into flippers, no hind limbs, and a horizontally flattened tail, like that of a whale, which they use to propel themselves through the water at a leisurely pace.

The sirenians are known from the Early Eocene of Hungary. Their evolution is something of a mystery, but many paleontologists believe that they may have developed from a sea cow closely related to the ungulates and descended from an ancestor shared with the elephants. This evolutionary connection between sea cows and elephants has been supported by recent molecular analysis.

Throughout the Eocene, the climate was relatively warm, and vast meadows of seagrasses—the main food of the marine sirenians—grew in the shallow tropical waters of the Mediterranean and Caribbean. However, these seagrass beds retreated in the Oligocene when the climate cooled. The manatees adapted to feed on freshwater plants in the rivers along the coasts of South America. Teeth have to be continually replaced to compensate for the extensive wear which the tough grasses inflict upon them.

NAME *Prorastomus*

TIME Middle Eocene

LOCALITY West Indies (Jamaica)

SIZE possibly 5 ft/1.5 m long

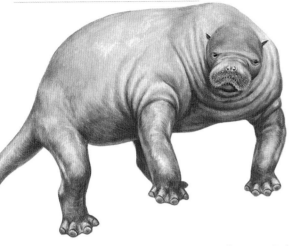

Prorastomus is the most primitive sirenian known. Only its skull and parts of its backbone and ribs have so far been discovered. The restoration is therefore speculative.

Prorastomus's skull indicates that it was not specialized for an aquatic lifestyle. It is quite likely that *Prorastomus* was still essentially a land-dweller. Its thick snout and double-crested cheek teeth suggest that it consumed a diet of soft vegetation.

NAME *Rytiodus*

TIME Miocene

LOCALITY Europe (France)

SIZE 20 ft/6 m long

By the Late Eocene, some 40 million years ago, dugongs were well established and resembled their present-day forms.

Rytiodus was an enormous beast—about twice the size of the single remaining modern marine species. It possessed all the typical sirenian features. Its body was fat and smooth, its hind limbs had disappeared, but it had a powerful tail for swimming, and its forelimbs had developed into flippers. The animal's bones, particularly the ribs, were thick and dense, and acted as ballast, helping to give *Rytiodus* just the right buoyancy for its submerged existence. It grazed on shallow coastal seabeds, and the pair of saber-like tusks in its upper jaw enabled it to root up seagrasses or seaweeds.

NAME *Hydrodamalis gigas*

TIME Pliocene to Recent

LOCALITY Arctic and North Pacific oceans

SIZE 26 ft/8 m long

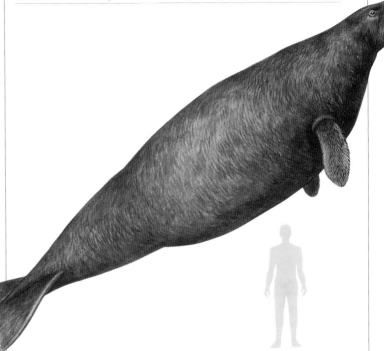

This enormous sirenian, only recently extinct, was known as Steller's sea cow, named after Georg Steller, the German naturalist who discovered it in 1741.

A former member of the dugong family, *Hydrodamalis gigas* evolved toward the end of the Pleistocene, about 200,000 years ago, but it became extinct (due to hunting by man) as recently as 1768. Its large size was probably an adaptation to life in the very cold waters of the creature's northern range. (A large animal retains heat better than a smaller one, which has a greater surface area relative to its size.)

Steller's sea cow had lost the thickened ribs of the other sirenians, and it had developed great layers of blubber, covered by a thick, bark-like skin, to serve as insulation against the cold waters of its habitat. As a result, the animal was probably too buoyant to dive.

Lacking teeth entirely, it fed on floating seaweed—a diet that is unique among mammals.

WHALES, DOLPHINS, AND PORPOISES

ORDER CETACEA

The whales, dolphins, and porpoises, sea creatures of magnificence and intelligence, are members of the only mammal order that have become thoroughly adapted to living their whole lives in the open oceans. The most specialized of all mammals with their sleek, streamlined bodies and fishlike shape, swim with ease, but they are denied any kind of life on land. However, they have retained the basic mammalian features of warm-bloodedness, the ability to suckle their young, and the necessity to breathe air.

There are about 140 known genera of fossil cetacean. The 40 living genera are found throughout the oceans of the world, and there are also freshwater dolphins living in the rivers of South America, India, and China. Many modern species are, however, threatened with extinction.

Cetaceans probably evolved from land-living early ungulates (see pp.378, 398) at the very beginning of the Tertiary, about 65 million years ago. Recent molecular analysis supports this assumption and groups the cetaceans with the even-toed ungulates (artiodactyls such as cattle, deer, and pigs) as the cetartiodactyls. This large group is in turn closely associated with the Carnivora and perissodactyls (horses). In detail the whales now seem to be most closely related to those aquatic ruminants, the hippos.

There are three suborders of whales: the primitive archaeocetes, all now extinct; the modern odontocetes, or "toothed whales," including the great sperm whale and all the dolphins and porpoises; and the modern mysticetes, or "baleen whales." The baleen group includes the largest animal that has ever lived—the mighty blue whale, *Balaenoptera musculus*, which reaches a length of 100 ft/30 m and a weight of some 144 tons/130 tonnes.

SUBORDER ARCHAEOCETI

The archeocetes were the first cetaceans to appear, in the seas of the Early Eocene about 54 million years ago. They evolved from amphibious mammals, and at first were small (never more than 10 ft/3 m long), four-legged, seallike creatures with few specializations for life in water. But by the end of the Eocene, some 15 million years later, they had developed into enormous, serpentlike animals, highly adapted for a marine life.

NAME *Pakicetus*
TIME Early Eocene
LOCALITY Asia (Pakistan)
SIZE 6 ft/1.8 m long

Pakicetus is the earliest-known whale. Although only part of its skull has been found, this has such primitive features that it is safe to assume that the rest of its body had few adaptations to a marine existence.

Pakicetus probably looked quite different from the modern whales. Its teeth were similar to those of the mesonychids, such as *Andrewsarchus* (see p.378), and the cheek teeth had the same triangular arrangement of cusps. This suggests that *Pakicetus* had evolved from flesh-eating terrestrial ungulates only a short time previously.

Its ears were not particularly well-adapted for functioning underwater, so *Pakicetus* probably spent much of its time on land. Discoveries of other land-living animals in the same deposits as this early whale seem to confirm this.

Pakicetus was probably rather seallike in general appearance. Its limbs were probably paddle-shaped, allowing it to move awkwardly on land, but making it completely at home in the rivers and estuaries along the eastern shores of the Tethys Sea. This expanse of water still existed along the southern edge of Asia in Early Tertiary times, about 50 million years ago.

NAME *Protocetus*
TIME Middle Eocene
LOCALITY Arica and Asia (Mediterranean area)
SIZE 8 ft/2.5 m long

Protocetus, which lived only some 8 million years after *Pakicetus*, had become much more whalelike in appearance. Its body was more streamlined, approaching the shape of modern whales. Its forelegs were flat and paddlelike, but the hind legs were greatly reduced, and while they may still have protruded outside the body, they would have been of little use in swimming.

A pair of horizontal lobes, called flukes, had probably developed on *Protocetus'* tail, to judge by the structure of the vertebrae in this area. Their up-and-down motion provided the propulsive force to drive the animal steadily through the sea.

The skull of *Protocetus* had become quite long, with a narrow snout. Its teeth were pointed and arranged in a zigzag pattern at the front of the jaws. These teeth held the prey, while the back teeth cut it up. *Protocetus* and other early whales doubtless hunted for fish in shallow coastal waters.

This whale's nostrils had begun to move back on the head, away from their position in earliest whales at the tip of the snout. *Protocetus* still had a good sense of smell, but vision was probably its most important sense for hunting prey. In contrast to *Pakicetus*, *Protocetus'* ears were adapted for underwater hearing, but it is unlikely that it had yet developed the sophisticated echolocation system used by modern whales.

NAME *Zygorhiza*
TIME Late Eocene
LOCALITY North America (Atlantic coast)
SIZE 20 ft/6 m long

Zygorhiza belonged to a family of early whales that developed extremely elongated, eellike bodies. *Zygorhiza*, however, was more whalelike than most of its relatives. Its body was about six times the length of its skull—the same proportion as in a modern whale. Unlike modern whales, its head was attached to the body by a distinct, short neck, made up of the usual mammalian complement of seven vertebrae.

Its paddle-shaped forelimbs could probably have been moved from the elbow (unlike those of modern whales, which have their forearm bones fused to the upper arm), which would have helped to haul their bodies from the water. Early whales probably still mated and bred on land, like their amphibious ancestors.

NAME *Basilosaurus*
TIME Late Eocene
LOCALITY North America (Atlantic coast)
SIZE up to 82 ft/25 m long

When the remains of this remarkable early whale were first discovered in the 1830s, they were believed to belong to some kind of dinosaur. This creature, which belonged to the same family as *Zygorhiza*, must have looked like a great sea serpent. Indeed, its bones were used in a famous sea serpent hoax about a century ago.

Basilosaurus' snakelike body was supported by a backbone of enormously elongated vertebrae. The ribs were short and confined to the front part of the body. The hip bones were still present, about two-thirds of the way down the animal, and the bones of the hind legs could still articulate with them. However, the limb bones were so small that it is difficult to imagine what use they would have been, or indeed if they showed outside the body at all.

Basilosaurus must have swum in the Eocene oceans by undulating its long body and tail. For the cylindrical body to have worked efficiently as a swimming organ, this whale probably had tail flukes.

The head of *Basilosaurus* was typical of the early whales, although it was small in proportion to the body. The nostrils were high up on the animal's snout, and the teeth were of a variety of shapes and sizes. The front teeth were pointed and conical, while the back teeth were saw-edged. (An obsolete name for this animal is *Zeuglodon*, which means "saw-toothed.") The dentition of this creature indicates that these large early whales must have hunted fish and squid in deep waters, as do the larger species of modern toothed whale, such as the sperm whale.

SUBORDER ODONTOCETI

The odontocetes—the toothed whales—probably evolved from the archeocetes in Late Eocene times, about 40 million years ago. Odontocetes make up the majority of the modern whales, including the sperm, beaked, and pilot whales, orcas, the belugas and narwhals, the dolphins and porpoises. All these modern species had appeared by Late Miocene times, some 10 million years ago.

The teeth of odontocetes tended to be simpler than those of the archeocetes, losing their cusps and becoming rounded pegs or cones. Some odontocetes had several hundred teeth in their jaws, while others were almost toothless.

NAME *Prosqualodon*

TIME Oligocene to Early Miocene

LOCALITY Australia, New Zealand, and South America

SIZE 7 ft 5 in/2.3 m long

Prosqualodon and its immediate family may have been ancestral to all the other toothed whales. It probably looked like a small modern dolphin, with a long, narrow snout armed with pointed, fish-catching teeth. But the teeth were primitive, since there were still triangular teeth at the back of the jaws, as there had been in the earlier whales, the archeocetes.

Prosqualodon's skull had become lightweight as a result of several modifications to the animal's front end. First, the neck had become very short, and the back of the head blended in with the body and needed less support and protection. Second, the complex jaw structure of earlier whales had been greatly simplified, due to the purely fish diet. And third, since the sense of smell was no longer the primary sense used in locating prey (sound having taken over), the complex olfactory apparatus was reduced.

In *Prosqualodon*, the nostrils were positioned on the roof of the head, between the eye sockets, where they formed a blowhole (as found in modern whales). The spent air that had accumulated during a dive was expelled explosively through the blowhole when the animal surfaced.

NAME *Eurhinodelphis*

TIME Middle to Late Miocene

LOCALITY Asia and North America (Pacific coasts)

SIZE 6 ft 6 in/2 m long

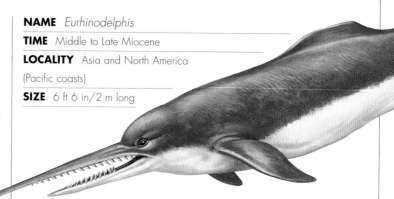

The odontocetes diverged into a number of groups during the Oligocene Epoch, about 30 million years ago. *Eurhinodelphis* was a typical member of the rhabdosteid family of long-snouted porpoises. The structure of its ears had become much more complex than in earlier odontocetes, so it is likely that this whale had developed the complex echolocation system seen in modern toothed whales.

Living whales rely on a form of ultrasonic sonar to help them track down and catch their prey and to find their way around underwater—they emit high-frequency clicking sounds that travel through the water and bounce off objects, and the echoes are analyzed by the animals' large brains to determine—with astonishing accuracy—the size, shape, distance, and speed of the object and, of course, its edibility.

Like that of a modern dolphin, the skull of *Eurhinodelphis* had become somewhat asymmetrical, with structures on one side different from those on the other. This arrangement might have been associated with the development of new abilities to cope with the demands of the creature's lifestyle, such as chasing fast-moving prey and navigating with increasing accuracy.

The most distinctive feature of *Eurhinodelphis*, however, was its elongated snout. The snout was toothless at the tip and may have been used in a way similar to the "sword" of the modern swordfish, to strike at and stun its prey, which was then seized in the animal's jaws.

SUBORDER MYSTICETI

The mysticetes, or baleen whales, are first known from marine rocks in New Zealand dating from Early Oligocene times, some 35 million years ago.

The fossils of their early forms occur along with rich deposits of plankton, the tiny creatures on which these huge creatures feed. The evolution of the baleen whales may have been triggered by the overall cooling of the southern oceans during the Early Oligocene, which encouraged the growth of the microscopic plants in the plankton and, in turn, the tiny, free-floating animals that feed on them. This rich food source is especially prolific in the southern oceans, where it is called krill. Despite the huge volume of water taken in and strained from each mouthful, these animals cannot swallow any large objects because the gullet is never any more than 22.5 cm/9 in wide, even in the largest of the baleen whales.

Baleen whales have evolved a unique method of feeding on the tiny, shrimplike animals in the plankton or tiny crustaceans in the bottom sediments. They have no teeth in their jaws. Instead, the jaws have become greatly modified to support great plates of a fibrous, horny substance, known as whalebone or baleen. The baleen plates hang from their upper jaws on each side and form a huge natural strainer through which the whale is able to strain the ocean's waters or bottom sediments in order to catch the the abundant planktonic organisms and crustaceans living there

Only eight genera survive today, and most species are under severe threat from hunting by man. The gray whale is the sole remaining species in the eschrichteriid family, while there are three species in the right whale family (the Balaenidae) and six species in the rorqual family (the Balaenopteridae). The right whales show the most extreme development of the baleen apparatus for filter feeding, and the plates may be more than 4.5 m/15 ft long. However, the diverse rorquals, which have 300 or so baleen plates on each side of the jaws, include the magnificent giant blue whale. Some 30 m/100 ft in length and 144 tons/146 tonnes in weight, it is the largest mammal that ever existed. In the feeding season these ocean grazers consume up to 4 tons/4 tonnes of planktonic crustaceans each day from the nutrient rich waters of the polar oceans.

The radiation of the living families dates from Miocene times, but their fossils are exceedingly rare until the Late Miocene, when the cetotheriids began to decrease in numbers. So it would appear that the living mysticetes replaced the cetotheriids.

NAME	*Cetotherium*
TIME	Middle to Late Miocene
LOCALITY	Europe (Belgium and former USSR)
SIZE	13 ft/4 m long

Cetotherium belonged to a family of early baleen whales that evolved in the Late Oligocene and reached their peak during the Miocene, some 15 million years ago. *Cetotherium* looked strikingly similar to the modern gray whale of the North Pacific, although it was less than a third of the gray whale's length. Its baleen plates were probably quite short, although this is difficult to determine, because baleen, like horn and hair, does not fossilize. The fossilized skulls retain the marks of blood vessels which would have kept the baleen supplied with blood during the creature's life, and much can be hypothesized from their traces.

Cetotherium and its relatives were probably preyed upon by a species of great white shark *Carcharodon* which, judging by the size of the teeth that are often found fossilized, reached a size approaching that of a small whale.

EARLY ROOTERS AND BROWSERS

Most ungulates ("hoofed animals") are large plant-eaters which root and browse among vegetation or crop grass. Early rooters and browsers were a diverse group of ungulates, most of which ate leaves, shoots, and roots, though some evolved into scavengers. Specialized grazers, such as horses, cattle, and deer evolved from these early ungulates. They rose to dominance during the Miocene, moving from the forest to exploit the feeding opportunities in the developing grasslands.

Some early ungulates were once regarded as members of the primitive order of carnivorous mammals, the creodonts. This confusion indicates the generalized nature of the mammals at the end of the Cenozoic Era.

ORDER ARCTOCYONIA

The members of this abundant and varied group were mostly small mammals, little bigger than today's domestic dogs. They had long, low skulls, and a complete set of rather uniform teeth (evolved for crushing rather than biting).

Family Arctocyonidae

This is the earliest and most primitive family of the order, and may be close to the ancestors of the later hoofed animals. Arctocyonids were mostly short-limbed, rather clumsily-built animals, up to the size of small bears.

NAME	*Chriacus*
TIME	Early Paleocene to Early Eocene
LOCALITY	North America (Wyoming)
SIZE	3 ft/1 m long

This agile climbing animal may have scampered through the tropical forests of Early Tertiary North America, eating insects, small animals, and fruit. It had powerful limbs, versatile joints, a semi-prehensile tail, and plantigrade feet (the full foot was placed on the ground) with long claws. The forelimbs may have been used for digging, but the hind limbs were those of a climbing animal.

ORDER ACREODI

When plant-eating mammals (excluding multituberculates) first flourished at the start of the Paleocene, no carnivores preyed on them. By the mid-Paleocene, however, over 60 million years ago, some primitive and generalized stock had developed into a new order, the Acreodi. This group of ungulates ranged from wolf-sized, up to 5–6 m long, far larger than any living terrestrial carnivore and matched in size only by the dinosaurs. Their closest affinities seem to be with the arctyocyonids and whales.

Family Mesonychidae

Among the Acreodi were mesonychids: wolf-like, hyena-like, or bear-like omnivores able to take advantage of this new source of food. They ranged from the size of foxes to the immense *Andrewsarchus*. Mesonychids flourished until the Early Oligocene, some 35 million years ago, by which time the creodonts and then the true carnivores had become the dominant flesh-eaters.

Similarities in the arrangement of bones in the base of the skull and in the teeth suggest that, despite their radically different habitats and lifestyles, the mesonychids may have given rise to the whales and dolphins (see pp.374–377).

NAME	*Andrewsarchus*
TIME	Late Eocene
LOCALITY	Asia (Mongolia)
SIZE	13 ft/4 m long

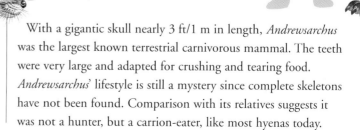

With a gigantic skull nearly 3 ft/1 m in length, *Andrewsarchus* was the largest known terrestrial carnivorous mammal. The teeth were very large and adapted for crushing and tearing food. *Andrewsarchus'* lifestyle is still a mystery since complete skeletons have not been found. Comparison with its relatives suggests it was not a hunter, but a carrion-eater, like most hyenas today.

ORDER PANTODONTA

This diverse group of extinct Early Tertiary browsers thrived in Paleocene and Eocene times, from 60 million to 40 million years ago. In Asia, a few pantodonts survived until the Early Oligocene, some 35 million years ago. This order is divided into some ten families, which were widely dispersed throughout Asia and North America. They diversified to fill many of the available plant-eating niches. Their origins and relationships are not clear.

Family Coryphodontidae

Though some members of this family were as small as rats, they were mostly bulky animals, some as large as rhinoceroses. The coryphodontid family led a semi-aquatic lifestyle, feeding by rooting up tubers, roots, and other vegetation.

NAME *Coryphodon*

TIME Late Paleocene to Middle Eocene

LOCALITY Widespread in North America, Europe, and eastern Asia

SIZE 7 ft 6 in/2.25 m long

Coryphodon was a large animal with canine tusks rather like those of a hippopotamus. These were especially well developed in the male. Like a hippopotamus, too, *Coryphodon* probably lived in swamps and marshes, where it may have uprooted plants with its tusks. The two prominent cross crests on its molar teeth suggest that *Coryphodon* browsed on jungle vegetation.

The upper section of the leg was longer than the lower, which would have provided the strength needed to support a massive body but could not have been suited to fast running.

Coryphodon's brain was very small and, at 3¼ oz/90 g per 1,100 lb/500 kg, probably represented the smallest ratio of brain to body weight in any mammal.

ORDER DINOCERATA

The largest mammals of the Early Tertiary were the dinocerates (meaning "terrifying horns"), also known as uintatheres. The name refers to the three pairs of bony protuberances on the skulls of these animals. Males in particular were armed with a pair of long, saber-like upper canine teeth.

Dinocerates were large, rhinoceros-like mammals from the late Paleocene and Eocene of North America and Asia, about 55 million years ago. Their evolution is something of a mystery.

Family Uintatheriidae

Except for one Mongolian genus, which had no skull protuberances or saber-like canines, all members of the order Dinocerata are included in this family.

The uintatheres were the largest land mammals of their time, with massive bones, heavy limbs, and broad, spreading feet. But their brains were very small—no larger in relation to body size than the brains of many of the dinosaurs. Uintatheres died out in the Oligocene, about 35 million years ago, and were replaced in their ecological niche as massive herbivores by the brontotheres (see pp.402–403).

NAME *Eobasileus*

TIME Late Eocene

LOCALITY North America (Wyoming)

SIZE 10 ft/3 m long; 5 ft/1.5 m high at the shoulder

Eobasileus looked rather like a rhinoceros with a pair of saber-like canine tusks in its upper jaw and six bony protuberances on its head. These blunt "horns" were probably covered with skin. It is likely that only the front pair on top of the nose were sheathed in "horns" of matted hair, as in rhinoceroses (see pp.406–409).

Incisor teeth were very small in the lower jaw, and missing entirely from the upper, which suggests that the tongue and tusks were the most important food-gathering organs.

EARLY ROOTERS AND BROWSERS CONTINUED

ORDER TILLODONTIA

The tillodonts were a small group of herbivores, about the size of modern bears, which have now become extinct.

The tillodonts may have been related to the pantodonts or to arctocyonids, but their origins and relationships to the other early mammals, and even their lifestyles, are still uncertain. However, paleontologists do know from fossil finds that they were once widespread across Paleocene and Eocene North America, eastern Asia, and Europe.

Family Esthonychidae

The large, bear-sized esthonychids are believed to have been the sole family within the order Tillodontia. They were one of a number of families of herbivorous mammals which evolved and radiated rapidly in early Tertiary times. Within the brief span of the Paleocene to Eocene (30 million years) they spread throughout the warm interior continental basins of North America and Eurasia only to die out and be replaced by another mammalian radiation.

NAME *Trogosus*

TIME	Early to Middle Eocene
LOCALITY	North America (Wyoming)
SIZE	4 ft/1.2 m long

From a distance, the squat body, short head and the flat feet of this large animal would have given it the appearance of a modern bear. However, as soon as *Trogosus* opened its mouth, its huge chisel-like incisors would have made it appear more like a gigantic rat or rabbit. As among rodents, the incisors were adapted for gnawing: the front surfaces were coated with enamel and grew continuously throughout the animal's life. The grinding teeth to the rear of the jaw were constantly being worn away, which suggests that *Trogosus* ate abrasive plant material, perhaps roots and tubers clawed out of the ground.

ORDER TAENIODONTA

These were another small group of Early Tertiary herbivores, now extinct, which were rat- to bear-sized and have been found only in North America. As with the tillodonts, the origins and relationships of the order Teaniodonta with other mammals remains obscure.

The Taeniodonta order evolved quickly—in fact, faster than any other mammal group is ever known to have developed—during Paleocene times, and became quite specialized as digging animals.

Family Stylinodontidae

Stylinodontids form the only family within the order Taeniodonta. Like the esthonychids, they were one of a number of rapidly evolving ammmal families in early Tertiary (Paleocene–Eocene) times within North America.

NAME *Stylinodon*

TIME	Early to Late Eocene
LOCALITY	North America (Wyoming, Colorado, and Utah)
SIZE	4 ft 3 in/1.3 m long

With its short powerful digging forelimbs and strong claws, *Stylinodon* was probably bear-sized, with a body like an aardvark and a pig-like face.

The fossil remains uncovered have given a detailed picture of the dentition of this animal. *Stylinodon* had no incisor teeth in its massive jaws, but the canine teeth had become greatly developed into huge, rootless, gnawing chisels. The peg-like cheek teeth were equipped with enamel on their surfaces which was arranged in a narrow band (the word taeniodont means "banded teeth"). The cheek teeth grew continuously throughout the animal's life, which suggests that *Stylinodon* had a diet of abrasive roots and tubers.

ORDER HYRACOIDEA

This order of herbivorous mammals was very diverse and abundant during the Early Oligocene Period, about 35 million years ago, having radiated from its origins in the Eocene into many ecological niches.

Some hyracoids looked similar to tapirs, some were similar to horses, while others resembled rabbits, as do modern hyraxes. Some grew as large as pigs, but most were smaller. The hyracoids seem to have declined as grazing animals expanded, and they are represented today by only seven species living in Africa and some parts of the Middle East. The most notable of these species is the rock hyrax.

The availability of living representatives of this group has allowed molecular analysis, which has shown that they are most closely related to the proboscids (elephants) and the sirenids (sea-cows).

Family Pliohyracidae

All the extinct forms of early Tertiary hyraxes are placed in this family. The later fossil hyraxes and all the living representatives of the order are placed in the family Procaviidae.

NAME	*Kvabebihyrax*
TIME	Late Pliocene
LOCALITY	Europe (Caucasus)
SIZE	5 ft 3 in/1.6 m long

The great difference between the fossil types of hyrax and the modern animals can be seen in *Kvabebihyrax*. With its stout body and small eyes set high upon the skull, *Kvabebihyrax* must have looked more like a small hippopotamus than a hyrax. The snout was short, and a pair of very large incisor teeth projected downwards. The two pairs of lower incisors were flattened and horizontal, the upper pair of incisors fitting between their points when the animal's jaw was closed.

ORDER EMBRITHOPODA

The extinct embrithopods are an Early to Mid Tertiary group of herbivores which were widely distributed throughout Asia, eastern Europe, and into North Africa. They do not easily fit anywhere into the evolutionary scheme and have no obvious ancestors or descendents, though the structure of their simple, small brains shows possible affinities with those of the elephants or sea-cows.

Family Arsinoitheres

The rhinoceros-like Arsinoitheres are the sole family in the order Embrithopoda.

NAME	*Arsinoitherium*
TIME	Early Oligocene
LOCALITY	Africa (Egypt)
SIZE	11 ft 6 in/3.5 m long; 6 ft/1.8 m high at the shoulder

Arsinoitherium's most memorable features were the two massive cone-shaped projections, fused at their bases, which covered the area from the nostrils to midway up its skull. In spite of its appearance, *Arsinoitherium* was only superficially like a rhinoceros. Its "horns" were in fact hollow, and traces of blood vessels on their surface suggest that they were covered in skin, at least when the animal was young. There were two smaller knob-like projections higher on the head that must have looked like a giraffe's skin-covered ossicones.

With its complete set of 44 unspecialized teeth forming a continuous series from incisors to last molars, *Arsinoitherium* was obviously a plant-eater, and probably browsed in the riverside forests. However, the high cross crowns of its cheek teeth suggest it may also have been able to chew tougher vegetation. From an ecological point of view, *Arsinoitherium* may well have been the African equivalent of the North American uintatheres (see p.379) and brontotheres (see pp.402–403).

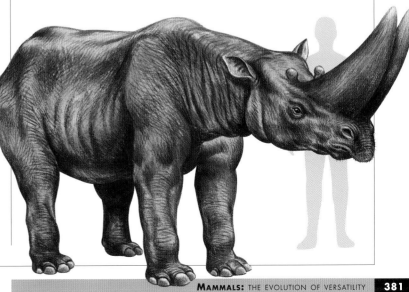

EARLY ELEPHANTS AND MASTODONTS

ORDER PROBOSCIDEA

The African and Indian elephants are the only two surviving species of a once diverse and widespread group called the proboscids. They are characterised particularly by developments of their teeth and adaptations of their limbs for supporting their increasing mass.

Recent analysis of elephant DNA has led to some significant changes in ideas about the affinities and relationships of the proboscids. Initially, the molecular data seemed to support the traditional grouping with the ungulates, but this has changed. Now the proboscids are grouped in a separate clade with just the sea-cows (sirenids) and hyraxes (hyracoids). It is thought that they evolved from a basal stock of primitive hoofed animals that also gave rise to the modern hyraxes (see p.381) and the aquatic sirenians (the dugongs and manatees; see pp.372–373).

From their origins in northern Africa in the Eocene as pig-sized creatures, like *Moeritherium,* without tusks or trunks, proboscids had evolved by Pliocene times, 50 million years later, into giants that had spread over all continents with the exceptions of Australia and Antarctica.

Their evolution involved a progressive increase in the size of the animals, the development of long pillar-like legs to support the immense weight. Associated with this is the development of flattened soles to spread the animal's weight evenly across the ground. This is so successful that a modern elephant will leave almost no footprint when it walks over firm ground, despite its great weight. In addition there was an extension of a proboscis or trunk, accompanied by the massive enlargement of the head, and a shortening of the neck. There was also a reduction of the teeth to a few grinding molars. The second upper incisors, which became the specialized tusks in later forms, are enlarged. The lower canines and first premolars are absent whilst the molars progressively develop as broad teeth with thickened cusps and ridges for chewing and breaking down coarse vegetation. The trunk and tusks were originally adaptations that enabled a tall, short-necked animal to reach food on the ground or in the trees, but they also function in display and courtship.

By Pleistocene times, about 2 million years ago, mammoths and mastodonts flourished over the northern continents, only to suffer mass extinction with the advance of the ice age. In Siberia, some mammoths have been discovered frozen in ice, with their flesh and fur perfectly preserved. The Elephantidae, the only family to survive, had already undergone rapid evolution in warmer climates to the south. Four families are known.

Family Moeritheridae

The name "moerithere" is derived from the word Moeris—an ancient Greek name for the lake in Egypt's Fayum province where its remains were found. The moeritheriids are one of a number of short-lived families of proboscideans which reflect the initial divergence of the group in Mid Tertiary times.

NAME	*Moeritherium*
TIME	Late Eocene to Early Oligocene
LOCALITY	Africa (Egypt, Mali, and Senegal)
SIZE	2 ft/60 cm high

This pig-sized, low-slung animal resembled a tapir or a pygmy hippopotamus more than an elephant. The external nostrils were at the front of the skull, which implies that it did not even possess a trunk, though it may have had a broad thick upper lip that helped it to root about among swamp vegetation. *Moeritherium* would have weighed about 450 lb/200 kg. It was probably partly aquatic in its habits, like the modern hippopotamus. As with the hippopotamus, its eyes and ears were high up on the skull so that it could keep watch at the water's surface while wallowing in the swamps.

But *Moeritherium* also displays several features that clearly indicate the development of an elephant-like lifestyle. Its skull was long and low, with a large area at the back for the attachment of strong neck muscles, and the lower jaw was deep. The teeth were primitive—small and almost complete—yet there were no lower canines. Even at this early stage in the evolution of elephants, two of the incisors were already tusk-like.

Although it showed many primitive features, *Moeritherium* itself was probably not the ancestor of the rest of the proboscideans. It was a long-lived genus, surviving into Oligocene times when several more advanced elephants were also around.

Family Deinotheriidae

Deinotheres were very large elephants with down-curving tusks in the lower jaw. They probably evolved in the Early Miocene in Africa but they soon spread into central and southern Europe and southern Asia.

The Deinotheres thrived almost unchanged throughout the Pliocene but then retreated back to Africa. They vanished altogether about 2 million years ago.

NAME *Deinotherium*

TIME Miocene to Pleistocene

LOCALITY Europe (Germany and Bohemia), Asia (India), and Africa (Kenya)

SIZE 13 ft/4 m high

The most remarkable feature of this elephant was its tusks, the purpose of which is still a matter of debate amongst paleontologists.

Deinotherium had no tusks in the upper jaw, but the lower jaw was curved downward at a right angle and gave rise to two huge curved tusks. Such a structure and shape seemed so unlikely that when scientists in the 1820s attempted the first reconstructions of a *Deinotherium* skeleton, they attached the animal's jaw upside down. The animal may have used its bizarre tusks for foraging for food—stripping the bark from trees or digging up tubers.

Surviving almost unchanged for 20 million years, *Deinotherium* was clearly a very successful animal.

Family Gomphotheriidae

The gomphotheres are one of three families in the suborder Elephantoidea. One is the Elephantidae, the family that contains the mammoths and true elephants. The other two families are browsing mastodonts: the gomphotheres themselves, and the more advanced mammutids. Elephantoids evolved rapidly during the Early Miocene. Several divergent and distinctive groups occurred, but all died out in the Pliocene and Pleistocene. The mastodonts appeared in the Early Oligocene about 35 million years ago. The early forms had quite long upper and lower jaws. Advanced forms had either a shortened upper jaw and an extreme elongation of the lower jaw into "shovel tusks," or a reduced lower jaw resembling that of modern elephants.

Gomphotheres were the dominant large mammals of the Miocene. They had spread from Africa into southern Europe and the Indian subcontinent by the Early Miocene, reaching North America by the Mid Miocene, and South America just before their extinction in the Pleistocene about 2 million years ago. Elephants gradually replaced them from about 5 million years ago.

NAME *Phiomia*

TIME Early Oligocene

LOCALITY Africa (Egypt)

SIZE 8 ft/2.5 m high

Phiomia evolved alongside its smaller, distant relative *Moeritherium. Phiomia* probably browsed in forests of the Fayum area, while *Moeritherium* wallowed in the swamps.

The upper and lower jaws were long, the flattened tusks of the lower jaw forming a spoon-shaped extension used for gathering food. The upper lip was probably extended to form a primitive trunk which worked in conjunction with this strange lower jaw apparatus. Shorter tusks in the upper jaw may have been used as defensive weapons.

EARLY ELEPHANTS AND MASTODONTS CONTINUED

NAME *Gomphotherium*

TIME Early Miocene to Early Pliocene

LOCALITY Europe (France), Africa (Kenya), Asia (Pakistan), and North America (Nebraska)

SIZE 10 ft/3 m high

This four-tusked mastodont was wide-ranging, its fossilized remains have been discovered on four continents—Europe, Africa, Asia, and North America. As a result of its occurrence in many places the same fossil animal has been given a variety of names by the people who unearthed it, including *Trilophodon* and *Tetrabelodon*.

The lower jaw of *Gomphotherium* with its parallel tusks, was greatly extended. The jaw was probably used in conjunction with an equally long trunk on the upper jaw for tearing and grasping leaves and other plant material.

Most members of the genus *Gomphotherium* ate the leaves from bushes, but one species was a swamp dweller and consumed soft water-plants.

As *Gomphotherium* evolved there was a progressive reduction in the number of teeth in the jaw, but those that remained developed a number of high ridges or cusps which served to increase the grinding area available in the animal's mouth.

This adaptation of the dentition was a necessary development to enable the teeth to cope with the large quantities of plant food that would have been required in order to maintain *Gomphotherium*'s immense bulk.

NAME *Platybelodon*

TIME Late Miocene

RANGE Europe (Caucasus Mountains), Asia (Mongolia), and Africa (Kenya)

SIZE 10 ft/3 m high

Platybelodon was another shovel-tusked browsing mastodont, similar to *Amebelodon*, which lived in Europe and Asia. The shovel arrangement of its tusks was shorter and broader than that of *Amebelodon*, and was indented at each side in order to make room for the tusks of the upper jaw.

Platybelodon evidently enjoyed much the same lifestyle as *Amebelodon*, wading through shallow rivers and dredging water weeds.

The fact that related types of proboscidean inhabited the continents of Eurasia and North America at this time suggests there was probably a migration route between the two landmasses—across a land bridge where the Bering Straits now lie.

The shovel-tuskers show an extreme specialization for a particular style of feeding. This means that, along with other highly specialized creatures, they were extremely vulnerable to environmental change because they were unable to adapt readily. As a consequence they were not a very long-lived group.

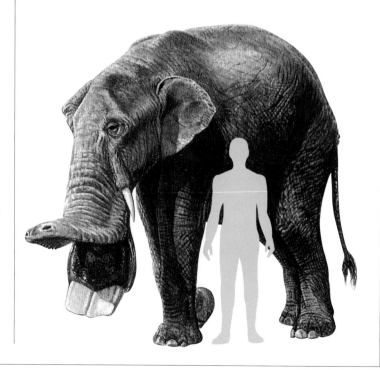

of the elongated lower jaw lay side by side, forming a shovel or trough which projected more than 3 ft/1 m to a spade-like cutting edge.

The water plants on which *Amebelodon* fed would have been gripped between the flattened trunk and tusks and ripped from the mud of the river bottom, then pulled up the trough to the mouth by the trunk.

NAME *Cuvieronius*

TIME Pliocene to Recent

LOCALITY North America (Arizona, Florida) and South America (Argentina)

SIZE 9 ft/2.7m high

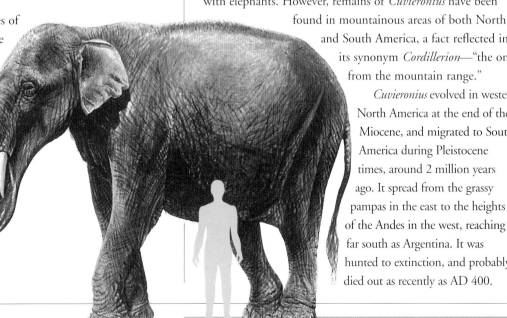

Cuvieronius was named for the great French paleontologist and founder of comparative anatomy, Baron George Cuvier (1769–1832). A fairly small gomphothere, *Cuvieronius'* most remarkable feature was its tusks, which were spirally twisted like those of a narwhal.

We do not usually associate the South American continent with elephants. However, remains of *Cuvieronius* have been found in mountainous areas of both North and South America, a fact reflected in its synonym *Cordillerion*—"the one from the mountain range."

Cuvieronius evolved in western North America at the end of the Miocene, and migrated to South America during Pleistocene times, around 2 million years ago. It spread from the grassy pampas in the east to the heights of the Andes in the west, reaching as far south as Argentina. It was hunted to extinction, and probably died out as recently as AD 400.

NAME *Anancus*

TIME Late Miocene to Early Pleistocene

LOCALITY Widespread in Europe and Asia

SIZE 10 ft/3 m high

With its short lower jaw and long, prehensile trunk, *Anancus* looked like a modern elephant; but it had shorter legs, and an extremely long pair of tusks which, at 10–13 ft/ 3–4 m, were almost as long as the rest of the animal.

Anancus seems to have adapted to woodland life. It could browse from high branches and root about among the leaf litter of the forest floor. It became extinct when grasslands replaced the woodlands.

NAME *Amebelodon*

TIME Late Miocene

RANGE North America (Colorado, Nebraska)

SIZE 10 ft/3 m high

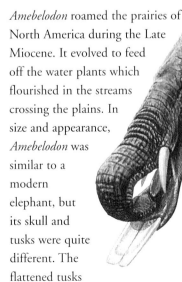

Amebelodon roamed the prairies of North America during the Late Miocene. It evolved to feed off the water plants which flourished in the streams crossing the plains. In size and appearance, *Amebelodon* was similar to a modern elephant, but its skull and tusks were quite different. The flattened tusks

MASTODONTS, MAMMOTHS, AND MODERN ELEPHANTS

NAME *Stegomastodon*

TIME Late Pliocene to Pleistocene

LOCALITY North America (Nebraska) and South America (Venezuela)

SIZE 9 ft/2.7 m high

Stegomastodon is another gomphotheriid but this creature must have looked like a shorter, stockier version of a modern elephant. It had a short lower jaw, no lower tusks, and the upper tasks curved upward.

Stegomastodon's cheek teeth were even more elaborate than those of its forebears. With their convoluted pattern of enamel, which provided a wide abrasive surface and an efficient grinding action, it is possible that these adapted teeth enabled *Stegomastodon* to eat grass.

Stegomastodon was one of the few proboscideans that reached South America, having migrated there around 3 million years ago once the Central American land bridge had become established. This land bridge was formed and broken again several times during Pleistocene times before it reached its present proportions. Each time the continuous chain of volcanoes and fold mountains appeared above the ocean, the way was opened for a new influx of migrating animals.

Stegomastodon became extinct in North America about 1 million years ago, but survived in Venezuela in association with early humans.

Family Mammutidae

Despite their names, these were not mammoths but mastodonts. Their cheek teeth are characterized by having a simple pattern of low, flattish-sided cusps arranged to form transverse ridges with open valleys between. This contrasts with gomphotherid teeth, which have much more complex cusps in transverse rows, and many smaller cusps filling the valleys between.

NAME *Mammut americanum*

TIME Late Miocene to Late Pleistocene

LOCALITY North America (Alaska, New York, Missouri)

SIZE 10 ft/3 m high

The American mastodont, *Mammut americanum*, was one of the most common of the North American proboscideans. Like the woolly mammoth, it was a cold-climate animal, covered with a coat of long shaggy hair. Some of the hairy skin is sometimes found with the skeletons. Its remains have been found as far north as Alaska, and south to Florida.

The head was quite long and held low, with a pair of massive upward-curving tusks. It browsed in herds in spruce woodlands, and may have been a contemporary of modern humans. Like the woolly mammoth, *Mammut* became extinct less than 10,000 years ago. Other mastodonts are known from Africa, Europe, and Asia, but these were not covered in hair.

Family Elephantidae

This is the family to which the modern elephants belong. They differ from their earlier relatives, the mastodonts, principally in the form of their teeth. True elephants have lost the tusks of the lower jaw, and this has enabled them to modify their method of mastication. Mastodonts ground up their food using a complex rotary motion, whereas elephants cut or shear it.

The change of chewing action has also affected the teeth, which are taller, with longer, more complex enamelled surfaces. In many species, there is only one grinding tooth at a time in each side, top and bottom.

Each of these four teeth has a series of up to 20 transverse loops of wrinkled enamel, infilled with softer dentine and separated from each other by thin bands of cement. The whole grinding surface thus forms a large, nearly flat area like the rasping surface of a file. The slight differences in hardness of the mineral phosphate between the enamel, dentine and cement result in variable rates of wear. Consequently the ridged and furrowed surface profile and its effectiveness in preparing plant material for digestion was maintained.

The mineral phosphate resists wear from grinding up the tough plant material which makes up the elephant's diet—hard and abrasive siliceous grasses, tree bark and tough twigs. Despite the structure, the teeth do get worn down by the wear of the animal's diet and need to be constantly replaced. Another tooth appears only when the earlier teeth have worn down.

The elephant's tusks are used for digging up roots while feeding or prising bark off trees, but they are also a weapon and in the males are used to display strength and size. The tusk themselves are greatly extended upper incisors and are made of a combination of dentine, cartilaginous material, and calcium.

Several members of the elephantid family survived the end of the Ice Age but became extinct shortly afterwards, some possibly as the result of being hunted by early human populations. These extinct elephant species include the Eurasian woodland elephant, *Elephas antiquus*; the dwarf forms, such as *E. falconeri*, which lived on the Mediterranean islands; and two mammoths, *Mammuthus primigenius* and *M. jeffersoni*. Populations of mammoths also became stranded on islands off the shore of southern California and the arctic coast of Siberia. This isolation and the intense competition for dwindling resources resulted in a general reduction in the size of individuals. Their cousin, the American mastodont *Mammut americanum*, joined them in extinction at this time.

Only two species of elephants survive today. The smaller Indian elephants inhabit forests in the Indian subcontinent, Indochina, Malaysia, Indonesia, and southern China. There are believed to be fewer than 50,000 remaining wild Indian elephants. The larger African elephant inhabits the grassland and forests of the African continent south of the Sahara. This species is the largest living land animal.

NAME	*Elephas antiquus*
TIME	Middle to Late Pleistocene
LOCALITY	Europe
SIZE	12 ft/3.7 m high

Elephas antiquus was a very large, long-legged and straight-tusked elephant. The tusks were long and straight, and slightly curved at the tip.

The bones of *Elephas antiquus* are relatively common in European Pleistocene deposits. During the Pleistocene Ice Age, the ice sheet advanced then retreated over large areas of the Northern Hemisphere. During the glacial retreats—periods of time known as the interglacials—the climate became much warmer. These interglacials tended to be warmer even than present-day climates, and subtropical conditions prevailed in places as far north as England. *Elephas antiquus* was one of the warm climate animals that frequented the lush woodlands that existed in these places at that time. The abundance of vegetation supported large populations of mammalian megaherbivores. The elephantids were accompanied by rhinoceroses, hippos, deer, horses, and bison. The top carnivores, the big cats that preyed upon the herbivores, were also present. The scene would probably have resembled that of a modern African game park. As each interglacial came to an end and the ice sheets advanced southward, *E. antiquus* moved southward as well. Its place in the northern lands was taken by the elephant group that was well adapted to cold conditions—the mammoths.

NAME *Elephas falconeri*

TIME Late Pleistocene

LOCALITY Mediterranean islands (Cyprus, Crete, Malta, Sicily, southern Calabria, and some of the smaller Greek islands)

SIZE 3 ft/90 cm high

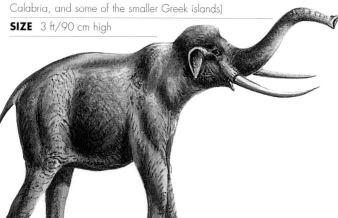

NAME *Mammuthus meridionalis*

TIME Early Pleistocene

LOCALITY Europe (Spain)

SIZE Up to 15 ft/4.5 m high

The genus *Elephas* includes the modern Indian elephant, *E. maximus*. The earliest members of the genus arose in Africa early in Pliocene times, about 5 million years ago, and radiated out into Europe and Asia. There are a number of interesting extinct dwarf elephants which may be separate species but were possibly varieties of their parent stock.

Elephas falconeri stood less than 3 ft/1 m in height and lived on the Mediterranean islands. Its ancestors, probably the European elephant *E. namadicus*, migrated out of Africa in the Early Pleistocene and spread west into central Europe and east to India and China, and even reached Japan.

During the lower sea levels of the glacial periods, this elephant was able to reach Malta, Cyprus, Crete, and Sardinia. With the rise of sea level as the glaciers melted in the interglacial periods, these areas became isolated as islands in the Mediterranean sea. In this isolation arose the dwarf form *E. falconeri*. Similar dwarf elephants arose on the Celebes Islands in Southeast Asia.

On islands such as these, natural selection would favor animals that made best use of smaller quantities of food, and dwarf varieties and species would evolve. A modern equivalent is the small Shetland ponies that have developed on the northern Scottish islands. There is a possible dinosaurian example, also, in the dwarf ankylosaur *Struthiosaurus* (p.303). The experience of very small animals such as rodents, however, is the exact opposite: rodents on the Mediterranean islands were often larger than elsewhere. In the absence of natural predators, there was little need to maintain a small and slender structure that could swiftly take refuge in holes and crevices.

The mammoths were a wide-ranging group of herbivorous animals that developed adaptations to a cold climate, and which radiated from Africa to Eurasia and North America during the Early Pleistocene Period.

Mammuthus meridionalis was one of the first of the cold-adapted mammoths, evolving in the open woodlands of southern Europe, where the climates were cool, but not severe, around 2 million years ago.

The ancestors of this creature probably came from farther east, or from Africa.

Mammuthus meridionalis resembled the modern Indian elephant in general appearance, but it possessed much larger, more impressive tusks. It may have been the ancestor of a number of more specialized mammoths which developed later, including the European *M. primigenius* and the North American *M. imperator*.

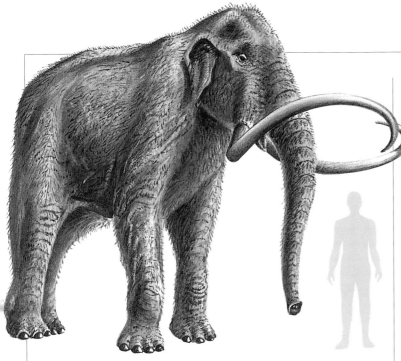

NAME *Mammuthus columbi*

TIME Late Pleistocene

LOCALITY North America (Carolina, Georgia, Louisiana, Florida)

SIZE 12 ft/3.7 m high

Mammuthus columbi was one of the American mammoths which migrated from Asia to North America, late in the Pleistocene, during a mild period, when it was possible to walk dryshod across the Bering Straits. *Mammuthus columbi* inhabited the warm grasslands in the south-eastern part of the continent and may even have moved as far south as Mexico.

Mammuthus columbi had twisted tusks, which perhaps distinguish it from the other American mammoth *M. imperator*, whose long tusks curled backward evenly. This latter species or subspecies had a more westerly range and its remains have been found in the tar deposits of Rancho La Brea, Los Angeles.

NAME *Mammuthus trogontherii*

TIME Middle Pleistocene

LOCALITY Europe (England, Germany)

SIZE 15 ft/4.5 m high

Mammuthus trogontherii was the steppe mammoth. It lived in the middle Pleistocene in central Europe, in much colder conditions than its ancestors, and because of this harsh environment *M. trogontherii* was probably the first to develop a hairy coat. It probably roamed in herds across the cold grasslands consuming the coarse grasses that grew there.

Mammuthus trogontherii was one of the largest mammoths. The spiral tusks, which were thicker in the males than in the females, were very long, some measuring about 17 ft/5.2 m.

NAME *Mammuthus primigenius*

TIME Late Pleistocene

LOCALITY Europe, Asia, and North America

SIZE 9 ft/2.7 m high

Mammuthus primigenius, the woolly mammoth, is what most people think of as the typical mammoth. Relatively small for a mammoth, it was a cold-climate tundra-dweller, with a thick shaggy coat and a fatty hump.

Paleontologists are quite familiar with the animal's soft anatomy and appearance in life, since several well-preserved remains have been found buried in frozen mud in Siberia and Alaska. There are also the eye-witness reports from early people who painted and engraved images of the animal on cave walls in France and Spain.

The woolly mammoth's coat consisted of long black hair, not red as in most restorations. The red coloration, seen in specimens in which the hair is preserved, was due to a chemical reaction in the hair after death. There was an undercoat of fine hair and a thick layer of fat to help the insulation. Behind the domed head was a hump of fat, evidently used as a source of nutrition when times were hardest during the winter.

Scratches on the ivory suggest that the characteristic curving tusks were used for scraping away snow and ice from the low tundra vegetation on which it fed.

Mammuthus primigenius survived until about 10,000 years ago, with a dwarf population surviving until 6000 years ago on Wrangel Island in the Arctic Ocean. The warming of the climate that accompanied the end of the last glaciation may have reduced its numbers. Overhunting by early humans probably hastened its extinction.

SOUTH AMERICAN HOOFED MAMMALS

During the Tertiary Era, South America supported as strange and unique a collection of mammals as Australia does today, and for many of the same reasons. Having once been part of a more or less unified landmass, continental drift and rising sea levels caused South America to become detached from North America and then from Africa and Antarctica. By early Tertiary times, roughly 50 to 60 million years ago, there was open sea, or possibly nothing more than a sporadic island chain, between North and South America.

At that time South America had three stocks of mammals on which evolution could act: marsupials (see pp.346–349), primitive edentates (anteaters, sloths, and hairy armadillos, see pp.350–353), and some early rooting and browsing ungulates (see pp.378, 398). But whereas North America subsequently acquired virtually all of the other evolving mammal stocks, due to its land connections with the Old World, South America gained only the rodents and primates.

For about 50 or more million years, from Paleocene until Pliocene times when the land bridge was re-established, the South American mammals were marooned on an island continent with no placental carnivores. As a result, the original stocks were given the opportunity to diversify into a variety of ecological niches which were filled elsewhere by other groups.

The animals described in the following pages are meridiungulates: the descendants of those stranded early rooters and browsers.

ORDER LITOPTERNA

Litopterns are mostly horse-like and camel-like animals. Their teeth are generally simpler than those of ungulates elsewhere in the world: their dentition remained more or less complete, and the gap (diastema) between front and cheek teeth was never as highly developed.

The legs and feet of the animals in this order are sometimes strikingly like those of the perissodactyls (the odd-toed ungulates, such as horses, tapirs, and rhinoceroses; see pp.398–409). There is the same tendency to a reduction in the length of the upper limb and an elongation of the lower limb. The hoofed toes, too, have reduced to three or one, with the weight of the body being carried on the third digit.

There are differences, though. The radius/ulna and tibia/fibula bones of the forelimbs and hind limbs did not fuse, as they have done in the horse, and the ankle bones are less complex (their name means "simple ankles").

Family Didolodontidae

It is not clear how this long-lived family should be classified. Some authorities place it with early rooting and browsing ungulates in the order Arctocyonia (p.378); other experts regard it as a litoptern. It is perhaps best considered as transitional between the two.

The earliest fossils are found from the Paleocene, around 60 million years ago, with examples still being found in the Mid-Miocene, 50 million years later.

NAME *Didolodus*

TIME Early Eocene

LOCALITY South America (Argentina)

SIZE Possibly 2 ft/60 cm long

The teeth of this creature were so much like those of the earliest hoofed animals that in life *Didolodus* may have resembled one closely.

A fleet-footed browser, which scampered through the undergrowth of the forests and ate the leaves of low-growing trees and bushes, *Didolodus*—or something closely related to it—may have been ancestral to most of the other hoofed South American mammals.

Family Proterotheriidae

The spread of the open grassy plains across the South American continent helped to induce the evolution of lightly-built running animals.

The proterotheres ("first creatures") were horse-like animals ranging from late Paleocene to late Pliocene times. Proterotheres appear to have undergone many of the same adaptive changes as the early horses in North America, sometimes in advance of developments elsewhere. It is unlikely that the proterotheres were able to graze, however, since their dentition remains that of browsing animals.

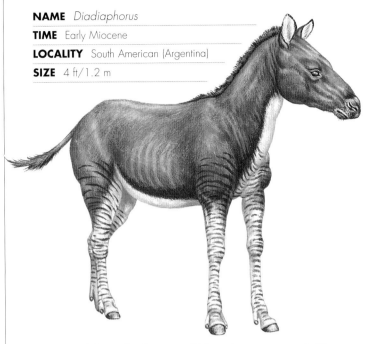

NAME *Diadiaphorus*
TIME Early Miocene
LOCALITY South American (Argentina)
SIZE 4 ft/1.2 m

The graceful *Diadiaphorus* would have been very much like a short-necked antelope or a pony in appearance. It was about the size of a sheep, but it had the feet of a three-toed horse.

Although the paired bones of *Diadiaphorus'* lower limbs (ulna/radius and tibia/fibula) never fused as they did in the later true horses, the animal's legs were long and slender. The middle toe (the third) had become very large and bore the animal's entire weight, while the toes to each side (the second and fourth) had atrophied.

The head was relatively short and deep, and the brain case was quite large. The low-crowned teeth, however, were quite different from a horse's and suggest that *Diadiaphorus* probably lived by browsing on the softer vegetation, bushes, and trees of Patagonia's plains.

NAME *Thoatherium*
TIME Early Miocene
LOCALITY South America (Argentina)
SIZE 2 ft 4 in/70 cm long

The smallest of the known litopterns, *Thoatherium* probably resembled a small gazelle. The feet and legs were very long for the size of the animal's body,

and it must have been a graceful runner. Although the paired bones of the lower limbs were reduced, they did not fuse. But the reduction of lateral toes which can be seen in both the true horses and in *Diadiaphorus* were taken to an extreme in *Thoatherium*. Indeed, the vestiges of its other two toes were even smaller than those of the single-toed horse of today. The dentition, too, remained primitive, so it can be assumed that *Thoatherium* lived on foliage rather than grasses.

Having achieved their greatest diversity in the early Miocene, the proterotheres became extinct in the Late Pliocene, about 3 million years ago.

Family Macraucheniidae

These curious camel-like litopterns, with rhinoceros-like feet, long necks and a proboscis, were once assumed to be extinct camels. This was not an unreasonable assumption because today the llamas and their close relatives in the camel family live in the same area (see pp.418–421). They are, however, quite distinct: any similarities that there are between the families are the result of evolutionary convergence—animals evolving in a similar way due to similar environmental pressures.

The macraucheniids were a long-ranging group and survived through much of Tertiary times and possibly the Pleistocene, only to become extinct in the last few thousand years.

NAME *Thesodon*
TIME Early Miocene
LOCALITY South America (Argentina)
SIZE 6 ft 6 in/2 m long

Trotting across the Pampas plains, this browsing and grazing long-necked creature would have looked much like a modern guanaco. The main difference would have been in the feet, which in *Thesodon* were three-toed and hence rather heavier. The position of the nostrils in the skull of *Thesodon* suggests that a trunk was also present, but this may have been no more prominent than the one carried by the living saiga antelope.

The lower jaw was very slim and the mouth had a full set of 44 teeth—the maximum for a placental mammal which is unusual for a plant-eater at such a late date in the Tertiary.

NAME *Macrauchenia*

TIME Pleistocene

LOCALITY South America (Argentina)

SIZE 10 ft/3 m long

Macrauchenia was a later and larger version of *Thesodon*, from which it may have evolved. The lifestyle of *Macrauchenia* ("large neck") is an enigma. It had certain camel-like features— including size, posture, small head, and long neck. But its three-toed, hoofed feet were rhinoceros-like, and it probably bore a substantial trunk, too, since the nostrils enter the skull high up between the eyes.

Some paleontologists have suggested that signs of a trunk imply a semi-aquatic lifestyle. Others regard it as evidence that the nostrils were simply surrounded by lips which could be closed to keep dust out. The presence of a trunk allied to high-crowned cheek teeth also suggests that *Macrauchenia* may have been able both to browse and to graze.

The legs were long, and the front legs were much longer below the knee than above it—a common feature of running animals. But, *Macrauchenia* would probably not have been a fast runner since the proportions of the hind limbs were reversed, as in non-running animals.

ORDER ASTRAPOTHERIA

A small but well-represented order, the astrapotheres were low-bodied herbivores which survived from the Late Paleocene through to the Middle Miocene. Some were as large as rhinoceroses, and had tusks and a small trunk.

Family Astrapotheriidae

It has been possible to reconstruct many complete astrapotheriid skeletons. Yet their lifestyle and their relationship to the rest of the South America ungulates is puzzling.

NAME *Astrapotherium*

TIME Late Oligocene to Middle Miocene

LOCALITY South America (Argentina)

SIZE 8 ft/2.5 m long

Except for its greater size, *Astrapotherium* was typical of the family. The head was quite short, with a dome over the forehead created by enlarged air sinuses.

The canine teeth grew throughout life and formed four tusks. The larger top pair of tusks sheared against the lower pair. The broad lower incisors protruded, and probably worked against a horny pad in the upper jaw to crop plants.

Evidence for a trunk is contradictory. The nose bones were very short, and opened high on the forehead, which suggest a trunk. Yet there seems to have been no clear reason for a proboscis: *Astrapotherium*'s neck was not particularly short, and its head could easily have reached the ground. It is possible that the "trunk" was really an inflated nose.

Astrapotherium had a long, low body with a weak back and legs, the hind legs feebler than the front ones. The feet were small and plantigrade (the weight borne on the flat of the foot).

The animal was probably largely aquatic, wallowing in shallow water and rooting about for water plants in a similar way to the amyndont rhinoceroses of the northern hemisphere (see p.408).

Family Trigonostylopidae

Paleontologists believe that the trigonostylopids may comprise a family of the astrapotherians, or that they may represent an order of their own. The principal resemblance of the trigonostylopids to the astrapotheres lies in their prominent canine tusks, but the remainder of the teeth suggest that they are more closely related to the litopterns.

NAME	Trigonostylops
TIME	Late Paleocene to Early Eocene
LOCALITY	South America (Argentina)
SIZE	Possibly 5 ft/1.5 m long

There are no remains of *Trigonostylops* other than its skull, so it is difficult to make any deductions about the animal's general appearance or its lifestyle.

The teeth are very primitive, but if *Trigonostylops* is an astrapothere—a deduction that is based on the large size of the lower canines—then the remainder of the body was probably something like that of *Astrapotherium*.

ORDER PYROTHERIA

The mammals of South America are excellent examples of convergent evolution—the development of similar structures and features among unrelated animals in response to similar environmental pressures. The pyrotheres were the South American "equivalents" of the elephants, but it is not known from which group they evolved.

Family Pyrotheriidae

This was the principal family of the order. They ranged from Argentina to Brazil, Venezuela, and Colombia, and are found from the Eocene to the early Oligocene.

NAME	Pyrotherium
TIME	Early Oligocene
LOCALITY	South America (Argentina)
SIZE	10 ft/3 m long

The remains of *Pyrotherium* were first found in the volcanic ash deposits of Deseado, Argentina: hence their name, which means "fire animal." Since that time, specimens have been discovered in many other parts of South America.

In life, *Pyrotherium* probably looked like the early elephant *Barytherium*, its African contemporary. *Pyrotherium* had a massive body supported on pillar-like legs, short broad toes, short thick neck, and a head equipped with a trunk and incisors enlarged to form tusks. There were two pairs of short, flattened tusks in the upper jaw and a single pairs of tusks in the lower jaw.

SOUTH AMERICAN HOOFED MAMMALS CONTINUED

ORDER NOTOUNGULATA

The notoungulates literally "southern hoofed animals" were the largest order of South American ungulates. There are about 100 genera grouped into four suborders. The suborders may already have diverged by the time South America was detached from North America at the end of the Paleocene.

The isolation of South America allowed the separate evolution of its mammal groups, many of which diversified into ecological niches taken, elsewhere in the world, by other groups.

Many notoungulates were small animals which looked and lived much like rabbits or beavers. Other, larger species came to resemble sheep, wart hogs, horses, rhinoceroses, and hippopotamuses. That they were related is confirmed both by the arrangement of cusps on the teeth and by ear bones, which are unique to the order.

Although most specimens are of South American origin, a few are also known from Late Paleocene and Early Eocene deposits in North America. The latter groups quickly died out, and from then the order existed only in South America.

The notoungulates achieved their greatest success as a group in the Oligocene, but they were still abundant early in the Miocene. Thereafter they declined. They have no surviving members. The last notoungulates became extinct in South America in the Pleistocene, about 1 million years ago, shortly after the emergence of the Panamanian isthmus opened the way to the invasion of mammal groups from the north.

SUBORDER NOTOPROGONIA

These are the most primitive notoungulates. When they first appear in the fossil record, members of all the suborders had primitive features. These include a complete dentition of all 44 teeth, low crowns to the teeth with little specialization, and no gap (diastema) between the front and cheek teeth.

The Notoprogonia were restricted to the Paleocene and Eocene: its members were extinct by about 45 million years ago.

Family Notostylopidae

Notostylopids were rodent-like, with prominent incisors at the front separated by a diastema from grinding premolars and molars at the back. However, the chisel-shaped incisors, which had roots and did not grow continually as those of a gnawing animal usually do, were adapted for nipping, not gnawing.

NAME	Notostylops
TIME	Early Eocene
LOCALITY	South America (Argentina)
SIZE	Possibly 2 ft 6 in/75 cm long

Notostylops was a rather rabbit-like animal which lived in the undergrowth, consuming herbaceous plants and other types of low-growing vegetation. The animal's body was probably fairly generalized with few adaptations to fit it for any particular ecological niche.

Notostylops would have had a short, deep face in order to accommodate the unusual rodent-like dentition that is characteristic of the family.

SUBORDER TYPOTHERIA

Typotheres have many features in common with rodents. Even their teeth are similar: the incisors and cheek teeth of advanced members of both groups are adapted for gnawing vegetation, and grow throughout life to compensate for the high rate of wear that the diet subjects them to.

Some members of the Typotheria suborder probably grew to about the size of the modern black bear, but most were smaller.

Family Interatheriidae

Most interatheriids were quite small, rodent-like mammals. They were a long-lived group, and fossil representatives have been found dating from Late Paleocene times through to the Late Miocene.

NAME *Protypotherium*

TIME Early Miocene

LOCALITY South America (Argentina)

SIZE 16 in/40 cm long

Protypotherium was about the size of a rabbit. It had a long tail and legs, and its rat-like head tapered to a pointed muzzle. All 44 teeth were present, and did not show specializations for any particular food. The neck was short and the body long, and there was a long and quite thick tail. The long, slender legs ended in paws which bore claws. *Protypotherium* probably ate leaves and scampered, rodent-like, over the Pampas.

SUBORDER HEGETOTHERIA

Like the typotheres suborder, in which they are often placed, hegetotheres include rabbit-like and rodent-like forms. They became effective gnawers. Later representatives have a diastema between incisors and cheek teeth. All teeth grew throughout life.

They emerged during the Middle Eocene, and did not become extinct until the Pliocene, about 3 million years ago.

Family Hegetotheriidae

Hegetotheriids include rabbit-like animals. Many members of the family had long hind limbs which would have enabled them to lope in the characteristic way.

NAME *Pachyrukhos*

TIME Late Oligocene to Middle Miocene

LOCALITY South America (Argentina)

SIZE 1 ft/30 cm long

Pachyrukhos shows certain similarities with the rabbits, whose ecological niche it filled in South America. It had a short tail, hind limbs that were considerably longer than its front limbs, and very long hind feet. It evidently moved about by hopping and leaping, like a rabbit.

The head was also rabbit-like, narrowing to a pointed muzzle. The teeth were adapted for a diet of nuts and tough plants.

Pachyrukhos had a well-developed

hearing apparatus, which probably means that the ears were long, and large eye sockets. These features suggest that the animal was nocturnal.

SUBORDER TOXODONTA

The suborder Toxodonta was widespread and varied during the Eocene, Oligocene and Miocene (when some reached the size of horses, or even rhinoceroses) and died out when the Central American landbridge was established.

The term "toxodont" means "bow tooth," a reference to a sideways curve in the cheek teeth. As in other notoungulate suborders, the teeth were low-crowned and complete in early genera, but became specialized later. The cheek teeth became large, and were coated in tough cementum. A diastema also appeared in many species.

Family Isotemnidae

The isotemnids evolved early and represent the most primitive family of toxodonts.

NAME *Thomashuxleya*

TIME Early Eocene

LOCALITY South America (Argentina)

SIZE 4 ft 3 in/1.3 m long

Thomashuxleya was named for the 19th century British naturalist and paleontologist, Thomas Huxley.

Robust and sheep-sized, *Thomashuxleya* appears to have been an unspecialized animal, with few adaptations to any particular way of life. The head was quite large in relation to the body, and all 44 teeth were present in the jaws.

The canine teeth, however, were enlarged into prominent tusks, so the animal may have rooted about in the undergrowth like a wart hog.

The strong limbs were like those of any primitive ungulate, and the relatively short feet were digitigrade—the weight was borne on the toes, not the soles. It is likely that *Thomashuxleya* was reasonably light on its feet, and perhaps not unlike a peccary (see pp.412–413).

Family Notohippidae

The term "notohippid" means "southern horse." Yet although it was once thought to be an ancestor of the true horses, the similarities (which lie chiefly in the shape of the skull and the cropping incisors) are a result of convergent evolution—when unrelated animals develop in a similar way due to similar evolutionary pressures. In fundamentals, everything is notoungulate. This family, like several other groups of notoungulates and litopterns were abundant in early to mid Tertiary times in South America. The notohippids evolved in mid Eocene times (some 43 million years ago) and survived through to the mid Miocene (some 14 million years ago).

NAME	Rhynchippus
TIME	Early Oligocene
LOCALITY	South America (Argentina)
SIZE	3 ft 4 in/1 m long

Rhynchippus (the name means "snout horse") presents a classic example of the convergent evolution of the South American ungulates with unrelated groups elsewhere in the world: in this particular case, with the horse. *Rhynchippus'* skeleton, with its deep body and its clawed toes, was not particularly horse-like, but the teeth were similar to those of a grazing animal such as a horse or a rhinoceros.

The animal's canine teeth did not form tusks, as they did in most of the other toxodonts. Instead they were the same size and shape as the incisors. These were tall and ideal for cropping vegetation. The large cheek teeth had a convoluted enamel surface, ideal for grinding up tough vegetation, and were coated in a cement.

Family Leontiniidae

The relationship of the Leontiniidae family to other groups is uncertain, but from the structure of the feet of the members it seems reasonable to include it among the toxodonts.

Leontiniids, were powerfully-built animals, and some may have had a rhinoceros-like horn.

NAME	Scarrittia
TIME	Early Oligocene
LOCALITY	South America (Argentina)
SIZE	6 ft 2 in/2 m long

Scarrittia is the only member of the Leontiniidae family that is known from a well-preserved skeleton.

In life, this bulky creature probably looked much like a lumbering, flat-footed rhinoceros. *Scarrittia* was a rather heavy animal with a long body and neck. It had stout legs, three-toed hoofed feet, and a very short tail. The tibia and fibula were partly fused at the top, which meant that the feet could not be turned sideways.

The animal's face was quite short and the jaws contained the full complement of 44 low-crowned, fairly unspecialized teeth.

Family Homalodotheriidae

A characteristic feature of the homalodotheriids is the presence of clawed toes. This characteristic is highly reminiscent of the chalicotheres which inhabited the Old World and North America (see p.404). The homalodotheriids, along with the loentiniids and toxodontids were abundant in mid to late Tertiary times in south America. The homalotheriids evolved in the early Oligocene and survived until late Miocene times.

NAME *Homalodotherium*

TIME Early and Middle Miocene

LOCALITY South America (Argentina)

SIZE 6 ft 6 in/2 m long

The llama-sized *Homalodotherium* is the only well-known genus of the Homalodotheriidae family.

Unlike other notoungulates, *Homalodotherium* had a claw instead of a hoof on the four "fingers" of each "hand." The animal's forelimbs were longer and heavier than the hind limbs; and whereas the hind foot was plantigrade (the weight was supported by the flat of the foot) the forefoot was digitigrade (the weight was supported on the digits). This characteristic would have made *Homalodotherium* higher at the shoulders than at the hips.

Such features made it likely that *Homalodotherium* was partly bipedal. It probably browsed on the leaves of low branches, rearing up on to its hind legs.

Family Toxodontidae

The toxodontids include animals the teeth of which were exceptionally high-crowned and curved. They had open roots so the teeth grew all the time in order to compensate for the wear that resulted from feeding on the tough Pampas grasses. The animals themselves looked similar to rhinoceroses and some species even possessed a horn on the snout. The toxodontids evolved around 30 million years ago in Oligocene times and survived into the late Pleistocene.

NAME *Toxodon*

TIME Pliocene and Pleistocene

LOCALITY South America (Argentina)

SIZE 9 ft/2.7 m long

Toxodon was a rhinoceros-like animal, with a heavy barrel-shaped body supported on short stocky legs. The creature's three-toed, hoofed, plantigrade feet were rather small, however. Since the hind legs were longer than the front ones, the body sloped forward to the shoulders.

The front of the head was quite broad, and may have had a fleshy prehensile lip. Immediately behind the snout the skull narrowed, as in a rhinoceros, then widened again. Its teeth suggest that *Toxodon* was a mixed browser and grazer, chopping and chewing the hard Pampas grasses, but also taking foliage.

NAME *Adinotherium*

TIME Early to Middle Miocene

LOCALITY South America (Argentina)

SIZE 5 ft/1.5 m long

Adinotherium looked rather like a sheep-sized, and less ungainly, version of *Toxodon*. The front legs were relatively longer than in some toxodontids, so the shoulders were about the same height as the hips, and there was no hump.

Adinotherium also had a small horn on the skull. This was probably some kind of display structure.

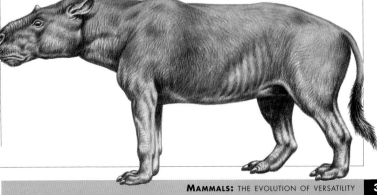

HORSES

...mmals—represent the main group of ...d animals living today. Their earliest ...rooters and browsers (see ... been dominant during Paleocene and ...–60 million years ago. Many evolved to take advanta... ...new opportunities presented by the formation of open grassy plains during the drier Miocene climates, about 20 million years ago.

Apart from the primitive rooters and browsers, ungulates can be divided into two great orders. The Perissodactyla or odd-toed ungulates (right) were represented by a large number of genera in the early Tertiary, but are now confined to horses, rhinoceroses, and tapirs. The other great group of modern ungulates, the even-toed *Artiodactyla* (see pp.410–425), have far more representatives now than in any previous period, including deer, sheep, goats and cattle, pigs and peccaries, hippopotamuses, giraffes, and camels and llamas.

Unlike early rooters and browsers, most of the advanced ungulates are adapted for fast running: a crucial advance for small and medium-sized animals threatened by swift predators. The upper leg tends to be short, with long, thin, fused lower-leg and toe bones, enabling the animal to gallop without twisting its ankle or wrist joints. The muscles are concentrated around the upper bone and their power is transmitted to the rest of the leg by a series of tendons. The ankle joint tends to be rigid, and the animals walk up on their toes. The toes are generally elongated and reduced in number—another weight-saving feature—and the hoof itself is an enormously enlarged toe nail.

In the odd-toed Perissodactyla, where one or three toes are usual, most or all of the weight is taken on the middle digit. Among the even-toed Artiodactyla, the weight is divided between the toes, usually two or four in number.

Other ungulate developments associated with grazing include batteries of enlarged grinding teeth, a complex gut suited to the digestion of cellulose (the complex carbohydrate present in plant food), and living in large herds. Several groups have also developed skull outgrowths, made of horn, bone, or even matted hair. The function of these growths varies, but includes defense and sexual display.

New molecular evidence for the affinities of the horses and other perissodactyls has produced another upset in the accepted view. Previously, the DNA data seemed to support a relationship of the perissodactyls with the hyraxes (hyracoids), elephants (proboscids), and sea-cows (sirenids). But they are now clustered with the cetartiodactyls (whales plus even-toed ungulates, such as pigs and cattle) and Carnivora. This association is better supported by the palaeontological evidence.

ORDER PERISSODACTYLA

The Perissodactyla order probably had its origins during Late Paleocene times about 55 million years ago.

There are three suborders. The Hippomorpha suborder contains the horses and the brontotheres (see pp.398–403), the Ancylopoda suborder (see p.404), and the Ceratomorpha suborder—the tapirs (see p.405) and rhinoceroses (see pp.406–409).

NAME *Palaeotherium*

TIME Late Eocene to Early Oligocene

LOCALITY Europe

SIZE 2 ft 6 in/75 cm high at the shoulder

Palaeotherium was first described by the great French anatomist Georges Cuvier in 1804. It is placed in the family Palaeotheriidae, which were an early to mid Tertiary (Eocene–Oligocene) group of European perissodactyls.

The tapir-shaped *Palaeotherium* inhabited the tropical forests that covered Europe during early Tertiary times. The animal's short, stocky build was well-suited to a forest-browsing lifestyle, and it is one that evolved several times in the evolutionary record among different mammal groups.

The long head and short trunk enabled the animal to browse from low bushes, while the narrow body and long legs allowed it to run between close-growing trees.

Unlike the horses, the palaeotheres did not reduce the number of toes as they evolved: all palaeotheres have four toes on the front feet and three on the hind. These would have given the animal spreading feet suited to walking on boggy forest soil.

Palaeotheres probably moved about in herds—evidence for this is that large numbers are often found fossilized together. Some palaeotheres grew as large as a rhinoceros.

Family Equidae

Equids have their origins in small, scampering animals, no larger than small terriers, which browsed in the forests of Early Eocene times. With the arrival of the generally drier climate of the Miocene, around 20 million years ago, humid forests began to give way to more open country, and in some parts of the world, notably in North America, to vast grassy plains. It is to such conditions that the modern equids—horses, zebras, and asses—are so well-adapted.

The evolution of the horses is often depicted as a straight line through time with increase in size, reduction in the number of toes, and changes in tooth morphology. Many of these developments are associated with changes of habit and habitat, from the small forest and woodland browsers to the fast running grazers of open prairie.

The true picture, however, is far more complicated and interesting. Very many different perissodactyls evolved through Tertiary times and an overall view of their "evolutionary tree" is much more like a many branched bush. There are as yet few clearly distinguishable "lines of descent" but, as the fossil record of the horses is often quite good, it is highly likely that the picture will become clearer as research progresses.

NAME *Hyracotherium*

TIME Early Eocene

LOCALITY Widespread in Asia, Europe, and North America

SIZE 8 in/20 cm high at the shoulder

In spite of its name, *Hyracotherium* is not in fact a close relative of the hyraxes (see p.381)—this is the result of mistaken identification in the last century. A more evocative name, *Eohippus*, the "dawn horse," has been suggested, but science retains the earlier term.

Hyracotherium, the earliest known equid, is believed to be ancestral to the rest of the horse line, and possibly to the palaeotheres as well.

This creature, however, was tiny compared to modern horses, only about 2 ft/60 cm in length. Its skull was elongated,

and the mouth had a full complement of 44 teeth, indicating how primitive the animal was. The teeth were low-crowned and suitable only for chewing the soft leaves of tropical forest trees and shrubs.

As with *Palaeotherium*, *Hyracotherium* possessed four toes at the front and three at the back, making the feet large and unlike those of a horse. Most of the animal's weight was carried on the third toe, anticipating the evolutionary pattern to come.

The body was long and arched, an would have given the animal a hunched appearance.

The relative size and complexity of the brain suggests that *Hyracotherium* was alert and intelligent, and this may have been a factor in the survival of the horse line as a whole.

Hyracotherium was widespread during Eocene times, but when the horse line died out in Europe and Asia during the Early Oligocene around 35 million years ago, further evolution took place on the North American continent.

NAME *Mesohippus*

TIME Middle Oligocene

LOCALITY North America

SIZE 2 ft/60 cm high at the shoulder

In areas where the forests were giving way to more open country, the horses were no longer confined to scampering among the undergrowth and began to develop the capacity to trot and run.

About the size of a greyhound, with a body some 4 ft/1.2 m long, *Mesohippus* was larger than any of its predecessors, but it had rather lighter three-toed feet. The central toe was larger than the others.

The premolar teeth began to resemble the molars, which increased the chewing surface and hence their efficiency, but they were still low-crowned. Its feeding habits were similar to those of *Hyracotherium* and it probably browsed off leaves from bushes and low trees. Such teeth needed only a shallow jaw, so the head was quite long and pointed.

HORSES CONTINUED

NAME Anchitherium
TIME Early to Late Miocene
LOCALITY North America and later Asia and Europe
SIZE 2 ft/60 cm high at the shoulder

The newly-evolved grasses contained abrasive silica in their cell walls, which made them difficult to crop and masticate. Teeth would have worn down faster had it not been for the acquisition of hard-wearing "cement" that coated their enamel crests and outer sides. It seems likely, therefore, that *Parahippus* ventured from the woodlands to take some advantage of the new source of nutrition—the spreading grasslands.

NAME Merychippus
TIME Middle to Late Miocene
LOCALITY North America (Nebraska)
SIZE 3 ft 3 in/1 m high at the shoulder

The evolution of the horse was not a simple "straight line" affair, and a number of side-branches developed which have left no descendants today. *Anchitherium* represents a very successful, but conservative, offshoot.

Anchitherium evolved in North America in Early Miocene times, around 25 million years ago. A three-toed browsing horse, much like *Mesohippus* in size and shape, *Anchitherium* browsed the tender vegetation of humid forests. Crossing the Bering land bridge that once joined modern Alaska to Siberia, it spread across Asia and Europe. There, it survived long after it had been replaced in North America by the first grazing horses during the Mid Miocene, some 15 million years ago. *Anchitherium* did not become extinct in China until the end of Miocene times, some 5 million years ago.

NAME Parahippus
TIME Early Miocene
LOCALITY North America
SIZE 3 ft 3 in/1 m high at the shoulder

Parahippus represents an intermediate stage in the evolution of the horse.

There were still three toes on the feet, and in appearance it was very similar to its ancestor *Mesohippus*. Its body was larger, though, as were its molars, which came to resemble millstones.

This latter change is highly significant.

Herds of *Merychippus*, the earliest horse to feed exclusively on grass, once roamed the prairies of what is now Nebraska.

Their teeth were tall-crowned—dental growth continuing for longer than had been the case hitherto—and interlined with cement. Continuing the development seen in *Mesohippus*, the premolars now had the same grass-grinding design as the molars. The tall teeth needed a deep jaw to contain them, so the head developed the heavy jawline of the modern horse.

Merychippus had a longer neck than its browsing ancestors, because it spent a great deal of its time with its mouth down in the grass. It also developed a strong ligament along the neck from the skull to the shoulder. The springiness of this ligament enabled the animal's heavy head to be raised with little effort, which meant that

Merychippus could stay alert to threats from swift predators, such as the early dogs and cats.

Merychippus still had three toes but now only the middle toe was used to bear the animal's weight (the two side-toes did not reach the ground).

In addition, an elastic tendon in the leg linking muscle to bone acted like a spring, further increasing the efficiency of movement and making possible a progressively lighter foot and lower leg. The compression of this tendon absorbed the shock of each step, thus saving the ankle from damage, then released the energy stored up in the process to spring the foot up into its next stride.

NAME *Hipparion*

TIME Middle Miocene to Pleistocene

LOCALITY Widespread in North America, Europe, Asia, and Africa

SIZE 4 ft 6 in / 1.4 m high at the shoulder

Once the plains-living grazing horses had evolved they, too, radiated into many different types. Of these, all but the *Equus* species are now extinct.

Hipparion represents one of the many grazing horses that evolved during the Miocene, around 15 million years ago. It was a particularly successful genus, spreading during the Miocene from North America into Asia, Europe, and Africa. In Africa, it survived until the Pleistocene about 2 million years ago.

This elegant creature resembled the modern horse, but like *Merychippus* had three toes, two of which were much reduced and did not touch the ground.

NAME *Hippidion*

TIME Pleistocene

LOCALITY South America

SIZE 4 ft 6 in / 1.4 m high at the shoulder

There seem to have been no horses in South America throughout the Tertiary Era. However, it cannot have been the environment that prevented their colonization of the region, since conditions in South America were able to support the evolution of horse-like litopterns such as *Diadiaphorus* (see p.391). When a land connection was re-established between North and South America during the Early Pliocene, 5 million years ago, horses were able to migrate to the south and thrive there.

Hippidion, which was probably a descendant of *Merychippus*, was one of these South American horses. It probably resembled a small donkey, with a fairly large head.

However, its long, delicate nasal bones were quite distinct from those of other horses, suggesting that *Hippidion* continued to evolve in isolation from the mainstream of horse evolution in North America until it became extinct around 8000 years ago.

The modern genus *Equus*, which includes the zebras and asses as well as the wild and domestic horses, seems to have evolved about 4 million years ago in North America, from where it migrated to Asia, Africa, and Europe.

Curiously, all the horses in North and South America died out about 8000 years ago, and did not reappear there until about 400 years ago—and then they appeared only as a result of deliberate introduction by human beings. Some paleontologists have speculated that the demise of the native American horse was caused by some devastating epidemic disease, possibly something like myxomatosis.

TAPIRS AND BRONTOTHERES

FAMILY BRONTOTHERIIDAE

Perissodactyls include two other groups of unusual extinct herbivores—the brontotheres and chalicotheres. The brontotheres are also called the titanotheres, or "thunder beasts," due to their great size. This group of rhinoceroslike creatures evolved in the Early Eocene, about 50 million years ago, in North America and eastern Asia from small animals similar to the first horses. Although they existed for only about 15 million years, about 40 different types have been described.

Brontotheres browsed on soft forest vegetation. Some forms evolved massive horns and large canines, and there was a common tendency to hugely increased bulk. But although they are often referred to as "horns," brontothere head growths did not contain any horn. Nor were they made of compacted hair, like those of rhinoceroses. They were more like the ossicones of giraffes: bony structures with a covering of thick skin. Since these knobs were larger in the males than the females, they were possibly used for display, or perhaps as weapons during fights.

Shortly after the brontotheres reached the peak of their monstrous development, climates became dryer and more open woodlands became plentiful. Evolution favored more lightly-built animals that could graze and live on the plains. Brontotheres became extinct in the middle Oligocene and were replaced by the rhinoceroses.

NAME Eotitanops
TIME Early to Middle Eocene
LOCALITY North America and Asia
SIZE 1ft 6in/45cm high at the shoulder

If you could travel back through time to watch a group of *Eotitanops* scampering through the undergrowth of an Early Eocene forest, at a glance it would be impossible to tell *Eotitanops* from its distant cousin *Hyracotherium*. Both were small browsing mammals, with four toes on the front feet and three on the hind. *Hyracotherium* gave rise to the elegant horses, but *Eotitanops* evolved into the huge, small-brained, lumbering brontotheres that failed to see out the Oligocene. It lived in North America in the early Eocene, but survived into the middle Eocene in Asia.

NAME Dolichorhinus
TIME Late Eocene
LOCALITY North America
SIZE 4ft/1.2m high at the shoulder

In appearance *Dolichorhinus* resembled a small hornless rhinoceros with a particularly long head. Indeed, with its low-crowned teeth, which were only suitable for chewing soft forest leaves, it probably lived very much like one of the modern rhinoceroses. The four-toed front feet and three-toed hind feet of its ancestors were retained, as they were through the whole brontothere line. The type of feet adapted for swift running, with reduced toes, as seen in the horses and antelopes, were never evolved in the brontotheres.

NAME Brontops
TIME Early Oligocene
LOCALITY North America
SIZE 8ft/2.5m high at the shoulder

As the Eocene passed into the Oligocene, the brontotheres became very large indeed—larger than any living rhinoceros—and developed the distinctive bony knobs on the snout.

Skeletons of *Brontops* have been found with partly healed breaks in the ribs, a fact which lends support to the theory the skull outgrowths were used in fights among males for dominance. The breaks suggest that the animal had received a heavy blow in the flanks from a rival, since no other animals of that time could have inflicted such damage. The movement of the ribs when breathing would have stopped broken bones from healing properly.

One of the most famous skeletons of *Brontops* was discovered in rocks that had formed in a bog. The animal had evidently lived in swampy woodland and had died by becoming swallowed up in the mud.

NAME *Embolotherium*

TIME Early Oligocene

LOCALITY Asia (Mongolia)

SIZE 8 ft/2.5 m high at the shoulder

The head of *Embolotherium* is typical of the grotesque shapes developed by the later brontotheres. From the back of the skull it swept forward in a deep hollow and then up to a massive single "horn" on the nose. The eyes were situated well forward, just behind the nostrils and at the horn's base. The shallow skull left little room for much of a brain; as in other large brontotheres, the brain was no bigger than a man's fist.

The occurrence of *Embolotherium* in the Gobi Desert of Asia gives an indication of just how widespread and successful were the brontotheres in their heyday.

NAME *Brontotherium*

TIME Early Oligocene

LOCALITY North America

SIZE 8 ft/2.5 m high at the shoulder

The bones of this giant mammal are quite common in the Badlands of South Dakota and Nebraska. The local Sioux tribes had always associated them with the creatures of mythology—the great horses that galloped across the sky producing storms—and so the term "brontothere," "thunder beast," was born.

Brontotherium itself was one of the largest—larger than the living rhinoceroses. Its nasal horn was Y-shaped and swept upward higher than the back of the head.

The vertebrae at the creature's shoulders had enormous upward-projecting spines. These spines were evidently used to anchor powerful neck muscles that must have been needed in order to support the animal's heavy head with its huge, flamboyant ornamentation.

There may have been fleshy lips and a prehensile tongue, enabling *Brontotherium* to select and nibble the juiciest twigs and leaves from the bushes; the animal's teeth were of relatively simple design and were able to deal only with tender vegetation.

Brontotherium seems to have lived, like other brontotheres, in large herds that wandered through open scrubby woodlands. They roamed along the foothills of the rising Rocky Mountains—which was an intensely active volcanic area at that time. Every now and again, a volcanic eruption would bury herds of *Brontotherium* in ash, and it is in these volcanic deposits that their fossilized skeletons are found today.

SUBORDER ANCYLOPODA

The second suborder of odd-toed ungulates, Ancylopoda, includes some bizarre animals, which have presented paleontologists with many enigmas.

There were two families within this suborder. The eomoropids were the first to evolve and generally resembled other primitive odd-toed ungulates. They lived in eastern Asia and North America during the Eocene and Early Oligocene, between 50 and 35 million years ago.

The second and most important family of ancylopods are the chalicotheres. They probably evolved in Eurasia during the Eocene and spread into Africa and North America during the Miocene. They survived until about 2 million years ago in eastern Asia and central Africa with little evolutionary change.

Family Chalicotheriidae

Whereas the rest of the ungulates have hooves on their toes, these animals evolved large claws instead and evidently would not have been able to run. The dentition and other features of some of the advanced chalicotheres, such as *Chalicotherium* from the Miocene of Europe, suggests that these animals were forest browsers and may have been able to rear up onto their hind legs in order to feed on the succulent leaves of the trees and shrubs above their heads.

Although fossil evidence is sparse, chalicotheres seem to have been a remarkably successful group, which flourished for almost 50 million years.

Paintings of animals which resemble chalicotheres appear as decorations on Siberian tombs dating from the 5th century B.C. Also, sightings are periodically reported in Kenyan forests of the so-called Nandi bear—a creature which allegedly has a gorilla-like stance, with forelimbs longer than its hind limbs, large bearlike claws, and a horselike face. It is little wonder, then, that claims are made that some chalicotheres still survive today.

NAME	*Moropus*
TIME	Early to Middle Miocene
LOCALITY	North America
SIZE	10 ft/3 m long

The chalicotheres have often been described as "horses with claws." The comparison is not a very apt one, however: although the head and body may have been somewhat horselike, the limbs were heavy and not suited for running. The teeth were low-crowned, showing that it was a browser rather than a grazer, eating the soft leaves of trees rather than tough blades of grasses.

Moropus' back sloped upward to the shoulders from heavy hips, while its forelimbs were long and armed wirh three long claws. The three toes of the hind foot had shorter claws. When the claws were first discovered, without the rest of the skeleton, they were thought to have belonged to some kind of anteater.

The function of the claws is something of a mystery. They may have been used by the animal for digging roots and tubers out of the ground, but the teeth do not show enough wear for a diet of this kind of food. Alternatively, *Moropus* may have stood on its hind legs and hooked branches down from the trees, but its elbow joints do not seem to have been flexible enough for this method to have been habitual. It is possible that *Moropus* could have fed either way, and the claws may also have been used as defensive weapons.

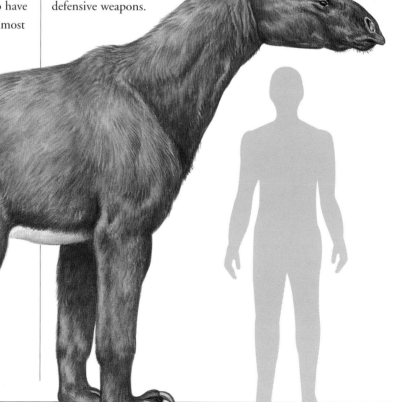

SUBORDER CERATOMORPHA

The final suborder of odd-toed ungulates contains the tapirs and the rhinoceroses (see pp.406–409).

The tapirs were among the first of the perissodactyls to evolve, appearing during Early Eocene times, about 55 million years ago, at about the same time as the first chalicotheres (see left) and the horses (see pp.398–401).

Bulky tropical browsers with short trunks, tapirs were widely distributed throughout Europe, Asia, and North America, but they were not discovered south of the equator until relatively recently. Tapirs managed to survive in the warmer areas of Europe, Asia, and North America until the Late Pleistocene Epoch, about 10,000 years ago.

Tapirs are among the most "conservative" of the mammals in terms of their evolution. In the 55 million years that they have been on Earth, the tapirs have changed remarkably little. Like the paleotheres (see p.398), the tapirs evolved a body shape that is ideally suited to a life foraging around in the dense tropical forests. Indeed, this low, compact body shape has been so successful an adaptation that it has evolved separately in several very different groups, such as the peccaries (see pp.412–413) and capybaras.

Family Helaletidae

One of the earliest families of tapirs, the helaletids were much like today's species, but were smaller and more lightly built.

NAME	Heptodon
TIME	Early Eocene
LOCALITY	North America (Wyoming)
SIZE	3 ft 4 in/1 m long

Heptodon, an early helaletid, had already evolved the characteristic tapir-shaped body, but had no trunk. The short trunk that is such a distinctive feature of modern tapirs was just beginning to evolve as a fleshy outgrowth of the upper lip in *Helaletes*, a relative of

Heptodon that lived during the Middle and Late Eocene in North America and Asia. The trunk is a valuable evolutionary adaptation, which tapirs used as a sensitive tool for pulling food within reach and handling the twigs and leaves on which they feed.

Family Tapiridae

The family to which the modern tapirs belong, the Tapiridae, can be traced back as far as Early Oligocene times, about 40 million years ago.

The four species of living tapirs are all placed in the single genus *Tapirus*. Two species occur in Central America and northern South America and two in Southeast Asia: none remains in the group's original northern stronghold.

This scattered "relict" distribution has often been cited by scientists as part of the evidence supporting the theory of the existence of the southern supercontinent of Gondwanaland. It is supposed that the animals reached their present, widely dispersed homes by migrating overland before the continents slowly drifted apart.

NAME	Miotapirus
TIME	Early Niocene
LOCALITY	North America
SIZE	6 ft 6 in/2 m long

The characteristic tapir features—a heavy body, short legs and tail, a large head with a short flexible snout, and a short neck—appeared early in the evolution of perissodactyls and have remained unchanged ever since.

Miotapirus was probably nocturnal, as are members of the living species *Tapirus*, and may have been just as versatile, adapting to many different environments—fossils of *Miotapirus* have been discovered in a range of sites from sea level up to heights of 15,000 ft/4,500 m.

RHINOCEROSES

Rhinoceroses and their closest relatives are odd-toed ungulates, members of the Perissodactyla. Unlike the later horses, which have eliminated all the lateral digits and now have only one toe, most rhinoceroses have three toes, the axis of weight-bearing passing through the middle or third digit.

Family Hyrachidae

The hyrachyids mark the transition between the tapirs (see p.405) and rhinoceroses. The latter evolved from a tapir similar to *Hyrachyus* during Late Eocene times, about 40 million years ago.

NAME	*Hyrachyus*
TIME	Early to Late Eocene
LOCALITY	North America (Wyoming), Asia (China), and Europe (France)
SIZE	5 ft/1.5 m long

Hyrachyus was generally a very similar creature to *Heptodon* (see p.405), but it was a little larger and more heavily built. It was a common and widespread animal. Many species have been discovered, ranging from the size of a modern tapir to that of a modern-day fox.

Hyrachyus appears to be ancestral to both the later tapirs and the rhinoceroses. Indeed, its resemblance to a primitive form of the latter group is so pronounced that it is often classed as rhinoceros, albeit a lightweight one.

SUPERFAMILY RHINOCERATOIDEA

Rhinoceratoids—literally "nose horns," from the Greek—make up the largest superfamily of the suborder Ceratomorpha. In fact, only one family, the Rhinocerotidae, evolved "horns," and

even these are not true horns. In fact they are outgrowths composed of highly compacted hair.

Rhinoceratoids evolved in Middle Eocene times and adapted to the change in conditions as the worldwide forests gave way to grasslands. The inability of their cousins the brontotheres (see pp.402–403) to do likewise soon led to extinction. Nevertheless the rhinoceroses have now passed their peak, with only five species still managing to survive today.

The evolutionary history of the rhinoceratoids is quite complex: they are grouped into three families.

Family Hyracodontidae

The hornless hyracodont rhinoceroses, of which there are about a dozen genera, were the earliest and most primitive family of the group. They probably evolved from a tapiroid close to *Hyrachyus*.

Their large, efficient cheek teeth were similar to those of the tapirs, but their incisors and canines were modified in various ways. Earlier hyracodonts were quite horse-like in build, with slender, elongated limbs. Later members of the family developed a more robust build.

NAME	*Hyracodon*
TIME	Early Oligocene to Early Miocene
LOCALITY	North America (Saskatchewan, Dakota, Nebraska)
SIZE	5 ft/1.5 m long

Hyracodon was a lightly-built fast-running animal, not unlike a pony. As with the horses, the number of its toes were reduced, so that the foot was lightened and could be moved quickly, and all the leg muscles were concentrated near the top. There were three toes on all feet.

The large and heavy head, however, seemed out of proportion to the body. No horns had evolved at this stage, and the only means of defence against such local meat-eaters as *Hyaenodon*, the last of the creodonts, or the early dogs would have been to flee. The back teeth were of a typical rhinoceros pattern, low-crowned and adapted for chewing leaves.

NAME *Indricotherium*

TIME Oligocene

LOCALITY Asia (Pakistan and China)

SIZE 26 ft/8 m long

It seems quite impossible that an animal as small, lightweight and fleet-of-foot as *Hyracodon* could have evolved into the largest land mammal known to have lived, but all of the evidence points in that direction.

Indricotherium—also known as *Baluchitherium* after the state in Pakistan in which major specimens were discovered—was an immense animal. With an estimated weight of 33 tons/30 tonnes, it was twice the weight of the largest known mammoth and more than four times that of the heaviest modern elephant. The skull itself was 4 ft 3 in/1.3 m long, but this was relatively small compared to the overall body size.

The vertebrae of the back and the long neck were sculpted into hollows and struts, like those of the largest dinosaurs,

which kept weight down while retaining the strength. The legs were elephantine, but the animal's entire weight would have been supported on only three toes—the normal rhinoceros pattern. Again, there was no horn; in fact, the nasal bones were quite weak.

The front teeth of the fossil rhinoceroses varied widely, but those of *Indricotherium* were very strange indeed. There were only two front teeth on top and two below: the upper pair pointing downward like tusks, while the lower pair pointed forward. Since there is some evidence that it had a large, flexible upper lip, such a construction would have enabled *Indricotherium* to browse giraffe-like from the tops of trees more than 26 ft/8 m from the ground.

Indricotherium probably lived in small family groups, taking advantage of the scattered trees found in dry open woodlands.

One skeleton was discovered in rocks formed from swamp mud. It is easy to imagine the difficulties such a huge creature would have had in a bog.

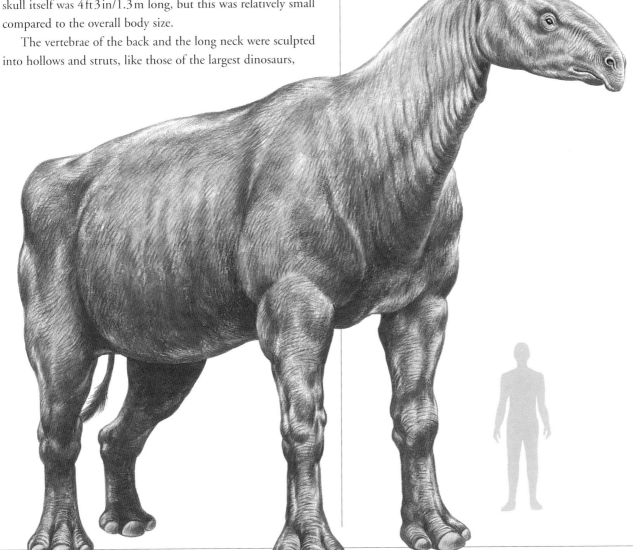

Family Amynodontidae

Amynodonts were a short-lived Eocene and Oligocene group of about 10 genera of hippopotamus-like, probably amphibious, animals with large bodies and short stout limbs. The canine teeth were short or absent in the two other rhinoceros families, but in the amynodontids they were huge, curved, and continually growing.

It seems likely then that amynodontids took the place in this habitat of the aquatic pantodonts such as *Coryphodon* (see p.379), and were eventually replaced by aquatic species of the rhinocerotid family, such as *Teleoceras* (opposite).

NAME *Metamynodon*

TIME Late Eocene to Early Miocene

LOCALITY North America (Nebraska, South Dakota) and Asia (Mongolia)

SIZE 13 ft/4 m long

Remains of *Metamynodon* and its relatives are found in rocks that were formed from river sands and gravels, indicating that these beasts were mostly aquatic by nature. *Metamynodon* was like a hippopotamus in appearance. It had a broad, flat head, a short neck, a massive barrel-shaped body, and short legs. The front feet were unique among rhinoceroses in having four toes.

The crest up the middle of the skull, may have anchored strong jaw muscles that evolved to cope with *Metamynodon's* tough, woody diet.

The hippopotamus-like enlarged canine teeth may have been used for grubbing about in the mud at the bottom of a river. It is also likely that *Metamynodon* had prehensile lips.

Another adaptation to an aquatic lifestyle were the eyes. Set high up on the skull, they allowed the animal to see all around while it was almost totally submerged.

Family Rhinocerotidae

This is the family to which modern rhinoceroses belong. They evolved in Late Eocene or Early Oligocene times and thrived throughout North America, Asia, Europe, and Africa. However, rhinoceroses began to decline during the Pliocene, and they had disappeared altogether from North America at the end of Miocene times, 5 million years ago.

Since this was about 2 million years before the Panama isthmus reformed, rhinoceroses never colonized South America. Neither did the woolly rhinoceros *Coelodonta* (opposite), which was once widespread throughout northern Eurasia, migrate across the Bering land bridge to reach North America.

Rhinocerotids adapted to a wide range of diets and habitats. Many were browsers, but some became specialized grazers. Some members of the family developed thick coats which enabled them to survive in northern regions even during the Pleistocene Ice Ages. Some also acquired "horns" composed of matted hair, which have not fossilized.

It seems likely that the continued decline of these animals, now the largest land mammals after elephants, is associated with changing climate, but also with the rise of humans. Out of about 50 genera, only five species are still alive.

NAME *Trigonias*

TIME Early Oligocene

LOCALITY North America (Montana) and Europe (France)

SIZE 8 ft/2.5 m long

The earliest well-preserved example of a rhinocerotid is *Trigonias*. It was already similar to the modern rhinoceroses in its general appearance, but *Trigonias* had no horn on the snout.

There were also more teeth in the jaw than are found in the jaws of any modern rhinoceros, though the actual number seems to have varied between different species. *Trigonias'* front feet had five toes, although the fifth was small and could not reach the ground. This suggests that the evolutionary line split away from the other rhinoceroses before the lightweight three-toed running forms developed.

NAME *Teleoceras*

TIME Middle to Late Miocene

LOCALITY North America (Nebraska)

SIZE 13 ft/4 m long

Like the amynodontids, the rhinocerotids developed hippopotamus-shaped forms as well. *Teleoceras* was typical of these. It had a long and massive body but short and stumpy legs. *Teleoceras'* legs were so short, in fact, that the creature's body would at times have dragged on the ground. It is likely that the legs were used to "pole" the animal along underwater rather than for walking on dry land.

The feature of this extraordinary animal that most distinguished it from the modern hippopotamus was the short conical horn on the nose. It is possible that this feature was confined to males, and was used for defense or display.

NAME *Elasmotherium*

TIME Pleistocene

LOCALITY Europe (southern Russia) and Asia (Siberia)

SIZE 16 ft/5 m long

As the forests of the Early Tertiary gave way to the grasslands of the Late Tertiary, many animal families adapted accordingly. Among the rhinoceroses, *Elasmotherium* shows the result well.

Elasmotherium had no incisors, and would have used its lips to pluck grasses. The creature's cheek teeth were like those of a huge horse—tall-crowned, covered in cement, and with

wrinkled enamel. Such teeth are adapted to eating tough, abrasive grasses. As the teeth wore down, the wrinkled enamel produced ridges that provided additional grinding surfaces. The teeth had no roots but grew continually to counteract wear.

Because of the lack of hiding places a grassland animal either needs to be very swift of foot to escape its predators, or so big and so well-armored that its predators are discouraged from attacking in the first place. As the largest known of the true rhinoceroses—it was almost as big as a modern elephant—*Elasmotherium* adopted the latter strategy.

Elasmotherium's "horn" was a truly remarkable structure, 6 ft 6 in/2 m long. Most rhinoceroses have their horns growing from the snout. In *Elasmotherium*, however, it grew from the forehead. There was a large dome of bone here, which presumably provided a more secure anchor for the massive structure than any foundation at the tip of the nose.

NAME *Coelodonta*

TIME Pleistocene

LOCALITY Europe (Britain) and Asia (eastern Siberia)

SIZE 11 ft/3.5 m long

Coelodonta had its origins in the Pliocene of eastern Asia, from where it migrated into Europe (but not into North America) and became the woolly rhinoceros of the Ice Age.

Coelodonta had a pair of huge horns on its snout, the front one growing to lengths of over 3 ft/1 m in old males.

Like the woolly mammoth (see p.389), *Coelodonta's* massive body and shaggy coat allowed it to withstand the harsh conditions of the tundra and steppe that bordered the great glaciers of the Northern Hemisphere. Although normally hair does not fossilize, the presence of the shaggy coat is known because of corpses found preserved in frozen gravels in Siberia. There are eye-witness accounts too. Early humans hunted this great beast, and depicted it on the walls of caves in southern France 30,000 years ago.

SWINE AND HIPPOPOTAMUSES

ORDER ARTIODACTYLA

The artiodactyls are the even-toed ungulates, and are the most widespread and abundant of today's running, grazing animals. They differ from their distant relatives the perissodactyls (odd-toed ungulates, such as the horses) in that they usually have four or two, rather than three or one, weight-bearing toes on each foot that form a semicircular hoof, giving rise to the "cloven hoof" typical of pigs, deer, and cattle.

Artiodactyls first appeared as small rabbit-sized herbivores in Eocene times, about 50 million years ago, and developed more slowly than the perissodactyls (see pp.398–409). Most groups had emerged by the close of Eocene times about 37 million years ago, when they rapidly outstripped their rivals.

Over the last few years, molecular analysis has emphasized the close relationship of the artiodactyls with the whales (cetaceans). New analysis confirms this and combines the two groups as the Cetartiodactyla, which is clustered with the Carnivora and horses (perissodactyls).

With the exception of the suines (pigs, peccaries, and hippopotamuses, below), the artiodactyls all ruminate: that is, they "chew the cud" to improve the efficiency of digestion. The ruminant stomach is divided into three or four chambers, the first of which is the rumen. Food is swallowed and passes into the first and second chambers, where it ferments until it is regurgitated for further chewing. It is only when this by-now fully masticated food is swallowed again that it makes the journey down the entire alimentary canal.

This complex digestive system increased the nutritional yield of the tough plants that were evolving in Miocene times. These, in turn, increased the range of habitats open to the artiodactyls, contributing in part to their success.

The importance of the ungulates, particularly artiodactyls, to human evolution and social development cannot be ignored. They were hunted, then more recently, several species were domesticated, which added to the resources available to humans, including milk, wool, transportation, and a source of energy for powering agricultural machinery. When harnessed to tools and machinery, ungulates enlarged the possibilities for the cultivation of crops.

SUBORDER SUINA

The word "suina," like swine, comes from the Latin for "pig." The suborder Suina includes the non-ruminant artiodactyls—the hippopotamuses, pigs, peccaries, and a number of other extinct groups.

These are generally considered the most primitive of the suborders of even-toed ungulates. Most have the simplest, almost complete teeth, and the least sophisticated digestive systems. Although the stomach may have two or three chambers, suines do not chew the cud.

Family Dichobunidae

Dichobunids are a family of small, primitive animals which must have looked more like rabbits than ungulates. Their classification as even-toed ungulates might seem to be inappropriate, since many had five toes on each foot. However, certain features of the skeleton indicate that this was the group from which all the others evolved.

NAME	*Diacodexis*
TIME	Early Eocene
LOCALITY	Europe (France), North America (Wyoming), and Asia (Pakistan)
SIZE	20 in/50 cm long including tail

The earliest-known of the artiodactyls, *Diacodexis* had simple teeth, and all five toes were present (though as in most artiodactyls, the third and fourth were the longest). There may also have been small hooves on the toes. *Diacodexis* must have lived in forest undergrowth, browsing leaves from bushes.

Diacodexis had much the same shape and general appearance as a muntjac deer, but with short ears and a long tail. The legs, too, were relatively longer than a rabbit's, and the forelimbs and hind limbs were equal in length. Such a build implies that *Diacodexis* ran rather than hopped and jumped. Indeed, it is the most highly adapted running animal known from Eocene times—the joints restricted the feet to an up-and-down movement, and the foot and lower leg bones were longer than the upper, a characteristic feature of fast-running animals.

Family Entelodontidae

These large pig-like animals, which probably originated in Asia in Late Eocene times, became common throughout Europe and Asia, and spread into North America. They were at their most prolific during the Oligocene but some survived in North America until the early Miocene, about 20 million years ago. Some members of the family were massive, reaching the proportions of a hippopotamus.

A prominent feature of the entelodontids was the presence of two pairs of bony knobs protruding from the side of the lower jaw.

NAME *Archaeotherium*

TIME Early Oligocene to Early Miocene

LOCALITY North America (Colorado) and Asia (China, Mongolia)

SIZE 4 ft/1.2 m long

Archaeotherium would have looked something like a modern wart hog with a narrow, crocodile-like head. Its skull was remarkably elongated, with long knobs of bone beneath the eyes and on the lower jaw. These protrusions may have been ornamental, or they may have anchored particularly powerful jaw muscles, which were used for grinding up the animal's diet of tubers and tough roots. The arrangement of *Archaeotherium*'s teeth suggests that, like a modern pig, this animal could eat just about anything, even scavenging on the corpses of animals.

The animal's shoulders were high, owing to a series of long spines on the vertebrae. These spines anchored the strong neck muscles needed to support the heavy head.

The creature's brain itself was tiny, but it did have large olfactory lobes, the areas of the brain associated with the sense of smell. *Archaeotherium* probably spent much of its time with its head down, snuffling and grubbing about in the soil of the Oligocene scrub in search of food.

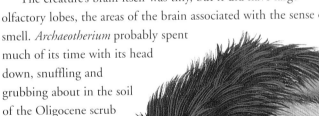

NAME *Dinohyus*

TIME Early to Late Miocene

LOCALITY North America (Nebraska and South Dakota)

SIZE 10 ft/3 m long

The entelodonts reached their maximum size in the omnivorous *Dinohyus* of North America. This animal was much like *Archaeotherium*, but about the size of a bull.

Although *Dinohyus*' bodily proportions were pig-like, the evidence of its long and heavy skull suggests that its face must have been quite different. For example, its nose was not flat, and the nostrils opened at the side of the muzzle rather than the front. Like *Archaeotherium*, it is thought that the long bony projections, on the zygomatic arch beneath the eye, and the bony knobs below the jaw were for the attachment of specialized muscles. These may have been for chewing but their function is not certain. What is certain is that like *Archaeotherium*, *Dinohyus* fed close to the ground, its long muzzle making up for its short neck.

Family Anthracotheriidae

The anthracotheres or "coal beasts," named for the deposits in which many have been found, may be related to the hippopotamus family. They were basically an Old World group, with many members appearing in Asia from the Eocene right up to the Pleistocene. They also migrated to North America, where they are mainly found in Oligocene deposits.

Like the hippopotamuses, which many of them resemble, anthracotheres were probably chiefly aquatic animals. It is possible that the hippopotamuses replaced them in the same aquatic niche.

NAME	*Elomeryx*
TIME	Late Eocene to Late Oligocene
LOCALITY	Europe (France) and North America (Dakota)
SIZE	5 ft / 1.5 m long

The hippopotamus-like *Elomeryx* had a long body and short stumpy legs, with a head which was long and superficially resembled that of a horse. Its teeth, however, were quite different, with elongated canines well adapted to hooking up the roots of water plants, and spoon-shaped incisors ideally suited for digging in the mud.

Unlike other even-toed ungulates, in which the toes are usually reduced to two, *Elemeryx* possed five toes (the first a "dew-claw") on its forefoot and four on its hind foot. Such broad feet would have been useful for walking on soft mud.

Family Hippopotamidae

The hippopotamus family is a recent group dating from the Late Miocene. They may have evolved from the anthracotheres (above), whose niche as swamp-living rooters they probably took over, or possibly from fossil peccaries.

The name of the family comes from the Greek for "river horse," referring to the semi-aquatic lifestyle of most of the family. Some, however, like the living pygmy hippopotamus, were forest dwellers. The only other living species is the almost entirely aquatic *Hippopotamus amphibius*.

NAME	*Hippopotamus*
TIME	Late Miocene to Recent
LOCALITY	Asia, Africa and Europe
SIZE	14 ft / 4.3 m long

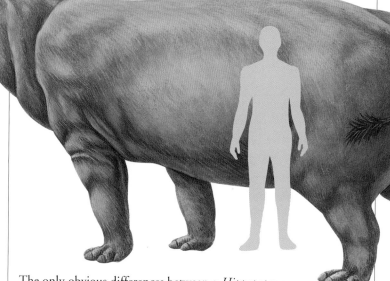

The only obvious differences between a *Hippopotamus gorgops* of Pleistocene East Africa and the living species *H. amphibius* were the great size and particularly prominent eyes of the former. These eyes probably protruded, periscope-like, above the skull on stalks, which would have afforded the animal good panoramic vision while it lay in the water with its whole body submerged and only its eyes, ears and nostrils visible.

These differences aside, *H. gorgops* had the same familiar shape as its modern counterpart, with a heavy body more at home buoyed up in the water than on land, short thick legs, and broad feet ideally suited for walking on mud. Its mouth, too, was wide, with the canine teeth forming the characteristic huge tusks used to dig up water plants.

Family Tayassuidae

The tayassuids, or peccaries, resemble their close relatives the pigs in so many ways that it is difficult to distinguish them in the fossil record. They are readily identifiable among living suines, however, because a peccary's canines do not protrude when its mouth is closed. Their feet, too, are different, having only two toes (with laterals reduced) in the place of a pig's four toes (with little reduction in the laterals).

Living peccaries are confined to South America and the south-western states of North America, but most of the fossil forms are found in North America, where the family evolved in the Oligocene. Fossil peccaries have also been discovered throughout Eurasia and Africa.

The tayassuids were, and continue to be, versatile creatures, successfully inhabiting a wide range of environments from virtual desert to tropical rain forest.

NAME *Platygonus*
TIME Pliocene to Late Pleistocene
LOCALITY North America (Great Plains) and South America
SIZE 3 ft 3 in/1 m long

Platygonus was larger than modern peccaries, and had longer legs. Like its modern relatives, it was primarily a forest animal. It also inhabited the more open Great Plains region, however, a fact which may help to explain its elongated limbs, which are suitable for running.

The nose was rather like a pig's snout, as in modern peccaries, consisting of a flat disk with forward-pointing nostrils. Such a nose was ideal for snuffling about on the ground looking for roots, grass, or fruit on which to feed.

Platygonus was herbivorous, as evidenced by a complex digestive system more like that of a cud-chewing animal than a pig's. Despite its diet, the canine teeth were almost those of a carnivore—long, straight, and needle-sharp. Such teeth could not have been necessary for a herbivorous diet, so it seems likely that they would have been used as weapons, perhaps for protection against attackers such as big cats.

Family Suidae

The suids, the pig family, evolved in the Old World, probably in Asia, in Oligocene times, and they appeared slightly later in Europe during the Miocene. The Suidae family, however, never colonized the Americas.

Although pigs are omnivores rather than herbivores, they seem to have filled the same ecological niches that were taken in the Americas by the peccaries. Fossil suids, like their living descendants, include animals that lived in a wide variety of habitats: from tropical rain forests to savannah woodlands, and even semi-aquatic environments.

Suid fossils are often relatively abundant and are of considerable use in helping geologists determine the relative age of terrestrial sediments. They have also proved of particular importance in matching and dating strata with fossil hominid remains in East Africa.

NAME *Metridiochoerus*
TIME Late Pliocene to Early Pleistocene
LOCALITY Africa (Tanzania)
SIZE 5 ft/1.5 m long

A contemporary of early humans, *Metridiochoerus* was a giant wart hog which inhabited eastern Africa.

Its head was large and heavy, and both its upper and lower canine teeth curled outward and upward to form great curved tusks. *Metridiochoerus'* cheek teeth were high with a complex pattern of cusps, indicating the omnivorous nature of this creature's diet.

OREODONTS AND EARLY HORNED BROWSERS

SUBORDER TYLOPODA

Tylopods—the word means "padded foot"—are a broad grouping of artiodactyls (even-toed ungulates). The suborder Tylopoda includes Old World rabbit-like cainotheres, the New World pig-like merycoidodonts and the camelids.

In many important respects, they stand midway between the swines (pigs, peccaries, and hippopotamuses; see pp.412–413) and the pecorans (giraffes, deer, and cattle; see pp.422–425).

The tylopods first appeared in the Late Eocene, around 40 million years ago, and were common through the Oligocene and up to Late Miocene times, 5 million years ago. Only the camelids—the camels, llamas, and their closest relatives—still survive (see pp.418–421).

Family Cainotheriidae

This is one of the most primitive families of the suborder. As in most primitive members of any group, the cainotheres were generalized animals, with few features to hint at the more specialized members that were to evolve.

Most members of the Cainotheriidae family were rabbit-like in size, appearance and in their bounding or leaping style of locomotion.

NAME *Cainotherium*

TIME Late Oligocene to Early Miocene

LOCALITY Europe (Spain)

SIZE 1 ft/30 cm long

Cainotherium was a small rabbit-like animal, with hind limbs longer than the front limbs. The parts of the creature's brain that were associated with hearing and with smell were well-developed.

This feature implies that *Cainotherium* was probably equipped with long rabbit-like ears and probably had a sensitive nose as well. As well as looking a little like a rabbit this animal must have lived in a similar way to a rabbit, scampering and hopping through the undergrowth, where it browsed on a variety of vegetation.

Yet *Cainotherium* was clearly an even-toed ungulate. Even at this early stage in its evolution, the animal's limbs had become slender, with only two toes and reduced lateral toes which ended in hooves.

Also, unlike the rabbit, *Cainotherium* did not have particularly specialized teeth. The full number of mammalian teeth (44) were present in its jaw. The teeth formed an almost continuous series with no gap (called a diastema) between the front and cheek teeth. However, the back teeth were quite broad, with five cusps, and were well-adapted for chewing and grinding up vegetation.

Cainotherium and its relatives may have competed with, and eventually lost the evolutionary competition to, the early rabbits and hares for the same ecological niches (see p.429). They were restricted to Europe and left no descendants beyond early Miocene times.

Family Merycoidodontidae

The suborder Tylopoda may well have evolved from the suborder Suina. This relationship can be seen from the Merycoidodontidae family which seems to combine some features typical of pigs with those characteristic of camels. Typically they were rather heavily built animals with short limbs and four toes on each foot. The merycoidodonts (the name means "ruminating tooth") are sometimes more euphoniously referred to as oreodonts—"mountain tooth," a reference to the type of terrain in which their remains were discovered. The teeth have advanced features which indicate relationships with the ruminants. The tooth was unbroken, without diastema or loss of teeth. The upper canine was a stout, somewhat projecting, chisel shape. The lower canine was reduced to the size of the incisors and the specialised cheek teeth were strongly selenodont (with pairs of crescent-shaped ridges). These features produced long-lasting grinding surfaces which were effective for the side to side chewing of vegetation.

A highly successful group of woodland and grassland browsers, the merycoidodonts evolved in North America during the Late Eocene, around 35 million years ago. The evidence suggests that they were particularly abundant throughout the Oligocene and into Miocene times. They then died out around 5 million years ago.

Members of the family may have diversified and adapted for existence in a variety of habitats. Some fossil merycoidodonts have been found with long tails and clawed digits similar to those of tree-climbing animals; others have the hippopotamus-like high eyes and nostrils, characteristics suited to life in semi-aquatic environments.

NAME *Merycoidodon*

TIME Early to Late Oligocene

LOCALITY North America (South Dakota)

SIZE 4 ft 6 in / 1.4 m long

Merycoidodon, which was a typical member of its family, probably looked something like a pig or peccary, but with a longer body and shorter legs.

Paleontologists believe that *Merycoidodon* probably would not have been able to run particularly well because there was no fusion of its limb bones. Also, the lower section of the animal's limbs were about the same length as the upper part, and the feet each had four toes.

The head, too, was pig-like, but with a full complement of 44 teeth. A significant feature of the dentition is that the lower canines had taken on the appearance of incisors—a characteristic which would continue to appear in the later camels and deer.

Another curious feature in *Merycoidodon* was a pit in the skull just in front of the eye which may have contained some kind of a gland. In fact modern deer have a gland here which they use to mark out their territories with scent. One theory to explain the pit is that *Merycoidodon* may have been a similarly territorial animal.

Vast numbers of fossils of *Merycoidodon* have been preserved in the Oligocene beds of the Badlands of South Dakota. The presence and numbers of the fossils imply that *Merycoidodon* probably roamed the woodlands and grasslands of the area in large herds.

NAME *Brachycrus*

TIME Early and Middle Miocene

LOCALITY North America (Great Plains)

SIZE 3 ft 3 in / 1 m long

Brachycrus was a merycoidodont that appeared quite late in North America. Although in some respects it was similar to its relative *Merycoidodon*, it was somewhat smaller and considerably more specialized.

The animal's skull and jaw were short—indeed, practically ape-like—and the eye sockets faced forward. The nostrils were placed far back on the top of the skull, a feature which suggests that the animal had a short tapir-like trunk. *Brachycrus* may have used this trunk in sniffing out and manipulating food in the undergrowth.

NAME *Promerycochoerus*

TIME Early Miocene

LOCALITY North America (Oregon)

SIZE 3 ft 3 in / 1 m long

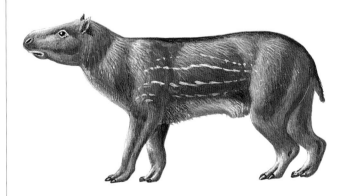

There are indications that some of the merycoidodonts were amphibious, pursuing a hippopotamus-like existence in the swamps and rivers of the time. *Promerycochoerus* may have been just such a semi-aquatic form since its body was particularly long and the limbs short and stumpy—features which often crop up in amphibious animals. There were two principal species: *P. superbus*, which had a long tapir-like face, and *P. carrikeri*, with a short, almost pig-like face.

Family Protoceratidae

Protoceratids—the name means "first horns"—were a family made up of about 10 genera of early animals that resembled modern deer but were actually more closely related to the camels. The Protoceratids inhabited the warmer, southern forests of North America for about 35 million years, from the Late Eocene to Early Pliocene times.

The most extraordinary features of these animals are their "horns" (which are in fact, bony outgrowths rather than true horns), which were well-developed in males, but either reduced or absent in females.

Some species simply manifested a variety of bumps and knobs on the skull (ossicones), but others had developed complex forked structures (antlers). The relative lack of development among the female animals implies that such horns were probably organs used primarily for sexual display rather than as weapons, although later protoceratids doubtless "sparred" with their rivals when competing for territory and/or mates.

The evolution of skull outgrowths in artiodactyls, whether horns, antlers, or ossicones, relate to changes in body size, social behavior patterns, and territorial structures.

Early ruminants were small, feeding on soft vegetation for which they had to range widely. They used their enlarged canine teeth for defense when necessary.

The ruminants moved out of the forests into the new scrublands that were developing, and adapted to feeding on the tougher vegetation that grew there. With this change, the amount of territory that the animal required to obtain sufficient food for its existence diminished in area.

As territorial boundaries shrank, so the importance of defending them increased. This evolutionary pressure meant that the difference between the sexes became more pronounced. The larger, heavily-armored males bearing antlers or horns defended a harem of females with many offspring, fighting off any challenges from outside. Protoceratids exhibit the beginning of these changes.

In some classifications, the ruminants are recognized as a distinct group and are given the same taxonomic ranking as the tylopods.

NAME	*Protoceras*
TIME	Late Oligocene to Early Miocene
LOCALITY	North America (South Dakota)
SIZE	3 ft 3 in/1 m long

This graceful little deer-like animal inhabited the upland woodlands of western North America. It was an early member of the family and was still quite primitive in having four toes on the forefeet and the hind feet.

The most remarkable and least deer-like feature of *Protoceras*, and indeed all the protoceratids, was the arrangement of horns on the face. Unlike the ornamentation of deer, these were not antlers and were not shed annually. Nor could they be rightly termed "horns," since they were not covered in horn. They were actually bony outgrowths that were probably covered with skin, like the ossicones of giraffes.

Protoceras had three pairs of knobs—one just behind the nostrils, one above the eyes, and one at the top of the skull. This arrangement was only present in the males. The females possessed only the top pair, and these were somewhat smaller than in the male. This arrangement of horns was evidently some kind of display structure for use in mating or for warning away rivals. These knobs would have probably been more effective seen from the side, rather than front on.

The earliest protoceratids retained the upper incisor teeth at the front of the jaw. However, by the time *Protoceras* had evolved, these teeth had been lost so that the lower cropping teeth worked against a bony pad in the upper jaw, just as in modern deer and cattle, to grind up the tough vegetation which made up its diet.

NAME *Syndyoceras*
TIME Early Miocene
LOCALITY North America (Nebraska)
SIZE 5 ft / 1.5 m long

Syndyoceras was more deer-like than its predecessor *Protoceras* in that the elegant running legs now had only two toes, each with a narrow pointed hoof.

The shape of the nasal bones suggests that the animal may have had an inflated muzzle similar to that of a saiga antelope. As in the other advanced protoceratids there were no incisor teeth in the upper jaw.

There was, however, a pair of canine tusks and these may well have been used for grubbing about on the ground in the search for food.

The head had a pair of horns at the snout and another long pair above the eyes. The snout horns were united at the base but grew forward, diverging and curling up and back. The rear pair of horns curved upward like those of cattle. These would not have been true horns and were probably covered in skin.

Whereas the horn arrangement of *Protoceras* would have been seen to best advantage from the side, that of *Syndyoceras* and the other advanced protoceratids would have been more spectacular when seen from the front. This suggests that the growths were used for sparring as well as for display.

NAME *Synthetoceras*
TIME Late Miocene to Early Pliocene
LOCALITY North America (Texas)
SIZE 6 ft 6 in / 2 m long

Synthetoceras was the latest and the largest of the family. Its long, shallow skull supported a pair of curving brow horns, similar to those of *Syndyoceras*. The horn at the animal's snout was long and Y-shaped. This flamboyant arrangement was only present in the males and was most probably used for sparring to protect mates and territory and for sexual display.

Synthetoceras browsed and grazed in herds.

Family Tragulidae

This family seems to link the suborder Tylopoda with the pecorans – the cud-chewing (ruminant) family that also contains the deer, the giraffes and the cattle (see pp.422–425). These animals possess four stomach chambers which allows the fermentation of vegetation, but it is not known whether the fossil forms possessed such a structure. Accordingly, there is much debate among paleontologists as to the true classification.

Always a rare group, the Tragulidae family consists of small, deer-like animals, which are hornless, but have strong upper canine tusks. Only two species survive today: *Hyemoschus*, the African water chevrotain which creeps though the undergrowth of the jungles of Central and West Africa, and *Tragulus* (spotted, lesser, and larger mouse deer) the chevrotain which is found in tropical forests and mangrove swamps in south and east Asia.

Members of the family tend to be small and secretive and all of the living species are active only at night.

NAME *Blastomeryx*
TIME Early Miocene to Late Pliocene
LOCALITY North America (Nebraska)
SIZE 2 ft 6 in / 75 cm long

This deer-like creature, which was not much bigger than a large rabbit, probably looked like and lived in a similar way to, the modern chevrotains. They were scampering, browsing forest animals, which were probably secretive in their habits. Their canine teeth had evolved into long sharp saber-like tusks, useful for rooting up food or for self-defense.

Blastomeryx possessed no horns, as is characteristic of the whole family. However, a late species from the end of the Miocene did have bony bumps on top of the skull, suggesting that horns may have been evolving; they also showed a reduction in the size of the tusks. This development is consistent with the modern "rule" that deer with tusks have no horns, and vice versa.

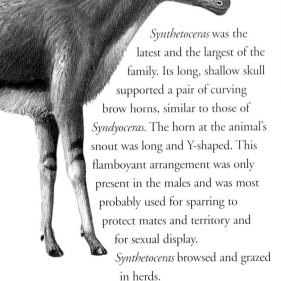

CAMELS

FAMILY CAMELIDAE

The modern camelids are found only where conditions are harsh. The camels are famed as "ships of the desert" capable of covering immense distances across difficult terrain in the most inhospitable of climates. Thanks to their extraordinary physiology, they can live for up to two months on rough grazing alone, without additional water, and can endure great changes of temperature. The South American camelids—the llamas and their relatives—are also found in challenging habitats, including that of the high Andes.

Modern camels have evolved a whole array of adaptations for coping with hot, dry environments. Most other animals, including humans, lose water steadily in hot, dry weather by sweating, panting, and breathing. As a result, their blood thickens, until eventually it circulates too slowly to remove heat from the body via the skin, and the animal suffers a sudden and dramatic rise in temperature that soon kills it. Camels avoid this danger by having unique blood that does not thicken. They also economize on water loss in a variety of ways.

Their thick coats protect them against becoming overheated and restricts water loss through evaporation from the skin. Their body temperature can fluctuate according to the outside temperature, so minimizing water loss through sweating. Camels also excrete very concentrated urine and dry feces, which contain very little water, and they store fat in their distinctive humps, drawing on this food reserve in times of scarcity. As they process it, the fat releases extra water. Finally, camels are able to drink remarkably quickly; they can take in as much as 25 gallons/115 liters of water. at a single session.

It is easy to think of camelids as specialized animals that can exist only in extreme environments, but modern camels are the remnants of a formerly widespread and diverse group. They first evolved in the Late Eocene, about 40 million years ago, not in Asia or Africa but in North America, and reached their peak in the Late Miocene, some 10 million years ago. It was not until the Pliocene, about 5 million years ago, that camels migrated into Eurasia and Africa, and llamas reached South America.

By the Pleistocene Ice Age, around 2 million years ago, the camelids tanged all over North America from Florida to Alaska. They had spread southward to South America across the Panama land bridge and eastward into Asia across the Bering land bridge.

Like some other animal groups that evolved chiefly in North America, such as the horses (see pp.398–401), the camelids survive today only on other continents—they became extinct in North America toward the end of Pleistocene times, about 12,000 years ago.

There are two living species of camel, the two-humped Bactrian camel and the one-humped Arabian camel or dromedary. Wild camels still inhabit the Gobi Desert, but the camels of Africa were introduced there by humans as recently as 2,500 years ago. Camels that are now feral in Australia were brought there just over 100 years ago. In South America the llama, alpaca, vicuna, and guanaco are the only representatives of the second remaining group.

Camelids have no horns or tusks, and their jaws have a reduced number of upper incisors. The lower incisors are flattened and project forward horizontally. They have elongated facial bones, so there are wide spaces between the front teeth that are left, and a wide gap—the diastema—between the front and cheek teeth. The cheek teeth are formidably large and hypsodont—that is, they have short roots but high crowns, as in horses. Such spiky front teeth enable the camelids to rip and tear at tough vegetation, while their cheek teeth are well-suited to "chewing the cud."

Like many other artiodactyls, the camelids ruminate—a process that involves chewing the partly digested food (the "cud") before swallowing it so that it undergoes a second digestion. The stomachs of camels are three-chambered, unlike those of more advanced ruminants, such as deer or sheep, which have four-chambered sromachs. The differences in the structure of their digestive systems suggest that they may have evolved the ruminant way of life independently from the other ruminants (convergent evolution). Another consequence of these differences is that the camelids are classified with the tylopods rather than the ruminants.

The camelids seem to have reduced the number of their toes much earlier than did most ungulate groups. Among the earliest camelids, the forelimbs had four toes, all of which touched the ground, but the second and fifth toes of the hind limbs were already vestigial (extremely reduced and insignificant). Indeed, the Late Miocene Procamelus already had legs that were probably almost identical ro those of a modern member of the family. The shanks were long and thin, there were two spreading toes on each foot, and the two metapodials had become elongated and fused at the top like an upside-down Y to form the cannon bone.

The later camelids thus walked in a characteristic way. Whereas other artiodactyls are unguligrade, walking on the tips of their hoofed digits, the later camelids are digitigrade: they have dropped down to walk on the entire underside of the splayed digits, and there is a rough pad beneath. Such developments have allowed modern camels to travel with ease across soft sand.

NAME *Protylopus*

TIME Late Eocene

LOCALITY North America (Utah and Colorado)

SIZE 20 in/80 cm long

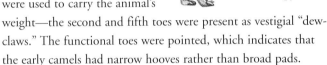

As in most groups of ungulates, the first camelids were small, rabbit-sized animals. The simple, low-crowned teeth were arranged along the jaw without any breaks—a primitive feature and one that indicates that the animal's diet was the soft leaves of the forest vegetation.

The forelimbs, which were shorter than the hind limbs, had four toes, all of which touched the ground. The hind limbs also had four toes, but only the third and fourth were used to carry the animal's weight—the second and fifth toes were present as vestigial "dew-claws." The functional toes were pointed, which indicates that the early camels had narrow hooves rather than broad pads.

It is unlikely the Protylopus was a direct ancestor of later camels, but it probably closely resembled, and was contemporary with, the earliest camels.

NAME *Poebrotherium*

TIME Oligocene

LOCALITY North America (South Dakata)

SIZE 3 ft/90 cm long

By Oligocene times, around 35 million years ago, the dense forests that once covered Dakota had given way to more open woodlands. Camelids became plentiful and began to look more like modern camels. At about the size of a sheep, *Poebrotherium* was

larger than Protylopus. Its head, with a distinctive narrow snout, was a smaller version of a llama's, and it may have had the llama's prominent ears as well.

Poebrotherium still had slightly longer hind legs than forelegs, and hoofed toes, yet its legs were clearly adapted for greater speed. These were relatively longer and more slender than those of Protylopus, they had lost their lateral toes, and the two central weight-bearing digits were beginning to diverge. Poebrotheriums teeth, too, show an advance on *Protylopus*. Dentition is still complete, but spaces were beginning to appear between the teeth. It seems likely that a number of different camelid lines radiated from *Poebrotherium*.

NAME *Procamelus*

TIME Late Miocene to Early Pliocene

LOCALITY North America (Colorado)

SIZE 5 ft/1.5 m long

Procamelus was either on the direct ancestral line to modern camels, or very close to it. It was much larger than any of the earlier camels, approaching the size of a modern llama. The head was very long but the braincase was quite small.

Procamelus still had incisors in the upper jaw, but only a single pair—and even these were reduced in size. Set in such a long jaw, the front teeth (one pair each of incisors and canines, and the first pair of premolars) had long gaps between them—a dentition that is adapted for tearing at vegetation. Crowns on the cheek teeth had grown to such an extent that they were now hypsodont, like those of a horse, and well-adapted for dealing with tough vegetation.

With *Procamelus*, the structure of the leg had almost reached that of the modern camel. The metapodials had partially fused and elongated to form a cannon bone, the shanks were long and thin, and there were two spreading toes. This splaying-out of the toes suggests that *Procamelus* may already have evolved a foot pad to spread the load when walking over soft terrain.

NAME *Titanotylopus*

TIME Pliocene to Pleistocene

LOCALITY North America (Nebraska)

SIZE 11 ft 6 in/3.5 m high at the shoulder

cope with the scarce supplies of food and water in the particularly hard environments inhabited by today's camels. Certainly the climate was cooling and becoming more dry throughout the Tertiary period in North America—climatic changes that caused forests to give way to scattered woodland and then to grasslands—but environmental conditions were still equable enough to relatively easily support a large number of different mammals. At this time, there was as yet no need for the development of such extreme food-storage devices as fatty humps and the camels' other moisture retentive physical adaptations.

NAME *Oxydactylus*

TIME Early Miocene

LOCALITY North America (South Dakota and Nebraska)

SIZE 7 ft 6 in/2.3 m long

Another offshoot from *Poebrotherium* was the line of giraffe-like camels with very long legs and necks—adaptations to browsing on high vegetation. The early Miocene landscape of central North America—grasslands with open scrub—must have been ideal for the evolution of such an animal. The toes were very narrow and bore slender antelope-like hooves, not the broad pads of the modern camels.

During Pliocene times, between 5 million and 2 million years ago, a number of very large camels evolved in North America. These huge camels were certainly closely related to *Procamelus* and may even have been derived from it.

Among them was *Titanotylopus*, which must have been taller than the elephants of the time (see pp.382–383, 387–388). However, in many other respects, this enormous creature was very similar to modern camels, with a narrow snout lacking upper incisors, a long neck, and splayed two-toed feet.

Despite its similarities with its modern relation, however, one distinctive feature of modern camels was almost certainly not present in *Titanotylopus*—their fatty hump. The hump in modern camels is an adaptation that has evolved in order to

NAME *Camelops*
TIME Pleistocene
LOCALITY North America (California and Utah)
SIZE 6 ft 6 in/2 m high at the shoulder

Camelops, which was another giant of the late Cenozoic Era and a contemporary of early humans, appears to have been the last camel to have survived on the North American continent.

It probably looked very much like the modern Asian camel, but certain parts of its anatomy indicate that it was more closely related to the South American llamas.

NAME *Stenomylus*
TIME Early Miocene
LOCALITY North America (Nebraska)
SIZE 3 ft/90 cm long

A number of side-branches of the camel family evolved in the Miocene, but became extinct soon afterward. *Stenomylus* and its relatives were small gazelle-like animals. They must have lived very much as African gazelles do today, browsing in herds on low vegetation and sprinting rapidly away from danger. The teeth of the lower jaw were unique in that the canines and the first premolars had taken the form of incisors, so the animal appeared to have 10 lower incisors. The neck was long and lightly built, and the legs were slender. The two toes on each foot had small, deer-like hooves.

NAME *Aepycamelus*
TIME Middle and late Miocene
LOCALITY North America (Colorado)
SIZE 10 ft/3 m high at the head

The giraffe-like camel line reached its climax in *Aepycamelus*, formerly known as *Alticamelus* because of its extraordinary height. The legs were long and stilt-like, and the two toes had very small hooves. *Aepycamelus*, then, had lost the running hooves of its ancestors and put in their place the broad pads of modern camels.

The modern camel moves both legs on one side of the body in the same direction at the same time. This method of walking is known as pacing, and is confined to camels and giraffes. Pacing is a very efficient method of traveling great distances across open terrain. An extremely long-legged animal such as *Aepycamelus* must have moved with a similar gait. Indeed there is some direct evidence for this in camel-like footprints that have been discovered in Miocene deposits.

GIRAFFES, DEER, AND CATTLE

FAMILY GIRAFFIDAE

Giraffes, like all other artiodactyls except the pigs and hippopotamuses (see pp.412–413) are cud-chewers, or ruminants. There are no incisor teeth at the top of the jaw, instead the lower incisors work against a bony pad at the front of the mouth. Having ripped off foliage from bushes and trees, the animal chews and then swallows it for the first time. The food then passes into the rumen, the first chamber of a complex, four-chambered stomach, where it is fermented by microorganisms. Once the food is partially digested, it is returned to the mouth and chewed again before its second journey back down the entire alimentary tract.

This method of digestion is very efficient at breaking down fibrous plant food, but the ruminant pays a price for this efficiency in that food takes a long time to pass through its gut, and it must spend a considerable proportion of each day chewing the cud.

There are two modern giraffes, both living in Africa, south of the Sahara. The more familiar is the tall, long-necked, long-legged giraffe *Giraffa* of the African savannah, which feeds from the tops of thorn trees. The other is the smaller, darker okapi, at home in the gloom of the African tropical forest.

With the exception of the camels, the ruminants typically have paired head ornaments. In the case of the giraffes these take the form of horn-like growths, called ossicones, which are covered in skin.

Both the giraffe and the okapi are two-toed browsers, the family having evolved before the grazing ungulates developed. The fossil record reveals a number of different forms, most of which were quite unlike the two surviving modern representatives of the family.

NAME	*Prolibytherium*
TIME	Early Miocene
LOCALITY	North Africa (Libya)
SIZE	6 ft/1.8 m long

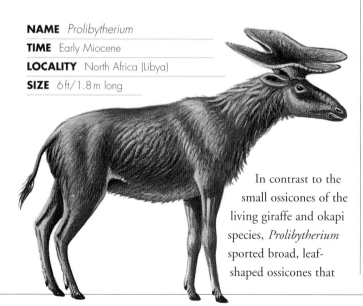

In contrast to the small ossicones of the living giraffe and okapi species, *Prolibytherium* sported broad, leaf-shaped ossicones that reached a span of about 14 in/35 cm.

Prolibytherium probably used the projections for display and in sparring contests between rivals, and it is possible that their covering of skin was shed annually. Apart from its flamboyant head ornamentation, *Prolibytherium* probably resembled the modern okapi.

NAME	*Sivatherium*
TIME	Pliocene to Late Pleistocene
LOCALITY	India (sub-Himalayas) and North Africa (Libya)
SIZE	7 ft/2.2 m high at the shoulder

Named in honor of Siva, or the Lord of the Beasts, who is one of the principal Hindu Gods, this massive animal would have appeared more like a moose than a giraffe.

The male of the species, at least, was ornamented with a pair of huge branched ossicones on the top of its skull, and a smaller pair of conical ones about the eyes—probably partly for display and defense. The body was quite stout, especially in the region of the shoulders, where strong muscles would have been needed to carry the animal's huge, heavy head.

Libytherium, which was a close relative of *Sivatherium*, lived in North Africa at the same time. Prehistoric human rock paintings that have been discovered in the Sahara Desert depict an animal that looks very much like *Libytherium*, so it is possible that sivatheres coexisted with early humans until as recently as about 8000 years ago.

Family Cervidae

Although the cervids, or true deer, were quite late to evolve they have become the principal browsing animals of the Northern Hemisphere and South America. Their diet includes leaves, grass, twigs, bark, and moss.

A characteristic feature of all living cervids is the presence of antlers in the males (and in females of the reindeer *Rangifer*) of virtually all species. The exceptions are the hornless musk deer *Moschus* and Chinese water deer *Hydropotes*. Antlers are branched bony outgrowths of the head which are used chiefly in display or for ritual sparring. They differ from the ornaments of the other ruminants in that they are shed and regrown each year. There is a swollen "burr" at the point at which they are shed. Each year the antler develops with another branch until the maximum for the species is reached.

NAME *Eucladoceros*
TIME Pliocene to Pleistocene
LOCALITY Europe (Italy)
SIZE 8 ft / 2.5 m long

Some deer evolved huge, flamboyant antlers. One of the most spectacular examples was *Eucladoceros*, whose antlers, each with a dozen points, or tines, had a total span of 5 ft 6 in/1.7m. Such a spread must have been something of a hindrance among the low branches of its forest home. As with *Megaloceros*, which had even bigger antlers, sexual selection probably sustained the development: the male that sported the most impressive antlers, and could spar most successfully in competitions for females during the breeding season, would have left the most offspring to continue his line.

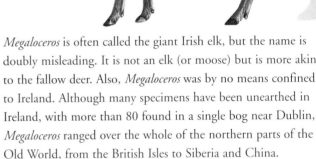

NAME *Megaloceros*
TIME Late Pleistocene
LOCALITY Widespread in Europe and Asia
SIZE 8 ft / 2.5 m long

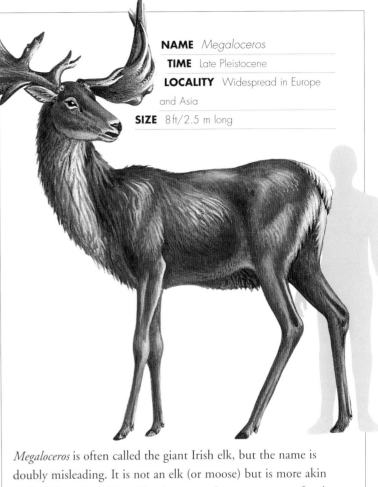

Megaloceros is often called the giant Irish elk, but the name is doubly misleading. It is not an elk (or moose) but is more akin to the fallow deer. Also, *Megaloceros* was by no means confined to Ireland. Although many specimens have been unearthed in Ireland, with more than 80 found in a single bog near Dublin, *Megaloceros* ranged over the whole of the northern parts of the Old World, from the British Isles to Siberia and China.

The largest deer that ever lived, *Megaloceros* is chiefly known for its antlers. They were truly monumental, reaching a span of 12 ft/3.7 m and weighing over 100 lb/220 kg—about a seventh of the weight of the entire animal. Even more remarkable, perhaps, is that these horns were probably shed and regrown annually, as in all true deer. A male *Megaloceros* must have expended a great deal of energy growing such structures.

The *Megaloceros* herds reached their peak during the last interval between the cold spells of the Pleistocene Ice Age, and began to decline about 12,000 years ago. They died out in Ireland about 11,000 years ago, but may not have become extinct in Central Europe until about 2500 years ago.

Evidence that early humans knew and hunted *Megaloceros* is provided by cave paintings depicting animals very like *Megaloceros* in Europe. One French cave painting shows the great deer with a small triangular hump on its back, like that of modern zebu cattle. This may have been a fatty structure, like a camel's hump, which was used as a food store during the harshest periods of the Ice Age winter.

Dwarf species of *Megaloceros* are also known, from Malta and the Channel Islands.

Family Antilocapridae

The pronghorn *Antilocapra* of North America is the only surviving genus of this family, but Miocene and Pliocene times saw the evolution of a large number of different types of antilocaprids. The other ungulates that evolved in North America—the camels and the horses—spread across to Asia and to South America and became extinct in their homeland.

The antilocaprids, on the other hand, remained in North America and spread nowhere else, although they were a very successful and varied group during the Pliocene and Pleistocene.

Antilocaprid head ornamentation consisted of a horny sheath, usually branched, around an unbranched bony core. The sheath was shed annually but the core was retained.

Most species had a single pair of horns, but others had as many as five or six, and some were bizarre in shape. In the living pronghorn, males have longer horns, with forward-pointing prongs below backward, pointing hooked tips—hence the animal's common name.

Although most of the even-toed ungulates have only two functional toes, the others being greatly reduced and not touching the ground, it is only in the pronghorns that all vestiges of the other toes have finally disappeared, with not even bony splints remaining. Their evolution of long, pointed hooves at the end of long, slender legs has enabled the family to be fast runners, (sometimes managing to reach speeds of up to 55 mph/86 kmph when escaping from predators).

Their hooves have also developed cushioning which acts as a shock absorber, protecting the animal's legs against the impact of leaping up to 26 ft/8 m in a single stride.

NAME *Ilingoceros*

TIME Late Miocene

LOCALITY North America (Nevada)

SIZE 6 ft/1.8 m long

The various antilocaprids differ from one another in the shape and arrangement of the horns. *Ilingoceros*, which was slightly larger than the living pronghorn, had a pair of spirally-twisted horns which grew straight up and ended in a slight fork.

Other forms include *Osbornoceros*, with smooth, slightly curved horns; *Paracosoryx*, with flattened horns widening to a forked tip; *Ramoceros*, with extraordinary vertical fan-shaped horns; and the particularly well-endowed *Hayoceros*.

NAME *Hayoceros*

TIME Middle Pleistocene

LOCALITY Nebraska

SIZE 6 ft/1.8 m long

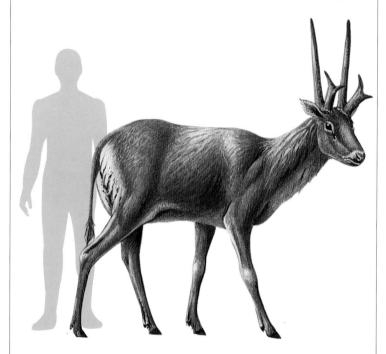

Hayoceros, which inhabited the grasslands of Nebraska in the Middle Pleistocene, was a particularly lavishly ornamented member of the Antilocapridae family. It had no fewer than four horns: one pair of broad, forked horns over its eyes, as in the pronghorn, and another much longer, narrower pair farther back at the top of its skull.

When two males were competing for mating partners, they probably adopted a sparring technique similar to that which is used by the living pronghorns. The competing males lock their forked horns and push until the weaker of the combatants withdraws. These ritualistic bouts, though they often appear to be quite violent, rarely seem to result in any permanent injury to either animal.

Family Bovidae

These are the true antelopes and the cattle. The head ornamentation of both males and females consists of bony horn cores covered with true horn that is not shed annually.

The bovids had evolved in the Old World by Miocene times around 20 million years ago but the older Mongolian genus *Hanhaicerus* from Oligocene deposits may also be a bovid. The earliest fossils, of gazelle-like bovids, have been found in France, the Sahara, and Mongolia. By the Late Miocene, about 10 million years ago, there was a huge increase in bovid variety, with 70 new genera appearing. By the Pleistocene, there were more than 100 genera, about twice as many as exist today.

Bovids are grazing animals, with high-crowned teeth adapted for chewing grass. Their lifestyle contrasts with most other even-toed ungulates, which eat soft leaves. They spend a great deal of time feeding and their digestive system is adapted to extract the maximum nutrition from the grass on which they feed.

They were restricted to the Old World until as recently as the Mid Pleistocene, about 1 million years ago, when they migrated across the Bering land bridge that existed at the time to reach North America. There they survive today as bison, bighorn sheep, and mountain goats. The vast majority of bovids, however, still live in the Old World, occupying a great range of habitats from forests and grasslands to swamps and even deserts.

NAME *Pelorovis*

TIME Middle to Late Pleistocene

LOCALITY East Africa

SIZE 10ft/3m long

This massive animal was a close relative of the modern African buffalo. The main difference between *Pelorovis* and its modern counterpart, apart from its sheer size, was the enormous set of horns that the creature carried on its head. Since the bony cores of the horns alone had a span of 6ft 6in/2m, in life the horns might have reached up to twice that size. (This has to be an estimate since horn itself decays rapidly after death and leaves behind no fossilized remains.)

Pelorovis survived in East Africa until as recently as about 12,000 years ago.

NAME *Bos*

TIME Pleistocene to Recent

LOCALITY Europe (Britain, Poland), Asia (India), and North Africa

SIZE 10ft/3m long

This is the genus to which modern domestic cattle belong. It may have evolved from a rather slim and antelope-like ox, *Leptobos*, found in early Pleistocene deposits in Eurasia. The ancestor of most of today's cattle was *Bos primigenius*, better known as the aurochs. It was larger than most of today's breeds and was first domesticated about 6000 years ago, although it was known to humans much earlier. Cave paintings at Lascaux, in central France, include dramatic and beautiful representations of these great cattle.

The aurochs spread during Pleistocene times from its center of origin in Asia. By the end of the last Ice Age it occupied a vast range in the Old World, from westernmost Europe to easternmost Asia, and from the Arctic tundras to North Africa and India. Despite their success, however, the aurochs eventually disappeared, succumbing to human hunting pressure. They became extinct in Britain by the 10th century AD, and the last surviving aurochsen died in Poland in 1627.

There are a number of surviving native species of *Bos* elsewhere such as the wild yak (*Bos grunniens*) of nothern India, Tibet, and China.

RODENTS, RABBITS, AND HARES

Traditionally, the rodents (guinea-pigs, rats, and mice) have been thought by taxonomists to be closely associated with the lagomorphs (rabbits, hares, and pikas). Recent molecular analysis, however, has rejected this association, instead indicating a surprising relationship for the lagomorphs with the primates and tree-shrews (Scandentia).

As a result of this reassessment of their relationships with other orders the rodents, whose uniqueness as a group had been questioned, are now restored as a natural group, but separated from the lagomorphs. It is now generally believed by paleontologists that the rodents are a relatively early and primitive group in the evolution of the mammals, and that the lagomorphs branched off before the radiation of the primates, artiodactyls, and Carnivora.

ORDER RODENTIA

The earliest-known rodents resembled small squirrels. They appeared in North America during the Late Paleocene, about 60 million years ago. Soon after their first appearance, the rodents diversified, adapting to take over the ecological niches abandoned by the similar-looking, although unrelated, multituberculates (see p.343), which were disappearing. The rodents have evolved into several major types, including squirrels, beavers, rats, mice, gophers, chinchillas, guinea pigs, and porcupines.

The rodents are by far the largest order of mammals today, with about 2,000 species in 35 families, making up 40 percent of all known living mammals. There are almost as many fossil genera again, and another 12 families.

Rodents are a highly successful group. They have spread over every continent, except Antarctica, and conquered a huge range of habitats, making them ecologically very important. Rodents can be found everywhere from tropical forests to freezing Arctic tundras, and from the hottest, driest deserts to the mountain tops. Rodents frequently live in close association with humans.

Although they have not managed to invade the seas, there are some freshwater rodents, such as beavers and water-rats. There are many tree-dwellers, too, notably the tree squirrels. Most rodents are, however, primarily terrestrial.

Given their versatility and impressively rapid rate of reproduction, it is not surprising that rodents have had a major impact on human history. They consume millions of tons of food every year—both crops and stored food—and carry fatal diseases such as typhus. The most notorious pests are the rats, which are believed to have accounted for more human deaths than all the wars in history. In the Middle Ages, plague borne by the black rat *Rattus rattus* killed around 25 million people—over a quarter of Europe's entire population.

The fossil record of the rodents is sparse, and much of what is known about their evolution is the result of studying tiny fossil teeth. Rodents were abundant throughout Tertiary times, and remains of their distinctive teeth can be used for dating and correlating continental sediments, just as the fossils of invertebrate shells are frequently used for dating and correlating marine sediments.

The chief distinguishing feature of rodents is their ability to gnaw using specially adapted front teeth. There is a single pair of large, curved incisors on the upper and lower jaws. These incisors are worn down with use but grow continuously from roots deep within the skull and mandible. Early members of the group had cylindrical gnawing teeth with enamel all round, but later forms had more triangular teeth with enamel confined to the front face. This keeps the edge sharp since the area behind wears down faster.

There are no canines, and even some of the premolars may be missing, so there is a large gap (diastema) between front and cheek teeth. The remaining cheek teeth form a battery of efficient grinding surfaces.

Rodents are generally small, the harvest mice being among the smallest of all mammals at 1½oz/40g. There are exceptions, however. The largest living rodent is the 110lb/50kg capybara which inhabits South America, but some extinct forms reached the size of a rhinoceros.

An interesting case study of gigantism among the rodents is provided by the giant Pleistocene dormouse *Leithia*, an inhabitant of several Mediterranean islands, including Malta and Sardinia. Except for its much greater size (10in/25cm long without tail), *Leithia* was indistinguishable from the modern dormouse *Muscardinus*.

Having been marooned on the islands when sea levels rose (possibly the result of the influx of the Atlantic into the Mediterranean basin or changing world temperatures during the Pleistocene Ice Age), the inhabitants of Mediterranean islands showed some unusual trends in body size. But whereas elephants (see pp.382–383, 387–388) and hippopotamuses (see p.412) became smaller, to make better use of the limited amount of food that was available, rodents such as *Leithia* became larger. In the absence of potential predators, the rodents had no reason to run and hide in cracks and crannies, as their smaller counterparts had to on the mainland.

The present classification divides the rodents into two suborders, differentiated by the arrangement of the bones and associated muscles of the lower jaw.

Suborder Sciurognathi

The sciurognaths (a name which means "squirrel-jaws") have a deep lower jaw on which the chewing (masseter) muscles are attached. This is by far the larger of the two suborders of rodents, and possibly the more primitive. The suborder includes the present-day families of squirrels, beavers, pocket gophers, hamsters, rats, and mice.

The sciurognath families seem to have diverged early in the evolutionary history of the rodents. Apart from their jaw and tooth structure, they have little else in common. Most are wholly vegetarian, but some are scavenging omnivores, and a few members of the Sciurognathi suborder eat insects.

A quarter of all mammal species today are rats, mice, and voles. Yet this immensely successful group only became ubiquitous at the beginning of the Pliocene, about 5 million years ago.

NAME	Ischyromys
TIME	Early Eocene
RANGE	North America
SIZE	2 ft/60 cm long

Ischyromys is among the earliest known of the true rodents. Mouse-like in appearance, this creature had many of the typical rodent head features, including the characteristic pair of upper incisors. The rest of the body was that of a typical rodent as well, with versatile forelimbs, strong hind limbs and five clawed toes on each of its feet.

While many of the other early Tertiary mammals were occupying the terrestrial niches, all the evidence suggests that *Ischyromys* and its more squirrel-like relative *Paramys* were taking advantage of the possibilities presented by trees.

As the most advanced climbing animals of their time, they eventually displaced the primitive rodent-like primates which had existed there from Paleocene times.

NAME	Epigaulus
TIME	Miocene
RANGE	North America (Great Basin)
SIZE	1 ft/30 cm long

Epigaulus is one of the oddest rodents known. It must have resembled a modern marmot, except that it possessed a pair of stout horns on the skull, small eyes, and its clawed hands were broad and paddle-like. The powerful claws were long and compressed from side to side. Clearly they were well-adapted for digging and so it seems likely that *Epigaulus* lived underground in burrows. The small eyes support this interpretation because many modern burrowing animals, such as the mole, have reduced eyes and limited eyesight.

No other known rodent had horns like these, placed on the snout just in front of the eyes and their function is something of a mystery. They may have been used for protection, sexual display, and combat between males. This interpretation is supported by the fact that not all fossils have horns; implying that those without were probably females. An alternative interpretation is that the horns may have assisted burrowing in some way.

Epigaulus and its closest relatives, the other primitive mylagaulids, died out when forests disappeared and were replaced by grassland in North America in Late Miocene times, about 5 million years ago.

NAME *Steneofiber*

TIME Early Miocene

RANGE Europe (France, Germany)

SIZE 1 ft/30 cm long

Suborder Hystricognathi

This is thought to be the more advanced suborder of rodents, despite the fact that the earliest known rodent probably belongs to this group.

The hystricognaths or "porcupine-jaws" have their chewing (masseter) muscles anchored on a bony flange which has developed from the lower jaw.

Although hystricognaths include some Old World species—for example porcupines, and the gundis and cane rats—most members of the suborder are natives of South America. No rodents have been found in South America prior to the Early Oligocene, when they occur in the far south of Patagonia.

South American hystricognaths include New World porcupines, cavies or guinea pigs, capybaras, pacaranas, chinchillas, agoutis, and coypus.

Beavers are well-represented in the fossil record from as far back as the Early Oligocene, around 35 million years ago. The early Miocene beaver *Steneofiber* was small, and lived on and near freshwater lakes, much as most living beavers do today. It is unlikely, however, that it could have felled large trees, as its modern counterparts do.

Many early species were more terrestrial, however, and some even burrowed. The Miocene deposits of Nebraska show strange vertical corkscrew-shaped burrows, 8 ft/2.5 m deep, which have been given the name "Daimonelix" or "Devil's corkscrews." These were excavated by the gopher-like beaver *Palaeocastor*, a close relative of *Steneofiber*.

Many beavers were giants, including the bear-sized *Castoroides* (7 ft 6 in/2.3 m long), found throughout North America during Pleistocene times.

NAME *Telicomys*

TIME Late Miocene to early Pliocene

RANGE South America

SIZE 7 ft/2 m long

Closely related to the guinea pigs and capybaras were the stout-tailed burrowing dinomyids ("terrible mice"), the pacarana family. The largest of these—indeed, probably the largest rodent which has ever lived—was *Telicomys*.

Teliocomys reached the size of a small rhinoceros, and would probably have looked rather like a hairy hippopotamus, or a giant capybara.

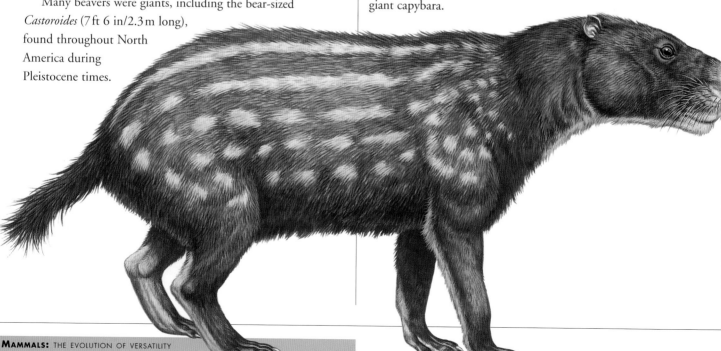

NAME *Birbalomys*

TIME Early Eocene

RANGE Asia (Pakistan)

SIZE 1 ft/30 cm long

Birbalomys is considered by some paleontologists to be the most primitive rodent, one which is probably close to the ancestry of the whole rodent group.

So little is known about *Birbalomys* that the restoration given (above) is highly speculative. *Birbalomys* may have resembled the North African gundis, creatures rather like guinea pigs which today inhabit desert or semi-desert habitats.

NAME *Eocardia*

TIME Miocene

LOCALITY South America

SIZE 1 ft/30 cm long

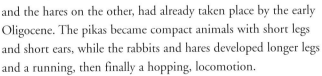

Cavioids are the most typical South American rodents and are closely related to the guinea pigs and the capybara.

Some cavioids became quite large. *Protohydrochoerus,* for example, was about the size of a tapir. However, *Eocardia* was more modest in size, reaching only 1 ft/30 cm tall and resembling the present-day guinea pig in appearance.

ORDER LAGOMORPHA

The lagomorphs—the pikas, rabbits, and hares—were once classed along with the rodents. Indeed, they seem to be very much like rodents, with their relatively small size and their continually growing, gnawing teeth.

The main difference between them lies in the fact that lagomorphs have two pairs of gnawing teeth in the front of the upper jaw, rather than the single pair found in rodents. These teeth have enamel all the way around them. Lagomorphs tend to have more cheek teeth than rodents (five or six, as opposed to five or fewer), and these are usually less ridged.

The chewing action is different too: lagomorph jaws work sideways, while those of rodents work backward and forward. The evidence that the lagomorphs are related to the rodents is ambiguous: their gnawing way of life might have developed through parallel evolution.

About 12 lagomorph genera survive today, although there have been four times that number since the order evolved. The earliest fossil representatives appeared possibly in eastern Asia, in the Late Paleocene or Early Eocene. Lagomorphs swiftly became a widespread vegetarian group, chiefly exploiting grassy plants and shrubs in rocky and desert areas.

Having been deliberately introduced in the 19th century into Australasia, where there were no natural predators, the rabbits' prodigious rate of reproduction and immense appetite for leaves and grain made it a serious pest.

NAME *Palaeolagus*

TIME Oligocene

RANGE North America

SIZE 10 in/25 cm long

The earliest lagomorph is *Eurymulus,* from the Late Paleocene of Mongolia. The separation of the group into the pikas on the one hand, and the rabbits and the hares on the other, had already taken place by the early Oligocene. The pikas became compact animals with short legs and short ears, while the rabbits and hares developed longer legs and a running, then finally a hopping, locomotion.

The skeleton of *Palaeolagus* is similar to that of a modern rabbit. However, the hind legs are a little shorter, suggesting that is was not yet the leaping animal so familiar today.

LEMURS AND MONKEYS

PRIMATES AND PRIMATOMORPHS

For over 150 years it has been recognized that humans are related to the apes. More recently, it became evident that this relationship extended to the monkeys, lemurs, and tarsiers, which are the survivors of a much more diverse group of fossil primates. The fossil record of the shared ancestry of humans and the primates is extremely patchy and fragmental. Consequently there is great difficulty in establishing relationships between the numerous groups and this is reflected in an often cumbersome, constantly changing and confusing classification.

The term primates—from the Latin word *primus*, meaning "first"—has traditionally been used to group together lemurs (Lemuridae), monkeys, apes, and humans (Anthropoidea), and their closest fossil ancestors. However, the recognition of the close association of the flying lemurs (called the Dermoptera and different from the Lemuridae) to the primates has resulted in the use of a wider definition under the term primatomorph, which is similar to an older classificatory term "prosimians." Several extinct fossil groups, such as the primitive form *Purgatorius* from the Late Cretaceous and the Plesiadapiformes, are also placed within this broader group of primatomorphs.

Molecular analysis broadens the morphological and palaeontological association of the true living primates with the tree-shrews (*Scandentia*), flying lemurs, and bats (*Chiroptera*). With the exception of the bats, the morphologically based association of the living primates, tree-shrews, flying lemurs, and their fossil ancestors is recognized as a superorder—the Archonta. But the exact nature of the relationships between all these groups is as yet unresolved.

ORDER DERMOPTERA

This group is based on the living flying lemurs. They do not fly but glide, using a membrane stretched between the limbs, body and tail. Until recently they had no fossil record, but recently an Eocene fossil flying lemur has been discovered in Thailand. The expanded concept of the order includes the extinct Plesiadapiformes, a fossil group of several families that radiated in the Early Tertiary of North America and western Europe.

Family Plesiadapidae

These are the best-known of the five families of Plesiadapiformes. Examples are plentiful from the Paleocene and Eocene of North America and Europe (roughly 65 million to 40

million years ago), a fact which indicates both a land connection between the continents and a uniformity of conditions between these areas at this time. It is possible that plesiadapids spread from North America to Europe via Greenland, which was at that time a warm, wooded "land bridge." Their features included a long tail, agile limbs with claws rather than nails, a long snout containing rodent-like jaws and teeth, and eyes placed on the sides of the head.

NAME *Plesiadapis*

TIME Late Paleocene to Early Eocene

LOCALITY North America (Rocky Mountains) and Europe (France)

SIZE 2 ft 6 in/80 cm long

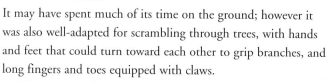

So many *Plesiadapis* remains have been found near Cernay in north-eastern France that it must have been a common animal at the time.

Plesiadapis was squirrel-like in build and about the size of a modern beaver. It may have spent much of its time on the ground; however it was also well-adapted for scrambling through trees, with hands and feet that could turn toward each other to grip branches, and long fingers and toes equipped with claws.

Nevertheless, the head of *Plesiadapis* was not that of a typical primate. The teeth resembled those of a rodent, with long gnawing incisors at the front, and a gap between them and the grinding molars in the cheek.

ORDER PRIMATES

The primates consist of some 200 living species, depending on how the order is defined. Modern humans are just one of these species. All primates are united by more than 30 characters that mostly relate to particular evolutionary adaptations for climbing in trees, prolonged parental nurture of offspring and high development of vision and intelligence.

Primates seem to have developed in a predominantly forested environment. In fact, many specific adaptations can be traced to the exacting demands of tree-dwelling, and to daylight living rather than nocturnal activity. Among these were interrelated developments in the enlarged, complex brain, the senses, and the limbs and digits. There was also a tendency toward a bipedal gait: the body became more erect, the feet and legs were specialized for movement, and the hands were adapted for holding and manipulating. Balance, touch, and grasp all improved, and there were two great developments in vision: the ability to see stereoscopically and in color.

Another critical development in such a precarious environment included a reproductive strategy that placed a premium on high parental involvement and protection and a small number of offspring.

The group includes a wide range of extinct and living forms from the fossil lemur-like adapids, to the lemurs (lemurids) and lorises (lorisids), which are clustered as the lemuriformes. Also, there are the tarsiers (tarsiids) and extinct omomyids, which are clustered as tarsiiformes, and finally the anthropoids—the monkeys, apes, and their fossil ancestors.

Family Adapidae

The lemur-like adapids were abundant in Eocene times, but then declined, becoming extinct in the Late Miocene about 10 million years ago. They were mostly European, but some lived in Asia and North America.

Adapids had several features that were a distinct advance on those of the plesiadapids. Their backs were more supple, which increased their mobility in trees, as did their longer, more flexible limbs (whose digits bore nails rather than claws) and grasping big toes and thumbs. They had shorter snouts, with eyes that had moved round closer to the front of the face. Their brains, too, were relatively large. Although it is possible that adapids could only cling and leap, it seems likely that they were advanced enough to walk and run on top of branches.

The lemur-like adapids and lemurids are sometimes grouped together as the Strepsirhini ("twisted noses") because their moist noses are divided vertically and laterally by slits.

NAME *Notharctus*
TIME Early to Middle Eocene
LOCALITY North America (Wyoming)
SIZE 16 in/40 cm long

This North American adapid was the last primate known from that continent. In appearance it was probably much like a modern lemur, and it was highly adapted for living in trees. It had eyes directed forward, which gave stereoscopic vision and

enabled it to judge distances accurately, long hind legs that allowed it to jump from branch to branch, and a long heavy tail to balance it in its acrobatics.

The first digit in the hand and on the foot formed a kind of thumb, a characteristic that enabled *Notharctus* to grasp both branches and food.

Family Lemuridae

Lemurs are similar to the adapids, but they have a long "comb" derived from the front teeth in the lower jaw, which is used for grooming.

About 50 million years ago, lemurs and their close relatives were found throughout Africa, Europe, and North America. Today, the lemurs, the Indri lemurs, and the aye-ayes survive only in Madagascar.

NAME *Megaladapis*
TIME Recent
LOCALITY Madagascar
SIZE 5 ft/1.5 m long

The largest-known lemur, with a massive body and short limbs, *Megaladapis* must have weighed about 110 lb/50 kg. Unlike its smaller relatives, it would not have been able to swing and leap about in the trees. It was probably a slow climber, clambering about in the tropical forest in search of leaves to eat. It was possibly finally wiped out by humans.

Family Omomyidae

This is the largest family of the tarsiers, and a group that still exists today (although in greatly depleted numbers) on some Southeast Asian islands, such as Sumatra and Borneo. The omomyids were abundant in Eocene times but declined during the Oligocene and had virtually died out by the beginning of the Miocene.

Tarsiers are grouped together as the Haplorhini (the "whole noses") because their noses are undivided.

Some paleontologists have considered that the tarsiers were the common ancestors of the monkeys and apes, though this seems unlikely given their extreme specialization.

NAME *Necrolemur*

TIME Middle to Late Eocene

LOCALITY Western Europe

SIZE 10 in/25 cm long

Necrolemur is the best preserved fossil member of the tarsier group. Its remains indicate that the animal had large eyes and ears, which enabled it to hunt at night. Its small sharp teeth were ideal for dealing with tough-shelled insects—which were its main food. *Necrolemur*'s body, too, would have been similar to the living species, with gripping pads on its long fingers and toes, long agile arms and legs, and a long tail that would have been used as a counterbalance when moving through the trees.

SUBORDER ANTHROPOIDEA

The suborder Anthropoidea contains two infraorders—the platyrrhines ("flat noses") or New World monkeys, and the catarrhines ("downfacing noses") or Old World monkeys, apes, and hominids. They evolved in North America or Eurasia around 40 million years ago. The two lines diverged soon after when a land bridge that linked North with South America once more disappeared.

New World Monkeys

The New World monkeys are distinguished from the Old World monkeys partly by their nostrils, which are placed wider apart and face outward rather than downward. There are also several other distinguishing anatomical features, including distinctive skull joints, or sutures, and the possession of one more pair of premolars than their Old World relatives.

Some species have an additional "limb" in the form of a prehensile tail—one that is able to support the body by coiling around branches. Curiously, this useful adaptation to tree dwelling never evolved in the Old World monkeys.

Modern representatives of this group include the delicate and often highly-coloured marmosets and tamarins, and the spider and howler monkeys. Together they constitute about one third of modern anthropoid genera.

NAME *Branisella*

TIME Early Oligocene

LOCALITY South America (Bolivia)

SIZE 16 in/40 cm long

This is the earliest-known monkey to have lived on the South American continent, but little can be said with confidence about *Branisella*'s lifestyle and relationships because the only fossil evidence of its existence are some fragments of jawbone.

The *Branisella*'s teeth were quite primitive, with many tarsier-like features. This would suggest that it evolved from the omomyids farther north. However, some other physical attributes seem to indicate that *Branisella* was quite close to the monkeys which were then living in Africa. So there is even the possibility that its ancestors may have reached South America by drifting across the Atlantic from west Africa on floating islands of vegetation.

NAME *Tremacebus*

TIME Late Oligocene

LOCALITY South America (Argentina)

SIZE 3 ft 3 in/1 m long

By the end of the Oligocene New World monkeys had become very much like the modern forms. *Tremacebus*, which is sometimes known as *Homunculus* because of its miniature humanoid form, must have resembled today's only truly nocturnal owl monkey, the *Douroucouli*.

Tremacebus is known from only a few specimens, including a skull, from Patagonia. The paucity of remains in this area suggests that the plains of Patagonia were as treeless then as they are now, so there was too small a woodland environment to support any greater monkey diversity.

Old World Monkeys

Old World monkeys, like apes and humans, differ from the New World monkeys in having nostrils that are close together and face downward, a bony canal leading from the exterior to the eardrum, and, in general, one fewer pair of premolar teeth.

Classed together in the family Cercopithecidae, these monkeys form the largest and most primitive group of catarrhines, and include among their modern representatives guenons, baboons, macaques, geladas, and the colobus monkey. Until recently the fossil record was confined to the last 10 million years. But now a 15-million-year-old possible ancestor to the cercopithecines, called *Victoriapithecus*, has been found in Kenya which links these catarrhines with the much older *Aegyptopitheccus* (see p.435).

The tail is never prehensile, and may be greatly reduced or absent, especially in ground-living animals. The tail is useful for tree-dwellers, however, since it improves balance and may allow a change of trajectory in mid-jump.

NAME *Mesopithecus*

TIME Late Miocene to Late Pliocene

LOCALITY Europe (Greece) and Asia (Asia Minor)

SIZE 16 in/40 cm long

Mesopithecus, which is also known as the "middle ape," was typical of the early cercopithecids. It was similar to the modern macaque monkey and was probably ancestral to the modern langur.

It was slim, had long muscular arms and legs, and long, nimble fingers and toes. Its limbs, like those of the modern macaque, could be used both for walking on the ground and for climbing in trees, which suggests that its environment was quite open.

Mesopithecus would have been active during the daytime rather than at night and would have eaten leaves and soft fruits.

NAME *Theropithecus*

TIME Middle Pliocene to Recent

LOCALITY South and East Africa

SIZE 4 ft/1.2 m long

The baboons are largely ground-dwelling monkeys that travel across open plains in family groups. They generally have dog-like faces and consume a wide range of foodstuffs. Although they tend to walk on all fours on the ground, baboons are still very adept at climbing, especially scrambling among rocks.

Theropithecus was a large baboon, the remains of which have been discovered in the Olduvai Gorge in Tanzania. For a baboon it had a short face, and there was a large crest of bone running along the top of its skull that must have held strong jaw muscles. It would probably have fed on tough dry-climate plant material.

APES

FAMILY OREOPITHECIDAE

The classification of the oreopithecids is problematical. Some paleontologists regard them as Old World monkeys related to *Mesopithecus*; but others point to their ape-like and even hominid-like attributes, such as their probable ability to brachiate (use their arms to swing from branch to branch) and even to walk upright. They are almost certainly an evolutionary blind alley, though, whose advanced features are a result of convergence. There is only one genus.

NAME	*Oreopithecus*
TIME	Late Miocene
LOCALITY	Europe (Italy)
SIZE	4 ft/1.2 m tall

Oreopithecus, the "mountain ape," has been jocularly referred to as "the abominable coalman" because the remains of this animal were found in the brown coal deposits of Tuscany in northern Italy, dated to about 14 million years ago. and because some of its features were almost human.

Oreopithecus had a monkey's snout, ape-like brow ridges, and monkey-like ankle bones.

The face was flat and small, the canines conical, and the patterns on the molar teeth resembled those of hominids. This mixture of monkey and human characteristics may be best explained by considering oreopithecines an independent lineage.

Since its remains were preserved in beds of soft brown coal, *Oreopithecus* probably lived in forested, riverside swamps. It is likely that it survived on a diet of leaves, shoots, and fruits of a wide variety of plants.

The animal's arms were rather longer than the legs, which indicates that it spent much of its time in the trees and probably moved about by swinging under branches. The spine and hip bones suggest that it was also able to walk, or at least to lope along in an upright stance.

SUPERFAMILY HOMINOIDEA

The only living hominoids—the word means "resembling humans"—are the apes (pongids) and our own species, *Homo sapiens*. They differ from the Old World monkeys in having no tails, and arms and shoulder girdles that are designed for hanging and swinging from branches.

In addition to the gibbons (hylobatids) and humans plus great apes (hominids), the group includes extinct forms such as the pliopithecids, which are regarded as a subfamily (along with the living gibbons) within the family Hylobatidae.

SUBFAMILY PLIOPITHECINEA

Although pliopithecids possessed some primitive features, including a long snout, a small brain case, and in some cases a tail. They are the earliest well-defined family of true apes. Advanced characteristics include ape-like teeth, jaws, and stereoscopic vision.

Pliopithecids almost certainly evolved in Africa, probably by the Early Oligocene, around 35 million years ago, and became extinct in the Miocene about 10 million years ago.

NAME	*Propliopithecus*
TIME	Middle Oligocene
LOCALITY	Africa (Egypt)
SIZE	16 in/40 cm long

In the Mid-Oligocene, over 27 million years ago, the Fayum region to the east of Cairo was not the dusty desert of today. The River Nile produced a swampy delta here, close to the shoreline of the now-vanished, Tethys sea. The forests of this delta once supported a large number of tropical animal types, including several primitive apes such as *Propliopithecus*

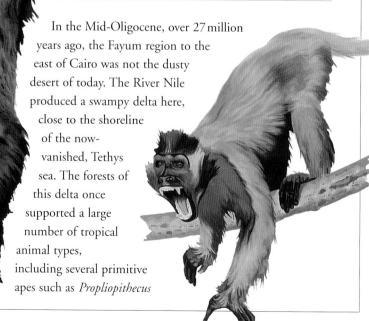

and *Aegyptopithecus*. (It is possible that both names apply to the same creature, in which case the former has priority.)

Propliopithecus was basically a quadrupedal animal, the size of a small gibbon, which ran on all-fours along tree branches in much the same way as the macaques do today.

The eyes were set in well-developed sockets and pointed forward to give stereoscopic vision. The dentition was adapted for eating fruit and was ape-like. *Propliopithecus* probably also ate insects and even small vertebrates.

NAME *Pliopithecus*
TIME Middle to Late Miocene
LOCALITY Europe (France and Czechoslovakia)
SIZE 1 ft/1.2 m tall

Opinions vary among paleontologists, but it now seems unlikely that *Pliopithecus* gave rise to the gibbons, as was once thought. Nevertheless, there are distinct similarities between the two creatures and they probably share a common ancestor in early Miocene times. The gibbon line may even extend back as far as *Propliopithecus* over 30 million years ago. *Pliopithecus* lived between 16 and 10 million years ago, when the Earth really was the "planet of the apes," with some 30 different, but contemporaneous, species most of which are now extinct.

Pliopithecus was gibbon-sized, with a short face, large eyes, and sharp canines. The body was long, and the limbs were equipped with long hands and feet. It may even have been able to brachiate. On the other hand, arms and legs were much the same length (the arms are much longer in gibbons), and there is evidence of a short tail, with 10 or more vertebrae. Its stereoscopic vision may not have been perfect either, because the orbits of the eyes were not directed fully forward.

NAME *Dendropithecus*
TIME Early to Middle Miocene
LOCALITY East Africa (Kenya)
SIZE 2 ft/60 cm tall

It is now widely thought that it was not *Pliopithecus* but one of its earlier relatives, the small eastern Africa apes such as *Micropithecus*, *Limnopithecus* or *Dendropithecus* that was ancestral to the gibbons. Remains of the slimly built *Dendropithecus* ("tree ape") have been dated to middle and early Miocene times, about 15 million to 20 million years ago. Although it had shorter arms and a longer tail than *Pliopithecus*, and was probably no better at brachiating, *Dendropithecus* was more gibbon-like in other respects, including its diet. *Dendropithecus* almost certainly inhabited a densely-forested area and enjoyed fruit, leaves, and flowers, just as the gibbon does today.

Family Hominidae

This family links humans (the subfamily Homininae) with the living great apes (the subfamily Ponginae) and their numerous fossil ancestors. Interrelationships within this broad group, however, are a matter of continuing development and debate as new fossil evidence begins to fill in what is still a very fragmentary fossil ancestry for both the humans and the great apes.

The family includes the largest of all primates at present, although in the past some other extinct primates, such as *Gigantopithecus*, have matched them for size. From fossil evidence and the molecular clock—a dating system based on the rate of genetic change—it is thought that the hominids originated at least 17 million years ago in Africa.

They subsequently diverged into two groups, one of which, the Ponginae, left Africa early in its development and migrated to Asia, where it is now represented by the still living but endangered orangutans. The other group, the Homininae, stayed in Africa until more recently.

SUBFAMILY PONGINAE

The Ponginae family includes the fossil and living apes. They are semi-bipedal, sometimes walking on four feet and sometimes upright on two, and have no tail. Today, the pongines are restricted to tropical Africa and South-east Asia, where two species of chimpanzee, and a single species each of gorilla and orangutan, survive.

Pongines were once a much more diverse group both in terms of the number of genera and in their geographical distribution. The earliest members date from the Early Miocene, around 25 million years ago.

In the past, almost every new specimen of hominoid was treated as a separate genus, and given a new name. This became confusing, and certainly held back the understanding of the broad lines of hominoid evolution. It is now increasingly accepted that many of these "near-people" were in fact closely related, in spite of subtle differences in their anatomies, and should perhaps be thought of as members of the same genus. (There are, after all, quite large anatomical differences among modern humans, too, yet we are one species.)

Until recent years, it was generally assumed that apes parted from the evolutionary line that resulted in australopithecines and humans around 15 to 20 million years ago. However, biochemical studies now suggest that this time period may be much too long.

Detailed investigations have been carried out into our mutual immune responses, and structural differences in DNA (the genetic material incorporated in every living cell) and complex proteins such as the haemoglobin in blood corpuscles. Given certain reasonable assumptions about the spontaneous rate of change of these molecules, it would seem that gibbons probably only split away from the ancestral line about 10 million years ago, with the orangutan parting shortly after.

Perhaps the greatest surprise, though, lies in what these studies imply about the relationship between modern humans and chimpanzees and gorillas. Although superficially we seem to be quite different from one another, in fact our biochemistry is too similar for much more than a period of between 5 million and 8 million years to have elapsed since we separated in evolutionary terms.

This theory about the interrelationships between the apes and man is still controversial, however, not least because fossil australopithecines have been discovered from as long ago as 3.5 million, and perhaps as long as 4 million to 5 million years ago. These seem too much like humans and too little like apes to be the product of only a few million years of evolution.

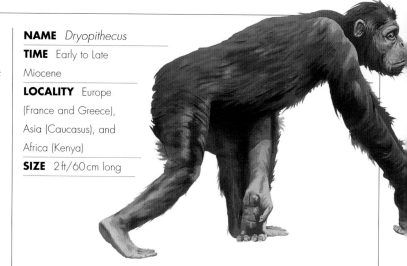

NAME	Dryopithecus
TIME	Early to Late Miocene
LOCALITY	Europe (France and Greece), Asia (Caucasus), and Africa (Kenya)
SIZE	2 ft/60 cm long

The evolutionary lines that developed into the modern apes and *Homo sapiens* may have begun with the widespread *Dryopithecus* ("tree ape") which lived about 12 million to 9 million years ago.

Dryopithecus evolved in East Africa, where the earliest remains have been found, and migrated to Europe and Asia (especially around the eastern end of the Mediterranean) when the continent of Africa fused with that of Eurasia.

The chimpanzee-like limbs show that it would have walked mostly on all-fours but could also walk on two legs. Its wrist was more like a monkey's than an ape's, so it probably walked on the flat of its hand, rather than on its knuckles as chimpanzees do. Its head, too, was rather chimpanzee-like, but it lacked the heavy brow-ridges.

Dryopithecus was definitely a climbing, tree-living animal adapted to eating fruit, since its cheek teeth were too thinly enamelled to chew tougher food such as roots or grasses. However, the environment of the time was developing into woodland mixed with open grass land, so it seems likely that *Dryopithecus* may also have moved about on the grasslands, probably in groups.

NAME	Sivapithecus
TIME	Middle to Late Miocene
LOCALITY	Southeast Europe, Asia, and Africa (Kenya)
SIZE	5 ft/1.5 m tall

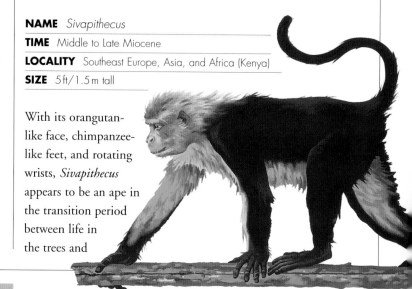

With its orangutan-like face, chimpanzee-like feet, and rotating wrists, *Sivapithecus* appears to be an ape in the transition period between life in the trees and life on the ground. This reconstruction showing a tail is speculative and that presented for the smaller *Ramapithecus* (which may be a sexual dimorph) is more accurate.

The evidence of its life habits are found in the dentition. The canine teeth were large and the molars had a thick covering of enamel—a dentition that is much more suited to the seeds, stems and roots that would have been found growing on the savannah than to the leaves and fruits of the forest.

It is clear that *Sivapithecus* ate drier, tougher foods than the dryopithecines could have managed. In fact, it is known that the climate was changing at that time, around 15 million to 7 million years ago. The forests were dwindling and the grasslands spreading, so it does seem likely that evolution would have promoted the animals that were adapting to these new environmental conditions.

Since important finds were made in India, *Sivapithecus* was named for Siva, one of the principal Hindu gods, sometimes known as Lord of the Beasts.

NAME *Gigantopithecus*

TIME Late Miocene to Middle Pleistocene

LOCALITY Asia (China, Pakistan, India)

SIZE 10 ft / 3 m tall

This enormous creature was a veritable King Kong of the fossil apes. *Gigantopithecus* must have weighed something like 650 lb/300 kg. A close relative of *Sivapithecus*, it is known mostly from fragmental remains of its jaws and teeth, which were about twice the breadth of the teeth of a modern gorilla. They first came to the attention of scientists when a paleontologist

saw four single molars in a Hon[...] Some complete lower jaws were dis[...]

Gigantopithecus was a ground-dwell[...] probably something like a gorilla in appeara[...] shorter jaw and relatively small incisors and can[...] ate roots, tubers, and seeds, but also small vertebra[...]

Gigantopithecus certainly lived until Pleistocene tim[...] 1 million years ago, and perhaps until even more recently. Indeed, it has been surmised by some that *Gigantopithecus* is no[...] extinct even today, but still survives in the remote foothills and mountain passes of the Himalayas, where it is occasionally sighted and identified as the Yeti.

NAME *Ramapithecus*

TIME Middle to Late Miocene

LOCALITY Asia (Pakistan) and Africa (Kenya)

SIZE 4 ft / 1.2 m tall

Ramapithecus —named for Rama, the Hindu god of chivalry and virtue—was originally thought to be a close relative of *Sivapithecus*, but a separate animal. The main distinguishing feature of its skeletal remains is that they are a little smaller in stature than *Sivapithecus*. They are now thought to be just sexual dimorphs, that is females of *Sivapithecus* and possibly some other similar genera.

Although the animal has elbows similar to those of modern apes, the arm bones are quite primitive and seem to indicate that movement by arm suspension was not a fundamental trait of the apes as has been thought. The face and skull share several features with the orang-utan which implies a developmental relationship between the two. If this is correct then this lineage has the potential to calibrate ape evolution.

The fossil evidence of the earliest occurrence of late Miocene Eurasian hominoids (such as *Sivapithecus* and *Dryopithecus*) is dated at around 12.5 million years in the Siwalik sedimentary sequence of Pakistan. Older strata show no evidence of any large hominoid so 12.5 million years is the minimum estimate for the timing of the orang-utan lineage and its divergence from the African bipedal hominids and apes. This can be used to calibrate the molecular clock and the genetic distance between the orang-utan and the African ape/human lineages.

inization," on
and cultural
fferences in
ges in way of
lations. Physical
on and posture,
egs longer than
pelvis and of
babies; increased
d the "precision
grip ————————————— ly between
thumb and forefinger; and modifications of the head.

Compared with less evolved primates, hominids have smaller
jaws and teeth, flatter faces, and more thickly enamelled teeth.
They have lost the ridges of bone over the eyes and the crest on
the top of the skull, but their brains are larger relative to the rest
of the body, and their brains are more complex.

Cultural developments have included the formation of
groups, cooperative work, tool-making, the harnessing of fire,
the making of sculpture and painting, and burial rites.

Each development should be seen as existing in a complex
feedback relationship with the others. For example, the freeing
of the hands from use in locomotion makes possible greater
facility in the production of tools, which encourages increased
hand-eye coordination and the development of the brain.

But tool-use also puts a premium on improvements in child-
rearing, social organization, and communication. A long-term
social group which prolongs infant care and supports its
members throughout adulthood is more capable of acquiring,
sharing, and accumulating experience. Groups that cooperate
intimately are also likely to use tools better, and to improve their
design and manufacture.

Many crucial cultural developments—such as language and
social structure—do not fossilize, so paleontologists can only
make guesses based on the activities which leave traces, for
example evidence of burial rites. And precisely because we have
such a selective record to go on, great caution must be exercised
in interpretation.

It is easy to let prejudice color the picture of the past. On
the whole, it is only hard objects which survive, so a lot is
known about stone tools but almost nothing about tools made
of animal and plant materials, such as leather and plaited-fiber
bags and baby slings. This type of bias in the fossil record could
lead to misunderstanding, not only of the nature of our
ancestors' diet but even their social life—if hunting is
emphasized, for instance, and the possible significance of
foraging for plants ignored.

SUBFAMILY HOMININAE

This subfamily unites humans and our fossil ancestors with the
extinct group of australopiths, meaning "southern apes." This
name reflects the discovery of these fossil hominids in southern
Africa. Since the discovery of the first australopith in the 1920s
by Raymond Dart, numerous other fossils have been found
throughout southern and eastern Africa from Pliocene and early
Pleistocene sediments. The fossil record from this area includes
the earliest known hominines dating from around 4.4 million
years ago, *Australopithecus ramidus*.

NAME	*Australopithecus afarensis*
TIME	Mid Pliocene
LOCALITY	Africa (Ethiopia and Tanzania)
SIZE	around 4ft/1.2m tall

One of earliest known
hominines, dating from
around 3.5 million
years ago, was
*Australopithecus
afarensis*—the "southern
ape from Afar." The partial
skeletons of this hominine, from
the Afar Triangle in northern
Ethiopia, match a slightly earlier
series of footprints in
volcanic ash near
Laetoli in Tanzania.
When it was
excavated in 1974, the
first skeleton was nicknamed "Lucy"
after a song by the Beatles.

The adults were small—not much
larger in height and weight than a six-
year-old child today. The skull and face
were not unlike a chimpanzee's, with
prominent brow ridges, but the
brain was a little larger (about
400cc). Lucy's teeth were chipped
in front, probably the result of using them to grip with.

The hips were quite narrow—implying that babies had
smaller heads relative to modern babies—but otherwise quite
human-like. The legs, too, signify that Lucy was fully bipedal:
she walked upright, albeit with a slight stoop, and with very
little of the chimpanzee's lurching gait. The footprints confirm

that the feet were essentially the same as modern human feet, but without a ball at the base of the big toe so that Lucy would have walked flat-footed, with the toes slightly curled in.

The combination of ape and human features makes *A. afarensis* a likely common ancestor of both modern humans and the robust australopithecines. Recent discoveries have, however, displaced *A. afarensis* as the oldest autralopithecine. In 1995 a new 4-million-year-old species, *A. anamensis*, was described, and in 1995 another, *A. ramidus*, at around 4.4 million years old. It is now the most primitive, also having features linking it to the later hominds. Both new species were discovered the Turkana region of East Africa.

NAME *Australopithecus africanus*

TIME Late Pliocene

LOCALITY African (Ethiopia, Kenya, South Africa, Tanzania)

SIZE 4 ft 4 in / 1.3 m tall

The skull of an infant specimen of *Australopithecus africanus*—"southern ape of Africa"—was unearthed in the Transvaal in 1924. It was largely disregarded at the time because anthropologists thought that the story of human origins lay with a fossil found some years earlier in Piltdown in southern England which was later proved to be a fake.

Australopithecus africanus is now regarded as a hominine, which probably descended from *A. afarensis* and was ancestral to *A. robustus*.

It lived around 3–2.5 million years ago. Even if *A. africanus* was not our direct ancestor, it was certainly very close. The brain was small by modern standards, being about the same size as a chimpanzee's (up to 400 cc), and the face still had heavy, ape-like jaws. The canine teeth were reasonably large, but in other respects the dentition was quite human.

Like *Australopithecus afarensis*, *A. africanus* was a slightly built creature, probably weighing about 65 lb/30 kg, which walked upright. More important than its overall appearance though, was its lifestyle. Some have claimed that *A. africanus* had moved from woodland to open savannah, and had already developed tools and cooperative hunting techniques, with a gang

of individuals hunting down and killing a singl[e]
chasing away another hunting animal from its kill. O[...]
that the evidence is equivocal. The bone "tools" are so ill-[...]
that they are probably nothing more than the remains of a
hyena's meal.

Although hunting was probably significant in human evolution, it is likely that plants—including seeds, nuts, fruit, leaves, stems, and roots—formed the major part of the diet.

NAME *Australopithecus robustus*

TIME Late Pliocene to Early Pleistocene

LOCALITY Africa (South Africa and Tanzania)

SIZE 5 ft 4 in / 1.6 m tall

A sideline of human evolution, *Australopithecus robustus* was, as its name suggests, a very large australopithecine ("southern ape") that lived from around 2.5 million to 1 million years ago. Whilst it is most likely to have descended from *A. africanus*, its relationship to other contemporary australopithecines, such as *A. boisei* and *A. aethiopicus*, is problematic.

Apart from its relatively large build (although it was still only about 110 lb/50 kg), the main difference between *A. robustus* and the other species was its ape-like face, massive jaws, and larger brain (about 500 cc).

Like its relatives, *Australopithecus robustus* seems to have left the forests and taken up a plains-dwelling existence. Almost certainly exclusively vegetarian, the fossil evidence suggests that *A. robustus* would have been the hunted rather than the hunter, since most of the best-preserved skeletons come from carcasses that were killed by carnivores. For example, a broken skull of *A. robustus* has been found with teeth marks that match up exactly to the fossilized teeth of a leopard.

The very large jaws of *Australopithecus robustus* were powered by strong muscles anchored to a crest over the top of the skull, a physical characteristic which gave rise to one of the early vernacular names for this creature— "nutcracker."

HUMANS CONTINUED

Homo

...ows that anatomical humans, ...merged over 2 million years ago, ...*afarensis* or *A. africanus*. Stone tool ...these earliest humans and there were at least t.. ...ry tool making species of *Homo* living in Africa around t.. ...me, *H. rudofensis*, *H. ergaster*, *H. habilis* and possibly *H. erectus*. The emergence of modern humans took place over 0.5 million years ago, with *H. heidelbergensis* from whom firstly the Neanderthals came then *H. sapiens* about 40,000 years ago.

Analysis of DNA from all different groups of living humans shows that we are all integrally the same and originated from a common ancestor—probably an African *H. heidelbergensis*.

NAME *Homo habilis*

TIME Early Pleistocene

LOCALITY Africa (Ethiopia, Kenya, Tanzania, possibly South Africa) and possibly Southeast Asia

SIZE 4 to 5 ft/1.2 to 1.5 m

By about 2 to 1.5 million years ago, several hominines existed alongside one another in East Africa. Some were close enough to modern humans to be classed in the genus *Homo*. The relationship of *H. habilis* to the other *Homo* species is not clear. *Homo habilis* was still quite short and light, with less massive jaws and brow ridges than its predecessors. Its head too was larger than that of its predecessors, as was its brain (up to about 800 cc). The brain was also more complex. There is even some evidence from the brain's structure that *H. habilis* would have been able to speak. However, the distinctive feature of *H. habilis*, or "handy human," is that it is one of the first hominines that is known to have fabricated and used tools. These tools mostly consisted of pebbles with a makeshift blade chipped out along one edge. There is also some evidence of the construction of simple shelters, scavenging, and the hunting of game by *H. habilis*.

NAME *Homo erectus*

TIME Early to Middle Pleistocene

LOCALITY Africa (Tanzania, South Africa, and Algeria), Europe (Germany, Spain, France, Greece, and Hungary), and Asia (Java and China)

SIZE about 5 ft 4 in/1.6 m tall

Homo erectus (the name meaning "upright human") was an outstandingly successful creature. Having evolved around 1.6 million years or more ago, it saw the extinction of all other hominids, including its possible ancestors. It survived until about 200,000 years ago and gave rise to our ancestor *H. heidelbergensis*. In its bodily appearance, posture and gait, *Homo erectus* must have been very similar to a modern human, although a little shorter. At 950 to 1,200 cc, the brain volume, too, was approaching the modern size, and areas of the brain associated with speech were well-developed. The head, however, still had heavy ape-like eyebrow ridges and protruding jaws. *H. erectus* was evidently a wandering gatherer and hunter, moving about in groups, but also creating settlements: a site in the south of France provides evidence of huts with brushwood walls supported on a framework of poles and anchored by stones. Tools found at the sites were sophisticated, and included spears, projectiles, blades, scrapers, and choppers made from wood, stone, antler, and bone. *H. erectus* is believed to have used fire for cooking and for defense.

About half a million years ago, *H. erectus* left its birthplace in Africa and spread throughout the tropical, subtropical and temperate parts of the Old World. Remains have been discovered in so many places that a multitude of confusing common and scientific names have been applied, including Java and Peking (Beijing) people, *Pithecanthropus* ("ape human") *Sinanthropus* ("China human"), and *Palaeanthropus* ("old human"). All are now placed together in the same species.

NAME *Homo sapiens neanderthalensis*

TIME Late Pleistocene

LOCALITY Europe (Mediterranean region) and Asia (Israel)

SIZE up to 5 ft 7 in / 1.7 m tall

Homo sapiens neanderthalensis, the "wise person from the valley of the River Neander," is named for a site in Germany where skeletons were discovered in 1856. However, it took more than 20 years for anthropologists to accept the significance of the find. Even when they did it was to portray the Neanderthals as very much "subhuman," primitive beings with low intelligence. Now it is known that they were powerfully built intelligent people some 30 percent larger and heavier than modern humans, with males weighing in at some 198 lb / 90 kg.

Many fossils have been discovered from Gibraltar and North Africa in the west, throughout the Near East, and east to central Asia.

Neanderthal people evolved around 250,000 years ago. They were very successful during the warm periods toward the end of the Pleistocene Ice Age, but probably died out around 30,000 years ago. Until recently, it was thought that Neanderthals may have interbred with the later, more advanced migrants from North Africa. But it now seems more likely that the Neanderthals represent the most recent extinct side-branch of the human family. Samples of DNA taken from the original Neanderthal fossils have shown that modern humans have not inherited any Neanderthal genetic traits. Apparently, Neanderthals and Cro-Magnons, the modern humans that replaced them, did not interbreed although they co-existed in some places for around 10,000 years. The DNA data also shows that Neanderthals and modern humans diverged from a common ancestor (*Homo heidelbergensis*) around 500,000 years ago.

From north of the Pyrenees populations of Neanderthals seem to have adopted certain "advanced" Cro-Magnon behavioral traits, whilst more southerly Spanish Neanderthals did not. They all became extinct between 34,000 and 3,000 years ago. It is not clear why.

Their bodies were short and powerfully built, and they had large hands and joints, a rather broad head, a flat or bulbous nose, and prominent eyebrows. The brain capacity, often in excess of 1,400 cc, was in fact on average greater than that of modern humans.

Neanderthal people were more sophisticated than previously thought, with a well-developed tool technology. They also show the beginnings of what has been thought of as a religious culture. For example, they buried the dead and clearly treated the cave bear, *Ursus spelaeus* (see p.361), with reverence.

NAME *Homo sapiens* "Cro-Magnon"

TIME Late Pleistocene to Recent

LOCALITY Worldwide

SIZE 5 ft to 6 ft / 1.5 m to 1.8 m tall

The modern subspecies of *Homo sapiens* is well known throughout the world from about 35,000 years ago. Artefacts and cave paintings found in central France, dating from about 30,000 years ago, testify to their cultural sophistication.

These remains of "Cro-Magnon people" suggest that they had a strong tribal system, made tools, gathered plant materials, hunted, fished and possibly herded animals, and built shelters and made clothing that enabled them to survive the last stages of the Pleistocene Ice Age. About 10,000 years ago, populations in many different parts of the world independently developed a farming lifestyle. Animals, such as pigs and sheep were domesticated, crops planted, a more sedentary lifestyle developed, and populations grew. The ability to modify the natural environment has led *Homo sapiens* to the dominant position that it currently enjoys.

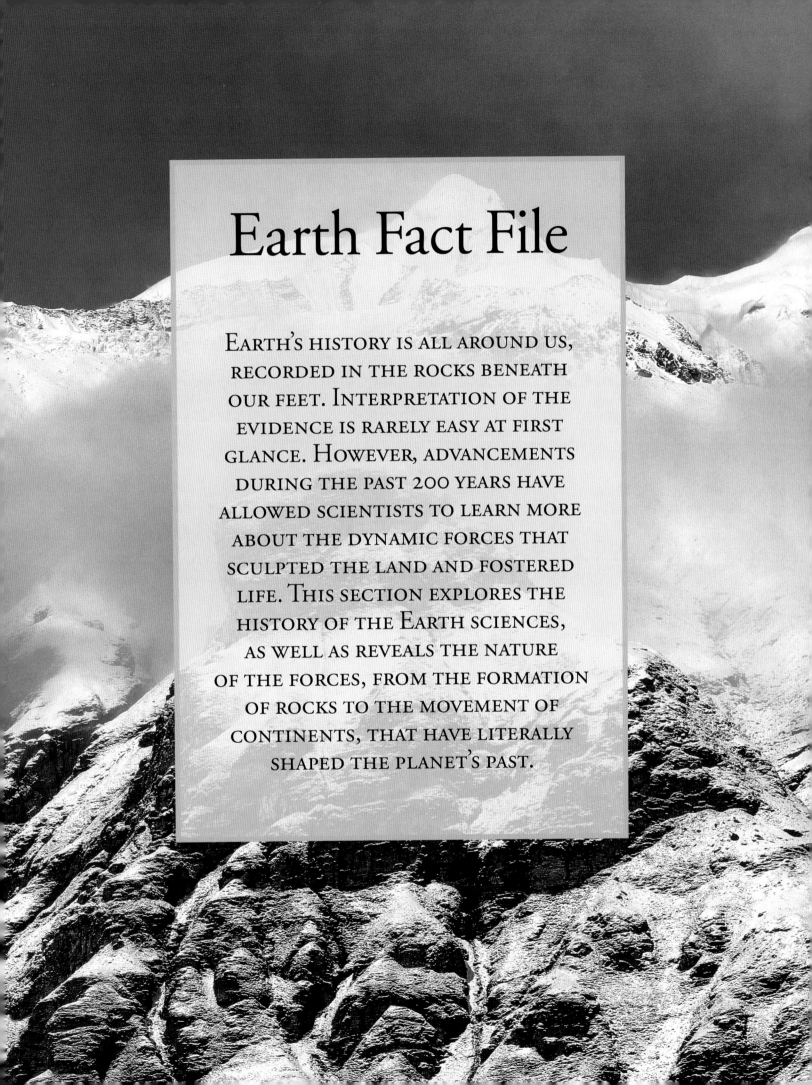

Earth Fact File

Earth's history is all around us, recorded in the rocks beneath our feet. Interpretation of the evidence is rarely easy at first glance. However, advancements during the past 200 years have allowed scientists to learn more about the dynamic forces that sculpted the land and fostered life. This section explores the history of the Earth sciences, as well as reveals the nature of the forces, from the formation of rocks to the movement of continents, that have literally shaped the planet's past.

Earth History: The Geological Timescale

The scientists who pieced together the Earth's history began without any geological "calendar" or "clock." Their task was like constructing a family tree from a mass of anonymous photographs; family likenesses, hairstyles, and fashions all point to relationships and chronology, but those limited clues can be misleading. The discovery of the Earth's distant past and the establishment of its broad chronology have been achieved only in the last 200 years. Now, thanks largely to radiometric dating, we can accurately date the formation of some rocks. We know with some certainty that the Earth is 4.6 billion years old.

English naturalist Charles Darwin's (1809–82) theory of evolution took little account of the fossil record because of its imperfections and lack of a timescale. His calculation of 300 million years for Tertiary times was a considerable overestimate, it lasted 65 million years.

A 6,000-YEAR-OLD EARTH

During the 17th and 18th centuries, attempts to determine the age of the Earth used the only dating techniques then available—historical documents, calendar systems, and astronomy. Even the greatest natural philosophers and mathematicians, such as Isaac Newton, believed that human history had prevailed through the same period in time as the history of the Earth. In 1650, James Ussher, Archbishop of Armagh in Ireland, calculated the date of the Earth's origin, according to biblical chronology, as 4004 BC. This age was generally accepted for nearly 200 years.

LAYING DOWN STRATA

Most early work on establishing a geological timescale focused on examining sedimentary strata—layers of rock formed by the deposition, or sedimentation, of mineral particles carried to the sedimentation site by water or wind. As early as 1669, the Danish natural philosopher and physician, Nicolaus Steno, formulated the "law of superposition." This stated that, in a given sequence of sedimentary strata, the bottom layers were laid down first, and layers become progressively younger toward the top. As a result of early investigations of superimposed strata, undertaken between 1780 and 1830, geologists gradually recognized that Earth processes, such as weathering, erosion, and transportation of sediment were incredibly slow. The accumulation of the great thicknesses of strata making up the layers of the Earth must, therefore, have taken a great length of time, much longer than the 6,000-year span allowed for by Christian theologians.

THE PRINCIPLES OF STRATIGRAPHY

Stratigraphy is a means of interpreting the history of the Earth's changing landscapes and seascapes. Past environments and their lifeforms are revealed by examining successive rock layers. These strata record deposition and erosion on land and at sea. It has taken 200 years to sequence, subdivide, match, and interpret these strata. The story of the last 600 million years is now known, but the history of the Earth's first 4 billion years is still uncertain.

PROBLEMS WITH STRATIGRAPHY

Stratigraphic layers do not always appear in chronological order. Many factors can cause older layers to appear above newer ones. The action of plate tectonics and mountain building can turn rock strata completely upside down (inversion).

In addition, volcanic igneous rock may intrude into sedimentary strata and other rock. When this happens, the igneous rock forms a relatively young layer between two older layers. This is an example of a cross-cutting relationship.

CROSS-CUTTING RELATIONSHIPS

A specific kind of cross-cutting relationship is called an angular unconformity. An unconformity represents a period during which no sediment is being deposited in an area. Folding, faulting, and erosion disrupt and displace the surface of the non-depositional area. When deposition is resumed, it cross-cuts the original surface to form an angular unconformity. The entire process can take millions of years, so unconformities represent major time gaps in the stratigraphic record. The most famous example of an angular unconformity, at Siccar Point in Berwickshire, Scotland, is known as Hutton's unconformity. Here, vertically inclined gray sandstone is overlain by gently inclined red sandstone.

THE FOSSIL RECORD

By the end of the 18th century, fossils were generally accepted as the remains of past, frequently extinct, forms of life. In the early 19th century, William Smith in England and Georges Cuvier and Alexandre Brongniart in France, discovered that successive layers of sediment contained fossils that were characteristic of certain chronological periods.

FOSSILS AND STRATIGRAPHY

The discovery of the relationship between fossils and certain geological time periods opened up the possibility of using fossil discoveries to establish a relative sequence of rock deposition

through time. In addition, the fossil deposits within sedimentary layers from different localities could be used to match and compare rock from diverse regions. When parts of separate sequences of strata were matched a general stratigraphic history gradually emerged.

THE FIRST BIOSTRATIGRAPHIES

William Smith was a practising engineer engaged in building canals in southern and central England, in the early 19th century. The economics of canal cutting required the accurate prediction of the nature of the underlying rock. From his practical experience Smith found that he could identify particular strata by their fossils. By measuring the inclination of strata he could also predict the next layers in the sequence. By a combination of taking vertical sections and identifying rock outcrops at the surface and noting their geographical distribution, he was able to map out the three-dimensional form of strata over large areas of countryside.

THE FIRST GEOLOGICAL MAPS

Smith extended his geological mapping across southern England, where most of the Secondary strata (now called Mesozoic) are gently inclined. Like the younger Tertiary strata of the Paris Basin (mapped by Georges Cuvier and Alexandre Brongniart in 1811), they have a relatively simple geological structure of folds and faults.

THE STRATIGRAPHIC COLUMN

By 1815, Smith published his remarkable map of the geology of England and Wales, one of the earliest of such large-scale maps in the world. He also produced a generalized stratigraphic column, extending from the youngest Diluvium strata

From left to right: Georges Cuvier, Roderick Murchison, and Adam Sedgwick, early 19th-century pioneers of "biostratigraphy," a method of using fossils to identify successive rock strata.

(now known to be Holocene and Pleistocene) at the top, down to the oldest undifferentiated Grauwacke strata of Wales. The geological complications of these older strata, almost completely unknown at the time, were unraveled by Roderick Murchison and Adam Sedgwick in the 1820s. As Murchison wrote, they were only able to do so by employing Smithian principles—identifying successive strata by their fossils.

ESTIMATING THE AGE OF THE EARTH

Attempts were made in the mid-19th century to calculate the age of the Earth using sedimentation and erosion rates. The British geologist, Charles Lyell, estimated the age of the Earth at about 100 million years. Charles Darwin, using similar methods, dated the length of time that had passed since the Cretaceous era at about 300 million years—a considerable overestimate.

THE RADIOACTIVE BREAKTHROUGH

By the 1890s, the main divisions of geological history, such as the Cambrian and Carboniferous periods, had been named and generally agreed upon internationally. But there was still no means of putting accurate dates on the geological calendar of the Earth. By the start of the 20th century, the radioactive decay of certain chemical elements was recognized as a natural and continuing process within the minerals of the Earth. Radioactive decay could be used to calculate absolute ages of rocks and minerals—and, therefore, of the Earth.

The Geological Timescale

By 1850, enough was known about the rocks of the Earth's surface to show that the total thickness of strata amounted to many miles. Fossils were found throughout many rock layers, even in some of the deepest and oldest strata. It had become clear that the Earth was much older than previously thought. In order to understand the complex history of the Earth's rocks and their record of past life, it was necessary to divide the rock record into recognizable phases. By the end of the 19th century, the basic divisions of "deep" time had been established around the world.

THE THREE GREAT ERAS

In the 19th century the periods of geological time thought to contain prehistoric life were grouped into three formal eras: the Paleozoic, (from the Greek *palaios,* ancient); Mesozoic (*meso,* middle); and Cainozoic (*caino,* recent). By 1860, John Phillips, professor of geology at Oxford, showed that distinctive plant and animal life (biotas) was associated with each great era.

FORMALIZED TIME

The divisions of the geological timescale are based on changes in fossils; boundaries between eras are marked by major extinction events. During the early 19th century, the entire geological time span was carved up into 16 periods, from the Cambrian to the Quaternary. Beneath the oldest fossil-bearing rocks of the Cambrian lay an earlier phase of Earth history. Since it was thought to have been devoid of life, it was called the Azoic ("without life," in Latin).

THE PRECAMBRIAN MYSTERY

By the end of the 19th century there was fossil evidence that primitive life may have evolved before Cambrian times. The discovery and use of radioactive dating in the early 20th century showed that the Precambrian era was much longer than had previously been thought. But without common fossils, the subdivision and correlation of Precambrian sequences of strata seemed impossible.

THE PRECAMBRIAN ERAS

In the last few decades there has been a remarkable change in understanding of the 4 billion years of Precambrian history. Three eras of Precambrian time are now recognized: the Hadean (4.6–3.8 billion years ago, or byr); the Archean (3.8–2.5 byr); and the Proterozoic (2.5–0.545 byr). Little is known about the early formation of the Earth as so few rocks of this age are preserved at the Earth's surface.

THE EARLIEST FOSSIL REMAINS

Archean times are now known to have the oldest known sedimentary rock and the first fossil remains, which are 3.7-byr chemical traces of organisms from Greenland. By 3 billion years ago stromatolitic organisms (blue-green algae) populated shallow seas.

THE PROTEROZOIC ERA

The youngest part of the Proterozoic era (Neoproterozoic 1000–545 million years ago, or MA) is divided into two well defined periods, the Riphean (1000–680 MA) and Vendian (680–545 MA). The Riphean saw the radiation of the eukaryotes, the build-up of atmospheric oxygen, and possibly the first multicellular organisms. Vendian times were marked by a major ice age with widespread glaciation (around 630 MA). This was followed by the diversification of multicelled organisms and the evolution of widespread and abundant marine, soft-bodied lifeforms, called Ediacarans. The extinction of these lifeforms and the arrival of the first shelly marine animals marked the beginning of Cambrian times and the Phanerozoic era.

THE PALEOZOIC ERA

The six periods of the Paleozoic, from the Cambrian to the Permian, span nearly 300 million years (545–248 MA). At first, distinctive Paleozoic lifeforms were largely confined to the marine realm. Early Paleozoic marine invertebrates were initially very small, but by mid-Cambrian times some predatory arthropods grew to about 3 feet (0.9 meters) in size. Gradually, a marine "arms race" developed. By the Silurian period predators equipped with teeth had evolved, and life was

The boundaries between each of the four great eras is marked by a drastic change in lifeforms preserved as fossils, signifying that great extinctions occurred at the end of each era.

EON	ERA	PERIOD	EPOCH	START OF INTERVAL	LIFEFORMS
Phanerozoic	Cenozoic	Quaternary	Holocene	0.01MA	Spread of modern humans
			Pleistocene	1.8	Appearance of first humans (*Homo*)
		Tertiary	Pliocene	5	Earliest-known hominids appear
			Miocene	24	Apes and whales; large browsing mammals
			Oligocene	34	
			Eocene	55	Grasslands begin to appear; ancestors of horse and camel appear
			Paleocene	65	First large mammals (dinosaurs die out)
	Mesozoic	Cretaceous	Upper		
			Lower	142	First flowering plants; placental mammals appear
		Jurassic		206	First birds and mammals Rise of dinosaurs
		Triassic		248	First flying reptiles and dinosaurs appear
	Paleozoic	Permian		290	First tetrapods with mammal-like features
		Carboniferous	Pennsylvanian	323	First reptiles
			Mississippian	354	Winged insects appear First forests appear
		Devonian		417	First tetrapods First tree ferns
		Silurian		443	First land plants and insects
		Ordovician		495	First freshwater animals First corals
		Cambrian		545	First fish; early shelled organisms
Precambrian	Proterozoic			2500	First colonial algae and jellyfish (soft-bodied invertebrates)
	Archean			3800	First multicelled organisms First life: algae and bacteria
	Hadean			4600	

forced to protect itself with shelly armor or escape down into the sediment.

PALEOZOIC LIFE

Distinctive Paleozoic groups included ancient arthropods, such as the trilobites and eurypterids. There were also plantlike graptolites, which were, in fact, colonial animals, and numerous straight and coiled cone cephalopods. There were also representatives of the more familiar snails, clams, sea urchins, starfish, and shrimplike arthropods.

THE FIRST VERTEBRATES

By 460 million years ago, the first vertebrate animals appeared—bizarrely shaped jawless fishlike animals (modern equivalents are lampreys and hagfish). By Silurian times the first jawed fish had evolved, intensifying the aquatic arms race.

LAND INVADERS

The Silurian period also heralded one of the major developments in the history of life—the invasion of the land, first by tiny plants only a few inches high. Altogether, life took over 3.4 billion years to conquer the land. Within 100 million years of the first arrival of life on land, extensive forests of tree ferns and clubmosses provided shelter for a diversity of animals.

THE FIRST COAL DEPOSITS

Early four-limbed vertebrates (tetrapods) included the ancestors of the amphibians, reptiles, and mammals. They preyed on abundant invertebrates—arthropods, such as the early millipedes, cockroaches, scorpions, and the dragonflies, the first flyers. Their fossil remains, buried in swamps and bogs, became the first coal deposits of the Carboniferous age (*carbo* being Latin for charcoal).

PALEOZOIC EXTINCTIONS

A number of extinction events occurred during the Paleozoic, but the Permo-Triassic extinction, which marked the end of the era, 248 million years ago, was the biggest extinction event of all time. Calculations suggest that nearly 70 percent of all marine species were wiped out at this time. The probable cause was a fall in sea level, which exposed the continental shelves, destroying shallow-water marine habitats.

THE MESOZOIC ERA

The Mesozoic era lasted some 183 million years (248–65 MA), from Triassic to Cretaceous times. Following the Permo-Triassic extinction event,

life took a long time to recover its diversity. The marine realm had been particularly devastated but gradually new mollusks and arthropods replaced the extinct forms. Bivalves replaced the brachiopods and new kinds of corals evolved. Marine reptiles, such as the ichthyosaurs and plesiosaurs, became the top predators in the oceans, feeding off abundant fish and cephalopods. The latter evolved new distinctive forms, the ammonites and belemnites. On land, cycads, gingkophytes, and conifers dominated the vegetation, providing the basis of the food chain.

GIANT PREY AND PREDATORS

Mesozoic forests fed the largest terrestrial herbivores ever—the giant sauropod dinosaurs and other reptilian herbivores. Many of these, in turn, fed the reptilian carnivores, especially the theropods, which ranged in size from the Triassic *Coelophysis* (5 feet/1.5 meters long) to the famously large tyrannosaurs of late Cretaceous times (up to 49 feet/15 meters long).

MESOZOIC INNOVATIONS

From Triassic times, the air was invaded by flying reptiles and then by a group of feathered dinosaurs. The extinct pterosaurs were the most successful of the flying reptiles, but then the more versatile birds took over. The birds from the late Jurassic age onward radically changed the nature of life on Earth. The emergence of small, warm-blooded, shrewlike mammals in the late Triassic and then the flowering plants (angiosperms) at the end of Jurassic times were both important developments. The birds, mammals, and angiosperms were to make their mark later when the ruling reptiles had gone.

EXTINCTION

The end of the Mesozoic was marked by another extinction event, which is particularly famous for a dramatic meteorite impact that coincided with the demise of the dinosaurs. The collision of the 6-mile (10-kilometer) meteorite with the Yucatan area of Mexico is thought to have increased the magnitude of the extinction event, although the importance of this impact is still being debated.

CLIMATE CHANGE

At the same time, a volcanic eruption caused a vast outpouring of basalt in the Deccan area of India that would also have produced a dramatic and long-lasting climate change. Certainly the dinosaurs and a number of reptiles became extinct at the end of the Cretaceous period. The marine ecosystem was also seriously disturbed at

this time, with the extinction of a significant proportion of planktonic microorganisms and the cephalopod ammonites.

THE CENOZOIC ERA

The Cenozoic era comprises the most recent 65 million years of geological time and extends from the Paleocene through to the present. The main, internationally recognized periods of Cenozoic time are the Paleogene, Neogene, and Quaternary, with further subdivision into seven epochs, from the Paleocene to the Holocene.

CENOZOIC MAMMALS

Although a large percentage of Cenozoic organisms are still in existence today, a visit to a Cenozoic landscape of 50 million years ago would have revealed many unfamiliar mammals,

Anahoplites, a Cretaceous ammonite and extinct fossil relative of the squid.

some resembling dogs or bears, others being pig- or hippolike. Some of these mammals took to the seas and were the ancestors of today's whales, seals, and dolphins. Mammal populations of the isolated continents of Australia and South America included many dog- and catlike marsupials, which evolved in parallel with the more advanced and modern placental mammals.

A FAMILIAR LANDSCAPE

Recognizable flowering plants, from herbs to trees, grew during the Cenozoic. Song birds evolved, and horses and deer grazed the extensive grasslands. The big planteaters were, in turn, hunted by carnivores, such as big cats, wild dogs, hyenas, and the newly emerging hominids. During ice ages, caused by changing climates toward the end of the Cenozoic era, cold-adapted species evolved, such as the woolly mammoth and rhinoceros. At the end of the last ice age, however, extinctions were caused by climate change and hunting by humans.

Methods of Dating: Innovations and Discoveries

Throughout the 19th century, there was no means of dating the geological past absolutely, therefore the age of the Earth was still a matter of speculation. The discovery of the radiometric "clock" at the beginning of the 20th century revolutionized our understanding of the deep history of the Earth, confirming what geologists had been claiming for decades—that it extended back over many hundreds of millions of years. Nevertheless, new, accurate dating methods posed further problems for the geologists; dates obtained by new techniques now had to be matched to the established, and widely accepted, divisions of geological time that had evolved in the 19th century.

Irish physicist Lord Kelvin (1824–1907) used physico-chemical principles to calculate the age of the Earth.

British physicist Ernest Rutherford (1871–1937), discovered the atomic nucleus and used radioactive decay to calculate the age of rocks.

FOSSIL CHRONOLOGY

Once the relationship between sequences of strata and successions of characteristic fossils had been established at the beginning of the 19th century, geologists soon discovered that there were very broad changes in the overall fossil content of strata. The three great geological eras, the Paleozoic, Mesozoic, and Cenozoic, could each be characterized by distinctive groups of fossils. Some fossils were so restricted in their distribution through time that they could be used to subdivide divisions of time more discretely.

ZONE FOSSILS

In the mid-19th century, Albert Oppel showed that detailed successive changes in ammonites could be used to recognize subdivisions (biozones) within sequences of Jurassic strata all over Europe. Oppel's method was enthusiastically taken up by other paleontologists. Charles Lapworth discovered that graptolites could be used to subdivide early Palaeozoic marine strata in the same way. Some ammonite and graptolite biozones can be recognized with durations of only one or two million years—a very short period in the context of the unimaginably long geological timescale.

ZONING TODAY

The biozonal method is still widely used, for instance in the subdivision of modern marine sediment and terrestrial deposits of the recent past. Foraminiferan microfossils, taken from deep-sea sediment cores, are one of the most useful ways of subdividing and matching oceanic deposits. On land, pollen and insect remains, such as beetle wingcases, are used for dating deposits from the last ice age.

KELVIN'S THEORY

In 1897, Lord Kelvin, the great Irish physicist, was one of the first scientists to use physico-chemical principles in calculating the age of the Earth at between 20 and 40 million years. He assumed that the mass of the Earth had cooled from an initial molten state. This estimate was far lower than geologists had expected, but Kelvin's prestige was high, and his figures were widely quoted. His calculations, however, had not taken into account the effects of both the convection of the Earth's mantle and of radioactivity, neither of which were known about at the time.

RADIOACTIVE DECAY

In the early 20th century, Ernest Rutherford and Arthur Holmes in England and Bertrand Boltwood in the U.S., realized that radioactive decay could be used to date minerals and rocks. In 1905, Rutherford used the decay of uranium to calculate a mineral's age at 500 million years old. This dating method depends on the fact that radioactive decay is random and unaffected by physical or chemical processes such as surface temperature or pressure variations.

RADIOMETRIC DATING

Radiometric dating is based on the amount of time it takes certain radioactive substances to decay. Atoms with identical chemical properties, but different weights, are known as isotopes of the same element. Most elements are mixtures of isotopes. Radiometric dating measures the proportions of certain chemical isotopes within minerals. Every isotope decays at a known rate, making it possible to calculate the age of rock formations. Radiometric dating allows each rock to be positioned more or less exactly at its correct time of formation in Earth history.

RADIOMETRIC DATES AND STRATIGRAPHY

Radiometric dating could originally be applied only to igneous rock, that is, rock formed as the result of crystallization of minerals from a molten material (magma) as it cooled. Until recently, sedimentary rock was not suitable for radiometric dating. This is because the age of a specific grain in a sedimentary rock, such as a sandstone, is the age at which the mineral formed in its original igneous setting and not when it was locked into the sedimentary deposit. The problem has been to relate radiometric dates from igneous rock to the stratigraphic record, with consists of sedimentary rock.

PROBLEMS WITH RADIOMETRIC DATING

Dating a zircon (a type of mineral) grain from a sediment illustrates the problems with radiometric dating. Zircon, a robust mineral, may have survived several cycles of erosion and many millions of years before being included in the sediment. But a new radiometric method can date tiny crystals that grow on zircon grains after deposition. As a result, it is now possible to date sedimentary rock, even if it does not contain fossils, such as Precambrian sandstone.

RADIOMETRIC ACCURACY

Volcanically extruded lava is one of the most useful rocks for radiometric dating. It is often interbedded with sedimentary deposits. The age of the lava is closely related to the time at which the sediment above and below it was deposited. This provides an accurate match between the radiometric dates and the dates taken from the stratigraphic timescale.

THE OLDEST MINERAL

The oldest known mineral on Earth, dated by the radiometric method, is a zircon, dated at $3,962 \pm 3$ million years, found in Archean granites from the Slave Province in northwestern Canada.

RADIOCARBON DATING

The decay of carbon isotopes within living organisms can be used to date organic materials such as charcoal, shell, and bone. Unfortunately, the radioactive isotope Carbon-14 decays relatively quickly (its half-life is only 5,730 years) so that the method is only of use for archeological or "sub-fossil" materials.

MAGNETOSTRATIGRAPHY

Many rocks, particularly igneous ones, but also a range of iron-rich sediments, contain magnetic minerals. These can be aligned with the Earth's magnetic field and become fixed in that magnetic orientation when the rock is formed. In an igneous rock, the magnetic minerals are locked in their magnetic orientation as the molten rock cools below temperatures of around 6,000°C.

MAGNETIC REVERSAL TIMESCALES

The Earth's magnetic field reverses sporadically. This gives rise to sequences of rocks that have "normal" polarity (their magnetic North is in the same direction as present-day magnetic North) and rocks with "reversed" polarity. Changes in the Earth's magnetic field, which occur roughly every half million years, generate a characteristic pattern over time. A particular reversal pattern in a rock sample may be matched, like a barcode, with the timescale of Earth's magnetic reversals to determine relative age. The magnetic reversal timescale is calibrated by radiometric dating.

MAGNETIC POLARITY OF SEDIMENT

As sediment is formed, tiny particles of magnetized iron within the grains of the sediment become aligned with the direction of the Earth's magnetic field. As the sediment solidifies into rock, this alignment is preserved. The establishment of the magnetic polarity of sediment has proved particularly useful in dating certain environments. It has helped to give age estimates for the important Miocene terrestrial sediments of the Siwalik region of northern Pakistan. A wide range of mammal fossils have been found there, including hominoids, but the age of the sediment was not known. Thirteen paleomagnetic reversals have been identified that help to place the sequence somewhere between 6.5 and 8.6 million years ago.

FISSION TRACK DATING

A number of new dating methods can be used in very specific situations. Fission track dating is based on the spontaneous fission (breaking apart) of the radioactive isotope Uranium-238, which produces trails of damage, a few microns long, near the site of the uranium atom within a mineral such as zircon. The number of trails increases over time, at a rate that is dependent on the uranium content of the mineral. The age of the mineral can be computed by measuring the density of fission tracks in a mineral and the uranium content. Fission track dating is used to verify radiometric dates. It has been particularly useful in dating the volcanic ashes interbedded in the hominid fossil-bearing strata of East Africa.

ATOMIC CLOCKS

Two innovative dating methods, electron spin resonance and thermoluminescence, both measure the number of electrons caught up in defects within minerals' atomic structure. These methods have proved particularly useful for dating a variety of inorganic materials, especially those in anthropological settings, such as burnt flints found in ancient hearths.

AMINO ACID RACEMISATION

Certain organic (carbon-based) chemicals exist in right- and left-handed forms, which are mirror images of each other. Amino acid racemisation, a new and sophisticated technique, depends on the slow chemical conversion of the left-handed amino acids naturally present in living organisms to their right-handed amino acid counterparts. This process is sensitive to environmental conditions, especially temperature. The method has proved particularly useful for dating some archeological materials, such as shells and bones, which are not suitable for dating by radiocarbon methods. This form of dating, however, can only extend back a few hundred thousand years.

OPPORTUNISTIC DATING

A useful, but rarely available, method of dating uses ash from volcanic eruptions, because it can be distributed over extremely wide areas instantaneously. Asteroid and meteorite impact events can spread tektites (glassy fragments formed from rock melted by the heat of the impact) over wide areas in a geological instant.

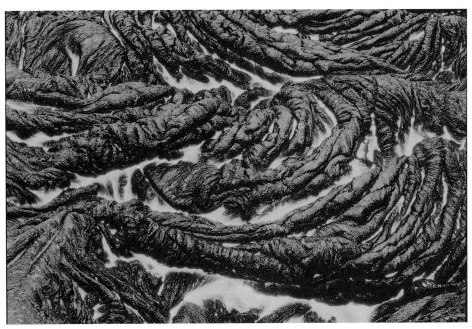

Lava, the result of volcanic eruptions, is a useful dating tool for geologists. Since it is igneous, it can be dated radiometrically, providing a useful chronological context for adjacent sedimentary rock.

Geological Controversies

Among the sciences, geology has a deserved reputation for controversy. Arguments have constantly arisen over interpretation of data, the quality of the information, and whether ideas can be tested adequately. Sampling of geological material is often difficult and sample sizes can be very small. When interpreting fossils, for example, entire species have been described on the basis of single specimens.

GEOLOGICAL INFERENCE

Many geological features and processes are not directly observable, especially those taking place within the Earth. They can only be inferred by interpretation of data from special kinds of exploration and analysis, such as geophysical methods of gravity or seismic measurement.

THE TIME FACTOR

For most sciences, testing theories in laboratory conditions is a crucial research tool. However, most of the major geological processes, such as mountain building and the folding of rocks, take place over many millions of years and it is not possible to replicate them in the laboratory using the same materials. Current geological challenges include the accurate prediction of earthquakes and volcanic eruptions. Since these complex, multifactor processes cannot be replicated by conventional scientific means, they require sophisticated mathematical modeling.

OBSERVING ROCKS

In the 18th century, most geological theories were based on arguments about previous ideas and lacked rigorous assessment of the quality of the information. Gradually, field studies of rock were accepted as necessary for understanding the geology of the Earth. One of the earliest attempts to relate direct observation of rock and strata to theory was attempted by Giovanni Arduino (1713–95), an 18th-century Italian professor of mineralogy at Padua. He divided the rock found in northern Italy into four groups: Primitive, Secondary, Tertiary, and Volcanic.

WERNER'S THEORY

Arduino's findings were incorporated into other Earth theories such as the one proposed by the German mineralogist Abraham Gottlob Werner, who claimed that the oldest (Primitive) rock was formed by precipitation from a universal ocean that had enveloped the Earth. Werner was a very successful teacher who attracted students from all over Europe. But he was very dogmatic, particularly as he grew older, and he became incapable of accepting new information and ideas.

THE NEPTUNIST THEORY

Werner's school of thought was characterized as Neptunist because of his reliance on the idea of a primitive ocean. He argued that "Primitive" deposits, including rocks such as granite, did not, therefore, contain fossils or sedimentary particles (clastic material). As the fluid level lowered due to the formation of this rock, continents emerged and became colonized. Rock formed in the liquid during this period was called Transition rock and included limestone and slate. The final and youngest "Floetz rock" was composed mainly of sediment, such as mudstone and sandstone.

THE PLUTONIST SCHOOL

Other observers came increasingly to support a different view, characterized as the Plutonist school, which looked to cooling magma, solidifying beneath the Earth's surface, as the main cause of rock formation. They supported the French geologist Nicolas Desmarest, who made a detailed study of the Auvergne volcanoes in central France in the mid-18th century. From field observations Desmarest suggested that basalt was igneous and came from volcanoes.

THE GEOLOGICAL CYCLE

Generally, the prevailing 18th-century view of nature and the Earth was centered on humans (anthropocentric). According to Werner's theory, continents were continually being

Abraham Gottlob Werner (1749–1817). He emphasized the importance of field and laboratory observations in geology.

The volcanoes of the Auvergne in central France were studied by French geologist Nicolas Desmarest. His discovery that basalt was igneous led to his refutation of prevailing 18th-century theories.

eroded. There was no renewal because the fluid from which the rocks had solidified had gone. Humans, therefore, were confronted with the threat of disappearing continents. This concern stimulated the Scottish natural philosopher James Hutton to present a new theory in 1785, which viewed geological processes as cyclical. Eroded material from the continents is deposited in the oceans, forming new sedimentary strata. When old continents are eventually worn down, the elevation of new rocks from the seabed forms new continents.

HUTTON'S UNIFORMITARIANISM

In direct opposition to the Neptunists, Hutton proposed that granite was formed from the solidification of molten igneous (volcanic) material and was younger than the adjacent strata. He also suggested that old continental rocks could be submerged and covered in new rocks, only to be elevated again. He believed that such processes were slow and repeated many times; the Earth was, therefore, very old. Hutton's theories came under attack in the first half of the 19th century. The development of stratigraphic rock sequences suggested that Earth history was not cyclical, as suggested by Hutton, but linear.

THE PROBLEMS OF CONTINENTAL DRIFT

One of the major arguments in the early 20th century within Earth Sciences concerned the question of how the continents could have moved around the surface of the Earth. Until very recently, there was no known physical process by which masses of rock and sediment

18th-century studies of the rock of the Giant's Causeway in Northern Ireland revealed that they were similar to erupted volcanic lava.

James Hutton (1726–97) is regarded as the founder of modern geology. He proposed that cyclical processes characterized Earth history.

the size of continents could have been moved over distances of thousands of miles. Yet a disturbing number of geological observations seemed to suggest that this had indeed happened in the distant past. It took a series of unsuccessful theories over the course of half a century before one theory emerged that could successfully explain these observations.

WEGENER'S THEORY

Alfred Wegener, a German meteorologist, suggested in 1915 that all the continents had once, in late Paleozoic times, been united as a supercontinent, which he called Pangea. He reconstructed the subsequent breakup of Pangea and the movement of the continents into their present positions in a remarkable series of maps. Wegener put forward a number of circumstantial arguments to support his theory: the shape of the coast on either side of the North Atlantic fits so closely together that it cannot be just a matter of accident; similar fossils are found in different continents now separated by large masses of water; evidence of a past ice age is found in India, southern Africa, South America, and Australia—this would be very unlikely in their present-day positions.

THE WEGENER DEBATE

Wegener's ideas were met with fierce opposition and ridicule from many geophysicists and geologists. The famous British geophysicist Harold Jeffreys argued that oceanic basalt was too strong to allow continents to move through

it. Some geologists, however, were prepared to go along with the idea. In 1928, Arthur Holmes proposed that mantle convection could drive continental movement. His idea was all but ignored. In 1937, the South African geologist Alexander Du Toit published a detailed article supporting the idea of continental drift and the conglomeration of the southern continents as one supercontinent, called Gondwana.

PALEOMAGNETIC REVELATIONS

In the early 1950s, opinions began to change. Paleomagnetic measurements on continental rocks of various ages showed that magnetic North had moved over time. In addition, measurements from separate continents mapped out different polar "wandering" paths for magnetic North. These findings suggested that the continents had been moving independently. Irregular magnetic patterns (anomalies) on the ocean floor were shown to be displaced by hundreds of miles—the observation demonstrated that large movements were indeed possible. In 1963 Fred Vine and Drummond Matthews showed that ocean-floor, magnetic anomalies were attributable to reversals in the Earth's magnetic field over time.

THE ACCEPTANCE OF PLATE TECTONICS

In 1962, Harry Hess suggested that continents do not move through the oceans but are attached to the ocean floors, and that both continents and ocean floor move over the Earth's mantle, driven by heat convection processes. He postulated that mid-ocean ridges are sites where the hot mantle rises to form new ocean crust in discrete, roughly linear zones. This fitted in well with the previous observations of symmetrical magnetic stripes on the ocean floor. The location and distribution of earthquakes and volcanoes on the Earth's surface was subsequently found to mark the boundaries where the various pieces of the Earth's surface layer, called plates, meet. At this point, in the face of overwhelming evidence, the theory of plate tectonics was born, 50 years after Wegener's formulation of continental drift.

ONGOING ARGUMENTS

It has been proposed that heat convection from the Earth's hot core through the mantle to the crust provides a driving mechanism for plate tectonics. However, there is good evidence that the mantle is layered into upper, transition, and lower zones and that the pattern of heat convection may be more complicated than previously thought.

Rock

Volcanoes, earthquakes, and glaciers are a constant reminder of the Earth's power to create rock. Igneous rock, cooled and crystallized from molten magma, may be ejected onto the surface through volcanoes, or cool farther deep within the Earth's crust. Metamorphic rock is transformed by high pressure and temperatures deep within mountains. Sedimentary rock is formed by long-term processes of weathering, erosion, and deposition.

In c. AD 125, the Romans built Hadrian's Wall across northern England, a distance of over 75 miles (120 kilometers). They built on top of a natural prominence formed by the Whin Sill, a horizontal intrusion of hard basalt, the result of volcanic activity during the Tertiary era.

IGNEOUS ROCK

Rock that cools and crystallizes from a magma, either on the surface (extrusive volcanic rock), or within the Earth's crust (intrusive), is known as igneous rock (from *ignis*, Latin for fire). The Earth's heat flows from the core through the mantle as rising convection currents. This heat flow drives plate tectonics and promotes melting at the base of the crust, a process known as igneous activity. The molten material generated in the crust by this process is known as magma.

AN IGNEOUS EARTH

Most of the Earth's surface is composed of igneous rock material that has been molten at some time during Earth's 4.6-billion-year history, especially during the early formation of the Earth over 4 billion years ago. Igneous rock forms the Earth's hot core and mantle, over 3,900 miles (6,300 kilometers) thick.

INTRUSIVE IGNEOUS ROCK

Intrusive igneous rock is formed from magma deep within the Earth's crust. Vast domes of granite, thousands of cubic miles in size, have invaded the roots of mountain chains. Walls and sheets of basalt have squeezed through cracks

only a few yards wide and yet run for hundreds of miles through the crust of the Earth. Both granite and basalt are intrusive igneous rock but each has a very different mode of formation.

GRANITE

Granite is generally a light gray, cream, or pink rock, made of large crystals of minerals such as feldspar, muscovite, and quartz. They have crystallized slowly from molten rock at depths of several miles within the root zones of mountain belts. The composition of granite can be changed by the incorporation and melting of the surrounding rock that it is intruding.

BASALT

Sheets of basalt rock are formed by volcanic activity and intrude the crust. Basalt is typically dark gray or greenish gray and is made up of very small crystals of silicate minerals such as feldspar, pyroxene, and biotite.

SOLIDIFIED LAVA

Sometimes lava does not reach the Earth's surface. Instead it solidifies (freezes or crystallizes) underground, and so is technically an intrusive rock. Vertical wall-like sheets of solidified lava are called dykes, horizontal sheets are called sills. Some dykes and sills are the channels through which lava flows onto the surface. Fissures like these are important in forming the mid-ocean spreading ridges, through which lava flows to form new ocean floor.

THE WHIN SILL

The famous wall across the north of England was built by Emperor Hadrian in c. AD 125 on top of a prominent basalt intrusion, the Whin Sill. The Romans used the Sill's blocky basalt rock in their construction. The Tertiary intrusion is related to volcanic activity in northwest Scotland.

EXTRUSIVE IGNEOUS ROCK

The intensity of surface volcanic activity has decreased enormously since the early evolution of the Earth's surface some 3.5 billion years ago. Nevertheless, rock that cools or crystallizes from volcanic lava is still the most common of all surface rock. Most lava is not visible because it forms the floor of the oceans, and the oceans make up some three-fifths of the Earth's surface.

PLATEAU BASALT

Volcanic rock is not confined to the ocean floor. Mantle plumes of heat flow also occur under the continents and produce outpourings of lava called plateau basalt; examples include the late Permian Siberian Traps in Russia, the late Cretaceous Deccan Traps in India, the early Tertiary Antrim lavas in northern Ireland and northwest Scotland, and the late Tertiary Columbia River Basalts in the U.S. Such large-scale outpourings of lava, ash, and gas have been linked with climate change and mass extinctions.

SEDIMENTARY ROCK

All the Earth's rock materials are brought to the surface by the processes of mountain building and are broken down into sediment by a cycle of weathering and erosion. The build-up of layers of sediment buries the deposits and compresses soft and loose sediment into sedimentary rock. Familiar sedimentary rock includes sandstone and limestone, used as building materials.

From top to bottom: igneous gneiss dyke intruded as a magma into metamorphic rocks. Feldspar, muscovite, and quartz are igneous minerals crystallized from molten magmas within continental crust rocks. Marble is a limestone that has been heated and compressed to form a metamorphic rock.

METAMORPHIC ROCK

Rock that is carried down into the depths of the Earth by geological processes is increasingly superheated and compressed the deeper it goes. As temperature and pressure increase with depth many rocks change their form (recrystallize) and, depending on their original composition, may be chemically reconstituted. The end-product of this process is metamorphic rock.

USES OF METAMORPHIC ROCK

Marble is metamorphosed limestone and is one of the most beautiful rock materials. It has been used by sculptors since classical Greek and Roman times. Slate is metamorphosed mud. It has been used as a natural roofing material for hundreds of years. Both rocks are the product of processes of heating and compressing during mountain building.

ROCK OF THE OCEAN FLOOR

The volcanic rock and deep-sea sediments of the ocean floor have been constantly recycled throughout Earth history. No ocean floor is much older than 180 million years—comparatively recent in geological terms.

PLATE TECTONICS AND ROCK FORMATION

The collision of the Earth's crustal plates not only pushes rock to the surface (mountain building) but also down into the Earth, where it is heated and compressed. At depth, rock may even melt to form new igneous rock.

IGNEOUS ROCK AND VOLCANIC ACTIVITY

All around the Pacific Ocean, the notorious "Ring of Fire" is a chain of volcanoes generated by the subduction of the ocean floor below the continental crustal plates. It stretches from New Zealand, through Japan and Alaska, and down the length of the west coast of the Americas. This dangerously explosive type of volcanic activity is generated by partial melting of rock at the base of the continental crust.

REVEALING EARTH'S MYSTERIES

The continental crust still preserves some of the oldest rock on Earth (dated at about 3,962 MA), most of which is metamorphosed igneous and sedimentary rock. In addition, a variety of younger sedimentary, volcanic, and igneous rock has been added to the older continental rock through time by geological processes. Over the last 300 years, geologists have dated and matched these rocks, slowly pasting together the history of Earth's environments and life.

Metamorphic and Sedimentary Rock

When the crustal plates that form the Earth's surface collide, they create mountains. The crust is wrinkled and thickened by the impact of the collision and rock is forced down as far as 40 miles (68 kilometers) deep into the Earth's crust where they are compressed by heat and transformed, a process called metamorphism. The Earth's crust is in constant slow motion and metamorphism is continually occurring, producing an infinite variety of altered rock, which geologists can use to decipher the conditions within the Earth. Sedimentary rock, on the other hand, is created by cyclical processes on the Earth's surface, such as weathering, erosion, and deposition.

Eroded material, carried by rivers and deposited at the river mouth, accumulates to create deltas. In the past, large-scale build up of plant material around fertile deltas has formed coal and peat deposits.

CONTACT METAMORPHISM

The process of metamorphism can take place on a very large scale, involving tens of thousands of cubic miles of rock. It can also take place on a relatively small scale. In either case, the process is ultimately driven by heat energy within the Earth. Localized heating at the base of the crust produces molten rock, or magma, which then rises up, or intrudes, the rock above. Sometimes the magma cools below the Earth's surface to form pods of igneous rock, known as plutons. Crustal rock intruded by igneous plutons is baked by the hot magma. The heating causes metamorphic changes to the minerals and appearance of the surrounding rock, a process known as contact metamorphism. The zone of altered rock is relatively narrow, from as little as a few inches to as much as a mile or so.

HOT-WATER METAMORPHISM

Hot fluids can also act as agents for metamorphism. At mid-ocean ridges, where oceanic crustal plates are moving apart (about 2 miles/3 kilometers underwater), molten rock is continually rising between the two plates and solidifying to form new seafloor (ocean crust). High temperature drives seawater through the brittle and fractured lava, a system known as hydrothermal circulation. Vast amounts of water (410 million tons per day) pass constantly through this global network of fractures and the hot 572°F (300°C) salty seawater reacts with the new ocean crust, changing or metamorphosing it. This metamorphism is often associated with the production of ore minerals such as iron sulfide.

METAMORPHIC VARIETY

Any type of rock—igneous, sedimentary, or even metamorphic—may be metamorphosed. The mineralogy and appearance of the end product depend on the original composition of the rock, and the conditions (temperature and depth) of the metamorphism. For example, a mudstone that is buried up to 6 miles (10 kilometers) deep is metamorphically compressed into a slate. The same mudstone buried to a depth of 12 miles (20 kilometers) and heated to 932°F (500°C) will become a silvery-colored rock with very pronounced layering known as a schist. This rock will contain aluminum-rich minerals such as muscovite, biotite, and garnet.

SEDIMENTARY ROCK

Sedimentary rock is created by processes that occur on the Earth's surface. Sedimentary material includes rocks created by the weathering of existing rock (sandstone), by ice (tillites), wind (eolian deposits) and rain, rock consisting of the organic remains of animals (limestones) and plants (coals), and rock deposited as a result of chemical reactions or evaporation (salt) at the Earth's surface.

THE RECYCLING PROCESS

Sedimentary rock, created by the reformation of existing rock, is the most common deposit. The parent rock, which may be igneous, metamorphic, or sedimentary, must first be broken down. The destruction of this rock may be a gentle dissolution by slightly acid rainfall, cracking by the expansion of freezing water, or vicious grinding by traveling glaciers. Rock particles, once created, are generally carried to another location before sedimentation and this transport may be by water, wind, ice, or snow.

THE POWER OF WATER

Water is the most common mode of transport for sedimentary particles. Boulders weighing several tons may be carried by mountain streams in flood, while slower-moving rivers running through flatter countryside carry smaller mud and silt particles, frequently in vast quantities. Flooding sometimes spreads this fine-grained sediment over the surrounding land. Eventually, rivers transport the particles to the sea where they are deposited in estuaries and deltas.

RIVER AND DELTA DEPOSITS

Terrestrial river sediment may build up to form great thicknesses of deposits. Over time, the sediment is squeezed and dried out by the weight of overlying deposits to form hard sedimentary rock, a process known as lithification. Such sedimentary rock preserves the story of how it was transported and where it was deposited. River deposits typically have winding channels filled with rippled sandstone. They are surrounded by thin layers of alternating siltstone and mudstone, which frequently contain fossil roots from the plants that colonized the river and delta floodplains.

Sand dunes are the result of the deposition of sand and fine rock particles by desert winds. Some dunes stand over 150 feet (45 meters) high, and extend for hundreds of miles.

DESERT SANDSTONE

Rock grains carried by wind generally finish their journey trapped in a river or stream, but if no water is available they may settle in a desert sand dune. The dry interiors of the great continents have little rain or plant cover, so loose rock particles are easily blown away by any strong wind, exposing fresh rock to weathering and further erosion by sand-laden wind. Blown sand builds up into dunes whose size depends on the strength and persistence of the wind.

MARINE SEDIMENTARY ROCK

Transportation by waves and currents redistributes land sediment along coasts and farther out to sea. The shallow water shelves that fringe the continents are the final resting place of most land-derived sediment. Over millions of years the continental shelves accumulate wedges of sediment several miles thick and extending for tens if not hundreds of miles into ocean basins. When continental shelf deposits solidify into rock, they typically form extensive sheets of sandstone, siltstone, and mudstone. These are often full of marine fossils, the remains of the great abundance of marine life and some land fossils brought down by rivers.

LIVING ROCK

In tropical environments, the abundance of life may be sufficient to build up reefs, which are made up of corals or other organisms such as stony sponges, moss animals (bryozoans), and calcareous algae. The surface of the living structure is then colonized by other organisms, which help strengthen and build it up. Because reefs are mostly made of limy minerals, such as calcium carbonate, which crystallize at normal atmospheric pressures and temperatures, they

can form massive sedimentary deposits that soon solidify into limestone rock.

SHALLOW SEAS

In past times of high sea level, shallow seas have flooded deep inland and produced vast continent-wide limestone deposits, such as the Silurian and lower Carboniferous (Mississippian) limestone of North America. Chalk rock is another form of limestone, which developed during Cretaceous times and forms the spectacular white cliffs of southern England and northwestern France. This carbonate rock is formed of millions of skeletons of single-celled microorganisms called coccoliths. The creatures lived in the plankton and, over a few million years, their skeletons piled up on the seabed to form carbonate mud, which is now limestone up to 1,000 feet (300 meters) thick.

SALTY DEPOSITS

The great salt mines of Siberia, which are 550 million years old, were formed by a process of evaporation. This process occurs when shallow marine basins or lagoons are intermittently connected to the sea. With a combination of high air temperatures and little input of freshwater from rivers or rainfall, evaporation rates are high. When the seawater evaporates, it leaves behind crystals of the minerals that make up seawater, especially sodium chloride (common salt).

DEEP SEA DEPOSITS

The deep sea is beyond the reach of most sand-sized sediment, except when a special type of current carries it there. Periodic turbidity currents, triggered by small earthquakes, transport great volumes of sand and mud from the edge of the continental shelves, down into submarine valleys which are cut into the shelf

slope. The valleys confine and channel the flow, like an avalanche, until it reaches the deep sea floor. The flows then spread out over thousands of square miles and deposit sheets of muddy sand up to a yard or so thick over time. These deposits can build up into piles of sediment many hundreds of yards thick in marginal ocean basins.

FROM DEEP SEA TO LAND

Since ocean floor crust is constantly recycled by the subduction process of plate tectonics, deep sea deposits are generally lost to the rock record. However, deposits formed by turbidity currents may be scraped off the ocean floor in great wedges and spliced onto the edges of the continents. Turbidite sandstone of deep-sea origin from the Tertiary era is found onshore in California as a result of this process.

INTERPRETING ANCIENT DEPOSITS

Any fossil content within a sedimentary rock will indicate its age and the type of environment in which it was deposited. Sedimentary rock often contains organic and inorganic materials. For example, early Jurassic black mudstone, found in the cliffs of Lyme Regis in southern England, contains organic material in the form of fish teeth and ichthyosaur bones. The mud itself is made of small inorganic rock particles, but its black color suggests a high carbon content, the result of decomposition of the soft body parts of animals.

THE CYCLE CONTINUES

Most sediment is deposited underwater, and is then buried farther before it becomes rock. The exposure of sediment above sea level is due either to tectonic processes, such as earthquakes or volcanic eruptions, or to a general decrease in sea levels. Once sedimentary rock is exposed, weathering begins, particles are transported, and the cycle begins again.

The largest biological structure in the world, Australia's Great Barrier Reef is an expanse of living rock 1,260 miles (2,027 kilometers) long.

Earth Processes: Plate Tectonics

Two hundred million years ago it would have been possible to walk on dry land from Australia to North America—many dinosaurs and other land-living vertebrates did just that. A map showing the distribution of continents and oceans at that time is almost unrecognizable today. The changes in locations and characteristics of the continents are a result of the geological processes known as continental drift and plate tectonics. The continents, which lie embedded in larger plates of ocean crust, have moved over the surface of the globe over geological time, and continue to do so.

The San Andreas Fault is where the edge of the North American continent slides past the plate that makes up the Pacific Ocean floor. The plates move relative to each other at a rate of 0.4 inches (1 centimeter) a year. Their irregular movements are the main cause of the large number of earthquakes in the region.

THE CONTINENTAL JIGSAW

One of the first observations leading to the remarkable theory of plate tectonics was made in 1756 by German priest Theodor Lilienthal, who noted that the facing coasts of many countries, for example the southern parts of the Americas and Africa, fitted together like pieces of a jigsaw puzzle, even though they were separated by oceans thousands of miles wide. This continental relationship continued to provoke a good deal of speculation, but it was not until the second half of the 20th century that progress was made.

SUBMARINE RELIEF

With the advance of ocean exploration, great lines of submarine volcanic mountains, called mid-ocean ridges, were discovered in the middle of all the major oceans. The mountain ranges rise nearly two miles (3.2 kilometers) from the ocean floor and link up to form the longest mountain chain on Earth, some 31,000 miles (50,000 kilometers) long. Chasmlike submarine trenches, up to 5 miles (8 kilometers) deep, border continental margins and island arcs. These topographic discoveries led H.H. Hess, an American geologist, to propose that the ocean floor was created at the mid-ocean ridges, then carried away from the ridges on top of convecting mantle currents. Eventually this conveyor belt process takes ocean floor to a deep-sea trench where it sinks, or is subducted, back into the Earth's mantle.

THE OCEAN FLOOR

The final proof for this process was provided when the study of ocean floor magnetism revealed that young ocean floor was always found close to the ridge volcanoes and old ocean floor near the coasts of the continents. The age of ocean floor increases away from the ridge, on either side. Scientists discovered that the entire ocean floor is less than 180 million years old.

PLATE TECTONICS

The theory of plate tectonics explains that the Earth's crust is divided into rigid pieces, called plates, that are moved around the surface by currents in the underlying mantle. The continents are embedded in ocean crust, and thus move along with the ocean floor. Many features of the Earth's geography and geology can be explained by plate tectonics. Earthquakes and volcanoes are more frequent around the rim of the Pacific Ocean (the Ring of Fire) and along mid-ocean

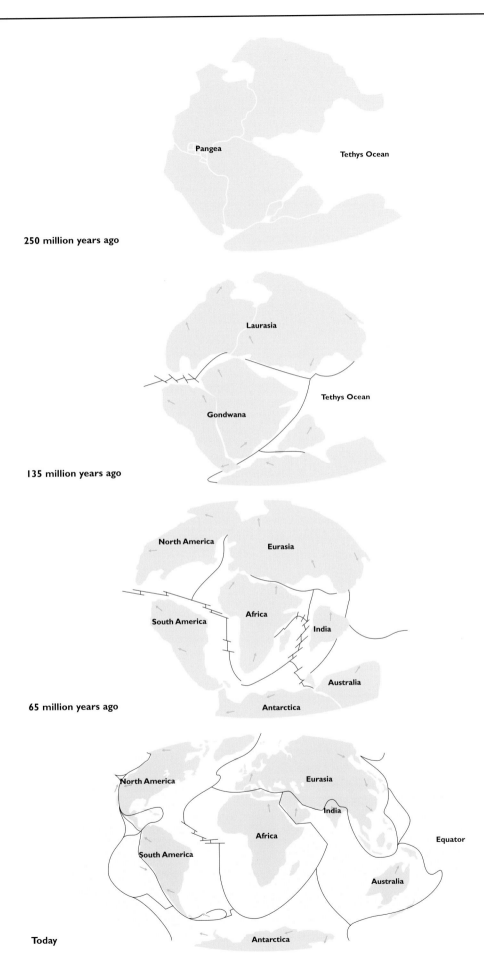

250 million years ago

Pangea
Tethys Ocean

135 million years ago

Laurasia
Gondwana
Tethys Ocean

65 million years ago

North America
Eurasia
South America
Africa
India
Australia
Antarctica

Today

North America
Eurasia
India
South America
Africa
Equator
Australia
Antarctica

A sequence of continental movements from 250 million years ago shows the supercontinent Pangea and its gradual break-up, resulting in the formation of the Atlantic Ocean.

ridges. The Ring of Fire marks plate boundaries, and seismic and volcanic activity is explained by the movements and collisions of the plates.

SUBDUCTING PLATES

When oceanic crust collides with continental crust at a plate boundary, the denser oceanic crust will sink (subduct) down into the mantle, and eventually melt. Deep trenches in the seafloor, such as the 6-mile- (10-kilometer-) deep Marianas Trench, are found where plates are subducting. Volcanoes and earthquakes are caused by this process.

FOLDING AND FAULTING

When two continents collide the crust "wrinkles" and thickens, folding and fracturing as the plates move toward each other. Wrinkling produces massive mountain belts like the Himalayas. Plates may also move horizontally, adjacent to each other, without colliding. As they slide past one another their contact is marked by a fault. Fault movement creates earthquakes, but few volcanoes.

OCEAN-FLOOR SPREADING

As oceanic crust is destroyed by subduction, it is replaced by mid-ocean ridge volcanoes. If this did not happen, the Earth would shrink. As the mid-ocean ridge is pulled apart, magma wells up and pours out as lava onto the ocean floor, where it hardens to form new ocean crust. New seafloor can spread from a mid-ocean ridge at up to 7.8 inches (20 centimeters) per year.

BUILDING SUPERCONTINENTS

Reconstruction of crustal plate movement shows that many, if not all Earth's crustal plates have joined to form supercontinents only to break up again. Break-up was almost certainly caused by rising mantle plumes, that have domed (forced up into a dome shape), stretched, and rifted the supercontinents apart. This happened in the case of Pangea, formed by the coming together of the ancient continents of Gondwana and Laurasia around 240 million years ago. A rising mantle plume caused doming and rifting along the join between the present-day continents of Africa and North America. Magma broke through the rift, forming new ocean floor lavas, eventually leading to the formation of the Atlantic Ocean.

Earthquakes and Tsunamis

Earthquakes are one of the most devastating of Earth's natural phenomena. On average, two major earthquakes, causing virtually total loss of property and heavy loss of life, occur each year. Part of the Earth's geological history, they are most frequently caused by the build-up of forces within the crust, the result of the inexorable movement of crustal plates. Earthquakes can also be triggered by the movement of molten rock below a volcano, or large-scale subsidence of strata deep within the Earth. Tsunamis, or giant waves, are most often the side-effects of earthquakes and can be equally devastating.

EARTHQUAKES AND FAULT LINES

Earthquakes are mainly generated by the breaking apart of the brittle rock in the Earth's crust. Stresses and strains are built up in the crust over hundreds to thousands of years by forces within the Earth, generated by the movement of crustal plates. The rock of the crust eventually breaks along fault lines. Faults can extend for hundreds of miles, both horizontally and deep into the crust. Frictional movement along the fault planes causes the rock to "judder" with such intensity that earthquakes are produced.

EARTHQUAKES AND SUBDUCTION

A different type of earthquake occurs when plates move toward each other. When a plate of oceanic crust collides with one consisting of continental crust, the higher density oceanic crustal plate sinks below the continental plate in what is known as a subduction zone. As the rigid ocean crust sinks through the mantle it sets off earthquakes that may originate up to 435 miles (700 kilometers) below the Earth's surface. The Pacific Ring of Fire is a string of subduction zones surrounding the Pacific Ocean.

SHAKING VOLCANOES

Not all earthquakes can be attributed to plate motion. When molten rock (magma) builds up or moves below the ground, or beneath a volcano, the Earth's surface stretches to accommodate the new material. This stretching induces earthquakes. Quake frequency is used in attempts to predict the date of the next volcanic eruption.

MEASUREMENT AND DAMAGE

Traditionally, the size of an earthquake has been measured on the Richter sliding scale of 1 to 10, which quantifies the energy released. Recently, the more practical and descriptive Mercalli scale, of 1 to 12 has been introduced. Most scientists still use the Richter scale—typically, a magnitude 3 quake involves fault movement of less than half an inch, and will be felt by some people sitting indoors, but causes no damage. Approximately 100,000 earthquakes of this size occur every year. A major earthquake of magnitude 8 releases 10 million times more energy than one of magnitude 3. Movements along fault planes are in the order of yards, causing widespread damage and loss of life.

EARTHQUAKE-PRONE AREAS

Some areas of the world rarely experience earthquakes. In Britain, for example, they are unusual occurrences, always of low magnitude, and cause little or no damage. Yet regions such as Japan or the west coast of California in the USA are regularly racked by small quakes, with large, catastrophic earth movements occurring every two centuries or so. This unequal global distribution of earthquakes can be explained by the location of the boundaries of the Earth's crustal plates. There is a marked coincidence of earthquakes with plate boundaries.

The 1906 San Francisco earthquake lasted for only 40 to 60 seconds; it caused 700 deaths and in its aftermath left 225,000 people homeless.

THE SAN ANDREAS FAULT

Different types of plate motion produce earthquakes with distinct characteristics. The San Andreas Fault, which slices up the western coast of North America is an example of a transform fault—a fault where two plates slide horizontally past each other. Transform faults produce shallow earthquakes. They emanate from a point, or focus, which is generally less than 18½ miles (30 kilometers) below the Earth's surface. The two plates involved in the San Andreas Fault system are moving past each other at a rate of 0.4 inches (1 centimeter) per year. The strains caused by the plates grinding together are absorbed until they reach a critical point. Then, suddenly, fracturing occurs, the rocks slip and an earthquake is released.

CALIFORNIA EARTHQUAKES

There have been several large earthquakes exceeding Richter magnitude 3 along the San Andreas Fault during this century. Only the first, which occurred in San Francisco in 1906, caused major devastation. This earthquake involved movement up to 23 feet (7 meters) along an 186-mile (300-kilometer) stretch of fault. The earthquake fractured the gas mains, leading to a firestorm that was almost impossible to quench, as the water mains had also been destroyed. Large parts of the city were completely wiped out, and 700 lives were lost.

JAPAN'S QUAKE-ZONES

Japan is located close to a point where three subduction zones meet, and is, therefore, very prone to earthquakes. Early documents record the Great Earthquakes of Ansei (1854–1855), and the 1891 earthquake that virtually split the country in two, destroying 200,000 homes. In 1923, over 143,000 people were killed, directly or indirectly, by an earthquake in Tokyo.

EARTHQUAKE MORTALITY

Most earthquake-related deaths are not caused by the earthquake itself, but by its side-effects. Fire, flooding, mud and rock avalanches, and the collapse of buildings can all cause fatalities at the moment of impact. Awareness and preparedness for these risks, as in Japan's 1995 Kobe earthquake, is reflected in relatively low mortality figures. In regions that are unprepared for the eventuality, many more people are killed by exposure, famine, and disease, the result of homelessness, poor water supply, and inadequate or absent sewage treatment before aid and supplies are available.

An earthquake struck the city of Kobe, Japan, in the early hours of January 17, 1995. A total of 5,000 people were killed and over 67,000 buildings collapsed causing tens of billions of dollars of damage.

SLEEPING GIANT

The first sign of the reawakening of the Mount Saint Helens volcano in Washington State was an earthquake of magnitude 4.2 that occurred on March 21, 1980. Constant low magnitude quakes during the following April are thought to have been triggered by the ascent of magma beneath the volcano. Then, on May 18 1980, a magnitude 5.1 earthquake triggered a rock avalanche that unbalanced the mountain and precipitated the explosion that blasted almost the entire northern flank of the volcano away.

TSUNAMIS

A side-effect of both volcanic eruptions and earthquakes are giant waves, or tsunamis, which may cause more destruction than the volcano or earthquake itself. Tsunamis can travel at speeds of up to 435 miles per hour (700 km per hour). They are caused by shock waves, mainly generated by submarine earthquakes or volcanic eruptions spreading through water.

PACIFIC WAVES

Most of the world's tsunamis are associated with ocean floor spreading in the Pacific. Since much of the Pacific region is underpopulated, or has been largely isolated from the rest of the world until this century, little is known about the historic frequency of tsunamis. The Japanese islands and Hawaii are both particularly prone to tsunamis. Out in the ocean, submarine shock waves produce small fast-moving waves that are barely noticeable. The waves gain height and destructive power when they move into shallower water near land. Sophisticated warning systems can now detect submarine earthquakes and predict where and when tsunamis might hit populated coasts.

THE KRAKATOA TSUNAMI

Perhaps the most famous tsunami in recent history was generated by the massive volcanic

The Krakatoan eruption in 1883 was heard 3,000 miles (4,800 kilometers) away. The tsunami it precipitated was 131 feet (40 meters) high.

eruption of Mount Krakatau (Krakatoa) in 1883 on an uninhabited Indonesian island, which was almost obliterated by the eruption. The tsunami was set up by the collapse of the island into the sea, creating a trench 5 miles (8 kilometers) wide, and over 600 feet (200 meters) below sea level. The wave spread out towards the neighboring islands of Java and Sumatra, and reached a height of over 130 feet (40 meters) when it approached land, swamping coastal settlements and killing some 36,000 people. Fishermen out at sea did not even notice the wave as it passed but returned to find their coastal villages, families, and livestock swept away. The tsunami caused more deaths than the eruption itself.

ALASKA PHENOMENON

Most tsunamis are initiated by earthquakes. These frequently occur under the sea, and the tsunami may harmlessly dissipate without damage. However, if the earthquake is large or unfortunately located, then the results can be catastrophic. An example is provided by the 1964 Alaska earthquake. This large earthquake, of magnitude 8.4, caused little damage in the sparsely populated surrounding area. Several vicious aftershocks, however, set off a series of 33-foot- (10-meter-) high tsunami waves. They spread out into the Gulf of Alaska and caused extensive damage to property.

TRAVELING TSUNAMIS

The waves generated by the Alaska earthquake were later observed off the coast of California, still 23 feet (7 meters) tall and still dangerous, as the deaths of 12 people in the region prove. Their journey continued to Hawaii, where they were still 6 1/2 feet (2 meters). By the time they reached Antarctica, on the other side of the globe, they measured 3 1/4 feet (1 meter).

A GIANT TSUNAMI

One effect of the 6 1/4-mile- (10-kilometer-) wide meteorite which hit the Yucatan peninsula, Mexico, at the end of the Cretaceous (65 MA), was the generation of a giant tsunami. The shockwaves from the impact were so great that the estimated height of the tsunami, which spread throughout the Caribbean and Gulf of Mexico, is about 3,000 feet (1 kilometer). There is geological evidence that ocean-floor sediments were ripped up and dumped onshore around the Gulf of Mexico. Such a wave would have destroyed all life around the coastal areas where it struck. It was probably one of the biggest tsunamis ever experienced on Earth.

Volcanoes

A volcano is a vent or fissure in the surface of the Earth through which molten, solid, or gaseous material erupts. The main products of eruption are molten or solidified mineral silicates and related gases. The type of erupted material varies greatly depending on prevailing physical conditions and the chemistry of the molten material generated deep within the Earth's crust (magma). Volcanoes are not found on Earth alone; on Triton, the larger of Neptune's two satellites, volcanoes spout fountains of nitrogen. On Io, the first satellite of Jupiter, plumes of sulfur dioxide and sulfur lavas are produced.

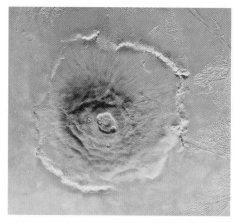

Volcanic activity is not restricted to the Earth. Olympus Mons on Mars, the largest known volcano, is over 15 miles (25 kilometers) high.

THE FORGE OF VULCAN

Not surprisingly, volcanoes, with their often catastrophically unpredictable behavior, have been invested with supernatural powers since prehistoric times. The term volcano is derived from the island of Vulcano, one of the Aeolian Islands off the north coast of Sicily. Because of its frequent eruptions, the Romans regarded the island as the forge of Vulcan, the god of fire and maker of weapons.

VOLCANO DISTRIBUTION

At present the Earth has more than 1,500 active volcanoes. They tend to be distributed around the edges of oceans, for example, on the edge of the continental landmasses around the Pacific rim (the Ring of Fire). There are some obvious exceptions to this, such as the volcanoes of the Hawaiian islands. The global distribution of volcanoes is largely controlled by plate tectonics—the movement of the upper 6 to 50 miles (10 to 80 kilometers) of the Earth's surface in a jigsaw of near-rigid plates.

PLATE BOUNDARIES

Some of these crustal plates are diverging, some are converging, and others sliding past one another. Volcanoes are generally found at the boundaries of the crustal plates, particularly at divergent and convergent margins. At divergent margins, the tectonic plates are stretched and thinned, allowing the hot, semi-molten mantle underneath to well up and melt further, forming magma. The magma may break through in a few places to form volcanoes such as Kilimanjaro, Mt. Kenya, and Oldoinyo Lengai, all found along the East African Rift Valley.

MID-OCEAN RIDGE VOLCANOES

Where plate divergence is extreme, the tectonic plate thins so much that it splits, allowing a more or less continuous chain of volcanic activity along the entire length of the fracture. This process forms the mid-ocean spreading ridges, such as the Mid-Atlantic Ridge, which runs down the middle of the Atlantic Ocean, from Jan Mayen, an island to the east of Greenland, to Bouvet Island in the South Atlantic. Small eruptions occur episodically all the way along the ridges, either from fissures up to about 9 miles (15 kilometers) in length or from more isolated volcanoes within a rift valley in the center of the ridge.

ICELANDIC ERUPTIONS

On the mid-Atlantic island of Iceland, where the mid-ocean ridge rises above sea level, most of the erupted magma, or lava, is fluid. But the volumes of lava expelled tend to be very large because the ridge coincides with an area of active upwelling from the mantle (a so-called mantle hot spot). In 1783–84, the Laki fissure erupted, emitting the longest flow of lava ever recorded—it traveled up to 43 miles (70 kilometers) from the source. Associated emissions of sulfurous gases caused climate change, leading to severe winters in northwest Europe. Crops and livestock were devastated in Iceland, leading to a disastrous famine. Disease and starvation killed 25 percent of the Icelandic population.

HOT SPOTS

Volcanic centers are also found above hot spots in the middle of tectonic plates, such as Hawaii, which lies in the middle of the Pacific plate. Most of the hot spot eruptions are moderately sized, but very long lived. The Pu'u'O'o eruption of Kilauea on Hawaii has been continuous for the last 16 years. The lava covers enormous distances because it is so fluid.

SUBDUCTION VOLCANOES

The volcanic eruptions that occur at convergent margins tend to be much more remarkable and devastating. The most volcanically active

The Ring of Fire, an extensive belt of volcanic activity stretching right around the Pacific Ocean, is the most seismically active area in the world. The volcanoes are located at plate margins, on the edge of continental landmasses. Most major cities have been affected by earthquakes or volcanic activity.

convergent margins are those where an oceanic plate is moving under a continental plate (a subduction zone). This is happening around much of the Pacific Ring of Fire. In these areas, the chemical composition of the magma makes it more sticky (viscous) than the magma produced at divergent margins. Consequently, the viscous lava tends to solidify below ground, forming solidified lava plugs in cracks and fissures. The trapped magma under the lava plugs continues to release gas bubbles, building up pressure. Eventually, either the pressure builds up too high or an event such as an earthquake dislodges the plug, forcing it out like a champagne cork.

MOUNT SAINT HELENS

After 123 years of inactivity, on March 21,1980, earthquakes started to be felt around Mt. Saint Helens, Washington State. On the north slope, a large dome of trapped magma grew at a rate of 5 feet (1.5 meters) a day. When, on May 18, 1980, a magnitude 5.1 earthquake caused the dome to slide away, the pressure that was holding back the underlying magma was released. A gigantic rockslide and avalanche ensued, as well as a major pumice and ash eruption. At least 17 different pyroclastic flows (flowing clouds of ash, rock, and gas), with temperatures of over 2,731°F (1,500°C) surged at over 60 miles per hour (100 km per hour) down the flanks of the volcano. Over 1,300 feet (400 meters) of the mountain peak was blown away.

Seismic activity gave ample warning of the eruption of Mt. St. Helens in 1980. Most of the area was evacuated and the mortality rate was comparatively low—even so, 57 people died.

In AD 79, the eruption of Vesuvius produced a pyroclastic flow which smothered the Roman town of Pompeii in hot ash and gas. The burned bodies left hollows which have been cast in cement.

VOLCANIC HAZARDS

The hazards arising from volcanoes are wide-ranging. Volcanic eruptions destroy housing, crops, livestock, and human lives. But the fertile soils produced by the weathering of lavas attract people to live and work on volcano slopes. The densely populated Soufrihre Hills on the Caribbean island of Montserrat, for example, were totally devastated by eruptions in 1997.

PYROCLASTIC DANGERS

A volcano's eruptive products, such as lava, ash, and pumice, may cause direct damage. Pyroclastic flows, which consist of superheated, suffocating ash, poisonous gases, and large blocks of rock, are particularly deadly. They can travel at 180 miles per hour (300 km per hour) or more over many square miles. Historically, the most famous pyroclastic flows erupted from Vesuvius in southern Italy in AD 79. Many citizens were overcome by flows of burning toxic gases and ash in the towns of Pompeii and Herculaneum.

VOLCANIC POLLUTION

An additional problem associated with large eruptions is the climatic effects of so much material entering the atmosphere. Some 74,000 years ago, the massive eruption of Toba in Sumatra ejected so much volcanic pollution into the atmosphere that its chemical composition was altered and the Earth was cooled.

ASH CLOUDS, MUDSLIDES, AND FLOODS

The side-effects of eruptions can also be dangerous. In 1985, hot ash from the small eruption of Nevado del Ruiz in Colombia melted ice and snow around the summit. Floods of meltwater, mixed with ash, formed rapidly moving mudflows, which poured down the mountainside destroying a small town and killing more than 20,000 people. The eruption of Grimsvvtn in Iceland in 1996 led to a colossal flood (called a *jokulhlaup*), releasing water at the rate of 65,393 cubic yards (50,000 cubic meters) a second.

BENEFITS FROM VOLCANOS

Volcanic activity is not all harmful. In Iceland, the geothermal heat created by the underground activity of the magma is used to generate electricity and to heat glasshouses in which to grow food that would otherwise be imported. Soils produced by the weathering of lavas are often very rich in mineral nutrients and can be highly productive when cultivated.

PREDICTING ERUPTIONS

It is essential to develop some means of predicting the timing and projected magnitude of volcanic activity to avoid catastrophes. Although it is possible to detect the early warning signs of an imminent eruption, it is very difficult to predict precisely when an eruption will begin, or in which direction lava and ash will flow. Eruption is controlled by many geological factors, not all of which are understood or can be monitored easily. Continual monitoring of seismic activity and volcanic gases may lead to a better understanding of some early warning signs, but it is unlikely that precise predictions of volcanic eruptions will be possible for a very long time.

Sedimentation

Submarine slides of rocks the size of city blocks, desert dust storms, avalanches of snow, ice, mud, or rock, incandescent flows of volcanic ash, and meteorite impacts are all occasional and catastrophic sedimentary processes. Although rare, they may have just as much, if not more, long-term impact as the steady settling of sedimentary particles on the floors of the world's oceans and seas. All of these sedimentary processes ultimately produce similar results—the deposition of sediments, in the form of layers of mineral and organic material, which may eventually become solid rock.

In this glacial avalanche in Alaska, suspended ice and snow particles thunder down the mountain. Its destructive power is greatly increased by dislodged rock material that is finally dumped downslope.

THE PROCESS OF SEDIMENTATION

The transport of sediment particles of any size from one place to another is known as sedimentation. Sedimentation may be fast or slow, taking seconds or decades. It may fill a small pond or a region of the ocean floor the size of a large country. Sedimentation can occur in response to catastrophic events, or be a steady, constantly occurring process. Sediment may be deposited on land or underwater, although sediment that forms underwater is by far the most likely to be eventually preserved as strata in the rock record.

GLOWING CLOUDS

One of the most impressive, violent, and destructive forms of sedimentation is the flow of volcanic ash and glass shards, carried in a stream of hot gas, down the side of a volcano. These flows, known as *nuée ardentes* (French for "glowing clouds") can move extremely fast, at up

to 180 miles per hour (300 km per hour), causing enormous amounts of damage and loss of life. In 1902, a *nuée ardente* erupting from Mount Pelee, a volcano on the Caribbean island of Martinique, completely destroyed the town of Saint Pierre, killing all but two of its 28,000 residents. The sediment produced by a flow of this nature is known as block and ash deposits. These flows are rare, producing only a very tiny fraction of the Earth's sediment.

ASH FALLOUT

The widespread fallout of ash from explosive volcanic eruptions is a much more common sedimentation process. Ash can be blasted through the atmosphere to heights of 25 miles (40 kilometers). Fine dust-sized particles are carried around the world by high-level winds, eventually raining down over vast areas. Very large individual volcanic eruptions, such as that of Krakatau in 1883, spread dust globally. Periods of

intense vulcanicity, such as the outpouring of the Indian Deccan lavas 65 million years ago, propelled enough ash into the atmosphere to actually change global climates and contribute to a major extinction event.

ASHFALL DEPOSITS

Larger ash particles are distributed more locally to form ashfall deposits, called tuffs, ranging from a fraction of an inch to hundreds of feet thick. Tuffs frequently contain minerals such as zircon, which can be dated radiometrically. When they are interbedded with normal terrestrial sediment, as in the Rift Valley of East Africa, they are, therefore, very useful for dating the deposits.

UNDERWATER AVALANCHES

Very similar flows of material are known to occur underwater. These flows, called turbidity currents, consist of sandy, muddy, and silty particles suspended in water. The suspension is triggered by earthquakes, or simply by the overbalancing of some of the vast piles of river-derived sediments that build up in lakes or on the edge of the continental shelves. Once the mass of particles is shaken up into a watery suspension, its density is greater than that of the surrounding water and gravity accelerates its flow below the main body of water, like an avalanche.

DEEP-OCEAN DEPOSITION

Turbidity currents can travel for hundreds of miles down the continental shelf before settling out in the depths of the ocean. On the deep-sea floor they spread out to form sediments known as turbidites. During the height of deposition several feet of sand and silt may be laid down in a very short length of time, ranging from several hours to days. A significant proportion of the sediment that reaches the oceans is eventually transported down the continental shelf by turbidity currents. Turbidite deposits form some of the most common deposits of ocean basins and are often preserved as sedimentary rock.

SPEEDING CURRENTS

An idea of the immense speed at which turbidity currents can move was provided by the earthquake that occurred close to Nova Scotia in 1929. The earthquake initiated a turbidity current, which proceeded, channeled by a submarine canyon. down the Grand Banks continental slope. The flow broke 13 submarine telegraph cables on its way. As the exact time of successive cable rupture was known, the speed of the flow was calculated at up to 60 miles per hour (100 km per hour). The area finally covered by the sediment carried within that single current was more than 108,000 square miles (280,000 square kilometers).

EXTRATERRESTRIAL IMPACT

When meteorites hit the Earth's surface, they melt the surrounding rock, which splashes up and out of the impact crater. The melted droplets, (tektites) may then be distributed over a wide area. Vaporization of the meteorite's outer layers leaves a trail of dust in the atmosphere, which can be distributed over a wide area, forming an almost instantaneous and identifiable deposit.

IRIDIUM DEPOSITS

Dust produced by the fragmentation of a meteorite has a unique chemical signature. It settles out to form a sediment containing traces of the rare element iridium. For example, the worldwide boundary deposits between the Cretaceous and Tertiary periods are enriched in iridium. They are related to the impact and fragmentation of a 6-mile- (10-kilometer-) wide meteorite in the Yucatan Peninsula of Mexico 65 million years ago. The dust cloud it created blocked out the Sun, killing vegetation and contributing to the extinction of the dinosaurs.

MOVING GLACIERS

The movement of glaciers can drastically modify landscapes and build up large deposits very quickly. A moving glacier grinds the underlying rock as it travels, and much of the pulverized material is incorporated into the frozen base of the ice flow. These fragments act like the abrasive grains on sandpaper, scratching and smoothing down rock surfaces.

GLACIAL DEPOSITION

When the ice melts, the mixture of boulders and rock fragments is dumped, forming moraines and boulder clay or tillite deposits, which contain a vast range of different materials of varying sizes, all surrounded by a muddy matrix. These sediments, which can be miles long, may be deposited in distinct ridges, parallel to the front of the glacier (terminal moraines), or parallel to the direction of flow of valley glaciers (lateral moraines). They are also deposited in sheets and molded into egg-shaped mounds (drumlins). Crag-and-tail deposits occur when a rock outcrop is too hard to be ground down, forcing the glacier to "climb" over it, dropping a "tail" of debris on its descent down the other side.

GLACIAL ERRATICS

Till deposits may contain a mixture of pebbles, which began their journey hundreds of miles apart, and house-sized boulders, known as glacial erratics, which are often left behind after the finer-grained material of the moraine has been eroded. Norwegian rocks have been transported by ice as far south as Norfolk on the east coast of England. Late Precambrian tillites, over 550 million years old, have been found in Canada, Ireland, and Scotland, indicating that ice ages have occurred throughout Earth history.

STEADY SEDIMENTATION

Many sediments are deposited continuously over the surface of the Earth: river-transported sediment builds up on beaches or deltas; coral and other fragments accumulate at the base of reefs; a steady "rain" of dust and organic particles falls in the abyssal plains of the deep sea.

DATING DEEP-OCEAN SEDIMENT

Sedimentary material that reaches the deep-ocean floor is varied. Volcanic ash, cosmic dust, and very fine sand blown by desert sandstorms make up the inorganic component, while the skeletons of swimming or free-floating organisms, which may be made of calcium carbonate or silica, make up the rest. Their skeletons are important for interpreting the deep-sea sediment record, but at great depths the skeletal calcium carbonate dissolves and is not deposited.

ENVIRONMENTAL CHANGE

Sedimentation in lakes with distinct seasonal climatic variations can provide very useful sedimentary records of changing environments in the past. For example, the 200,000 to 400,000-year-old sedimentary rocks now found in the Parana Basin of Brazil record the passage of each year in the form of a pale layer, formed during summers, and a dark layer, rich in the remains of living creatures, that formed during winters.

AFTER DEPOSITION

Once sediment is deposited, it is eroded or transformed by a range of processes. In water, waves may reduce the size of existing particles or winnow through a mixed sand and silt deposit, removing finer material, to leave a sandstone. Once covered by other sediments, grains may react with the water trapped beneath. On land, wind, frost, and rain erode or remove any sedimentary deposits.

HUMAN DEPOSITION

Today, the human race is leaving behind a wide range of indestructible deposits—especially the huge waste deposits rich in bottle glass and plastics and contaminated by a potentially toxic chemical cocktail. They will be examined by future geologists who will be able to decipher them in the same way that they interpret ancient environments from sedimentary rock.

The crater at Canyon Diablo, Arizona was formed about 50,000 years ago, by a nickel-iron meteorite 197 feet (60 meters) in diameter.

The Perito Moreno glacier, Patagonia, Argentina. During the last ice age glaciers were well beyond their present limits; today are retreating.

The Present as a Key to the Past

How are mountains formed? Why are shells of sea-dwelling animals enclosed in hard rock, uplifted thousands of feet above sea level, and seemingly carried hundreds of miles inland to form mountains? How are rocks bent and folded as if they were made of soft clay? What turns soft sand and mud into hard rock? Even these basic geological questions have only been satisfactorily answered in the last 200 years. The most important key to the geological past was an understanding of present processes.

Richard Owen (1804–92), anatomist, paleontologist, and pioneer of dinosaur reconstruction. He made extensive studies of extinct vertebrates, and campaigned for a Natural History Museum in London.

CATASTROPHISM

While many geological processes are infinitely slow, some are fast-acting and often dangerously dramatic or even catastrophic. In the past, powerful events such as earthquakes and volcanic eruptions were thought to be responsible for the opening up of valleys and elevation of mountains. For a long time, European natural philosophers believed that the creation of life and history of the Earth followed the Old Testament version of events. The Great Flood was seen as particularly important in shaping Earth's geology. Gradually, as geological understanding developed, this ancient view had to be modified to include successive large-scale catastrophic events.

GRADUALISM

A quite different view came to dominate geological thinking throughout much of the 19th century. Geological processes were seen as both incredibly slow and inexorable and, given enough time, capable of producing the structures observed in rocks and mountains. The models for many of these processes were in fact the common, everyday processes that can be observed all over the Earth's surface.

OBSERVATION AND CALIBRATION

For the first time, geologists observed and measured the processes of weathering and erosion on mountainsides, the sediment-carrying capacity of streams and rivers, the features of deposition by wind, water, ice, and river, and the character of their deposits. Given enough time, these familiar processes were evidently capable of destroying mountains and recycling their rocks into layers of sediments. Just how the mountains were built was still not clear, but many of the intermediary processes were.

A STABLE UNIVERSE

The methodology of this approach was to use the present as a key to the past. Behind these ideas were two famous Scottish geologists, James Hutton (1726–97) and Charles Lyell (1797–1875). Hutton observed the ceaseless and repetitive nature of Earth processes, which fitted an even older Newtonian view of a stable and cyclic universe. Lyell took up this Newtonian approach; natural phenomena could only be reasonably explained by agencies that are seen to be effective. Explanations should always be in terms of actual causes, since only the present can be directly observed and witnessed.

VICTORIAN PRAGMATISM

Victorian geologists were intent on describing and obtaining the facts of the natural world as much as theorizing about them. They initiated the first mapping of the distribution of strata at the Earth's surface, and there was a realization that the layering of strata reflected a historical sequence of events. By drawing vertical sections through the layers, it was possible to work back through time from the youngest, uppermost deposits, into successively older strata. By the 1860s it had become evident that even older strata and, therefore, a deeper past remained to be plumbed.

THE DIRECTION OF LIFE

Adhering to his cyclic view, Lyell expected to find fossil representatives of all kinds of organisms, even in some of the oldest rock. But by the middle of the 19th century it was becoming apparent that there was some overall development of plants and animals from the primitive to the more advanced throughout geological history. Lyell, initially unsympathetic, was converted to Charles Darwin's theory of evolution by the persuasive advocacy of the English biologist, Thomas Henry Huxley.

OLD-WORLD GEOLOGY

Many of the early developments in geology were made in Europe during the 18th century, and in Britain, France, and Germany in particular. For such a small geographical area, the geology of Britain contains a remarkable sample of Earth history, from the Precambrian era through to the present. Several major subdivisions of geological time, such as the Cambrian, Ordovician, Silurian, and Devonian, were named by British geologists, The often abundant fossils of these strata allowed British and European paleontology to advance very quickly in the early part of the 19th century.

NEW-WORLD VISTAS

When it came to larger-scale geological phenomena, however, Europe could not provide a full sense of the geological possibilities. The global scale could only be determined by the vastness of the New World, as revealed by the North American geological pioneers in the latter part of the 19th century. Charles Lyell visited North America four times between 1841 and 1853 and used his new experiences to illustrate subsequent editions of his famous book *Principles of Geology* (which was first published in 1830).

MOVING MOUNTAINS

One of the most important contributions by the North American geologists was to the understanding of the geological complexities of mountain belts. Not only were they sites of enormous thicknesses of sedimentary strata, but structurally they could be complicated by large-scale folds and faults, with an order of magnitude greater than anything seen in Britain. Some of these structural mountain belts, such as the northeastern Appalachians, terminated abruptly with ocean margins. The puzzle was finally resolved by the discovery of plate tectonics, which explained their continuation in the Caledonian Mountains of Ireland and Scotland on the other side of the Atlantic.

THE BRITISH DINOSAUR

The first dinosaur remains were discovered and described as such from very fragmentary and incomplete fossil remains. The bones were found in Mesozoic strata from the south of England in the first few decades of the 19th century. The first full-scale dinosaur reconstructions were undertaken by anatomist and paleontologist, Richard Owen.

REPTILE RECONSTRUCTION

When Owen attempted to reconstruct this new group of reptiles, the only models available to him

This model of an *Iguanodon* was created for the 1854 Great Exhibition at London's Crystal Palace by the artist Benjamin Waterhouse Hawkins under the supervision of paleontologist Richard Owen.

were the living reptiles, especially the lizards, crocodiles, and newly discovered iguanas. This was an instance where the simple application of present models for the past did not work at first. Owen realized that it was not possible to simply scale them up to elephant size, so he partly employed mammal-like models. The result was a curious hybrid; massive and lumbering rhinoceroslike reptiles.

THE HEROIC AGE

The discovery in America of more complete dinosaur skeletons suggested that all were not the lumbering quadrupedal beasts that Owen had envisaged. The center of dinosaur investigations shifted away from Europe. In 1858, Joseph Leidy found a skeleton in New Jersey, which he reconstructed in a two-legged, kangaroolike posture. By the 1870s, two schoolmasters, Arthur Lakes and O. W. Lucas, found even better dinosaur remains in Colorado and started what has been called the "heroic age" of dinosaur discovery. As paleontologists have realized the limitations of the comparative anatomy approach, the image of the dinosaurs has continued to evolve slowly.

THE NEW CATASTROPHISM

In the last decade or so, geologists have come to understand the potential power of catastrophic events such as storms, floods, gravity flows, tsunamis, and meteorite impacts. The impact of rare natural events, both on land and at sea, can be greater than the cumulative effects of the intervening slow and gradual processes.

COSMIC IMPACT

The most dramatic catastrophic events are the large meteorite impacts that occur at intervals of hundreds of millions of years. Some, such as the Chicxulub impact, which took place 65 million years ago in Mexico's Yucatan Peninsula, are claimed to have been responsible for mass extinctions. The realization that such events are more common than had previously been thought and that they will recur in the future has added a new interest to the study of catastrophic events of geological significance.

A painting of marine reptiles by Benjamin Waterhouse Hawkins (1809–89), assistant to Richard Owen. Pictures such as these helped popularize the "denizens of the abysmal slime."

What Next? Future Plate Movements and Their Consequences

The study of the Earth's geological history shows an extraordinary record of dynamic change. Oceans have repeatedly opened and closed. Continents have moved about the Earth's surface like pieces of an enormous jigsaw puzzle, colliding with one another, joining up, and then breaking apart again. Understanding of these movements is based on the geological interpretation of the Earth's 4-billion-year-old rock record. There is no indication that these processes have slowed down in recent geological history and it is likely that they will continue into the distant future. Eventually, the gradual cooling and thickening of the lithosphere, the rigid outer layer of the Earth, will slow down the plate tectonics processes. The Earth will lose its dynamic drive and begin to die.

THE PAST AS A KEY TO THE FUTURE

It is possible to use some of the methods employed by geologists to determine the past configurations of the continents to calculate the direction of future continental movements. The basic assumption is that the rate of present movement will continue. The fundamental driving force behind Earth's dynamic processes is the formation of new ocean floor at mid-ocean ridges. Measurement of plate movement is not simple and depends on calculating the rate at which new ocean floor is generated. Two basic methods are used, mapping and measurement of paleomagnetic reversals and radiometric dating of the ocean floor rocks.

PALEOMAGNETIC REVERSALS

The Earth's magnetic field is generated by convection currents in the molten iron of the Earth's core. Every so often, the direction of the Earth's magnetic field reverses and magnetic North becomes magnetic South and vice versa. As new ocean floor lavas are forced out and solidify at the mid-ocean ridges each newly formed strip of lavas records the magnetic field at that time. Continued generation of lavas records any changes in the magnetic field in the form of a linear pattern like a barcode. Two symmetrical linear patterns mirror each other on either side of the spreading ridge. These patterns have been mapped by ship-towed instruments and can be fitted to particular segments of the global history of reversals.

PROVIDING A TIMESCALE

Samples of ocean-floor lava retrieved by submersible can be dated radiometrically. Their ages of formation provide a contextual timescale for the history of magnetic reversals. With an accurate knowledge of when the reversals took place, the precise rate at which the ocean floor is spreading can be calculated. Using this method, it is also possible to see where changes in plate motions have occurred.

MEASURING FAULT MOTION

The measurement of fault movement during an earthquake is another way of calculating present-day plate motion. By recording earthquakes over a period of time in a particular area and using a global network of seismometers, it is possible to determine rates of strain within the Earth's crust, providing a clue to present plate movements.

SPACE OBSERVATIONS

Satellites now provide another method of measuring plate movement. By recording the change of position of particular points in the crustal plates over a period of time, the rate of movement of these points relative to one another can be calculated.

The East African Rift, an incipient mid-ocean ridge. Within 10 million years, the northern rift may have opened out, looking like the Red Sea.

TIME TREK

A computer program called Time Trek has been developed at the University of Cambridge in England to show past plate motions and to predict plate movement, although some unpredictable events, such as rises in sea level caused by global warming and glaciation, cannot be taken into account. The sequence of future scenarios, which reveal that within 20 million years from now (a geologically short period) the surface of the Earth may look very different, can be summarized as follows:

+20 MILLION YEARS: AFRICA DIVIDED

Eastern Africa and Madagascar have split off from the rest of Africa and in the process are opening a new ocean. Spain has cut its connection with France and rotated clockwise slightly. Australia, New Zealand, and Papua New Guinea have moved so rapidly northward, that northern Australia now lies on the equator. The Black Sea is now completely cut off from the Mediterranean Sea and the Gulf of Aqaba has opened up all the way north to Turkey.

+40 MILLION YEARS: WIDENING ATLANTIC

The Persian Gulf is now cut off from the Indian Ocean and the Black Sea has halved in size, on the way to being completely closed. Africa continues its inexorable move northward and is gradually closing the Mediterranean Sea. Sicily has pushed north and is lying offshore within sight of Rome. Spain continues its move clockwise, away from France. East Africa is still pushing eastward away from the rest of Africa, while Australia continues its northward journey towards Southeast Asia. The Americas move farther away from Europe, and the Atlantic Ocean widens.

+50 MILLION YEARS: CALIFORNIA SPLIT

North America (with Greenland) moves further away to the west and starts to rotate clockwise and move southward. From now on, Greenland will begin to be truly green as it creeps south below 60°N. Part of California has finally split away from mainland America, along the line of the San Andreas Fault and is heading northeastward.

+80 MILLION YEARS: DISAPPEARING MEDITERRANEAN

New Zealand has lost any vestiges of Alpine snow

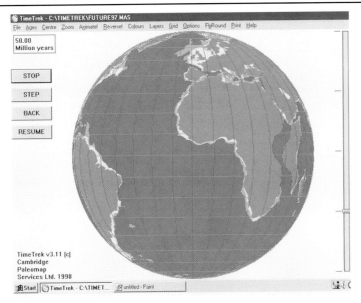
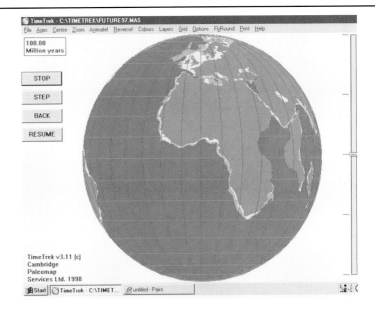
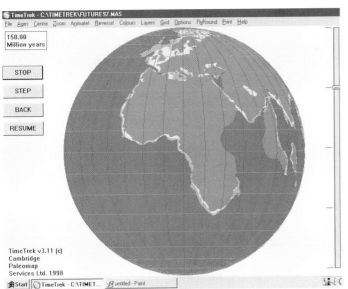
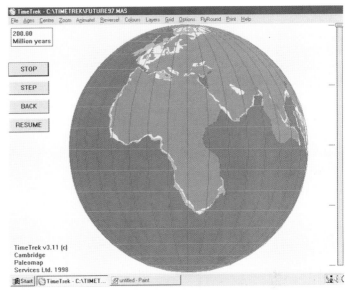

Future scenarios from the Cambridge University Time Trek program monitor the gradual widening of the Atlantic Ocean. Top left +50 million years, top right +100 million years, bottom left +150 million years, bottom right +200 million years.

as it moves into the tropics. Meanwhile, Australia has collided with Japan. Antarctica has started to move toward Australia. Africa has finally collided with southern Italy and Spain, closing the Mediterranean, and destroying the remains of the classical world. The impact is starting a new phase in the long history of mountain building in the Alps.

+90 MILLION YEARS: AMERICAS DIVIDED

North and South America have finally split apart. The southward movement of North America is bringing it alongside South America.

+150 MILLION YEARS: TROPICAL NEWFOUNDLAND

The large continent of Greenland is now entirely south of 60°N and enjoying a climate it last experienced in early Tertiary times (200 million years before the present). Newfoundland is entering the tropics, Mexico now lies on the equator, with Florida a few degrees north. South America is moving southward, leaving Peru at about 30°S.

+200 MILLION YEARS: EQUATORIAL ANTARCTICA

Antarctica now lies very close to Mexico and together they straddle the Equator. Once again Antarctica is luxuriously vegetated as it was in early Mesozoic times (400 million years before the present). East Africa has finally collided with India while Madagascar has moved eastward to join Indonesia in Southeast Asia. Newfoundland, at about 10°N, is moving toward the Equator, which Florida has crossed as it moves south.

South America has rotated clockwise through 90°, so that Argentina lies along the latitude of 60°S. During these last 200 million years, the British Isles and Scandinavia have moved slowly southward and eastward.

THE END OF EARTH'S STORY

Tectonic plates are comprised of the brittle and rigid outer layer of the Earth, the crust and upper mantle, known as the lithosphere. Since the Earth is slowly cooling, the lithosphere will become thicker and more resistant to movement. Ocean-floor spreading will slow and subduction of the oceanic crust beneath the continents will cease. The Earth will lose its dynamic drive and start to die. It will take many millions of years for this to happen, but when it does, Earth will eventually become as barren as Venus or Mars.

Fossils: Classification

Scientific attempts to classify the tens of millions of organisms that have lived on Earth both now and in the distant geological past have developed out of very ancient traditions. Scholars of the Classical Greek and early Christian worlds handed down various schemes in which life was organized into hierarchies that progressed from the most primitive to the most advanced (humans). Within these hierarchies, natural divisions of organisms, such as worms, insects, plants, fish, birds, mammals, and humans, were recognized, and have been crystallized in our language for many centuries.

In 1836, English naturalist Charles Darwin (1809–82) embarked on a surveying voyage to South America and the Pacific islands on board the *Beagle* (above). His observations of the geology, fossils, and living organisms that he encountered on his journey led him to develop his theories of evolution, which were later formulated in his controversial work *On the Origin of Species* (1859).

INHERITED CHARACTERISTICS

Human reproduction, family history, and the ancient skills of breeding domesticated plants and animals provided a basic understanding of life processes and their genealogical implications. Cereals, vegetables, and ornamental plants have been bred and cultivated over thousands of years to improve yields and appearance. Similarly cattle, horses, dogs, and cats have been "improved" by human intervention. Although the mechanisms were not understood, it was clear that generally "like begets like." Inheritance of characteristics was understood, at least at a pragmatic level.

CLASSIFYING LIFE

Since 1735, the standard biological method of organizing and grouping plants and animals has been based on the scheme outlined by the Swedish naturalist Carl Linnaeus (1707–78) in his *System of Nature*. Linnaeus believed that species are real and discrete biological units that are unchanged from one generation to another.

NAMING LIFE

Linnaeus adopted a hierarchical system of classification with four ascending levels: species genus, order, and class. Linnaeus introduced the still-used method of giving each species two Latinized names, the first referring to the genus and the second to the species. The human genus, for example, is characterized as *Homo,* and the species as *sapiens*. Linnaeus placed the genus *Homo* in the Order Primates, along with the apes, monkeys, and lemurs. These, in turn, were placed within the Class Mammalia, as part of the Kingdom Animalia.

THE DARWINIAN REVOLUTION

Despite initial criticism, the Linnaean method of classification was generally adopted by scientists. It was, and still is, constantly expanded and modified to accommodate the discoveries of biology. For early 19th-century naturalists, it was a representation of the natural order. However, the publication of the theory of evolution, developed jointly by Charles Darwin and Alfred Wallace in 1858, changed all that. The impact of *On the Tendency of Species to form Varieties; and on the Perpetuation of Varieties and Species by Natural Selection* is still being felt today.

EVOLUTIONARY LINKS

According to the theory, there should be evolutionary links, or transitional forms, between groups of organisms as one evolved into another through time. But Darwin realized that it would be difficult to find support for his proposals from the fossil record. His knowledge and experience of geology indicated that the fossil evidence was too fragmentary to back up his theory. The fossil record seemed to preserve such a small sample of past diversity that it was unlikely that the intermediary links would be found. In the light of subsequent methods of dating and analyzing fossils, Darwin would doubtless have been amazed by the extent to which the fossil record has supported his revolutionary theory of the mid-19th century.

THE PREHISTORIC "FAMILY TREE"

The 19th-century German biologist Ernst Haeckel (1834–1919) was one of the first scientists to portray the complete succession of prehistoric changes in life on Earth through time. He described the history of life as a connected genealogy, or extended family tree, with humans forming the highest branch.

COMMON ANCESTORS

Haeckel also developed the concept of the phylum (from the Greek for "stem"), a new and high rank of classification. All classes of organisms within a phylum are descended from a common ancestor. This concept gave the Linnaean classification a new dimension. All species, living or extinct, could be portrayed somewhere on the phylogenetic tree, with their lines of descent ideally being traced back to a common ancestor.

THE TIME DIMENSION

Darwin and Haeckel developed the classification of organisms into a genealogy in which species evolved through time. The growing understanding of the nature of the fossil record generally supported this view. The different nature of fossils and living organisms, however, often creates problems of affinity. The test of a living species, whether it can breed viable young, cannot be applied to fossil species.

CLADISTICS

Cladistic analysis is a recent development in the understanding of evolutionary and biological interrelationships between organisms. Pioneered by the entomologist (expert on insects) Willi Hennig, it is a formal method of assessing the extent to which organisms, both living and fossil, share characteristics. With this method, the importance of the dimension of time is reduced. The closeness of relationships between species

Analysis of genetic similarity has suggested to some researchers that whales should be grouped with even-toed hoofed mammals (artiodactyls) such as hippopotamuses, although other scientists feel there may be insufficient data to support this conclusion.

and their most recent common ancestor is represented by a branching diagram, a cladogram.

SHARED CHARACTERS

A cladogram is constructed by assessing characteristics that are shared between two species exclusively (called shared derived characters, or synapomorphies). The succession of branching points (nodes) on a cladogram shows the relative order in which synapomorphies arise.

MEANINGFUL COMPARISONS

By showing the order in which shared derived features evolved, cladograms can be useful for several purposes. Groups that share more or fewer synapomorphies are considered more or less closely related to each other. Also, the sequence of acquisition of novel abilities or behaviors (for example how birds evolved wings) can be elucidated. It is also important to compare a large number of features and organisms.

THE DNA TREE

The ability to analyze and describe the genetic code (DNA) of organisms has created a new measure of the interrelationships, at the molecular level, between major groups of living

organisms. Molecular phylogeny, the assessment of fundamental relationships between organisms, is based on the information held in the genetic code. Measures of the similarity between organisms at this level can be used to check the morphological classification (based on the form and structure of organisms). Assessments of genetic similarity have helped to resolve outstanding questions, such as showing that chimps and humans are probably closer to each other than either is to gorillas.

TESTING THE FOSSIL RECORD

Although this method cannot be used for extinct groups, it provides useful information that can be used to test the fossil record. An accurate assessment of the genetic distance between major invertebrate groups (phyla) such as annelids, mollusks, arthropods, and echinoderms, can be used to estimate how far back in time they diverged. Since representatives of these phyla of multicellular organisms (metazoans) are known from Cambrian strata, it has been estimated that the metazoans must have originated some 800 million years ago in the late Precambrian. This is significantly further back than the fossil record indicates, and paleontologists are now actively trying to test this claim.

Fossil Formation

Fossils are the most direct evidence of past life and its 3.8-billion-year history on Earth. But fossils record the existence, actions, and behavior of a very small sample of that past life—mainly those organisms with preservable hard parts like shells and bones. How representative of past life is the fossil record? Can it be relied upon to give a true picture of past life, the "family" histories of the plants and animals alive today, and all those that are extinct? To assess the shortcomings of the fossil record, it is necessary to understand the process of fossilization.

THE DIVERSITY OF LIFE TODAY

There are some 10 million species of organisms alive on Earth today, with an enormous diversity and size range, from viruses and bacteria to giant redwood trees and mammalian blue whales. The majority (some 63%), however, are relatively small arthropods and most of these are insect arthropods (over 85%). Given the plenitude of life today, the fossil record potentially should contain even greater numbers of species. Since species do not exist forever, perhaps between 1 and 15 million years, there has been considerable turnover of life during the Earth's history.

FOSSIL SAMPLE SIZE

Taking the average species duration as 10 million years, there have been over 50 complete turnovers during the 500 million years from the Cambrian to the present. Assuming the same level of diversity of ten million species over that time, there should be in the order of 500 million fossil species buried in the stratigraphic record. So far, paleontologists have described only a few hundred thousand fossil species. At less than 0.01 percent, this represents a very small sample of the estimated total.

FOSSIL RECORD BIAS

In general, organisms without mineralized hard parts are not readily fossilized, discounting from the fossil record most of the single-celled creatures and other microorganisms (bacteria, protists, fungi), algae, vascular plants without woody tissues, worms, jellyfish, and so on. The insects in particular are poorly represented in the fossil record, considering their present phenomenal diversity and numbers.

PRESERVING BODIES

The vast majority of fossils are shells, bones, teeth, pollen, and carbonized plant material, which are the toughest, most easily preserved parts of animal and plant bodies. The organisms most commonly fossilized are marine creatures (such as clams, snails, corals, brachiopods, echinoderms, trilobites, crabs) and most of these live, or have lived, in shallow seas. The original organisms were very abundant, and their remains are resilient and frequently buried by sediment.

VERTEBRATE PRESERVATION

Bony parts of the backboned animals (vertebrates), especially teeth, vertebrae, and skeleton fragments, are all fairly tough and preserve quite well, provided they are buried quickly in sediment. Bone is a mixture of a limy mineral (calcium phosphate) held together by an organic "cement," which can be degraded by bacteria, fungi, and oxidation. The organic component of bones left on the surface of the ground or seabed can, therefore, rot away in a few months or years. Tissue in vertebrate bodies attracts scavengers, and in any case, most soft tissue, such as flesh and organs, starts to decay within hours of death. Consequently, the fossil remains of land-living vertebrates, such as dinosaurs and humans, are relatively rare.

DRYING

Drying, especially in desert environments, can preserve tissues such as skin, hair, and even muscle. Some land-living vertebrate fossils have been preserved by this type of desiccation and there are rare examples of fossilized dinosaur skin impressions. Some entire dinosaur skeletons, buried by desert dust-storms, have been found in Mongolia in late Cretaceous sandstone.

AMBER

Amber is one of the best-known natural preserving mediums. It is a complex aromatic resin produced in the Baltic by araucarian pine trees, and has fungicidal properties that help to prevent the biological degradation of organisms that become trapped in it. As a fossil resin, it is most common in Cenozoic deposits, such as

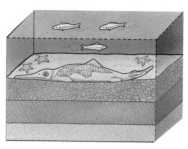

An ichthyosaur dies and is buried in soft sediments on the sea floor.

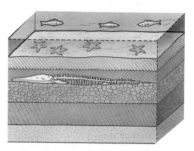

The flesh decays, and the bones, covered by layers of sediment, are mineralized.

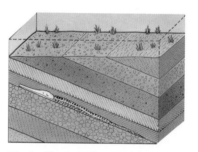

The fossilized skeleton is compressed by the weight and movement of the land.

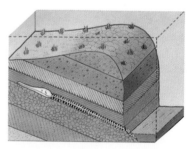

A stream's eroding action exposes the tail, some bones drop into the stream bed.

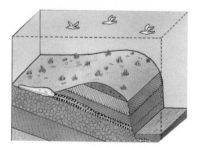

The forces of erosion wear away the land's surface and the skeleton is exposed.

those of the Baltic (30–40 MA) but older Cretaceous amber (up to 120 MA) is known from the northeastern U.S., Siberia, Lebanon, and the Isle of Wight in England.

PRESERVED IN AMBER

A great range of organisms from toadstools to feathers and insect parasites has been found in amber, and since amber persists in the rock record as an organic mineral, entrapment in amber is true fossilization. Although most amber fossils are invertebrate and predominantly insects, a number of small vertebrates (tree-living frogs and lizards) have also been found.

FREEZING

Freezing in permafrost conditions can preserve blood and body organs for tens of thousands of years. Complete bodies of ice age mammoths and other animals such as the woolly rhinos, horses, wolverines, and bisons of Siberia and Alaska (and the occasional human such as the Ice Man of the Tyrol) have been preserved in this way. Although not permanently fossilized, because permafrost will not last indefinitely, they provide an invaluable source of information about ice age conditions. The most remarkable find was the 1977 discovery of the complete baby male mammoth (between 6 and 12 months old), Dima, who lived about 40,000 years ago.

BUGS AND MUD

Bacteria are fundamental to the natural recycling of organic material. They are present in huge numbers in almost all environments on Earth, from the depths of the oceans to hot-water springs on land and even in polar ice. Most bacteria degrade and break down the complex chemicals of organic matter into simpler liquids and gases. In certain circumstances, however, especially where there is a lack of oxygen, bacterial action can enhance fossilization of soft tissues by setting off chemical reactions.

ANAEROBIC PRESERVATION

Conditions where bacterial action enhances fossilization often arise in fine-grained muds at the bottom of lakes or the sea. Minerals are produced, such as calcium phosphate and iron pyrites, that cover and replicate in very fine detail tissues such as muscle fibers, skin, feathers, intestines, and even delicate gill tissues. The early Cambrian Burgess Shale of Canada is a famous fossil locality with this kind of preservation—arthropods with legs and gills, soft-bodied worms, and chordates were all found there.

Fossils are a direct record of the evolution of life on Earth. From top to bottom: a late Eocene turtle, *Praecoris*, an ant bug trapped in amber, and *Sabalites*, a fossilized palm frond of early Tertiary age.

A MARINE ENVIRONMENT

Seashore environments, abundant in all kinds of life, are rich in the fossils of common marine invertebrates. Paleozoic marine sandstone is typically full of brachiopods, fragments of trilobites, sea lilies and moss-animals (bryozoans), with occasional snails, clams, and cephalopods (nautiloids). Mesozoic sandstone contains clams, snails, cephalopods, sea lilies, and brachiopods. Cenozoic sandstone contains many different kinds of snails and clams, fragments of echinoderms (sea urchins, starfish), and crabs.

FOSSIL FUELS

Plant remains are generally carbonized during fossilization. They are gradually transformed by increasing pressure and temperature within the Earth's crust from an initial peatlike condition, through lignite to coal and anthracite. This process also releases gases that, under certain geological conditions, may be trapped. Despite intense exploitation throughout the 19th and 20th centuries, coal and gas still form major global reserves of fossil fuels.

PLANT MINERALIZATION

Some woody plant tissues may be altered in different ways by lithification (transformation into solid rock) and replacement by various minerals, from calcium carbonate and iron pyrites to opal or chert. Surprisingly, these modes of mineralization can provide remarkably detailed information on the cell anatomy of extinct plants, many millions of years old.

BURIAL

Fragments of organisms that can be preserved must be buried in sediment in order to become fossils. Most marine preservation takes place in the accumulated sediment on the shallow marine shelves around the continental margins. The land is subject to weathering and erosion, so the preservation of sediment and fossils is dependent on trapped sedimentary deposits, found in inland seas or lake basins, the flanks of rising mountain chains, or fault-bounded troughs such as rift valleys. These environments, known as depositional traps, accumulate so much sediment that, despite later uplift and erosion, some strata, with their buried fossils, remain.

Fossil Discoveries: Reconstructing the Past

Today, fossils are readily accepted as the remains of once-living organisms, brought to life in films, books, and animated museum displays as dramatic reconstructions. Even a hundred years ago, such vivid representations of the life of the past would not have been possible because much of the scientific evidence on which they are based was not available. Fossil discoveries over the last few decades continue to reveal new and often unsuspected aspects of the distant past. We are still just scratching the surface of Earth's 3.8-billion-year-old fossil record.

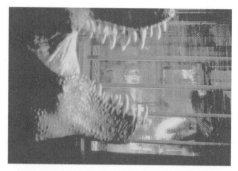

Steven Spielberg's *Jurassic Park* is famous for its lifelike and animated dinosaur reconstructions.

THE FIRST FOSSIL DISCOVERIES

Fossils have been objects of fascination since they were first discovered by early humans, several thousand years ago. Fossil shells, clearly valued by our prehistoric ancestors, were used as objects of personal adornment and were buried along with their owners. The first discoveries of large fossil bones were generally construed as belonging to some mythical beast or giant.

SEEKING AN EXPLANATION

Within the Biblical tradition of the Western world, the story of the Great Flood provided a persuasive explanation for these enigmatic fossil remains. The apparent explanatory power of this story was so strong that it was not dislodged until the early part of the 19th century. Many eminent early geologists were convinced that there was good geological evidence for the Flood and, therefore, support for the historical truthfulness of the Bible account.

REMNANTS OF THE FLOOD

When the bones of a variety of large animals, such as those of elephants, were found in northern Europe and North America, far beyond the animals' known geographical range, it was assumed that the beasts had been drowned and swept there by the Flood. In addition, the event seemed to provide a reasonable explanation for the discovery of fossils closely resembling the shells and bones of sea creatures buried in rocks found far inland and sometimes even high on mountains. It was not until the mid-19th century that there was a general acceptance that this interpretation was mistaken.

EARLY INTERPRETATIONS OF FOSSILS

Our present well-developed understanding of the nature and history of the fossil record is little more than 300 years old although ancient Greeks such as Aristotle (384–322 BC) and Romans, such as Pliny the Elder (c. AD 23–79) did make enormous progress with accurate observations and deductions of the natural world. Much of this classical learning was not rediscovered until medieval times and it was not until the Renaissance in Europe that much more progress was made.

MEDALS OF CREATION

The location, collection, and illustration of fossils became an accepted pastime and matter of study. From the middle of the 17th century, fossils were increasingly accepted as the genuine remains of once-living creatures rather than objects formed by some force or fluid within the ground in which they were found. The collection and study of fossils was acceptable as long as they could be seen as "medals of creation," which confirmed the prevailing doctrine and world view based on the version of the Creation as presented in the Old Testament of the Bible.

REASSESSING THE PAST

By the early 1800s great thicknesses of fossiliferous strata had been discovered and it became clear that they could not all have been produced by a single flood, however catastrophic. Furthermore, the duration of the Earth's early prehistoric development could no longer be confined within a restricted period of some 6,000 years. In 1650, the Protestant Archbishop of Armagh in Ireland, James Ussher, had used the genealogical accounts in the Old Testament to calculate the date of the Creation as 4004 BC. As the slow rates of many geological processes of erosion and sedimentation became understood, the age of the Earth had to be extended into millions of years. The geological investigation of the Earth's long history now revealed that the burial of organic remains in accumulating layers of sediment was continual, and that types of fossil organisms changed throughout the known succession of strata.

REASSESSING BIBLE NARRATIVES

At this time, scholarship was showing up the many contradictions within the Bible. It was becoming clear that the Bible was not a simple historical document of fact but a complex cumulation of historical narratives of different age that required interpretation. For many Christian divines who were actively involved in the investigation of the natural world and particularly the search for the fossil remains of past life, these

revelations were not particularly problematic. New discoveries could still be viewed as the "wondrous works of a benevolent and munificent God." However, cracks were soon beginning to appear, even in this liberal view.

THE PROBLEM OF EXTINCTION

From the latter part of the 18th century, fossil finds of the remains of large and often unrecognizable vertebrate animals were being made in different parts of the world. In 1739 elephantlike bones (named *Mastodon* in 1806) were found on the banks of the Ohio River in North America. In 1796, fossil remains from Paraguay were described as those of a giant ground sloth and named as *Megatherium*. The "Beast of Maastricht," a giant marine reptile, was found in 1786 (finally named as *Mosasaurus* in 1823). The sea dragons of Lyme Regis (*Ichthyosaurus* and *Plesiosaurus*) were first recovered in the early decades of the 1800s. Even by then, the world was sufficiently well explored for naturalists to have to face up to the possibility of extinction. But questions remained; if they were not victims of the Great Flood, how could a benevolent creator allow any of his creations to be somehow deficient enough to die out? The problems of extinction were to pale into insignificance compared with the growing problem of evolution.

CREATING THE IMAGE OF THE DINOSAURS

The first discovery, early in the 19th century, of very fragmentary fossil remains of some large animals that did not compare with any living reptiles, was initially little more than a biological puzzle, of interest to only a small number of the academics and natural historians. But when Richard Owen, an English professor of anatomy, interpreted the fossils as the remains of dinosaurs, a group of extinct reptiles new to science, everything changed. Richard Owen could not have realized what he was creating in 1842. He was to generate a whole new realm of fact and fiction and a renaissance in animal fantasy.

REVIVING THE DEEP PAST

Both the study of fossils (paleontology) and the rocks in which they are found (geology) are academic disciplines which largely belong to the 19th-century development of the sciences. The raw data and information on which this revivification of the "deep" past is based is generally incomplete, often no more than a collection of petrified, broken, and distorted fossil bones. From these unpromising beginnings fossils are brought to life by paleontologists, modelers, and scientific illustrators as convincing animals, often dramatized as ferocious and predatory. The resulting image is generally accepted without much question. But the images, no matter how realistic they might look, are still interpretations with varying degrees of possible resemblance to the original organisms. Their realism depends entirely on the quality of the fossil data and the availability of an appropriate living model.

THE SIGNIFICANCE OF DINOSAURS

The meaning and image of the Dinosauria have changed, almost beyond recognition, since they were first invented by Richard Owen. From being the dragonlike "lowly creeping serpents" of the Bible, dinosaurs have become an extraordinary array of beasts ranging from bird-sized and birdlike to vast lumbering monsters, whose size and strength seem to defy the laws of biology and physics. Some dinosaurs are now thought to have been highly active, warm-blooded killers. Long dead, the dinosaurs have never been observed in action by human beings, so they offer enormous potential for speculative reconstruction. Even so, no matter how fanciful the interpretation, there is still the unalterable proof, provided by the fossil record, of their existence and size. There is no doubt that some dinosaurs really were the largest terrestrial plant-eaters and meat-eaters to have ever existed on the planet.

PREHISTORIC MONSTERS

Furthermore, the dinosaurs were influential and instrumental in helping to destroy a number of the preconceptions of Victorian society. With beasts of such size, it was no longer possible to argue convincingly for the continuing hidden existence of a colony of mysterious monsters in an unexplored region of the Earth—although this notion still persists today in stories of the Loch Ness monster and other refugees from the geological past.

Evolution and the Fossil Record

In the early decades of the 19th century, geologists such as Roderick Murchison and Adam Sedgwick discovered that the fossil remains of past life could be found not just in young rock strata near the surface, but also in older strata beneath, stretching far back into the depths of time. The fossils demonstrated that extinction had not just happened once but many times. The idea of a single Flood as the cause for extinction was abandoned, in the same way the idea that the Earth was only a few thousand years old had to be revised. Life had acquired a long history.

Found in Upper Jurassic limestone deposits in Solenhofen, Germany, *Archaeopteryx* shows a mixture of bird and reptile features (bony tail and feathers).

TRANSMUTATION

Growing evidence that individual species and groups of animals and plants appeared in, and disappeared from, the geological record at different times raised questions about just how fixed in form the species were. After all, if new varieties of life could be produced by human intervention in the interbreeding of species, could one species transmute or change into another over the course of time? Ideas about transmutation had been circulating since the end of the 18th century among natural philosophers, such as Georges-Louis Leclerc de Buffon (1707–88) and Jean-Baptiste de Monet de Lamarck (1744–1829) in France and Charles Darwin's grandfather, Erasmus Darwin (1731–1802), in England.

SELECTIVE BREEDING

A species is distinguished by its ability to produce viable young that are fertile. Humans have bred improvements into crops and animals over thousands of years, and it has long been known that by selective breeding of offspring, the chances of increasing particular characteristics can be improved significantly. Most of the different breeds of cattle, dogs, cats, pigeons, and flowers, for example, have been artificially bred in this way. Although the detailed mechanism was not understood, it was clear that over successive generations living organisms could change.

COMMON PATTERNS EMERGE

The idea of a hierarchical succession of life, arranged from the most primitive to the most advanced, has ancient classical roots. But since the time of Linnaeus and his system of classification of organisms, marked similarities between the great apes and humans became evident. Questions arose as to whether apes could be "civilized" and attempts were made to do so. Furthermore, structural comparisons have been made between all the vertebrate skeletons, revealing a common underlying pattern.

COMPARATIVE ANATOMY

The science of comparative anatomy, founded by the Scottish surgeon John Hunter (1728–93) and the French naturalist Georges Cuvier (1769–1832), enabled scientists to reassemble the fragmentary and mixed fossil bones of extinct creatures into anatomically viable animals. The acceptance of a common skeletal plan among all vertebrates was the basis for reconstruction. The basic form of a lizard's thigh bone or upper arm bone, for instance, is fundamentally similar to that of a frog or a human.

CUVIER'S MODELS

Cuvier made some of the most innovative and startling reconstructions of extinct mammals, ranging from the giant ground sloth (*Megatherium*, 1796) that lived within the last 2 million years in South America to some of the then earliest known primitive mammals of the Tertiary era from the strata of the Paris basin, including an extinct marsupial mammal (1804) and the tapirlike *Palaeotherium* (1804). However, the widely accepted connection between the skeletal structure of all vertebrates did not immediately lead to an acceptance of the emerging theories of species evolution.

THE DARWINIAN REVOLUTION

Charles Darwin was tutored in geology and paleontology by Adam Sedgwick in Cambridge and Wales and by his reading of Charles Lyell's newly published *Principles of Geology*. Darwin also gained firsthand experience of geology during his voyage on board the *Beagle*. He soon realized that the sample of past life provided by fossil evidence was, and still is, fragmentary. In *On the Origin of Species* (published in 1859), he speculated that evolutionary links, or transitional forms, should be found between different groups of organisms as one evolved from another. But the fossil record was such a small sample of the diversity of past life that the likelihood that such intermediaries would be preserved was small, and Darwin largely avoided the fossil evidence.

THE MISSING LINK

In 1860, the discovery of one particular fossil, a single feather in some Jurassic lithographic limestone in Bavaria, Germany, was a breakthrough. Six months later a virtually complete bird skeleton was found. The English biologist and exponent of Darwin's theories, Thomas Henry Huxley (1825–95) realized that this new find, named as *Archaeopteryx* (Greek for "ancient wing"), showed a mixture of reptilian and bird characteristics. It therefore provided the first, surprisingly good, fossil example of a transitional form that clearly linked one major group of animals (the birds) to the ancestral group (the dinosaur reptiles) from which it had evolved in the past.

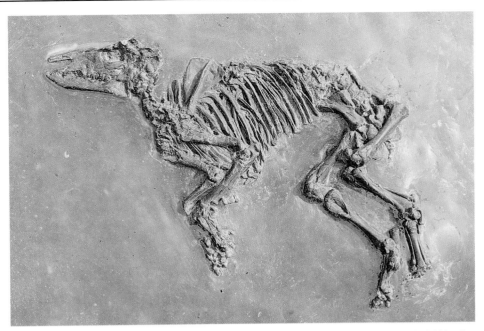

A fossilized horse (*Propaleotherium*) from Eocene deposits in Germany. Paleontologist Othniel Marsh showed that horses' foot bones follow an evolutionary pattern through time for faster running.

CHANGING HORSES

Another, and in some ways even better, example of evolution was provided by the fossil record of horses. A French expedition in the 1850s recovered large numbers of horse leg bones from terrestrial deposits at Pikermi in Greece. In the 1860s, a provisional family tree for the evolution of the horses was drawn up by linking the Greek find with previous finds from France. The oldest known form, *Palaeotherium,* was a small ungulate mammal with three toes of nearly equal length. The younger *Hipparion* from Greece still had side toes but they were nonfunctional as they were too small to reach the ground. It was therefore identified as an intermediate between *Palaeotherium* and the modern horse *Equus*, which has an enlarged single-hoofed toe and side toes reduced to insignificant splints. The story of horse evolution was further elaborated in the 1870s by American paleontologist, Othniel Marsh, who discovered a number of other horse species in the Tertiary deposits of North America.

MICRO-EVOLUTION

In the last decade or so, paleontologists have discovered sequences of strata that are exceptionally rich in particular fossil groups. These deposits record detailed changes in the evolutionary lineages within these organisms. Outstanding samples of evolutionary change are provided by Ordovician trilobites from Wales, Silurian graptolites from Poland, Tertiary snails and cichlid fish from East Africa, and recent deep-sea sequences of microfossils.

KEEPING TRACK

Large samples made up of hundreds or even thousands of specimens belonging to successive generations of fossil species can be tracked over millions of years. They appear to acquire and lose characteristics at varying rates, and independently of other closely related lineages. The cichlid fish, which took advantage of the formation of a number of large lakes, show how evolutionary developments can happen very quickly. Even Charles Darwin would have been impressed by the quality of the fossil data. By comparison the fossil records of dinosaurs or hominids are sadly deficient.

LIFE'S PARISH REGISTER

Not long ago, an eminent biologist claimed that so much was known about evolutionary relationships from living organisms that all the fossil record had to contribute was to "fill in the parish register of life." But in the last decade, fossil discoveries have actually provided vital information. In vast areas of the world that have not been geologically explored in any great detail, the fossil sample of the past is very small. Paleontologists now have a much better understanding of the circumstances under which soft tissues can be preserved. Consequently, it is possible to review the past record for new examples of such conditions. The greatest stretch of *terra incognita* in the past is still the Precambrian period, over three billion years of the history and evolution of life about which we know very little.

Fossils and the Molecular Clock

The real missing link for Darwin and Wallace's theory of evolution was the understanding of the underlying mechanisms of inheritance. Even the fundamental patterns by which characteristics are passed from one generation to the next was not generally realized until the turn of the century, after the death of Darwin and Wallace, although these hereditary patterns had, in fact, been discovered in the 1860s by an Austrian monk, Gregor Mendel (1822–84). He had published the results of his botanical breeding experiments with garden peas, but they went unnoticed by the rest of the scientific community and were not rediscovered until some years after his death. Armed with Mendel's discoveries, Darwin would have been able to promote his revolutionary theory with greater confidence.

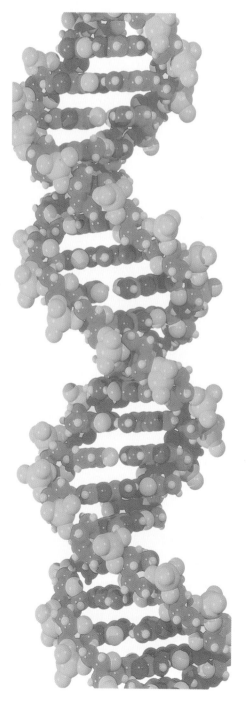

UNDERSTANDING INHERITANCE

At the turn of the century, independent breeding experiments by the British zoologist William Bateson (1861–1926) and Dutch botanist Hugo de Vries (1848–1935) revealed that repeated ratios of inherited characteristics, called "dominant" and "recessive," are distributed among offspring. But scientists had still not discovered the deeper mechanism that actually controls the way in which reproductive cells combine and exchange the information that determines the mixed inheritance of parental characters in the offspring.

CRACKING THE CODE

The underlying mechanism of inheritance, encoded within the chromosomes of each body cell, is replicated during cell division by duplication of the double helix structure of deoxyribonucleic acid (DNA), the main constituent of the chromosomes of all organisms. The genetic code is the order in which the nitrogenous bases of DNA are arranged within the molecule, which then determines the type, and amount, of protein to be synthesized in the cell. This mechanism was finally discovered in 1953 by the American James Watson (1928–), and the Englishman Francis Crick (1916–). They built on the pioneering work of many other scientists working toward the same goal.

EVOLUTIONARY RELATIONSHIPS

The detailed genetic code of each body cell determines the uniqueness of every individual organism. Similarity of cellular codes between organisms determines their ability to interbreed.

A section of the DNA molecule, which is twisted in a double-stranded helix. DNA is responsible for the transmission of hereditary characteristics from parents to offspring.

The analysis of detailed sequences of genetic information encoded within each cell of an organism allows the closeness of evolutionary relationships among living organisms to be assessed. This analysis has confirmed the genetic proximity of humans and chimpanzees.

OUR NEAREST RELATIVES

In the 1960s and 1970s molecular biologists found that chimpanzee genes are closer to those of humans than expected. The fossil record had seemed to indicate that the evolutionary split between the higher apes and humans occurred approximately 15 million years ago. If that had been the case, then there should have been a greater genetic distance between humans and the higher apes than is actually found.

THE MOLECULAR CLOCK

The idea of the molecular clock was based on experimentally determined rates of genetic mutations in living organisms. These rates differ among different biological molecules. At first the hypothesis was tested that mutations occurred at a constant rate through time, but extensive tests in living organisms have shown that different molecules change at different rates. Studies now suggest that some molecules are not very reliable as "clocks," whereas others may keep fairly regular time. In each case, inferences about molecular rates of evolution between groups must be tested against information from the fossil record and elsewhere.

MAMMALIAN RELATIONSHIPS

Despite knowing a great deal about the biology of the different mammalian groups, biologists still puzzle over their interrelationships. For instance, how closely related are the living primitive mammals, the egg-laying monotremes (for example, the duck-billed platypus) and marsupials (for example, the kangaroos) to the more advanced placental mammals (eutherians)? Traditional thinking, based on assessing their form and structure, has suggested that monotremes are far more primitive. New molecular data suggests that monotremes and marsupials may be closer to each other than to the placentals.

USING FOSSILS PLUS MOLECULES

Molecular differences by themselves cannot tell us when groups of organisms diverged from each other. They have to be calibrated against fossil records. For example, based on the first known extinct members of the lineages leading to crocodiles and to birds, the date of crocodile and bird divergence has been estimated at 225 million years ago. Assuming molecular changes have accumulated gradually and regularly over time, molecular studies can then provide an estimate of the divergence times in various bird and crocodile subgroups. New molecular studies have sometimes proposed relatively earlier or later divergence dates than have been known from the existing fossil record, and subsequent fossil discoveries have often supported these molecular estimates. Working in concert, a clearer picture of the relationships of groups and their times of divergence has begun to emerge.

ANCIENT DNA

The problem with genetic analysis is that, despite the recent claims highlighted by Michael Crichton's story *Jurassic Park*, DNA cannot be extracted from fossils of any great age. Most large biological molecules, such as DNA and proteins, break down very rapidly after the death of an organism, unless the tissue is preserved in some unusual way, such as by rapid freezing.

EXPERIMENTING WITH AMBER

The apparently perfect preservation of organisms that are trapped in amber had led to hopes that their DNA would also be preserved. Numerous attempts have been made to extract DNA from insects embedded in amber and there have been claims of success. But all attempts at replication of the analysis have failed, indicating that the samples were contaminated by modern DNA.

FROZEN IN TIME

Rapid freezing of the tissue of extinct organisms happened during the last ice age, when animals such as the woolly mammoth became preserved in permanently frozen ground. Their DNA has been preserved and analyzed; however the cadavers are only some tens of thousands of years old. It may be possible to combine the preserved DNA of these ice age remains with that of modern species, to recreate an "Ice Age Park," populated by animals such as hybrid elephants and mammoths.

The edentate (toothless) armadillos (top) have long been regarded as the most primitive placentals, but analysis of new molecular data suggests that the insectivores, such as the hedgehog, may be the most primitive. Another remarkable molecular discovery suggests that the lagomorphs (such as rabbits) may be closely related to the primates, whereas they were previously classified with rodents, such as rats.

"Progress" and Catastrophe

The fossil remains of the past tell us that the history of life on Earth has been full of dramatic changes of fortune. Entire groups of organisms have come and gone through a wide range of natural causes. The fossil record is punctuated by 54 extinction events over the last 500 million years, which have wiped out 10 percent or more of fossil genera. Climate has always changed, ice ages have come and gone, and we humans will have to continue to adjust to such change in order to survive. Knowledge about the processes that have disrupted life in the past equip us to assess our impact on the planet more accurately; we tamper with climate change at our peril unless we want to follow the dinosaurs into oblivion.

The surface of the Moon is pitted by meteorite impact and volcanic activity—there is no erosion or sedimentation. The large Copernicus and Tycho craters were formed 800 to 400 million years ago.

EVOLUTIONARY DEVELOPMENT

Traditionally, the history of life has been portrayed as one of progress and advance, from the lowest, most primitive organisms to the highest, most advanced organisms. The mammals and, in particular, the hominid primates, have been seen as the high point of this progression. Since the early 20th century and the development of the Darwinian theory of evolution, genetic mutation has been regarded as the driving force behind the potential fitness and adaptation of organisms. The environment and other organisms provide the selective forces that allow the best adapted organisms to survive and reproduce.

NUCLEAR WINTER SCENARIOS

Recently, catastrophic events have been reassessed as factors that may have contributed significantly to the history and development of life and may do so again in the not-too-distant future. One of the effects of the cold war was the development and modeling of nuclear winter scenarios, which predict the aftermath of a nuclear holocaust. These models suggested that during such a catastrophe, so much rock dust from the explosions would be thrown into the atmosphere that winter conditions could prevail for long enough to have a drastic effect on life. Plant growth at the base of the food chain would be damaged, affecting life at all levels.

FLOOD BASALTS

Cold War scenarios made scientists think about other catastrophic events, such as large-scale volcanic eruptions and extraterrestrial impacts on Earth. The geological evidence of lava and ash layers in the stratigraphic rock record shows that both are natural types of events that recur throughout Earth history. There have been 11 vast eruptions of flood basalts over the last 250 million years, taking place at average intervals of 22 million years. Most of the eruptions have coincided with extinction of lifeforms, which is recorded by loss of fossil organisms.

VOLCANIC IMPACT

Volcanic eruptions on a large scale throw out great volumes of ash and gases, especially carbon dioxide, which is a natural greenhouse gas. It allows shortwave solar radiation to enter the Earth's atmosphere, but stops longwave radiation from escaping, a process that traps heat and raises the Earth's temperature. A major eruption can cause initial cooling because of low light levels and acid rain, followed by global warming. All these effects can have a disastrous impact on life on Earth, especially on plants.

LUNAR IMPACT

The pockmarked surface of the Moon is an object lesson in the history of Earth. Both have suffered continuous bombardment from space by a range of extraterrestrial bodies of varying size and composition. However, the surface of the Moon preserves the impact craters, while the geologically dynamic Earth tends to conceal the evidence as its surface is constantly recycled.

EXTRATERRESTRIAL EVENTS

Nevertheless, several hundred measurable impact events have now been identified, spread

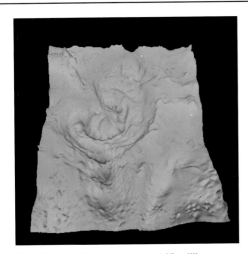

The Chicxulub impact occurred 65 million years ago in the Yucatan Peninsula, Mexico. It is the only impact that has made a crater bigger than 60 miles (100 kilometers) in diameter.

out over the last 500 million years. Thirty of these have involved objects that have made craters larger than 6 miles (10 kilometers) wide, and events of this magnitude occur with a frequency of less than 10 million years.

EXTINCTION EVENTS

Of the 54 extinction events that have occurred over the last 500 million years, 15 have involved the extinction of 30 percent, or more, of the Earth's genera. Scientists have realized only in the last decade or so that extinction events have been so frequent in the history of life.

THE END OF THE PALEOZOIC

The Permo-Triassic extinction event, which marks the end of the Paleozoic, is the most drastic event in the history of the Earth. It is now known that at least 57 percent of all families of marine organisms died out and possibly as many as 95 percent of all species disappeared. The hardest hit were the common shelly fossils, which lived attached to the seabed in shallow water such as the brachiopods (lamp shells), bryozoans (moss animals), and crinoids (sea lilies). But terrestrial animals also suffered. While it is surprising that life continued at all, it is a reflection of the resilience of living organisms, both plants and animals, that they not only recovered but continued to diversify.

ENVIRONMENTAL FACTORS

The cause of the Permo-Triassic extinction is generally thought to have been environmental. It may well be linked to climate change and the outpouring of the Siberian plateau basalts around 250 million years ago. The involvement of the

impact of an extraterrestrial body has also been suggested, but this catastrophic cause has not been verified, and no large impact crater or impact-related debris has been identified of this exact age. The disappearance of species seems to have been drawn out over a period of some 10 million years. A major factor is likely to have been the global assembly of the continental plates to form the supercontinent of Pangea.

FALLING SEA LEVELS

Plate assembly was accompanied by a major fall in sea level. Consequently, the extensive shallow seas that surrounded the continents withdrew oceanward. Living conditions for a great diversity of marine creatures were altered so quickly that many were unable to adapt, especially those that lived attached to the seabed and within reefs built upon it.

ICE AGE EXTINCTION

The most recent extinction event is associated with the last ice age. As the zone of permanently frozen ground spread south across northern Asia, Europe, and North America, glaciers developed in the mountains and sea-ice spread into the Atlantic. The large mammals were forced to retreat southward. Many of them were able to adapt to the cold and therefore survived on the windswept tundra and grassland steppe of Asia and North America.

EVIDENCE OF CLIMATE CHANGE

It is known that woolly mammoth and rhinoceros, bear, wolves, wolverines, giant deer, horses, big cats, and many other mammals occupied the cold regions of Asia, Europe, and North America during the last ice age because their fossils, including butchered bones, remain. There is also the evidence of the vivid Paleolithic cave paintings of western Europe. They shared these habitats with one of the most effective predators of all time, humans.

THE HUMAN IMPACT

Undoubtedly, the rapid climate change and consequent disruption to vegetation that characterized the end of the last ice age was largely responsible for the demise of animals such as the woolly mammoth. In the northern hemisphere the pressure of human hunting on the dwindling population stocks probably soon reduced them to an unsustainable level. Recent genetic analysis suggests that modern Cro-Magnon humans may also have been responsible, albeit indirectly, for the extinction of the

Neanderthals. Certainly there is no evidence of Neanderthal genes within our genetic makeup, as would have been the case if there had been any interbreeding.

BAD LUCK AND SURVIVAL

Some paleontologists argue that extinction may well have played a significant and highly unpredictable role in the process of evolution. Evolution has been portrayed as a board game in which chance, or bad luck, is a controlling factor. At irregular intervals extinctions, with their random levels of destruction, impact on the progress of life. Recovery and further progress may depend on which organisms have survived. Their ability to make the best of the opportunity and exploit the vacated ecological space may then determine the direction of evolution until the next random extinction.

PERSISTENCE AND SURVIVAL

Other paleontologists, however, disagree and point to the persistence of certain lineages of more advanced and complex organisms through time. The vertebrates, for instance, that developed from the chordates in the early Cambrian, have survived through the known 54 extinction events and still prospered. Whatever the cause of extinction events, our own survival depend on our learning from the distant past.

Mountains of ivory tusks are burnt in Nairobi National Park, Kenya. Humans, the Earth's most effective predators, are endangering the remaining megaherbivores of Africa and Asia.

The fossil vertebrate animals described in the animal fact file are grouped in the following classification. They are not arranged in evolutionary sequence; see the evolutionary charts at the beginning of each main section in the animal fact file to see the relationships between groups. This classification is intended to show to which group a particular animal belongs. In most cases, the animals are classified to family level.

FISHES (see pp.162–189)

PHYLUM CHORDATA (vertebrate ancestors)

SUBPHYLUM CEPHALOCHORDATA

(Acraniata): *Pikaia*

SUBPHYLUM VERTEBRATA (Craniata)

CLASS AGNATHA

SUBCLASS MYXINOIDEA (hagfish)

SUBCLASS PETROMYZONTIFORMES (lampreys)

SUBCLASS CONODONTA: *Promissum*

SUBCLASS UNNAMED

    ORDER HETEROSTRACI: *Arandaspis, Drepanaspis, Doryaspis, Pteraspis*

    ORDER THELODONTIDA: *Thelodus*

    ORDER GALEASPIDA

    ORDER OSTEOSTRACI: *Boreaspis, Dartmuthia, Hemicyclaspis, Tremataspis*

    ORDER ANASPIDA: *Jamoytius, Pharyngolepis*

CLASS CHONDRICHTHYES

(cartilaginous fishes)

SUBCLASS ELASMOBRANCHII (sharks, skates, rays)

    ORDER CLADOSELACHIDA: *Cladoselache*

    ORDER SYMMORIIDA: *Cobelodus, Stethacanthus*

    ORDER XENACANTHIDA: *Xenacanthus*

    ORDER EUSELACHII: *Hybodus, Tristychius*

    ORDER NEOSELACHII: *Scapanorhynchus, Sclerorhynchus, Spathobathis*

SUBCLASS HOLOCEPHALI (chimaeras or ratfish)

    ORDER CHIMAERIDA: *Deltoptychius, Ischyodus*

CLASS ACANTHODII (spiny sharks)

    ORDER CLIMATIIFORMES: *Climatius*

    ORDER ACANTHODIFORMES: *Acanthodes*

CLASS PLACODERMI (armored fishes)

    ORDER RHENANIDA: *Gemuendina*

    ORDER PTYCTODONTIDA: *Ctenurella*

    ORDER ARTHRODIRA: *Coccosteus, Dunkleosteus, Groenlandaspis*

    ORDER ANTIARCHI: *Bothriolepis*

    ORDER UNCERTAIN: *Palaeospondylus*

    ORDER ACANTHOTHORACANS

CLASS OSTEICHTHYES (bony fishes)

SUBCLASS ACTINOPTERYGII (rayed-finned fishes)

    ORDER PALAEONISCIFORMES: *Canobius, Platysomus, Cheirolepis, Moythomasia, Palaeoniscum, Saurichthys*

    ORDER PERLEIDIFORMES: *Perleidus*

    ORDER SEMIONOTIFORMES: *Dapedium, Lepidotes*

    ORDER PYCNODONTIFORMES: *Pycnodus*

    ORDER ASPIDORHYNCHIFORMES: *Aspidorhynchus*

    ORDER TELEOSTEI: *Berycopsis, Enchodus, Eobothus, Hypsidoris, Hypsocormus, Leptolepis, Pholidophorus, Protobrama, Sphenocephalus, Thrissops*

SUBCLASS SARCOPTERYGII (lobe-finned fishes)

INFRACLASS RHIPIDISTIA

    ORDER ONYCHODONTIFORMES: *Strunius*

    ORDER POROLEPIFORMES (rhipidistians): *Gyroptychius, Holoptychius*

    ORDER OSTEOLEPIFORMES (rhipidistians): *Eusthenopteron, Osteolepis*

INFRACLASS ACTINISTIA (coelacanths): *Macropoma*

INFRACLASS DIPNOIFORMES

    ORDER DIPNOI (lungfishes): *Dipnorhynchus, Dipterus, Griphognathus*

AMPHIBIANS (see pp.190–201)

CLASS AMPHIBIA

    Family Acanthostegidae: *Acanthostega*

    Family Ichthyostegidae: *Ichthyostega*

    Family Baphetidae: *Eucritta*

    ORDER UNCERTAIN: *Crassigyrinus, Greererpeton*

    ORDER TEMNOSPONDYLI

    Family Colosteidae

    Family Eryopidae: *Eryops*

    Family Dissorophidae: *Cacops, Platyhystrix*

    Family Peltobatrachidae: *Peltobatrachus*

    Family Capitosauridae: *Paracyclotosaurus*

    Family Plagiosauridae: *Gerrothorax*

    ORDER ANTHRACOSAURIA

    Family Eogyrinidae: *Eogyrinus*

    ORDER SEYMOURIAMORPHA

    Family Seymouridae: *Seymouria*

SUBCLASS LEPOSPONDYLI

    ORDER AISTOPODA

    Family Ophiderpetontidae: *Ophiderpeton*

    Family Phlegethontiidae: *Phlegethontia*

    ORDER NECTRIDEA

    Family Keraterpetontidae: *Diplocaulus, Keraterpeton*

    ORDER MICROSAURIA

    Family Pantylidae: *Pantylus*

    Family Microbrachidae: *Microbrachis*

INFRACLASS LISSAMPHIBIANS

    ORDER PROANURA (early frogs and toads)

    Family Protobatrachidae: *Triadobatrachus*

    ORDER ANURA (modern frogs and toads)

    Family Ascaphidae: *Vieraella*

    Family Palaeobatrachidae: *Palaeobatrachus*

    ORDER URODELA (newts and salamanders)

    Family Karauridae: *Karaurus*

    ORDER GYMNOPHIONA (caecilians)

REPTILIOMORPHS

    Family uncertain: *Westlothiana*

    ORDER DIADECTOMORPHA

    Family Diadectidae: *Diadectes*

REPTILES (see pp.202–231)

CLASS REPTILIA

SUBCLASS ANAPSIDA

    ORDER CAPTORHINIDA

    Family Protorothyrididae: *Hylonomus*

    Family Captorhinidae: *Labidosaurus*

    Family Procolophonidae: *Hypsognathus*

    Family Pareiasauridae: *Elginia, Pareiasaurus, Scutosaurus*

    Family Millerettidae: *Milleretta*

    ORDER MESOSAURIA

    Family Mesosauridae: *Mesosaurus*

    ORDER TESTUDINES [CHELONIA] (turtles, tortoises, terrapins)

SUBORDER PROGANOCHELYDIA

    Family Proganochelyidae: *Proganochelys*

SUBORDER PLEURODIRA

    Family Pelomedusidae: *Stupendemys*

SUBORDER CRYPTODIRA

    Family Meiolaniidae: *Meiolania*

    Family Testudinidae: *Testudo*

    Family Protostegidae: *Archelon*

    Family Trionychidae: *Paleotrionyx*

SUBCLASS UNCERTAIN

    ORDER PLACODONTIA

    Family Placodontidae: *Placodus*

    Family Cyamodontidae: *Placochelys*

    Family Henodontidae: *Henodus*

    ORDER UNCERTAIN

    Family Claudiosauridae: *Claudiosaurus*

    ORDER NOTHOSAURIA

    Family Nothosauridae: *Ceresiosaurus, Lariosaurus, Nothosaurus*

Family Pistosauridae: *Pistosaurus*
ORDER PLESIOSAURIA
SUPERFAMILY PLESIOSAURIDEA
Family Plesiosauridae: *Plesiosaurus*
Family Cryptocleididae: *Cryptoclidus*
Family Elasmosauridae: *Elasmosaurus*, *Muraenosaurus*
SUPERFAMILY PLIOSAUROIDEA
Family Pliosauridae: *Kronosaurus, Liopleurodon, Macroplata, Peloneustes*
ORDER ICHTHYOSAURIA
Family Shastasauridae: *Cymbospondylus, Shonisaurus*
Family Mixosauridae: *Mixosaurus*
Family Ichthyosauridae: *Ichthyosaurus, Ophthalmosaurus*
Family Stenopterygiidae: *Stenopterygius*
Family Leptopterygiidae: *Eurhinosaurus, Temnodontosaurus*
SUBCLASS DIAPSIDA
ORDER ARAEOSCELIDIA
Family Petrolacosauridae: *Petrolacosaurus*
Family Araeoscelididae: *Araeoscelis*
ORDER UNCERTAIN
Family Weigeltisauridae: *Coelurosauravus*
ORDER THALATTOSAURIA
Family Askeptosauridae:*Askeptosaurus*
ORDER CHORISTODERA
Family Champsosauridae: *Champsosaurus*
ORDER EOSUCHIA
Family Tangasauridae: *Hovasaurus, Thadeosaurus*
SUPERORDER LEPIDOSAURIA
ORDER SPHENODONTIDA (tuataras)
Family Sphenodontidae: *Planocephalosaurus*
Family Pleurosauridae: *Pleurosaurus*
ORDER SQUAMATA (snakes and lizards)
SUBORDER LACERTILIA [Sauria] (lizards)
Family Kuehneosauridae: *Kuehneosaurus*
Family Ardeosauridae: *Ardeosaurus*
Family Varanidae: *Megalania*
Family Mosasauridae: *Platecarpus, Plotosaurus*
SUBORDER SERPENTES (snakes)
Family Dolichosauridae: *Pachyrhachis*

RULING REPTILES (see pp.232–313)

INFRACLASS ARCHOSAUROMORPHA
ORDER RHYNCHOSAURIA
Family Rhynchosauridae: *Hyperodapedon*
ORDER PROLACERTIFORMES
Family Protorosauridae: *Protorosaurus*
Family Tanystropheidae: *Tanystropheus*
SUPERORDER ARCHOSAURIA
Family Proterosuchidae: *Chasmatosaurus*
Family Erythrosuchidae: *Erythrosuchus*
Family Rauisuchidae: *Ticinosuchus*
Family Phytosauridae: *Rutiodon*
Family Stagonolepididae: *Stagonolepis*

Family Euparkertidae: *Euparkeria*
Family Ornithosuchidae: *Ornithosuchus*
Family Lagosuchidae: *Lagosuchus*
Family uncertain: *Longisquama*
SUPERORDER CROCODYLOMORPHA
ORDER CROCODYLIA (crocodiles)
Family Sphenosuchidae: *Gracilisuchus*
Family Saltoposuchidae: *Terrestrisuchus*
Family Protosuchidae: *Protosuchus*
DIVISION MESOEUCROCODYLIA
Family Teleosauridae: *Teleosaurus*
Family Metriorhynchidae: *Metriorhynchus*
Family Bernissartiidae: *Bernissartia*
SUBORDER EUSUCHIA
Family Crocodylidae: *Deinosuchus, Pristichampsus*
ORDER PTEROSAURIA (pterosaurs)
SUBORDER RHAMPHORHYNCHOIDEA
Family Dimorphodontidae: *Dimorphodon*
Family Eudimorphodontidae: *Eudimorphodon*
Family Rhamphorhynchidae: *Anurognathus, Rhamphorhynchus, Scaphognathus, Sordes*
SUBORDER PTERODACTYLOIDEA
Family Dsungaripteridae: *Dsungaripterus*
Family Pterodaustriidae: *Pterodaustro*
Family Pterodactylidae: *Cearadactylus, Pterodactylus*
Family Ornithocheiridae: *Pteranodon, Quetzalcoatlus*
ORDER SAURUSCHIA ("lizard-hipped" dinosaurs)
SUBORDER THEROPODA
INFRAORDER CERATOSAURIA
Family Ceratosauridae: *Ceratosaurus*
Family Podokesauridae: *Procompsognathus, Saltopus, Coelophysis*
DIVISION MANIRAPTORA
Family not named: *Protoarchaeopteryx*
Family Coeluridae: *Coelurus*
Family Compsognathidae: *Compsognathus, Sinosauropteryx*
Family Ornithomimidae: *Dromiceiomimus, Elaphrosaurus, Gallimimus, Ornithomimus, Struthiomimus*
Family Oviraptoridae: *Oviraptor*
Family Dromaeosauridae: *Deinonychus, Dromaeosaurus, Saurornitholestes, Velociraptor*
Family Saurornithoididae: *Saurornithoides, Stenonychosaurus*
Family Baryonychidae: *Baryonyx*
INFRAORDER CARNOSAURIA
Family Megalosauridae: *Dilophosaurus, Eustreptospondylus, Megalosaurus, Proceratosaurus, Teratosaurus*
Family Allosauridae: *Allosaurus, Yangchuanosaurus*
Family Spinosauridae: *Acrocanthosaurus, Spinosaurus*
Family Tyrannosauridae: *Albertosaurus,*

Alioramus, Daspletosaurus, Tarbosaurus, Tyrannosaurus
SUBORDER SAUROPODOMORPHA
INFRAORDER PROSAUROPODA
Family Anchisauridae: *Anchisaurus, Efraasia, Thecodontosaurus*
Family Plateosauridae: *Massospondylus, Mussaurus, Plateosaurus*
Family Melanorosauridae: *Riojasaurus*
INFRAORDER SAUROPODA
Family Cetiosauridae: *Barapasaurus, Cetiosaurus*
Family Brachiosauridae: *Brachiosaurus*
Family Camarasauridae: *Camarasaurus, Euhelopus, Ophistocoelicaudia*
Family Diplodocidae: *Apatosaurus (=Brontosaurus), Dicraeosaurus, Diplodocus, Mamenchisaurus*
Family Titanosauridae: *Alamosaurus, Saltasaurus*
ORDER ORNITHISCHIA ("bird-hipped" dinosaurs)
INFRAORDER ORNITHOPODA
Family Fabrosauridae: *Echinodon, Lesothosaurus, Scutellosaurus*
Family Heterodontosauridae: *Heterodontosaurus, Pisanosaurus*
INFRAORDER PACHYCEPHALOSAURIA
Family Pachycephalosauridae: *Homalocephale, Pachycephalosaurus, Prenocephale, Stegoceras*
Family Homalocephalidae: *Homalocephale*
Family Hysilophodontidae: *Dryosaurus, Hypsilophodon, Othnielia, Parksosaurus, Tenontosaurus, Thescelosaurus*
Family Iguanodontidae: *Callovosaurus, Camptosaurus, Iguanodon, Muttaburrasaurus, Ouranosaurus, Probactrosaurus, Vectisaurus*
Family Hadrosauridae: *Anatosaurus, Bactrosaurus, Corythosaurus, Edmontosaurus, Hadrosaurus, Hypacrosaurus, Kritosaurus, Lambeosaurus, Maiasaura, Parasaurolophus, Prosaurolophus, Saurolophus, Shantungosaurus, Tsintaosaurus*
SUBORDER THYREOPHORA
Family Scelidosauridae: *Scelidosaurus*
INFRAORDER STEGOSAURIA
Family Stegosauridae: *Kentrosaurus, Stegosaurus, Tuojiangosaurus, Wuerhosaurus*
INFRAORDER ANKYLOSAURIA
Family Nodosauridae: *Hylaeosaurus, Panoplosaurus, Nodosaurus, Polacanthus, Sauropelta, Silvisaurus, Struthiosaurus*
Family Ankylosauridae: *Ankylosaurus, Euoplocephalus, Saichania, Talarurus*
SUBORDER CERAPODA
INFRAORDER CERATOPSIA
Family Psittacosauridae: *Psittacosaurus*
Family Protoceratopidae: *Bagaceratops,*

Leptoceratops, Microceratops, Montanoceratops, Protoceratops

Family Ceratopsidae: *Anchiceratops, Arrhinoceratops, Centrosaurus, Chasmosaurus, Pachyrhinosaurus, Pentaceratops, Styracosaurus, Torosaurus, Triceratops*

BIRDS (see pp.314–325)
CLASS AVES
SUBCLASS ARCHAEORNITHES
    Family Archaeopterygidae: *Archaeopteryx*
    Family Alvarezsauridae
    Family Iberomesornithidae
SUBCLASS ENANTIORNITHES
SUBCLASS ODONTORNITHES
    ORDER ICHTHYORNITHIFORMES: *Ichthyornis*
    ORDER HESPERORNITHIFORMES: *Hesperornis*
SUBCLASS NEORNITHES
DIVISION PALAEOGNATHAE
DIVISION NEOGNATHE
    ORDER STRUTHIORNITHIFORMES: *Aepyornis, Dinornis, Emeus*
    ORDER COLUMBIFORMES: *Raphus*
    ORDER CICONIIFORMES: *Argentavis, Harpagornis, Limnofregata, Osteodontornis, Palaelodus, Pinguinus*
    ORDER GRUIFORMES: *Diatryma, Neocathartes, Phorusrhacus*
    ORDER ANSERIFORMES: *Presbyornis*

MAMMAL-LIKE REPTILES
(see pp.326–337)
SUBCLASS SYNAPSIDA
    ORDER PELYCOSAURIA
    Family Ophiacodontidae: *Archaeothyris, Ophiacodon*
    Family Caseidae: *Casea*
    Family Edaphosauridae: *Edaphosaurus*
    Family Sphenacodontidae: *Sphenacodon, Dimetrodon*
    Family Varanopseidae: *Varanosaurus*
    Family Eothyrididae
    ORDER THERAPSIDA
    SUBORDER EOTITANOSUCHIA
    Family Phthinosuchidae: *Phthinosuchus*
    SUBORDER DINOCEPHALIA
    Family Titanosuchidae: *Titanosuchus*
    Family Tapinocephalidae: *Moschops*
    SUBORDER GORGONOPSIA
    Family Gorgonopsidae: *Lycaenops*
    SUBORDER DICYNODONTIA
    Family Galeopsidae: *Galechirus*
    Family Cistecephalidae: *Cistecephalus*
    Family Robertiidae: *Robertia*
    Family Dicynodontidae: *Dicynodon*
    Family Kannemeyeriidae: *Kannemeyeria*
    Family Lystrosauridae: *Lystrosaurus*

SUBORDER THEROCEPHALIA
    Family Ericiolacertidae: *Ericiolacerta*
SUBORDER CYNODONTIA
    Family Procynosuchidae: *Procynosuchus*
    Family Galesauridae: *Thrinaxodon*
    Family Cynognathidae: *Cynognathus*
    Family Traversodontidae: *Massetognathus*
    Family Tritylodontidae: *Oligokyphus*
SUBORDER BIARMOSUCHIA

MAMMALS (see pp.338–441)
CLASS MAMMALIA
SUBCLASS PROTOTHERIA
    Family Morganucodontidae: *Megazostrodon*
    Family Haramiyidae: *Haramiya*
    ORDER MULTITUBERCULATA
    Family Ptilodontidae: *Ptilodus*
    ORDER MONOTREMATA (platypus, spiny anteaters)
    ORDER DOCODONTA
    ORDER TRICONODONTA
    ORDER SYMMETRODONTA
    Family Dryolestidae: *Crusafontia*
SUBCLASS THERIA
INFRACLASS METATHERIA
    ORDER MARSUPIALIA (marsupials)
    SUBORDER DIDELPHOIDEA
    Family Didelphidae: *Alphadon*
    Family Borhyaenidae: *Borhyaena, Cladosictis*
    Family Thylacosmilidae: *Thylacosmilus*
    Family Argyrolagidae: *Argyrolagus*
    Family Necrolestidae: *Necrolestes*
    Family Thylacoleonidae: *Thylacoleo*
    Family Macropodidae: *Procoptodon*
    Family Diprotodontidae: *Diprotodon*
    Family Palorchestidae: *Palorchestes*
INFRACLASS EUTHERIA (placentals)
    Family Zalambdalestidae: *Zalambdalestes*
COHORT EDENTATA
    Family Metacheiromyidae: *Metacheiromys*
    ORDER XENARTHRA (armadillos, sloths, anteaters)
    Family Dasypodidae: *Peltephilus*
    Family Glyptodontidae: *Doedicurus*
    Family Megalonychidae: *Hapalops*
    Family Megatheriidae: *Megatherium*
    Family Mylodontidae: *Glossotherium*
    Family Myrmecophagidae: *Eurotamandua*
ORDER PHOLIDOTA
    Family Manidae: *Eomanis*
COHORT EPITHERIA
    SUPERORDER INSECTIVORA (hedgehogs, shrews, moles)
    ORDER LEPTICTIDA
    Family Pseudorhyncocyonidae: *Leptictidium*
    ORDER LIPOTYPHLA
    Family Palaeoryctidae: *Palaeoryctes*
    SUPERORDER ANAGALIDA

ORDER ANAGALIDA
    Family Anagalidae: *Anagale*
    SUPERORDER GLIRES
    ORDER LAGOMORPHA (rabbits, hares)
    Family Leporidae: *Palaeolagus*
    ORDER RODENTIA (squirrels, rats, beavers)
    SUBORDER SCIUROGNATHI
    Family Paramyidae: *Ischyromys*
    Family Mylagaulidae: *Epigaulus*
    Family Castoridae: *Steneofiber*
    SUBORDER HYSTRICOGNATHI
    Family Ctenodactylidae: *Birbalomys*
    Family Dinomyidae: *Telicomys*
    Family Eocardiidae: *Eocardia*
    SUPERORDER ARCHONTA
    ORDER CHIROPTERA (bats)
    Family Icaronycteridae: *Icaronycteris*
"PRIMATOMORPHS"
    Family Paromomyidae: *Pargartorius*
    ORDER DERMOPTERA (FLYING LEMURS)
    Family Flagiomenidae: *Planetetherium*
    SUBORDER PLESIADAPIFORMES
    Family Plesiadapiae: *Plesiadapis*
    ORDER PRIMATES (LEMURS, MONKEYS, APES, AND HUMANS)
    INFRAORDER ADAPIFORMES
    Family Adapidae: *Notharctus*
    INFRAORDER LEMURIFORMES
    Family Lemuridae: *Megaladapis*
    Family Lorisidae
DIVISION HAPLORHINI
    Family Omomyidae: *Necrolemur*
    Family Tarsiidae
    SUBORDER ANTHROPOIDEA
    INFRAORDER PLATYRRHINI
    Family Cebidae: *Branisella*
    Family Atelidae: *Tremacebus*
    INFRAORDER CATARRHINI
    SUPERFAMILY CERCOPITHECOIDEA
    Family Cercopithecidae: *Mesopithecus, Theropithecus*
    Family Oreopithecidae: *Oreopithecus*
    SUPERFAMILY HOMINOIDEA
    Family Hylobatidae (gibbons)
    Family Pliopithecidae: *Dendropithecus, Pliopithecus,Propliopithecus*
    Subfamily Ponginae (fossil and living apes): *Dryopithecus, Gigantopithecus, Ramapithecus, Sivapithecus*
    Family Hominidae (humans and great apes): *Australopithecus, Homo*
    Subfamily Homininae (humans and fossil ancestors)
    SUPERORDER FERAE
    ORDER CREODONTA (creodonts)
    Family Hyaenodontidae: *Hyaenodon*
    Family Oxyaenidae: *Sarkastodon*

ORDER CARNIVORA (true carnivores)

Superfamily Miacoidea

Family Miacidae: *Miacis*

Superfamily Feloidea (cats, mongooses)

Family Viverridae: *Kanuites*

Family Hyaenidae: *Ictitherium, Percrocuta*

Family Nimravidae: *Nimravus*

Family Felidae: *Dinofelis, Eusmilus, Homotherium, Megantereon, Panthera, Smilodon*

Superfamily Canoidea (dogs, bears, pandas)

Family Mustelidae: *Potamotherium*

Family Canidae: *Canis, Cerdocyon, Cynodesmus, Hesperocyon, Osteoborus, Phlaocyon*

Family Procyonidae: *Chapalmalania, Plesictis*

Family Amphicyonidac: *Amphicyon*

Family Ursidae: *Agriotherium, Hemicyon, Ursus*

SUBORDER PINNIPEDIA (seals, sealions, walruses)

Superfamily Phocoidea (eared seals)

Family Phocidae: *Acrophoca*

Superfamily Otarioidea (fur seals and sealions)

Family Enaliarctidae: *Enaliarctos*

Family Desmatophocidae: *Desmatophoca*

Family Odobenidae (walruses): *Imagotaria*

Family Otariidae

SUPERORDER UNGULATA
(hoofed mammals or ungulates)

ORDER ARCTOCYONIA (condylarths)

Family Arctocyonidae: *Chriacus*

ORDER ACREODI

Family Mesonychidae: *Andrewsarchus*

ORDER TAENIODONTA

Family Stylinodontidae: *Stylinodon*

ORDER PANTODONTA

Family Coryphodontidae: *Coryphodon*

ORDER TILLODONTIA

Family Esthonychidae: *Trogosus*

ORDER DINOCERATA

Family Uintatheriidae: *Eobasileus*

ORDER ARTIODACTYLA
(even-toed ungulates)

SUBORDER SUINA (pigs, peccaries, hippopotamuses)

Family Dichobunidae: *Diacodexis*

Family Entelodontidae: *Archaeotherium, Dinohyus*

Family Suidae: *Metridiochoerus*

Family Tayassuidae: *Platygonus*

Family Anthracotheriidae: *Elomeryx*

Family Hippopotamidae: *Hippopotamus*

SUBORDER TYLOPODA (oreodonts, camels)

Family Merycoidodontidae: *Brachycrus, Merycoidodon, Promerycochoerus*

Family Cainotheriidae: *Cainotherium*

Family Protoceratidae: *Protoceras, Syndyoceras, Synthetoceras*

Family Camelidae: *Aepycamelus, Camelops, Oxydactylus, Poebrotherium, Procamelus,*

Protylopus, Stenomylus, Titanotylopus

SUBORDER RUMINANTIA (deer, giraffes, cattle)

Family Tragul: *Blastomeryx*

Family Cervidae: *Eucladoceros, Megaloceros*

Family Giraffidae: *Prolibytherium, Sivatherium*

Family Antilocapridae: *Hayoceros, Illingoceros*

Family Bovidae: *Bos, Pelorovis*

ORDER CETACEA (whales, dolphins, porpoises)

SUBORDER ARCHAEOCETI

Family Protocetidae: *Pakicetus, Protocetus*

Family Basilosauridae: *Basilosaurus, Zygorhiza*

SUBORDER ODONTOCETI (toothed whales)

Family Squalodontidae: *Prosqualodon*

Family Eurhinodelphidae: *Eurhinodelphis*

SUBORDER MYSTICETI (baleen whales)

Family Cetotheriidae: *Cetotherium*

ORDER TUBULIDENTATA (aardvarks)

ORDER PERISSODACTYLA (odd-toed ungulates)

SUBORDER CERATOMORPHA (tapirs, rhinoceroses)

Family Helaletidae: *Heptodon*

Family Hyrachyidae: *Hyrachyus*

Family Tapiridae: *Miotapirus*

Family Hyracodontidae: *Hyracodon, Indricotherium*

Family Amynodontidae: *Metamynodon*

Family Rhinocerotidae: *Coelodonta, Elasmotherium, Teleoceras, Trigonias*

SUBORDER ANCYLOPODA

Family Chalicotheriidae: *Moropus*

SUBORDER HIPPOMORPHA (horses, brontotheres)

Family Palaeotheriidae: *Palaeotherium*

Family Equidae: *Anchitherium, Hipparion, Hippidion, Hyracotherium, Merychippus, Mesohippus, Parahippus*

Family Brontotheriidae: *Brontotherium, Brontops, Dolichorhinus, Embolotherium, Eotitanops*

SUPERORDER MERIDIUNGULATA (South American hoofed mammals)

ORDER LITOPTERNA

Family Didolodontidae: *Didolodus*

Family Proterotheriidae: *Diadiaphorus, Thoatherium*

Family Macraucheniidae: *Macrauchenia, Theosodon*

ORDER NOTOUNGULATA

SUBORDER NOTIOPROGONIA

Family Notostylopidae: *Notostylops*

SUBORDER TOXODONTA

Family Isotemnidae: *Thomashuxleya*

Family Homalodotheriidae: *Homalodotherium*

Family Leontiniidae: *Scarrittia*

Family Notohippidae: *Rhynchippus*

Family Toxodontidae: *Adinotherium, Toxodon*

SUBORDER TYPOTHERIA

Family Interatheriidae: *Protypotherium*

SUBORDER HEGETOTHERIA

Family Hegetotheriidae: *Pachyrukhos*

ORDER ASTRAPOTHERIA

Family Astrapotheriidae: *Astrapotherium*

Family Trigonostylopidae: *Trigonostylops*

ORDER PYROTHERIA

Family Pyrotheriidae: *Pyrotherium*

ORDER HYRACOIDEA

Family Pliohyracidae: *Kvabebihyrax*

SUPERORDER TETHYTHERIA

ORDER EMBRITHOPODA

Family Arsinoitheriidae: *Arsinoitherium*

ORDER PROBOSCIDEA

Family Moeritheriidae: *Moeritherium*

Family Deinotheriidae: *Deinotherium*

SUBORDER ELEPHANTIODEA
(elephants, mastodonts, mammoths)

Family Gomphotheriidae: *Amebelodon, Anancus, Cuvieronius, Gomphotherium, Phiomia, Platybelodon, Stegomastodon*

Family Mammutidae: *Mammut*

Family Elephantidae: *Elephas, Mammuthus*

ORDER SIRENIA (dugongs, manatees)

Family Prorastomidae: *Prorastomus*

Family Dugongidae: *Rytiodus, Hydrodamalis*

ORDER DESMOSTYLA

Family Desmostylidae: *Desmostylus*

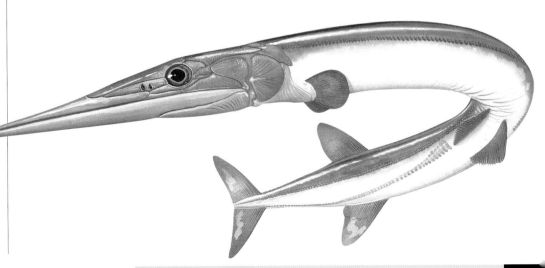

Biographies

Douglas Louis Agassiz (1807–1873) Swiss-American naturalist and glaciologist. He trained as a doctor in Germany, attended **Georges Cuvier**'s lectures in Paris, and made important studies on fossil fish, describing more than 1,700 new species. He was one of the first scientists to argue that there had been a recent ice age. He went on to teach at Harvard in 1846 and was an opponent of **Charles Darwin**'s theory of evolution.

Roy Chapman Andrews (1884–1960) American explorer and museum scientist who led the first expedition, from the American Museum of Natural History in New York to the Gobi Desert of Mongolia in the 1920s. The expedition discovered many new dinosaurs, including *Protoceratop*s, *Oviraptor, Velociraptor*, and the first nests of dinosaur eggs with hatchlings.

Mary Anning (1799–1847) The most famous member of an English family of professional fossil collectors. The Annings recovered fossils of ichthyosaurs, plesiosaurs, fish, and many invertebrate fossils from the early Jurassic strata in the seacliffs around the coastal town of Lyme Regis in southern England.

Luis (1911–1988) and Walter (1940–) Alvarez American father and son team who in 1980 claimed that the thin layer of clay (enriched with the rare element iridium) found at the boundary of Cretaceous and Tertiary rocks (K-T Boundary) marks the impact of a large extraterrestrial meteorite. They also claimed that this event, 65 million years ago, was responsible for the extinction of the dinosaurs. Luis Alvarez was an astrophysicist and Nobel prize-winner for physics in 1968.

Elso Barghoorn (1915–1984) American paleontologist who in 1956 discovered the 2-billion-year-old Precambrian gunflint microfossils. In 1968, he showed that chemical fossils such as amino acids can be preserved in rocks as old as 3 billion years.

Joachim Barrande (1799–1883) French engineer and naturalist who studied with **Georges Cuvier** and then worked as a tutor to the exiled French royal family. He devoted his life to describing early Paleozoic fossils in Bohemia.

Hugo Benioff (1899–1968) American seismologist (earthquake expert) who gave his name to the Benioff zone. He found that the subduction (see glossary) of oceanic plates causes earthquakes, and that the farther inland this happens, the deeper the center of the earthquake.

Bertram Boltwood (1870–1927) American chemist who showed that measurement of the ratio of the isotopes (see glossary) of lead and uranium in rocks can be used to date them.

Alexandre Brongniart (1770–1847) French naturalist and pioneer of stratigraphy (see glossary). He worked with the naturalist **Georges Cuvier**, mapping the strata around Paris and collecting local fossils.

Adolphe Brongniart (1801–1876) Son of **Alexandre Brongniart**, he was mainly a botanist who pioneered botanical techniques for the investigation of fossil plants. They provided a model for future studies.

Jennifer Clack (1947–) English paleontologist who revised the way we view the first vertebrate animals with legs (tetrapods). Her detailed studies of Devonian fossils showed that legs initially evolved for swimming in fast-moving water. Only later were they adapted for walking on land.

Edwin Colbert (1905–2001) American expert on Triassic dinosaurs who found and excavated the Ghost Ranch site in New Mexico with its remarkable abundance of *Coelophysis* skeletons.

Edward Drinker Cope (1840–1897) American naturalist who collected mammal and dinosaur fossils and was a great rival of **Othniel Marsh**. Cope's large collection is now in the American Museum of Natural History in New York.

Georges Cuvier (1769–1832) French founder of comparative anatomy, Cuvier was one of the greatest naturalists of his day. He showed how a fossil vertebrate animal can be reconstructed from a few bones and deductions made about its way of life. With **Alexandre Brongniart**, he discovered the principles of stratigraphy (see glossary). He believed that catastrophes occurred at various points in the history of the Earth and that these greatly affected the progress of life.

James Dwight Dana (1813–1895) American geologist who was a collector for the Wilkes Pacific expedition. His reports on the geological and zoological specimens he gathered are famous for their excellent insight and accuracy. He also reported on volcanoes, coral reefs, and the formation of mountain ranges. Dana supported **Charles Darwin**'s theory of evolution.

Raymond Dart (1893–1988) Australian-born zoologist who discovered the first fossil *Australopithecus* (meaning "southern ape") ancestor of humans. The small but well-preserved skull, nicknamed the "Taung child," was found in 1924 in cave deposits in Botswana, southern Africa. Dart's claim that it represented a link between fossil apes and humans was not generally acknowledged until the late 1930s.

Charles Darwin (1809–1882) English naturalist who studied geology and both living and fossil organisms, especially during his five-year round-the-world expedition on *HMS Beagle*. He developed a now widely accepted theory of the evolution of life through natural selection. The outline theory was first published in 1858 with Alfred George Wallace, who had reached the same conclusions independently. Darwin then developed the theory into his famous book *On the Origin of Species by Natural Selection*, published in 1859. The theory met with considerable opposition, especially when he applied his ideas to *The Descent of Man* in 1871. Many of the scientists of the time, such as **Adam Sedgwick**, were bitterly opposed to the theory.

Louis Dollo (1857–1931) French-born paleontologist who studied the famous *Iguanodon* skeletons in Belgium with Louis de Pauw. Dollo made the first reconstruction of *Iguanodon*, modeled on bird and kangaroo skeletons. He also published a theory of irreversibility in evolution in which specialized creatures cannot evolve into unspecialized ones.

Dianne Edwards (1942–) Welsh paleobotanist who found the earliest fossils of vascular plants (see glossary) in Silurian rocks in Britain. She showed how these first land plants evolved and colonized the land.

Maurice Ewing (1906–1974) American marine geologist who showed that ocean crust is thinner than continental crust. In 1953 he discovered the worldwide extent of mid-ocean ridges (see glossary) with **Bruce Heezen**. Then he found the central rift in the mid-Atlantic Ridge and showed that the ridge is being pulled apart.

Martin Glaessner (1906–1989) Australian geologist who produced the first detailed descriptions (from 1958) of the late-Precambrian soft-bodied, Ediacaran fossils from the Flinders Range mountains in South Australia. The fossils had originally been discovered by R.C. Sprigg in the late 1940s.

Stephen Jay Gould (1941–) American paleontologist and evolutionist who developed the idea of "punctuated equilibria" in evolution. This proposes that new species have evolved in rapid bursts followed by periods of little change.

James Hall (1811–1898) American pioneer of the study of Paleozoic fossils, especially in New York State, and mountain building in the Appalachians. He later became director of the Museum of Natural History in Albany.

Bruce Heezen (1924–1977) American oceanographer who showed that powerful, submarine turbidity currents with speeds of up to 55 mph (85 kph) could carry vast amounts of land-derived sediment hundreds of miles out into deep ocean basins.

Harry Hammond Hess (1906–1969) American geologist who advanced the understanding of the geology of the oceans. In 1962, he suggested that molten rock material constantly rises from the mantle to the surface along mid-ocean ridges (see glossary). From there it spreads out horizontally and forms new ocean floor. The farther away from the ridge the ocean floor is, the older it is.

James Hutton (1726–1797) Scottish naturalist whose *Theory of the Earth* (1788) claimed that the Earth was of great age with "no vestige of a beginning, no prospect of an end" and that geological phenomena can and should be explained by the study of present-day processes. This approach was taken up and developed by another Scottish geologist, **Charles Lyell**.

Donald Johanson (1943–) American paleoanthropologist who, in 1973, discovered the knee joint of an australopithecine in Ethiopia. From the bones, he was able to show that these hominid ancestors walked upright in a similar way to modern humans. The following year he found "Lucy" (*Australopithecus afarensis*). This partly complete fossil skeleton was the earliest known human ancestor, some 3.1 million years old.

Mary Leakey (1913–1998) English paleoanthropologist who lived and worked in Kenya. She led the expedition to Laetoli, Tanzania, which found the oldest known australopithecine footprints, dated as 3.6 million years old.

Inge Lehmann (1888–1993) Danish geophysicist who discovered that the Earth's inner core is solid.

Carolus Linnaeus (1707–1778) Swedish physician and naturalist, whose *Systema naturae* of 1735 formed the basis for the classification of organisms. Linnaeus' system grouped organisms with shared characteristics in which the basic unit is the species. He used Latin names for the different groupings from species to genus and order to kingdom.

Katherine Lonsdale (1903–1971) Irish crystallographer who pioneered the study of crystal atomic structure, especially that of organic, carbon-based crystals, using X-rays. Her work helped progress toward unraveling the structure of proteins such as DNA.

Charles Lyell (1797–1875) Scottish barrister and geologist whose *Principles of Geology* (1830–1833) laid down the beginning of the modern approach to the study of Earth science and was particularly influential on the development of **Charles Darwin**'s evolutionary theory. Lyell was opposed to **George Cuvier**'s catastrophist views and supported **James Hutton**'s approach. He showed how the study of present-day processes can be applied to geological phenomena and divided Tertiary time into epochs—Paleocene, Eocene, Oligocene, Miocene, and Pliocene.

Othniel Marsh (1831–1899) American professor of natural history at Yale, Marsh was one of the great pioneers of dinosaur studies. He described 19 new genera of dinosaurs and competed with his rival **Edward Cope** to collect new dinosaurs from the American Midwest. He also worked on vertebrate evolution, especially that of horses.

Drummond Matthews (1931–1999) English co-discoverer, with **Frederick Vine,** of symmetrical patterns of magnetized ocean floor lava on either side of mid-ocean ridges (see glossary). The patterns showed alternating normal and reversed magnetization, reflecting a history of reversals in the Earth's magnetic field, and showed that the ocean floor is formed at mid-ocean ridges.

Motonori Matuyama (1884–1958) Japanese geologist who in 1929 discovered that some sedimentary rocks are magnetized with a reversed polarity, concluding that the Earth's magnetic field must have changed in the past. This helped develop the idea that plates have moved over the surface of the Earth throughout geological time.

Stanley Miller (1930–) American chemist who in the early 1950s created complex organic substances such as amino acids by passing an electrical charge through simple gas mixtures that replicated the early atmosphere of the Earth. His results showed how the first lifeforms on the planet could have been created.

Andrija Mohorovicic (1857–1936) Croatian geophysicist who in 1909 discovered differences in the speed with which earthquake waves travel through the Earth. He realized that the Earth's crust overlies a denser mantle that lies about 19 miles (30 kilometers) beneath the surface.

Sir Roderick Murchison (1792–1871) Retired Scottish military officer who pioneered the mapping and study of Paleozoic rocks, defining and naming the Silurian System in 1835, the Devonian System (with **Adam Sedgwick**) in 1839, and the Permian System in 1841.

Alexander Ivanovich Oparin (1894–1980) Russian chemist who pioneered a chemical approach to the origin of life. He argued that simple organic substances were present on the Earth's surface before life itself evolved. His approach influenced **Stanley Miller**.

Richard Owen (1804–1892) English anatomist who first coined the name "dinosaur," in 1842. Owen supervised the first life-size reconstructions made for the world's first theme park—the Crystal Palace Gardens in London. Owen also described *Archaeopteryx*, the oldest fossil bird, but was opposed to **Charles Darwin**'s theory of evolution.

Henry Fairfield Osborn (1857–1935) Paleontologist with the U.S. Geological Survey and former president of the American Museum of Natural History in New York. He promoted **Charles Darwin**'s theory of evolution, and in 1905 described and named *Tyrannosaurus rex* (although the specimen was actually found by the "bone hunter" Barnum Brown in the late Cretaceous sediments of Hell Creek, Montana).

Catherine Raisin (1855–1945) English geologist and one of the first women to become head of a university department in Great Britain (1890). She made advances in the study of minerals and rocks, especially serpentinites, using a microscope. These rocks are important as fragments of ancient ocean floor that have been caught up in mountain building.

Charles Richter (1900–1985) American geophysicist who in 1935 developed a scale (which bears his name) for measuring the absolute strength of earthquakes. The largest earthquakes this century have registered 8.9 on the Richter scale; the earthquake that destroyed San Francisco in 1906 would have registered 8.25.

Adam Sedgwick (1785–1873) English cleric and Woodwardian professor at the University of Cambridge (from 1818). He mapped the Lower Paleozoic strata of Wales and defined the Cambrian System in 1835 and the Devonian System (with **Roderick Murchison**) in 1839. Subsequently Murchison lowered the base of his Silurian System into Sedgwick's Cambrian, and a bitter dispute broke out which was not fully resolved until after both men had died.

William Smith (1769–1839) English canal engineer and self-taught pioneer of geological mapping and stratigraphic geology (see glossary). He discovered and used the principle that the layers (succession) of strata can be characterized by the fossils they contain. Different fossils are buried at different times. The same principle was independently worked out by **Georges Cuvier** and **Alexandre Brongniart** in France. Smith produced the first geological map of England and Wales in 1819.

Marie Stopes (1880–1958) English paleobotanist who showed how plant remains alter to become coal. She subsequently became better known for promoting women's health issues.

Frederick Vine (1939–) English co-discoverer in 1963, with **Drummond Matthews**, of magnetic anomalies across mid-ocean ridges (see glossary). They measured and mapped the repeated symmetrical patterns of polarity reversals in magnetized lavas on either side of the mid-ocean ridges. This provided support for the suggestion by **Harry Hammond Hess** that new ocean floor rocks are formed at spreading ridges (see glossary).

Charles Doolittle Walcott (1850–1927) American paleontologist who specialized in the study of fossil arthropods, especially those of Cambrian times. He discovered the rich Cambrian deposits of the Burgess Shale in British Columbia, Canada, in 1909. Over several years Walcott excavated some 70,000 specimens and had them shipped back to the Smithsonian Institute, of which he became head in 1907. Administrative work left him little time to devote to the study of this remarkable find.

Alfred Wegener (1880–1930) German meteorologist and geophysicist who developed the theory of continental drift. He collected all the available evidence from rocks and fossils to show that South America, Africa, India, Antarctica, and Australia had once been joined together as a supercontinent, which he named Pangea in 1912. However, he could not suggest an acceptable mechanism by which the continents could have moved such great distances over the surface of the Earth. The theory was not widely accepted until the 1960s, when plate tectonic theory (see glossary) provided hard evidence that the continents had indeed moved.

Abraham Gottlob Werner (1749–1817) German mineralogist and teacher who proposed the Neptunist theory of geology, in which minerals that had dissolved in an ancient ocean that covered the whole Earth were gradually deposited as solid rock (precipitated). The lowest and oldest were "Primitive" granites and slates, followed by "Transition," "Flötz" or stratified rocks, then "Alluvial" sediments. His teaching was highly influential at the time.

John Tuzo Wilson (1908–1993) Canadian geophysicist whose work helped develop plate tectonic theory (see glossary). He showed that oceanic islands become progressively older the farther away they are from mid-ocean spreading ridges (see glossary), and in 1965 proposed the concept of "transform" faults that break up mid-ocean spreading ridges into sections. Wilson also suggested the existence of "hot spots" (see glossary) with heat plumes rising within the mantle.

John Woodward (1665–1728) English professor of medicine who collected "natural objects" including fossils and minerals. He left his collection to the University of Cambridge, where it can still be seen in the Sedgwick Museum.

GLOSSARY

A

ADAPTATION: A biological modification that makes an organism better suited for a particular way of life—for example, to feed on a specific diet.

ADAPTIVE RADIATION: The divergence of an ancestral stock into forms (species, families, etc.) for distinct lifestyles or ecological niches. For example, primitive shrewlike mammals evolved into organisms as varied as bats and whales.

ADVANCED (of a feature of an animal): More modified, specialized, and complex forms.

AGNATHANS: A group of jawless and toothless fishlike vertebrates that includes many extinct sea and freshwater forms. Only the hagfish and lampreys survive. (Ordovician to recent.)

ALGAE: The general name given to several unrelated groups of simple organisms that live in moist or wet environments and include some of the most primitive organisms known. There are both single and multicelled forms and, like plants, they need sunlight to build their cells. Fossilized algae first appeared some 3.5 billion years ago.

AMBER: A sticky, scented resin produced by certain trees since Jurassic times as protection against disease. Insects and other organisms can become trapped in the resin and fossilized when it hardens into amber.

AMMONITES: An extinct group of cephalopod mollusks that lived in coiled shells and are often found as fossils in Mesozoic strata. (Jurassic to end Cretaceous.)

AMNIOTES: Living and fossil vertebrates whose embryos develop within a special protective membrane—the amnion. The group includes some early tetrapods, reptiles, birds, and mammals, but not amphibians.

AMPHIBIANS: A major group of vertebrates that includes all the tetrapods with gills for breathing in water when young, but lungs for breathing air as adults. Amphibians develop into tadpoles from an unprotected egg laid in water and then change into the adult form. (Mid-Carboniferous to recent.)

ANAPSIDS: A member of a group of reptiles characterized by having no openings in the skull behind the eye, including turtles, tortoises, and some other primitive groups.

ANGIOSPERMS: Commonly referred to as the flowering plants, this major division of the plant kingdom includes deciduous trees, shrubs, grasses, and weeds as well as flowers. The seeds are enclosed in an ovary. (Late Jurassic to recent.)

ANKYLOSAURIDS: A family of armored dinosaurs with horny beaks for plant-eating. Bony plates and spikes covered the neck, shoulders, and back, and the tail was armed with a bony club. (Mid- to end Cretaceous.)

ANNELIDS: Soft-bodied worms with bodies divided into segments. They have left a fossil record of trace fossils, some calcareous tubes, and organic toothlike structures. (Late Vendian to recent.)

ANTHRACOSAURS: A group of fish-eating, lizard-shaped tetrapods that includes some land-living and some water-dwelling creatures; they may include the ancestors of the reptiles. (Early Carboniferous to Permian.)

APPALACHIANS: An ancient mountain range on the eastern seaboard of North America with a complex geological history extending back to late Precambrian times.

ARACHNIDS: A large group of mostly land-living carnivorous arthropods including the scorpions, mites, and spiders. The earliest fossil forms are Silurian scorpions, with spiders first appearing in the Devonian period.

ARCHAEBACTERIANS: Primitive, single-celled microscopic bacteria, many of which can live in extreme conditions such as acid or very hot water. They are thought to be among the earliest lifeforms to have evolved, around 3.5 billion years ago.

ARCHAEOCYATHANS: An extinct group of early Cambrian spongelike organisms that grew attached to the seabed to form the first reefs. The animals lived in cup-shaped calcium carbonate structures with porous walls and are thought to be related to the sponges.

ARCHEAN: The earliest part of the Earth's Precambrian rock record, dating from about 3.8 to 2.5 billion years ago.

ARCHOSAURS: A group of reptiles that includes the dinosaurs, pterosaurs, and living crocodiles. They originated in the early Triassic; many became extinct in late Cretaceous times.

ARMORICA: An ancient chunk of continental crust made up of the lands that now form France, Switzerland, southern Germany, and parts of Eastern Europe. Originally Armorica was part of the southern supercontinent of Gondwana, but it broke away and drifted northward from Ordovician times.

ARTHROPODS: The biggest group of animals (over a million living species) that includes many extinct groups such as the trilobites and eurypterids, and living groups such as the crabs, insects, and spiders. They have jointed limbs and a hard skin that has to be periodically shed to allow growth. (Lower Cambrian to recent.)

ATROPHY: To wither away; become useless.

AUSTRALOPITHECINES: An extinct group of small but upright-walking, apelike human ancestors that lived from 4.5 to 1.4 million years ago.

AVALONIA: An early Paleozoic crustal plate consisting of Newfoundland, England, Wales, southeast Ireland, and part of western Europe that broke away from Gondwana in Ordovician times and joined Laurentia at the end of Silurian times.

B

BACTERIA: A large, diverse group of microorganisms consisting of single cells whose nuclei do not have well-defined membranes around them. Together with the blue-green algae, they make up the prokaryotes, organisms that were among the first and most primitive to evolve, 3.5 billion years ago.

BALTICA: An early Paleozoic crustal plate made up of northwestern and central Europe and part of Russia. The plate collided with Laurentia to form the Caledonian mountain belt in Ordovician times.

BASALT: A volcanic rock formed either in sheets on the surface, when lava flows from a vent or fissure in the ground, or underground when lava is injected into cracks in the surrounding rocks. Cracks filled with basalt are called dykes when they are vertical and sills when they are horizontal.

BED: A layer of sediment (a stratum) deposited by wind, water, or gravity-controlled flow to form a more or less flat-lying sheet.

BELEMNITES: An extinct group of squidlike sea creatures with a solid, bullet-shaped structure embedded in the end of the body. (Jurassic to Cretaceous.)

BIOZONE: A subdivision in geological time, characterized by the presence in a series of rock strata of fossils of the same, or a group of, species.

BIPEDAL: Standing, walking, or running on two legs. See also **QUADRUPEDAL.**

BRACHIATE: To swing through the trees, moving from branch to branch using the hands.

BRACHIOPODS: Shellfish, common in the Paleozoic, that were similar to the bivalved mollusks but distinguished by different body organs. (Early Cambrian to recent.)

BROWSER: A plant-eating animal that selects leaves and twigs from shrubs and trees. Compare: **GRAZER.**

BRYOPHYTES: Plants, including the mosses and liverworts, that lack true roots and cannot grow much above ground level. They are thought to have been the first plants to have colonized the land, in Ordovician times.

BRYOZOAN: See **MOSS ANIMAL.**

BURGESS SHALE: A mid-Cambrian marine deposit in British Columbia famous for the diversity and preservation of its fauna.

C

CALCIFICATION: Deposition of calcium minerals, which stiffen cartilage and form bone.

CALCIUM CARBONATE: A naturally occurring mineral that can form at the Earth's surface; used by many animals (corals, trilobites, clams) to build or reinforce their skeletons.

CALEDONIDES: The Paleozoic mountain chain that extends from Scandinavia through the northwest British Isles into Newfoundland, the result of the collision between Avalonia and Laurentia at the end of the Silurian period.

CAMBRIAN: The first geological period of the Phanerozoic Era, from the end of the Precambrian (545 million years ago) to the beginning of the Ordovician (495 million years ago). A time when most of the main invertebrate groups (phyla) appear in the fossil record, along with the first chordates.

CANINE TOOTH: Conical mammal tooth between the incisors and premolars, well-developed and sharp for piercing prey. Absent or vestigial in many herbivores. There is a pair in each jaw in both the milk set of teeth and the adult set.

CARAPACE: The hard, protective shell or shield enclosing the body of animals such as the invertebrate arthropods and some reptiles such as the turtles.

CARBONIFEROUS: The period of geological time from the end of the Devonian (354 million years ago) to the beginning of the Permian (290 million years ago.) In this time the first extensive forests developed, leaving coal deposits and the remains of the first land-living vertebrate communities of reptiles and amphibians. Divided into Mississippian and Pennsylvanian.

CARNASSIAL TEETH: Upper and lower cheek teeth modified for meat-shearing.

CARNIVORES: A group of mammals that have well-developed, dagger-shaped canine teeth for eating meat. (Early Tertiary to recent.)

CARNIVOROUS: Describing an animal that eats the flesh of vertebrate animals but is not necessarily a true carnivore. See also **HERBIVORES, INSECTIVORES.**

CARNOSAURS: A group of large carnivorous dinosaurs with large skulls and teeth, many of the biggest being bipedal. (Early Jurassic to end Cretaceous.)

CARTILAGE: Gristly, flexible material that makes up the skeleton in many fish. It is also present in more advanced animals in the embryo and in bone joints. May become stiffened by calcification.

CATASTROPHISM: A theory that claims that the history of the Earth and its life are influenced by sudden catastrophic events. Originally associated with the Biblical Flood, the theory has now been modified to include extraterrestrial impacts and environmental events.

CAUDAL: Related to the tail.

CEPHALOPODS: A large group of sea-dwelling animals, including octopus, squid, and cuttlefish, with a well-developed head surrounded by tentacles. (Cambrian to recent.)

CERATOPSIANS: A group of about 20 species of rhinoceroslike, plant-eating dinosaurs protected by bony head shields and horns. (Late Cretaceous.)

CERVICAL: Related to the neck.

CHALK: A soft limestone formed from a "mud" of calcium carbonate, often made up of the shells of tiny marine organisms, as in the Cretaceous chalk deposits of Western Europe.

CHEEK TEETH: Teeth lying in the cheek region of the jaw. For example, mammalian molars.

CHELONIANS: A large group of reptiles, including the turtles and tortoises, that have short, broad bodies protected above and below by shields composed of bony plates overlain by plates of tortoiseshell. (Late Triassic to recent.)

CHERT: A silica-rich mineral deposit that can form in seabed sediments and enclose and then fossilize the remains of organisms, especially microbes. Precambrian chert provides much of the fossil evidence for primitive life.

CHORDATES: Animals with a notochord or backbone. (Mid-Cambrian to recent.)

CLASS: A high-level grouping of similar organisms. A class contains one or more orders; similar classes form a phylum.

CLUBMOSSES: A group of plants that included large, coal-forming trees in Carboniferous times and still survive as much smaller forms. Their stems are covered in small, leaflike structures; they reproduce by means of spores, grouped in conelike structures. (Devonian to recent.)

COAL: A carbon-rich deposit formed from the remains of plants. At first the material becomes peat; as this becomes more and more compressed, it turns into lignite (brown coal), then harder forms such as anthracite. Each successive form contains more carbon and less water.

COELACANTHS: Primitive bony fish with large single and paired fins, thought to have died out in Cretaceous times until the living coelacanth, *Latimeria*, was found in 1938. (Late Devonian to recent.)

COLLISION ZONE: A region where two crustal plates collide, leading to folding and faulting (mountain building) of the rocks and often subduction of one plate, depending on the type of crustal plates.

COLONIAL: A group of animals or single cells of the same species living together to form an organism. Some colonies, like corals, sponges, and graptolites, have a shared skeleton, but others, like the insects, may have a close social organization in which some individuals are specialized for certain specific duties.

COLONIZATION: The "invasion" of a new habitat or ecological niche. May displace existing animals. For example, North American mammals caused extinction of many South American species when the Panama land bridge was established.

CONIFERS: A large group of woody plants with needle or scalelike leaves and single-sex cones for reproduction. (Carboniferous to recent.)

CONODONTS: An extinct group of small, jawless sea creatures with mouths filled with several pairs of tooth-bars made of bonelike material; recently considered to be chordates or possibly primitive jawless vertebrates. The fossil teeth have considerable use in dating strata. (Late Cambrian to end Triassic.)

CONTINENTAL BREAK-UP: Splitting apart of continental crustal plates, caused by large-scale heat flow within the Earth's mantle, to form a rift valley. Volcanoes and fissures erupt dense basalt lavas in the valley bottom and build a ridge that continuously subsides as the rift valley splits apart. Eventually, the low-lying valley floods with seawater, forming a new ocean. See also **MID-OCEAN RIDGE.**

CONTINENTAL CRUST: The uppermost, brittle rock layer of the Earth that forms the continents and varies in thickness from 16 to 56 miles (25 to 90 kilometers); it has an overall composition of granite, but includes a wide variety of metamorphic, igneous, and sedimentary rocks.

CONTINENTAL SHELF: The margin of the continents that is covered by shallow seas and shelves steeply down to the ocean floor at its outer edge; floored by thick piles of seabed and delta sediments, it is home to many important groups of marine life.

CONVECTION (MANTLE): Heat-carrying currents in the Earth's semimolten mantle. Material becomes hot near the Earth's core and slowly rises through the mantle. At the same time, cooler material descends toward the core. The heat transferred in this way can melt rocks in the crust to produce magma.

CONVERGENT EVOLUTION: The phenomenon whereby animals evolve similar structures in response to the same environmental pressures—the wings of bats, birds, and pterosaurs, for example.

COPROLITE: Fossilized animal droppings.

CORALS: A group of soft-bodied and primitive sea creatures that build a supporting calcareous skeleton. They vary in size and shape from small cups (less than an inch in size) to branched and dome-shaped structures up to 3 feet (1 meter) in diameter. Modern corals, called scleractinians, need light and mostly live in shallow, tropical waters; they evolved in Triassic times from Palaeozoic species that are now extinct. (Ordovician to Permian.)

CORE: The dense, hot center of the Earth, 4309 miles (6940 kilometers) in diameter, composed of the metallic elements iron and nickel in two layers forming an outer liquid and solid inner core.

CRANIAL: Related to the skull.

CRETACEOUS: A period at the end of the Mesozoic, after the Jurassic and before the Tertiary, that lasted from 142 to 65 million years ago.

CRINOIDS: See **SEA-LILIES.**

CROCODILIANS: An ancient but surviving group of reptiles that are often armored with bony scales. They have front legs shorter than hind and an elongated body with a laterally flattened tail for swimming. (Late Triassic to recent.)

CROWN: The exposed part of a tooth, normally coated with enamel.

CRUST: The hard and brittle surface rock layer of the Earth that overlies the mantle and varies in thickness and composition depending on whether it is continental or oceanic crust.

CRUSTACEANS: A large class of marine, freshwater, and occasionally terrestrial arthropods (over 35,000 living species), including the crabs and shrimps. They are protected by a tough outer layer, called a carapace. (Late Cambrian to recent.)

CUSP: The high point on a mammalian tooth. The number and pattern of cusps is characteristic.

CYCADS: Palmlike seed plants with massive stems and a crown of fernlike leaves. They may be short or treelike, growing to 65 feet (20 meters) high. (Permian to recent.)

CYNODONTS: An extinct group of advanced reptilelike tetrapods, abundant in Triassic times, that includes the ancestors of the mammals. (Late Permian to late Jurassic.)

D

DELTA: The mouth of a river where it meets the sea and deposits its sediment, often in huge delta shapes many miles across, depending on the strength of the current flow and its ability to carry sediment. The fossil remains of abundant plant and animal life buried in ancient tropical deltas have formed deposits of coal, oil, and gas.

DENTICLE: Pointed scales of many cartilaginous fishes; may be covered in enamel.

DENTITION: Set of teeth.

DEVONIAN: An Upper Paleozoic period of geological time, 417 to 354 million years ago, between the Silurian and Carboniferous periods. Named for the county of Devon, in southwest England, where rocks of this age are well exposed.

DIAPHRAGM: Sheetlike muscle and tendons separating the thorax from the abdomen; only found in mammals. Its movement helps draw air into the lungs and expel it.

DIAPSIDS: A member of a major group of animals that includes the dinosaurs, extinct marine reptiles, crocodiles, lizards, snakes, and birds, characterized by a pair of openings in the skull immediately behind the eye socket. (Upper Carboniferous to recent.)

DIASTEMA: A natural gap in a row of teeth; often seen in herbivores, such as that between the incisors and the cheek teeth of a rodent, where it separates functions of biting from chewing.

DICYNODONTS: An extinct group of advanced reptilelike tetrapods with two prominent, downward-pointing tusks. (Permian to Triassic.)

DIGITIGRADE: Walking on the underside of fingers or toes, as in a cat or dog, rather than flat of the hand/foot. See also plantigrade and unguligrade.

DINOSAURS: The so-called "terrible lizards," members of an extinct and diverse group of land-living reptiles that flourished from the late Triassic to the end of the Cretaceous and may have given rise to the birds.

DIPROTODONTIDS: An extinct family of Australian marsupial mammals. Most were plant-eaters and some grew to the size of hippos. (Late Tertiary to Quaternary.)

DISTAL: Away from point of attachment, usually away from body. Opposite of proximal.

DNA: Deoxyribonucleic acid, genetic material that determines the inherited characteristics in most living organisms. When a cell divides, its DNA is duplicated so that each new daughter cell receives the same genetic DNA code. See also **NATURAL SELECTION.**

DORSAL: Related or near to the back or upper part of the body.

DRIP TIP: An elongation of the tip of a leaf to form a lip that helps shed heavy rain and avoid damage to the leaf; characteristic of rain-forest plants.

DROMAEOSAURIDS: An extinct group of birdlike theropod dinosaurs 4 to 10 feet (1.2 to 3 meters) in length; active predators, they had light, agile bodies, long fingers, and a long claw on one toe. (Mid- to late Cretaceous.)

DUNE: A large body of sand piled up by the flow of water or wind. Dunes vary enormously in shape, but their form often indicates the direction of flow. Some extend for tens of miles and on land may reach heights of 100 feet (30 meters.)

DYKE: A vertical, wall-like body of igneous rock that has been squeezed (intruded) into older rocks from a magma chamber deep within the Earth. Some dykes of volcanic origin reach the surface and pour out molten lava.

E

ECHINODERMS: Sea-dwelling invertebrates, including the starfish (asteroids), sea urchins (echinoids), sea lilies (crinoids), sea cucumbers (holothurians), and some extinct forms dating back to Cambrian times. They have an unusual, five-rayed symmetry. Many grow a hard, chalky skeleton and form common fossils.

ECOLOGICAL NICHE: A particular "role" played, or position occupied, by an organism in its environment; determined by such factors as type of food, predators, and tolerance of climatic conditions. Ecological niches tend to be exclusive, with no two closely related species occupying the same niche in a particular area. The same niche in different areas may be filled by different species. See also adaptation.

ECOLOGY: The study of the relationships between organisms and the environment in which they live.

ECOSYSTEM: A unit in nature made up of a community or communities of organisms and the environment within which they live and interact.

EDIACARANS: A group of soft-bodied organisms found fossilized within Vendian seabed sediments. Many of them are extinct. It is not yet clear what kind of organisms they were, but some seem to belong to living groups such as the seapens. Named after the Ediacaran Hills in the Flinders Range of South Australia where the fossils are well preserved.

EMBRYO: An animal in its earliest stage of development, between fertilization and hatching or birth.

ENAMEL: The hard layer that covers the crown of teeth and denticles; mostly calcium salts.

ENVIRONMENT: The sum total of all the factors—climatic, geological, biological, etc.—in which a creature lives.

EOCENE: See **TERTIARY.**

EROSION: The removal of rock material that has already been broken down by weathering through the transport processes of wind, water, gravity, or ice.

EURYPTERIDS: An extinct group of scorpionlike arthropods that lived in both salty and freshwaters from early Ordovician to end Permian times; some grew to 10 feet (3 meters) in length.

EVAPORITE: A sedimentary deposit of minerals, such as salt and gypsum, formed when salty water has evaporated under a hot, dry climate.

EVERGREEN: A plant that retains its leaves throughout the year. The leaves are generally small to reduce water loss and are shed after a year or two.

EVOLUTION: The process of development and change in life that has been going on since life began on Earth. The fossil record shows that from primitive and tiny single-celled creatures life has gradually become larger and more complex. Evolution results from a combination of genetic change or mutation, reproduction, and the interaction of organisms with their environment, and is a process in which some species change and survive while others die out. The first scientific statement of the theory of evolution was made by Charles Darwin and Alfred Wallace in 1858.

EXOSKELETON: The tough and protective "skin" on the outside of arthropods such as insects, crustaceans, and spiders. It is made of soft material that hardens into a shell. Some arthropods, such as the living crabs, have to molt their exoskeleton periodically and produce a new, bigger one.

EXTINCTION EVENT: A geologically brief time when an abnormal number of organisms die off. Causes may be changes in sea level, climate change driven by movement of the Earth's crustal plates, extraterrestrial meteorite impact, or changes in the amount of heat coming from the Sun.

F

FAMILY: A taxonomic grouping of similar organisms. A family contains one or more genera; similar families form an order.

FAULT: A fracture in rocks caused by the build up of pressure within the Earth, so that rock on one side of a fault moves relative to rock on the other side. Individual movements, often associated with earthquakes, may be only of a few feet, but over time they may add up to many miles. The San Andreas Fault in California, for example, has moved over 186 miles (300 kilometers) over the last 30 million years.

FEMUR: See **PENTADACTYL LIMB.**

FERNS: A large group of terrestrial plants that includes many living and extinct species, Ferns originated in Carboniferous times (although fernlike plants are found from early Devonian times) and are still abundant. They have large, divided, frondlike leaves that usually carry the reproductive spore-producing organs.

FERN SPIKE: An abundance of fern pollen found in a single layer within rock strata, indicating that ferns had formed the main plants in the landscapes of the time.

FIBULA: See **PENTADACTYL LIMB.**

FLASH FLOODS: Unpredictable, powerful, and often catastrophic deluges of water that occasionally flow down dry stream valleys after torrential storms, carrying sediment and drowning anything in the path of the flood.

FLOOD BASALT: Volcanic lava that pours out over the surface of the land in huge quantities from deep cracks (dyke fissures) in the crust; often produced by mantle "hot spot" plumes rising from deep within the Earth.

FLOOD PLAIN: Flat landscape around a river, formed when the river bursts its banks and dumps its load of sediment on the surrounding countryside. Repeated flood layers of sediment can build up very thick deposits.

FOOD CHAIN: A way of linking different organisms together according to what each eats, and what each is eaten by. For example, microscopic plants living near the ocean surface are eaten by small swimming animals such as shrimps that, in turn, are preyed on by small fish who are then eaten by bigger fish.

FOSSIL: The remains or trace of a once-living organism, preserved in rock strata. A fossil may be a chemical trace of an organism, a trace of activity, a bit of the original body, or a mineral replica of it.

G

GENERALIZED (of an organism): showing few specific adaptations to a particular ecological niche. A generalized organism tends to be similar to its remote ancestors. See also **PRIMITIVE.**

GENUS: A group of closely related organisms (species). For example, *Homo* is the genus to which both the living species *Homo sapiens* and the extinct species *Homo neanderthalensis* belong.

GINKGOS: Living fossils of a group of primitive plants, with fan-shaped leaves and woody stems, that were much more common in the geological past. Represented today by one surviving species—*Ginkgo biloba*, the maidenhair tree. (Permian to recent.)

GLACIAL: A cold phase within an ice age when glaciers advance. See also **INTERGLACIAL.**

GLACIATION: The covering of part of the Earth's surface by ice sheets or valley glaciers and the accompanying processes of landscape erosion and deposition of glacial debris.

GLACIER: A mass of ice and snow, usually infilling a valley, that can flow slowly downhill, erode the landscape, and carry vast amounts of rock debris.

GLOSSOPTERIDS: An extinct group of plants whose fossil leaves are common in Permian and Triassic strata in the lands that once made up the supercontinent of Gondwana. The distribution of the distinctive strap-shaped fossil leaves in India, Australia, South Africa, South America, and Antarctica was part of the original evidence for the existence of the supercontinent. (Permian to Jurassic.)

GONDWANA: A supercontinent formed in the southern hemisphere by the joining together of several large crustal plates (Australia, South America, Africa, Antarctica, India) and numerous smaller crustal fragments such as Florida; the pieces were assembled in Cambrian times and joined by Laurasia in the Permian to form the even bigger supercontinent of Pangea, which began to break up in Jurassic times, having lasted for some 300 million years.

GRANITE: A hard, crystalline igneous rock formed from a molten rock (magma) deep in the continental crust and made up of particular minerals such as quartz, feldspar, and mica.

GRAPTOLITES: An extinct group of tiny animals that lived in the seas of Paleozoic times (Cambrian to Permian) and built tubular skeletons of organic material. Their fossils look like pencil markings on rock surfaces and are useful for telling the age of marine sedimentary rocks.

GRASSES: Flowering plants (family Gramineae) whose evolution in Tertiary times was closely linked to the increase in grass-eating (grazing) mammals, especially ruminants (cud-chewers) such as the deer, cattle, and horses.

GRAZER: A grass-eating animal—mostly mammals but also some birds—that can crop, chew, and digest grass. The vegetation wears down teeth and requires slow fermentation in the stomach.

GREENHOUSE STATE: A time of warm global climates; increased quantities of carbon dioxide and other gases in the atmosphere trap a greater proportion of the energy in sunlight than usual, causing global warming. The gases can be released by human activities, such as burning fossil fuels, or by natural processes, such as volcanism. Compare: **ICEHOUSE STATE.**

GYMNOSPERMS: A group of seed plants such as ferns and conifers whose seeds are not enclosed in ovaries. (Late Devonian to recent.)

H

HADROSAURIDS: A group of large two- and four-legged ornithopod dinosaurs. They had horny beaks for browsing vegetation and batteries of cheek teeth for chewing. (Mid- to end Cretaceous.)

HATCHLING: A baby animal that has just emerged from an egg. Some are well developed and can soon leave the nest (precocial); others first need parental feeding and care (altricial).

HERBIVORES: Animals that feed on grass and other plants, usually with a specially adapted stomach and teeth for eating and digesting tough plant material.

HOMINIDS: A family of primates that includes humans and their fossil ancestors, the australopithecines. Experts argue as to whether the group should include the higher apes such as chimpanzees. (Pliocene to recent.)

HOOF: A massively enlarged toenail adapted to take the weight of ungulates; made of keratin.

HORN: A tough substance made of the protein keratin. A bony projection of the skull is properly called a horn if it is covered with horn (as in cattle), but those that lack a horny covering are called antlers (as in deer) or ossicones (as in giraffes). The "horn" of a rhinoceros is made of compacted hair.

HORSETAILS: Members of the family Calamitaceae that were among the most common of the Carboniferous coal-swamp plants. Some were tree-sized, growing to over 60 feet (18 meters) with hollow stems, tiny scalelike leaves, and branches arranged in circlets. (Mostly late Devonian to early Triassic, but with a few surviving species.)

HOT SPOT: An area in the upper part of the Earth's mantle between 70 and 140 miles (100 and 200 kilometers) wide, from which molten rock (magma) rises in a plume to form volcanoes. The volcanic islands of Hawaii were formed by a hot spot.

HYDROTHERMAL VENT: A small, volcanolike opening from which hot water flows and may deposit minerals. Most vents are located along mid-ocean ridges and recirculate seawater enriched with minerals to form unique seabed communities independent of sunlight.

HYPERDACTYLY: A condition in which there are more than the usual number of digits, as in an ichthyosaur's paddle.

HYPERPHALANGY: A condition in which there are more than the usual number of joints in the digit, as in a plesiosaur's paddle.

HYPSILOPHODONTIDS: Ornithopod dinosaurs 6 feet (1.8 meters) high. Fast-moving and ostrichlike but for their long stiff tails, they browsed plants with horny beaks and cheek teeth. (Late Jurassic to end Cretaceous.)

I

IAPETUS: An ocean that grew between Laurentia and Gondwana in early Cambrian times; it was closed and the ocean floor subducted during Ordovician times as continental fragments such as Avalonia broke away from Gondwana and moved north, opening a new ocean, the Rheic.

ICE AGE: A period of several million years with alternating warm and cool global climates leading to the development of polar icecaps, glaciers, changing sea levels, and climatic zones.

ICECAP: A flat, dome-shaped mass of ice that develops over the poles during ice ages and spreads outward, flowing under its own weight.

ICEHOUSE STATE: A period of Earth history with cool climates and ice ages, connected to low intensities of volcanic eruption and low levels of "greenhouse" gases, such as carbon dioxide, in the atmosphere. Compare: **GREENHOUSE STATE.**

ICHTHYOSAURS: An order of fast-swimming and predatory marine reptiles with dolphin-shaped bodies. (Early Triassic to late Cretaceous.)

IGNEOUS: Rocks formed from a molten material (magma).

IGUANODONTIDS: A group of plant-eating ornithopod dinosaurs that walked on two legs. One of the first groups of dinosaurs to be recognized as fossils in the early 19th century by Gideon Mantell in England. (Late Jurassic to late Cretaceous.)

IMPACT EVENT: The result of the collision of a body from outer space with a planet, forming a crater and, depending on the size of the impact, causing extinction among plants and animals.

INCISORS: The cutting teeth at the front of a mammal's mouth.

INSECTIVORES: A group of small and mainly nocturnal mammals, including the living hedgehogs, moles, and shrews, that feed on insects. This group evolved at the end of the Cretaceous and developed enormously during the Tertiary period.

INSECTIVOROUS: All those organisms, including some plants, that feed mainly on insects.

INTERGLACIAL: A warm phase between cold glacials within an ice age.

INTRUSION: An igneous rock that has been injected below ground into the surrounding rocks, often forming wall-shaped dykes, horizontal sills, or rounded plutons.

INVERTEBRATES: Animals without backbones, from single-celled organisms to the arthropods. The invertebrate echinoderms show some relationship to the vertebrates in the development of their larvae.

IRIDIUM: A rare metal element in the Earth's crust. It is present in meteorites and other debris from outer space.

ISLAND ARC: A chain of volcanic islands formed over a subduction zone where ocean crust has been partially melted with the molten rock magma forcing its way to the surface to erupt explosively through volcanoes.

ISOTOPES: Differing forms of the same chemical element, having the same number of protons but different numbers of neutrons in their nuclei. Some of the isotopes of various chemical elements are radioactive (unstable). The individual atoms of these unstable isotopes "decay" (spontaneously convert) into more stable daughter forms at a steady rate. Measuring how much daughter isotope is present in a rock indicates when it was formed.

JK

JURASSIC: The middle period of the Mesozoic era from 206 to 142 million years ago between the Triassic and the Cretaceous period. Named after the Jura Mountains in Europe.

KERATIN: A strong fibrous protein, occurring in outermost skin layers of vertebrates. Forms nails, claws, hoofs, feathers, hair, and horn.

K-T BOUNDARY: The boundary between the Cretaceous and Tertiary periods. The abbreviation is derived from "K" for *kreide*, German for chalk, a widespread late Cretaceous deposit, and "T" for Tertiary. The boundary is dated at 65 million years ago and is marked by a mass extinction.

L

LANCELETS: Small sea creatures that can swim by flexing their bodies sideways, using paired muscles on either side of a stiff internal rod called the notochord. The presence of the notochord identifies them as chordates and ancestors of the vertebrates.

LAND BRIDGE: A narrow stretch of low-lying land that appears when sea levels are low and connects land masses, allowing land animals to cross but preventing the migration of sea creatures.

LATERAL: Related to the side of an organism.

LAURASIA: The supercontinent formed in the northern hemisphere by the closure of the Iapetus Ocean in Ordovician times and the joining of Laurentia and Asia (excluding India).

LAURENTIA: The name for the ancient continent of North America that formed around the Precambrian Canadian Shield.

LIGAMENT: An elastic fibrous tissue that joins bones together at a joint.

LIMESTONE: A sedimentary rock made from calcium carbonate minerals, often as the shelly remains of sea creatures.

LUNGFISH: A group of primitive bony fish (dipnoans) with both gills and lungs for breathing in water and air. (Devonian to recent.)

M

MAGMA: Naturally occurring molten rock formed deep within the Earth's crust that can flow upward toward the surface and sometimes erupt as lava.

MAMMALS: Warm-blooded and hairy vertebrates that feed their young. The group includes animals living in a variety of habitats from water to land and air. They arose from reptilelike cynodonts in Triassic times.

MAMMARY GLAND: A skin gland of female mammals specialized to produce milk.

MANDIBLE: Lower jaw.

MANTLE: The layer of hot, solid rock that lies below the Earth's crust and above the core and is some 1800 miles (2900 kilometers) thick. Heat circulates from the core to the crust through the mantle in rising zones known as convection cells and mantle plumes.

MANTLE PLUME: A rising column-shaped zone of heat through the mantle that spreads out sideways when it reaches the base of the crust. A plume heats the crust, causing it to expand, dome upward, and crack, allowing magma to erupt at the surface through volcanoes and fissures.

MARSUPIALS: Mammals that give birth to small, undeveloped young that are nurtured in a skin pouch on the mother's stomach until they can better fend for themselves. They originated in Cretaceous times and survived in Australia and the Americas.

MAXILLA: The largest of the tooth-bearing bones of the upper jaw.

MEMBRANE: A thin sheet of tissue.

MESOZOIC: The middle era of life, from 248 to 65 million years ago, between the Paleozoic and Cenozoic (comprising the Tertiary and Quaternary). Subdivided into the Triassic, Jurassic, and Cretaceous periods.

METACARPAL: See **PENTADACTYL LIMB.**

METAMORPHISM: A process whereby rocks are altered by heat and pressure within the crust, especially during mountain building.

METATARSAL: See **PENTADACTYL LIMB.**

MICRODIAMOND: Microscopic diamonds formed by the explosive melting of carbon-rich minerals such as limestone as a result of large meteorite impacts.

MID-OCEAN RIDGE: A submarine mountain range of volcanic rocks that rises from the ocean floor, and is often the site of new seafloor creation.

MILK DENTITION: The first of a mammal's two sets of teeth. Includes no molars.

MIOCENE: See **TERTIARY.**

MISSISSIPPIAN: See **CARBONIFEROUS.**

MOLARS: The back teeth of a mammal, usually adapted—for grinding, crushing, or meat-shearing. Not present in milk dentition.

MOLECULAR CLOCK: An estimate of the timing of evolution based on known rates of genetic change in particular groups of organisms.

MOLLUSKS: A large group of soft-bodied animals that includes the living snails, clams, squid, octopus, and the extinct ammonites and belemnites. They appear in the fossil record in early Cambrian times and must have evolved before that. Many of them build calcium carbonate shells that are commonly preserved as fossils.

MONOTREMES: A group of primitive mammals with reptilelike features such as egg-laying. Only the platypus and spiny anteater (echidna) survive. (Mid-Cretaceous to recent.)

MOSASAURS: A group of very large and powerful sea-living reptiles. They grew to 33 feet (10 meters) long and were ferocious predators. (Mid- to late Cretaceous.)

MOSS ANIMALS: Tiny animals that live in colonies resembling rafts of moss or seaweed. The colonies form geometric patterns and can contain thousands of individuals, or zooids. The colonies cling to the surfaces of plants such as kelp. (Ordovician to recent.)

MOUNTAIN BUILDING: The process of forming mountains on land by the thickening of crustal rocks during the collision of crustal plates. As plates collide, continental crust is both pushed down into the mantle and up into the air.

MULTITUBERCULATES: The earliest plant-eating mammals, having chisel-shaped front teeth and ranging from mouse to beaver size. (Late Jurassic to mid Tertiary.)

N

NATURAL SELECTION: The key evolutionary process whereby organisms with the most appropriate adaptations to their environment are more reproductively successful. In this way the environment is seen to "select" the characteristics of species or individuals that succeed best within that environment.

NEANDERTHALS: An extinct group of humans (*Homo neanderthalensis*) who evolved about 150,000 years ago in the eastern Mediterranean region, spread into Europe and western Asia, and died out around 35,000 years ago. Genetic analysis suggests they did not interbreed with modern humans.

NICHE: The space in the environment occupied by a particular organism and defined by its characteristics such as temperature tolerance, feeding habits, and predators.

NOTOCHORD: A flexible rod within the body of chordate animals. Running from head to tail, it forms the basis of the backbone in vertebrate animals.

O

OCEAN CRUST: A thin but dense layer of volcanic rocks, 4 to 7 miles (6 to 11 kilometers) deep, that forms the floor of the oceans. None of the ocean crust of today is more than 180 million years old. New ocean crust forms at a mid-ocean ridge and then moves slowly away from the ridge.

OCEAN FLOOR SPREADING: The process by which a new ocean forms. A rising plume of hot material from the Earth's mantle stretches the continental crust above, in time opening volcanic rifts on the surface. The rifts widen into a valley that eventually floods and becomes a new ocean as it continues to spread.

OCEANS: Large bodies of salty water that now cover about 60 percent of the surface of the Earth. They first formed around 2 billion years ago and have opened and closed, and risen and fallen, as the continents have moved and the climate has changed.

OLIGOCENE: See **TERTIARY.**

OMNIVOROUS: An animal able to eat material of plant or animal origin.

OPPOSABLE (of the thumb, etc.):The ability to be brought up to meet or touch the tips of the rest of the digits; e.g., to grasp an object between big toe and other toes, as among chimps, or to grip an object between thumb and index finger.

ORBIT: Cavity in vertebrate skull that houses the eyeball.

ORDER: A taxonomic grouping of similar organisms. An order contains one or more families; similar orders form a class.

ORDOVICIAN: A period of early Paleozoic time, 495 to 443 million years ago, between the Cambrian and the Silurian periods. The name comes from an ancient British tribe, the Ordovices.

ORNITHISCHIANS: One of the two main orders of dinosaurs. They have a birdlike pelvis and are entirely plant-eating. They include groups such as the ornithopods, stegosaurs, and ceratopsians. (Early Jurassic to late Cretaceous.) See also **SAURISCHIANS.**

ORNITHOPODS: A group of ornithischian dinosaurs that walked predominantly on their hind limbs and had three-toed, birdlike feet. Examples include iguanodonts and hadrosaurids.

OROGENY: A period of mountain building, caused by the collision of continents. The great mountain chains of the world have all been created this way. Some orogenies, including the Alpine-Himalayan, are still active today.

OSSICONE: A "horn" found among giraffes and possibly some fossil species, consisting of a bony core permanently covered in skin.

OSSIFICATION: The formation of bone; a process which involves calcification.

P

PALATE: The plate of bone roofing the mouth. See also secondary palate.

PALEONTOLOGY: The scientific study of fossils, their formation and preservation; the formulation of theories and the history and evolution of ancient life that the fossils represent.

PALEOCENE: See **TERTIARY.**

PALEOZOIC: The era of ancient life extending from 545 to 248 million years ago, from the beginning of the Cambrian period, through the Ordovician, Silurian, Devonian, and Carboniferous periods, to the end of the Permian period.

PANDERICHTHYIDS: A small group of fish with two pairs of lobed fins and a particular pattern of skull bones. They are considered ancestral to all tetrapod vertebrates. (Late Devonian.)

PANGEA: A global supercontinent formed by the joining of Gondwana, Laurentia, Baltica, and Siberia at the end of Triassic times. Pangea stretched almost from pole to pole, but soon began to break up as the Atlantic Ocean opened.

PANTHALLASSIC OCEAN: Large ocean that surrounded the supercontinent of Pangea, occupying more than half of the Earth's surface.

PARALLEL EVOLUTION: The independent development of similar shapes or behavior in closely related organisms in response to similar environmental pressures. See also convergent evolution.

PECTORAL: Related to the shoulders.

PELVIC: Related to the hips.

PELYCOSAURS: A group of reptilelike tetrapods that show some mammalian features such as different tooth shapes. Some pelycosaurs had webbed sail structures on their backs supported by bone that may have helped the animals to warm up or cool off. (Late Carboniferous to late Permian.)

PENNATULACEANS: See **SEAPENS.**

PENNSYLVANIAN: See **CARBONIFEROUS.**

PENTADACTYL LIMB: Literally "five fingers"); basic structure of forelimb and hind limb found among the tetrapods. Consists of single bone in upper limb (humerus or femur), two bones in lower limb (radius and ulna, or tibia and fibula), five joint bones in the wrist or ankle (carpals or tarsals), five rodlike bones in the palm or sole (metacarpals and metatarsals) tarsals), and digits (fingers or toes). Digits are made up of small bones arranged end-to-end, the phalanges. They may be modified to fewer or more than five digits in course of adaptive radiation.

PERMAFROST: An area of permanently frozen ground on the fringe of the polar icecaps. The surface may thaw briefly during summer to allow the growth of some hardy plants.

PERMIAN: The last period of the Paleozoic era, 290 to 248 million years ago, from the end of the Carboniferous to the beginning of the Triassic.

PHALANGES: See **PENTADACTYL LIMB.**

PHANEROZOIC: The current eon of historical time, covering the last 545 million years, during which there has been abundant life. Follows the Proterozoic eon (2,500 to 545 million years ago).

PHOTOSYNTHESIS: The formation of organic compounds by plants to build their body tissue, using light energy from the Sun, carbon dioxide from the atmosphere, and water. Photosynthesis also releases oxygen into the atmosphere.

PHYLUM (plural, phyla): A high-level grouping of similar organisms. A phylum contains one or more classes; similar phyla form a Kingdom.

PLACENTALS: Mammals that develop a special tissue (placenta) by which embryos can exchange nutrients and waste products with their mothers. The placenta supplies nutrients for growth until the offspring are born. (Mid-Cretaceous to recent.)

PLANKTON: Microorganisms that inhabit the surface waters of lakes and oceans and form the basis of the food chain of these environments.

PLANTIGRADE: Walking on the flat of the foot, as in humans. See also **DIGITIGRADE** and **UNGULIGRADE**.

PLATES: The huge slabs into which the rocks of the Earth's crust are divided up, ranging from continent-sized fragments to many smaller pieces. A typical plate includes continent, shelf sea, and ocean areas.

PLATE TECTONICS: The geological process in which the Earth's crustal plates move over its surface, driven by currents within the semimolten mantle. The plates may diverge to form oceans, slide past one another along major faults, or crash into one another forming island arcs and mountain ranges.

PLATEAU LAVA: A great area of basalt lava that has poured out over the continents above rising mantle plumes through rifts in the continental crust.

PLESIOSAURS: A group of marine reptiles, 10 to 40 feet (3 to 12 meters) in length, that lived in Jurassic and Cretaceous times. Many were long-necked, but there were also short-necked varieties called pliosaurs. (Jurassic to Cretaceous.)

PLIOCENE: See **TERTIARY.**

PLUTON: A mass of igneous rock that has solidified below the surface of the Earth.

POLLEN: Microscopic spores and grains produced in huge numbers by the male reproductive organs of flowering plants (angiosperms) and seed-bearing plants (gymnosperms) for reproduction.

PRECAMBRIAN: An era of the Earth's history from its formation, 4.6 billion years ago, until

the beginning of the Paleozoic era, 545 million years ago.

PREMOLARS: Mammalian teeth situated between the molars and the canines. May be enlarged or "molarized" for grinding, or simplified for meat-shearing. Unlike molars, they are present in the milk teeth.

PRIMATES: A group of mammals that includes living monkeys, apes, and humans, and their fossil ancestors. They evolved from small, four-legged, tree-living insect-eaters in early Tertiary times.

PRIMITIVE: Of a feature of an animal, having changed little from the condition in its ancestor. Opposite of advanced.

PROBOSCIS: A tubelike muscular extension of the nostrils, like an elephant's trunk, adapted to forage, grasp, suck water, etc.

PROXIMAL: Situated on the same side as the point of attachment; usually toward the body. Opposite of distal.

PTEROSAURS: An extinct group of flying reptiles. Their wings were formed out of skin that stretched from the body over the forelimbs and along elongated fourth fingers that acted as supporting ribs. (Late Triassic to late Cretaceous.)

QR

QUADRUPEDAL: Walking on all fours.

QUATERNARY: The most recent period of Earth history, 1.8 million years ago after the Tertiary, marked by a major ice age.

RADIUS: See **PENTADACTYL LIMB.**

RHEIC OCEAN: An ocean that opened up as the crustal plates of Avalonia, Armorica, and Iberia rifted away from the northern edge of Gondwana and swept northward toward Laurentia during Ordovician and Silurian times.

RIFT VALLEY: A valley formed by the sideways stretching, sagging, and then fracture of brittle crustal rocks along two parallel fault lines so that the central area between the fault lines drops down to form a valley floor; often accompanied by volcanic eruptions, and sometimes the precursor to continental break-up.

RODENTS: A group of small mammals including squirrels, beavers, rats, porcupines, and their extinct ancestors. Rodents have sharp, chisel-shaped front teeth that grow continuously for gnawing tough grains and seeds. (Early Tertiary to recent.)

S

SACRAL VERTEBRAE: Vertebrae attaching the backbone to the hips.

SANDSTONE: Rock made up of mineral fragments deposited and layered as sediment by the action of gravity, wind, or water, and then compressed.

SAURISCHIANS: One of two major orders of dinosaurs. They had a reptilelike pelvis and include the large, plant-eating sauropods that walked on four legs, and the generally smaller carnivorous theropods that walked on their two hind limbs. (Early Jurassic to late Cretaceous.) See also **ORNITHISCHIANS.**

SAUROPODS: Saurischian, plant-eating dinosaurs with small heads, long necks and tails, massive bodies, and four trunklike legs. (Early Jurassic to late Cretaceous.)

SAVANNA: Open tropical landscapes in which grasses are the main plants due to a yearly dry season and wildfire. Savannas first developed in early Tertiary times and have provided plant food for large herds of grazing mammals.

SCABLANDS (CHANNELED): Landscapes molded by large-scale torrential floodwaters that carve channels in the bedrock several miles wide and up to a hundred feet deep. The floodwaters also form huge sediment ripples on the channel bed.

SCAPULA: A bone in the shoulder girdle, the shoulder blade.

SCAVENGER: An animal that consumes the flesh of dead animals which it has not itself killed. See **CARNIVOROUS**.

SCUTE: A plate of bone or horn, embedded in the skin.

SEA-LILIES: Plant-shaped echinoderms that live attached to the seabed by roots. They have a long stem ending in a cup with arms, and are made of jointed plates of calcium carbonate. (Early Ordovician to recent.)

SEAPENS (PENNATULACEANS): Soft-bodied, feather-shaped creatures that live rooted in the seabed by a stalk. They are related to the sea-anemones and corals. (Vendian to recent.)

SEA SQUIRTS (TUNICATES): Soft-bodied animals that live attached to the seabed as adults but have free-swimming, tadpolelike larvae. The presence of a notochord in the larva shows that they are chordate animals. (Early Cambrian to recent.)

SECONDARY PALATE: A sheet of bone separating the mouth and nasal passage.

SEDIMENTARY ROCK: Rock that was originally laid down, usually by water or wind, composed of particles that were eroded from existing rocks. Sometimes sedimentary rock incorporates material of organic origin, such as shells. See **LITHOGRAPHIC LIMESTONE**.

SEED FERNS: An extinct group of gymnosperms called pteridosperms with fernlike leaves on which seeds are developed. (Late Devonian to late Cretaceous.)

SEED PLANTS: Plants with naked seeds (gymnosperms). These contrast with the flowering plants (angiosperms), which have enclosed seeds. The gymnosperms were the dominant land plants until the angiosperms took over in Cretaceous times. (Late Devonian to recent.)

SHOCKED QUARTZ : Grains of the silicate mineral that have had their atomic structure distorted by very high pressure such as that produced by an enormous explosion from a meteorite impact or volcanic eruption.

SILL: A horizontal sheet of igneous rock found between older rocks deep underground. The igneous rock is formed from magma.

SILURIAN: The period of Paleozoic time, 443 to 417 million years ago, that followed the Ordovician period and preceded the Devonian. Named by Roderick Murchison in 1835 after an ancient British tribe, the Silures, for a series of strata in the Welsh Borderlands.

SPECIALIZED, SPECIALIZATION: To become adapted to a particular lifestyle and habitat; to become restricted to a specific ecological niche.

SPECIES: A group of closely related organisms that can interbreed and produce fertile young.

SPREADING RIDGE: See **MID-OCEAN RIDGE**.

STEREOSCOPIC VISION: The ability to judge depth and distance; having both eyes pointed forward and able to focus on an object.

STERNUM: Breastbone of vertebrates, to which most ribs are attached.

STRATA: A sheet of rock formed from sediment deposited through the action of wind, water, or simply gravity. Successive layers of sediment are layed over each other, buried, and compressed to form level strata of sedimentary rock. Subsequently strata can be folded and faulted by geological processes such as mountain building.

STRATIGRAPHY: The study of rock strata, especially their relative ages, character, and correlation across different locations.

STEGOSAURS: A group of plant-eating ornithischian dinosaurs that walked on four legs. Stegosaurs had rows of bony plates or spikes along the back, which were probably for sexual display and perhaps heat regulation. (Mid-Jurassic to late Cretaceous.)

STROMATOLITES: Layered mound structures, several feet high, built up over many years in shallow and warm tropical waters by sheets of bacteria growing over the seabed and trapping sediment. Stromatolites first formed in Precambrian times 3.5 billion years ago.

SUBDUCTION: A plate tectonic process in which dense rocks on the ocean floor are pushed down beneath lighter continental rocks when crustal plates collide. The process releases huge amounts of energy, in the form of earthquakes. In addition, some of the subducted rock melts to become magma that rises to the surface of the continental plate and erupts from volcanoes.

SUPERCONTINENT: The joining together of continental crust plates to form a bigger continental mass, such as Gondwana or Pangea.

SYNAPSIDS: A group of extinct tetrapods with mammalian characteristics, including the pelycosaurs and therapsids, which have a single pair of openings low down in the skull behind the eyes. (Mid-Carboniferous to mid-Jurassic.)

TU

TECTONIC THEORY: See **PLATE TECTONICS**.

TELEOSTS: A very large group of some 22,000 species of bony fish such as cod, salmon, and eels. They are dominant in both the marine and fresh waters of the Earth today. (Late Triassic to recent.)

TENDON: A cord or band of strong tissue connecting muscle to bone or to other muscles.

TETHYS OCEAN: A largely tropical ocean that separated Laurasia and Gondwana between Permian and mid-Tertiary times and was closed by the northward movement of Africa and India.

TERRANE: A fragment of continental crust that has a different origin to the rest of the surrounding rocks. Terranes have always originated some distance away from their final destination. They were moved into position by plate tectonic movements.

TERTIARY: The period at the beginning of the third era of life after the Cretaceous period and before the Quaternary, between 65 and 1.8 million years ago. It was subdivided by Sir Charles Lyell in 1833 into five epochs— Paleocene, Eocene, Oligocene, Miocene, and Pliocene.

TETRAPODS: A major group of vertebrates including all four-limbed vertebrates. Tetrapods evolved in late Devonian times, and their descendants include the amphibians, reptiles, mammals, and birds. Some early tetrapods cannot be assigned to any of these groups, notably reptilelike tetrapods with some mammalian characters such as the therapsids.

THERAPSIDS: A group of late Permian to early Triassic reptilelike synapsid tetrapods that include the ancestors of the mammals.

THEROPODS: A diverse subgroup of saurischian dinosaurs. They were large and walked on their hind limbs. They were also mostly carnivorous, and included the tyrannosaurs. The theropods make up 40 percent of all known kinds of dinosaurs. (Late Triassic to late Cretaceous.)

THORAX, THORACIC: Region of vertebrate body containing heart, lungs, etc.; the "chest."

TILLITE: A rock that is a glacial deposit left when ice melts. Tillite is composed of mud, sand, and rock debris mixed together without any size sorting. The larger rocks are often scratched by ice. Tillite strata are characteristic of past periods of glaciation.

TRACE FOSSIL: A mark left on or in sediment by the movement of an animal or plant and preserved in the rock.

TREE-FERNS: An ancient group of ferns that grew to the size of trees. There are a few surviving representatives such as *Dicksonia*. (Late Carboniferous to recent.)

TRENCH (SUBMARINE): A deep submarine valley in the ocean floor that in places may descend to depths of more than 36,000 feet (11,000 meters). Trenches are formed where the ocean floor is pushed down (subducted) below a plate of continental crust in a plate collision zone.

TRIASSIC: The earliest period of the Mesozoic era, lasting from 248 to 206 million years ago, before the Jurassic period and after the Permian period. The Triassic was named in 1834 by Friedrich von Alberti to describe a threefold division of strata in Germany.

TRILOBITES: An extinct and abundant group of Paleozoic sealiving arthropods with a distinct threefold division of the body and hard, shell-like exoskeletons. The skeletons had to be molted for the animals to grow and their remains were readily fossilized. (Early Cambrian to late Permian.)

TSUNAMI: A surface wave caused by earthquakes, submarine faulting, or a large meteorite impact; can travel at speeds of up to 550mph (900kph) across oceans, gaining height and destructive power as it approaches land.

TUNICATES: See **SEA SQUIRTS**.

TYRANNOSAURS: An extinct group of large-headed theropod dinosaurs. Tyrannosaurs walked on their hind limbs and had unusually short arms and two-fingered hands. They lived in late Cretaceous times and were distributed through North America and eastern Asia.

ULNA: See **PENTADACTYL LIMB**.

UNGULIGRADE: Walking on the tips of the toes, which bear thickened hoof, as in horses or cattle. See also **DIGITIGRADE** and **PLANTIGRADE**.

VW

VARISCAN: A phase of mountain building stretching eastward from the Atlantic seaboard of North America through the southern British Isles and into Germany in late Carboniferous and early Permian times. It resulted from the closure of the Rheic Ocean as Avalonia and northern Gondwana collided.

VASCULAR PLANTS: Plants with special cells for carrying water and nutrients from the soil through a root system, up the stem, and usually to the leaves. The cells are generally strengthened to allow upright growth away from the ground toward the light.

VENDIAN: A late Precambrian period of Earth history, 600 to 545 million years ago, before the beginning of Cambrian times.

VERTEBRAL COLUMN: A long jointed skeletal structure that allows the body to be flexed and supports the head, internal organs, and paired limbs. Commonly known as the backbone in vertebrates.

VERTEBRATES: A major group of animals that have an internal bony skeleton made up of a backbone and paired limbs. (Mid-Ordovician to recent.)

VESTIGAL (of an organ): Small, undeveloped, with little or no obvious function; it has become diminished from its former state. For example, the lateral toes of modern horses and the human appendix.

VETRAL: Related to the lower surface of an organism.

VIVIPAROUS: Bearing live young that have been nourished by a placental connection to the mother. See also **PLACENTAL**.

VOLCANIC ASH: Small particles of solidified magma, rock fragments, and mineral crystals that are blasted into the atmosphere during volcanic eruptions and fall back to Earth to form a sediment. Some dust-sized particles may be carried by winds around the globe before falling.

WILDFIRE: Naturally occurring forest and prairie fires caused mostly by lightning, particularly during dry seasons. Wildfires are important for renewing plant growth.

BIBLIOGRAPHY

GENERAL:

Benton, M. J. (ed.), *The Fossil Record 2*, Chapman & Hall, UK, 1993

Benton, M. J., *Vertebrate Palaeontology*, Chapman & Hall, UK, 1997

Benton, M. J., and Harper, D., *Basic Palaeontology*, Longman, UK, 1997

Benton, M. J. (ed.), *Phylogeny of the Tetrapods*, Oxford, UK, 1988

Benton, M. J., and Osborne, R., *Atlas of Evolution*, Viking, UK and US, 1996

Briggs, D. E. G., and Crowther, P. R., *Palaeobiology: a Synthesis*, Blackwell Scientific Publications, UK, 1990

Buffetaut, E., *A Short History of Vertebrate Palaeontology*, Chapman & Hall, UK, 1987

Carroll, R. L., *Vertebrate Paleontology and Evolution*, W. H. Freeman, UK, 1988

Carroll, R. L., *Patterns and Processes of Vertebrate Evolution*, Cambridge University Press, UK, 1997

Chernicoff, S., and Fox, H., *Essentials of Geology*, Worth Publishers, US, 1997

Condie, K., and Sloan, R., *Origin and Evolution of Earth: Principles of Historical Geology*, Prentice Hall, US, 1998

Conway Morris, S., *The Crucible of Creation: The Burgess Shale and the Rise of Animals*, Oxford University Press, UK, 1998

Dingus, L., *Next of Kin: Great Fossils at the American Museum of Natural History*, Rizzoli, US, 1998

Elsom, D., *Earth*, Macmillan, US, 1992

Gould, S. J. (ed.), *The Book of Life*, Ebury Hutchinson, UK, 1993

Gould, S. J., *Wonderful Life: The Burgess Shale and the Nature of History*, Hutchinson Radius, UK, 1990

Hallam, A., and Wignall, P. B., *Mass Extinctions and their Aftermath*, Oxford University Press, UK, 1997

Hublin, J., *The Hamlyn Encyclopaedia of Prehistoric Animals Hamlyn*, UK and US, 1982

Imbrie, J., and K. P., *Ice Ages*, Harvard University Press, US, 1986

MacDougall, J. D., *A Short History of Planet Earth*, John Wiley & Sons, US, 1996

McFarland, W. N., Pough, F. F. H., Cade, T. J., and Heiser, J. B., *Vertebrate Life*, Collier Macmillan, US, 1979

McGowan, C., *Dinosaurs, Dragons and Spitfires,* Harvard University Press, US, 1991

Norman, D., *Prehistoric Life: the Rise of the Vertebrates*, Boxtree, UK, 1994

Osborne, R., and Benton, M. J., *The Viking Atlas of Evolution*, Viking, US, 1996

Palmer, D., *Life Before Man*, Reader's Digest, UK, 1997

Patterson, C., *Evolution*, British Museum (Natural History), UK, 1978

Press, F., and Siever, R., *Earth (4th edition)*, W. H. Freeman, US, 1986

Romer, A. S., *The Vertebrate Story*, University of Chicago Press, US, 1974

Scarth, A., *Volcanoes*, UCL Press, UK, 1994

Schaal, S., and Ziegler, W., *Messel*, Oxford University Press, UK, 1992

Skelton, P. (ed.), *Evolution: a Biological and Palaentological Approach*, Addison-Wesley, UK, 1993

Skinner, B., and Porter, S. C., *Physical Geology*, John Wiley & Sons, US, 1987

Taylor, P., *Eyewitness Guides: Fossil*, Dorling Kindersley, UK, 1990

Van Andel, T. H., *New Views on an Old Planet: A History of Global Change*, Cambridge University Press, UK, 1994

Walker, C., and Ward, D., *The Eyewitness Handbook of Fossils*, Dorling Kindersley, UK, 1998

Whitfield, P., *From So Simple a Beginning: The Book of Evolution*, Macmillan, US, 1993

FISHES:

Janvier, P., *Early Vertebrates*, Oxford, UK, 1996

Long, J. A., *The Rise of Fishes*, John Hopkins University Press, US, 1995

Maisey, J. G., *Discovering Fossil Fishes*, Henry Holt, US, 1996

REPTILES:

Benton, M. J., *The Reign of the Reptiles*, Kingfisher, UK, 1990

King, G., *Reptiles and Herbivory*, Chapman & Hall, UK, 1996

Rowe, S. R., Sharpe, T., and Torrens, H. S., *lchthyosaurs: A History of Fossil Sea Dragons*, National Museum of Wales, UK, 1981

RULING REPTILES:

Alexander, R. McN., *Dynamics of dinosaurs and other extinct giants*, Columbia University Press, US, 1979

Alvarez, W., *T. rex and the Crater of Doom*, US, 1997

Archibald, J. D., *Dinosaur Extinction and the End of an Era*, Columbia, US, 1996

Bakker, R. T., *The Dinosaur Heresies*, Morrow, US, 1986

Benton, M. J., *Penguin Historical Atlas of Dinosaurs*, UK and US, Viking, Penguin, 1996

Carpenter, K., Hirsch, K. F., and Horner, J. R. (eds.), *Dinosaur Eggs and Babies*, Cambridge University Press, UK, 1994

Charig, A. J., *A New Look at the Dinosaurs*, Heinemann, UK, 1979

Colbert, E. H., *Dinosaurs: An Illustrated History*, Hammond, US, 1986

Currie, P. J., and Padian, K. (eds.), *Encyclopedia of Dinosaurs*, Academic Press, US, 1997

Czerkas, S. J., and Olson, E. C., *Dinosaurs Past and Present*, Natural History Museum of Los Angeles County, US, 1987

Farlow, J., and Brett-Surman, M. (eds.), *The Complete Dinosaur*, Indianapolis University Press, US, 1997

Glut, D., *The New Dinosaur Dictionary*, Citadel, US, 1982

Lambert, D., *The Ultimate Dinosaur Book*, Dorling Kindersley, UK, 1993

Lambert, D., *Collins Guide to Dinosaurs*, Collins, UK, 1983

Norman, D., *The Illustrated Encyclopaedia of Dinosaurs*, Salamander, UK, 1985

Norman, D., *Dinosaur!*, Boxtree, UK, 1991

Russell, D., *An Odyssey in Time: The Dinosaurs of North America*, University of Toronto Press, Canada, 1989

Thulborn, R. A., *Dinosaur Tracks*, Chapman & Hall, UK, 1990

Weishampel, D. B., Osmolska, H., and Dodson, P., *The Dinosauria*, University of California Press, US, 1990

Wellnhofer, P., *The Illustrated Encyclopedia of Pterosaurs*, Crescent Books, US, 1991

Wilford, J. N., *The Riddle of the Dinosaurs*, Faber & Faber, UK, 1985

MAMMAL-LIKE REPTILES:

Hotton, N. III, Maclean, P. D., Roth, J. J., and Roth, E. C. (eds.), *The Ecology and Biology of Mammal-like Reptiles*, Smithsonian Institution Press, US, 1986

King, G., *The Dicynodonts: A Study in Palaeobiology*, Chapman & Hall, UK, 1990

BIBLIOGRAPHY

BIRDS:

Dingus, L., and Rowe, T., *The Mistaken Extinction: Dinosaur Evolution and the Origin of Birds,* W. H. Freeman & Co., US, 1998

Feduccia, A., *The Age of Birds,* Harvard University Press, US, 1980

Feduccia, A., *The Origin and Evolution of Birds,* Yale University Press, US, 1996

Shipman, P., *Taking Wing: Archaeopteryx and the Evolution of Bird Flight,* Weidenfeld & Nicolson, UK, 1998

MAMMALS:

Aiello, L., *Discovering the Origins of Mankind,* Longman, UK, 1982

Benton, M. J., *The Rise of the Mammals,* The Apple Tree Press, UK, 1991

Clutton-Brock, J., *Domesticated Animals from Early Times,* Heinemann/British Museum (Natural History), UK, 1981

Halstead, L. B., *The Evolution of the Mammals,* Peter Lowe, UK, 1978

Jones, S., and Martin, R. (eds.), *The Cambridge Encyclopedia of Human Evolution,* Cambridge University Press, UK, 1992

Kemp, T. S., *Mammal-like Reptiles and the Origin of Mammals,* Academic Press, US, 1982

Lambert, D., *The Cambridge Field Guide to Prehistoric Life,* Cambridge University Press, UK, 1985

Lambert, D., *The Cambridge Guide to Prehistoric Man,* Cambridge University Press, UK, 1987

Leakey, R. E., *Human Origins,* Hamish Hamilton, UK , 1981

Lewin, R., *Human Evolution: An Illustrated Introduction,* Blackwell Scientific Publications, UK, 1984

Lillegraven, J. A. S., Kielan-Jaworowska, and Clemens. W. A., *Mesozoic Mammals,* University of California Press, US, 1979

Lister, A., and Bahn, P., *Mammoths,* Macmillan, UK, 1994

MacFadden, B. J., *Fossil Horses,* Cambridge University Press, UK, 1992

Napier, J. R., and P. H, *The Natural History of the Primates,* British Museum (Natural History), UK, 1985

Reader, J., *Missing Links, the Hunt for Earliest Man,* Penguin, UK, 1988

Savage, R. J. G., and Long, M. R., *Mammal Evolution: An Illustrated Guide,* British Museum (Natural History), UK, 1986

Scott, W. O., *A History of Land Mammals in the Western Hemisphere,* Macmillan, US, 1967

Simpson, G. C., *Splendid Isolation: The Curious History of South American Mammals,* Yale University Press, US, 1980

Stringer, C. B., and McKie, R., *African Exodus: the Origins of Modern Humanity,* Cape, UK, 1996

Szalay, F. S., Delson, E., *Evolutionary History of the Primates,* Academic Press, UK and US, 1979

Szalay, F. S., Novacek, M. J., and McKenna, M. C., *Mammal Phylogeny,* Springer-Verlag, Germany, US, 1993

Tattersall, I., Delson, E., and Van Couvering, J. (eds.), *Encyclopedia of Human Evolution and Prehistory,* Garland Publishing, Inc., US, 1988

White, M., *The Flowering of Gondwana,* Princeton University Press, US, 1990

Young, D., *The Discovery of Evolution,* Cambridge University Press, UK, 1992

INTERNATIONAL MUSEUMS

The museums listed below are among those that contain outstanding collections of fossils of the prehistoric creatures described in this book.

ARGENTINA Buenos Aires: Museo Argentino de Ciencias Naturales La Plata; Museum of La Plata University

AUSTRALIA Brisbane, Queensland: Queensland Museum
Sydney, New South Wales: Australian Museum

AUSTRIA Vienna: Natural History Museum

BELGIUM Brussels: Royal Institute of Natural Sciences

BRAZIL Rio de Janeiro: Museo Nacional

CANADA Calgary, Alberta: Zoological Gardens
Drumheller, Alberta: Tyrrell Museum of Paleontology,
Edmonton, Alberta: Provincial Museum of Alberta
Ottawa, Ontario: National Museum of National Sciences
Patricia, Alberta: Dinosaur Provincial Park
Quebec: Redpath Museum
Toronto, Ontario: Royal Ontario Museum

CHINA Beijing (Peking): Beijing Natural History Museum; Institute of Vertebrate Palaeontology and Palaeoanthropology
Beipei, Sichuan: Beipei Museum
FRANCE Paris: National Museum of Natural History

GERMANY Berlin: Natural History Museum, Humboldt University
Darmstadt: Hesse State Museum
Frankfurt-am-Main: Senckenberg Natural History Museum Munich: Bavarian State Institute for Paleontology and Historical Geography Stuttgart: State Museum for Natural History

Tubingen: Institute and Museum of Geology and Paleontology

GREECE Athens: Department of Geology and Paleontology, University of Athens

INDIA Calcutta: Geology Museum, Indian Statistical Institute

ITALY Bologna: Q. Capellini Museum Genoa: Civic Museum of Natural History Milan: Civic Museum of Natural History Padua: Museum of the Institute of Geology Rome: Museum of Paleontology, Institute of Geology Venice: Museo Civico di Storia Naturale di Venezia

JAPAN Osaka: Museum of Natural History
Tokyo: National Science Museum

KENYA Nairobi: Kenya National Museum

MEXICO Mexico City: Natural History Museum

MONGOLIA Ulan-Bator: State Central Museum

MOROCCO Rabat: Museum of Earth Sciences

NIGER Niamey: National Museum

POLAND Chorzow, Silesia: Dinosaur Park Warsaw: Institute of Palaeobiology

RUSSIA Leningrad: Central Geological and Prospecting Museum; Museum of Geology Moscow: Paleontology Museum

SOUTH AFRICA Capetown: South Africa Museum
Johannesburg: Bernard Price Institute of Palaeontology
SWEDEN Uppsala: Paleontology Museum, Uppsala University

UNITED KINGDOM
Birmingham: Birmingham Museum
Cambridge: Sedgwick Museum, Cambridge University
Cardiff, Wales: National Museum of Wales
Edinburgh, Scotland: Royal Scottish Museum Elgin, Scotland: Elgin Museum
Glasgow, Scotland: Hunterian Museum
Leicester: The Leicestershire Museums
London: British Museum (Natural History)
Crystal Palace Park Maidstone: Maidstone Museum
Oxford: University Museum
Sandown, Isle of Wight: Museum of Isle of Wight Geology

UNITED STATES OF AMERICA
Boulder, Colorado: University Natural History Museum
Buffalo, New York State: Buffalo Museum of Science Cambridge, Massachusetts: Museum of Comparative Zoology, Harvard University
Chicago, Illinois: Field Museum of Natural History
Cleveland, Ohio: Natural History Museum
Denver, Colorado: Denver Museum of Natural History Jensen, Utah: Dinosaur National Monument Los Angeles, California: Los Angeles County Museum of Natural History
New Haven, Connecticut: Peabody Museum of Natural History, Yale University
New York, New York State: American Museum of Natural History
Pittsburg, Pennsylvania: Carnegie Museum of Natural History Princeton, New Jersey: Museum of Natural History, Princeton University
Salt Lake City, Utah: Utah Museum of Natural History Washington DC: National Museum of Natural History, Smithsonian Institution

ZIMBABWE Harare: National Museum of Harare

INDEX

ACKNOWLEDGMENTS

Picture credits

t=top, b=bottom, c=center, l=left, r=right

1 François Gohier/Ardea; 2 Vaughan Fleming/Science Photo Library; 4 P. Morris/Ardea; 6l Simon Conway Morris, 6c Sinclair Stammers/Oxford Scientific Films, 6r François Gohier/Ardea; 7l Vaughan Fleming/Science Photo Library, 7c The British Museum, 7r P. Morris/Ardea; 8t The Natural History Museum, London, 8b François Gohier/Ardea; 9t John Reader/Science Photo Library, 9b François Gohier/Ardea; 10-11 Tony Stone Images; 48-49 P. Morris/Ardea; 50t B. Murton/Southampton Oceanography Centre/Science Photo Library, 50b Sinclair Stammers/Science Photo Library; 51 Jean-Paul Ferrero/Ardea; 52 François Gohier/Ardea; 53 Breck P. Kent/Oxford Scientific Films; 54t Simon Conway Morris, University of Cambridge, 54b Dr Peter Crimes; 55t Dr Peter Crimes, 55b Simon Conway Morris, University of Cambridge; 56 Jean-Paul Ferrero/Ardea; 57 Shuhai Xiao and Andrew Knoll, Harvard University; 58l Simon Conway Morris, University of Cambridge, 58r Simon Conway Morris, University of Cambridge; 59t Simon Conway Morris, University of Cambridge, 59b Simon Conway Morris, University of Cambridge; 60 Dr Peter Crimes; 61 Dr Peter Crimes; 62t Simon Conway Morris, University of Cambridge, 62b Royal Ontario Museum; 63t Simon Conway Morris, University of Cambridge, 63b Dr Derek E.G. Briggs, University of Bristol; 64 Simon Conway Morris, University of Cambridge; 65l Simon Conway Morris, University of Cambridge, 65tr Dr Derek E.G. Briggs, University of Bristol, 65br Dr Derek E.G. Briggs, University of Bristol; 66t Gary Bell/Planet Earth Pictures, 66b Simon Conway Morris, University of Cambridge; 67 NHPA; 68t William Campbell/DRK Photo, 68b Jens Rydell/Bruce Coleman; 69t Martin Land/Science Photo Library, 69b Volker Steger/Science Photo Library; 70 Richard Aldridge, University of Leicester; 71t BD/IPR/19-7 British Geological Survey © NERC. All rights reserved, 71b The Natural History Museum, London; 72t Manfred Schauer, 72b Martin Land/Science Photo Library; 73t The Natural History Museum, London, 73b The Natural History Museum, London; 74l Sinclair Stammers/Science Photo Library, 74r Department of Earth Sciences, Cardiff University, Wales; 75l Kaj R. Svensson/Science Photo Library, 75r Sinclair Stammers/Science Photo Library; 76t Breck P. Kent/Oxford Scientific Films, 76b The Natural History Museum, London; 77t Eric and David Hosking/Corbis, 77b The Natural History Museum, London; 78 Zig Leszczynski/Oxford Scientific Films; 79 University Museum of Zoology, Cambridge; 80t G.I. Bernard/NHPA, 80b Sinclair Stammers/Oxford Scientific Films; 81t Sarah Finney, 81b The Manchester Museum, The University of Manchester; 82l Andrew Mounter/Planet Earth Pictures, 82r University Museum of Zoology, Cambridge; 83 National Museums of Scotland; 84 P. Morris/Ardea; 85 Prof. Dr Carsten Brauckmann/Institut für Geologie & Palaeontologie, Clausthal; 86t David Muench/Corbis, 86b The Field Museum, Chicago Neg. No. GEO 81284; 87t David M. Dennis/Oxford Scientific Films, 87b Chip Clark; 88l Dr David Norman, 88r Luiz Claudio Marigo/Bruce Coleman; 89 The Field Museum, Chicago Neg. No. GEO 81027; 90 The Natural History Museum, London; 91 François Gohier/Ardea; 92t P. Morris/Ardea, 92b Sinclair Stammers/Science Photo Library; 93t Specimen: Staatliches Museum für Naturkunde Stuttgart/Dr R. Wild; 93b Specimen: Museo Civico di Scienze Naturali "E. Caffi" Bergamo, Italy/Dr R. Wild; 94 François Gohier/Ardea; 95 Neg. No. 329319 Photo by Bolton Courtesy Dept. of Library Services American Museum of Natural History; 96 The Natural History Museum, London; 97t Geoscience Features Picture Library, 97b James D. Watt/Planet Earth Pictures; 98t David M. Dennis/Oxford Scientific Films, 98b P. Morris/Ardea; 99t François Gohier/Ardea, 99b Vaughan Fleming/Science Photo Library; 100 Robert Harding Picture Library; 101 P.Morris/Ardea; 102b Mary Evans Picture Library; 103t Ken Lucas/Planet Earth Pictures, 103b Peter Scoones/Planet Earth Pictures; 104 The Natural History Museum, London; 105l Ken Lucas/Planet Earth Pictures; 105 François Gohier/Ardea; 106 John Fields/Nature Focus; 107 Anthony Bannister/NHPA; 108t Tony Stone Images, 108b The Natural History Museum, London; 109t François Gohier/Ardea, 109b François Gohier/Ardea; 110 Steve Hutt; 111 Vivek Sinha/Oxford Scientific Films; 112l François Gohier/Ardea, 112r The Natural History Museum, London; 113l The Kobal Collection; 113r Brigham Young University; 114t David Sanders, 114b François Gohier/Ardea; 115t E.R. Degginger/Oxford Scientific Films, 115b Ken Lucas/Planet Earth Pictures; 116 François Gohier/Ardea; 117 François Gohier/Ardea; 118 Jonathan Blair/Corbis; 119 François Gohier/Ardea; 120 Jean-Loup Charmet; 121 Natuurhistorisch Museum Maastricht; 122t François Gohier/Ardea, 122b Paul A. Souders/Corbis; 123t Dr David Kring/Science Photo Library, 123b E. Hanumantha Rao/NHPA; 124 The Natural History Museum, London/Dorling Kindersley; 125 J. David Archibald; 128t P. Morris/Ardea, 128b François Gohier/Ardea; 129t David C. Fritts/Oxford Scientific Films, 129b Wolfgang Kaehler/Corbis; 130t The Stock Market, 130b Ken Lucas/Planet Earth Pictures; 131t Photo: Senckenberg, Messel Research Department, 131b Photo: Senckenberg, Messel Research Department; 132 Photo: Senckenberg, Messel Research Department; 133 Photo: Senckenberg, Messel Research Department; 134 Kevin Schafer/NHPA; 135 Krafft/Planet Earth Pictures; 136t Kathie Atkinson/Oxford Scientific Films, 136b Dr Paul Selden, University of Manchester; 137t David Dilcher and Ge Sun, 137b Steve Hopkin/Planet Earth Pictures; 138t Alex Kerstitch/Planet Earth Pictures, 138b George Poinar; 139t Vaughan Fleming/Science Photo Library, 139b David Maitland/Planet Earth Pictures; 140 NHPA; 141 David Maitland/Planet Earth Pictures; 142 David Paterson; 143 NASA/Science Photo Library; 144t Adrian Warren/Ardea, 144b John Reader/Science Photo Library, 145t John Reader/Science Photo Library, 145b James Balog/Tony Stone Images; 146 Christopher Ratier/NHPA; 147 Anthony Bannister/NHPA; 148 Copyright 1995, Worldsat International and J. Knighton/Science Photo Library; 149 Tony Stone Images; 150t Anup Shah/Planet Earth Pictures, 150b Kenneth W. Fink/Ardea; 151l John Reader/Science Photo Library, 151r Gerald Cubitt/Bruce Coleman; 152t Harald Sund/The Image Bank, 152b Dr D.P. Lane, University of Keele; 153t Mike Newton, 153b Peter Parks/Oxford Scientific Films; 154 Novosti Photo Library; 155t B & C Alexander/NHPA, 155b Jean Vertut; 156 Grotte Préhistorique de Rouffignac; 157t The Natural History Museum, London, 157b The British Museum; 158/159 Images Colour Library; 158t Richard Coomber/Planet Earth Pictures, 158b J.G. Paren/Science Photo Library; 159t Frank Spooner Pictures, 159b Dick Mol; 442-443 David Paterson; 444 Stuart Westmorland/Tony Stone Images, 444 inset Bettmann/Corbis; 445l Bettmann/Corbis, 445c Hulton-Deutsch Collection/Corbis, 445r Hulton-Deutsch Collection/Corbis; 447 David Bayliss/Geoscience Features Picture Library; 448l Bettmann/Corbis, 448r Bettmann/Corbis; 449 G. Brad Lewis/Tony Stone Images; 450t Archiv für Kunst & Geschichte, Berlin/AKG London, 450b Herve Gloaguen/Network; 451t Corbis, 451b The Stock Market; 452 M. Angelo/Corbis, 452 inset Oliver Benn/Tony Stone Images; 453 Corbis; 454 Yann Arthus-Bertrand/Corbis; 455t David Muench/Corbis, 455b Yann Arthus-Bertrand/Corbis; 456 Craig Lovell/Corbis, 456 inset Kevin Schafer/Corbis; 458 Bettmann/Corbis; 459t John Dakers; Eye Ubiquitous/Corbis, 459b Mansell/Time Inc.; 460 World Perspectives/Tony Stone Images; 461t Bettmann/Corbis, 461b Prof. Stewart Lowther/Science Photo Library; 462 Tom Bean/Tony Stone Images; 463l François Gohier/Ardea, 463r Robert van der Hilst/Tony Stone Images; 464 Mary Evans Picture Library; 465t The Natural History Museum, London, 465b The Natural History Museum, London; 466 C. Weaver/Ardea; 468 Sinclair Stammers/Science Photo Library, 468 inset Mary Evans Picture Library; 471t Tom Bean/Corbis, 471c George Poinar, 471b Buddy Mays/Corbis; 472 The Kobal Collection; 474 Geoscience Features Picture Library; 474 T.A. Wiewandt/DRK Photo; 476 Richardson/Custom Medical Stock Photo/Science Photo Library; 478 Lick Observatory; 479b Robert Hadley/Impact Photos; 484-512 Ken Lucas/Planet Earth Pictures

If the publishers have unwittingly infringed copyright in any illustration reproduced, they would pay an appropriate fee on being satisfied to the owner's title.

Illustrators

Graham Allen 106/107, 149t, 196–297, 477; David Bergen 84/85, 100/101, 124/125, 126/127; Richard Bonson 134/135, 142/143, 158/159; Robin Bouttell 78/79, 110/111, 146/147; Jim Channell 60/61, 74/75, 154/155; Bill Donohoe 52/53, 56/57, 70/71, 104/105; Malcolm Ellis 172–181; Eugene Fleury 90/91; Vana Haggerty 18/19, 46/47, 58/59, 88/89, 170/171, 182/183, 194/195; Gary Hincks 157; Steve Holden 148, 196–297; Rob Jakeway 50/51; Steve Kirk 60–169, 96/97, 184–193, 196–297, 472/473; Kuo Kang Chen 470; Colin Newman 20–57, 64/65, 82/83, 137; Luis Rey 94/95, 118/119, 140/141; Andrew Robinson 149c & b, 196–297; Peter David Scott 88/89, 116/117, 120/121, 132/133; Dick Twinney 477; Andrew Wheatcroft 156/157, 196–297

Maps

Three-dimensional maps produced by Lovell Johns Limited, Witney, using illustration by Hardlines Limited, Charlbury, and based on data supplied by Paleomap Services Limited, Cambridge. Two-dimensional maps by Eugene Fleury.

The publishers would like to thank the following people for their kind help during the production of this book:

Dr. Alan Smith, Department of Earth Sciences, University of Cambridge
Dr. Norman Macleod, Natural History Museum, London